Feetwashing during the love feast of the Manheim Brethren, late nine-teenth century. Drawing by Alice Barber Stephens in *The Ladies' Home Journal* (July 1898)

Fruit of the Vine
A History of the Brethren, 1708-1995

Donald F. Durnbaugh

Brethren Press®
Elgin, Illinois

Copyright © 1997 by Donald F. Durnbaugh

All rights reserved. No portion of this book may be reproduced in any form or by any process or technique without the written consent of the publisher, except for brief quotations enbodied in critical articles or reviews.

00 99 98 97 96   5 4 3 2 1

Library of Congress Cataloging-in-Publication Data
Durnbaugh, Donald F.
    Fruit of the vine : a history of the Brethren, 1708-1995 / Donald F.
    Durnbaugh.
        p.   cm.
    Includes bibliographical references and index.
    ISBN 0-87178-003-8
    1. Church of the Brethren—History.   I. Title.
BX7815.D83   1997
286".5—dc20   96-22415

Manufactured in the United States of America

To

students in classes at Juniata College, Bethany Theological Seminary, and Elizabethtown College, and our times of shared learning.

CONTENTS

PREFACE

According to the first historian of the Brethren, Alexander "Sander" Mack, Jr., the movement began when "eight persons covenanted and united together as brethren and sisters...to form a church of christian believers." Their next step was to consult "authentic histories" where they found that the Christians of the first and second centuries were uniformly "planted into the death of Jesus Christ by a threefold immersion into the water-bath of holy baptism." They checked this with the New Testament and found all "perfectly harmonizing." This then led them to the baptisms in 1708 which marked their beginning.[1]

An interesting aspect of this account is the reference to "authentic histories." Surprisingly, the early band turned first to history and only afterward to the scriptures to decide on the method of baptism. Of course the entire course of their faith enterprise was saturated in biblical study.

Many of their latter-day descendants have been less avid in pursuing and perusing the historical record as orientation. It is startling to recognize that the present book is one of very few attempts ever made to write a comprehensive history of the movement we know now as the Church of the Brethren, despite a raft of books and articles on Brethren history.

The best information we have on Brethren in the colonial period is found in the compilations by a Baptist author, Morgan Edwards (1770ff.) A comparable collection of data was published by Howard Miller over a century later as a *Record of the Faithful* (1882), based on his work as a US census taker for plain groups. Valuable as both are, neither could be called histories.[2]

Pioneer nineteenth-century publisher Henry Kurtz undertook to write one but never got past the pre-history with the Waldenses. The Annual Meeting in 1895 authorized the publication of a church history, but M. G. Brumbaugh got his book out first and the project was dropped by S. Z. Sharp, who contented himself with writing the first history of Brethren education.

A number of Brethren authors about the turn of the century were competing to publish the first history; Brumbaugh won the race, aided by his personal purchase of the foundational collection of Abraham Harley Cassel. Although Brumbaugh called his pioneer work the *History of the German Baptist Brethren in Europe and America* (1899), it really covers only the eighteenth century, with a few fragments added dealing with the nineteenth century.

His rival George N. Falkenstein, whose book contains a sharp critique of Brumbaugh (though unnamed), called his history *The German Baptist Brethren or Dunkers* (1900), but it focuses on the early story of Germantown where he was a pastor. Another rival of Brumbaugh, the Progressive leader Henry R. Holsinger, came closest to compiling a comprehensive history (1901); after describing the early shared history, he dealt with the three major groupings of the time but the book is most complete on his own Brethren Church and most valuable for his biographical sketches.

Otho Winger's history of the Brethren (1919, 2nd ed. 1920) is a useful short text written for instructional purposes, as was that of C. Ernest Davis (1923). Both J. E. Miller (in 1941, rev. ed. 1957) and Virginia Fisher (in 1958, rev. ed. 1974) wrote popular Brethren histories, but they were designed for young people and were quite brief. Because Floyd E. Mallott taught Brethren history at Bethany Biblical Seminary for many years, one could have reasonably expected a comprehensive history from his pen. He did, in fact, produce a lengthy manuscript, which, however, was shortened at the direction of the publishing house and printed under the title *Studies in Brethren History* (1954), indicating a focus on selected topics. The admirable book *Brethren Society* (1995) by Carl F. Bowman comes closest to a comprehensive assessment of Brethren history, but by design focuses on the cultural transformation of the Brethren from 1850 to the present. Because of the excellence of his study of change in church life and practice, gaps in this study may be remedied, in part, by reference to his insightul and well-documented book.

John M. Kimmel (of the Old German Baptist Brethren), Albert T. Ronk (of the Brethren Church), and Homer A. Kent, Sr. (of the Grace

PROLOGUE

It was early August in the year 1708; the site was a tiny village called *Schwarzenau* (Black Meadow) in the modest principality of Wittgenstein in central Germany. Five men and three women gathered in the early morning along the Eder Brook to perform an illegal act. Their intent? To carry out an un-authorized series of baptisms. Under imperial law such "rebaptisms"—for all eight had been routinely baptized as infants in the established churches according to immemorial practice—were capital offenses. Understandably, there were no witnesses to their dangerous undertaking nor any written record kept of it.

One man, whose name was never revealed, baptized the leading personality of the small group. His name was Alexander Mack, a former miller from the Palatinate, recognized as one who possessed strong gifts of preaching and shepherding. Mack baptized his baptizer and then the remaining three men and three women. Each person kneeled in the waters of the brook and pledged a covenant of discipleship to the Lord Jesus Christ. Each was then firmly and completely immersed three times in the successive names of the Trinity. Following each baptism Mack urgently sought in prayer God's blessing for the participant.[1]

This daring action of civil disobedience signaled the emergence of a religious movement which in time grew to considerable size and widespread, indeed, world-wide involvement. By the late 20th century, over 300,000 adult believers in more than 2,000 congregations in many nations looked back to the Schwarzenau baptisms as the origin of their church affiliation. Including those linked in some way with these churches the number surpassed 600,000. Several distinct but related denominations stem from that Wittgenstein beginning; all of them include the biblical term *Brethren* in their official names to express their sense of community.[2]

The following chapters will sketch the background of the Schwarzenau baptisms, the immediate outcome of these acts, the shift in locale from Europe to North America, and the subsequent developments through the centuries on several continents.

1

Background for the Brethren

To grasp why a movement such as the Brethren began, it is necessary to know the context in which it occurred. Some knowledge of the political, social, economic, and particularly the religious conditions of the times is essential if the behavioral forms and religious beliefs of the early members are to be understood. Most of those persons who became Brethren originated in the area known as the Palatinate, which had its own special character. In addition to the underlying warp and woof of Protestant Christianity, there were two formative strands woven into the fabric of the early Brethren pattern; they were called Anabaptism and Radical Pietism. They need to be briefly defined and described. In particular, it is important to gain an overview of Radical Pietist activities, because it was directly from these that the Brethren were formed.

POLITICAL CONDITIONS

Historians speak of "the Germanies" in the early 1700s because that part of Europe that we now call Germany was then a patchwork of more than three hundred splinter states, free cities, and territories. There was indeed an overall political entity known as the Holy Roman Empire, German Nation, which basically included the Germanies and Austria, but it was a loose and ineffectual organization. To repeat the quip of Voltaire, it was neither holy, nor Roman, nor an empire.[1]

Given this comparative vacuum in central authority, local rulers took power into their own hands. They made much of the regnant political theory, that of the divine right of kings, which maintained that hereditary rulers were ordained of God to rule over their subjects. Their authority was understood to be derived directly from God and therefore was not to be limited by any lesser agency. This is the opposite of the theory of social contract in which power is understood to be delegated from the citizenry for limited and specific purposes.

The arbitrary and glorious rule of the French *Sun King*, Louis XIV, at his impressive palace at Versailles was taken as the model. Each petty monarch in the hundreds of German states aped this pattern, attempting to create a glittering French-speaking court, mighty army, and ornate palace. Without the economic strength of France, the result was shocking fiscal oppression of each subjugated populace.

These problems were the more painful because the German states had not fully recovered from the effects of the destructive and intolerably protracted Thirty Years War (1618-1648). By the best estimate, fully one-third of the population of the German states perished during the war. Although recent scholarship has tended to play down the extent of overall destruction, certain areas were devastated.

Armies at that time were totally dependent for their supplies upon requisitions from the areas where they were quartered. In most cases this amounted to brutal plundering. For this reason, whether the armies were "friendly" or "enemy" made little practical difference to local residents. Thousands of villages and towns were destroyed and depopulated by occupation, fighting, looting, and disease.

Parts of the Germanies, struggling to rebound from these crises, were hit again by warfare at the end of the seventeenth century. While the emperor was busy battling the Turks who besieged Vienna from 1683 to 1699, Louis XIV sent his troops into the Palatinate to seize territory under thinly based hereditary claims. When the French armies were forced to withdraw, they practiced a scorched-earth policy. Heidelberg, Speyer, and Worms were burned, Mannheim was leveled, and scores of villages completely razed. Crops were destroyed, vineyards uprooted, and livestock slaughtered. Residents were tortured to induce them to reveal the location of foodstuffs and hidden treasures.[2]

A second invasion in 1693 repeated the tragedy, ruining anything missed in Heidelberg earlier, including the castle. The Treaty of Rijswijk (1697) brought an end to the war in the Palatinate, but fighting soon flared up again to become the first truly world-wide conflict as the War of the Spanish Succession, which ended finally in 1713-14. Again the Palatinate suffered as rival armies marched through, pillaging as they went. The Northern War dragged on until 1721. The period when the Brethren emerged was thus one of continual warfare. It is not surprising that from the beginning they took a firm stand against war and violence.[3]

SOCIAL AND ECONOMIC CONDITIONS

The hardships of these wars had a profound effect on social conditions. Thousands of peasants and townspeople were reduced to begging or thieving because of the loss of their fields, homes, and trades. The rough soldateska had left disease and corrupted morals behind them when the undisciplined armies moved on. Vulgarity and coarseness set the general tone.

There were great gaps between the social classes. The rulers succeeded in gathering around them the lesser nobility and the cultivated part of the populace. Court life was brilliant and showy but corrupt, immoral, and shallow. Common people were considered to be brutish, little better than animals. Occasionally, they would be allowed to come to the court, only to be made the victims of cruel jokes. On the other hand, some of the middle class maintained a rather high standard of moral living. Towns were controlled by a few intermarried families, primarily of the mercantile class.

Continual warfare had almost ruined the economies of the German region. Peasants lost interest in replanting fields that were repeatedly overrun and destroyed. Great sections of the land lay idle for lack of workers to till it. Townspeople were impoverished through the effects of plundering or through paying ever heavier taxes.

Commerce was hampered by steep fees imposed at each of the many borders that goods had to cross. A ship sailing down the Rhine River from Strasbourg to the Dutch border had to pass customs thirty times and be offloaded and reloaded twice. The mouths of all of the German rivers were controlled by foreign powers, who blocked German trade or exacted exorbitant tolls. The confused currency system made trade even more difficult.

The peasants, as serfs, were forced to give more and more time to work on their lords' estates. In some areas they had to work five days for their masters and on the sixth earn enough to feed themselves and pay the burdensome taxes. Children of the peasants had to serve their masters a certain number of years without pay and were often badly mistreated. Nobility trampled fields during the many hunts that they enjoyed. Although wild animals damaged seeds and crops, there were drastic penalties preventing farmers from killing the destructive game.

RELIGIOUS CONDITIONS

The religious wars of the sixteenth century had resulted in the toleration of the Lutheran faith, despite the best efforts of Roman Catholics to roll back the gains of the Reformation. At the end of the Thirty Years' War the Reformed (Calvinist) faith was also recognized. In 1700 there were, therefore, three official churches in the German states—Roman Catholic, Lutheran, and Reformed. These were state churches, which means that they were integral parts of the government in their areas and subject to political control.

The compromise settlement at the Treaties of Westphalia (1648) confirmed the earlier principle that the ruler determines the religion of the territory—the slogan was "as the prince, so the religion"—but limited its effective sway. Church properties were to be re-established as they were in 1624. When divided church loyalty had existed in a certain territory in 1624, this situation was in theory to be maintained after 1648, a provision often ignored or twisted. Lutherans and Calvinists agreed that a change in ruler to one or the other faith after the day of signing the peace treaty should not affect the religion of subjects.

Otherwise, sovereigns were free to choose one of the three as the official religion in their respective lands. Clergymen were state employees and were chosen by the ruler, who was the final authority on matters of church government and even of dogma. This was less true for the Catholic countries, where the pope continued to exercise his authority, although not as completely as before. Subjects of any land were in theory free to migrate if their own faith was not tolerated. In practice, this was often not permitted.

Dissenters were not tolerated in the German states and were subject to banishment or punishment if caught. The most numerous among them were the Anabaptists or Mennonites; they had originated in several places in the early sixteenth century, especially in the Swiss cantons, Southern Germany, and the Low Countries. They were tagged as "rebaptizers," because they rejected the customary baptism of infants, convinced by their study of the scriptures that only the baptism of adult believers was valid.[4]

They rejected the state church and its coercion in affairs of faith, maintaining stoutly the revolutionary principles of religious freedom and voluntarism. Though Anabaptists soon became dedicated to complete nonresistance, some marginally connected groups believed that force was justified in what they considered to be the last days before Christ's second coming. All Anabaptists were tarred with their errors.

Anabaptists stressed the necessity of strict ethical lives, using church discipline to keep their ranks unspotted by open immorality. One of their basic tenets was that Christian faith must be demonstrated in daily living. Despite the exemplary conduct of most Anabaptists, they were condemned as heretics and harshly suppressed. The sufferings of thousands were later recorded in a martyrology known commonly as *The Martyrs Mirror*, first published in 1660 in Dordrecht. Dutch Mennonites won relatively early toleration in the freer air of the Netherlands and thus had access to the printing press.

Although dissenters were still liable to the death penalty under imperial law, by the early 1700s German society was generally tired of shedding blood for religious reasons, so that expulsion and banishment, along with other (often harsh) penalties, were more common sentences. Although the three official faiths were still deadly enemies of one another, they combined to suppress those daring to have dissident religious opinions. There were a few islands of tolerance where dissenters, especially Mennonites, were allowed to reside because of their value as good farmers and industrious craftsmen.

Catholics controlled Southern Germany, Austria, and several German bishoprics. Northern, Central, and Eastern Germany were Lutheran, and the Reformed were dominant in some territories along the Rhine, including the Palatinate.

Because of this intense religious rivalry, each faith paid attention to solidifying its defense by drawing ever more precise theological boundaries. The effect on church life was deadening; it became increasingly cold and sterile in the view of its critics. The intense religious fervor of the Reformation era and of the Catholic Counter Reformation had hardened, they contended, into lifeless doctrines. Instead of the bread of life, worshipers received the crusts of dogma. Protestant clergy jealously guarded the purity of the "true faith"—the creeds and theological statements of the sixteenth century—and the Catholics concentrated on elaborate ritual to hold their people.

Sermons in the Lutheran and Reformed churches were often violent attacks against other faiths or dealt with obscure points of doctrine. Dogmatic formulations were spun out to fantastic lengths and logical extensions in what has become known as Protestant Scholasticism. There were, of course, notable exceptions to these generalizations in parishes where conscientious pastors worked faithfully to shepherd their flocks.

Strict attention was paid to regular church attendance by the religious and secular authorities acting in concert. Absence from divine worship was immediately noticed and the culprits haled before the church council. If the miscreants were stubborn enough to ignore the disciplinary actions of the church, they were turned over to the secular officials who took drastic action to correct the crime.

A fixed system of church taxes, often paid in kind, provided the support for the clergy. Given the generally unsatisfactory state of religious affairs, compounded by political, social, and economic straits, many earnest searchers found refuge in spiritualistic and millenarian speculations.

THE PALATINATE

The religious condition of the Rhenish Palatinate, where most of those who became Brethren lived, was especially disturbed. It became Lutheran in 1546 but converted to the Reformed faith in 1560. Four more flip-flops took place by 1648. Six switches of the official religion thus occurred within 150 years and change was not yet over![5]

The wise Elector Karl Ludwig (ruled 1648-1680) followed a policy of toleration as part of his attempt to rebuild his devastated country. He permitted limited numbers of Mennonites to settle as farmers and artisans, with the proviso that no conversions were to be allowed and their faith was to be limited to their families in private. Even Hutterian communities were tolerated, as for example in Mannheim. Waldensian refugees from persecution found asylum there as well.

Although his successor continued this relatively generous policy, with the successor's death in 1685 that line of the family was terminated. The land then went over to the Catholic line. It was this circumstance that Louis XIV seized upon as the opportunity to make his claims to the territory and later invade, as previously reported.

During the French occupation (1688-89), the Roman Catholics seized control of many of the church buildings and other properties that had been theirs before the Reformation. A clause in the Treaty of Ryswick provided that the Roman party should retain possession of all property in their hands at the time of the peace in 1697.

The new Palatine sovereign, Elector Johann Wilhelm (ruled 1690-1716) followed a pro-Catholic policy. Although he could not openly force his country to return to the mother church (because of the provisions of the Treaty of Westphalia), he pursued a regimen that repressed Protestants. His Catholic officials knew how to administer the outwardly tolerant regulations so as to benefit their party. Although the Catholics were numerically small, a commission awarded them five-sevenths of the church property.

A unique feature of the Edict of Toleration of 1698 was the order that Lutheran, Catholic, and Reformed services must be held alternately or successively in those villages where there was only one church building. In those disturbed times, this supposedly generous edict led to endless bickering among the three faiths. If the first took too much time for its Sunday service in a village, then the second had to cool its heels in waiting, and the third might not get into the church at all. Bitter complaints were exchanged, in some places leading to open violence, even at funerals.

Protestants were especially unhappy that the Elector made them observe Catholic holy days and kneel when Roman processions passed by on the streets. Their complaints to the Protestant nations (such as Brandenburg-Prussia and England) led to a compromise in 1705, which mitigated some of the worst abuses in Protestant eyes. To show his displeasure at this event, the Elector moved his residence to Düsseldorf.

These were the conditions which created in the hearts of many earnest souls the desire for reform. The continual violence of war led some to believe that the world was coming to an end, and this made action seem more urgent. Unbearable oppression by tyrannical rulers, harsh dogma and rigid orthodoxy in the churches, brutality and outrage from marauding soldiers, all caused great unrest and discontent; on the other side, there was a wider distribution of the scriptures in the German language, as well as increased educational possibilities. These factors, both positive and negative, enter into the rise to prominence in German church life of the movement known as *Pietism*.

PIETISM AND RADICAL PIETISM

PIETISM

An early recorded use of the term Pietist was in 1689, cited by a professor in Leipzig: "The name Pietist is known all over the city. What is a Pietist? One who studies God's word and leads a holy life in accord with it. This is well done, indeed, it would be good for every Christian."[6]

Early developments of Pietism in the Germanies came in the Reformed church in the North, influenced by previous reform movements in the Netherlands. They in turn had been largely caused by impulses from Puritan England. It is, however, within the Lutheran Church that the greatest leaders of German Pietism emerged. Johann Arndt, a pastor in Braunschweig, was the first noted advocate of Pietist reform. This came through his devotional book, the *Six Books of True Christianity* (1605-1620). This work became for centuries the best-loved and best-known inspirational work for those reading the German language and is still cherished.

Later in the seventeenth century the Alsatian-born pastor Philipp Jakob Spener introduced Pietistic practices in his parish in Frankfurt/Main. In 1670 he gathered small groups of his congregation about him to discuss recent sermons and to study the Bible; these study groups were called *conventicles*. In 1675 he wrote a foreword to a new edition of Arndt's devotional book in which he called for reforms in church life; he entitled the foreword *Pia Desideria*, that is, *Pious Desires*. This brief essay, often republished, struck a responsive chord in the hearts of Christians all over the Germanies.

Spener urged a six-point program of improvement: 1) more intensive Bible study; 2) more lay activity; 3) Christianity to be practiced in daily life; 4) freedom in religious matters; 5) reform of theological training; and 6) more edifying preaching instead of rhetoric about dogmatic issues. The fact that these suggestions (which today seem rather mild) raised a storm of criticism shows better than anything else the state of religion of the time. Spener accepted high positions first in Dresden and later in Berlin, whence he exerted great influence through his many publications, extensive correspondence, and personal recommendations of worthy young men to fill churchly positions.[7]

One of these younger associates of Spener was August Hermann Francke. As a young graduate student, Francke attended private meetings of theological students at the University of Leipzig to study the Bible, trying to learn what it meant for everyday life. Later while studying biblical interpretation at Lüneberg, he experienced a profound conversion. Returning to Leipzig as an instructor, Francke's biblical lectures became so popular that he was forced out by senior faculty members, who accused him of heterodox teaching but were really jealous of his success. After holding several other positions, with the aid of Spener he found his life work at Halle on the Saale River, where he became a pastor and professor of theology at the recently founded university (established in 1694).

Armed with little more than faith in God's providence, indomitable willpower, and a flair for what a later age would call public relations, Francke created an amazing complex of institutions, known over the years as the Francke Foundation. He began by taking a few orphans into his own home, and by the time of his death his schools were training over two thousand pupils. He established orphanages, hospitals, schools, seminaries, and famous Bible and foreign missionary societies. The University of Halle became the theological center of Pietism and the Francke institutions the center of practical action. The Francke Foundation became internationally known and respected; it still exists and since the reunification of Germany has become the center for research on Pietism.[8]

RADICAL PIETISM

Some Pietists were dissatisfied with the pace of reform progress. They came to believe that leaders like Spener and Francke compromised with the evils of the day and depended too much on the church's institutional framework. Moreover, in many areas the authorities would not permit the slightest deviation from the orthodox line. Those gathering for Bible study were treated like desperate criminals. Quite often the state's heavy-handed repression precipitated separation. To be true to their high calling, these Pietists felt that they had to break with the church. They were called Radical Pietists or Separatists.[9]

They were encouraged in their separatism by the earlier writings of the mystic Jakob Boehme, who had a strong underground influence within Europe, despite long-standing suppression. The shoemaker-philosopher experienced illuminations about the deepest mysteries of life and the cosmos, expressed in what was called theosophy. His most famous works were *Aurora* (1612) and *The Way to Christ* (1624). Boehme was a scathing critic of the institutional church, which he called the "great harlot;" he urged earnest Christians to flee this "Babel," the anti-Christ.

Particularly offensive to the established church were Boehme's ideas about Divine Wisdom, the Heavenly Sophia. Those seeking the deepest spiritual experience—union with Sophia—should forego human marriage. In his understanding, the fall of humankind came with the desire of Adam for sexual relations. Celibacy (or at the most companionate marriage) was the superior path to God. These ideas were among those with which the early Brethren struggled; they remained constituent for the Ephrata Society in colonial Pennsylvania. Contemporary feminist writers have revived some of Boehme's ideas about Sophia.[10]

The best known and most influential of the Radical Pietists was Gottfried Arnold. Born a part orphan in 1666, he earned money for his education by tutoring. His unusual abilities can be seen from the fact that he was awarded a master's degree at the age of twenty. As a student at Wittenberg, he avoided the customary raucous student life and immersed himself in the study of theology and church history. He was much influenced by Spener, who helped him following his graduation to several positions as tutor and chaplain for private families of the nobility. A position in Quedlinburg brought him into contact with mystical-spiritualistic circles, who were strongly critical of the church.

In 1696 he published his first weighty book based on his patristic studies, called *The First Love, That Is, The True Portrayal of the First Christians*. His comprehensive mastery of early church writers enabled him to depict the lives and worship of the Christians of the first three centuries, which he held up as models for all later Christians. He stressed the informal nature of the early church, without hierarchy, dogma, church buildings, and liturgy. The fall of the church came in the fourth century with the change under the Emperor Constantine that made it first a protected and later the established church.

So popular was the work that it was republished five times before 1732 and translated into several foreign languages. It won him an appointment as professor at the University of Giessen near Frankfurt/Main.

After less than one year of teaching, Arnold suddenly resigned the prestigious position. His explanation, which appeared in print (and was republished six times in two years), was that it was impossible to be a real Christian in such a secular and pagan atmosphere. University education corrupted youths and led to vanity. Arnold withdrew to the home of a friend and devoted himself to further intensive study.

The result of his labor was his most important work, the multivolumed *Impartial History of the Church and Heretics* (1699-1700). The chief contribution of this massive study was that, for the first time, someone had attempted to write about the dissenters whom the church had pronounced heretical by using sources from these movements themselves, rather than by relying upon the often distorted and repetitive accusations by orthodox writers. For this reason Arnold has been called the father of modern church history and his books are still read.

The striking thesis of these volumes was that the heretical movements had actually perpetuated the true church, while the orthodox church that had persecuted them was, in reality, the anti-church. In Arnold's words, "The Church has always flowered best under the cross; it was never the majority and the persecutor but rather the minority and the persecuted. The anti-Christian false church has always found its work and its holiness in outward things, symbols, shadows, sacraments, manners, and ceremonies."

The test of the true church, asserted Arnold, was not in its orthodoxy (correct doctrine) but rather in its orthopraxis (true life or behavior). This position understandably called forth a mighty stream of protest from vindictive orthodox clergy, who succeeded in pointing out a few factual errors in the comprehensive history, but did not inhibit Arnold's work from becoming the source book for all those movements that sought to model themselves after the early Christians.

Arnold eventually returned to the Lutheran Church and became a pastor. Shortly after recovering from a severe illness, he was conducting a Communion service when recruiting agents broke into the liturgy and dragged off several young men for the Prussian army. Arnold died in 1714 from the shock this caused.[11]

Gottfried Arnold was the intellectual leader of Radical Pietism, but Ernst Christoph Hochmann von Hochenau was its evangelist. Hochmann was a friend of Arnold and the spiritual father of many early Brethren. Born in 1670, he came from a noble family living near Hamburg in northern Germany and enjoyed a good education in law at several German universities. His promising career was abandoned in 1693, however, when he was "awakened" or converted in Halle by Francke.

Soon in trouble with the authorities because of his enthusiastic and ecstatic preaching, Hochmann left Halle and began a lifelong itinerant ministry, calling on his hearers to repent and learn to know Lord Jesus. His preaching followed three themes: 1) he had been called by Christ to preach the gospel; 2) there is a spiritual church; and 3) the kingdom of Christ is at hand.

A nobleman of spirit as well as of birth, Hochmann was equally welcome and at ease at the table of the high nobility and in the hut of the peasant. He was humble and loving in manner and preached in simple words with amazing power. Many became his followers throughout the German states and even in the Netherlands and Switzerland. He was imprisoned more than thirty times for his evangelistic activity and once was held for a year in Nürnberg. Often shamefully mistreated (he was driven from one territory by an official whose horse trampled Hochmann's feet), he was always cheerful and gentle. As a condition for his release from the prison at Detmold in 1702, he wrote a brief creed; known to the Brethren, it was reprinted in America.

Hochmann had a small hut built for his use at Schwarzenau/ Eder in the county of Wittgenstein. He called it his "castle of peace." Here he retreated for study and meditation after his strenuous journeys. At one point, he began a community that lived in the so-called Laboratory near the river, but this did not last long. He died in 1721 and was buried near his hut. The great Reformed Pietist hymnwriter Gerhard Tersteegen, on later visiting Schwarzenau, composed a moving epitaph and had a gravestone erected.[12]

RADICAL PIETIST ACTIVITY

Documents exist in scattered archives in Europe which tell of Radical Pietist activity in the early eighteenth century. Some of these involve persons who later became Brethren. They show how inoffensive gatherings to study and discuss the Bible were suppressed by the official church and how this led to complete separation. Among the most relevant are the stories of activities in Strasbourg, Basel, Württemberg, Kassel, and the Palatinate.[13]

The first historical sketch of Brethren origins was penned by Alexander (Sander) Mack, Jr., son of the first minister. It was a preface to the second edition of his father's writings, published in

Germantown, Pennsylvania, in 1774. He described the process of awakening and subsequent separation of those who became Brethren in these words:

> It pleased the good God in His mercy at the very beginning of this present century to support His saving grace, which appears to all men, through some voices calling for repentance and awakening. In this way He awakened many people from the death and sleep of sin. They then sought to find righteousness in Christ. However, they immediately saw to their sorrow great decay almost everywhere. Therefore they felt impelled to give many sincere testimonies of truth about this. Here and there private meetings (in which the newly-awakened souls sought their edification) were established alongside of the usual church organization. However, because of the spiritual envy of the clergy, the hearts of the authorities were embittered, and persecution began to take place here and there.[14]

ACTIVITY IN STRASBOURG

An active Pietist group developed early on in the border city of Strasbourg on the Rhine River. This was one of the historically important German cities but had been taken over by the French in 1681. The group there was made up of pastors, theological students, and townspeople and centered around Michael Eckerlin. A respected citizen, he was a tailor and capmaker by trade; after 1696 he represented the tailors' guild on the larger city council.

In 1700 a Radical Pietist named Johann Heinrich Kraft came to Strasbourg and began to hold meetings in Eckerlin's house. Church officials gathered evidence against the meetings, and in March 1701 Kraft was driven out. Eckerlin's wife had died in the summer of 1701 and he proceeded in November 1702 to take as his second wife Anna Grimman from Switzerland, who had been Kraft's maid. She was a strong separatist.

Eckerlin was given a strict warning not to participate in the conventicle. Nevertheless, all of those involved continued to meet.

Johann Friedrich Haug (who later became famous as the editor of the *Berleburg Bible*, 1726-1742), other theological students, and pastors persisted in carrying on the meetings at Eckerlin's house near the cathedral. The testimony of spies and intercepted correspondence resulted in their again being called before hearings held in 1705 by the church council.

From the hearings it was learned that Eckerlin was considered to be a godly and well-read man, highly regarded by conventicle members. Upon a special order from the king of France at his Versailles palace, Eckerlin and the others were driven from Strasbourg in March 1705 by guards armed with battle axes. He took his wife Anna and his children to Schwarzenau, where they became members of the Brethren movement. Although Eckerlin died there before 1720, his widow and children migrated to Pennsylvania, where the Eckerlin sons later became leaders in the Ephrata Society.

Activity in the Basel Area

Andreas Bohni (or Boni) was one of the first eight at the founding of the Brethren movement in 1708. A native of a village near Basel, Switzerland, he was baptized and confirmed (1690) in the Reformed Church. Young Bohni traveled to Heidelberg after he had passed his test as a journeyman weaver. There, he and his wife, Maria Sarah, became citizens in December 1702. While in the Palatinate, Bohni came into contact with Anabaptist and Pietist ideas. After his wife died in 1705, he returned to his Swiss home and began to tell others of his newly found religious beliefs, especially his brother Martin.

The local pastor quickly complained (June 1705) to the Basel authorities that the Bohni brothers refused to carry weapons or appear at military drill, rejected the swearing of oaths, and did not attend Holy Communion. When they were examined, the Basel clergy recommended that they not be punished but rather be given more instruction. Andreas soon returned to Heidelberg, while Martin indicated that he would take to heart the clerical admonitions.

When Andreas Bohni came back to his parents' home one year later during the fall of 1706, he became even more active in spreading his convictions. The village mayor demanded that some action be taken; many people were becoming interested in Bohni's views "because it has a good outward appearance and meets with rather favorable response...." The local pastor complained that at an infant baptism that he was conducting, Bohni had pulled out his New Testament (which he always carried with him) and had challenged the pastor to show him where this practice was therein commanded. None of the reasons which the pastor gave to defend the rite impressed Bohni, who countered with logic and biblical passages, the "usual Anabaptist excuses."

The Basel city council had both of the Bohni brothers arrested and imprisoned in the Spalen Tower, where they underwent long interrogations by both the secular and churchly authorities. The prisoners refused to name those who had previously visited them and those whom they had visited. Andreas Bohni called the clergy hirelings and said that every Christian who received the Holy Spirit was privileged to teach the congregation. The Basel church officials added in their report that the reasons such false teaching occurred were that open sins were not punished and that often the pastors and the officials themselves practiced what they publicly criticized.

Andreas Bohni was expelled and threatened with severe punishment if he dared to return to the Basel area. In a letter to the mayor he said that the authorities should punish the wicked and protect the good; it may be necessary at times for the Christian to disobey man if obeying would mean disobeying God (Acts 5:29). Bohni did return once more to Basel and was again imprisoned. From his cell he wrote a long letter to the mayor and council calling on the city to repent of its terrible sins "in these last terrible and disturbed times." He was expelled for the second time after being placed in the stocks in April 1707. Bohni then found his way to Schwarzenau.

Activity in Württemberg

Separatist activity in Württemberg centered around Johann and Johanna Kipping. A mason from Oberstenfeld, Johann Kipping came to public attention in August 1706 when he refused to permit his third child to be baptized. As a result he was imprisoned in a tower in Beilstein and his infant baptized against his wishes.

At this hearing, Kipping stated that he could not believe that the baptism would be of any use to his child. True baptism required a believing baptizer and a believer receiving the baptism. An infant child, however, could not yet have any faith; moreover, he did not consider the pastor who baptized this child to be truly converted. He could not observe that either old or young who were baptized as infants had been changed in their lives. The apostles had neither commanded nor practiced infant baptism, which, in fact, came from the anti-Christian practices of the pope. Kipping stated that he had been led to these views by an old Anabaptist book borrowed from a local Pietist.

It was revealed at the hearing that three years before this incident, Kipping had been a member of a Pietist conventicle at nearby Bottwartal. A leading figure there was Eberhard Ludwig Gruber, who later became a leader of the Inspired. Another influence was the Radical Pietist itinerant Johann Georg Rosenbach. Kipping testified that these leaders had convinced him that the state church could not be the true church, because so many godless people were members of it. Therefore, he could not himself attend or take Communion. Instead, he believed that the true church was to be found in those who had Christ in their hearts.

The consistory sent theologians to reason with Kipping; they hoped to reclaim him because other propertied Pietists had already left the province to settle in Wittgenstein. When this approach failed to achieve any result, the authorities expelled Kipping from Württemberg. His children were detained, to be cared for by local officials. At that point Kipping's wife decided to stay to care for the children; according to this account she did not agree with her husband's religious views. This may have been a false perception, because only two years later Johanna Kipping became one of the first members of the Brethren at Schwarzenau.

ACTIVITY IN HESSE-KASSEL

Two Radical Pietist evangelists—Heinrich Horch (Horche) and Samuel König—itinerated through Hesse-Kassel at the beginning of the eighteenth century. They were able to awaken a number of persons, who came to question the validity of the state church structure, the practice of infant baptism, and the irregular lives of church members and leaders. The ruler, Landgrave Karl, issued a stern edict in September 1702, attacking this Pietist incitement to separation.

A central figure in Hessian Pietism was Georg Grebe of Kassel. He was a respected and wealthy craftsman, having secured the position of gunsmith at the Hessian court. His generosity was evidenced by the hospitality he gave to five ladies, all sisters, from the Von Callenberg family of nearby Rothenstein. Because of their attachment to Pietism, they were harshly treated by their relatives and found refuge in Grebe's home in Kassel.

When Grebe made his way to Schwarzenau to find toleration, the ladies Von Callenberg followed. Lady Clara Elizabeth moved into Grebe's humble dwelling near Schwarzenau and left a record of her life there. She later became well known in Pietist circles as the wife of the French nobleman and mystic Charles Hector Marquis St. George de Marsay. Several of the Von Callenberg sisters fell in with the notorious cult led by Eva von Buttlar, also from Hesse, who had moved shortly before this to a village near Schwarzenau. Portraying herself and two associates as the Holy Trinity, she led deluded members in orgiastic ceremonies to achieve ritual purity. When the scandalous practices of the outwardly benevolent community were revealed, the reputations of all Pietist movements were harmed.

Activity in the Palatinate

It was late in 1700 that the first complaints about the "new sect of the so-called Pietism" were heard in the Palatinate. An official report asserted that the movement was infiltrating virtually everywhere and infecting Palatine subjects and servants. Two years later specific evidence was found in the village of Lambsheim near Frankenthal, west of Mannheim. A laborer, Mattheis Baumann, had influenced several others to break with the established church. After several confrontations with the authorities, about 1719 Baumann immigrated to Pennsylvania where he organized a perfectionist group called the New Born.

In 1706 four members of the Reformed Church in Lambsheim—
Johannes Traut, Jacob Bossert, Jacob Berg, and Adam Pfarr—came
to the attention of the government as Pietists when they refused to
swear the customary oath of loyalty expected of all subjects. The
four were arrested and later expelled; they emerged later as members of the Brethren movement.[15]

Attention shifted during the same year to Schriesheim, a village
about five miles north of Heidelberg. The central figure in the Pietist
activity there was Alexander Mack, later to become famous as the
leading figure among the Brethren. Mack was born in 1679 as the
eighth child of Johann Philip Mack, a prosperous and respected
miller, member of the local council and mayor, and elder of the
Reformed Church.

When the oldest son of the Mack family died, the ten-year-old
Alexander had to learn the miller's trade in order to help his older
brother Hans Jacob. It is, therefore, unlikely that he received more
than an elementary education. In early 1701 Alexander Mack married Anna Margaretha Kling, the daughter of another propertied
and influential citizen, Johann Valentin Kling.

It is not completely clear how Mack became estranged from the
Reformed parish in which he grew up. It is known that he came
under the influence of Hochmann von Hochenau, the Radical
Pietist leader. In 1705-06 Mack met Hochmann in the Marienborn
area (near Büdingen), one of the few areas of comparative religious
tolerance in the Germanies. Mack invited the charismatic speaker to
visit him in Schriesheim. This took place in the summer of 1706 with
the arrival of Hochmann and a companion.

Hochmann began to hold meetings in the large room of Mack's
mill, also preaching in the streets to workers who were returning to
their homes in the village after laboring in the fields. According to
local officials, more than fifty had joined the Pietistery and hundreds more would have come if the visitors had not been driven
from Schriesheim.

Some of the party dispersed to small villages nearby and later
to Mannheim where they were arrested. Mack himself was almost
imprisoned there when he demanded to see his brethren.
Hochmann and the others were sentenced to hard public labor on a

bread and water diet. The punishment, however, backfired, for many churchgoers from Mannheim flocked to the embankments where Hochmann was working, so that they could hear him speak. Beatings failed to stop the nobleman from preaching and only earned him more sympathy from the onlookers.

The foreign prisoners were soon released and expelled from the Palatinate, although the Palatine subjects were still detained. The Elector Palatine, Johann Wilhelm, issued a harsh edict mandating that anyone suspected of Pietism was to be arrested without trial and put to hard labor. Energetic action was thought necessary because of the "hypocritically good appearance" of the sect.

This forced Mack to decide whether to persist in following the new teaching or not. He decided to stay loyal to his new-found faith and determined to leave his home. During the previous spring he had sold his half of the mill to his older brother; the two had been granted the mill four years before because of their mother's death and their father's unease about the troubled times in which they were living. In October 1706 Mack sold most of the inheritance from his father, who had died four months earlier. He, his wife, and two sons then left for Schwarzenau, which he had heard offered religious freedom.[16]

Despite the expulsion of Hochmann and the departure of Mack, Pietist activities continued. Mack's father-in-law Kling became the leader of the small conventicle at Schriesheim. He broke with the Reformed church when the pastor demanded that he sign a statement denouncing his son-in-law. Kling continued to hold meetings in his home and refused to attend the local parish church. In May 1708 Kling and three others were seized as they sang a psalm in Kling's home. Eventually, following a long hearing, they were released.

The experience did not prevent them from continuing their meetings. One year later (April 1709) some of the same group were arrested in the home of the buttonmaker Martin Lucas in Heidelberg. Again the prisoners were closely questioned by a commission. They were forced to tell the names of others of their group in the Palatinate. They testified that they had been impelled to leave the Reformed Church because of the sinful lives of the laity and clergy. They knew two men who had the apostolic gift of interpreting the scriptures, Alexander Mack and Hochmann von Hochenau.

When asked about the nature of their meetings, they described them in this way:

> When they come together they sing two or three hymns, as God moves them; then they open the Bible and whatever they find they read and explain it according to the understanding given to them by God, for the edification of their brethren. After they have read, they fall to their knees, raise their hands to God, and pray for their authorities that God might move them to punish the evil and protect the good. Then they praise God that He has created them for this purpose.[17]

The authorities were determined to crush the gathering of Pietists. Some were expelled and placed with a military regiment in the Brabant. Martin Lucas and his wife were expelled; their children were seized and their home sold to defray the costs of raising the children. Most of those involved with Pietist activities in the Palatinate found their way to the Wittgenstein or Marienborn areas and many were later brought into the Brethren movement. Kling, however, remained in Schriesheim.

Radical Pietist activity in several places in the Germanies led to suppression and often to expulsion of those participating in it. Many of those driven out made their way as religious refugees to Wittgenstein. Once there, in comparative safety, they passionately discussed the next stage of their pilgrimage.

2

Formation of the Movement

Religious refugees in the early 1700s had heard of one territory where they might be able to find freedom of religion and a secure residence. This was the country (*Grafschaft*) of Wittgenstein, now located in the southeastern tip of the state of North-Rhine-Westphalia. Although otherwise an unimportant and poorly favored land, Wittgenstein was made famous by the policy of toleration in religious matters maintained by its sovereign Henrich Albrecht (ruled 1698-1723). The ruling family was divided into two branches—one led by Henrich Albrecht residing at Laasphe to which the village of Schwarzenau/Eder belonged, the other led by the Countess Hedwig Sophie and her son Casimir at Berleburg.

Wittgenstein was a hilly, even mountainous, area with a stony soil. It was bounded on the west, north, and south by mountains. Two rivers, the Eder in the north and the Lahn in the south, originated on its western border and ran through the land to the east. Their valleys provided the county with its best farmland; the waterways also opened the region to travel. The rolling hills were covered with evergreens which provided lumber and also fuel for the making of charcoal. Slate mines provided another source of revenue but as a whole the county was poor.

Henrich Albrecht's father Gustav Otto (ruled 1683-98), of the Reformed faith, accepted a colony of French Reformed (Huguenot) refugees in the latter part of the seventeenth century, following the expulsion in 1685 of French Protestants by Louis XIV. This generous act helped to set a precedent for Henrich Albrecht's policy of toleration.

Upon his father's death the forty-year-old Henrich Albrecht became the ruler of the small county. While remaining a nominal member of the Reformed Church, he was himself favorably impressed by Pietism and often invited Pietist leaders to his castle at Laasphe or to the manor house at Schwarzenau. Four of his sisters became Pietists and actually married commoners, a shocking act in that era of stringent class distinctions.

His policy of toleration was probably also influenced by economic concerns. He needed to attract settlers to his thinly populated county, still seeking to recover from the devastation of the Thirty Years War. A scholar reported, "As a consequence of the terrible tax burden and the other miseries of the war, the [Wittgenstein] peasants abandoned their farms, fled into the woods, or were victims of the military events."[1] The "repellent poverty" of Wittgenstein around 1700 was notorious.

Religious dissenters had the reputation of being hardworking artisans and farmers, thus a policy of toleration and mild usage could encourage their immigration. Henrich Albrecht promised newcomers land on long-term lease; they were freed from the usual burdensome fees and personal services, including military obligations. There was only one modest yearly tax levied on their land.

Schwarzenau and its surrounding area were set aside as a center of settlement, attracting religious refugees from many German states and several foreign nations. A report to the imperial cameral court (*Reichskammergericht*) of 1710 complained that "from all over the world—Halle, Hesse, the Palatinate, Switzerland, Holland, and England—vagabonds, Pietists, Anabaptists, Quakers and Mennonites, had banded together, in number about four hundred, and had filled the lands of Berlebourg and Wittgenstein."[2]

At the turn of the century the village of Schwarzenau consisted only of a mill, a few small houses, and the imposing manor house. Most of the new settlers were given land on the wooded hills overlooking the village. There they built crude shelters and cabins. One clearing above Schwarzenau on the path to Berleburg was settled by those who later became Brethren. It is still known as the Valley of Huts (*Hüttental*).

The Valley of Huts (*Hüttental*) above Schwarzenau/Eder. The Alexander Mack Museum is contained in the long building in the upper-left portion of the photograph. *BHLA Collection.*

Preparation for the First Baptism

Those gathering in and around Schwarzenau were a colorful lot whose only common characteristic was distaste for the established churches. These separatists came from a variety of church backgrounds, from Catholic to Unitarian. Not surprisingly there emerged among them sharp differences in religious views. Some became hermits and isolated themselves in the forest, living on a minimum of food. Most carried on some trade such as weaving or devoted themselves to lumbering and farming.

Some of those in Schwarzenau became concerned about the problems that religious freedom brought with it. They recalled the

scandalous excesses of the Eva von Buttlar society in nearby
Sassmannshausen, so recently exposed (1704). There were those
who became so disillusioned about disunity in Wittgenstein that
they returned to their original homes to rejoin the state churches.

Others, however, had an ardent desire to follow Christ's teachings in all things and came to the prayerful conclusion that they had
to create some new form of church community. Thus wishing to
obey Christ's commandments, they called attention to the eighteenth chapter of Matthew's Gospel, where, in dealing with discipline, the text enjoins followers to settle disputes in the church.
They reasoned that they could not follow this command if there
were no church community.

As this small group considered how necessary obedience in faith
was for salvation, they were confronted with the New Testament
command to be baptized. They had learned from Hochmann von
Hochenau that infant baptism was not scriptural. As early as 1703
some of his followers had urged, "You men, dear brethren; we must
be baptized according to the teachings of Jesus and the apostles."
The opposition they encountered prevented them from carrying this
out at that time, but they did not forget this imperative.

Then, according to an early account, in 1706 two "foreign
brethren" visited them and spoke of the baptismal necessity. The
visitors may have been members of the Dutch Collegiants, a contemporary immersionist party with whom the Brethren later had
close connection. Response to this catalyst revealed that some of
them had been pondering baptism for some time without recognizing that others shared their concern.

This realization was followed by a lengthy period of intensive
Bible study to be sure that their wish was solidly based upon the scriptures. They also pored over the works of Gottfried Arnold to learn
about the practices of the early Christian church. The result was "They
found in trustworthy histories that the early Christians during the first
and second centuries were planted into the death by crucifixion of
Christ, according to the commandment of Christ, through trine immersion" (Sander Mack). As had the Anabaptists before them, those who
became Brethren concluded that they must cast off traditional religious
observances to model their lives and worship on the primitive church.[3]

INVITATION TO THE FIRST BAPTISM

Following this period of intense preparation, the small group of religious refugees at Schwarzenau decided to act. In the eloquent words of Sander Mack,

> Finally, in the year 1708, eight persons agreed together to establish a covenant of good conscience with God, to accept all ordinances of Jesus Christ as an easy yoke, and thus to follow after their Lord Jesus—their good and loyal shepherd—as true sheep in joy or sorrow until the blessed end....These eight persons united with one another as brethren and sisters in the covenant of the cross of Jesus Christ as a church of Christian believers.[4]

Early in July 1708 they wrote to Hochmann von Hochenau for his advice about their intention to form a congregation through baptism. He answered them from his Nürnberg prison in a letter addressed to Georg Grebe and Alexander Mack. It was his firm conviction that infant baptism could nowhere be found in scripture and that believer's baptism by immersion after a confession of faith was expressly commanded.

He cautioned them, nonetheless, that they must carefully test their desire before God to make sure that it was truly a divine leading. They must "count the cost" to see if they were ready to suffer the trials that would undoubtedly come. (As they had all been baptized as infants, a new baptism fell under the rigorous penalties of existing law.) His further concern was that they must be careful not to become sectarian by insisting that everyone must be baptized, for "promptings on this matter are varied." His attitude was the same about the observance of the Lord's Supper and feetwashing.[5]

During this period the eight persons who became the first Brethren sent out an open letter to Pietists in the Palatinate (the former home of many of them), after drawing lots to determine who should compose the letter. The anonymous writer began by describing how their conviction had grown about their need to be baptized in apostolic manner, quoting the Great Commission (Matthew

28:19-20) and calling for obedience to the commandment of the Lord Jesus Christ. Baptism was a covenant of a good conscience with God (1 Peter 3:21); they were to be baptized into the death of Jesus (Romans 6). The letter concluded, saying, "As Christ, our head and keeper, had lowered Himself into the water, so must we of necessity, as His members, be immersed with him."

Obedience required following Christ's precepts and example. Similarly, obedience demanded the exercise of church discipline for the correction of those in error and the preservation of good order. If these commandments were followed, then it would be possible to commune with integrity. The writer invited readers of the letter to join with them in the planned baptism:

> So, then, if some more brethren wish to begin this high act of baptism with us out of brotherly unity according to the teachings of Christ and the apostles, we announce in humility that we are interceding together in prayer and fasting with God. We will choose him, whom the Lord gives us as the baptizer as God will reveal to us.

The last sentence reveals a serious problem facing the earnest group. Who was to baptize them? They called upon Alexander Mack to perform this, as he was their leader in teaching the word. Mack, however, considered himself to be unbaptized and first needed to be baptized correctly before he could baptize others. The Mennonites were a possible source, for they practiced the baptism of adult believers, but they practiced baptism by pouring. The Schwarzenau eight had become convinced through study of the scriptures and of church history that three-fold immersion was the apostolic mode.[6]

THE FIRST BAPTISMS PERFORMED

They found strength in this dilemma in Jesus' promise that "where two or three are gathered in my name, there am I in the midst of them" (Matthew 18:20). After additional fasting and prayer, they drew lots to see which of the brothers would baptize Mack. After this was done, they went to the clear waters of the Eder Brook early one summer morning of 1708. The brother chosen by lot immersed Mack, who baptized his baptizer and then the other six. They promised never to reveal who had performed the first baptism so that no one could ever call them by that person's name. They left no record of the month or the day, but an analysis of early records reveals that it took place sometime during the first two weeks of August.

The eight participants were Alexander and Margaretha Kling Mack, Andrew and Johann Nöthiger Bohni, Johann and Johanna Kipping, Georg Grebe, and Lukas Vetter (like Grebe, from Hesse-Kassel). The account by Sander Mack reports, "After they had all emerged from the water..., they were all immediately clothed inwardly with great joyfulness. This significant word was then impressed upon them through grace: 'Be fruitful and multiply' (Genesis 1:28)." Their immediate reaction was to spread widely the word of their new initiative, first in the Schwarzenau area and then farther afield. A contemporary record stated that the response was so great that there was no hall large enough to contain their meetings, forcing them to hold meetings outside. A lot is still pointed out in Schwarzenau as the "Anabaptist lawn" (*Täufer Garten*) where this took place.

Sander Mack explained that "after this the...eight persons were more and more powerfully strengthened in this newly begun obedience in faith to witness publicly about the truth in meetings. The Lord especially imparted His grace in them too, so that more became obedient to the faith." A critical Swiss writer corroborated this result, stating, "In these muddied waters the New Baptists (*Neutäufer*) fished after 1708 with success, inasmuch as they found it easy to win the over-excited people to their teachings." By 1715 a large congregation was reported to be active at Schwarzenau.[7]

REACTION OF THE AUTHORITIES

News of the illegal baptism and the rapid growth in Wittgenstein did not go unnoticed by the rulers of surrounding territories, who were indignant at Henrich Albrecht for permitting religious dissent. One especially, a brother-in-law named Carl Ludwig, did all he could to make trouble for the Wittgenstein count. He wrote directly

Brethren visitors to Schwarzenau in the early twentieth century, among the first of many to make the pilgrimage to the site of the first Brethren baptisms. *BHLA Collection.*

to Henrich Albrecht and to the count's relatives, complaining in strong language about the latter's policy of toleration. He then wrote to all of the neighboring nobility, a great number of other rulers, and repeatedly the imperial officials whose duty it was to enforce the regulations of the Holy Roman Empire, German Nation. He also complained to Henrich Albrecht's liege lord, the landgrave of Hesse-Darmstadt, who responded with a threatening letter to Wittgenstein.

Henrich Albrecht rejected all of the charges out of hand, pointing out that he was responsible only to the imperial government on such matters. Furthermore, he argued, those settlers who had come to his land were a quiet-living and devout folk who did not deserve to be treated as criminals. Fortunately for the new Brethren, the imperial bureaucracy was so ponderous that officials did not get around to investigating the charges made in 1710 until ten years later. By that time the Brethren had left the Schwarzenau area.

REACTIONS OF THE SEPARATISTS

The dramatic baptismal initiative of the Brethren met with both interest and criticism on the part of Radical Pietist separatists, their recent associates. Hochmann von Hochenau heard about the baptisms in November when he reached the Marienborn area after being released from the Nürnberg prison. His former followers immediately asked for his opinion of this act. In a letter to the Pietist-minded Count of Solms he wrote that when he heard of the baptism, he "brought the matter before God in prayer, and therefore came to the conclusion that I should remain in impartial Christian love with all, the baptized as well as the nonbaptized." He emphasized the necessity for an inner baptism without which the outward baptism was meaningless.

In a second letter to Christian Liebe in the Palatinate, he repeated the above statements, again warning against their making of baptism a cause of division; he stressed the need for love and tolerance in these matters. Later, he was to become much more critical of the Brethren because he felt they, indeed, had become sectarian: "A person who has not been baptized at all but is truly humble would be much more preferable to me than such an arrogant saint who insists only on dipping and despises others on that account."[8]

Another separatist and disciple of Jakob Boehme, Johann Georg Gichtel, who lived in Amsterdam, commented about the Brethren in some of his many letters to associates in Germany. Gichtel said of the Brethren that they baptized by immersion and held feetwashing and communion but refused to let anyone participate in the latter who was not first baptized by them. He said that one of the Brethren (no doubt Mack) shared his considerable means with others and thereby gained followers. Gichtel predicted that the movement would be short-lived. The separatist movements were as critical of each other as they were of the state churches.

Yet another critic was Eberhard Ludwig Gruber, the former pastor and theologian from Württenberg with whom Johann Kipping earlier had Pietist connections.[9] Gruber had lost his church position because of his separatist views and found asylum, first, in the Marienborn area and, later, in Schwarzenau. In 1713 he directed a long questionnaire to the Brethren with forty probing questions in order to obtain their "opinions more fully and authentically" on the "new baptism and church." The young Brethren movement accepted the challenge and published the questions with responses written by their leader Alexander Mack in July 1713 as *Basic Questions*. This is the first known Brethren publication.[10]

Two years later Mack wrote a more extended treatise, composed in the popular style of a conversation between father and son. The title may be translated as *Rights and Ordinances of the House of God* (1715). In the book, the son is made to complain that he has been attacked because of his beliefs on baptism; he would like to hear from his father the reasons for it. The father replies, using both Old and New Testaments and church history. The range of topics in the book besides baptism is broad: communion, separation, the ban, oathtaking, excuses of nonbelievers, and rewards for believers, among others. These reflect the major criticisms of the Brethren by their separatist opponents.[11]

EXPANSION OF THE BRETHREN

In the wake of the Schwarzenau baptisms, a number of congregations were established by the zealous Brethren, including the Wittgenstein area itself, the Marienborn area, the Lower Rhine area, the Netherlands, the Palatinate, Hamburg-Altona, and Switzerland.

THE WITTGENSTEIN AREA

Following the first baptism, the eight immediately became zealous in witnessing to their newly found faith. They were convincing because they were convinced. Often their radiant lives impressed onlookers and attracted growing interest, which often ripened into the desire to join a group of that character. Their zeal was translated into a period of intense growth.

uproar. The officials ordered Naas and the participants to leave, but the count postponed the order to allow for another meeting of the church consistory to pass on the event.[16]

Gottfried Neumann (one of those baptized) later wrote a letter describing the Brethren to the Pietist leader August Hermann Francke at Halle to explain why he joined the movement. He later left them to join the Inspired, only to move on to the Moravians. Here is an excerpt from his letter, written in 1719, which well captures the contemporary atmosphere:

> At this time a special awakening arose in the hearts of many among the friends in this land, who did not wish to remain longer in such division and indifference. They therefore began to unite in prayer and edify one another from the Holy Word. They were called New Baptists [*Neue-Täufer*] because they practiced, among other well-seeming ordinances, baptism of adults by immersion. They were mostly single-minded and good souls.
>
> They displayed at first a great earnestness and zeal in their behavior and conduct, through which many were moved and were drawn into their circle. Finally, they were also able to affect me through their affectionate and humble manner, and through their strong "magic," they induced me to be baptized.[17]

The tempest caused by these fourth baptisms might have subsided, as had the preceding ones, had it not been for the arrival of the Inspired or Community of True Inspiration (the group which later founded the Amana colonies in Iowa). Curiously, a key leader was Eberhard Ludwig Gruber who had severely criticized the Brethren as sectarian just one year earlier.[18]

The excitement aroused by this dramatic movement soon overshadowed that caused by the Brethren, for the latter were generally very quiet, coming only under public gaze through their baptisms. The Inspired believed that their leaders had the gift of divine prophecy; they called them Instruments (*Werkzeuge*) of God. When seized by inspiration, they went into a trance accompanied by violent bodily motions and odd cries. After a time in this state, they delivered coherent speech or testimony, speaking as if they were God.

In these prophecies they often critiqued individuals, especially the rulers. When this happened publicly, naming Karl August, the count lost all patience and decreed that all settlers who did not abandon open demonstrations (which included baptisms) must leave the county. This posed a great problem for the Brethren in the Marienborn area. Must they give up their homes once again because of their faith? The count's decree permitted them to remain if they would limit their activities to small groups meeting privately in homes.

They decided to leave. If they could not practice their newly won beliefs in their entirety, including conducting the baptisms that were so meaningful to them, they must seek another place where they hoped to enjoy greater freedom. In faith they trusted that the Lord would provide an asylum. The local officials provided them with a passport which certified their good character—"They have so conducted themselves in their civil lives that no one can reasonably bring anything against them." The only problem was their insistence on holding public meetings, which the count would not permit. "As they are resolved to leave here and transfer their residence elsewhere, we therefore warmly recommend to everyone to aid them in their undertaking as evidence of our good will."[19]

THE LOWER RHINE AREA

As the Brethren left they headed in a northwesterly direction, their destination the town of Krefeld on the Lower Rhine, not far from the Dutch border. They had heard that this was another of the few places of toleration among the German states. In the seventeenth century Krefeld had been the property of the house of Nassau-Orange and thus shared in the liberal religious policy of the Netherlands. Between 1697 and 1702 it had been independent, and after 1702 it came under Brandenburg-Prussian rule.

Krefeld had prospered by allowing Mennonites to settle there, who introduced a flourishing textile industry. The Prussian rulers were more pragmatically tolerant than many of the other monarchs in the Germanies; for the sake of economic development, they were willing to relax laws against religious dissenters, despite repeated complaints from the Reformed clergy along the Lower Rhine. The Mennonites in Krefeld enjoyed sufficient toleration to own their own meetinghouse but had lost some of their earlier vitality as they became successful business people. The zealous Brethren had much in common with them; partly for this reason many Mennonites were attracted to this newer and more active group. A Swiss separatist visiting the area wrote back to his friends about the Brethren: "As they had completed their harvest in Marienborn, the Palatinate, Schwarzenau, and around those areas, they came to this district....They have a great zeal to impress their beliefs upon the conscience of men through the authority of the Holy Scriptures. They are gathering a great number of poor people...." Even one of the Mennonite lay pastors was evidently baptized by the Brethren in the Rhine River in 1724.[20]

Another Mennonite pastor preached a sermon (the text of which has been preserved) at Krefeld in 1716 to uphold the traditional Mennonite practice of adult baptism by pouring water over their heads. He granted that immersion was the original form of baptism of the early church but doubted that it was necessarily always practiced in this fashion. He accepted as valid the mode of immersion on which the Brethren insisted, though he maintained that several forms were acceptable and therefore appealed for moderation on this point.

A census of Krefeld residents taken about 1716 lists several Brethren—Johannes Naas, Hans Jakob Preiß, Peter Becker, Martin Lucas, Lukas Vetter, and Daniel Ritter. The last two named were on relief, a reflection of the hardships entailed in their relocation from the Marienborn area. Brethren names that can be established from other records include Stephan Koch, Johannes Preiß, J. Tilmann Haecker, Peter Schilpert, and Christian Liebe.[21] Several other Brethren families known to have left the Marienborn area may also have resided in or near Krefeld but their names have not been discovered (the Stumpf and Keim families may be listed under different spellings). Existing marriage records show that Johannes Naas was their pastor (literally "teacher"). In one record he is listed as acting as a character witness for two young couples from the congregation.

At nearby Duisburg, three Brethren—Johannes Naas, Peter

Schilpert, and a man named Höcker (perhaps J. Tilmann Haecker) —were called before the church consistory there for baptizing a number of people in the Rhine River in January 1717; they had also conducted love feasts and feetwashing services. They were accused at the consistorial hearing of misusing the toleration extended to the inoffensive Mennonites for their own evangelistic purposes. The three accused men gave as their rationale the Great Commission and the invalidity of infant baptism. After a severe interrogation, they were released but warned not to return.

The official Reformed Church of the area was very troubled by Brethren proselytizing. Clergymen pointed out in almost all of their synodal meetings after 1716 that the Brethren were not only winning converts from the Mennonites but also from their own Reformed parishes. The Krefeld pastors were delegated to secure from the Brethren living there answers to certain questions. The answers—this "creed" as they called it—were sent to the king of Prussia, in an attempt to convince him that the local officials should be ordered to suppress the heretical Brethren. The Reformed clergy were not successful in their appeal.

Solingen, not far from Krefeld and famous for its steel production, was also a center of activity. This was the home of Brethren who were sentenced to life imprisonment at hard labor because of their faith. Their story will be recounted later.

THE NETHERLANDS

Brethren also traveled in the Netherlands seeking converts, concentrating on but not limited to the Frisian areas. A Quaker journal records an encounter at Twisk in 1715 between an Anabaptist (from the description a Brethren adherent) and a traveling member of the Society of Friends, Thomas Story. Story reproved in his public testimony a respected local resident who advocated water baptism, contending that true baptism was by the Holy Spirit. The resident brought to a later meeting a stranger from Groningen to defend his cause.

According to Story's account, the stranger "began slily and smoothly to move some Conference about Matters of Religion, and more especially drew on towards the Subject of Baptism." Story was alert to the challenge when the stranger asserted that Jesus Christ had instituted a new baptism, a baptism by water, that replaced the baptism of John the Baptist. Story countered with Paul's statements in Ephesians (4:5) and 1 Corinthians (12:13) that there was but one baptism and that was the spirit of truth.

As the discussion continued, many more biblical passages were brought forth on both sides, including the question of Peter's (Acts 10:47) regarding the baptism of the centurion: "Can anyone forbid water?" The visiting Quaker insisted that water baptism was not commanded but rather a baptism of the Spirit, and, according to his account, he was able to silence both advocates of water baptism, who went away "under a Disappointment."[22]

Brethren activity continued in the Netherlands in the 1720s, particularly when the Schwarzenau congregation relocated there for nearly a decade. This story and that of Brethren remaining in the United Provinces after most of the former Schwarzenau congregation immigrated to Pennsylvania will be told later.

THE PALATINATE, HAMBURG/ALTONA, AND SCANDINAVIA

Scattered "lovers of the truth" were located in the Palatinate but because of the limitations placed upon Pietism there by the Catholic Electors Palatine, it was impossible to develop ongoing congregations. Those attracted to the Brethren generally migrated to the Marienborn or Schwarzenau areas. There is one later reference to the baptism of a sickly woman, conducted sometime before 1722 by Johannes Naas in the Rhine River near Mannheim. Although discouraged by her friends and family who feared that the exposure would mean her death, the invalid (who had been bedridden for years) insisted upon her baptism. According to the account, she arose from the water a whole and healthy individual who provided hospitality for the assembly.[23]

There were also Brethren at Altona, near Hamburg, at that time under Danish rule. It was known as a place of some toleration. Already by 1650 there was a group associated with the Mennonites who practiced immersion baptism and were therefore called *Dompelaars* (a Dutch term that could be translated as Dunkers). They continued during and after the Brethren era and may well have had some connection. Several individuals in Altona are known to have been Brethren. The most interesting story involves Jürgen Barthold Petersen, a fisherman. While serving in the army he became seriously concerned about the salvation of his soul. Upon his release he sought out a Protestant pastor, who evidenced little interest. When Petersen persisted, the pastor finally gave him a Bible and told him that everything necessary for his salvation was found in it. Although illiterate, Petersen persuaded some children to teach him how to read; within two weeks he was able to study the scriptures.

Becoming convinced from this study that the first Christians were baptized by immersion, he sought a religious fraternity that practiced baptism in that manner. Someone told him about such a group in Krefeld. He traveled there immediately and after some inquiry found a member of the Brethren congregation. This man welcomed him and urged him to stay there until the next Sunday when the request for baptism could be properly brought before the entire congregation. Petersen insisted upon immediate baptism and pleaded so vigorously that his host agreed to perform the ordinance. As it was wintertime, a hole had to be chopped in the ice before the act could be performed. Petersen returned to Altona where he remained until his death, keeping in touch with other Brethren from time to time by visits and correspondence.[24]

Two Danish brothers from Copenhagen named Simon and Søren Bølle, it is said, were baptized in Altona by Brethren from Krefeld. In the early 1740s the brothers founded separatist groups in Copenhagen and in Drammen, Norway. Søren Bølle, along with a shoemaker named J. Halvorsen, baptized eight adults in the Drammen River in 1742. Although the baptizers were immediately imprisoned, two other laymen from their circle, a schoolmaster Jørgen Kleinow and a Niels Markussen, baptized another twenty-five men and women the next year. The four leaders were expelled to Altona, with forty-eight sympathizers accompanying them. Some of the group later returned to Drammen; others remained in Altona. Søren Bølle returned to the state church of Altona in 1749. In the twentieth century, the Danish-led group Christ's Assembly (*Christi Menighed*) traced its connection to the Schwarzenau and Krefeld Brethren through the Bølle brothers.[25]

THE SWISS AREAS

That Brethren were active in the Swiss cantons has also been documented, although the history of actual congregations there is hazy. Christian Liebe was on a tour to Bern in 1714 to visit the "local brethren" when the authorities captured him. It is not clear whether this referred to a Brethren congregation or to the Mennonites living there. According to an account circulated within Pietist conventicles, a confrontation occurred in Switzerland between Mack and Hochmann von Hochenau. The latter had come to a meeting of the Brethren to demonstrate his impartial love, although he had become increasingly critical of Brethren practices of church discipline. The account has Mack responding to Hochmann's overture by calling him in the open meeting a hypocrite and false prophet. After the close of the meeting, Hochmann is said to have embraced and kissed Mack, saying, "Dear Brother Mack, when you are in heaven, and see me arrive there too, then you will rejoice and say 'Oh, look! There comes also our dear Brother Hochmann!'"[26]

It is likely that Brethren activity in Switzerland centered about Basel, the home area of Andreas Bohni. There are records of Anabaptists there in the early 1720s, but it is not known definitely whether the group was specifically connected with the Brethren. Several Swiss noblemen had close connections for a time with the Brethren.

An article in a Brethren publication in 1876 reported on a "body of religious people that very much resemble the Brethren." In the 1870s a member of the Brethren from Lena, Illinois, visited the group, who lived in the Swiss Alps, and interviewed their bishop. Although they had changed from a three-fold immersion baptism to a single immersion and no longer practiced feetwashing, it appeared to the visitor that they had descended from the Brethren in Germany. "It seems that when the persecution in Germany arose against Alexander Mack and his brethren, that some of them fled into the mountains of Switzerland for safety, and there, shut out from the busy world, have remained to this day, and now have a considerable number in the community." Although the editor of the journal was making further inquiry, nothing more is known about the Swiss group.[27]

Andreas Bohni was imprisoned in the *Spalentor* (Spalen Gate) in Basel, Switzerland, for disobeying the authorities. Wilbur Brumbaugh photo, *BHLA Collection.*

The total number of early Brethren in Europe is uncertain, because of the sparsity of reliable documentary evidence. Estimates have ranged from two hundred adult members to one thousand. Perhaps the figure of five hundred would be a safe estimate. Regardless of the exact numbers, the contemporary sources are unanimous in describing the great evangelistic zeal and vigor of the early Brethren. They were dedicated to sharing without ceasing the good news of their newly won faith. Originating with eight persons in 1708, their numbers grew remarkably in little more than a decade despite many outward restrictions.

NATURE OF BRETHREN BELIEFS

Because the Brethren were in reaction to what they considered to be an overly creedalized and dogmatic state church, they opposed any effort to spell out their beliefs in a systematic and complete fashion. It is therefore necessary to derive their beliefs from fragments secured from court records, letters, contemporary descriptions, and their own few publications.[28]

The first point that needs to be made is that the Brethren basically shared the orthodox Protestant beliefs established in the Reformation—especially the authority of scripture and the priesthood of all believers. Under questioning, the Solingen Brethren stated that they could accept all of the tenets of the Heidelberg Confession of the Reformed Church except those dealing with infant baptism, oath-taking, and the Calvinistic interpretation of justification by faith. Their differences with the established churches were not over doctrine; they were about religious freedom and the failure of the laity and the clergy of the churches to live moral lives.

The main contours of specific Brethren belief may be discerned as centering about the following themes: discipleship and obedience, restitution of the church, nonconformity and separation, church discipline, mutual aid, biblicism, and nonresistance. Their distinctive ordinances were important, but that will be discussed in a later chapter. This list does not exhaust their convictions but it is representative of their leading beliefs.

DISCIPLESHIP AND OBEDIENCE

All early Brethren writings expound the necessity of obedience as disciples to Jesus Christ their Lord. The only passage emphasized by italics in Mack's early treatises refers to the imperative of following the commandments of the Master: "[T]hat has always been the true faith and the true love of all saints and believers." Again, "If it is to be a saving faith, it must produce works of obedience."[29]

The unknown author of the open letter to the Pietists urged readers to join them in their baptismal intent, writing, "What is then better than being obedient and not despising the commandments of the Lord Jesus Christ, the King of all Glory!" The historical sketch by Sander Mack, based on conversations with his father and other early members, explained that "it was emphatically opened to them in their hearts how necessary is obedience in faith if a soul wishes to be saved."[30]

RESTITUTION

The concept of restitution has been defined as the "recovery of the life and virtue of the early church."[31] The early record is clear that Brethren accepted this Anabaptist concept of the church. In the account of the origins by Sander Mack, he described how the first eight members "felt powerfully drawn to follow again the footsteps of the first Christians"; they then asked Mack as their leader to baptize them "upon their faith after the example of the *first and best* Christians." We have seen that they studied the history of the early church as well as the New Testament to learn about the original form of baptism.[32]

A critical Swiss separatist, describing them in a letter of 1719, stated, "Their foundation, as is well known, rests on the mere letter of the scripture, and is an imitation of the early Christians." Brethren sought in their own patterns of worship and church life to follow in the footsteps of primitive Christianity.[33]

NONCONFORMITY

It was clear to the early Brethren that discipleship and restitution on the pattern of the early church would of necessity bring them into conflict with the general practices and expectations of society. They therefore emphasized the necessity of nonconformity and separation from the world. Brethren drew clear lines of conduct that would show everyone that they followed a different Master.

Although we do not have a complete picture of their early lives because of the lack of documentation, some clues are suggestive. From the beginning, Brethren restricted the appellations Brother and Sister to those who had been baptized into the community. All others were referred to as Friends, however saintly and pious they might be. There were several references to the male members wearing beards, a sign of nonconformity then as well as later; they were known as the "Bearded Ones" (*Bartleute*) in early documents. There is no mention of a specific style of dress in the early years.

CHURCH DISCIPLINE

Connected with this form of separation is that occasioned by church discipline, which loomed large in early Brethren discussion. Lengthy passages in Mack's *Rights and Ordinances* dealt with separation and the ban, because it was one of the points most disputed by Radical Pietists. The question followed, Why can a Christian not keep in fellowship with someone in sin, who persists in it despite loving admonition? The sin, after all, would rest on his shoulders. Would it not be more loving to stay in touch with him? In his answer Mack demanded absolute separation, saying that it was truly love (rather than feigned love) because it called sinners to repent instead of resting in their wickedness. He used the stark dichotomies of the Old Testament to document his point.

In *Basic Questions*, Mack had to respond to the question, Were they not "much more loving, meek, [and] humble" before their baptism than afterwards? Mack replied by condemning the kind of "pernicious, hypocritical love" they had learned while "still among the Pietists." They now realized that genuine love "hates and punishes wickedness and evil." In doing so, it is in fact more loving than a weakly tolerant love. That parent truly loves the child who disciplines it rather than allowing it to follow its own whims to destruction.[34]

So important was this part of church life to the early Brethren that they stressed it in their open letter of invitation to the baptism. "There is...an exact relationship and brotherly discipline, according to the teaching of Jesus Christ and His apostles. When a person does not better himself, after faithful warning, he must be expelled and cannot be treated any more as a brother." The hope, of course, was that this stringent action would bring former members to themselves, so that restoration and reconciliation could take place.[35]

MUTUAL AID

In a way surprising to modern ways of thinking, Brethren—along with other Anabaptist-minded groups—considered church discipline to be another and helpful form of mutual aid. Certainly, they would care for the physical needs of their sisters and brothers. But to care for the outward necessities and then neglect the inward spiritual need would not be a truly loving action.

All of the contemporary accounts related how much sacrificial care the early Brethren extended to their fellows. Mack, Sr., as we have seen, is said to have spent his patrimony helping out those in need. A Radical Pietist sneered that when Mack's money ran out, the movement would fall apart. When persecution came upon them, the Brethren braved great distances and difficulties to visit and comfort those imprisoned. Some visitors even offered to take the place of prisoners for a time so that the latter could regain their health.

The Brethren attitude toward property was that one "owned" material goods only in the sense of being a steward over them. Those in greater need had better claim to those things. Although mutual aid was directed first of all at the members of the community, it was not limited there. Brethren were known for their generosity to anyone in need.

3

Suppression and Migration

Because the formation of the Brethren movement was an act of civil disobedience to religious and political authorities, members met with varying degrees of suppression in the provinces in which they resided or traveled. Even in the relatively tolerant areas of Wittgenstein, Marienborn, and the Lower Rhine where they were able to found congregations, they were not completely free. Sander Mack summed up their early experience:

> Although on the one hand they found favor with God and the people, they also encountered enemies of the truth. Now and then persecution occurred for the sake of the Word. Some endured with joy the confiscation of their property. Others, however, had to endure bonds and imprisonment. Some spent only a few weeks, but others several years in prison....All were freed, however, with clear consciences through the miraculous providence of God.[1]

All of these incidents were not recorded, but in several cases, at least, there is surprisingly ample documentation.

An often repeated story of hardship involved Brethren leader Johannes Naas. He was said to have been seized by recruiters for the king of Prussia while traveling with Jakob Preiß near Krefeld. Naas was "a man of great physique and commanding personality" which made him attractive for the crack troop of the royal body-guard. Despite excruciating torture, Naas refused to accept enlistment. According to the story, he was then dragged before the king, who demanded to know the cause for rejection. Naas replied that he could not enlist because he was already enrolled in the service of Jesus Christ. The king is said to have accepted this reason and even rewarded him for his fidelity.[2]

A remarkably similar story is recorded of another Brethren man; it may have been the basis of the received Naas account:

> One John Fisher from Hall, who had been baptized, they would force against his conscience to [en]list in the king's service, and tormented him terribly for ten days together, [in] different ways. [B]ecause he would not comply with their wills, they tied his hands and feet together and by them hung him up, thrusting and beating him with sticks and pricking his body with pins to such a degree that his shirt became stiff with blood, and when he was quite faint and could stand no longer on his legs, they put him over a deep water and he tumbling into it, they pulled him out again by his legs, but at last when they had tired themselves with tormenting...him, and he still refusing to swear to the colours and take arms, they threw him into a hole....

He was delivered from this predicament by a prince who saw him and demanded his release.[3]

CHRISTIAN LIEBE ON THE GALLEYS

In the early summer of 1714 Christian Liebe with a companion (probably Andreas Bohni) traveled to Bern, Switzerland; his stated purpose was to "visit the local brethren, to minister, to solace, and to baptize someone if the occasion arose." As it happened, the Bernese city fathers had recently decided to institute draconian punishment for any Anabaptists, especially leaders, in their jurisdiction. For years they had been trying to suppress this persistent movement, using a variety of procedures. They were particularly exasperated that Anabaptists were returning to their area after being expelled. They decided that any able-bodied Anabaptist males caught should be sentenced to the galleys of the king of Sicily, others to be imprisoned for life.[4]

Despite the pleas for mercy from the Swiss Reformed clergy, "five Anabaptists [including Liebe] and one notorious thief" held in the prison-tower (*Käfigturm*) in Bern were forged into chains in late July 1714 to begin the arduous march over the Alps to Italy. When they reached Turin they were set to hard labor to spend the winter, before being sent on to the galleys. One of the Mennonites died there because of the harsh treatment.

They were not, however, abandoned to their fate. Andreas Bohni went to Turin to support them. He sent word to the Mennonites in Krefeld, who in turn passed on the information to their Dutch brethren. German and Dutch Mennonites immediately sent money to the prisoners in Turin, so they could purchase food from their jailors. The Dutch Mennonites also had good connections with the Estates General, the government of the Netherlands; they asked it to intervene with the Swiss authorities on behalf of the prisoners. The Estates General pointed out to the Bernese city fathers that both governments were currently applying diplomatic pressure on the French government because the latter had sentenced French Huguenots to the galleys. How could they expect the French to release the Huguenots if they found out that the Bernese were doing the same thing? Although the Bernese excused their action because of the stubbornness of the Swiss Anabaptists, they agreed to allow the release of the galley slaves if the Dutch Mennonites would guarantee that the prisoners would never return to the Canton of Bern.

While this diplomatic effort was underway, two Swiss noblemen of Pietist persuasion heard of the case and interceded with the Bernese authorities on their behalf. One named Nicolaus Samuel de Treytorrens became especially active. He was affiliated with the Brethren in Schwarzenau in 1709 before returning to Switzerland. After a friend had presented a petition from Christian Liebe's mother to the authorities, they promised to recommend Liebe's release from the Sicilians if a messenger would take the petition to them. De Treytorrens volunteered to do so.[5]

Aid was offered from yet a third side. An archbishop of the Church of England had heard of the case and offered to send money to aid the prisoners. In the meantime the prisoners had been transferred from Turin to Palermo in Sicily. There another of their number died, leaving but three—two Mennonites and Liebe. An agent of their Swiss Pietist friends reached them in Palermo, provided them with more funds, and arranged for better treatment.

Through the agent, in November 1715 the remaining prisoners sent an appeal, written by Christian Liebe, to the Dutch Mennonites; they expressed their willingness to avoid Bernese territory (the condition of their release) and urged the Dutch to expedite the diplomatic actions at Bern. Liebe wrote,

> We are greatly obliged to God and to the dear friends in Amsterdam, whom we shall repay as our strength allows....There are only three of us left, who warmly greet their dear friends who are concerned about us or ask about us in love....Let the dear friend Gossen Goyen [in Krefeld] know that we are still minded to hold out through the teachings of Jesus Christ....If we should not see or speak with each other in this world, may then God prepare both of us for His eternal Kingdom, where we can see one another with joy.[6]

After several complications and delays, the communication was finally sent from Bern to the king of Sicily asking for the release of all three prisoners. To effect this they were sent from Italy to Nice, France; De Treytorrens met them there and arranged transportation for them to Turin. Their weakened condition made it necessary to travel slowly. In Turin they received their final release. The two surviving Mennonites went to a refuge in western Switzerland, and De Treytorrens and Liebe went to Germany.

THE SOLINGEN BRETHREN

An equally well-documented story involves six young men from the steel-making town of Solingen in the Lower Rhine area.

The narrative describing their experiences is the most heartwarming of early Brethren history. The six were Johann Lobach, Johann Friedrich Henckels, Wilhelm Knepper, Gottfried Luther Stetius, Jacob Grahe, and Wilhelm Grahe. Wilhelm Grahe wrote the extended account of their arrest, trial, and imprisonment; it was treasured among Pietists who read it in their conventicles for its edifying quality and handed it down over the decades.[7]

Early in 1717 these six men were arrested in their native Solingen-Wald upon complaint of the Reformed clergy, as they had all been baptized into that faith as infants. News of their conversion through baptism by Brethren from nearby Krefeld and their subsequent private meetings for worship had been noised about. On February 1, the six were bound and marched off under heavy guard to Düsseldorf, where they were to be tried. Their joyful hymn singing attracted much attention among the Solingen citizens, who tended to sympathize with the prisoners.

They were accused of separation from the state church and of creating a new religion. They replied that their faith was not new but simply that of Jesus Christ. If their conduct seemed strange, it was only because the church "had strayed far from the truth and the right way." The judge told them that their conduct was blameless but that they must rejoin one of the three tolerated faiths—Lutheran, Catholic, or Reformed. They were to be given time to reconsider.

Six weeks passed in prison and then they were asked if they were ready to recant. Upon their refusal, they were held another six weeks. When this passed they were threatened with severe measures if they did not repent. Prisoners were tortured in the vicinity of their cells to shake their nerves, and then they were brought themselves to the door of the torture chamber; when the prisoners failed to respond, they were returned to their cells without harm. It had been a ruse to break their wills.

They were tormented in petty and severe ways by their jailors, but they stayed firm. Clergymen from all three established faiths visited them repeatedly to persuade them to change their minds, again to no avail. The prisoners spent most of their time reading and writing. They drafted a confession of faith which Wilhelm Knepper put into rhyme. He wrote some four hundred hymns during their captivity, nearly one hundred of which were included in the first Brethren hymnbook.

Finally, their case was sent to three theological faculties for judgment. The Roman Catholic faculty recommended the death penalty, the Lutheran faculty the galleys, and the Reformed faculty life imprisonment at hard labor. This last "milder" punishment was the one adopted. They were sentenced to spend the rest of their lives at hard labor at the fortress of Jülich near the Dutch border.

An armed escort marched them off from Düsseldorf early in December 1717. It took them three days to complete the thirty-mile trek because their legs were weak from their ten-month detention. Wilhelm Grahe related an incident of the trip, which sheds light on the attitude of the Solingen Brethren:

> It so happened as we were walking along toward Jülich that some of us with a few guards had gone ahead, and some others had lagged behind...so that I walked alone in the middle of the field far from both parties, and had no guards beside me. A man came from the side of the field and fell in with me. He saw then the first group going along with guards and asked what kind of people they might be. Then I said that I belonged to them too, and explained the situation to him. He was astonished that I was walking along alone and had no guards with me. I answered him that they did not worry about our running away. That was not necessary for us, for we did not fear any man, because Jesus, His truth and teaching were our protection and solace. I had many opportunities to escape;...I could have gone wherever I pleased, but the love of the truth and for my brethren kept us together.[8]

When they arrived at Jülich they were placed in the common dungeon known as the Bacon Pantry, a grim reference to the rodents infecting it. Twelve hardened criminals lodged there made their life miserable, taking delight in placing vermin in the clean clothes of the newcomers. They demanded an initiation treat of liquor, which the Brethren refused. What depressed the Brethren even more was that they were forbidden to sing in prison, and their Bibles were taken from them.

They were soon separated into three different cells. Through the efforts of the father of one of the prisoners, they were reunited in one dungeon located under the gate called *Paradise*. There they stayed nearly two years. Their cell was four feet deep in the ground, with walls ten feet thick. The slit for light was so narrow and the grating so thick, the sun shone in only three or four weeks of the year. While imprisoned together they organized their householding duties efficiently. They took turns cooking and cleaning the cell. They were able to supplement the prison ration of bread by purchasing peas, beans, and other legumes from the canteen. This they paid for with gifts from their visitors and by making buttons, a skill they learned from Johann Lobach. This handwork, of course, was only possible after their long days of hard labor.

In the summertime they had to work for six hours in the forenoon and six hours in the afternoon; in the wintertime, with its shorter days, the workday was also shorter, allowing more time for button making. During the first winter, they had to excavate dirt from a hole forty feet deep for the purpose of strengthening the fortification. In the spring they worked outside of the fort collecting trash. Much of the time they spent breaking up stones. Their worst task came in the late fall of 1718, cleaning debris out of the moat, so that none of the soldiers could escape. They had to work waist deep in cold waters for two weeks.

The treatment they received from the guards varied with the personnel. In general they won a remarkable degree of trust. As long as any two of them were inside the fortress, the others were allowed to move freely outside; it was well known that the love they bore each other would prevent anyone from escaping.

Despite this measure of freedom, their life was not an easy one. The summer of 1719 was extremely hot. All of the Brethren became seriously ill because of the continual change between their frigid dungeon and the heat in which they had to work. They were near death until the local physician arranged for them to be moved to better quarters. Because of their limited diet they developed scurvy so badly that their gums grew over their teeth. Once, Wilhelm

Grahe was almost crushed when a heavy framework he was helping to construct fell on him.

In 1720 the prisoners were often ill. Johann Lobach's letter in April describes their condition, though without a hint of complaint: "Brother Knepper suffers now daily from chills. Brother Henckel's legs are swollen, but not as much as usual. Brother Wilhelm Grahe still has pains in his legs. Therefore the other three of us, that is Brother [Jacob] Grahe, Stetius, and I go to work, but the others stay in the prison." Two months later the prisoners were separated; Wilhelm Grahe was placed in the common dungeon again, where he had to suffer at the hands of the other prisoners. "Each morning I had all I could do from six o'clock to ten o'clock to kill the lice and fleas. I was also maltreated in other ways."[9]

From the first days, the surprisingly high morale of the prisoners was maintained by numerous visits from Brethren and Mennonites, mostly from Krefeld. If the visitors were willing and able to pay the high costs of meals, it was usually possible for them to visit for several hours with the prisoners in the canteen. Once two of the visitors were allowed to stay overnight with the prisoners, but on another occasion, when two visitors offered to trade places with two of the ailing prisoners until they could regain their strength, their request was denied. The townspeople of Jülich were amazed at the number of visitors. Among the Brethren who came were Alexander Mack, Stephan Koch, Wilhelm Müller, Peter Becker, Johannes Naas, and Michael Eckerlin.

Late in 1719 two Dutchmen, who proved to be instrumental in securing the release, visited the Solingen prisoners. The men were Jan and Gilles de Koker, members of the Collegiant movement in the Netherlands. Upon their return home, they took up the case of the Solingen Brethren with the Dutch government. Another Dutchman heard of the prisoners while traveling in Germany and also appealed on their behalf to the Estates General.

The initial efforts of the Dutch government had no effect, because the German ruler, the Elector Palatine, was fully within his legal rights in punishing the prisoners because of their refusal to rejoin one of the three established faiths. The Dutch, nevertheless, persisted. As it happened, a representative of the Elector Palatine arrived in The

Hague seeking financial aid from the Estates General. He was told that as long as the Brethren were imprisoned solely because of their religious convictions, he could expect no satisfactory answer to his appeal. His report back to his superiors had the desired effect. The Elector issued a decree freeing the prisoners. There were two conditions of their release. Because the Solingen Brethren had been metalworkers, they were made to promise not to reveal secrets of their trade outside of their original home area. They also had to promise not to return to the Elector's territory. The prisoners agreed.

Finally, the day of release came on November 20, 1720, a few months short of four years of incarceration. The Solingen Brethren distributed most of their meager possessions to the remaining prisoners and said farewell to others. "Many rejoiced with us, yes, even officers and priests clapped their hands and wished us much blessing upon our freedom." Friends from Krefeld helped them to hire a horse and wagon to carry those too weak to walk. After three days of traveling they arrived in Krefeld and were greeted with much joy by the Brethren and Mennonites.[10] It is likely that such cases of suppression helped to convince the Brethren that they would do well to consider migration to more favorable locations. This they proceeded to do.

MIGRATIONS OF THE BRETHREN

Between the years of 1719 and 1740 almost all of the Brethren emigrated to North America. Traditionally, persecution suffered by the group as just recounted has been offered as the sole reason for the exodus. The promise of religious freedom in the New World must have sounded attractive to these harried dissenters. Yet, while the effects of governmental suppression should not be minimized, this does not fully explain their decision to leave their homeland. Toleration, after all, was still available to them in several places in Germany and more fully in the Netherlands.

The economic factor also played a considerable role in the decision to leave. Contemporary accounts invariably mention the difficulties the Brethren faced in making a living. The areas sheltering them were not especially prosperous. We have observed that Mack spent his patrimony in relieving the needs of his poor brethren.

Several of the Brethren families in Krefeld were listed on the relief rolls. The lure of cheap land in America was doubtless as attractive to the Brethren as it was for many other natives of German lands who made their away to America in the eighteenth century. Certain internal divisions also seemed to have played a role in their departure. A church squabble in Krefeld was cited by the Ephrata chroniclers as the reason for the first migration; although this was a biased source, eager to disparage the Brethren, it can not be entirely discounted.

It is not surprising that the Brethren chose Pennsylvania for their new home. There need have been no specific invitation to them, as sometimes claimed, to cause the eyes of the Brethren to turn to the "Island of Pennsylvania." William Penn had circulated extensive promotional materials about the charms and benefits of his colony through his agents on the continent. More effective even than these publications were personal communications arriving in Germany from those who had earlier made the journey. The perils of the risky ocean voyage and the hardships of resettlement were often forgotten or minimized in these letters, as the new Americans praised the freedom, abundant land, and healthy climate of the Middle Colonies. They advised potential immigrants to avoid both New England and the Southern colonies because of the harsh climatic conditions and oppressive state churches there.

An immediate connection for the Brethren was that between Pennsylvania and Krefeld. The first mass migration of German speakers traveled on the *Concord* in 1683. They established Germantown, which then became the port of entry for many later immigrants arriving from the German states. The Krefeld emigrants were of Mennonite background, but most had joined the Quakers shortly before their departure. It was natural that they reported back to their homeland about the conditions they experienced in the New World.[11]

THE KREFELD SCHISM AND THE FIRST MIGRATION

The congregation of Brethren in Krefeld flourished after the first members had arrived from the Marienborn area in 1715.

Unfortunately, a dispute about whether a member could marry outside of the congregation led to a major division. More than one hundred persons on the point of joining the congregation, it is said, were put off by the dissension. One of the leaders, Johannes Naas, who had taken the side of lenience in the quarrel, is thought to have withdrawn from the Brethren for a time.

For whatever reason, a large number of Krefeld Brethren, under the leadership of Peter Becker, did decide in 1719 to migrate to Pennsylvania. Tradition has it that twenty families accompanied him, including most of those who had been active in the Marienborn area. It is said that they left from Friesland on a large Flemish vessel, which experienced a severe storm underway. When the despairing captain observed the fervent prayers of the Brethren, he took heart again, because he believed that "the Almighty would not, for their sakes, permit them to perish in the deep."[12]

The departure of the Brethren from Krefeld occasioned delight and relief on the part of the Reformed clergy of the Lower Rhine. They had been greatly exercised about the loss of their members to the Brethren. The Moers Synod of July 1719 heard the report that these people, "who have been most damaging to our church, are said to have departed by water and sailed away to Pennsylvania." Similar reports and expressions of pleasure were recorded for the synods of Cleves and Berg, revealing the extent of Brethren activity in the region.[13]

THE KREFELD BRETHREN WHO REMAINED

Not all of the Brethren in Krefeld left for America. A nucleus remained, including most of the Solingen Brethren. Christian Liebe, the former galley slave who had been one of the protagonists in the schism, also stayed in the area. The Ephrata chroniclers claimed that he dropped away from the congregation, but there is evidence that he remained active. In 1736 Andreas Bohni recommended him to relatives as a person who would help them in the course of their emigration. To his death in 1757, Liebe remained in close correspondence with the Pennsylvania Brethren.

In 1733 Johannes Naas sent greetings to the brethren in Krefeld; named were Grahe, Schmitz, Liebe, Lobach, Müller, Rahr, Lingen,

Zwingenberg, and also Frau Benders and Frau Mummert. A Krefeld document of 1737 created during the allegiance ceremony at the ascension to the throne of Friedrich II has a separate list at the end of Mennonite names, certainly referring to the continuing Brethren congregation. Names mentioned there are Johann Georg Schmitt, Johannis Zwingenberg, Willem Brun, Wilhelmus Müller, Wilhelmus Grahe, and Lotter [Luther] Stetius. These names may represent many of the continuing congregation.

A reference in a communication from the Krefeld Reformed consistory in 1737 complained that "the *Täuffer*, as is well known, are placed on the same level and are treated as Mennonites in this town." Scattered evidence in the Krefeld archives reveals that the congregation was in existence into the 1740s. After that time, members tended to die off, join the Mennonites, or drift back into religious separatism.[14]

Most is known about two of the Solingen Brethren, Johann Lobach and Gottfried Luther Stetius. For a time they lived together in a small house there. Until the authorities suppressed it in 1731, along with one from the Catholics, Lobach conducted a school for children in the congregation; authorities also confiscated his extensive library, which was auctioned off in 1739. Stetius married their housekeeper, and after her death, remarried. He became a member of the Mennonite congregation, the church of his second wife. Both Lobach and Stetius were well known in Pietist circles for their spiritual gifts. They were close friends of the Reformed Pietist writer and counselor Gerhard Tersteegen, who often corresponded with them.

Lobach's correspondence was considered so edifying that it was collected, copied, and circulated among Pietist circles for many years. It was extensive, even reaching North America. His special correspondent in Pennsylvania was Stephan Koch, member of the Brethren at Germantown and later a brother at Ephrata. In 1750 a local Pietist wrote the Wittgenstein Pietist Charles Hector de Marsay that "our dear Brother Johannes Lobach passed into eternity last week with a serene, joyous spirit, after lying ill with a fever about five weeks." A friend penned a long poem, "A Rhymed Consideration of the Christian Life and Blessed Passing of Johann Lobach in Krefeld, 1750," which circulated among Pietist conventicles.[15]

The Brethren Leave Schwarzenau

One year after the departure of the Krefeld group to America, the larger congregation at and around Schwarzenau left Wittgenstein for Friesland. They stayed there for nine years before they left in 1729 for Pennsylvania. It is not completely clear why they chose to leave Schwarzenau in 1720. The usual explanation is persecution, but the ruling count there, Henrich Albrecht, continued his policy of religious toleration until his death in 1723, several years after the Brethren departed. To be sure, in 1719 he had been forced to give up part of his sovereignty to a younger brother, who had no sympathy for his brother's religious policies. Early in 1720 he complained to the imperial court that the settlers in Wittgenstein were damaging the forests and endangering the game. It could well be that the Brethren saw the handwriting on the wall, when this count attained complete rule.

Economic considerations also played a role. Wittgenstein was a poor land, with little fertile land and little industry except for char-coal burning. As the Ephrata chroniclers described the situation, Mack "devoted all his earthly possessions to the common good, and thereby became so poor that at last he had not bread enough to last from one day to the next." A contemporary observer agreed, giving this account of their departure in 1720: "When they were tired of promoting their cause in the Upper Rhine area, or rather, when they could not find sufficient livelihood, and moreover, met with all kinds of resistance from the awakened, they turned to the area of the Lower Rhine, even to Friesland, and still farther to America."[16]

The Brethren trek to Friesland in the eastern Netherlands was made possible in part by the assistance of the Dutch Collegiants. In 1719 Brethren received 8,000 guilders, sent to help the "needy Schwartzenauers." Sometime between April and June 1720 they left. The route probably went to Siegen, and thence to Köln, where they could board ships to take them down the Rhine River.[17]

Shortly after the Brethren departure, a local official responded to a query about them from the imperial solicitor, which had been years in the works. He said of them,

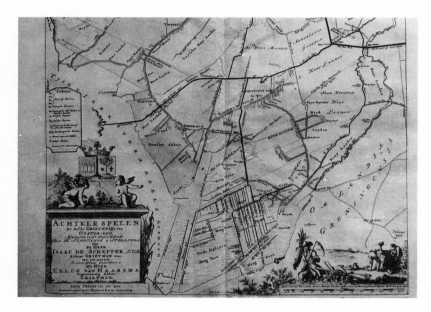

An eighteenth-century map depicting the Surhuisterveen region. The illustration in the lower right-hand corner shows workers gathering peat. *Durnbaugh Collection.*

> [M]any pious people resided here for a time, about whom one heard nothing evil, but rather perceived that they conducted themselves quietly and devoutly in all things. No person has ever complained about them. From this group, forty families, numbering about two hundred persons, recently left this county permanently. They were said to have been Anabaptists.[18]

Some real estate records refer to their leaving. Georg Grebe, for example, was listed as selling his extensive land holdings in the Stüntzel area because "he, and his wife Juliana, intend to migrate to Friesland with the other Anabaptists." Mack sold his cabin to Christoph Sauer, who himself emigrated to Pennsylvania in 1724.[19]

Count August, who took full control of Wittgenstein in 1723, was not a popular ruler; in fact, a number of his subjects rioted against him and others left. In 1725 he had his officials draw up a list of 389 subjects who had either left secretly for Pennsylvania or planned to do so. From other records it is known that the list was not complete.

THE BRETHREN IN FRIESLAND

The Schwarzenau Brethren found a new haven in the village of Surhuisterveen in Friesland. The word *veen* in the name reveals its nature as a marshy area in the process of being drained by canals to create land suitable for farming. It had been settled by Mennonites, and the Brethren were widely considered to be a Mennonite sect. It is likely that Surhuisterveen had been recommended to the Brethren as a relatively secure place for settlement. It was isolated and generally safe from religious repression, although laws antagonistic to Anabaptists still remained on the books. Active Collegiant groups existed in the nearby city of Groningen as well as in the capital of the province, Leeuwarden. Members of these groups may have helped the Brethren resettle.

Aside from economic pursuits, Brethren kept largely to themselves in Surhuisterveen. Their meetings for worship were held in a building across from the Mennonite meetinghouse. They baptized in a clear pond called *Kortewolde*, not far from the village. Local tradition has it that the Brethren introduced the growing of potatoes to the district. They were also said to be suspicious when they first saw ice skating; they thought such rapid movement must be from the devil. The only archival record of the Brethren stay in Friesland consists of four marriage records registered between 1721 and 1724.

The *Chronicon Ephratense*, always glad to report anything negative about the Brethren, claimed that at a public meeting in Friesland, Georg Grebe accused Mack of being sectarian. This was supposedly recorded by Wilhelm Knepper, one of the Solingen Brethren, who joined them in Friesland after being released from imprisonment in Jülich.

Sander Mack reported later in his life that the Brethren had close connection with the Collegiants, asserting that "many Dutch friends joined the Brethren" in West Friesland. He listed them by name, ten in all. Brethren and Collegiants shared the practice of immersion baptism; they differed in that the Collegiants were a loosely structured society. It was quite possible and usual that members of the Collegiant society were also active in other denominations, especially the Mennonites. On the list was the figure of Adrian Paauw (or Pfau), a wealthy Dutchman well known for his philanthropic spirit.[20]

Also listed were three men from the De Koker family, other members of which had been active in effecting the release of the Solingen Brethren. The De Kokers were a prosperous merchant and professional family in Rotterdam. One of them, Jan de Koker, had hosted John Wesley when this founder of the Methodists visited the Continent. They remained in correspondence for many years. When Andreas Bohni wrote in 1736 giving counsel to relatives on how they should emigrate, he instructed them to call on Pieter de Koker in Rotterdam at the *Kornmarkt*, who would provide them with jobs or other assistance.

Despite all of the aid that Brethren received from Collegiants in Friesland, they still were in an uncertain economic position. Surhuisterveen was a poor area, and it was difficult to become self-sufficient. A Quaker scholar who interviewed Brethren in Pennsylvania to secure facts about their early history, gave this summary of what he had learned about their situation in the Dutch territory:

> [S]ome of them commemorate that in great poverty they frequently experienced the special providence of God, but since they could never gain strength enough in Europe to eat their own bread, although in Holland good friends were moved to assist them and actually did shew them great love, they were continually longing for a place, where by the blessing of God, they might be able to maintain themselves by the labor of their hands, and to pass the rest of their time in perfect liberty of conscience, which nowhere in Europe they could enjoy together. In their native country they had not full liberty of conscience, nor in Holland, besides there, many could not

maintain themselves, but were helped by others, which
made them all come over [to America] by degrees....[21]

They received encouraging word from the Krefeld contingent
who emigrated in 1719, in particular about the religious awaken-
ings after 1723. In the fall of 1724 the Germantown Brethren sent
their brethren in Friesland a full report, telling of the revival which
was "daily increasing."

Following the decision to leave Friesland for Pennsylvania,
almost all of those who had gone there with Mack from
Schwarzenau departed from Rotterdam in 1729, probably assisted
there by the De Koker family. They sailed on the *Allen*, captained by
James Craigie, master. After the usual customs checks, they left
English shores from Cowes on July 7.

BRETHREN REMAINING IN THE NETHERLANDS

As had been the case in Krefeld, not all of the Brethren in the
Netherlands joined the emigration to Pennsylvania. An unknown number stayed in Friesland and Holland. In 1736 Count Zinzendorf wrote to
an acquaintance about his connections in Holland. In mentioning a
number of persons, he noted Johann Friedrich Henckels of the
Anabaptists as being reputed to be an honest person. In 1743, when he
returned from his Pennsylvania sojourn, Zinzendorf brought back with
him two Brethren leaders, Andreas Frey and Joseph Müller, it is said, to
help him contact and influence the Brethren there. According to one
contemporary writer, Zinzendorf had "urged Frey to travel with him,
because of the other *Täufer* in Holland." Müller wrote late in life in an
autobiographical statement about this time, that he was sent to Holland,
"from where I visited Friesland and Groningen and the Mennonites and
Brethren there." After several days, he visited Gernfield in Germany,
where he "visited Brethren and Mennonites." It is known that Jan de
Koker had warm relationships with the Moravians.[22]

When Morgan Edwards wrote of the Brethren in 1770, he
described Brethren as being Arminian in theology, but not "Arians
nor Socinians, as most of their Brethren in Holland are." He may
have been thinking of Collegiants, who were liberal in their beliefs.[23]

OTHER MIGRATIONS

The major Brethren migrations were in 1719 and 1729, but some came in smaller groups or as individual families. The family of Michael Eckerlin left Schwarzenau in 1725 for America; the father had died before 1720, but his widow and their four sons (who were to play a large role in Ephrata) went on their own. Lukas Vetter, one of the first eight at Schwarzenau, arrived with three children in 1731. One year later Abraham Dubois crossed the Atlantic with his wife and son.

The best documented journey involves the leader Johannes Naas. He and some of his family sailed on the Pennsylvania Merchant, arriving in Philadelphia in September 1733. He wrote a long letter to his son Jakob Wilhelm that described the ocean passage in great detail. The difficult journey took three months to complete, alternating severe storms with glassy calms. Ten deaths, especially among small children, saddened the voyage. During one of the storms Naas fell from the deck to the hold, the accident requiring bed rest for two weeks. He penned a vivid description of one storm, which provides insight into the hardships experienced by travelers in that day:

> Then came a powerful storm-wind from the northwest, so that the sea or ocean rose so high that when one looked at it, it was as if one traveled in high mountains, where all mountains were covered with snow. One mountain or wave after another struck the ship....The water came into the ship with such force that many people's bedrolls which lay by the portholes were completely wet. In great haste, all holes were quickly closed, the rudder bound, and the ship set...against the wind with close-rigged sails so that it did not roll so much to both sides. The storm continued throughout the night with great force. All could see without fear that it was not the strength of the ship that endured such blows, but rather the almighty hand of the Lord who preserved it in order to make known His might to the people—to Him be above all and before all the honor. Amen.

> Not a person remained on the deck of the ship, except a sailor tied to the rudder who held watch....The ship lay for a time at the mercy of the wind, always on its side so that it shipped water, but the water always ran off again. Around midnight, the waves struck so hard on the aft portholes that two porthole boards broke loose, and as the people lay partly in sleep and slumber the water poured in through the portholes, a stream as large as the hole, and immediately into the beds, which caused a great panic among those who lay near the porthole. The water took a board with rope completely away again. We leaped up, because the friend who lay near the porthole had not tied the board tightly enough, and this misfortune could have been great; we took a wool sack close at hand and stuffed the porthole shut again, and the other porthole with the remaining board.
>
> The storm began to let up a little bit, also the fear of the people decreased, and around two o'clock in the afternoon the sky cleared, the wind died down, the portholes were opened, and there was quiet, beautiful weather.

Not surprisingly, it was with heartfelt joy that they were reunited with their Brethren in Philadelphia. Naas reported that "brethren and sisters came to meet us in small boats with delicious bread, apples, peaches, and other refreshments of the body, for which we praised the great God publicly on the ship with much singing and resounding prayers."

He further reported that the Pennsylvania Brethren were all well established. They were doing well, "one better than the other." Summarizing his experience, Nass maintained that the most difficulty came when people really did not want to make the journey, or when all members of the family were not agreed on the trip. Also a problem was the lack of sufficient provision for victuals, because the ship's rations were miserable. Despite the hardships and storm reported, Naas recommended that his son and family should migrate as well. They decided to do so, arriving in 1735.[24]

With the momentum of the Brethren movement now shifted to North America, the story shifts to their experiences in the New World. After a delay to become settled in their new homes, to resolve past squabbles, and to secure an adequate living, they turned again to their religious concerns.

4

Settlement in Pennsylvania and Beyond

The first Brethren arrived in the colony of Pennsylvania almost forty years after its founding. In 1681 the aristocratic Englishman William Penn, a convert to the Religious Society of Friends, became the proprietor and governor of forty thousand square miles of wilderness in the New World. The English monarch Charles II granted the immense holding to him in lieu of a monetary payment for the services of his father, who was an admiral in the king's navy. The forested territory was called "Penn's Woods" in honor of the elder Penn, with the euphonious Latin equivalent becoming the accepted form.[1] As early as 1671 and again in 1677 Penn had traveled in the Low Countries and within the German states to further the Quaker cause. He was impressed by the sturdy qualities of the Mennonite and other German sectarians whom he met and subsequently made special efforts to inform these German dissenters about the opportunities his new colony presented. He had descriptive treatises, some of which he wrote himself, translated into German and Dutch and then distributed widely. His promises of complete religious liberty (for all except atheists) and comparative lack of interference from government, combined with the offer of fertile and inexpensive land, came as the voice of Providence to many oppressed German farmers and craftsmen and their families.

The first group of German buyers to secure land from Penn had organized the Frankfurt Company. Most of the original founders of the company were from the Pietist circle that Spener had formed.

Although none of the founders ever actually went to Pennsylvania, their agent Franz Daniel Pastorius, a young university graduate from Bad Windsheim, emigrated to the new country in 1683. He became the leading figure (though not himself among the first residents) in the founding of Germantown, just north of Philadelphia, the site which became central in the history of German emigration to Pennsylvania.[2]

THE 1683 KREFELD MIGRATION

Shortly after Pastorius landed, there arrived thirteen Krefeld families who had also purchased real estate. Although of Mennonite stock, almost all of them had become members of the Society of Friends before they left. This migration marks the first mass movement of German settlers to North America, though isolated German emigrants had preceded them from Virginia to New England.

The Krefeld immigrants settled in Germantown, at that time little better than a wilderness. Despite the initial rugged conditions in the new settlement, which caused the village to be known as the "poor town" or "beggars town" (*Armentown*, a pun on Germantown), the newcomers soon prospered, in particular because of their introduction of fine weaving. Members of the Germantown settlement have been honored for issuing in 1688 the first public protest against the institution of slavery in North America; this was at a time when the "best people" accepted the degrading system as a matter of course, including wealthy Friends. (A later critic said of these early Friends that they had gone to Pennsylvania to do good and ended up doing quite well!)

As emigration from German states increased, in 1727 the colonial assembly passed a measure requiring all immigrants arriving in Pennsylvania to swear or affirm allegiance to the king of England and the provincial government of Pennsylvania. The stream of immigrants from Germany, especially from the southwest, persisted so strongly that leading politicians such as Benjamin Franklin worried openly that the English population would be submerged by what he called "Palatine boors." This issue became prominent in later Pennsylvania politics.[3]

The "old Dunker parsonage" at Germantown, Pennsylvania, was sketched in the early 1860s and later drawn on zinc by John Richards; the building was demolished in 1907. J.F. Sachse, *Quaint Old Germantown in Pennsylvania* (Lancaster, Pa.: 1915), plate XX, *BHLA Collection.*

THE BRETHREN MIGRATION OF 1719

It was to Germantown that the first large party of Brethren came in 1719 from Krefeld, under the leadership of Peter Becker. As their arrival preceded the requirement for registrations mentioned above, exact information about their names and number is not available. A Philadelphian wrote in 1719, "We are daily expecting ships from London which bring over Palatines, in number about six or seven thousand." Because so many Germans were leaving the Palatinate during these years, it became customary for all those arriving from German states to be called Palatines, regardless of their actual homelands in Hesse, Württemberg, Saxony, or elsewhere. It is possible that the Krefeld Brethren were numbered among the thousands referred to in this quotation.[4]

Some of the Brethren settled in Germantown itself—Peter Becker for example—but most of the new arrivals penetrated further inland to the north and west along the Schuylkill River to seek cheaper land. They moved into such areas as Skippack and Oley. That they prospered through hard toil can be seen in the statements contained in a letter to Germany in 1724 written by a new arrival from Wittgenstein (who had traveled with Christoph Sauer).

He had been met by Brethren at the port of Philadelphia and helped to settle in the new land. Johann Gumre (also Gomorry) gave him and his family a place to stay until he found something for himself; Johann Heinrich Traut hauled his baggage without charge. The newcomer wrote back to Count Casimir in Berleburg that his host Gumre had come to Pennsylvania with but small savings; within five years he had a valuable property and great numbers of livestock. Others who had arrived with Gumre had on average properties worth twice or three times as much as he did and quantities of livestock. When Johannes Naas arrived in 1733 he also reported that the Brethren were well off. This speaks well of their capacity for hard work and adaptability.[5]

For several years after the arrival in 1719 of the Krefeld Brethren, the immigrants seemingly made little attempt to gather for worship. The writers of the *Chronicon Ephratense*, always glad to report friction among the Brethren, explained the delay as a lingering effect of the dispute in Krefeld. They quote the Brethren as complaining that the previous affection they held for one another was lost on the long and hazardous ocean voyage: "[W]e have become strangers one to the other, and nearly all love and faithfulness have been lost among us." The great freedom enjoyed in America caused them to become more interested in worldly things, by this reckoning.[6]

Another explanation may be more relevant. The newly arrived Brethren had first to concentrate their energies upon wresting a living from the wilderness. Migration is always a difficult process, but under pioneer conditions in a strange land it makes supreme demands upon those brave or desperate enough to attempt it. As has been noted, the Brethren quickly became substantial landowners. After they had achieved a degree of economic security, they could direct their attention to their spiritual needs.

That Brethren had not totally lost their sense of community is documented by a land transaction of 1719-20, soon after their arrival. Johann Gumre bought a plot of land along the Wissahickon Brook in his name and in the name of "the congregation of Brethren." It was on this property that the first baptisms took place late in 1723.[7]

RENEWED RELIGIOUS ACTIVITY

In the fall of 1722 Peter Becker and two companions took the initiative in reuniting the scattered Brethren. They set out to visit their friends in Germantown and the surrounding territory. They made their way first on foot to the Skippack region, and then on to the Perkiomen Valley, Falckner's Swamp, and as far as Oley. They returned to Germantown by way of the Schuylkill River valley where many of the Brethren lived.

Everywhere they went they told of their desire to begin meeting as a congregation again and invited the others to meet with them. After their return home they began to worship regularly, alternating the meetings between the homes of Peter Becker in Germantown and Johann Gumre along the nearby Wissahickon River. Winter interrupted their meetings, but they began again in the spring of 1723.

In August the rumor spread that Christian Liebe had arrived in Philadelphia. A number of settlers along the Schuylkill journeyed to the city to see the Brethren leader, well known for his eloquence as a preacher and his grueling experience as a galley slave. They were disappointed to learn that the rumor had no factual basis. Nevertheless, they were gratified by the invitation to meet and worship with the Germantown Brethren. The *Chronicon* reported that the visitors heard "so much of the Germans' awakening, that they went home very much edified." Soon after, "a second visit was made to Germantown, by which both parties were so much edified that the Germantown Baptists promised them a visit in return, which they also made four weeks afterward with great blessing."[8]

The upshot of these visits was the request by the Schuylkill Brethren of the Germantown folk to receive them into fellowship by baptism. This posed a problem for the latter, for they had no regular minister and did not consider themselves to be a fully organized congregation. They consulted by letter with the Brethren still in Friesland, who encouraged them to organize with Becker as minister and to proceed with the baptisms.

Because of the time involved in transatlantic communications in this era, this could not take place until Christmas Day, 1723. Peter Becker baptized the following in the Wissahickon River: Martin and Catherine Reist Urner, Hans Heinrich and Elizabeth Hirt Landes, Frederick Lang, and Johann Mäyle (Meyle), all of whom were from the Schuylkill Valley in what became the Coventry congregation. In the evening following the momentous baptism, the Germantown congregation welcomed the "first fruits"—as the newly baptized were called—through participation in the first love feast in North America. This consisted of the examination service, feetwashing, Lord's supper, and bread and cup eucharist.[9]

RELIGIOUS REVIVAL AND EXPANSION

News of the first American baptism by Brethren spread among the German population in Pennsylvania. Others began to attend the meetings in Germantown that continued, weather permitting, into the spring of 1724. By that time, the awakening reached such proportions that onlookers spoke of a revival. Later historians have called the Brethren initiative the forerunner of the *Great Awakening* among the American colonies which looms so large in religious history. In 1813 a well-informed and rather critical Lutheran cleric rehearsed the story in the context of the broader revival among German-speaking churches:

> The first tempestuous movement to cause excitement came about among the old Brethren (*die alten Täufer*), who resided from the Germantown area on into the country. The Brethren have always been diligent proselyters, and had recruited many who had belonged in Germany to all kinds of Brotherhoods....[T]hey were kind, loving people, full of good works which they performed, and the spirit of grace had his fire and hearth among them. They travelled, they preached as far as Virginia, they visited the brethren, spoke of repentance and conversion, and of the inward life, and considered themselves to be the centerpiece of the kingdom of God.[10]

In the fall of 1724 the Germantown congregation decided to send out the entire male membership on evangelistic visits to all those formerly affiliated with the Brethren and others whom they could contact. Fourteen men set out on foot and on horseback on October 23, 1724, following much the same route Becker and his companions pursued two years previously. They went to Skippack and Falckner's Swamp, where they held a meeting and love feast; from there they visited the newly baptized members along the Schuylkill to organize the Coventry congregation. Under the leadership of Martin Urner, meetings had already been held there, and two persons were ready for baptism. These took place on November 8 and were followed by a love feast.

THE CONESTOGA AREA

The Germantown Brethren heard of religiously interested persons in the Conestoga area, in what later became Lancaster County. They decided to push on to visit them and held a meeting at the home of Heinrich and Christina Höhn, where "great revival powers were manifested" as the Ephrata chroniclers phrased it. Five persons from that area asked for baptism, which, upon due examination, was provided. A sixth person was so impressed by the baptisms that she spontaneously asked to be immersed, which also took place.[11]

There was an onlooker at these dramatic events. This was Conrad Beissel, later to become famous as the founder of the Ephrata Society. Born in 1691 in the Palatinate after his father died, he became a complete orphan in 1699 when his mother died as well. After a worldly, music-loving early life as a journeyman baker, Beissel fell under the sway of Pietists in Heidelberg and began to live a converted life. This brought him into difficulties with the authorities and led to his expulsion. He contacted both the Inspired in the Marienborn area and the Brethren in Wittgenstein, without permanently joining either. In 1720 Beissel emigrated to the New World.

He intended to join a Radical Pietist community living along the Wissahickon River after 1694 but found to his disappointment that it had disbanded. Being at loose ends, he apprenticed himself to Peter Becker to learn weaving. His restless nature, however, led him to leave before the agreed time to join some comrades in a hermitage in the "bush" in the Conestoga area. Thus it was that he witnessed the baptisms conducted by Becker, his former master, and the other Germantown Brethren.

This event threw Beissel into a spiritual dilemma. On the one hand he felt powerfully drawn to ask for baptism as well, but on the other hand he considered the Germantown Brethren to be inferior to his own spiritual attainments. While struggling with this, the insight came to him that even Jesus Christ had allowed himself to be baptized by someone lesser than himself. There was no reason why he could not do likewise. He then submitted to water baptism at the hands of Peter Becker and thus became a member of the Brethren. This incident characterizes, as well as any, the personality of the ambitious and talented Beissel who was to cause the Brethren so much soul-searching trouble.[12]

The customary love feast was celebrated with the new Conestoga members in the evening of the day of baptism,

November 12. Other meetings and baptisms followed in the area during the next few days. A meeting at the home of Sigmund Landert and his wife resulted in the couple asking for baptism. The minister Peter Becker is reported to have said at that occasion,

> These two persons have applied to us for baptism, but as they are unknown to us in their walk and conversation, we make this announcement of the fact to all men here present, especially to their neighbors. If you can bear favorable witness concerning their lives, it is well and we can baptize them with the greater assurance. But if you have any complaints to bring against them, we will not do it.

This comment clearly reveals both the evangelistic zeal of the Brethren, who were glad to baptize seekers, even with limited instruction, as well as the requirements of sober conduct and behavior expected of all members. The emphasis upon conversion was linked to high ethical expectation.[13]

Before the Germantown Brethren left the Conestoga area, they counseled at length with the new members there about the organization and conduct of their church life. They told them that the great distance between Conestoga and Germantown would necessitate the former to bear great responsibility in arranging their congregational life. Members chose Conrad Beissel as minister of the flock at Conestoga, thus becoming the third congregation in Pennsylvania, following Germantown and Coventry. The choice was to prove fateful for the development of the Brethren movement in the New World, for Beissel's impetuous leadership resulted in the first major division among the Brethren in America. Details of this development will be recounted later with the story of the Ephrata Society.

After the tension between Germantown and Conestoga led to a rupture in 1728, the remnant remaining loyal to the "mainline" Brethren proceeded to build up its ranks and restore its church life. Under the strong leadership of Michael Frantz the Conestoga congregation not only survived the defection of the Beissel followers, it actually flourished. The body numbered perhaps twenty when

Frantz became its leader in 1734; it had increased ten-fold by the time of his death.

Able successors followed Frantz, including Michael Pfautz, who added nearly sixty members in the first year of his eldership and one hundred more within six more years. A large number of daughter congregations were spun off from Conestoga over the years and scores of members migrated to other regions, permitting some to call it the "mother church" of the Brethren, although Germantown has most usually been so termed because of its chronological priority.[14]

THE 1729 IMMIGRATION

Word of these striking developments was soon sent across the sea to the former Schwarzenau congregation, which from 1720 to 1729 lived at Surhuisterveen in Friesland. The promising reports about religious renewal in Pennsylvania thus received were undoubtedly encouraging to the Frisian congregation as they considered emigration themselves. They also pondered the uncertainty about the extent and duration of religious toleration in Friesland; although the situation was much safer there than in most German states, laws still on the books forbade Anabaptist activity. Moreover, the economic situation in Surhuisterveen was hardly better than that at Schwarzenau. It was a poor area, consisting largely of marshes, with digging of peat for fuel the major occupation.

Under the leadership of Alexander Mack, Sr., nearly sixty families left the Rotterdam area in the summer of 1729, sailing on the *Allen.* As was obligatory, they stopped at the English port of Cowes to pass customs, before sailing from the Isle of Wight in early July; they arrived in Philadelphia in September.

The newcomers proceeded to register and affirm their allegiance to the king of England and the provincial government on September 11, 1729. Unlike the case in 1719, there is an exact listing of the heads of families preserved in the Pennsylvania archives. Only a few names among the 126 listed are clearly not linked with the Brethren movement. Unfortunately, additional information such as that featured in some of the lists—which provide ages, hometowns, and professions or trades—was not recorded in this instance.[15]

Mack's party was met with great joy in Philadelphia by those Brethren who had arrived ten years earlier. Not only were their numbers greatly increased, with the new arrival they were reunited with their leader and first minister. Peter Becker at once graciously stepped aside to allow Alexander Mack, Sr., to assume pastoral leadership of the Pennsylvania Brethren.[16]

The 1729 arrivals followed in the footsteps of the earlier immigrants: some, such as Alexander Mack, Sr., remained in Germantown but most sought out land in the surrounding areas. Although details are lacking, it is probable that their relocation went rather smoothly because they could count on the counsel and assistance of the Brethren who had arrived earlier, now well established in the New World.

There is some indication that the language used by the Brethren in Germantown was that used in Krefeld, described as "broken Hollandisch." Mennonites in Krefeld used a version of Dutch, which the Brethren arriving there from the Marienborn area could have learned. The Schwarzenau Brethren spent nearly a decade in Friesland and no doubt became fluent in that variation of Dutch as well. If this was the case, it was peculiar to Germantown and did not last there long, for later records in the colonial period were all written in German.[17]

OTHER EARLY CONGREGATIONS

The Brethren continued their effort to call new congregations into existence following the unusual campaign of 1724. Because of the proximity of Skippack to Germantown, the creation of a separate congregation in that area was delayed until 1785; it was long considered part of the original church. Those in the Skippack area became known as the Indian Creek church; it was later to produce many stalwart preachers and pastors, in particular members of the Preiß (Preisz), or Price, family.[18]

A leading figure here was Johann Jakob Preiß, who had been active among the Marienborn Brethren; he settled briefly in Krefeld and then joined the first Brethren migration to Pennsylvania. In 1720 Preiß and his family secured land adjoining the Indian Creek. Preiß attended the first Brethren baptism on Christmas Day, 1723, and hosted the Germantown Brethren as they began their missionary forays into the Philadelphian hinterland.

A son of Johann Jakob was Johannes Preiß. According to family tradition Johannes married a woman of mixed European and Indian parentage, with whom he had two sons, Daniel and John; the latter was born after his father's premature death. Johannes Preiß is best known as a poet; some of his many compositions were published by the Sauer press in 1753 as *Geistliche und andächtige Lieder* ("Spiritual and Devotional Hymns").

A grandson, also named Johannes Preiß, became the longtime elder of the Indian Creek congregation. He was a dear friend of Sander Mack; they often exchanged correspondence. When Preiß married a Mennonite woman, Elizabeth Weidner, in 1780, she was expelled from her congregation for marrying out of the faith. Mack protested the action in a letter to the wife's brother, a Mennonite minister. The letter, appealing for tolerance in religious matters, has often been cited and republished.

A number of Brethren settled in the Oley region (Berks County), where a congregation (the fourth) was established by 1732. In the next decades a large proportion of the membership moved away to find better land, keeping the numbers small. Oley is notable because a well-proportioned stone meetinghouse was built for the membership in 1777 by Martin Gaube, located in present-day Pricetown; it is the oldest unaltered church building of the Brethren. A meetinghouse had been built seven years earlier for the Brethren in Germantown, but this has been changed and augmented over the years.

Great Swamp in Bucks County was established in 1733, with their minister Johannes Naas, who lived in New Jersey. Naas had settled in Amwell, where the first congregation outside of Pennsylvania was created, also in 1733. Two famous names in American finance, John Wanamaker and John D. Rockefeller, were descendants of member families there. Another early congregation was set up in White Oak (1736) in the Conestoga region. This became and has remained one of the strongest, predominantly rural congregations among the Brethren.

Several early congregations across the Susquehanna River in York County were Little Conewago (1738), Conewago (1740), Swatara (1756), Little Swatara (1757), Codorus (1758), and Bermudian (1758). An early congregation farther west in present-day Somerset County was Stony Creek (Glades, Brothersvalley), with settlement in the 1750s and possible congregational organization by 1762. It is not always clear, in the few records that have been preserved, which dates refer to first settlement by Brethren families and which to actual organization as a congregation by outside Brethren elders, following regular practice. Reputedly Peter Leibundgutt (Livengood), an Amishman, was the first settler; many of the Glades Amish became Brethren.

The primary source for the early records of Brethren church activity in Pennsylvania and the other colonies are the research records of the Baptist pastor/historian Morgan Edwards. Because of his interest in unity among Baptist-minded groups, he included in his records German-speaking bodies such as the Brethren and Mennonites, along with his English-speaking Baptists. He sought out as best he could the early histories of each church body through interviews with members and checking of documents; in each case he listed ministers and members by name as of 1770. At times Edward's research was limited by his inadequate mastery of the German language; this is often reflected in the curious spellings of names. Only two of his manuscripts were published, for Pennsylvania (1770) and for New Jersey (1792), but his compilations on other colonies were preserved and later brought to print.[19]

According to his reckoning, by 1770 Brethren had fifteen congregations in Pennsylvania, with twenty-one ministers and exhorters, and one in New Jersey, with two ministers, for a total adult membership of over eight hundred. He calculated that, counting family members, some 2,200 individuals were involved. Edwards missed the Antietam congregation of Frankin County in Southern Pennsylvania (because of its link with the Maryland congregations) and the Ten Mile church in Western Pennsylvania.

Parchment deeds and indentures of the Germantown congregation created during the eighteenth century. *BHLA Collection.*

Further Expansion Southward

It was not long before Brethren pushed southward into the fertile valleys of Maryland, establishing early settlements in the Conococheague and Monocacy river valleys; the former region overlapped in its territory with Franklin County in Pennsylvania. Among the early congregations were Conococheague (1743), Middle Creek (1747), Monocacy (1749), Pipe Creek (1751), and Beaver Dam (1747) in Frederick and Carroll counties. Early leaders were the second Martin Urner, Jacob Danner, and especially Daniel Leatherman. Edwards was impressed by the intense activity and wide responsibilities of Leatherman, whom he called a "bishop," a term not customary in Brethren usage.

By 1770 congregations had been well established in the Shenandoah valley of Virginia, largely by migration from Pennsylvania and Maryland. The first Brethren settlers came in the wake of outposts from the Ephrata Society. Their residence was transient, largely because of the insecurity of the area owing to Indian raids. The first permanent Brethren settlements probably came in the 1750s, centering in the Flat Rock area (Shenandoah County) and the Blackwater River area (Franklin County). John Garber and Jacob Miller were prominent leaders.[20]

Brethren settlement began in North Carolina in the 1750s along Killian's Creek in what became Lincoln and Catawba counties. About the same time some members also settled along Crane Creek in Rowan County and along the Uwharrie River in what became Randolph and Davidson counties. A leading early minister was Jacob Stutzman. In the 1770s Elder Gasper Rowland led Brethren from York County (Pennsylvania) and Frederick County (Maryland) into the Yadkin River valley in what became Davie County. Sporadic Indian troubles led some of the early Brethren to seek shelter near the Moravian settlements of the Wachovia district (Salem and Bethabara), where they are noticed in the excellent Moravian church archives.[21]

Brethren may have begun settlement in South Carolina as early as 1748. The initial Brethren congregations in South Carolina bore allegiance both to Germantown and Ephrata; it is not always possible to distinguish clearly their alignment. Individual congregations in the South varied from time to time in their allegiance. Georg Adam Martin, a controversial figure in colonial Brethren history, is thought to have established an early congregation on the Beaver Creek in Fairfield County in the late 1750s. Emanuel Eckerlin, one of the four Eckerlins involved in Ephrata's history, owned land in the territory and is said to have founded a congregation along Germantown Brethren lines.

By the 1770s when Morgan Edwards recorded the Brethren status, David Miller was the leading minister in the Carolinas. Other ministers bore English names—Elijah Padget, James Warren, John Pearson, Joseph Summers, Giles Chapman, and Elijah Lynch—and probably came from Baptist and Quaker backgrounds. These congregations left the Brethren fold in the post-Revolutionary War era to become Universalists, as will be recounted later.

There are fleeting references in the contemporary records to early Brethren in Georgia. A Moravian record of 1737 describing German religious groups in the Americas speaks of the *Tumplers* or Brethren, who had in Pennsylvania and "in Georgia several congregations where more is to be found than with the others." Several of the early colonizing attempts in Georgia failed because of the climate and poor soil. Possibly, this was the fate as well of Brethren who attempted to settle there.

Based on the statistical records of Morgan Edwards, it may be that, at the end of the colonial period, there were some 1500 adult members of Brethren congregations in North America. Counting family members as well, perhaps five thousand people had Brethren connections toward the end of the eighteenth century.

5

The Ephrata Schism

The aggressive expansion of the Germantown Brethren following the renewal of religious activity in 1723 led, as we have seen, to the planting of congregations in eastern Pennsylvania and across the Delaware River in New Jersey. Some of the most exciting, if not always the most edifying, developments came with the Conestoga congregation. It was here that Conrad Beissel deigned to allow himself to be baptized by Peter Becker. His evident spiritual talents immediately led to his selection as the minister of the young congregation.

It soon became clear that his restless and demanding genius would not long permit him to play a subordinate role to the Germantown elders. Although the rupture was several years in coming, it was not long before differences began to accumulate. Two major problems developed: the first was Beissel's inclination to introduce Judaizing practices, from observing Saturday as the day of rest and worship to the elimination of all those foods from the diet (such as pork) that were banned by Old Testament laws. Some of Beissel's followers even circumcised themselves, though he told them that went too far.

The second problem was his insistence that his own divine revelations took priority over the scriptures. As the Ephrata chroniclers expressed it, although both movements had a base in Radical Pietism, they depended on different authorities: "Those who knew how the affairs stood between the two congregations, know also that a close union between them was impossible; for they were born of diverse causes, since one had the letter for its foundation, and the other the spirit; and while both had the same Father, they had different mothers."[1]

As reported in the *Chronicon Ephratense*, Beissel "conducted all meetings...with astonishing strength of spirit, and used so little reflection over it, that even in the beginning he was not suffered to use a Bible; so that the testimony in its delivery might not be weakened by written knowledge." For the biblicist Brethren, this was inadmissable.[2]

Added to these basic differences was Beissel's increasing emphasis upon the virtue of celibacy, which led to the breakup of families as several wives left their homes to live near Beissel. After hearing Beissel preach, Elder Martin Urner clung to his wife and exclaimed, "Oh, my dear wife! I pray you for God's sake, do not leave me!" Beissel was called a seducer and sorcerer.[3] Differences became clear in 1726 at a love feast held at Pentecost at Coventry; as Peter Becker could not come, Beissel was asked to preside. His spiritual powers were much in evidence, bringing about great renewal. It was said that "quite extraordinary powers of eternity manifested themselves, such as were never known before or after...." The singing was especially moving, so that some claimed they heard angels' voices.[4]

In the summer of 1727, the increasingly uneasy Germantown Brethren sent a delegation to the Conestoga area. They restored on their own authority a member who had been placed in the ban by Beissel, which heightened the tension. About the same time the Conestoga and Germantown Brethren tangled over some awakened persons in the Falckner's Swamp area. Both sought to make converts there. Beissel and some colleagues succeeded in baptizing a number of families. When the Germantown Brethren visited, seeking to win the allegiance of the group to their side, Beissel's standpoint saw this as an underhanded ploy.

Finally, in 1728 the break occurred, so long in coming. Because Beissel could not accept his indebtedness to Germantown, whose leader had baptized him, he decided to "give back" the baptism. He accomplished this by having a follower rebaptize him once more; he then proceeded to baptize his baptizer and then another brother and four sisters. (Christoph Sauer pointed out that made four baptisms that Beissel had experienced—once as an infant, once by his own hands, once by Germantown Brethren, and now the last.) Some of his

The Ephrata Cloister in the early twentieth century before restoration. E. G. Hoff photo, *BHLA Collection.*

LATER DEVELOPMENTS AT EPHRATA

Beissel lost no time in eradicating all traces of the Eckerlin dynasty. He collected the voluminous writings, published and unpublished, of Israel Eckerlin and cast them on a bonfire. Mysteriously, most of the mills built up so painfully and carefully fell to ashes at the hands of unknown arsonists. Even a vast orchard of bearing fruit trees was uprooted. Beissel believed that poverty and economic struggle made for higher spiritual gains; conversely, economic well-being would prove inevitably unhelpful, even ruinous, for the life of the spirit.

A relative from Beissel's homeland brought a contingent of additional members to Ephrata in the so-called Gimbsheim revival. Through correspondence, relatives of Beissel became aware of the portentous happenings on the Cocalico. In the years 1749 to 1751 several of the Beissel family, as well as the Kimmels and Lohmanns, arrived to swell the numbers at Ephrata.[20]

EPHRATA'S CULTURAL ACCOMPLISHMENTS

Lasting recognition of Ephrata has come largely through the bountiful life of artistic creation that flourished there. In literature, art, and music, its record has been highly acclaimed. This was, of course, not the original intent of the community, but rather a byproduct of their intense spiritual pursuit.

Some writers, it is true, have downplayed the merit of the literary production at Ephrata, considering it to be banal and repetitious. On the other hand, John Joseph Stoudt, an authority on mysticism, claimed that Beissel could even be ranked with the great medieval mystics Tauler and Eckhart, and with Boehme. "Here in this one small Pennsylvania German community there were as many poets as there were English poets in all Colonial America." He considered the quantity of poetry produced there to be "astonishing" and of a quality unmatched by their English-speaking contemporaries.[21]

Very little of Ephrata's literary output has been published in modern times and even less translated. The chief reason is that it was written with a specialized vocabulary, based upon the theosophical writings of Jakob Böhme. The baroque embellishments seem foreign and even offensive to modern eyes. A recent assessment of research on Conrad Beissel and Ephrata pointed out that Beissel's literary style has never been studied in depth; some of his verses, they say, compare favorably to those of the lyrical Angelus Silesius or Gottfried Arnold. The authors of the assessment called on professors of the German language in America to turn their attention to detailed studies of German-American writers "among whom Conrad Beissel and his fellow believers at Ephrata form a distinguished group."[22]

The artistic accomplishments of Ephrata's members are not as controversial as are the literary. The unworldly beauty of its manuscript illustration—the *Fraktur*—is universally recognized. Even minor examples of this art are avidly collected. A noted authority said of this work, "Fraktur illumination not only appeared in America first at the Ephrata Cloister...but also reached its greatest perfection there." This assessment has been seconded by many others expert in this distinguishing genre of Pennsylvania-German art.[23]

It may be said with good reason, however, that music was Ephrata's greatest accomplishment, even surpassing its literary and artistic genius. Contemporaries could not find words adequate to praise the singing developed there and the original compositions. Morgan Edwards, Baptist pastor and historian, remarked that "their singing is charming; partly owing to the pleasantness of their voices, the variety of parts they carry on together and the devout manner of their performance."[24] Jacob Duché, the cultured and knowledgeable Anglican divine from Philadelphia, recorded his impressions after a visit in 1771, when the Cloister was already in decline:

> I shall at present remark but one thing sure, with respect to the Dunkers, and that is, the peculiarity of their music. Upon a hint given by my friend, the sisters invited us into their chapel, and seating themselves in order, began to sing one of their devout hymns. The music had little or no air or melody, but consisted of simple, long notes, combined in the richest harmony. The counter, treble, tenor, and bass were all sung by women, with sweet, shrill, and small voices, but with a truth and exactness in the time and intonation that was admirable.

Duché continued with a statement of the impact of the music on his own spirit:

> It is impossible to describe...my feelings upon this occasion. The performers sat with their heads reclined, their countenances solemn and dejected, their faces pale and emaciated from their manner of living, their clothing exceedingly white and quite picturesque, and their music such as thrilled to the very soul. I almost began to think myself in the world of the spirits, and that the objects before me were ethereal. In short, the impression this scene made upon my mind continued strong for many days, and I believe, will never be wholly obliterated.[25]

It is clear from the record that Beissel placed great priority upon music, directing the choir himself after the early work of Ludwig Blum and developing his own unique theories of composition. Christoph Sauer wrote to Europe about it, stating that the choir had to "sing from notes very precisely, and not only in four-part harmony but in six, and only melodies which Beissel has composed. For this they all have very large hand-written books, and those who know something about music say that they have never heard such beautiful music." Beissel's unique musical theories were incorporated into the novel *Dr. Faustus* by the noted German author Thomas Mann during the American exile in the 1940s of the anti-Nazi author.[26]

The Decline of Ephrata

It was difficult to maintain the spiritual zeal of Ephrata indefinitely. Even the chroniclers admit that the later years of the society were troubled by disputes and personal tensions. Beissel himself was seen "in the likeness of one who is drunk," which they explained as a sign of his intense mystical activity or as a test of the loyalty of his followers. There were even accusations of sexual improprieties by the leader with the sisters.[27]

He died in 1768, when the zenith of Ephrata's popularity had already passed. He left the leadership of the community in the capable hands of Johann Peter Müller. The latter far surpassed Beissel in intellectual gifts, scholarship, and attractive personality but did not have the intensity or charisma of the late superintendent. There were few new accessions under his leadership, although he enjoyed warm personal relationships with leading Pennsylvania figures. He was elected, for example, a member of the prestigious American Philosophical Society. The paper he read for this occasion was scarcely a mystic masterpiece; instead he wrote about the cultivation of peas.

When the storms of the Revolution arrived in the 1770s, Ephrata hoped to be spared, but that was not its fate. The first blow came when commissioners of the rebel American forces arrived to confiscate a store of paper at Ephrata. They even seized unbound sheets of *The Martyrs Mirror*. This alarmed the brothers and sisters, who were nonresistant pacifists. They well knew that the commissioners would use paper for gun-wadding. This profane purpose shocked those at Ephrata so much that they made an effort to buy back the sheets, with some success.

A more serious impact upon the cloistered life came in the aftermath of the bloody battle at nearby Brandywine. Cartloads of wounded American soldiers were transported over the rough roads to Ephrata. Several large buildings were given over to their care as improvised hospitals. In sacrificial labor, sisters and brothers cared for the casualties. Camp fever swept the buildings, despite their best efforts, causing the deaths of 150 soldiers and a number of society members. Buildings had to be burned to quell the spread of the contagion.

The care given to the wounded found appreciation. An American officer expressed the gratitude of the men in this statement:

> I came among this people by accident, but I left them with regret. I have found out...where we expected to be met with a cold reservedness, we may sometimes be surprised by exhibitions of the most charming affability and disinterested benevolence. They all acted the part of the Good Samaritan to me, for which I hope to be ever grateful; and while experiencing the benefits of their kindnesses and attentions, witnessing the sympathies and emotions expressed in their countenances, and listening to the words of hope and pity with which they consoled the poor sufferers, is it strange that, under such circumstances, their uncouth garments appeared more beautiful in my eyes than ever did the richest robes of fashion...? Until I entered the walls of Ephrata, I had no idea of pure and practical Christianity. Not that I was ignorant of the forms, or even of the doctrines of religion. I knew it in theory before; I saw it in practice then.[28]

A musical pageant currently produced for summer visitors to Ephrata is built around a fictional romance between a wounded American soldier and one of the Ephrata sisters.

Even as the community declined they were bitterly attacked by their orthodox Protestant opponents. An example of this polemic is the anonymous (and now rare) *Testimony of One Re-Born against an Anabaptist Blasphemy* (*Das Zeugniß eines Wieder-Gebornen gegen eine Wieder-Täufferische Läster-Schrift*) published in 1792. It was an answer to an Ephrata publication of 1791.

By 1814, the numbers had dwindled to a handful of celibate sisters. In that year, the society was reorganized to form a church denomination, principally among the descendants of the householders. They continue today in small numbers in several places in Pennsylvania, under the name of Seventh Day German Baptist Brethren.

OFFSHOOTS OF EPHRATA

During the apogee of Ephrata's life, Beissel and his associates were concerned with extending the life and witness of the Cloister to other areas. These included attempts in Falckner's Swamp, Nantmill, and Coventry, as well as Amwell in New Jersey, which had no permanence; those awakened in these areas made their way to Ephrata. Similar efforts at Bermudian and Stony Creek in Pennsylvania and in the Shenandoah Valley of Virginia survived but became associated with the mainstream Brethren movement.

The single exception to these abortive developments took place in Franklin County at Quincy, Pennsylvania, a few miles north of Waynesboro. This was the Snow Hill Society, often referred to as the Snow Hill Nunnery. Although never as vibrant and creative as Ephrata, this daughter colony actually survived as a monastic institution longer than did its parent. It grew out of the Antietam congregation of Brethren developed by Georg Adam Martin; when he was placed under discipline by the Germantown Brethren, he associated himself with Ephrata.[29]

Snow Hill took its name from the Schneeberger family. Barbara and Andreas Schneeberger were the initiators, with the wife taking

The main building of the Snow Hill Nunnery in Quincy, Pennsylvania. *Durnbaugh Collection.*

the lead, the husband reluctantly following. With the advice and counsel of Johann Peter Müller, they moved toward a celibate posture, finally establishing the community on their land in 1798. Peter Lehmann was the first strong leader at Snow Hill. The threefold pattern of Ephrata was followed at Snow Hill, with celibate brothers and sisters, as well as householders living in farms in the vicinity. They held their worship services in a stone meetinghouse, located by a stream behind the main building. This evolved in three stages to form one very long (150 feet) brick structure, sufficient to house the celibates. Singing here, as at Ephrata, was highly praised by visitors who liked to attend the love feasts as onlookers. The celibates also practiced calligraphy, which, while attractive, lacks the ethereal and delicate beauty of Ephrata *Fraktur.*

One of the last of the brothers, Obed Snowberger, was a practical printer, using one of the original Ephrata presses. He reprinted many of the Ephrata broadsides, often in English translation, as well as a periodical for the Sabbatarian Baptists. The common dining room closed in 1889; the last two monastics died in 1893 and 1894. With their passing the spirit of Ephrata also ceased, although the small German Seventh Day Baptist denomination attempts to preserve the memory of Ephrata and Snow Hill to the best of its ability.

As Ephrata rose to a flourishing and famous position in colonial America, the Brethren with whom they were once affiliated pursued their own pursuits. Not as exotic as the spirituality and art of the solitary mystics at the Cloister, they developed their own distinctive patterns of worship and church government in the colonial period.

6

Brethren Worship and Polity

A German Pietist known only by the initials J. B. S. sketched a graphic description of leading religious bodies active in Pennsylvania in the mid-eighteenth century. His pen portraits of the Friends, Mennonites, Brethren, and Ephrata Society appeared in his "vision" as grouped on a square in a well-populated city. After describing the Friends as the "most powerful and the richest in the city," he turned his attention to the Brethren:

> On the left across from this house there stood the second house, not as large, to be true, but it struck the eye because of its beautiful paint. Above the door was a lamp which had been overturned, with this inscription:
>
> > "We sing and preach with great outcry;
> > If only the Spirit could be thereby."
>
> These people seem rather peaceful and modest in their conduct. Their clothing is middle-class [*bürgerlich*]. Most of the men wear beards. They do not tolerate infant baptism. When they become adults, and wish to be baptized, they go to where there is water and are immersed three times. They hold communion or love feast often. Their meetings are zealous and their preaching and praying often take place with great clamor, as if their God were hard of hearing. One hymn chases another as if they lacked [inner] silence. They teach their cherished truths after the letter.[1]

Despite the satirical tone of these remarks, derived from the Radical Pietist orientation of the writer, several comments are noteworthy. Brethren enjoyed a good reputation; their conduct was well respected. Love feasts were held often, an interesting point because the traditional pattern of the nineteenth century Brethren was to hold them annually in each congregation. These were, however, ordinarily arranged at different times so that members could visit neighboring or distant congregations to commune, thus being able to participate several times per year.

Brethren at mid-eighteenth century were pictured as wearing the normal dress of the citizenry. This indicates that the severely plain garb that later became typical for them had not yet become standardized, although it is probable that their garb was quite simple in style. Most of the men wore beards, as did the Mennonites. This is corroborated by other records in America and in Europe, where the Brethren were referred to as the "bearded ones."[2]

The zeal and liveliness of Brethren worship, though satirized by the author, were often noted by contemporaries. Their singing was energetic and many hymns were used. This fervor was often mentioned by converts as the reason they joined the Brethren, as for example, many Mennonites and Amish did throughout the eighteenth century. According to J. B. S., Mennonite "meetings are often sleepy affairs"; some of them found more spiritual food for their souls with the Brethren.[3]

MEETING PLACES

Through much of the eighteenth century, Brethren met in homes, following apostolic practice as they understood it. The Baptist historian Morgan Edwards counted only four meetinghouses in 1770, when he took a census of Brethren congregations. He quoted them as explaining their lack of formal meeting places by preferring "rather to meet *from house to house* in imitation of the primitive Christians." As late as 1855 the Annual Meeting answered a query whether it was "conforming to the world to build meetinghouses"; the answer was that it was not "if built without unnecessary ornaments, and only for the worship of God."[4]

Price's meetinghouse at North Coventry, Chester County, Pennsylvania, built in 1817. *Durnbaugh Collection.*

Brethren in Germantown met in private homes until 1760. According to Brethren historian Abraham Harley Cassel, the separatist printer Christoph Sauer made the second floor of his spacious stone house on Germantown Avenue available to the Brethren for worship services, though not himself a member. From 1760 to 1770 Brethren used a room in the log structure known as the Pettikoffer house in Germantown as their place of meeting. The complicated line of ownership of this building can be traced in the surviving parchment deeds. Interestingly, a room and kitchen in the structure were set aside as dwelling for a poor widow. When the congregation outgrew this arrangement and built a new meetinghouse, the entire house was given over to housing for widows until it was razed in 1861.[5]

In 1770 a solid stone meetinghouse was built next to the Pettikoffer house. It still stands, though much altered, as part of the churchhouse at 6611 Germantown Avenue. It was erected in the same year as the Mennonite meetinghouse located several blocks south on the same street; the two buildings closely resemble each other and may have been constructed by the same builders.

The Germantown meetinghouse has served over the decades both as a facility for the local congregation and also as a museum and information center for visitors. Members of all Brethren bodies stemming from Schwarzenau have looked upon it as the "mother church" and have enjoyed viewing the building, its appurtenances, and the adjoining burial ground. This was the last resting place for many members, after being placed into use in 1793. The remains of Alexander Mack, Sr., joined those of his son when the former were transferred from an older burial place in 1894.

Visitors to Germantown usually trek as well to the nearby site on the Wissahickon River where Brethren met in 1723 for the first baptisms. In May, 1955, young people of the Eastern Region of the Church of the Brethren erected a memorial plaque there "To honor those who have passed this way...To inspire all who seek to follow."[6]

The oldest virtually unchanged Brethren meetinghouse is located at Pricetown in Berks County. It was constructed in 1777 as a gift from the local elder Martin Gaube. The simple but handsome lines of the stone structure can be found repeated by many meetinghouses erected during the nineteenth century. The starkly bare interior had no decoration or frills, save for racks with pegs for the broad-brimmed hats of the male members. Benches without backs were positioned across the long axis of the building for seating. As was the custom for all denominations of the time, men and boys took places on one side of the central aisle, women and girls on the other.

The Pricetown meetinghouse is noted for a stone annex, the outside door of which served as a separate women's entrance. The annex contains a hearth and still-existing wooden crane, which was used for preparing the broth for love feasts. The hearth at Germantown was in a different location, on a lower level beneath the meetinghouse proper. Because of these facilities for cooking, at least one Brethren historian claimed that the Brethren were the first American denomination to feature kitchens in their places of worship, now almost universal in church plants across the nation.[7]

The Klein meetinghouse near Harleysville, Pennsylvania, part of the Indian Creek congregation, stands as one of the oldest

Brethren frame structures. It was constructed in 1843 and features the typical two outside doors on the long side of the building that provide separate entryways for men and women. As at Germantown and Pricetown, the interior is barren of anything but benches and a preachers' table.[8]

All three meetinghouses are noteworthy in having the area where preaching took place situated on the same level as the benches of the worshiping congregation. Ministers took seats on a bench placed behind the simple trestle table on which they could rest their Bibles and songbooks. The lack of elevation for speakers was to symbolize the equality of all members. An often repeated statement in sermons emphasized that "at the foot of the cross of Jesus Christ all stand on the same level."

One adaptation of this feature may be seen in some early meetinghouses. In these, the floor of the house slopes upward from the preaching bench and table in such a way that seated members were eye-to-eye with preachers when they stood to speak. Ordinarily benches in early meetinghouses were in rows along the long axis of the structures, but in some cases they were placed along three sides of the building's interior, thus allowing face-to-face worship. In Brethren understanding the Holy Spirit was present throughout the church body, not confined to a specific site such as an altar.

As churchhouses were built throughout the nineteenth century, they tended to follow the simple lines of the early meetinghouses, differing primarily in their greater size. Some have likened them in general appearance to the substantial barns that Brethren farmers erected on their lands. Stories of individual congregations included in the series of district histories compiled in the twentieth century repeat similar accounts of the members' pooling resources and labor to raise these simple structures, ordinarily constructed under the direction of a master carpenter and often completed without plans.

Dunkers accepted the values underlying severe simplicity, as expressed by an entry in the almsbook of Mennonites in Lower Montgomery County, Pennsylvania, who were about to build a new meetinghouse. In translation, it reads, "There shall be no intent to erect a proud and magnificent temple according to the principles of ornamentation and pride, no superfluities, nothing unnecessary. Instead, the purpose shall be to erect only that which is serviceable, orderly, becoming, and lasting."[9]

Brethren leaders found virtue in simple meetinghouses because they welcomed the common people. This view was forcefully articulated in the chapter on nonconformity written by R. H. Miller in his influential book *The Doctrine of the Brethren Defended* (1876). Following his advocacy of ministers who used plainness and simplicity in their preaching, he wrote,

> We do not only need a ministry suited to preaching the gospel to the poor, but we must have a meeting house, a place of worship, built in such plain and humble style that all may come, even the poor,...where they can feel welcome and feel at home; not a house built in the highest style and fashion of the day, costing from one to two hundred thousand dollars, and finished in the most costly manner, with painted glass, and cushioned pews to be sold to the highest bidder to pay the high salary of the great minister, whose family must be kept in the highest circle of society....

Miller continued in a pungently egalitarian style to condemn the robed choirs and costly organs common in the fancy churches to "harmonize with the gewgaw style of ribbons, feathers and furbelows which adorn the gay assembly as it meets for pleasure and display." Miller complained that this drove away from the church the poor who live "in sound of its tolling bell, and die with old age without ever hearing the gospel preached, because the style of such a church forms a circle in society too high for their poverty and too grand for their families."[10]

WORSHIP SERVICES

As is the case with other topics of colonial Brethren history, we lack detailed descriptions of Brethren worship practice. It can be inferred from some early accounts of devotional gatherings among the Pietists in the German states, from scattered accounts, and from the

The Pfoutz meetinghouse of the Marsh Creek congregation near Gettysburg, Pennsylvania, built in 1833 and enlarged in 1883. S. S. W. Hammers photo, *Durnbaugh Collection.*

practice of the Brethren in the nineteenth century. Because Brethren were at pains to retain their order over the decades, it is generally safe to extrapolate earlier practices from those followed later.

The simple pattern of worship typical of Brethren in America had been foreshadowed by the meetings of Pietism from which they sprang. Gatherings of Pietists met for mutual edification and support. When they came together, they sang, prayed, read the scriptures, and heard interpretations of these verses from those whom they discerned to have this gift. In a hearing of Heidelberg Pietists in 1709 their interrogators asked them if it was their belief that unlearned artisans of their day were given the same grace as God gave the apostles. They responded that "the door of grace is open for all people, and God is still the same God, which He was from eternity, who can give them grace as He did to the twelve apostles." Upon further query, they answered that they knew of two men who had this apostolic grace, the nobleman E. C. Hochmann von Hochenau and Alexander Mack, formerly of Schreisheim, then at Schwarzenau.[11]

During Brethren worship in the later eighteenth century and through most of the nineteenth century, the ministers, sitting on a bench behind the preacher's table, conferred among themselves as to who would deliver the main sermon. It was customary for them to "pass the liberty" from the most senior to the most junior of the multiple ministry; one willing to speak would stand and read a scripture. Ministers from a distance were given priority in speaking. After the extended sermon, ordinarily well over an hour and usually delivered in a chanting manner, two or three other ministers would speak to corroborate what had been presented, at times expanding on points touched only briefly in the main sermon. The service of worship would ordinarily take several hours to complete, following which those attending would linger in fellowship.[12]

In earlier years it was not the custom for services to be held in each congregation each Sunday. Because congregational districts covered considerable territory, it was not possible for all members to reach the preaching point on foot, on horseback, or by horse and wagon on every Lord's Day. These places were alternated around the territory to make more equitable the amount of traveling required of each member.

By the nineteenth century, it was common for preaching schedules for several months to be printed and circulated. One congregation might have as many as twelve or fifteen preaching points and several meetinghouses; without such a guide it was difficult to recall where services would be held on a specific Sunday. Members were admonished not to choose favorite speakers and attend on that basis, but this sometimes happened.

FORMS OF MINISTRY

While Brethren placed great importance upon the equality of all persons under God, they were also concerned about conducting their community in good order. For this reason, from the beginning they "set aside" those of their number to carry out ministerial duties. These men neither possessed formal theological studies nor desired such. What they did have were substantial self-taught biblical knowledge and innate skills in pastoral care. They were often referred to as *Lehrer*, that is teachers, those who could instruct their fellows in God's word, or *Prediger*, that is preachers, those who could expound God's word. Also important for the congregation as a basis for ministerial selection was the personal character of this leader and his reputation in the broader community.

Again, it was Morgan Edwards who provided information about the method by which these ministers were selected. By his 1770 account, Brethren permitted every brother "to stand up in the congregation to speak in a way of exhortation and expounding." When by this means the congregation identified someone "eminent for [biblical] *knowledge* and *aptness* to teach," he was selected as a minister. He was ordained by the laying on of hands, "attended with fasting and prayer and giving the right hand of fellowship."[13]

Additional calls were given to what Edwards termed exhorters, those who were licensed to minister their gifts "statedly," that is, by special appointment. Brethren gradually came to identify three orders or levels of ministry: the ministers in the first degree, the second degree, and ordained elders. The last named were proven and tested ministers, who were given the oversight over one or more congregations ("housekeeping"). They also visited adjoining congregations to preside over the election of new ministers or to adjust difficulties. Edwards used the term bishop; although that term is found in nineteenth-century Brethren usage, the term *elder* was more common in Brethren vocabulary.

Another level of leadership was found in the deacons and deaconesses ("ancient widows"), who served the material needs of any members requiring assistance such as the ill and elderly. Deacons also were involved in the annual visits before love feasts to ascertain whether unity prevailed in the congregation.

Morgan Edwards observed that all grades of ministry served without compensation ("though they admit their right to pay"), considering it more blessed to give than to receive. He concluded that the ministers, as well as their flocks, were a body of "meek and pious Christians," whose "acquaintance with the Bible is admirable."[14] Not all contemporaries admired the Brethren in this way. They experienced criticism, in particular from the German Lutheran and German Reformed clergy, who were often disgruntled about the goodly number of their parishioners who left to join the Brethren in the free air of Pennsylvania and other colonies. Typical of many was the harsh comment of Heinrich Melchior Mühlenberg, who organized the Lutheran Church in Pennsylvania and other colonies.

He pointed out that the Quakers and the German plain groups had an economic advantage by arriving early in the colonies' existence. Because they were not dependent on any government to organize and maintain their congregations, they were able to adjust much more quickly to the freedom of religion and absence of state church establishment found in Pennsylvania. Further, the church folk had no adequate pastoral leadership for many years. For these reasons, many Lutheran and Reformed who wished to "have prestige can find no better opportunity than to go over to their side," that is, to the plain folk. Here is Mühlenberg's comment about the Brethren following his appraisal of the Ephrata Society:

> If one wants to be master of his own property and land, and still become something special, which has a better appearance than the usual church system, then one can be converted to the belief of the so-called Sunday Baptists [in contrast to the sabbatarians at Ephrata]. All one needs to do is to memorize several verses from the Revelation of John about Babel, the Beast and the Harlot, present along with this a good outward appearance, and be publicly baptized by them by immersion. Their lessons are very comfortably and easily learned. All that is necessary is to mock infant baptism, and condemn all others who do not agree with them, especially the clergy and church people.[15]

Beneath the harshness of this observation can be discerned several significant points. Brethren opposed the established or state-church system and followed the voluntary system of religious freedom. The language of their critique (*Babel, Beast, Harlot*) was taken from Radical Pietist vocabulary. They held infant baptism to be invalid and nonscriptural and emphasized the immersion baptism of adult believers. They placed importance on moral character (good outward appearance). Members were respected in the broader society (could become something special). Although considered sectarian and narrow, the Brethren presented an attractive option for many German immigrants.

CHURCH POLITY

Because Brethren emerged in reaction to a highly organized and bureaucratized state church, they were slow to develop a carefully articulated church government. They were content to develop in an informal and largely unstructured manner. They were a movement rather than an institution. As problems arose, leaders met or communicated with each other to reach a unified position. Brethren were never completely congregational in polity; rather, they always emphasized the connectional spirit of unity among and between the several congregations.

One major challenge to Brethren identity and self-understanding seems to have stimulated the emergence of what was later to become the centerpiece of Brethren church organization; this was variously called the Yearly Meeting, Great Meeting, Annual Meeting, and finally Annual Conference. Its roots go back to the early 1740s. The stimulus was the arrival in North America in late 1741 of the charismatic leader of the Renewed Moravian Church, Count Nicholas Ludwig von Zinzendorf.[16]

Count Zinzendorf had two ambitious goals in America: to bring Christianity to the Native Americans and to institute a unique form of church union, especially among the German-speaking sects and churches. He believed that the New World with its comparative religious freedom offered an excellent opportunity to put his plan into effect. Far from the stuffy chancelleries and raging doctrinal disputes of Europe, he would bring a new ecumenical vision to demonstrate that a God of love could "make all things new."

He had a base from which to operate; the Associated Brethren of the Skippack formed in 1736 a loosely-knit fellowship of separatists and believers from several denominations, who met once a month to edify themselves and to seek closer Christian unity. They were disturbed by the growing secularization in the colony; increasingly residents were careless about religious affiliation and activity. It said of those indifferent to the faith that they had "the Pennsylvania religion." The Associated Brethren sought religious renewal in the colony.

Zinzendorf had been well informed of the association by one of their number, his advance agent, Augustus Gottlieb Spangenberg. Beginning early in 1742 Zinzendorf called together a series of meetings soon called the Pennsylvania Synods, eventually seven in number. An average of one hundred participants attended each gathering, coming from nine different denominational backgrounds. Brethren were represented by five persons, especially Georg Adam Martin, Andreas Frey and Joseph Müller; the last two named took leading roles.

Despite this initially favorable reaction, Brethren abandoned the meetings after the third synod, which met in the Oley region in February 1742. They had two main grievances. First, they sensed that the count was overly dominant during the proceedings, manipulating events and conclusions. Second, they were perturbed when three Indian converts were baptized at Oley by sprinkling rather than by what they considered to be the apostolic manner of immersion. By his own account, Georg Adam Martin returned from the Oley synod convinced that Zinzendorf was using the conferences as "snares" in order to bring the naive and inexperienced "back to infant baptism and church-going," that is, to "erect the old Babel again." He took counsel with his elder, Martin Urner of Coventry, who had sent him to the synod as a representative. They agreed, again by Martin's account, to summon Brethren leaders to hold their own conference so as to unite in opposition to Zinzendorf's program. This gathering, in late spring 1742, is thus "the beginning and foundation of the Great Assemblies of the [German] Baptists."[17]

Although the Brethren withdrew, the final judgment upon them by the Moravian-led synod was rather positive. Although held to be "without illumination," they were considered a "congregation of

God-fearing folk...who are earnest and therefore appealing people." If some persons "make up their minds to live among them and be loyal to them, they are happy...." The ecumenically minded synod recommended that the Brethren and Mennonites come to an agreement about the method of baptism and then unite, thus making "one less sect in the country."[18]

The two Brethren most active in the synods, Joseph Müller and Andreas Frey, were persuaded to accompany Count Zinzendorf back to Europe. Frey soon became disaffected and left for North America but Müller stayed until 1749, when he also returned to Pennsylvania. He thereupon sought to persuade former Brethren to make common cause with the Moravians. This brought about another large gathering of Brethren leaders, likely to be considered another Yearly Meeting, though held in February 1750. They firmly rejected Müller's appeal, considering him now a "friend" not a brother, and requested him in a firm manner to renounce his mistakes and "fables." If he would do that, then they would consider him to be a "brand plucked from the burning." This communication was signed by thirty-one ministers, who had evidently been called together in a special meeting to make this decision.[19]

Another serious challenge arose more than a decade later around the visions after 1762 of a young Brethren woman, Catherine Hummer of the White Oak congregation in Lancaster County. She was the daughter of Peter Hummer, the first minister within the bounds of the congregation. The heaven-sent visions, as she understood them, created a major stir among the Brethren and others; they were supported by Peter Hummer as divine in nature. Many of the curious flocked to hear the reports of the visions. The Germantown separatist and former inspired leader Johann Adam Gruber reported to correspondents in Europe that Catherine Hummer had seen "many hundred persons baptizing in eternity," that is, in paradise.

A Yearly Meeting in May 1763 discussed the difficulties caused by the "astonishing occurrences and various transactions...since the exercises, visions, and actions...of Sister Catherine Hummer" took place. Those who gathered came from their "different places of residence in the fear of the Lord in heartfelt and compassionate brotherly love" to address the question. They chose not to pronounce on the validity of the visions as such, but did pronounce against the disunity which reports of the visions had caused. They disapproved of the unusual activities connected with it and asked all members to be tolerant of those with conflicting opinions for the sake of unity:

> Now, if one or the other thinks that we have not suffi-
> ciently judged the occurrence, let him consider that we
> cannot in the least give cause for a separation for con-
> science' sake. Therefore we felt constrained not to criti-
> cize or judge this strange happening but rather urge
> everyone to a God-like impartiality and patience, lest
> someone judge before the time when the Lord comes,
> who will also reveal the hidden things of darkness and
> will make manifest the counsel of the heart.[20]

This conclusion was signed by twenty-two leading ministers, including Sander Mack. He later expressed much the same point of view in an often-quoted communication. This was contained in a letter included as an appendix in a second edition (1774) of the doc-trinal treatises of his father. It described a serious difference of opin-ion in the Germantown congregation about the correct order of the elements of the love feast, in particular, at which time the feetwash-ing should take place.

Sander Mack reported that in his experience the ordinance had been performed at different points, according to the biblical under-standing of the time. When better understanding was forthcoming, the timing was changed. He was especially concerned that the love and unity of the church not be lost. He reminded his readers that Jesus Christ did not say that his disciples would be recognized by the manner of feetwashing or breaking of bread, but rather that all "shall know that you are my disciples, that you have love for one another." Inasmuch as they are to be so minded to submit to each other in "love and peace and humility," it would be scandalous if a service of humility should lead to hard feelings. "Oh, how Satan could mock us if we were to quarrel with one another about the time when the feet should be washed, and love would be destroyed...."

Mack concluded his ardent discussion with these classic words: "Therefore, dear brethren, let us watch and be careful, and *above all preserve love, for thus one preserves light.* The spirit of truth testifies in 1 John 2:10: 'He who loves his brother abides in the light, and in him there is no cause for stumbling.' "[21]

CHURCH DISCIPLINE

As these examples make clear, Brethren were very concerned with the unity of the body, and this could only be maintained, they believed, by loving church discipline. This concern had been present at the very beginning of the movement. As we have seen in the open letter to Palatine Pietists, the unnamed writer had placed this at the forefront of the invitation to join in the first baptisms: "There is also an exact relationship and brotherly discipline, according to the teaching of Jesus Christ and his apostles."[22]

This was one of the points of debate between the early Brethren and their former associates among the Radical Pietists. The latter contended that the Brethren were falling into sectarianism by this emphasis upon discipline. The former held, for their part, that the "false love" and tolerance of the Pietists was not taking discipleship seriously. In fact, Brethren efforts to maintain "the law of Christ" (Matthew 18:15ff.) resulted in much tension within their ranks; it was not always possible, they found, to "speak the truth in love" to the satisfaction of all members.

Among the few Brethren records preserved from the colonial era, several deal with cases of church discipline. Even the families of church leaders felt the sting of disapproval. In a letter in 1776 to his dear friend Johannes Preiß, Sander Mack revealed that his daughter Hannah had been shunned apparently for having sexual relations with her fiancé before marriage. He also reported that his daughter Sarah was denied the holy kiss of peace and participation in communion because she married outside of the church. A daughter of Johannes Naas had suffered the same penalty because of a moral indiscretion. Discipline was also exercised over cases of slave holding, military involvement, and heretical teachings, to name some of the most grievous infractions.[23]

BRETHREN ORDINANCES

Brethren rejected the traditional emphasis of institutional churches on the sacramental system. In this understanding the chief elements of religious faith were receiving the rite of infant baptism to remove original sin and the bread and cup in the eucharist as bearers of God's grace. Brethren were concerned about following the ordinances, that is, those special actions commanded by Jesus Christ, as an integral part of their lives of discipleship and obedience. In their understanding, these ordinances included baptism of adult believers by three-fold immersion; the love feast involving the three-fold elements of feet-washing, the Lord's Supper or meal of fellowship, and the communion of bread and cup; the holy kiss; anointing of the ill or those suffering from brokenness of relationship with God or others; and laying on of hands. In a negative sense, refusing to swear oaths and refusing to perform military duties were virtually seen as ordinances.[24]

The commonly used nicknames of Dunkers or Dunkards for the Brethren recall the emphasis they placed upon an apostolic form of initiation into the church. They were convinced of the validity of this method through their study of the scriptures (Matthew 28:19 and elsewhere) and of histories of the early church. They may have also been influenced by the earlier immersionist movements, the Dompelaars and the Collegiants.

Because of their insistence on this practice, Brethren found themselves in debate with leaders of the church folk, especially Lutherans, Reformed, and Anglicans, all of whom continued and justified theologically the traditional practice of infant baptism. Although Brethren agreed completely with the Mennonites about the merits of believers' baptism, as contrasted to infant baptism, they contended that the Mennonite modes of pouring or sprinkling were not as biblical as theirs of three-fold and complete immersion. In conversations with the Friends, Brethren defended the importance of the outward form of baptism of believers, over against the Quaker emphasis upon the inward baptism with the fire of the Holy Spirit. Friends acknowledged that the Brethren usage was biblical but considered it to be unnecessary for those who had attained greater maturity in the spirit life.

In addition to their peculiar form of baptism, the Brethren practice of the love feast was quite distinctive. Indeed, the Moravian Brethren had a "love feast" but this consisted of serving coffee and rolls at special morning services and fell short, in the Brethren view, of appropriate biblical observance. A Brethren love feast took most of two days, not counting the travel time to attend, which could be lengthy.[25]

They gathered on a Saturday afternoon for a service of examination; this had been preceded by the annual visit of the deacons, who ascertained whether all members were at peace and unity with one another. Any differences or tensions that became evident during the visits were to be resolved, so that the communion could take place worthily. It was not unknown in cases of serious difficulty for the love feast to be postponed until harmony prevailed. In other cases, individuals not in unity would be asked to refrain from communing, so as to avoid bringing condemnation upon themselves (Matthew 5:23-24). To be set back from the love feast was an important part of the practice of church discipline.

When the service of examination was concluded, tables were prepared for the evening service. It was important to Brethren that the Lord's Supper be held in the evening, following the precedent of Jesus in the upper room. With appropriate reading of John 13 and instruction, members engaged in feetwashing. Originally, this was followed in the so-called single mode, which entailed each brother or sister washing and drying the feet of his or her adjacent brother or sister, who then repeated the action, until all had both received and given the service.

The predominant method later in the eighteenth and throughout the nineteenth century was the so-called double mode. In this method, two brothers or two sisters went down the line, one washing and the other drying the feet of those ministered to. After several had been served in this manner, two other brothers or sisters took up the tasks, until all had been served. With this procedure, all communing had their feet washed and dried, but all did not themselves participate in the washing and drying.

A simple meal of fellowship followed, ordinarily consisting of a broth prepared from lamb meat. It was customary in early times for participants to dip from common bowls, at least four to a bowl. A deep and sacred silence was maintained during the meal. This was followed by the holy kiss, sister to sister and brother to brother, around the tables.

The high point of the love feast was the communion of bread and cup. Unleavened bread, prepared by the deaconesses, was broken between male communicants to commemorate Christ's broken body. (The officiating minister broke the bread for the sisters communing.) A large cup containing wine was passed from which members drank to commemorate Christ's blood shed for the remission of their sins (1 Corinthians 11:23-26). Following scriptural narrative, the service was ended by the singing of a hymn, after which communicants left in silence. Those from a distance were invited to the homes of local members or were accommodated in the loft of the meetinghouse, often reached by a ladder on the outside to a gable door. During the following forenoon, the usual lengthy worship service was conducted, often made more memorable by the presence of many visiting members and ministers.

The holy kiss was often commanded by Jesus (Romans 16:18, 1 Corinthians 16:20 and elsewhere) as an expression of the love which should exist between members of the church. Besides the solid scriptural authority, Brethren found the practice documented for the early church (Acts 20:37) and by early church fathers such as Justin Martyr and Cyprian. As has been seen, the ordinance was an important element in the full love feast. Brethren also observed the practice, separated by gender, when meeting in homes and in public gathering for worship. Conversely, withholding the kiss was used in church discipline to indicate estrangement.

Anointing (after James 5:13-16) was a significant part of Brethren church life. As Morgan Edwards explained, they "anoint the sick with oil for recovery." This was ordinarily limited in earlier Brethren practice to cases of mortal illness, as in the Roman Catholic rite of extreme unction. In more recent Brethren usage, anointing can be used in any instance of physical illness or spiritual distress. Because the passage in James speaks of confession, Brethren gave the person being anointed the opportunity to confess sins or make a statement of faith. It has been used in cases of brokenness between individuals to restore the relationship.[26]

Laying on of hands was practiced by Brethren in colonial America principally in three settings: first, at the time of anointing; second, at the baptism of new members; and, third, at the time of setting aside members for advanced ministry. They found the tradition cited in both Old and New Testaments as conveying the sense of blessing or benediction and consecration.

MUSIC AND HYMNALS

Brethren were much influenced in their worship patterns by the Pietist movement which helped to form them. One of the chief contributions of Pietism was a renewal of congregational singing and a renaissance of new hymn writing. In their gatherings for worship, Brethren often used the standard Pietist hymnal, the *Geistreiches Gesang-Buch* ("Spiritual Songbook"), originally published in 1704 by J. A. Freylinghausen.[27]

The first Brethren-sponsored hymnal used the same name, *Geistreiches Gesang-Buch*; it was printed in 1720 in Berleburg, near Schwarzenau. It can be identified as Brethren by several points: it identifies its sponsors as *Taufgesinnte* ("baptism-minded"); it mentions the inclusion of some 100 hymns written by Brethren imprisoned for their faith, a clear reference to Wilhelm Knepper of the Solingen Brethren. It includes the hymn "Count the Cost," known to have been written by Alexander Mack, Sr. Some of its 295 hymns are devoted to distinctive Brethren ordinances, such as the love feast, feetwashing, and immersion baptism.

A puzzling question is why the hymnal is so little known. No reference to it or of its use has been found in Brethren literature. Only five copies have ever been found. At present one remains in Germany and four in North America, located in recent years. A possible explanation, but still speculative, is that the Brethren commissioned the printing of the *Geistreiches Gesang-Buch*, but it only came off the press after they had to leave in 1720 for Friesland.

A much more important hymnal was issued in Pennsylvania in 1744; this was *Das kleine Davidische Psalterspiel* (The Small Davidic Psalter). Brethren had it printed on the Sauer press for their use, because the presence of so many different hymnals at worship was confusing. They intended it as well for use by other Christians, which in fact occurred. It was widely used by a number of different German-speaking bodies and often reprinted. Members of the Sauer printing family reprinted it, with slight changes, five times (1760 to 1797); other printers in other locations republished it eight times before a stereotype edition came out in 1830.

The *Psalterspiel* received a small supplement in 1792, *Die kleine Harfe*; it was published twice by Samuel Sauer, a grandson of the first Sauer printer, near Philadelphia. Containing only 58 hymns, it was notable for including eight hymns composed by five different Brethren authors. They are identified in the second printing. Some other hymn-poems by Brethren were included in smaller, non-hymnbook publications, especially by the Sauer press.

The first Brethren hymnal in the English language appeared in Germantown in 1791; this was *The Christian's Duty*, published by another Brethren printer, Peter Leibert. Some of its 352 hymns were selected from a hymnbook issued by Elhanan Winchester, a leader of the Universalist Church, who had some association with the Brethren in the Philadelphia area. Three later editions were published at Germantown and another at Canton, Ohio.

Strangely, there was almost no congruence between the rich amount of Brethren hymnody in the German language and the growing number of English language appearing in the nineteenth century. It has only been in recent years that some of the early poetry in hymn form has been rediscovered, translated, and placed again in Brethren hymnals. None of these hymnals included musical notes, following the custom of the time. The titles of well-known hymn tunes were indicated, allowing the song leaders to begin the congregational singing. Often the meters (long, short, common, etc.) were also indicated.

Hymns were "lined," that is, the *Vorsänger* (songleader) announced the melody and then read out or sang several lines of the hymn, which the congregation then sang. This was repeated until the hymn was finished. The practice of lining was initiated because of the lack of hymnals in early times; later, even when books were plentiful, lining of hymns continued, partly from long tradition, partly to emphasize community, and partly because those singing could meditate on the meaning of the words for a longer time.

7

The Sauer Press
and Brethren Literature

Of all the persons connected with the colonial Brethren, Christoph
Sauer (Saur, Sower) and his like-named son are the best known in
general American history because of the broad influence they
wielded with German immigrants all along the Atlantic seaboard
through the medium of their printing press in Germantown. Their
integrity was such that their counsel in social and political matters
was widely followed. Most famous for their printing of not one but
three editions of the first complete Bible in a modern language in
America (long before an English Bible appeared), they also published the first successful German-language newspapers, almanacs,
and religious periodicals in North America. Their press was also the
first colonial enterprise to cast type in quantities. Thousands of
copies of their imprints, especially religious and educational books,
poured off their press from its inception in 1738 until the turmoil of
the American Revolution put an abrupt stop to its activity in 1777.[1]

Although Johann Christoph Sauer, Sr., to give him his full
German name, was never a member of the Brethren movement, he
was intimately connected with it. As we have seen, he made the second floor of his spacious residence on Germantown Avenue available as a place of worship for the Brethren until they constructed a
meetinghouse. He attended their meetings and often defended
them publicly. As a religious separatist, he abstained from membership in any faith but was more closely linked with the Brethren than
with any other religious body.[2]

SAUER'S EARLY LIFE

Sauer was born in 1695 in the Palatine village of Ladenburg, only two miles from Schriesheim, the birthplace of Alexander Mack, Sr. Sauer's father, a minister in the German Reformed church, died when the son was only six years old. The bereaved family moved to the Wittgenstein area, where young Christoph learned the tailor's trade and later married. His only son, Christopher II, was born in Laasphe in 1721. Three years later the family—father, mother, and son—migrated to Pennsylvania, settling first in Germantown.

In 1726 the Sauers moved to the Mill Creek valley in what is now Lancaster County, where they purchased fifty acres of uncleared land. This was the area where Conrad Beissel led the Conestoga congregation of the Brethren, before the final division occurred in 1728. Beissel and Sauer had known each other in Wittgenstein and were now neighbors. Israel Eckerlin, one of the sons of the Strasbourg Pietist Michael Eckerlin, recorded that he was taken to a meeting of the Brethren by Sauer.

When Beissel began to evidence signs of his curious doctrines and exalted claims of personal authority, Sauer became critical. This was intensified when the brilliant but erratic Beissel persuaded Sauer's wife, Maria Christina, to leave her family and join his ranks. She later became the assistant superintendent of the sister's house, using the cloistered name of Sister Marcella. She did not rejoin her husband and son until 1744.[3]

THE GERMANTOWN PRINTING PRESS

Sauer returned to Germantown after his wife's desertion. There he worked at a number of crafts; an extremely gifted man, he learned without apprenticeship at least twenty-six trades. His ingenuity is confirmed by contemporaries as well as by his own account. Despite this prowess, which brought with it economic plenty, Sauer longed to establish a printing press to benefit his fellow Germans. He tried but failed to obtain a press and type from the Pietist center at Halle, who saw no need for a printing establishment in the "West Indies." Through the assistance of a separatist colleague in Hesse, he was able to secure the necessary fonts from a well-known typecasting firm in Frankfurt/Main owned by a Dr. Heinrich Luther.

The Germantown craftsman may have acquired a used printing press from Berleburg in Wittgenstein, which he adapted and put into working order. (Sauer also wrote of crafting his own press.)[4] Sauer explained his motivation for this unusual publishing effort in a 1740 letter to Dr. Luther: "My small printing shop, now started, is dedicated to God, and I hope that during my and my son's lives that nothing shall be printed except that which is to the glory of God and for the material or eternal good of my neighbors." Tradition has it that this sentiment was also expressed in a dedication hung in the shop, *Zur Ehre Gottes und des Nächsten Bestes* ("To the glory of God and my neighbor's good").[5]

A glimpse of Sauer's achievements and abilities is seen in a letter of an associate, written one year following the initiation of the printing enterprise:

> Our friend Sauer is a wise and much esteemed man here in this country. He has built a two-story stone house in Germantown, besides a lathe and a glazier workshop, which is very spacious. This summer he erected a building for his book-printing establishment, and also a place to burn lampblack, which he needs partly for his printing press [for ink], the remainder being sold retail and wholesale. He currently carries on six trades, namely: 1) surgeon and bloodletting, plus a small apothecary shop, which I reckon only as one; 2) clock-making...; 3) the lathe-shop...; 4) the glazier shop...; 5) the printing press, wherewith he has already earned at least 1000 florins...; 6) the lamp-black manufacturing etc.[6]

SAUER'S INFLUENCE

The initial product of the Sauer press in 1738 was the first issue of his famous and popular almanac, containing many kinds of practical information. In 1739 he began his influential newspaper, which continued under several different names, formats, and frequency of appearance until 1777. As his readers knew that Sauer could neither be bribed nor intimidated, they trusted his reports and comments implicitly. This gave Sauer great political power, which he used to support the peace-loving policies of the Quaker bloc in the Assembly. His strong pacifist principles often brought him difficulties when he commented acidly on current events. He wrote, for example, that there was no difference between a soldier and a common criminal: "One commits murder with the sanction of the government, the other without. Both are alike in eternity."[7]

In 1748 the father of Lutheranism in America, Heinrich Melchior Mühlenberg, summarized Sauer's role in a report to his sponsors in Halle: "The Quakers, who are the foremost party in this province, have on their side the German book publisher Christoph Sauer, who controls the Mennonites, Separatists, Anabaptists [Brethren], and the like with his printed works and lines them up with the Quakers. All of these speak and write against the war and reject even the slightest defense as ungodly and contrary to the commands of Jesus Christ."[8]

In 1765 Mühlenberg wrote in the same vein, stating that "the Germans had been so inculcated with the idea that if they failed to keep the Quakers in the government and elected in their place Englishmen from the Episcopal or Presbyterian churches, they would be deprived of their ancient rights and liberties and then they would be saddled with laws forcing them to engage in military drill to assist in defense against enemies, and also to pay a tithe to the ministers of the Episcopal church." The German sectarians provided the swing vote in several elections, and Sauer largely guided them in this direction.[9]

As a convinced separatist, the deeply religious Sauer was very critical of religious organizations. He delighted in reporting the failings of the inept and often immoral Lutheran and Reformed clergy in Pennsylvania; quite a number of them came to the colonies when scandals at home ruined their reputations. They proceeded to prey upon rather than pray for their flocks. Later, when better order was brought into their ranks, Sauer was more gracious, although he still maintained his deep suspicions of professional clergymen. For him religion was a deeply personal matter, and no one should receive pay for performing religious ritual.

His starkly separatist stance motivated his political and religious opponents to attempt to create a counterweight by setting up a less independently minded German-language press. Benjamin Franklin tried several times, with little success, to establish a rival press during the lifetime of the first Sauer. It was not until 1762 that Johann Heinrich Müller (Miller), a sometime Moravian, succeeded in large part in breaking the monopoly of the Sauer press, then directed by Sauer II. Müller lost no time in aligning himself with the so-called Presbyterian party that was gaining influence in the Commonwealth. As the tensions between the American colonists and the British government intensified, Müller became openly pro-independence. His press was the first to publish the Declaration of Independence.

The Charity School Scheme

A celebrated case illuminating these struggles was that of the Charity School scheme of the 1750s. Benefactors in England and on the Continent were persuaded to donate funds ostensibly to provide instruction in English for the benighted children of German immigrants in Pennsylvania. The plan won the support of Lutheran and Reformed clergymen (the potential schoolmasters) as it seemed to offer another means of support not dependent on the whims of reluctant parishioners. Sauer immediately attacked the plan on two grounds. In the first place, he denied the picture painted by proponents that the Germans were wretchedly ignorant and a menace to society. In the second place, he noted that the project's supporters were the political opponents of the Quakers and suspected that the plan was a device to gain support for the war party. As Sauer wrote, the real purpose was to get the "Germans to stick their necks out by serving in the Militia" in order to protect the property of leading politicians, including Franklin, "who care very little either for religion or for the cultivation of the Germans."[10]

Proponents of the Charity Schools quickly established a rival German-language press, one of the first issues of which was a German translation of the royal articles of war. Sauer pointed out that this was a curious production for a program ostensibly dedicated to the religious instruction of children. The Charity School program soon failed, in part because Sauer turned public opinion against it. Lutheran and Reformed clergy also turned away from the plan when one of its major backers, the Anglican divine William Smith, revealed his intention to incorporate the members of their churches into the Church of England.

THE GERMANTOWN BIBLE

Sauer's greatest single undertaking was the publication in 1743 of the entire German Bible (including the Apocrypha) in the Martin Luther translation, with minor additions from the Radical Pietist Berleburg Bible. As an agent of German-language Bibles printed in the homeland, Sauer was aware of the demand for scriptures among the increasing number of German immigrants. He had a keen desire to further the cause of religion among the German element, despite his standing criticisms of churchly bureaucracy. He was concerned that the poor among them were barred from possession of Bibles because of their high cost. For these reasons, only three years after beginning his printing shop, he announced his intention by releasing a prospectus, with a sample page of the Bible on the reverse side.

Early in 1742 he further publicized the ambitious venture through a notice in the *American Weekly Mercury* issued in Philadelphia, in particular seeking to learn how many copies of the Bible he could reasonably publish:

> Whereas Numbers of the Dutch people in this province, especially of the Newcomers, are thro' mere poverty unable to furnish themselves with Bibles in their own language, at the advanced price those which are brought from Germany are usually sold at here; Therefore Christopher Sauer of Germantown, proposes to print a High Dutch Bible in large Quarto, and in a Character that may be easily read even by old Eyes.[11]

The now-demolished residence of Christoph Sauer I and his son at 4645-4653 Germantown Avenue with the printshop and bindery behind it. In   M.G. Brumbaugh's *A History of the German Baptist Brethren in Europe and America* (Elgin, Ill.: 1899), p. 355.

He solicited contributions for the project so that the Bibles could be sold at reduced prices to the poor, including servants. Sauer noted that some benefactors had already pledged to make such donations; he promised full public accounting of the contributions received. The anticipated price was fourteen shillings without subsidies, less if sufficient gifts were forthcoming. He hoped to begin work in April and anticipated completion within a year's time (it actually took fifteen months). A similar announcement was included in his almanac for 1742.

By the fall of 1743 some 1,200 copies of the Bible had been print-ed, with 1,267 pages in each. The last copies of the edition were sold five years after Sauer's death in 1758. The handsome title page was printed in two colors with red and black ink. Sauer announced with some pride in a preface that more than 100 typographical errors in the Luther text were corrected in his edition. Unfortunately, the title page had to be reset for later copies and in this version, one of the reprinted words lacked a letter.

The reason for the change in the title page had to do with the reception of the Bible by the Lutheran and Reformed faiths. Even though the 34th edition of Luther's translation (printed at Halle) had been used as the text of the Germantown Bibles, the clergy of those churches had warned their flocks against their purchase. The pastors had smarted under Sauer's critical attention to the many problems among their parishes. They were not eager for their parishioners to give their patronage to the "arch-separatist" Sauer. Cynics also pointed out that they were themselves agents for German-language Bibles imported to Pennsylvania and had therefore an economic interest in Bible sales.

Their eagle eyes searched for grounds for criticism and found them. A phrase on the title page stated that the new Bible featured the "usual appendix." In fact, Sauer had included in the Bible an appendix to the Apocrypha from the Radical Pietist Berleburg Bible (not contained in the Halle edition) and a brief passage in Job (19:25-27) with both Lutheran and Berleburg versions. He had also included a brief descriptive statement at the end of the New Testament with some of his own views on scripture. To mollify these critics, Sauer reset the title page to omit the phrase "usual appendix," thus creating the possibility for the embarrassing typographical error.

This notwithstanding, experts agree that the Germantown Bible of 1743 is a true masterpiece of the printer's art, the more remarkable for its production by a pioneer press. When the international Gutenberg Museum of printing in Mainz, Germany, was rebuilt and rededicated after World War II, the US government donated one of the Sauer Bibles as its gift for the important event; to this day the 1743 Germantown Bible is featured in the museum.

After completing this tremendous feat of printing, Sauer sent a shipment of twelve of the Bibles to his patron in Frankfurt, Dr. Luther, from whom he had purchased his type fonts. The ship carrying the Bibles was captured by pirates off the French coast and the cargo sold at public auction. By accident (or providence), Dr. Luther heard about the sale, traced the buyer, and acquired the Bibles. He had a Latin dedication printed which explained the origin and adventurous journey of these "Apostle Bibles," as he called them. These dedications he pasted in the Bibles, which he then donated to leading public and aristocratic libraries in major European cities, some copies of which still remain. The dedication reads in part, in translation,

> This Holy Book is up to this time without example in the West Indies, as it has previously been published there neither in the English, Dutch, nor any other language....The publisher of this novelty and rarity, Christopher Sauer, a most famous man in that area because of his talent and industry, entrusted this book with eleven other copies to a ship sailing across the ocean to Europe....So go forth then, Book, distinguished with the name "apostle" because of your miraculous fate, and embellish and increase, with your brothers which have been won back to freedom, the most flourishing libraries....[12]

CHRISTOPH SAUER II

The great founder of the Germantown press died on September 25, 1758. His son, who had been active as a bookbinder, hesitated to take over the responsibility of the press. In the first issue of the newspaper under his own authority, the second Sauer wrote, "Even though I have not received, nor probably ever will, such a rich measure of gifts [as he had], yet I shall faithfully serve with that which I will be given. And since I know that I, like my father and even much more than he, will have to pass through many good and bad judgments, I have already prepared myself even for that and neither one thing nor another will prevent me from doing what I believe is right and good."[13]

In fact he built up the press to a peak of productivity and prosperity surpassing that of his father. He pushed two more editions of the German Bible through the press in 1763 and 1776 and introduced the first solely religious periodical in North America, *Ein Geistliches Magazien* (The Spiritual Storehouse) in 1764. Published irregularly until 1773, the periodical when completed consisted of sixty-five issues in two volumes. Because Sauer was doing well financially with his newspaper, he distributed the periodical to sub-scribers free of charge. It contained edifying essays, poems, and nar-ratives, including some original compositions by Brethren. Sauer also engaged himself in the political process when he thought it essential and became nearly as influential as had been his father, although his stance was not as aggressive.[14]

Unlike his father, the younger Sauer was an active member of the Brethren. Baptized in 1737, he became a deacon in 1747, a min-ister in 1748, and an elder in 1753. He was a key figure in the Germantown congregation and in the broader church. Through his publications, he made Brethren principles known on a great num-ber of public issues such as peace, education, and morality. He attacked, for example, the practice of slaveholding (as had his father before him), then widely defended by respectable businessmen even in the northern colonies. A friend of public schooling, he was one of the most important sponsors of the well-known Germantown Academy.

BRETHREN LITERARY ACTIVITY

For a relatively unlettered folk, the Brethren in colonial America engaged in a surprising amount of literary activity. If the total pro-duction of the press of Sauer, father and son, were to be included, the extent of publication would be huge. This, however, would be inappropriate because the Sauer press was not a church undertak-ing (as some historians have claimed) but rather a private venture. The Brethren, indeed, did feel in some ways responsible for the pub-lications of Sauer II as a member of the faith. On occasion they sent church leaders to him on disciplinary visits because of their dis-pleasure with some of the material he printed, in particular that sponsored by the Lutheran and Reformed churches.[15]

A bibliographical listing of Brethren publications lists over fifty items issued before 1800, only a few of which were released in

Europe.[16] Some were reprints and later editions, but many were new creations. A typical item was a 1747 booklet called *Ein Geringer Schein des verachteten Lichtleins* (A Humble Gleam of the Despised Little Light of the Truth), written in answer to a German-language Quaker tract. The three points covered were "On the Holy Scriptures," "On the True Conversion," and "On the Baptism of Christ."

The first section begins, "The Holy Scriptures are a letter of God which He has written to the human race through the operation of his Holy Spirit." The unknown author presented in clear language the Brethren viewpoint on disputed points, with strong emphasis upon the necessity for baptism of true believers by a three-fold immersion, thus rebutting the Quaker view that denied the need of outward baptism but rather called for an inward baptism of the spirit.[17]

ALEXANDER MACK, JR. AND MICHAEL FRANTZ

The most prolific of the Brethren writers during the colonial period was Alexander (Sander) Mack, Jr. At his death (1803) Sander Mack left many unpublished poems and manuscripts.[18] His two most ambitious published efforts were polemical in nature, defenses of Brethren doctrines on believer's baptism, church discipline, and other basic tenets. He replied to the critiques of a Lutheran divine, the Reverend Dr. Johann Christoff Kunze of Philadelphia and New York. The first of these publications by Mack was (in English translation) the *Apologia or Spiritual Vindications* (1788), which linked Kunze's critique of Brethren baptismal practices with running rebuttal in dialogue form. A spirited rejoinder by Kunze motivated Mack's second response, the *Appendix to the Conquered Anabaptist* (1788), which is as valuable for its historical material as for its line of reasoning.[19]

In addition, Sander Mack maintained a lively personal correspondence with Brethren in several colonies, primarily to give spiritual counsel; those letters which have been preserved reveal his character as one of deep piety and personal concern. A spirit of amity, tenderness, and care for others shines through his written work, especially his poetry and correspondence.[20] After 1772 it was his practice to write a poem on each anniversary of his birth. The last was written in 1802 shortly before his death in 1803. He composed his own epitaph: "God, who us of dust did make/And us again to dust will take—/His wisdom, like the sun, shall break/When in his likeness we awake."[21]

An important doctrinal treatise, written by the Conestoga elder Michael Frantz, appeared in print in 1770, more than twenty years after Frantz died. Under fifty pages in length, it is partly in prose and partly in verse. Among the themes he discusses are Brethren emphases such as nonconformity, the ordinances, the congregation, not taking oaths, church discipline, and simplicity of life; he also treats basic theological topics such as the foundation of faith, incarnation, unity with God, and resurrection of the dead. Personal concerns include marriage, celibacy, poverty and wealth, work, and recreation. Frantz also deals with issues relating to church and state, such as citizenship and military participation, in the surprisingly full if concise collection. Taken altogether, it is the most comprehensive summary of Brethren beliefs of the colonial period.

Something of the spirit of Frantz's writings can be gleaned from the following passage dealing with the relationship between the outward and inward communion with God:

> If the inward communion with God has been truly realized, it will issue in outward communion as described above, with all kinds of virtues of love, for when the name of the word of congregation or communion is spoken in truth, then the words "mine" and "yours" must no longer be heard. That is to say [that] no one is to own or possess anything by himself any longer. To this extent "mine" and "yours" may be spoken on this basis, that this is mine and that is yours to administer and keep until a time of need for the poor and suffering in and outside of the congregation. To love one's neighbor as one's self shows clearly what communion is.[22]

ALEXANDER MACK, SR. AND ANDREAS FREY

The most substantial Brethren publications during this period were printed in 1774; they were the second editions (issued in one volume) of the foundational writings of Alexander Mack, Sr., published in Wittgenstein, the so-called *Basic Questions* and *Rights and Ordinances*. Of especial importance to Brethren history was an introduction to the work written by Sander Mack. Based partly on papers derived from Mack, Sr., and Peter Becker and partly on conversations with these and other early Brethren, the introduction is the first historical account of Brethren beginnings. Given the lack of original records and the sparsity of contemporary descriptions, the pages by Mack are of inestimable value for their accurate facts and revealing insight into the religious orientation and manner of the founders of the Brethren movement.[23]

These books by Mack, Sr., were published in a third edition by Samuel Saur in Baltimore in 1799. Saur was a grandson of the first Christoph Sauer; after the Revolution he published books and almanacs in Chestnut Hill near Philadelphia before moving to Baltimore in 1795 where he became better known as a typefounder. A fourth edition followed in Lancaster in 1822. The first complete English translation of the *Rights and Ordinances* and *Basic Questions* appeared in Philadelphia in 1810.[24]

Most widely noticed of Brethren-authored publications of the eighteenth century was an exposé of the Renewed Moravian Church by Andreas Frey. His book of 1748, *Andreas Freyen seine Declaration, oder Erklärung* describes his experiences among the Moravians, following his involvement with the ecumenical Pennsylvania Synods of 1742 led by Count Zinzendorf. Frey was chosen by lot to be one of the leaders of the synods and decided to accompany the count when he returned to the Continent. Frey resided for a time in the Moravian colony of Herrnhaag near Büdingen; this was at the peak of the antinomian excesses called by Moravian historians the "Sifting Time." The sober Anabaptist Frey was repelled by the merriment and childish rites led by Zinzendorf's son and reacted badly to the teasing his objections brought him. He returned to Pennsylvania and wrote his exposé.

Because of the international controversy surrounding the Moravian initiatives, Frey's report met with intense interest. It was reprinted three times in Germany and given Dutch (1750) and English (1753) translation. The full title of the English version provides a summary of its contents: *A True and Authentic Account of Andrew Frey, Containing the Occasion of his coming among the Herrnhuters or Moravians, his Observations on their Conferences, Casting Lots, Marriages, Festivals, Merriments, Celebrations of Birthdays, Impious Doctrines, and Fantastical Practices.* As late as 1950 it was drawn on heavily as an "honest witness" by a Roman Catholic author in his critique of the Moravians.[25]

OTHER PUBLICATIONS

The most popular of Brethren publications was the 1744 hymnbook, *Das kleine Davidische Psalterspiel* (*The Small Davidic Psaltery*), described earlier. It went through fourteen more editions by 1830, when it was first issued in stereotyped form for rapid republication. The hymnal was used widely among the German-speaking population in North America, not only by the Brethren. Their first English-language hymnal, *The Christian's Duty* (1791), was also "Recommended to the Serious of all Denominations" by the "Fraternity of Baptists." It won four reprintings in Germantown and in Canton, Ohio.

An interesting imprint of the press of the second Christoph Sauer was the path-breaking primer on pedagogy drafted by the colonial teacher Christopher Dock. After his arrival in Pennsylvania the "pious schoolmaster" taught in a subscription school in the Mennonite settlement at Skippack, interspersed with years of farming. Christoph Sauer I had been much impressed by Dock's kindly and effective methods of teaching and discipline and urged him (through a mutual friend) to write an essay explaining them. Unlike most pedagogs of the time, Dock motivated his pupils not by fear of punishment but by encouragement and reward for achievements.

Dock did produce a manuscript, with the proviso that it could not be published before his death. Nevertheless, shortly before he died he was convinced to permit its publication. In 1770 Christopher Sauer II printed the *Schul-Ordnung* (School Management), the first published discussion of teaching methods in America. Also noteworthy were Dock's articles "One Hundred Necessary Rules for Children's Conduct" and "One Hundred Rules for Children," both guides to behavior and deportment that reflect the manners and ways of life of colonial German homes; these were published in the religious periodical of the second Sauer.[26]

If the prolific output of the schismatic Ephrata Society were to be classed as well with Brethren literary activity, the publishing record would be formidable. The Beissel-led group established its own printing press, when the first Sauer raised questions about some language that he felt praised Beissel too highly. There is in fact an overlap, because Sander Mack was the author of several Ephrata imprints during his stay at the cloister.

As mentioned earlier, he translated from the Dutch language a portion of *The Martyrs Mirror*, a massive anthology of martyr accounts first released by Mennonites in 1660; Mack's near-decade-long stay in Friesland had given him the linguistic tools for this project. In 1748/49, after three years of unrelenting effort, the Ephrata monks produced for the Pennsylvania Mennonites the largest book printed in the American colonies in the eighteenth century, the complete German version of the martyrology. It was subsequently reprinted in Lancaster (1814) and thereafter many times in German and English translation for the Mennonites and Amish in North America.

BRETHREN POETRY

Brethren also made strong contributions in poetry during the century. Already mentioned were the prolific Sander Mack and Michael Frantz, who placed some of his important points in poetic form. Among other names of known Brethren poets are Heinrich Danner, Jacob Danner, Peter Becker, Johannes Naas, Christoph Sauer II, Johannes Preiß, and Jacob Stoll. Although not often studied or appreciated, some of their work has been preserved as hymnody. Almost all of their poetry, unfortunately, dropped from view when the Brethren ceased speaking German. The compilers of the nineteenth-century Brethren hymnals in the English language neglected this part of the Brethren cultural heritage. A few of their contributions have been recovered in the mid-twentieth century in translated form.

The scholar John Joseph Stoudt included these writers in his anthology of Pennsylvania German poetry. He particularly favored the productions of those living at Ephrata, especially that of Conrad

Beissel, but found Brethren poets able as well. In general, Stoudt felt that the literary achievements of the Pennsylvania Germans had been slighted. According to him, the Germans in America were writing "literate poetry executed in literary patterns of an ancient cut, of a quality which their Anglo-Saxon neighbors could not match, and in a quantity so astonishing that English poetry pales by comparison."[27]

Despite the impressive numbers of persons involved and total of publications, it must be admitted that no literary genius appeared among the Brethren. An early student of these works was John S. Flory of Bridgewater College. His characterization of 1908 bears quoting: "They were earnest, thoughtful, practical men, who had to face stern facts and harsh realities, and to them life was a very intense and serious matter. When they wrote they wrote because they had something to say; and the bulk of their writing is characterized by an earnest, sincere, rugged directness that gives it a positive aim, and directs it to some definite mark."[28]

In early Brethren writing there is little to be found of literary grace and style. They were plain men and wrote in a plain style, often with pleasing results, but there was not a John Woolman among them. An exception to this judgment may be found in the literary production at Ephrata, which notably included the graceful and devout thoughts of the sisters. Their work, however, was primarily intended for internal consumption and failed to achieve a broader readership during their own time and since, because it was couched in the theosophical language of Arnold, Boehme, and Gichtel.

These internal developments were abruptly interrupted by broader political events—the turmoil leading up to the rebellion mounted by militant American colonists against the British crown. Although Brethren tried to stay aloof, they were inexorably drawn into the turbulent waters of the Revolution by the flood of political events.

8

War and Revolution

Early Brethren emerged in the midst of wars and from the beginning held a strong nonresistant position. As those attempting to follow the example of the primitive Christian church, they accepted the pacifist stance of early Christianity. Both of the movements that shaped them most profoundly, Anabaptism and Pietism, were peace-oriented. Although the very first Anabaptists held a variety of positions on war, by the end of the first decade of its existence the movement had adopted a thoroughgoing nonresistant stance. They then all agreed with the early statement of Conrad Grebel that "true Christians use neither the worldly sword nor engage in war since among them taking human life has ceased entirely, for we are no longer under the Old Testament." Their direct descendants, the Mennonites, held this position firmly.[1]

In one of the strongest statements in the doctrinal treatises of Alexander Mack, Sr., he praises Mennonite peacefulness, contrasting that to the "bestial outcome" of the state churches, Catholic, Lutheran, and Reformed:

> The Jews and the Turks are scandalized by the horrible wickedness of these three religions. Not even with gallows and torture can they keep them, who are of one faith, from murdering one another in their homes....What is still more horrible, they go publicly to war, and slaughter one another by the thousands.

Although Mack was critical of the decline in religious vitality he observed in the Mennonites, whom he knew well from personal visits, he maintained that none "will be found in war" and that "the majority of them are inclined to peacefulness."[2]

Pietism as well had a strong orientation toward nonresistance. E. C. Hochmann von Hochenau, who had a great influence on Mack and other dissenters who became Brethren, was noted for preaching against warring Christians. He knew the works of Quaker theologian Robert Barclay, who featured the peace testimony in his writing. Among the Radical Pietists awakened by Hochmann, peace was important. Their testimony at an interrogation at Heidelberg revealed that love of enemy was central for their understanding of Christian life.[3]

Most of the dissenters who became Brethren came from the Palatinate, which had been devastated in the destructive Thirty Years War and again repeatedly at the end of the seventeenth century. As previously noted, these early Brethren had experienced the horrors of war, military requisitions, and family tragedies. Schriesheim, the birthplace of Alexander Mack, Sr., had suffered grievously during this period, although not completely leveled as were some neighboring villages and towns. Thus, it was from a combination of their theological convictions and life experiences that the Brethren from their inception as a movement held to a consistent peace testimony.

The Brethren in America

For several decades after Brethren began arriving in America, they experienced no problems because of their peace principle. Most lived in Pennsylvania where the founding Friends had strong political influence. The first article of the *Fundamental Constitutions*, the basic document of the colony, pledged that peaceable residents "shall have and enjoy the free possession of his or her faith and exercise of worship towards God, in such way and manner as every person shall in conscience believe is most acceptable to God...."

Quaker leaders had welcomed the German sectarians such as the Brethren and Mennonites, in part, because of their shared peace witness. In the 1760s a Quaker writer wrote of the Brethren, "They hold it not becoming a follower of Jesus Christ to bear arms or fight

since their true Master has forbidden his disciples *to resist evil...*,"
basing this, as other principles, on the authority of the New
Testament. A Baptist historian compared the Brethren way of life to
that of the Friends, saying "like them, they will never swear or
fight."[4]

Unfortunately for these peace-loving peoples, the American
colonies were caught up in the repercussions of the near-century-
long struggles of the major European powers—Austria, Prussia,
England, Spain, and France. As the last three all had territorial
claims in North America, wars in Europe also resulted in conflicts
in the New World, especially on the frontier. The English and
French rivalry over control of North America was especially
intense, lasting from 1689 until 1763 when the French were driven
from the region. A long series of conflicts on the borders were given
names in America such as King William's War, Queen Anne's War,
King George's War, and the French and Indian War, corresponding
to the broader and more bloody wars elsewhere.

A sharp test came in the early 1740s when trade tensions
between England and Spain led to demands by the Pennsylvanian
governor for a militia. The Quaker-dominated, anti-proprietor party
was unwilling to permit this, as the soldiers raised in this way could
be sent far afield. They were also unwilling to give up legislative
authority to the executive. This issue was raised repeatedly during
the eighteenth century, with many settlers on the frontier demanding additional military protection.[5]

Members of the peace groups ordinarily lived in harmony with
the indigenous peoples, who were well aware of their nonresistant
principles. However, as raiding parties of Indians (often from a distance) struck isolated farms, at times nonresistants fell victim along
with other settlers. Those Dunker families who had followed the
Eckerlins into Virginia were directly affected. Others in the
Carolinas left their holdings to find shelter with the Moravians at
Salem and Bethabara.

In 1756 pressures had built up so much that most peace-loving
Quaker representatives in the Pennsylvania Assembly resigned,
opening the way to the passage of an act authorizing a militia. Stiff
fines were demanded under the law for those unwilling to drill.

ECKERLINS ON NEW RIVER AND CHEAT RIVERS

Brethren nonresistance was severely tested between 1754 and 1763 with the outbreak of the French and Indian War (known in Europe as the Seven Years' War). Some Brethren living close to or on the frontier were swept up in the turmoil. While the whole story has not been documented, a number of instances have been preserved that illustrate the Brethren response. One of the most interesting involves Israel and Gabriel Eckerlin, who had left Ephrata in the autumn of 1745 for the Virginia frontier. They had established a settlement of 900 acres and sought to bring others there from Germantown and Ephrata.[6]

Although the brothers had enjoyed good relationships with the local Indians, increasing white settlement led to friction. Apprehension about Indian raids may have stimulated the Eckerlins' decision to move to another frontier location, which they did in 1750. After first selecting a location in western Pennsylvania, they found a new settlement on the Cheat River in Virginia (now West Virginia), at a site still called Dunkard Bottom. They sought permission from the appropriate tribes for their new residence, nearly two thousand acres, established in 1752. A Dunker, Daniel Hendricks from Virginia, joined them there as a hired man.

When the French authorities staked out claims in the Ohio Valley by building a series of forts in the early 1750s, the English government responded in 1755 by sending inland a strong expeditionary force under General Edward Braddock. This cumbersome army of redcoats needed logistical support; some of the nonresistants (including Brethren and Mennonites) were willing to hire their wagons out to transport supplies for the effort, but drew the line at hauling ammunition. After Braddock's humiliating defeat near Fort Duquesne (Pittsburgh), the army was withdrawn precipitately, opening the Pennsylvania interior to damaging Indian attacks.

To the mounting suspicions of the nervous frontier settlers, the Eckerlin hermitage on the Cheat River was strangely spared. They suspected that the Eckerlin brothers were actually spies for the French and their Indian allies. When several raids took place in areas only recently visited by the brothers, the suspicions seemed confirmed. Samuel Eckerlin, who traveled the most, sought to dispel these fears in visits to the Virginia capital. This proved to be insufficient; in the late fall of 1756 the governor of Virginia ordered the army to bring in the brothers. Samuel was forced to guide a military unit to the Dunker settlement, on the way being handled roughly by the soldiers, who were convinced of his guilt. Their suspicions were only abandoned when the party arrived at the site to find it in ruins and the two Eckerlins and Hendricks gone. They had been seized by a party of Ottawa Indians, led by a French officer; the ensuing report read, "Captain McKenzie, who was sent out for the Dunkers,...found nothing on the Spot they inhabited but Spears, broken Tomahawks, and the Ashes of their Hutts. The Spears were of French Make."[7]

Undergoing considerable maltreatment, Israel and Gabriel Eckerlin, along with their servant, were forced by the raiding party to travel to Montreal. After arriving, they were at first mistaken by the French as Augustinian monks. An officer who interrogated them there, reported, with some inaccuracies perhaps attributable to the language barrier,

> [T]here arrived at Niagara two hermits of sorts captured by a party of Ottawas on the upper Monongahela. These two men were settled there for almost 20 years with the consent of the Belle-Rivière nations. They told Mr. Pouchot that they followed the Roman rite in their prayers, that they had three convents in Pennsylvania, consisting of 1,500 members and that their founder was Friedsam Gottrecht. They added that the English had tried to force them into war service. Most of them had to disperse into the woods. They were three brothers. The English had first removed them from their wilderness and held them in prison for a long time to find out if they had contacts with the French and their savages but as nothing was discovered, they were released with the exception of the third brother who was still held as a prisoner at Williamsburg. These people seem very close and trustworthy. They were revered by the savages in those parts.

Hendricks, the Eckerlin's servant, escaped from his captors and made his way back to the English settlements, and then on to the Shenandoah area; there he related his story to the remaining brother, Samuel Eckerlin, who sought aid through government sources for news about his brothers.[8]

The prisoners were transferred to a prison in Quebec, where they endured a harsh winter. They were permitted to beg on the street and became the objects of pity to the residents. From Quebec they were sent with other prisoners by ship to Rochelle in France. One brother may have died on shipboard and the other after reaching port. The records are unclear. Samuel Eckerlin attempted to secure more information on their fate from Benjamin Franklin in 1764, but there is no record of a reply.

THE BRETHREN IN THE REVOLUTION

The American Revolution not only set American against Briton but American against American. It was a civil war as well as a rebellion. It is reliably estimated that but one-third of the colonists were pro-revolution (Whigs). Somewhat fewer than one-third wished to stay loyal to the crown (Loyalists or Tories); the remainder attempted to stay neutral although it was often impossible. This meant that in town and countryside the events leading to the Declaration of Independence and to the war found friends and neighbors, even members of the same families, on opposite sides. As the fortunes of politics and war rose and fell, emotions ran at fever pitch.

For the Brethren there were many reasons for trying to stay neutral, to stay aloof from the conflict. First, they were deeply religious people whose parents had risked migration to worship as they thought right. Their beliefs made them biblical nonresistants and forbade participation in warfare and bloodshed. Like the early Christians, after whom they modeled themselves, they considered themselves to be a colony of heaven, strangers in an alien land, in the world but not of it. Their traditional position had been one of noninvolvement in worldly affairs. Only with reluctance did some participate in elections, and then only to ensure that the peace-loving Quaker party stayed in power in Pennsylvania.[9]

As they surveyed the scene at the dawn of the Revolution, they noticed that the outspoken voices for revolution came from just those persons most antagonistic to them and to their beliefs—from the anti-Quaker Presbyterians, some of the urbane Anglicans, and the stern Puritan Congregationalists. Because the Brethren were largely rural folk, they had little interest in the mercantile policies of the British which had caused so much of the strife. Tea and other luxuries were not essentials for them.

Moreover, they, along with the Friends, Mennonites, Amish, Schwenkfelders, and Moravians, owed a great debt of gratitude to the British government for their years of peace and prosperity in the New World. Many of them had suffered persecution in Europe but had found religious freedom and economic sufficiency in the American colonies. There was enough toleration of religious divergence in most of the colonies that the worst burdens of church establishment were spared them, especially in Pennsylvania where so many of them lived.

When they, or their forebears, had emigrated to North America, they had taken pledges or affirmations of loyalty to the crown. True to their understanding of the proper relationship of church to state, shaped by Romans 13 and 1 Peter 2, they thought themselves subject to the authority established by God, except where conscience drew the line.

They believed in rendering unto Caesar what was owed him, and, for them, George III of England was the current Caesar. As a crucial pronouncement of the 1779 Yearly Meeting of the Brethren put it, "Inasmuch as it is the Lord our God who establishes kings and removes kings, and ordains rulers according to his own good pleasure, and we can not know whether God has rejected the king and chosen the [American] state, while the king had the government; therefore we could not, with a good conscience, repudiate the king and give allegiance to the state."[10]

Many of their contemporaries, even some religious leaders, viewed this stance with suspicion. Heinrich Melchior Mühlenberg, although he himself inclined to neutrality, wrote at that time, "Now many of the inhabitants are again in a predicament, especially the Quakers, [Ana]Baptists [that is, Mennonites and Brethren], etc., who

have been hoping all along that the might of England would con-
quer the land and protect these sects in their former liberties and
accumulated possessions, leaving them undisturbed and settled on
their lees, while only the Protestant church people would be turned
into slaves."[11]

A visiting Moravian bishop understood the position better.
When again returned to Germany, he contradicted a published
claim that the peace groups had been belligerents *vis à vis* England:

> Pennsylvania is full of Quakers, also of various kinds of
> [Ana]Baptists and other denominations who hold that
> they dare not bear arms with a good conscience. All of
> these groups have remained true to their principles from
> beginning until end. No Anabaptist, no Quaker took up
> arms. What is more, all of these people were so sympa-
> thetic and loyal to the government of Great Britain that
> they could not be persuaded to abjure the king of Great
> Britain and his heirs in the required manner, even though
> the authorities would have been content with their con-
> scientious affirmation, in the place of an oath.[12]

THE ASSOCIATIONS

An early test of the nonresistant groups was the organization of
Associations, set up as quasi-governments to organize resistance to
the British. Although completely illegal, they reflected the attitudes
of a loud minority who captured the public voice. One of their chief
occupations was to form military units for drilling. Largely because
of the well-known peace position of the Quakers and their involvement in politics, most colonies had provisions respecting conscientious objection. Those who would not drill were required to pay a
fine or penalty.

As emotions rose, this exemption was questioned. What happened next is illustrated by turmoil in Lancaster County. Those
administering the Association issued a handbill attempting to allay
the animus against the Nonassociators. The committee reported
that these had been "threatened by some violent and ill-dispos'd

people in the county of Lancaster, notwithstanding their Willingness to contribute chearfully to the Common Cause, otherwise than by taking up of Arms." The attempt backfired against the authors. A mob gathered that accused them of taking bribes from the peace people to escape duty; the committee members resigned their posts under this pressure.[13]

The first task of the newly reorganized Lancaster County Committee was to involve the nonresistants in payment, if not in presence: "Resolved, to recommend it to such Persons, whose religious Principles debar them from associating, [tak]ing up, or furnishing Arms, and who shall be deemed by the Township Committees of sufficient Abilities to pay into the hands of the Committee's Treasurer the Sum of £ 3-10-0, to be applied to such Uses as to this Committee shall appear most advantageous to the public [Int]erest." An additional tax, on the order of the regular provincial tax, was further to be assessed on those "who from Scru[ples] of Conscience, are averse to associating, and taking up Arms," meant to equalize the sacrifice made by those who were drilling.[14]

The plain people of Lancaster County—Amish, Mennonites, and Brethren—met with the Committee to inform them of an appeal to the Congress. This, in part, resulted in the Congressional resolution of July 18, 1775, which stated, "As there are some people, who, from religious principles, cannot bear arms in any case, the Congress intend no violence to their consciences, but earnestly recommend it to them, to contribute liberally in this time of universal calamity, to the relief of their distressed brethren in the several colonies, and to do all other services to their oppressed Country, which they can consistently with their religious principles."[15]

This sounds generous, but the crux of the matter lay in the interpretation of the phrase "contribute liberally...to the relief of their distressed brethren." The intent, increasingly of the revolutionary committees, was to make the nonassociators pay for the supplies and wages of the military. The peace groups, including the Brethren, tried to designate their forced contributions for the relief of the needy, although they were astute enough to know that this direction would not always be respected.

The elder of the Conestoga congregation, Jacob Stoll, revealed the hesitation in his letter to Sander Mack, obviously replying to a query from the latter about how the Lancaster County Brethren were handling the issue:

> [Y]ou would like to know how we have given our money, [whether] 'for protection money' or 'for the needy.' Let this serve as an answer that in part it has been given for both. There seemed to be no other alternative than to give something in order to be safe, for the fire was too much ignited. Therefore, we gave our money, and told the man to whom we gave it that we were giving our money for the needy....[W]e therefore did as we were ordered and had no further scruples as to how the Committee used it. For we gave it in good faith for the needy and the man to whom we gave it gave us a receipt stating that the money would be used for that purpose.[16]

TAXES AND OATHTAKING

Other Brethren took the same tack when pressed for contributions to the revolutionary cause. In 1777-78 a Germantown militia company asked the public for financial support. Christoph Sauer II headed the list of donors with a large sum, but with the designation "for the poor widows and children."[17] During the course of the war the amounts demanded increased sharply. In case of principled refusal to pay the fines, the revolutionary officers were quick to requisition goods, livestock, and other chattel, often in far greater amounts than needed to pay the fines.

Ordinarily the Brethren took the position that such fines were to be considered taxes and thus to be paid. However, there were those who considered the voluntary giving of such money to be contributing to the shedding of blood. Of them, the Yearly Meeting of the Brethren in 1781 said, "[Y]et, if one does not see it so, and thinks, perhaps, he for his conscience' could not pay it, but bear with others who pay, in patience, we would willingly leave it over, inasmuch as we deem the overruling of conscience to be wrong." The Brethren agreed that members should not volunteer to hire substitutes in lieu of military service. Lists of Brethren who refused to drill and muster and were therefore liable to pay fines, have been preserved, especially in Maryland and Pennsylvania.[18]

A stronger line was taken by the Brethren against any members taking loyalty oaths or *attests* as they were known. This problem arose because the revolutionary cadres in all of the American colonies were determined to force their opponents into the open. They passed increasingly stricter laws demanding that all residents must renounce allegiance to the king and swear loyalty to the new regimes. A recent historian noted some of the reasons: "To smoke out the dissenters and extract from them pledges of conformity undoubtedly had the effect of frightening the timid into silence and discouraging open opposition from the bolder Tories." The peace groups, with some few exceptions, consistently refused to take these oaths, despite harsh legal and financial penalties levied against them. Although some Brethren took the attest, by action of Yearly Meeting (1778-79) they were to be placed under church discipline for doing so.[19]

Other measures of the revolutionary authorities weighed heavily on the Brethren. In some colonies the regular taxes were doubled and tripled (and for a time in North Carolina were as much as sevenfold). When the military needed blankets, clothes, or food, they went first to the sectarian groups for their requisitions. This was for several reasons: first, it was easier to seize these goods from the nonresistant pacifists, because they often met with fierce resistance from the patriots; second, it was felt appropriate to punish them in this way for their tacit resistance to the new era. Scattered cases of brutality have been recorded against the Brethren. Usually the local agents and petty officials were harsher than the higher authorities.

CHRISTOPH SAUER II AND CHRISTOPH SAUER III

For no Brethren did the American Revolution bring more misery than that of the family of Christoph Sauer II of Germantown. He was the best-known member of the church. A wealthy and influential figure, the second Sauer had very early seen the dangers on the horizon. At the time of the Stamp Act (1765), he had warned against violent reaction to it and called for a convention to work out peaceable solutions to tension points. For several years before the first shots were fired in anger at Lexington and Concord, he had used the motto "Wars and Rumors of Wars" on his popular German-language almanac.[20] Because of his long-standing opposition to those political factions heading the rebel cause, he was targeted for special harassment. His son, Christoph Sauer III, later wrote that he and his father "became so obnoxious to the rebel rulers that they were obliged several times to secret themselves from the fury of the mobs which were exerted to seize on their persons and threatened to tar and feather them and otherwise to treat them with the utmost indignity."

Perhaps wearying of the struggle, in 1776-77 Sauer turned over the direction of his printing establishment to his sons Christoph and Peter. When the sons took over editorial control of the press, they changed the political tack of their father. He was committed to neutrality; they chose to become open Tories, although Christoph Sauer III seems to have been for a time a partisan of the revolutionary cause. The sons had perhaps been angered by the unfair treatment that their father received. At any rate, when the British seized control of Philadelphia, they established a press there where they published newspapers and tracts on behalf of the English, using bitter language.[21]

In December 1777, Christoph Sauer III accompanied British soldiers to Germantown, then a contested area between the two armies. (One of the hottest battles had been fought there near the Dunker meetinghouse two months earlier.) He was captured by an American patrol but was soon released in exchange for a powder manufacturer in the hands of the British. When the occupying army left Philadelphia, Christoph and Peter Sauer went with them to New York. While there Christoph Sauer III had occasion to visit a prison ship and found to his astonishment the American captain who had taken him captive in Germantown. Sauer attended to his needs and secured his release along with two of his companions, this time without an exchange of prisoners.

Christoph Sauer III played an important behind-the-scenes role in New York. High-ranking British officers after the war praised his efforts to rally support for the monarch. A later historian summarized his activities under three headings: he attempted "to rouse and encourage the Loyalists" in Whig-held areas; he procured intelligence for the British forces; and he tried "to persuade the home government to take such steps as would aid in detaching the mass of people from the Patriot leaders." A rather complete account of his efforts was been preserved in the papers of the British high command. Sauer figures prominently in the narrative of the conspiracies of Benedict Arnold and Major André.[22]

Sauer III was particularly active in identifying and enlisting support for the Tory cause among the rural areas of several colonies. In his own words he "opened a correspondence with his friends in Pennsylvania, Maryland and the Delaware counties...to encourage them to persevere in their loyalty." This included peace group leaders as well as church people.[23]

In 1780 Sauer published a strong appeal to the German population in the colonies, encouraging them to realize that their real interests lay with the British government. It was a direct response to Thomas Paine's influential tract *Common Sense*, which did much to rally public opinion to the rebel cause. Sauer was convinced that the motivations for the Revolution were to be found in the economic and political interests of a small group of plotters:

> It was not the taxes on the tea and other duties to the king...that laid the foundation for the downfall of your previous benign government. No! Rather, it was many of your merchants who had squandered their wealth in debauchery that has caused your misfortune. The debts which they had incurred with the merchants in England had become burdens to them, which they partly could not, and partly would not, repay. There was, of course, no other way out than to scheme for independence from Great Britain in order through it to cancel at the same time the debts from their books.[24]

Some historians of the American Revolution have made similar interpretations. It was clear to Sauer that New Englanders were behind the unhappy rebellion:

> As rebels, they were driven out of their fatherland many years ago, and the poison of rebellion had perpetuated itself in their grandchildren. Before the outbreak of the rebellion they sent men of keen minds into all the provinces to investigate the feelings of the leading people. Indeed, they even sent out preachers...to scatter from the pulpit the poison of rebellion to the innocent. And unfortunately, many of our German preachers defiled the pulpit with the poison of rebellion and washed their hands in innocent blood![25]

Sauer also played shrewdly on the Germans' concern for sound money, pointing out that the worth of the paper money issued by the Continental Congress was rapidly diminishing: "The sum of the matter is this: *you give paper in taxes and receive for your products a new and freshly printed paper made by a new and fresh fraud.* This is the truth about the money with which you must conduct a war and which is nowhere of any value except where the Congress doles it out at the point of a bayonet." There are several contemporary records of incidents when Brethren and Mennonite farmers were punished for insisting on hard money as they sold their produce.[26]

For these and other services, Sauer was finally awarded a large postwar compensation from the crown, after going to England to press his claims. He was also awarded the post of king's printer in New Brunswick, where many of the American Loyalists settled. Here he also engaged in politics (where he fared poorly) as well as printing. In 1799 he traveled to Baltimore intending to resettle his family there and to assist his brother Samuel but died before this could be effected. His family did relocate in Baltimore in 1801.[27]

LOYALIST PLOTS IN PENNSYLVANIA AND MARYLAND

One of the most ambitious projects of Christoph Sauer III involved the organization of Loyalist resistance within the boundaries of the American forces. Potentially one of the most serious threats to the Revolutionary cause was a widespread underground movement known as the Associated Loyalists of Pennsylvania and Maryland.

William Rankin in Pennsylvania and Hugh Kelly in Maryland were its leaders.[28]

Rankin, a propertied man and justice of the peace in York County, was an early supporter of the revolution. He was made colonel of the York militia. However, when it became clear that Congress had independence in view, he returned to his prior loyalty. To maintain protective cover, he retained his military position. Using it, he was able to protect some Loyalists and also to secure military intelligence.

In 1778 he conveyed word to the British commander in New York that he had gathered a "great number" of men in his area willing to take up arms against the rebels. Although many, like himself, were serving in the American military, they had given their oaths of allegiance to the crown. He was advised by the British leaders that his help was welcome but that he must wait for orders before taking any action. He was to remain in contact with the army headquarters through Christoph Sauer III, then recently arrived in New York.

Sauer was the conduit for messages back and forth between the English officers and Colonel Rankin. One of the messages he forwarded to headquarters was the so-called "Christian Musselmann report." Sauer characterized it as stating that the "Mennonites and German Baptists (the latter in derision called Dunckers) in the different parts of Pennsylvania, have long wished to know from Authority how to conduct themselves during the present Rebellion, that they might not give offense to His Majesty or to His Representatives in America." According to Sauer, the groups held several meetings to consider their reaction to the growing crisis, at one of which he himself was present.

Several ministers and leading men on that occasion drew up a petition to the king. They wished to set forth their "Happiness while under his Government, their desire to be reinstated in the enjoyment of their former Blessings, and their readiness to assist with their Goods and Chattels" to bring about a restitution of the prior status. Sauer said that he knew all of the leading Mennonites and Dunkers and many of the laity; he considered them to be the "most loyal People in the World." The printer estimated the Mennonites to consist of two to three thousand families and the Brethren of three thousand members. "In political matters they are ignorant to an extreme and glory in being so. The aged of both societies profess to be conscientiously scrupled of bearing arms...."[29]

As time went on and the number of Associated Loyalists grew to as many as 6,000, they grew impatient to act. In 1780, going over the heads of the slow-moving British generals, they sent an appeal through Sauer to the British king. Later Sauer himself carried a similar appeal to London and delivered it to the hands of the secretary of George III. Despite this and many other urgent appeals, the order to proceed never came to the Loyalists. In 1781 Rankin was arrested on suspicion of anti-patriotic activity but escaped to the British lines.

The Associated Loyalists in Maryland were also frustrated. The ringleader, the Irishman Hugh Kelly, began as early as 1775 to enlist a force pledged to resist the Revolution. By 1781 he had 1,300 men sworn by an oath of allegiance to rise on behalf of the British cause. He further enlisted nonresistants, including Quakers, Mennonites, and Dunkers—those "who do not take an Oath or personally bear Arms." They affirmed, rather than swore, "true and faithful Allegiance" to their "Lawful Sovereign the King of Great Britain." It appears that they expressed willingness to aid the Loyalist cause by hauling provisions and in other noncombatant ways.

Through misadventure, the plot in Maryland was revealed and participants arrested. Seven leaders were condemned to the ancient and barbaric sentence for the crime of high treason: they were "to be drawn to the Gallows of Frederick Town and be hanged thereon, that they be cut down to the Earth alive, that their Entrails be taken out and burnt while they are yet alive, that their Heads be cut off and their Bodies be divided into four Parts and that their Heads and Quarters be placed where his Excellency the Governor shall appoint." It was a sardonic twist that Americans guilty of treason in the eyes of their former king now applied this old English penalty against those attempting to remain loyal to the crown!

The sentences were reduced before execution: three men were hanged and four condemned to service on a French man-of-war. One of those hanged was a man named Peter Suman (Sueman) thought to have been a Dunker; other Brethren may have been sentenced to lesser punishment for their participation in the plot. The ringleader, Hugh Kelly, escaped trial. He hid in the forest for six months and grew a long beard. Thus disguised, he donned simple garb and made his way through the American-held territory until he reached the British lines. He was once arrested in Carlisle but convinced his captors that he was a simple Dunker and was then released.[30]

The Fate of Christoph Sauer II

Although the second Sauer did not participate in any overt Loyalist actions, as did his sons, he was made to suffer for his nonresistant beliefs. He had, during the winter of 1777-78, unwisely relocated to his sons' residence in Philadelphia, then occupied by the British armies. When he returned to his home in Germantown in the late spring of 1778 he was seized by a troop of American soldiers.

As they marched him to army headquarters at Valley Forge they mistreated and tortured the elderly man. His clothes were stripped from him, his hair and beard mutilated, his body painted with garish colors; clad only in rags, he was prodded by bayonets along the way. His Quaker acquaintance, John Pemberton, reported, "I visited Christopher Sauer, who had been taken prisoner by the Americans, stripped naked, and painted in different colors, confined at camp for some time, and at length released with a few rags given him."[31] Although released from the provost, he was forbidden to return to his home. Instead, his extensive real and personal properties were auctioned off for the benefit of the rebel cause; many patriots did well by acquiring valuable property with debased Continental currency. The reason given for this outrage was that he had been pronounced a traitor to the American cause during his residence in Philadelphia and had not appealed it.

Sauer protested that he had been in arrest during the time the appeal was to be made. He also said that it went against his religious principles to go to law on this matter. To his dying day he held the seizure of his property to have been unjust, a judgment supported by some of the scholars who have studied the case. His question was, "If a man is openly declared a traitor without a cause, without hearing or trial, when he was not absent and might have been heard, is it just to let him forever lie under that reproach?" Sauer II died a poor man in 1784, having expressed gratification that he had been able to repay all the debts he had incurred following his incarceration.[32]

In some sense the Sauer press continued its Brethren connections. A trustee of the Germantown congregation and formerly one of Sauer's apprentices, Peter Leibert, bought much of the auctioned printing equipment. At the end of the war, he, together with his Lutheran son-in-law Michael Billmeyer, revived the Germantown newspaper and almanac under the original names. In 1787 they dissolved their partnership and each continued with his own printing press. Leibert published many of the postwar Brethren books and hymnals.

So far as is known, the Sauers suffered greater property loss than any other Brethren family. However, others experienced hardship as well. One night a mob at Germantown stoned the house of Elder Peter Keyser. The next morning, while cleaning the debris, Keyser found a slip of paper dropped by one of the rioters; it bore the name of a neighbor. Elder Keyser returned the paper to the neighbor, saying, "You paid me a visit last night."[33]

Toward the end of the war another Brethren elder received a visit. This was Martin Urner of the Coventry congregation. Early one winter morning in 1783, Urner opened his home to three travelers. At the breakfast table they recounted that they were escaped British prisoners attempting to reach the British lines. Urner tried to persuade them to give themselves up and wait for a prisoner exchange, but they insisted on going on. A few weeks later, the same men returned, this time with a troop of American soldiers, who arrested Elder Urner. It turned out that the men were covert agents sent out to discover those partial to the British cause.

Martin Urner was sentenced to receive 117 lashes for his supposed misdeed, later commuted to a severe fine of £150. He made three appeals to the Supreme Executive Council, asking that the fine be reduced. He had suffered from great depredations by General Smallwood's brigade, who had ruined his farm and seized his horses and wagons. Moreover, the Continental Army had for nearly five years owed him money for forage. He defended his actions in assisting the freezing travelers, saying that "he did it not because they were British, but because they were men." He concluded one petition with this notable statement: "Worthy Gentlemen, I begg your *pardon* to Act according to the Golden Rule."[34]

A legend about Johann Peter Müller, leader of the Ephrata Society during this period, illustrates something of the spirit of the nonresistants. According to the account, Müller walked a great distance to plead for the life of a Tory condemned to death by hanging. He reached the place of execution just before the verdict was to be carried out. The commanding officer, impressed by the venerable appearance of Müller and his plea for clemency, remarked that Müller must be a close friend of the prisoner. When he was told that far from being a friend, the prisoner was Müller's worst enemy, the officer set the accused free. It is known that Müller interceded with the authorities on behalf of Mennonites and others accused of Toryism.[35]

CHARITABLE ACTIVITIES

Along with the other peace groups, Brethren were concerned about balancing their refusal to perform military service by willingness to meet human need. They provided foodstuffs from their rich farms to feed the hungry of both sides of the conflict. They gave freely of their means to aid those in need. The spirit of the Brethren is best caught in the language of a petition sent by Brethren and Mennonite elders to the Pennsylvania Assembly in November 1777. Along with a polite but firm reaffirmation of their nonresistant stance, they stated, using the male-related language of the day,

> The Advice to those who do not find Freedom of Conscience to take up Arms, that they ought to be helpful to those who are in Need and distressed Circumstances, we receive with Chearfulness towards all men of what Station they may be—it being our Principle to feed the Hungry and give the Thirsty Drink—we have dedicated ourselves to serve all Men in every Thing that can be helpful to the Preservation of Men's Lives, but we find no Freedom in giving, or doing, or assisting in any

> Thing by which Men's Lives are destroyed or hurt—We
> beg the Patience of all those who believe we err in this
> Point.[36]

AFTERMATH OF THE WAR

The stresses of this difficult period served to underscore the Brethren tendency of withdrawal and nonparticipation. Those, such as the Sauer family, who had begun to participate actively in secular affairs, were seen to suffer heavily. Some were so disillusioned with the outcome of the revolution that they emigrated to Canada to stay under the rule of the crown; a small colony of these Brethren found their way to Lower Ontario. Some of them later moved southward to Ohio, Michigan, and Indiana.

They were known in Canada as Tunkers; this has caused confusion because of the arrival after the war of members of the River Brethren, also known as Tunkers. Both nicknames came, of course, from their practice of baptism by immersion. The River Brethren had asked for this apostolic rite from the Brethren in Lancaster County. On learning that this could be performed only if those applying wished to become converts, the River Brethren proceeded to conduct their own baptism, much as had the Brethren in Schwarzenau in 1708. The River Brethren (later to be known as the Brethren in Christ) accepted other Brethren usages.[37]

Most Brethren stayed, however, in the newly constituted United States. They were happiest in small, isolated, rural enclaves where they could be by themselves. They were characterized in this period by an Anglican traveler, who commented about the religious conditions of Maryland. He described the

> Mennonites and Dunkers, who seem to have been broken
> off by so contracted a scheme of discipline as clashes
> with the common methods of government and civil soci-
> ety; not that they intend any disturbance or innovation,
> for they are remarkably peaceful and passive and there-
> fore are readily tolerated and excused....As to their
> morals in general, they are like those of other industrious

people. They are not addicted to the dissipating vices....They exhibit but little of what is called taste, and take much more pains to grow rich than to appear fine.[38]

Differences with civil authorities were not the only problems for the Brethren. In the colonial and early national periods, they also faced interaction with other religious bodies. With some they shared common values, at times making it difficult to draw clear boundaries. In other cases, new and aggressive religious movements impinged upon their membership. It was not always possible to remain in isolated enclaves, much as the Brethren might have preferred it.

9

Relations with
Other Religious Bodies

Brethren were not living in a vacuum in a religious sense. From their beginning in 1708, they related either in positive or negative ways to other religious bodies. The most strained relationships were with church establishments, such as the Lutheran, Reformed, and Catholic. The warmest (with occasional strains) were with Mennonites and Collegiants in Europe and with Mennonites and Quakers in North America.

Brethren, Mennonites and Friends

As has been seen, Brethren and Mennonites had been welcomed to Pennsylvania by members of the Religious Society of Friends. The mutual feelings of kinship had been deepened by the support given by the German sectarian groups to the policies of Friends in the Pennsylvania Assembly and to their philanthropic efforts to aid the American Indians.

Over the decades, Brethren had the closest relationships with the Mennonites. Although of "like precious faith" (as a phrase popular in the nineteenth century had it), the more zealous Brethren were often able to win converts from the more staid Mennonites. Many family names appearing in Brethren annals as staunch Dunkers, prove, if investigated, to be originally of Amish or Mennonite derivation. This was true of their very first converts in America and remained the case throughout the colonial and early national eras.[1]

It was difficult for contemporaries in Europe and America to distinguish clearly between the Brethren and Mennonites, so much alike were they, except that the Brethren were recognized as more zealous. An otherwise critical Radical Pietist writer commented about developments in eighteenth-century Germany:

> The congregations of the Old Anabaptists [Täufer] had undergone an improvement and enlargement from the New Anabaptists....The Old Anabaptists do not seek to enlarge themselves outside of their family, but rather remain in their old simplicity, the simple lay ministry, administrations of the sacraments, and the lowly farming and artisan life, etc. The New Anabaptists, however, want to make themselves large and broad among the awakened souls with powerful teaching and converting to the new baptismal peculiarity and necessity.[2]

We recall that, at the conclusion of the Pennsylvania Synods of 1742, Count Zinzendorf urged the Brethren and Mennonites to unite, inasmuch as in his view their only difference was in the mode of adult baptisms. A German traveler who visited Germantown in 1783-84 noted that a sect of Tumblers lived at Germantown: "They wear beards and a simple dress but not after the manner of the Quakers. They are similar to the Anabaptists [Mennonites], but I cannot say how they are distinguished in creed or opinions...."[3]

One distinguishing characteristic was that Brethren were more active not only in seeking converts, but also in defending their faith stance. In a published debate carried on in the late 1780s by Sander Mack and a Lutheran divine, Mack's opponent made it clear that "the Mennonites have no part in our dispute. They are for the most part peaceful and patient people who leave their fellowmen in peace." He had harsh words for the positions of both Brethren and Ephrata members.[4] Brethren and Mennonites were often found as neighbors; there are many accounts that relate friendly interchange at communal gatherings, especially at funerals. Intermarriage brought conversion one way or the other, as it was not customary at that time for spouses to hold different religious views; it was precisely because of the great similarity of beliefs that from time to time polemical exchanges took place. It was not uncommon for these differences to find their resonance in sermons.

On occasion the tension found publicized form. One example was a book by the Mennonite author Christian Burkholder addressed to the youth; its title is *Nützliche und Erbauliche Anrede an die Jugend* (Useful and Edifying Address to the Youth), published in 1804. Included in it is a strong critique of immersion baptism. This was answered two years later by the publication of Christian Longenecker, a Brethren elder in Lancaster County, called *Eine Vertheidigung der Wahrheit, Geboten Gottes und der Heiligen Taufe* (A Defense of the Truth, God's Commandments, and Holy Baptism). This in turn calls for a rebuttal from the Mennonite Melchior Brenneman, *Auslegung der Wahren Taufe Jesus Christi* (Exegesis of the True Baptism of Jesus Christ), in 1808. A comparable interchange flared up in Virginia several decades later.[5]

There were also contacts between the Brethren and Friends; in some areas of Pennsylvania, Maryland, and the Carolinas, they lived together and had neighborly relations. We have noted the fact that several "distinctive" and long-used Brethren practices were actually borrowed from the Religious Society of Friends, such as meetinghouse architecture and the term *query* for questions brought to the Yearly Meetings.[6]

In other instances traveling Quakers recorded in their journals encounters with Brethren. A British Friend Emanuel Howitt met Dunkers living near Lewistown, Pennsylvania, most likely in the Spring Run congregation. He found that "their mode of living, and brotherly unity" were based on the principles of the early church, which they indeed resembled, in his view. His description was favorable:

> These people occupy a considerable part of the big valley. They have a most patriarchal appearance, wearing their beards and habited in clothes of the utmost plainness. They have little intercourse with the world. They do not court its acquaintance, but seek tranquility and seclusion. Their character stands high for honesty, and they are generally

wealthy. They bear a testimony against oaths and war, refuse to go to law, and lend their money without interest.

Friend Howitt provided further detail on their manner of life:

> Providence seems to have allotted them here, a land adapted to their dispositions, and industry secures them in their prosperity....Their houses are generally small, but their barns comprise everything necessary for a complete farmyard. On the first floor are stables, cow-houses, store rooms, on the second, a large granary, which projects on every side eight or nine feet.[7]

Another British Friend traveling in the United States was struck by the "venerable" appearance of Brethren men; their large bushy beards made them look to him like fathers of the church. He was, nonetheless, disappointed that he received no sound rationale for the custom when he asked them for it.[8]

The noted American Friend Samuel Janney encountered a Dunker minister named Myers in Clear Springs, Maryland, "whose mild countenance" greatly interested him. Upon hearing that the visitor proposed holding a religious meeting, Myers immediately took steps to make that possible. They found that they agreed on many points of religious doctrine, "bearing a testimony against oaths, slavery, and a stipendiary [salaried] ministry." The Lutheran church building was made available to Janney for the service, but "Brother Myers sat with us on a bench under the pulpit, not being willing to go into it," reported Janney, "which was agreeable to my feelings, as it was too much decorated for us."[9]

UNIVERSALISM

In the early national period, several newly developed denominations became active and posed new challenges for the Brethren. These were the Universalists, the Restoration Movement (Disciples), the Adventists, and the Spiritualists.

In the liberal atmosphere of post-Revolutionary America, the liberal tenets of Universalism became popular. Thomas Jefferson, himself a deistic free-thinker, conjectured that the movement would sweep the country. Together with its more aristocratic cousin, Unitarianism—a liberal evolution of New England Congregationalism—Universalism seemed to be well suited to the vigorous expansionism and positive attitude of the new nation, now freed from English control.[10]

Universalism, although early deemed to be a heresy by orthodox Christian dogmaticians, has rootage in the New Testament and the early church. A passage in the book of Acts (3:19-21) reads, "Repent therefore, and turn to God so that your sins may be wiped out, so that times of refreshing may come from the presence of the Lord, and that he may send the Messiah appointed for you, that is, Jesus, who must remain in heaven until the time of universal restoration that God announced long ago through his holy prophets." Several verses in the Pauline letters speak of the fall of humankind through Adam's disobedience and the reconciliation "of all things, whether on earth or in heaven" through the obedience of Jesus Christ (Col. 1:20; 1 Cor. 15:21-23; Rom. 5:18-19).

The doctrine of universal restoration was prominent in the teachings of Radical Pietism; it was certainly known to the early Brethren. It appears in the writings of Alexander Mack, Sr., who considered it to be biblical but easily misunderstood and likely to be misapplied. In dealing with eternity and punishment of the wicked, Mack wrote, "...that it should last for eternity is not supported by Holy Scripture." He feared that some might be misled, believing that sin would not always need to be avoided by the thought that punishment would have an end: "Therefore, that is a much better and more blessed gospel that teaches how to escape the wrath of God than the gospel which teaches that eternal punishment has an end. Even though this is true, it should not be preached as a gospel to the godless."[11]

Well-informed contemporary writers in Pennsylvania noticed this teaching. Lutheran patriarch Heinrich Melchior Mühlenberg wrote of the Brethren that members "must also be able to believe...that the Devil and the damned should be saved again from Hell." The Baptist historian Morgan Edwards commented of the Brethren, "General redemption they certainly hold; and withall, general salvation; which tenets, though wrong, are consistent."[12]

Unlike some of the more extreme Universalists who denied any penalties or rewards in the afterlife, Brethren expected judgment and punishment. Where they differed with Calvinistic theology was their understanding that a God of love would not condemn erring ones for all eternity.

Brethren knew and had contact with Dr. George de Benneville, considered to be the pioneer Universalist in America. Both in the Oley region and near Germantown, they were in touch with this celebrated and talented figure.[13] A somewhat younger personality was Elhanan Winchester, a former Baptist preacher who became an outstanding exponent of the Universalist doctrine. He became acquainted with the Germantown Brethren and preached for them in 1781; he later wrote about them in glowing terms:

> They are industrious, sober, temperate, kind, charitable people; envying not the great, nor despising the mean. They read much, they sing and pray much, they are constant attendants upon the worship of God. Their dwelling-houses are all houses of prayer. They walk in the commandments and ordinances of the Lord blameless, both in public and in private. They bring up their children in the nurture and admonition of the Lord. No noise of rudeness, shameless mirth, loud vain laughter is heard within their doors. The law of kindness is in their mouths. No sourness or moroseness disgraces their religion; and whatever they believe their Savior commands, they practice without enquiring what others do.

One reason for Winchester's heaping praise upon the Brethren was that he wished to use them as an example. A common complaint about the Universalist doctrine was that adherents would not follow a moral life, trusting in the eventual forgiveness of God and consequent salvation. The highly ethical life of the Brethren, who accepted the Universalist belief, proved that the criticism was unfounded, in Winchester's view. Brethren were active in republishing Winchester's books well into the mid-nineteenth century.[14]

This rationale was recognized by another late eighteenth-century observer, the well-known physician Dr. Benjamin Rush, who wrote of the Brethren and other sectarian groups that advocated universalism: "The singular piety and exemplary morality of these sects has been urged by the advocates for the salvation of all mankind, as a proof that the belief of that doctrine is not unfriendly to the morals and the order of society, as has been supposed."[15]

There were more direct connections. In 1826 a former Universalist pastor, Timothy Bangor, became the minister of the Brethren in Philadelphia and served them until his death in 1847. Nevertheless, Brethren were loathe to emphasize their belief in universal restoration. It was strong meat and not meant for babes in the faith. They would not accept being identified as Universalists. Richard Eddy, a leading Universalist historian, recounted the statement of a Dunker minister he once visited: "If I were to say to my neighbors I have a Universalist preacher stopping at my house, they would say: 'How do you dare to have such a character under your roof?' But if I should say, 'I have a friend with me who preaches universal restoration,' they would say, 'Have you? I am glad; I would like to come in and see him.'" Much the same was reported by a member of the Brethren in Pennsylvania. This was Jacob Meyers who became a Universalist leader; he was active in bilingual (German/English) meetings and became the editor of a Universalist journal, *Der fröhliche Botschafter*.[16]

Not all Brethren were strongly opposed to Universalism. This is reflected in controversies in the Carolinas at the turn of the century. These came to the repeated attention of the Yearly Meetings in 1794, 1798, and 1800, indicating that the belief was held stubbornly by a number of members. It seems that a minister referred to as "John H." (possibly Ham or Hendricks) was teaching that there was neither heaven nor hell nor a literal devil and that God punished no person because of sin.[17]

Brethren pronouncements against this heresy helped to precipitate migrations from the Virginias and Carolinas to the upland South (Kentucky, Tennessee, and Missouri) and to the Old Northwest (Ohio, Indiana, and Illinois), in which regions the Far Western Brethren were formed (see Chapter 10). The doctrine of universal restoration was held firmly by Brethren in these areas for many years. Because Brethren settlement on the West Coast came predominantly from this area, the controversy was taken there as well.

Belief in universal restorationism persisted for decades as a sore point between Brethren on the then frontier and those remaining in the East. As late as 1878 the Annual Meeting had to rule on the issue, directing Brethren not to distribute Winchester's books and not to preach openly on the belief. It could, however, be held privately. It was in this way that the well-informed Brethren editor and debater James Quinter spoke of it some years before, in the context of correcting a published description of the Brethren: "It is by no means universal among us. And the Brethren as a body have never announced it to be one of their tenets. Consequently, where it is held, it is held as an individual, and private opinion." As Quinter's careful language makes clear, some Brethren believed in the doctrine, but the church did not allow it to be maintained publicly.[18]

In South Carolina perhaps as many as eight Dunker congregations had gone over to the Universalist camp by 1835. Leading ministers there were David Martin, Elijah Lynch, Joseph Summers, and Giles Chapman. Universalist historians give credit to John Ham and John Stansel (Stansill)—both identified as Dunkers—for spreading universalist doctrine in North Carolina. Members of congregations there in turn migrated westward as far as Texas. Virtually the entire southern bloc of Universalism stemmed from the Dunkers in the Carolinas. Later Universalist congregations in Kentucky, Illinois, Missouri, and Oregon also had Brethren roots.[19]

RESTORATIONISM (DISCIPLES)

Also using the term restoration but in quite a different sense was the movement that produced the Disciples of Christ and the Churches of Christ. Led by former Presbyterians Alexander Campbell and Barton W. Stone and derived from dissenters from several different churches that grew out of the Second Great Awakening, the Restoration movement expanded rapidly in the nineteenth century, especially in the Midwest and Southwest. It intended to restore the primitive church, taking as its motto the wish to be "Christians and

Christians only." Some have called it a uniquely American church movement. Because it had a programmatic bias against "denominations," it was only gradually that it took on structured form. Members were often called "Campbellites," after Alexander Campbell who emerged as a pre-eminent leader.[20]

There came to be close connections of Brethren with the Restoration movements in the Ohio Valley. Both were biblicist, immersionist, and noncreedal, although Brethren insisted on a threefold forward immersion, while the Restorationists promoted a single, backward immersion following Baptist practice. They also differed about the correct method of observing the Last Supper, which was observed by Restorationists every Sunday. The outcome of this development found many Brethren congregations in southern Ohio, southern Indiana, and Kentucky lost to the Restorationists. This included at least 15 churches and 2,000 members.

The process took place in two stages. In the first a number of Dunker congregations in the region led by Adam Hostetler and Peter Hon created an organization independent of the Annual Meeting, the Association. The next found its leaders connecting ever more closely with the emerging Restoration movement. The specific reasons for the division remain obscure, but it is evident that Association leaders were unwilling to conform to all the rules observed by the Brethren on the eastern seaboard.

The most likely issues were the openness of the Ohio Valley Dunkers to revival meetings and to single-immersion baptism, as well as a disinclination to adhere to a uniform style of dress. In Kentucky some Brethren also held slaves, forbidden by Brethren principles. Two major church councils were held to attempt to reconcile the differences. These efforts failed, with the result that between 1816 and 1826 Hostetler, Hon, and their following were disfellowshipped by the eastern Brethren (although not by official Yearly Meeting action).

The Annual Meeting held in Somerset County, Pennsylvania, in 1821 dealt with the question of single-immersion baptism, responding to a query about the acceptability of this mode. The answer was rather flexible; while restating the Brethren conviction that true gospel baptism required the threefold method, the assembled Brethren concluded about single immersionists that "if such persons would be content with their baptism and yet acknowledge the Brethren's order as right, we would leave it over to them and receive them with the laying on of hands and prayer." The palm branch thus proffered seemed not to have been accepted because the Association moved quickly toward acknowledging only the single-immersion form.[21]

Leading figures in the alignment with the Disciples or Restorationists were the "boy preacher" Joseph Hostetler, a nephew of Adam Hostetler, and Peter Hon (Hahn). Hostetler became dissatisfied with the traditional Brethren through reading Alexander Campbell's publication *The Christian Baptist*. He wrote a letter to Campbell in 1825, which the latter published. Among other points, Hostetler wrote,

> A sincere desire to know the truth as it is in Christ, is the sole cause of these lines....I belong to a church called "German Baptists," sometimes "Dunkards," whose government is the New Testament only. They are not the same in principle or faith with those of the old connexion in Pennsylvania, Virginia, Maryland, and Ohio, but an order that took rise from them in Kentucky, by one *Teacher* [Adam Hostetler] in Shelby [County] about six years ago, amounting now to about two thousand, having about 24 teachers, and increasing fast.

Hostetler contended that some of Campbell's positions were not correct. Why did he not accept feetwashing and the holy kiss? Why not the biblical form of threefold immersion baptism? The tenor of the editor's response was that several traditional practices still accepted by Joseph Hostetler were social customs of the early church and should not be made mandatory church rituals. His preference was for the single immersion. Campbell's reasoning was persuasive to the young Hostetler, who soon dropped his remaining objections to the Restorationist practice.[22]

A comparable development can be observed with the colorful Kentuckian and frontier evangelist Peter Hon, who was credited with baptizing 3,000 converts. He had traveled to Illinois with

Adam Hostetler to ordain George Wolfe II. He organized churches both in Kentucky and in Ohio, where they were called "Honites" by the Brethren, and preached widely in southern Indiana. A letter about a meeting held at the Union Meeting House near Sharpsburg, Kentucky, "usually known by the appellation of the Tunker Church," was written in 1842 by a Restorationist colleague; it describes Hon and his shift in affiliation:

> When brother Peter Hon first commenced his labors there, his zeal, piety, and devotion induced many to turn to the Lord, who even then, according to the laws of these Brethren, were received into the church by being immersed three times, face forward, in a kneeling position.
>
> Brother Hon has continued his labors constantly from the first up to this time, and being one among a thousand of our race who seeks the truth for the love of it, he has always been willing to give up error for the sake of truth, and in love instructs his brethren who might differ with him.
>
> Since the commencement of this reformation he has nobly abandoned and laid aside two of his immersions, and through love and truth persuaded all the churches under his care to do the same.[23]

An encounter between Alexander Campbell and Timothy Bangor in Philadelphia did not go so well for the Restorationist leader. According to a nineteenth-century history, Campbell sought to recruit the "Keyserites" for his cause. (Peter Keyser was the senior Brethren pastor in the Philadelphia congregation.) According to the account, Bangor replied to Campbell's invitation: "We are both for baptism by immersion, and I do not see any reason why *we* should join *you*, that would not equally require *you* to join *us*." To this Campbell replied, "*You* celebrate the Lord's Supper twice a year, whereas *we* celebrate it every Lord's Day." Bangor replied that that simply increases the number of times it is observed, without touching the principle. "What do you say concerning the washing of feet? *We* do that: do *you*? Besides we hold to the restitution of all things. Do *you*?" Campbell replied negatively to both questions, prompting Bangor's conclusion: "Our testimony is altogether the largest and grandest, and vainly do you try to argue us into relinquishment of it."[24]

At some crucial meetings of the Ohio Valley Association during this period Joseph Hostetler persuaded other former Dunkers to accept the new line. He and his colleagues joined forces with a former Quaker named John Wright (who also had Brethren ties), calling themselves simply *Christians* in good Restorationist style. An early history of Indiana Disciples said of Wright: "His greatest work was in aiding his brother Peter,...[and] other pioneers, in uniting more than three thousand—Baptists, New Lights, and Dunkers—in one body, on the word of God in a single day." Out of this union eventually emerged the strong Disciples church in southern Indiana. Also active with Hostetler were Solomon and Abraham Kern, the Peter Hon mentioned above, and George H. Hon. These former Brethren became leading figures among the Disciples, traveling widely.[25]

Probably in response to this development, the Annual Meetings of the late 1820s and early 1830s drew an increasingly hard line on the accepted form of baptism. Single immersion was not to be accepted at all; those baptized in this form would have to be rebaptized "correctly" if they wished to be Brethren in good standing. Those Brethren leaders on the frontier who left the fold for the Restorationists evidently wanted to be more open to cooperate with other Christians and to practice their faith as they saw fit without restriction from the eastern Brethren. Their independence, in turn, had the effect of stiffening the conviction of the Eastern Brethren in holding the now traditional lines.

That relations were not always strained is indicated by a report in a Disciples periodical of 1851; it was written by a Disciples evangelist in Western Pennsylvania: "We are all very busy in our evangelistic labors in this county....I have to speak often in German, which I find is absolutely necessary in many regions, where almost all the preaching is done in that language. The German brethren (Dunkards) have invited us in all directions to preach for them. They are very numerous here, numbering some 2,000 or more in Somerset county. They have the largest and most commodious meeting-houses I have seen in America."[26]

LATTER-DAY SAINTS (MORMONS)

Another popular American religious movement originating in the early nineteenth century was the Church of Jesus Christ of Latter-day Saints, commonly called the Mormons. It was initiated by the charismatic Joseph Smith in upstate New York. His *Book of Mormon* (1830), alleged by Smith to have been divinely inspired, described the adventures of the lost tribes of Israel on the South and North American continents. Smith's followers developed communities in Kirkland (Ohio), Jackson County (Missouri), and Nauvoo (Illinois) in the face of great hostility, before the great trek to Utah where they founded the kingdom of Deseret at Salt Lake City.

The controversy surrounding the Mormons developed from Smith's claims to prophetic powers, his political ambitions, his attack on traditional denominations, and unorthodox social practices such as polygamy, adopted first secretly and later openly by Smith, and, at his insistence, by other leaders as well. The Latter-day Saints were intensely missionary-minded, sending their messengers across the United States and to Europe to recruit immigrant followers.

In the course of their journeys, Mormons encountered Brethren as well, some of whom were won to the cause. This was the case with the influential Abraham Hunsaker (Hunsiker) family of Adams County, Illinois, and the Pfautz family of Pennsylvania. A descendant of the latter family, John Faust, became one of the highest Latter-day Saints leaders with the rank of an apostle. The Pfautz family were residents of Franklin County, Pennsylvania, near Waynesboro, which was the site of an attempted Mormon colony in the mid-1840s under the leadership of Sidney Rigdon. Some two hundred of the Saints converged there, some from distant regions, others being local converts; all resided on a large farm spanning the Conococheague Creek. When millennial expectations waned, the colony disbanded, many travelling westward and the disillusioned returning to their former affiliations.[27]

Mormon historians have noted that a number of Utah settlers bore typical Brethren names: Hoff, Groff, Hess, Harley, Rodebaugh, Preuss (Price), Koch (Cook), and the like. Two women from the Bigler family, with Brethren connections, were plural wives of

Bishop John Hess. Margaret Harley Randall, a polygamous spouse, came from the Harley family of Montgomery County, Pennsylvania. She was a cousin of the well-known historian and collector Abraham Harley Cassel.

A well-documented link with the Brethren occurred in the Clark family. Joshua Reuben Clark, an active Mormon, was a son of Hendricks Clark, a noted Dunker minister who lived near South Bend in St. Joseph County, Indiana. Originally from West Virginia, the Clark family lived for a time in Stark County, Ohio, before moving to northern Indiana. The son defied the Brethren nonresistant position and sorely grieved his mother by joining the Union Army in the Civil War. At its end, he went west, participating in the gold rush in Montana, before settling in Utah.[28]

His diary records a trip back to northern Indiana and his encounters with his mother and siblings there, as well as with former acquaintances. He was soon reconciled with his sister Rebecca, but her husband, his brother-in-law, carried on long discussions with him. When he attended a funeral meeting held at the Dunker Church and a family sale, he was engaged in debate by several persons. "I had one discussion with J. R. Brown, M.D., and gave him as good as he sent...." According to Clark, the doctor "was very abrupt and got quite angry but finally cooled down...."

Clark talked with Brethren member Daniel Whitmer but avoided religious themes to reminisce about old times. Several persons requested more information about the Mormons, without debating the controversial points. Clark noted his attendance at the local Dunker congregation with his family to hear John Wise from Pennsylvania preach on the second coming, finding that his "exhortations were very good."

A document dismissing a member of a Philadelphia congregation because of her Mormon connection has been preserved:

> Philadelphia, April 4th, 1841
> To Mary McMinn, Dearly Beloved
>   At a meeting of the members of the German Baptist church held in their church in Crown st. below Callowhill st. It was by a unanimous voice agreed that

you be Excommunicated from said Church, and that in future you shall have no right or Tittle to the ordinances Immunities or anything Belonging to the German Baptist Church here or else where in consequence of you[r] abstaining yourself from the same and joining the Mormons.

Signed on behalf of the Members of said meeting: Peter Keyser, James Lynd; Committee: John Fox, Thos. Major.[29]

On occasion Brethren leaders debated Mormons; in Illinois, D. B. Sturgis, a physician and elder, is said to have debated with Mormon leader Sidney Rigdon. His colleague George Wolfe II was active in countering the mission activity of Mormons when they were centered at Nauvoo, not far from the large Brethren settlement in Adams County.[30]

In Virginia, sometime Brethren minister William C. Thurman debated a Mormon spokesman. A few of Thurman's disillusioned followers joined the Mormons. Later in the nineteenth century Brethren periodicals regularly included articles critical of Mormon belief and practice. Some Mormon literature claims connection with the Brethren by virtue of the former's adoption of immersion baptism.[31]

Somewhat similar in belief structure to that of the Mormons was the British-Israel movement. It contended that the ten lost tribes of Israel did not come to the Western hemisphere, as Latter-day Saints believed, but rather found their way to the British Isles. Thus Anglo-Saxons are the true heirs of Yahweh's covenant with ancient Israel. The argumentation is complicated but depends in large part on word linkage; for example, the Hebrew words *B'rith* (covenant) and *ish* (man) were thought to be the source of the English word *British*.

Some early advocates did not deny that the Jews were Israelites but held that they were but a small minority compared to the millions of Anglo-Saxon British and Americans; others, like M. M. Eshelman, did deny it. In twentieth-century Radical Right groups in the United States, the idea has provided an argument for anti-Semitism. Their claim is that the Jews, through intermarriage, lost the promise and have no claim to the Abrahamic covenant, now inherited by Anglo-Saxons. British-Israelism provides the basis for the violent Christian Identity movement.

A leading proponent of British-Israelism in North America was the Dunker publisher and promoter M. M. Eshelman, who first heard of it from an aged English immigrant. Eshelman's book on the subject, *Two Sticks: Or the Lost Tribes of Israel Discovered* (1887), was expanded from a fourteen-part series of articles published in *The Gospel Messenger* from February to May 1887. The title was derived from the image in Ezekiel 37:15ff. His thesis is indicated by a sentence in the preface: "That the Anglo-Saxons possess a large number of the qualities ascribed to Israel in her preparatory state, prior to entering the Holy Land, cannot be successfully denied." Eshelman's book was influential in spreading the concept in the United States but seems to have had little lasting influence among Brethren, with whom he remained active.[32]

ADVENTISM

This millennialist movement was instigated in North America by a Baptist layman named William Miller in New England. Becoming fascinated by the doctrine of last things (eschatology) and building on prophetic passages in the Old Testament, Miller calculated that the Second Coming of Christ would take place between March 21, 1843, and March 21, 1844. Aided by slick promotional work by Joshua V. Himes, a New York businessman, the Advent ideas swept the country, attracting thousands of adherents.

As the stated time approached, believers readied themselves for the millennium, settling their affairs and making right any unresolved personal problems. When March 21, 1844, came and went, a disappointed Miller recalculated, announcing that October 22, 1844, must be the day. When this too passed without visible action, many followers became disillusioned. A large number, however, rallied to form the Seventh Day Adventists under the leadership of Ellen Gould White.

The chief Brethren involvement came through a former Southern Baptist named William C. Thurman. He came to the attention of the Brethren during Civil War days with an excellent biblical treatise on nonresistance. Thurman joined the Brethren in 1862 and soon developed a following. Before long, he came into conflict with church leaders because of his outspoken criticism of the Brethren pattern of feetwashing. He promised not to agitate the issue but was finally expelled from the church in 1867 because he did not keep his promise.[33]

Even before this, Thurman had provoked additional tension in the church with his millennial calculations. He had been pursuing his studies for some years. In 1863 he informed Brethren editor Henry Kurtz of his interest when the two met at the Annual Meeting of 1863. Kurtz's initial reaction was favorable, saying that "we would be very glad to have something from our brotherhood which may have a tendency to make this interesting subject both plain and practical." Brethren periodicals of the time contain numerous articles about Thurman's idea, both positive and strongly negative. One of the longest, by R. H. Miller of Indiana, was a critique stretching over four issues of the *Christian Family Companion* (1865).[34]

The publication Thurman had in mind was an extensive book, *The Sealed Book of Daniel Opened*, which enjoyed four editions in the year of its publication, 1864. Henry Kurtz printed favorable reviews from other periodicals in *The Gospel Visitor* but later apologized for not recognizing the errors it contained. Adventist publications promoted the very erudite book, drawing on Thurman's calculations from various scholarly disciplines.[35]

Like William Miller, Thurman too had little success in finding the right date: he suggested successively in sermons and print 1868, 1875, and 1878. To spread his views he traveled extensively in New England, Illinois, and especially Virginia where a number of Brethren joined the "Thurmanites." Among his outspoken adherents were Benjamin Bowman and John F. Flory. In Philadelphia, he was strongly supported by Sister Margaret Worrell. A letter from Bowman to Worrell was dated "13th of 10th month 5993 [1864]," based on Thurman's calculations. Bowman reported both support and strong objections to Thurman's millennial views. He received a letter from outspoken D. P. Sayler of Maryland, who directed him to stop sending any more of Thurman's writings: "It is useless to send any of Thurman's stuff to me. I have plenty of pine planings to kindle with...." Bowman later joined the Mormons.[36]

One of Elder John Kline's last letters (April 11, 1864) was sent in answer to Sister Worrell's communication about Thurman. Writing in the midst of the "ungodly war," Kline was cautiously positive about some of Thurman's views, as far he understood them: "That the latter days are fast a drawing on, no one who is a bible reader and an observer of passing events can deny." He thought that Thurman was wrong in some of his ideas.

Stories were told of the disappointments suffered by those who accepted "timeism," that is the calculation of specific dates for Christ's return. Those who had accepted his April 19, 1875, prediction were reported to have "sold their possessions and assembled themselves in a hall where they...observed Feet-washing and the Lord's Supper, and then spent the time in singing, prayer, and religious conversation, waiting for the end until after midnight." When it became clear that the great event had not occurred, the "poor deluded people left the hall, many hardly knowing whither to go, the victims of bitter disappointment."

Understandably, skeptics tended to poke fun at those followers who believed implicitly in Thurman's work. One anecdote, recalled or embellished later, involved residents of the northern part of Augusta and the lower part of Rockingham counties in Virginia:

> One Sunday afternoon the Thurmanites met on a farm between Bridgewater and Harrisonburg to be off for the glory land....Their rolling stock was parked some distance from an old strawstack in the center of that particular field. A large crowd of curiosity-seekers was present to see the Thurmanites off....The Thurmanites mounted the strawstack and prayed long and loud. After a time a small cloud came in the sky over Pendleton County. This increased their faith. They again entered into a long season of prayer. During this second period of prayer, one of Peck's bad boys set the strawstack on fire. Up went the haze and smoke and down came the Thurmanites. One of them shouted, "In Hell, just as I expected!"[37]

Not only was Thurman learned, he made a favorable impression in public. A contemporary described him: "In person, he was of ordinary height, with a fine head, square shoulders, and of prepossessing appearance. He had a pleasant voice and persuasive manners in conversation. His manner of speaking was argumentative and he was a good reasoner and debater." Thurman excelled in debates. Two have been recorded, of which one was with the Latter-day Saints. They intended to discountenance Thurman by pointing out his error in predicting the Second Coming. To their discomfiture, in his opening statement Thurman acknowledged his mistake. He continued, however, by stating that he had made one error, but that "Mormonism was born in error, continued in error, and would die in error at the last day." Another debate was with a Seventh Day Adventist, who advocated sabbatarianism. It was reported that after nine days, Thurman had a complete victory for the Lord's Day. In his travels in New England, he convinced some Seventh Day Adventists of the truth of threefold immersion baptism; a congregation holding this tenet was still active in Maine in the early twentieth century.

Thurman died in the poorhouse in Richmond, Virginia, in 1907. The obituary read, "Rev. William C. Thurman, who, while preaching in Rockingham and Augusta Counties, predicted the world would come to an end in 1868, died a few days ago in the Alms House at Richmond. Shortly before his death he said he had misread the Bible dates, and that the end would come in 1917." A number of his earlier Brethren followers maintained themselves as a congregation until they joined the Progressive movement in the 1880s.[38]

SPIRITUALISM

Of lesser impact was another widespread American religious movement of the 1850s, that of Spiritualism. There was intense interest in communicating with the dead. The Fox sisters were famed for their table tipping and rappings. Eventually they revealed that they had begun it as a joke and showed their methods for the "communications." For a time there was a movement in the Union Bridge area of Maryland but the strong stand of Elder D. P. Sayler discouraged the enterprise. Those leading seances were discomfited by the exposés.

When a local man, "Samuel G.," reputed to be a medium, called at Sayler's mill, the elder asked him if he would "call up a friend" from the spirit world for him. The neighbor, calculating that it would be a feather in his cap if he could convert Sayler, agreed to do so. Sayler then said that a friend would like to communicate with his aged mother. The medium shortly thereafter established connection with the spirit of the mother, using the rapping of a stool as the means of communication. Thereupon Sayler asked a long series of detailed questions about how long she had been dead, whether her husband was dead, and about the number and health of remaining members of the family, to which the medium gave detailed replies.

Sayler finally said that he was satisfied and left briefly to secure a letter. On his return, he announced, "Samuel, I received a letter yesterday from my friend in Ohio. He tells me that he is well, and I will read it to you." The letter recounted that all were well, that they had just had another baby son, making two children in all, that he had recently heard from his mother who lived in an adjacent county, that she was in good health, and that her husband had recently left the Methodists to join the Brethren,

Sayler then said to the medium: "Samuel, I think that when I answer this letter, they will be surprised when I tell them that it has been revealed from the spirit world that they are the parents of six children, that two of them are dead, and that his mother has been dead seven years and is happy with old Brother S. in the spirit world. Now, Samuel, quit this deviltry and *go home and repent*." The following Sunday, according to the account, Sayler preached a strong sermon in the Beaverdam church "against the lying spirits and the strong delusions that were overspreading the land."[39]

The Annual Meeting dealt with the issue in 1852, referring to a minister who was accused of attending "spiritual rappings," asking questions of departed spirits, and inviting the medium to the homes of congregational members. The answer of the gathering was a firm rejection of rappings as a "lying wonder and delusion," forbidden in both Old and New Testaments. Any minister or member involved was to be admonished and made to make "satisfactory acknowledgments" of error to the church.[40]

THE RISE OF DEBATES

Mention was made of debates by Wolfe, Sturgis, and Thurman. This points to a development in Brethren contention with other denominations that came to the fore in the mid-nineteenth century and flourished for several decades. It reflected a pattern of religious discussion in the United States that gained great popularity during this period. It became quite common for representatives of contending religious persuasions to engage in formal public debates, often attracting large numbers of hearers. They were a form of public entertainment, although they often had a serious impact on gain or loss of church membership.

Once a challenge had been given and accepted, committees representing both sides met to establish the meeting date, place, format, moderator, and duration. It was common for such debates to extend for a week or longer, with upwards of one thousand persons attending. Often the daily routine and business of a town would be suspended to allow residents to attend the discussions. The format ordinarily involved statement of theses or resolutions, with one side affirming, the other denying. Although efforts were made to preserve courteous decorum, it was not unknown for participants and onlookers to become heated.

Henry R. Holsinger reported on a debate between James Quinter and a Lutheran minister that took place in 1853 in Blair County, Pennsylvania. He described the tactics of the Lutheran preacher as designed to "break down his opponent [Quinter] by provocation." Accordingly, he "taunted him, ridiculed him, and did everything that he thought might provoke Brother Quinter and throw him off guard...." Quinter, in Holsinger's view, "showed his Christian manhood and strength of purpose to perfection"; his equanimity was such that he "appeared to be clothed with a coat of mail, proof against the darts of his enemy. Nothing but the grace of God could sustain a man under such trial." According to his daughter, Quinter "did not greatly enjoy this work, yet when urged to defend the truth as he believed it to be taught in the Gospel, he was always ready to do so." He preferred to call them "discussions."

Quinter's ability as a defender of Brethren doctrine was one reason he became an outstanding leader during this period. He also was respected as an author, editor, preacher, and educator. Noted as a gentleman of deep spirituality, Quinter died on his knees, leading a prayer at the Brethren Annual Conference held at North Manchester, Indiana, in May 1888.

That partisanship could work both ways is clear in another debate reported by Holsinger. This again involved James Quinter and a lawyer who was a member of the Disciples or Christian Church, held in 1868 in Cumberland County, Pennsylvania. Holsinger was asked to introduce one of the sessions with a devotional exercise. In his prayer, Holsinger asked for a special blessing upon Quinter "that he might be enabled to successfully defend the truth." Then to "show impartiality," he prayed also for the lawyer, asking "that the Lord would give him light to see his error and accept the better way." Quinter remonstrated later with the younger Holsinger that in such public discussions, including the prayers, as a "matter of courtesy and consistency" impartiality must be displayed. Each participant must "grant the possibility of himself being in the wrong and his opponent in the right...."[41]

Although Brethren were at first hesitant to become involved in such contentious affairs, true to their belief in nonresistance, it seemed impossible for them to avoid such interchanges completely. At least forty debates are known to have taken place between 1840 and 1890. Several Brethren leaders became noted for their skill in defending distinctive Brethren practices, especially their threefold method or "mode" of believer's baptism.

Quinter, the editor and educator, and R. H. Miller, preacher and writer from Indiana, were considered pre-eminent in this field. Others who developed reputations were Isham Gibson, D. B. Sturgis, B. F. Moomaw, S. H. Bashor, George W. Studebaker, and J. W. Stein. As late as 1935 B. E. Kesler, leader of the 1926 division which became the Dunkard Brethren, was active in debates.[42]

The father-in-law of R. H. Miller, who was of Baptist background, described in a letter how a debate might originate; this involved a challenge from a Disciples minister in 1861:

> A reformer preacher wants Robert to preach on baptism[;] he offered his meetinghouse to the Brethren for that occasion....Robert is agoing to prove the Trine Immersion rite by history, then by Grammer, and then by Scripture that the forward motion is nearer rite than the backward motion. they think he cant. he will deceave them bad when they hear him. he is an able debater in Scripture.[43]

Miller was noted for his logically organized presentations, his thought evidently honed by previous legal training. He was known to have conducted at least nine public debates.

Formal debates became especially prominent in the later nineteenth century, but earlier Brethren had also engaged in doctrinal defenses. The early treatise by Alexander Mack, Sr., known in English as *Basic Questions* (1713), responded to pointed questions by a critic, as did two of the late eighteenth- century publications of his son Sander Mack, involved with a Lutheran divine. In 1750 Jacob Danner had a written exchange with a German Reformed leader. Brethren elders contended in print with Mennonite ministers in Pennsylvania and Virginia in the early nineteenth century over the biblical form of baptism and the Lord's Supper. George Wolfe II engaged in a well-publicized debate with a Catholic priest ca. 1818.

Many of the nineteenth-century debates took place with churches sharing many common beliefs, for example, between Brethren on one side and Restorationists (Disciples, Christian Churches), Baptists, or Mennonites on the other. In these cases quite often the methods of baptism and church order were argued. In debates with Lutherans or Reformed, the issue was most often the validity of infant baptism as opposed to adult or believer's baptism. Brethren also debated Latter-day Saints, Methodists, United Brethren, and Adventists. Other issues in question were the love feast, feetwashing, the holy kiss, secret (fraternal) societies, and millennialism.

Stenographic reports of debates involving Brethren were often reproduced verbatim in Brethren-sponsored periodicals, because of their length extending over many issues. A number of special interest were published in book form and enjoyed great popularity.

Typical among them are these titles: *Is Immersion the Mode of Christian Baptism Authorized and Proved by the Bible? A Debate between Elder James Quinter of Ohio and Rev. S. P. Snyder of Indiana* (1867); *The Waynesboro Discussion on Baptism, The Lord's Supper, and Feetwashing, Between Rev. P. B. Bergstresser, of Waynesboro, Pa., and Elder S. H. Bashor, of Ashland, Ohio* (1880); *The [J. W.] Stein and [D. B.] Ray Debate: A Church Discussion Between the Brethren and the Baptists* (1881); and *The [R. H.] Miller and [Daniel] Sommer Debate* (1889).

A debate was understood by some Brethren as an evangelistic tool, not only as a defense of Brethren doctrines and practices under attack, but also as a way of promulgating the church's understanding of faithfulness to the New Testament. There was, however, an underlying uneasiness of some Brethren about the contentiousness involved, as reflected by queries about them directed to the Annual Meetings.

Members were specifically forbidden to take part in lyceums or societies that held debates. On the other hand, a query about Brethren engaging "in public discussions with other professors upon religious or other subjects" was answered positively: "Considered, that we think it right to defend the Gospel, when interrogated (or assailed) either in private or public; but that we should not engage in worldly or political subjects, at least not to discuss them publicly" (1861).[44]

By the early twentieth century it was uncommon for Brethren to engage in public debates, with certain noted exceptions. The decline in activity probably reflected the decline in its popularity across the land as denominations began to cooperate much more in missionary, educational, and other outreach activities. In these decades Brethren began cautiously to participate in ecumenical work.

Whereas in Europe the Brethren had to contend with the state church system and state regulation, in the United States the issue was the competition of the large number of aggressive religious bodies, able to seek converts freely under the separation of church and state. Interestingly, to at least one outspoken foreign visitor, the acid-tongued Englishwoman Mrs. Frances Trollope, the Brethren were counted among the significant players. She wrote about the necessity for a Christian believer to be affiliated with a specific denomination to have social standing: "Besides the broad and well-known distinctions of Episcopalian, Roman Catholic, Presbyterian, Calvinist, Baptist, Quaker, Swedenborgian, Universalist, Dunker, etc.... there are innumerable others springing out of these, each of which assumes a church government of its own." In the face of such variety, the visitor concluded that the established Church of England was far superior.[45]

It became obvious during this period that Brethren were being changed by the altered state of affairs in the newly created and rapidly expanding nation. This necessitated a variety of changes within the church as its members adapted to this new environment.

10

Brethren in the New Nation

The history of the Brethren in America in the eighteenth and nineteenth centuries is one of immigration, consolidation, and further migration. With Germantown north of Philadelphia as the springboard, the Brethren expansion was largely westward and southward in the early decades. The Amwell congregation in New Jersey is the exception to this rule. By the 1760s the Brethren had pushed well across the Susquehanna River into southern, central, and western Pennsylvania. Three centers of Brethren expansion were Morrisons Cove in Bedford and Blair counties, the Antietam section of Franklin County, and the Glades or Brothersvalley area of Somerset County.

The movement southward was along the Cumberland Valley, following the Blue Ridge Mountains of the Piedmont in Maryland, Virginia, and the Carolinas. Although scattered Brethren were found early on in Virginia, it was not until the Revolutionary War era that lasting settlements were established there. These were in the Shenandoah Valley (Rockingham County), the Roanoke Valley (Botetourt and Roanoke counties), and the Blackwater River region (Franklin County). Brethren settled in that part of Virginia that became West Virginia along the Potomac River and Beaver Run. The oldest congregation, Sandy Creek, was organized in 1825. The Thomas and Fike families provided leadership there over the years.

From these bastions along a large stretch of the Appalachian Mountains, Brethren proceeded to move westward in large numbers in the post-Revolutionary, early national period of American history. Many came from the Carolinas or Virginia, others from the older settlements in Pennsylvania. They pushed steadily westward toward the retreating frontier. In certain areas, such as southwestern Ohio (Miami Valley), northwestern Indiana (Elkhart County), and southern Illinois (Union County), Brethren pioneers were among the very first settlers. By mid-century, some adventurous Brethren had reached the West Coast, bypassing the Great Plains by traveling via the Isthmus of Panama to California or journeying along a northern passage to Oregon.

Doubtless a mixture of motives precipitated these moves, always full of toil and uncertainty and, occasionally, danger. Individual Brethren had suffered greatly during the storms of the Revolutionary era because of their unwillingness to take up arms and their unseasonal gratitude to the British crown for the benefits that they had enjoyed after their arrival in North America. Relocation in more isolated areas may well have seemed attractive to them, as they hoped for greater tranquility and freedom from molestation.

More important, surely, was the attraction of cheap and fertile soil. The land policies of the new United States government encouraged westward movement. Because Brethren with few exceptions were farm families, the presence and promise of new land were persuasive. Their families tended to be large, and it became increasingly difficult to find enough farmland in the East to provide for all offspring. A sheer love of adventure and the wish to see new sights may also have been present among them, as it certainly was for many Easterners moving west.[1]

TRANS-APPALACHIAN SETTLEMENTS

Brethren found their way to the dark lands of Kentucky by the turn of the nineteenth century; the earliest Brethren settlements by 1800 were along Hinkston Creek (Bourbon and Nicholas Counties) and Drakes Creek (Warren and Simpson Counties). Somewhat later Brethren came to Shelby and Muhlenberg Counties. Elder Gasper Rowland, formerly of North Carolina, was the first recorded minister in Kentucky, perhaps preaching there as early as 1795. There seems to be some Brethren linkage to the famous Boones, originally a Quaker family from Berks County, Pennsylvania, who later lived near Brethren in North Carolina before moving to Kentucky. Brethren met for worship in homes and barns before they built any meetinghouses for such use.[2]

After 1810 Brethren from Virginia began to settle in Tennessee along the Holston River; the first congregation was organized in 1811 at Knob Creek, which became the mother congregation for the state. Brethren were also active in the west in Wilson and Rutherford counties. Ministers from Virginia traveled periodically into Tennessee to care for love feasts and to ordain ministers.[3]

Even earlier (late eighteenth century) Brethren had moved directly west from Pennsylvania into Ohio, when the lingering resistance of Indians fighting for their homelands had been mercilessly crushed. The first congregations along the Ohio River were in the Virginia Military Tract, with Stone Lick claimant to be the first congregation (between 1795 and 1802). Many churches were organized in the Miami Valley region in southwestern Ohio after 1805; this has remained a strong Brethren center.[4]

Elders from this area were active in establishing congregations in south-central Indiana (Wayne and Union Counties). Possibly the first organized Protestant congregation in the Indiana territory was founded about 1802 by Jacob Stutzman, who had previously resided in Chester County, Pennsylvania; Frederick County, Maryland; and Rowan County, North Carolina, before moving to Clark County. Some Brethren moved overland from the Pittsburgh area into northeastern Ohio (Stark County); more, however, chose to use the Ohio River system with its tributaries from Pittsburgh to float westward. Somewhat later Brethren found their way into northwestern Ohio, in the Great Black Swamp area.

Isaac Leedy wrote in 1906 his remembrances of life in Knox and Richland Counties in the 1830s. He recalled the wilderness, with log houses scattered here and there, out of sight of each other, visited primarily by wild turkeys, deer, wolves, and bear:

> I fancy I can see all my uncles, aunts and cousins and the Winelands, Baringers, Yunkers, Caufmans, Shir[k]ys, Bralliers, Beels, Garbers, Teeters, Brumbaughs and a host of strangers coming...to one of these ancient meetings in

father's large barn, all dressed in the plainest garments made out of coarse, home-made linen goods, and many of the boys and girls, and some of the older folks came on foot, and barefoot at that. Some came in their large farm wagons, drawn either by a yoke of oxen or a span of horses, large groups of young men and young women came riding on horses, either side by side or two, a boy and his girl riding the same horse, the girl usually taking the rear seat.

At the appointed time all were seated and engaged in [the] song service. Oh how I admired those melodious, inspiring dutch [German] hymns. I fancy I see from three to a dozen of preachers seated behind the table and about the same number of deacons in front, facing the preachers. The services were rather tedious, several discourses were delivered in the German language, and as many in English, after which the deacons bore testimony to what the preachers said.

After the religious services were over the laborious task of feeding the multitude began. Two tables were erected the entire length of the barn floor, loaded with the choicest bread and butter, pickles and fruit, good enough for a king. All seemed to enjoy this ancient meal, judging from the attitude of some, one could not resist the conclusion but that they cared more for the "loaves and fishes" than for the preaching....

Judging from their general appearance and warm greetings and the many "God bless you" expressed by those pioneers, there was a more tender regard for each other, more genuine love, affection, friendship, and sociability existing among those ancient pioneers though poorly clad and dwelling in little huts, than is existing among us of the twentieth century with all our modern improvements....[5]

The Ohio River route allowed several possibilities for settlement: Kentucky, Ohio, Indiana, Illinois, and Missouri. By the early decades of the nineteenth century, there were congregations in all of these states or territories. Brethren reached Missouri by 1795, southern Ohio by 1795, Indiana by 1801, northern Indiana by 1830, southern Illinois by 1809, and northern Illinois by 1842. Other midwestern states experienced later Brethren migration; Iowa came as an extension of Illinois in 1844, but Wisconsin (1854), Minnesota (1858), and Michigan (1868) were relatively late and never became as strongly settled by Brethren as other states.

There were earlier Brethren in Ontario and the Detroit area. Some loyalist-minded Brethren from York County, Pennsylvania, and Frederick County, Maryland, had been sufficiently distressed by their unhappy experiences during the Revolutionary period that by 1788 they left the new nation and moved to an area still under British control, that is to Upper Canada, later known as Ontario. Among them were members of the Eiler (Iler), Arnold, Schneider, and Weigel (Wigle) families. Few of the Dunkers remained long in Ontario, most—including notably the Eiler family—relocating to Ohio and to Indiana. (Early in the twentieth century twelve congregations of the Church of the Brethren were established in the provinces of Alberta and Saskatchewan through colonization but dwindled over time; in 1968 the two remaining churches became part of the United Church of Canada.)[6]

Joseph Moore, a traveling Quaker lay minister, visited the Detroit area in 1793. He records his friendly encounter with a number of German speakers, including John Messemer, a member of "the religious society called Dunkers." Messemer was featured as a frontier preacher visiting Philadelphia in an anecdote recorded by a Baptist historian:

> 'While visiting my brethren in these parts,' said the Tunker in his broken English, 'I thought I would go to de city of Philadelphia, and hear some of de preachers there. I first went to hear de Universalists; and I found dey preach *no hell* dere, but dey seem have no religion too. I next go to hear de Methodists, and dey preach *all hell*, but dey seems have good deal religion too. I next go to hear de Baptists, and dey preach some *hell* and some *heaven*, and dis I thought was de rightest way.'[7]

Because the Brethren method of holding the important Yearly Meetings was dependent on the hospitality of local congregations, some insight into the strength of Brethren settlement can be derived by observing the locations of these annual conferences. These assemblies were held in Ohio by 1822 (the first west of the Alleghenies), Indiana by 1848, and Illinois by 1856. The last named was held near Lena, Illinois, at the farm of Michael Reber. Records show that the cost of the conference was $881.58; the four sponsoring congregations were left with a balance of $183.00, made possible by great amounts of volunteer labor and donations.[8]

THE WOLFE FAMILY

The story of the Wolfe family has often been told as representative of others of this time frame. In 1787 George Wolfe I moved over the Alleghenies with his family to the vicinity of Uniontown in Fayette County, Pennsylvania. Thirteen years later he built a flatboat and floated his family and possessions down the Monongahela River to the Ohio River, and thence to Logan County, Kentucky. As was commonly done, upon arrival the travelers took the boat apart and used the lumber for lodging. The senior Wolfe was active in gathering other Brethren to establish church life in the new area. He died in the early Illinois town of Kaskaskia while on a preaching trip.[9]

His two sons, George Wolfe II and Jacob Wolfe, along with Abraham Hunsaker (the brother-in-law of George I) explored the forested land in southern Illinois, then part of the Indiana Territory, it is said, as early as 1803; in 1808-09 they moved there with their families, thus becoming the first white settlers in what became Union County. Their names loom large in the chronicles of the area. J. H. Moore described their first task, constructing cabins:

> The logs had to be cut, brought together, notched at the ends and put together in order. Clapboards for roofing had to be split, punching split and dressed down for the floors, fireplace built and plastered with clay, and all this done without the driving of a nail....With an ax the logs could be cut and notched. With a frow, the clapboards

could be split, and in the absence of a drawing knive, smoothed a bit with the ax. Any place a nail was a real necessity a hole could be bored with the auger, and a pin, whittled out with the ever present jack-knife, driven in. With these simple tools the pioneer could construct his log cabin without paying out one cent of money.[10]

Following the great earthquakes of 1811-12 near New Madrid, Missouri, there was a tremendous revival of religion across the frontier areas. After early involvement as leader of a Methodist class meeting, the younger George Wolfe led his neighbors in bringing together a Dunker congregation; they chose him as their first minister of the small congregation in Union County. Elder John Hendricks of Kentucky was the visiting elder to effect the organization in 1812.

Wolfe was ordained one year later and went on to become an important figure among the Brethren, traveling throughout Illinois, Kentucky, Missouri, and Iowa. He was the outstanding leader of the so-called Far Western Brethren, who developed in a way different from the Eastern Brethren. His influence was always cast on the side of maintaining union and harmony, while at the same time preserving the unique positions of the Brethren on the frontier.

An associate and another important pioneer leader, D. B. Gibson, characterized Wolfe in these words:

> Bro. Wolfe was almost gigantic in proportions; six feet or more in height, very broad shoulders, slightly round, deep chested, heavy limbed and weighed, I should judge, about two hundred and seventy-five pounds. His head was large, very broad and protruding brows, indicated strong intellectuality; forehead receding, high and full. Hair rather auburn until whitened by age. Nose aquiline but not large. Mouth broad and jaws wide. Lips flexible. Eyes blue and deeply set under over-arched brows.[11]

He was a stalwart defender of traditional Brethren practices over against other aggressive religious bodies. He is known to have held debates on these points with Baptist and Catholic opponents. A seal chosen for Union County three decades later commemorates the irenic spirit in which the Baptist-Brethren religious discussion was held. It shows Wolfe and the Baptist spokesman shaking hands at the end of their meetings. According to the record, the debate with a Catholic priest at the Catholic stronghold of Kaskaskia was less cordial.

In what was probably his last public sermon, during a funeral, Wolfe was recalled to have stated,

> I have preached the gospel for over fifty years. I labored much when Illinois was a wilderness. My work is now nearly done. I have, like Paul, finished my course, and if when eternity shall dawn, and as I gaze with enraptured vision on the mighty hosts of the redeemed, if in that mighty throng one soul should be numbered with the blest because I worked, prayed, and preached, I shall be fully requited for all my labors.[12]

Wolfe also became influential in secular affairs. He was well known by leading politicians, including Governor Shadrach Bond, who had high praise for his oratorical skills. He served on the committee chosen to select a permanent seat for the county government, which was called Jonesboro, and on the first grand jury. Wolfe is credited by some historians with keeping slaveholding out of the territory, thus extending Brethren values beyond the borders of the church. He is also said to have convinced the state government to permit the Brethren to maintain their nonresistant principles in the wake of the Black Hawk War of 1832.

In later life George Wolfe II moved with his family from Union County to a site near Quincy in Adams County, in west-central Illinois, which became a center of Brethren activity as the Liberty congregation. This was in 1831; a number of Brethren formerly living in Union County had preceded him in the relocation. About ten years later Brethren established a strong center in northern Illinois in Carroll and Ogle counties; unlike the Wolfe-led settlements, these did not come by way of the South but directly westward from Central Pennsylvania. Christian Long from Franklin County, Pennsylvania, was one of the patriarchs.

A portrait of the midwestern patriarch George Wolfe II. From Elgin P. Kintner, *BHLA Collection.*

While maintaining a home base in Adams County, George Wolfe continued to travel widely, visiting Brethren and organizing congregations as far as Iowa before he died in 1865 at the age of 85. A son David served in the state legislature before becoming a minister among the Brethren. A nephew Jacob W. Wigle reached Oregon by 1853. Another nephew, also named George Wolfe and thus often referred to as "George Wolfe III" reached the Pacific Coast in 1856 by way of the Isthmus of Panama. Two years later he organized the first Brethren congregation in Pajaro Valley near Gilroy, California. Thus in three generations of one family, Brethren moved from Pennsylvania to Kentucky, to Illinois, and then across the continent to the West Coast.[13]

BRETHREN MIGRATIONS

The extent of this relocation is unusual within such a short span of time. A more typical example of Brethren relocation is found in a local history of Indiana, with reference to the early settlement of Brethren in northwestern Indiana in what became Elkhart and St. Joseph counties. The account involved Martin Weybright, Jr., who moved there from Montgomery County, Ohio, where he had also been a pioneer. With Weybright was Daniel Cripe, the Brethren patriarch in this area. Called the first Protestant minister in Elkhart County, he died in 1859 in his 87th year. According to the account,

> In 1829...Mr. Weybright sold his farm in Ohio and came to Elkhart county, making the journey with a yoke of oxen and a three-horse team, and being on the way seventeen days. In the spring of that year they first settled on the land...and put out a crop of seed corn. Two weeks later he moved to the farm...on the southwest side of the prairie.
>
> The first night the family slept under the spreading branches of a huge oak tree and the next day the neighbors met together to assist Mr. Weybright to build a log cabin. This was erected and places cut out for a door and window; mother earth was the floor to the cabin and continued as such until the fall. The bedstead Mr. Weybright

A Brethren "circuit rider" of the nineteenth century leaving his home for an extended ministerial journey. *Durnbaugh Collection.*

made by driving stakes in the ground in one side of the cabin and covering them with poles and split clapboards. On this was then spread blankets and comforts until it was very comfortable, and in this huge bed the entire family slept until better arrangements could be made.

The account continues, describing Weybright's religious activities as preacher for the Dunkers and his worldly success. By the time of his death at the age of 58, he had given each of his children 160 acres and he himself owned a fine farm of 400 acres, totaling 2,000 acres in all. "The improvements on his farm were all first class for those days, the house being log, but plastered, and the barn being also a large log structure. He set out a good orchard, and being progressive and enterprising, reaped rich returns."[14]

It was customary for Brethren families to begin holding meetings in their homes as soon as they erected their rude cabins. Often preachers were involved in these early relocations. If not, other persons would lead out. Actual congregations would be organized during the visits of ministers from a distance. For this reason, the beginning dates of individual congregations may be difficult to establish. It ordinarily took place several years, or even much longer, after the first settlement of Brethren.

Some possible places of settlement investigated did not result in actual migration. One such is recorded in the annals of the communitarian Harmonist Society who lived from 1814 to 1824 in the extreme southwestern corner of Indiana. According to a note in a letter (December 1814) from the commune's leader, Georg Rapp, some Dunkers visited the colony and took dinner there. Rapp reported, "They were looking for land for 200 families. I told them about our region and they expressed the opinion they would [come] again and select a piece of from 12 to 14,000 acres near us."

In other cases, members of Brethren families were attracted to other religious groups. One account, often reprinted, relates the experience of Jacob Bower of Kentucky. He had moved with his family from Lancaster County, Pennsylvania, to Kentucky while in his teens. He was first attracted to the Universalists, thought of joining the Brethren because of family background, but finally decided to go with the Baptists. His tale well illustrates the religious situation on the frontier:

> About this time [1812] I had a great desire to be united with some society of Christians. And in those days there were no societies in that part of Kentucky but Baptists, Tunkars, and some Methodists, and for a time I could not decide which of them to offer myself for membership....I

first thought of Uniting with the Tunkars. And if Mr. [John] Hendrix (their preacher) had come into the vicinity, I would have been baptized by him (by trine immersion). I thought that it must be the right way, or Father would not have been baptized that way. But I could not arrive at any decision on the subject. I therefore resolved to read the new Testament, and go the way it pointed out to me, and unite with that church which practised, and walked nearest to the divine rule. I commenced at the first chapter of Mathew, determined to read the Testament through and thought again & again till I could be able to decide. I had a German Testament, and when I could not well understand the English, the German would explain it to me.

Bower was welcomed in baptism by the Hazle Creek Baptist congregation in March 1812 and later became a Baptist preacher in Illinois.[15]

The manner of life of these migrating Brethren proved appealing to their neighbors and many were attracted to the movement by it. They were known for their neighborliness and their honesty and industry. This is revealed in a backhanded way in an anecdote contained in the autobiography of the well-known Methodist frontier preacher Peter Cartwright. He had a run-in while serving in the Illinois legislature with a lawyer from Union County where many of the Brethren lived.

In Cartwright's somewhat doubtful recollection, the lawyer wished to pass a law that would favor Brethren, excusing them from paying taxes, working on roads, performing military duty, serving on juries, etc. (Brethren certainly did not object to paying taxes or working on roads; they would have objected to military duty and serving on juries.) Cartwright vigorously opposed these waivers, contending that if the Brethren would not bear arms, they "were unworthy of the protection of government"; if they would not work on roads, they should not be allowed to travel on them; if they would not pay taxes to support the government, they "should be declared outlaws."

At this, the representative from Union County angrily drew a contrast between the Brethren and the Methodists. "He said that the Dunkers were an honest, industrious, hard-working people"; their preachers worked for their own support, making it unnecessary to carry "the hat round in the congregation for public collections" to support the preachers, as was done among the Methodists. Cartwright won the argument, he recalled, but the characterization of the Brethren in Union County remains.[16]

A winsome description of the Brethren way of life on the frontier was penned by the English author Harriet Martineau, whose travel in June 1836, by stagecoach from La Porte to Michigan City in northwestern Indiana was interrupted by bad weather. A Brethren family offered the travelers shelter. "We perceived by a glance at the beard and costume of our host, that there was something remarkable about him. He was of the Tunker sect of Baptists..., a very peculiar sect of religionists." According to the traveler, he "explained, without any reserve, his faith, and the reason on which it was founded." Martineau was charmed by her host's wife who "won our hearts by the beauty of her countenance, set off by the neat plain dress of her sect." Although she was ill, she and her husband made the unexpected guests "thoroughly comfortable, without apparently discomposing themselves." The family had sixteen living children, of whom two sons and five daughters were living at home; the youngest was three years old.

The house was of logs, consisting of three rooms, "two under one roof" and another evidently added later. Cooking and eating went on in one room; one room was made available to the traveling ladies and some small children; the third accommodated the rest of the family and the men who were in the traveling party. "Huge fires of logs blazed in the chimney; two or three of the little ones were offered us as hand-maidens; and the entire abode was as clean as could be conceived. Here was comfort!" As the soaked travelers warmed and dried themselves by the chimney, they "looked upon the clear windows, the bright tin water-pails, and the sheets and towels as white as snow."

The farm contained 800 acres, much as yet untilled and covered with huckleberries. The farmer said that he had paid $1.25 per acre three years previously when he came from Ohio and that he was currently being offered $40.00 per acre because of its advantageous location.

Having slept well "amid the luxury of cleanliness and hospitality," the travelers took breakfast and then went on their way. "When it had come to saying farewell, our hostess put her hands on my shoulders, kissed me on each cheek, and said she had hoped for the pleasure of our company for another day," wrote Harriet Martineau, expressing her wish for it as well if she passed that way again.[17]

TRANS-MISSISSIPPI SETTLEMENTS

The Whitewater Creek congregation near Cape Girardeau in Missouri was the first Brethren church to be established west of the Mississippi River, under the leadership of Daniel Clingingsmith. The first love feast was held at the home of Joseph Niswinger in 1810, conducted by Elder John Hendricks from Warren County, Kentucky, who was active in much of the Ohio Valley region before his death in 1813. His son James Hendricks continued his father's work.

Brethren families, including the Bakers, Millers, and Niswingers, came by wagons on the Mission Road through the Cumberland Gap from North Carolina, continuing the trip on flatboats via the Ohio River. This took place between 1795 and 1800, when that area was still under Spanish administration, prior to the assumption of American control in 1803. The settlers had come from the Carolinas by way of Kentucky. It was not until several decades later that other Brethren congregations were established in Missouri, and these were then planted in the western area of the state.

Visiting Brethren from Illinois like George Wolfe II had been holding meetings in Iowa for some time before formal organization took place. The first known congregation was in Jefferson County, Iowa, in 1844. In the mid-1850s a substantial Brethren settlement centered about Waterloo in Black Hawk County. A colony of Brethren from Indiana moved into Minnesota in Winona County in 1856. As indicated earlier, Brethren were on the West Coast in the 1850s, thus jumping across two thousand miles. The first Brethren

there, from Illinois, arrived in California in 1856; in the same year
Brethren organized a congregation in Oregon.

The major transplantation west of the Mississippi took place in
later decades. This came through the transcontinental connection of
the railroads following 1869. The transportation companies competed to attract farmers to settle along their tracks. They needed the business of transporting settlers, but they needed more the freight business of transporting the crops of settlers. As Brethren were known as
a sober and hardworking people, the railroad companies competed
to attract them as settlers. This story will be told later in more detail.

TENSIONS AND DIVISIONS

All of this expansion did not come without a price, which can be
seen in the emergence of several parties with divergent convictions
about church practices and doctrines. Three of the most important
were the Far Western Brethren, the Congregational Brethren, and
the Church of God (New Dunkers). In all three instances there was
division and separation; in the first case the schism was temporary
and reconciliation was eventually accomplished; in the second and
third cases the division became permanent.

The term Far Western Brethren refers to a substantial group of
Brethren ministers and laity in the Ohio Valley, especially in western Kentucky, Illinois, Missouri, and Iowa—later extended as well
to California and Oregon; they were active between 1800 and 1860.
The division had its origins in the ministry of John Hendricks in the
Ohio Valley region, who taught the doctrine of universal restoration. Congregations in this area were less responsive to the direction
of the Yearly Meetings. As westward settlement proceeded, thus
creating greater distances between these congregations and those
farther east, different practices became more apparent.

Differences tended to cluster around the manner of conducting
the love feast. One of the troubled issues came from the manner of
washing feet; the Far Western Brethren followed the practice of the
single mode whereas the eastern Brethren (except for Germantown)
had developed the practice of the double mode. The Far Western
Brethren also originally performed the ordinance following the

Lord's Supper, although correspondence with eastern leaders convinced them to place the rite before the meal. In some congregations of the Far Western Brethren, women broke bread and passed the cup instead of being served individually by the elder, as was followed in the East.

As has been seen, Peter Hon came to teach a different method of baptism; he contended it should be a single, backward immersion. This Baptist method was communicated through the Restoration (Disciples) movement, led by Alexander Campbell, who had been associated earlier with Baptists. For a time, between 1821 and 1834 the Yearly Meeting accepted this form as a valid baptism, but later returned to the long-standing insistence on the threefold forward mode as the only valid form.[18]

Elder George Wolfe II and Isham Gibson became the leaders of the Far Western Brethren after the death of John Hendricks. Wolfe especially desired a closer connection with the Eastern Brethren. As increasing numbers of Eastern Brethren settled among the Far Western Brethren in states like Illinois, there was more pressure to come to complete union. In 1850 and 1851 the issues were discussed at the Annual Meetings, without resolution. In 1856 a committee of elders worked out articles of agreement of the points at issue; basically the compromise was that the Far Western Brethren could retain their single mode practice of feetwashing if they were willing to use the double mode when they visited with congregations who followed the latter practice. A minister from Germantown gave testimony that indicated that the mother congregation had always used the single mode; this undercut the attempt of the committee to banish the practice. In 1859 Elders Wolfe and Gibson sent letters of submission to the Annual Meeting, acknowledging that the Annual Meeting held final authority on church matters.

It soon became apparent, however, that all had not been completely settled. Universal salvation was still a troublesome issue, and some congregations in the West insisted on using only the single mode. The Annual Meeting began sending committees to visit congregations that were not "in the order"—this led to the expulsion and disfellowshiping of many Brethren in the Midwest, among whom Isham Gibson was the leading personality.

These actions led eventually to the formation of the Congregational Brethren in 1872, which sought to unite a number of smaller, disaffected groups such as the Leedy Brethren, Bowman Brethren, Christian Brethren, Hoppingite Brethren, and the followers of W. C. Thurman and John Cadwallader. Although differing on several points, they shared resistance to Annual Meeting "despotism" and the practice of the single mode of feetwashing; they also tended to permit their members to participate more actively in the broader society than did the mainline Brethren. Andrew P. Gibson of Missouri, son of Isham Gibson, and George Wolfe III of California, nephew of George Wolfe II, were prominent leaders in the movement. In 1883 the Congregational Brethren merged with the Progressive Brethren to form The Brethren Church.

THE CHURCH OF GOD (NEW DUNKERS)

The Church of God (New Dunkers) first emerged in 1848 as a dispute at the Bachelor Run (Lower Deer Creek) congregation in Carroll County, Indiana; factionalism developed through the teaching of two Brethren ministers George Patton and Peter Eyman (also Oyman). The two leaders began to advocate practices differing slightly from traditional Brethren customs. They used the single mode of feetwashing before the meal was placed on the table at love feasts. Probably more bothersome was their greater leniency about the involvement of members in secular society; the elders permitted them to vote in elections, serve on juries, and join secret societies.[19]

Representatives of the Annual Meeting interceded in an attempt to reconcile differences in the congregation and made some progress; deciding that those on both sides had made errors, they promised restoration to fellowship of all those who would admit error. Eyman and Patton, however, were not willing to concede their position. They met in Eyman's house in 1848 to organize a new church, choosing to be called the Church of God, but were often called the New Dunkers or Dunkards. The movement spread to some other parts of the state after Eyman's death some four years later.

The movement was evangelistic and held meetings in the open

air, in tents, in schools, or wherever possible, at times attracting numbers of attendants from other denominations. The New Dunkers developed a number of congregations, almost all in Indiana. Despite attempts over the years to unite with other denominations such as the Church of God in North America and the Brethren Church, the small body maintained itself until 1962, when it voted to disband.

CONSOLIDATION OF DISCIPLINE AND POLITY

The early national period of American history saw, besides westward expansion, a consolidation of Brethren forms of discipline and church government or polity. Because of the emergence of the Brethren as a movement in conscious opposition to the highly institutionalized state churches, Brethren organization had remained informal for many decades. Important decisions on matters of doctrine and practice could be decided by face-to-face meetings of church leaders at the Annual Meetings or other specially called gatherings. As members pushed through the wilderness to the ever extending frontiers, such informality no longer served to retain unity. By mid-century, church leaders determined that more highly developed forms of discipline and government were necessary.

DRESS CODE

How the increasing formality came to be practiced can be observed in the tighter control on the manner of Brethren dress. By 1860 this became a symbol of Brethren conduct and discipline and was (revealingly) often simply referred to as the Order. All conservative religious bodies of Anabaptist background make much of the totality of behavior and ethical codes, often communicated orally and at least in part in writing. Willingness on the part of members to submit to direction on the style of dress is often considered to be basic to preserving the order. Although at times conceded to be of relatively minor importance in itself, the posture of humility and obedience to church regulations it represents is held to be of the highest value.[20]

As has been seen, there is little evidence in the first years of Brethren activity of a mandatory form of dress. By the end of the eighteenth century, there was a recognizable garb or dress style. The first minute of a Yearly Meeting dealing with wearing apparel came in 1804; the concern expressed was with members who "gratify too much the lust of the eye," "conforming therein themselves to the world," especially the young people. The meeting ruled that church leaders and parents should use "all diligence" to curb the spread of new fashions, in particular in regard to those who apply for church membership. Aspiring members must "deny themselves" and permit themselves to be instructed on this point, so as to reject that "contrary to wholesome doctrine."[21]

Thirteen years later a similar concern was extended to members who were found to be conforming to the world "in wearing fashionable clothing"; any member "found guilty" of this "should be admonished." If the admonition were not heeded, then such a member could not be held "in full fellowship, inasmuch as the Savior says, 'That which is highly esteemed among men, is abomination in the sight of God' (Luke 16:15)." Twelve more decisions on the same point were concluded by Annual Meetings before 1865, demonstrating both the increased specificity of church discipline regarding wearing apparel and also the recurring incidence of members testing the limits of the order.[22]

The 1861 decision used a phrase that was to be heard increasingly in this discussion; that is the requirement that members follow "the order in dress as generally practiced by the old brethren and sisters." This opened the door to the critique that the church was not depending on the clear word of scripture as the basis of authority but rather on human decisions. In the latter decades of the nineteenth century, this complaint would be heard more often and in more aggressive tones. For more than a half-century, however, Yearly Meeting minutes had appealed to the counsel of the "old brethren" or to the "ancient brethren." It was an understandable and natural approach for those seeking to maintain unity and conformity within the church, but also a stance that irritated members seeking to renew or reform the church.

ANNUAL MEETING REQUIREMENTS

In the course of the first half of the nineteenth century, a discernible trend was under way; this involved a shift toward greater formalization of the authority of the Annual Meeting. Whereas previously decisions of the gathering had the weight of the concerted conclusions of church leaders, which were taken seriously by individual members and individual congregations, increasingly the Meeting was seen as a legislative body passing laws. This became obvious in the language and also in the enforcement procedure.

Arrangements for Annual Meetings varied from time to time, as thought appropriate and necessary. It became customary to meet at the time of Pentecost each year, accepting invitations from individual congregations. Ordinarily a farm would serve as the site of the meeting, with barns as the largest buildings available for meetings. Those attending would be accommodated in the homes of members living nearby. This meant that ordinarily only those congregations with substantial membership would be in a position to host the meetings.

Earlier in the nineteenth century, Brethren would gather in the vicinity by Thursday evening, ready to begin consultation on Friday. Meetings would conclude with worship gatherings on Saturday and Sunday, including a love feast on Sunday evening. By 1832 this pattern was changed to have worship first on the weekends, with business dealt with in the council meetings on Monday and Tuesday. The purpose of the shift was to allow greater privacy for discussion of church issues, without the presence of nonmembers.

A minute of the meeting of 1841 provides a good summary of the plan for holding Yearly Meetings in the first decades of the nineteenth century:

> The unanimous counsel of this meeting and desire of the old brethren is to follow the track of the apostles as closely as possible. Therefore the council meeting ought to consist of the elders and all the members of the church which receives the meeting, and of such teachers, ministers, or (private) members, who may be sent as delegates from the other churches. It is considered necessary that

every church, or, where the distance is too great, several churches together, should send two, three, or more delegates to the annual meeting.

The yearly meeting is to take place as heretofore on Pentecost or Whitsuntide, and the council-meeting to be held on Friday and Saturday before, to which end the delegates ought to arrive in the neighborhood on Thursday evening. The public meeting begins on Sunday, when a love feast is to be held, and the church is at liberty to invite thereto also neighboring churches as usual. The proceedings of the council meeting should be immediately recorded in writing, and as much as possible communicated to all the churches.[23]

In 1846 the decision was to invite the "Western Brethren" to host the Annual Meeting every other year with the "Eastern Brethren" admonished to attend; the Allegheny Mountains provided the boundary between East and West. Because of the continuing westward movement, in 1860 the boundary line was later shifted to the Ohio River, evidently meaning the border between Pennsylvania and Ohio. It was in 1846 that the terminology Annual Meeting replaced the earlier Yearly Meeting, signaling a change from a more informal gathering for worship and fellowship to one designed to transact business.

As a result of some tension and question, in 1847 greater specificity was introduced into the manner of conducting the Annual Meeting. Congregations were directed to send one or two delegates to represent them, bearing a written certificate. Delegates were to bring with them queries to be presented to the meeting. Whereas heretofore decisions were made by consensus of those present, the 1847 minute introduced the principle of voting by a two-thirds majority to decide issues. (This latter action proved, in fact, to be too much of a departure, for it was withdrawn at the next Annual Meeting to permit seeking of unanimity; the practice of voting became more common in the 1870s but was not officially endorsed until 1882.) A minute passed in 1847 encouraged congregations to settle those problems locally that pertained to themselves alone, so "as not to embarrass the councils of the Annual Meeting with such local cases."[24]

Because of the increasingly large numbers present at the Annual Meeting and attendant crowding, it was decided in 1851 to omit holding love feasts on the Saturday or Sunday evenings prior to the meeting for business. A continuing concern through these decades was how to cope with the presence of nonmembers during deliberation of church business.

Continuing dissatisfaction with some aspects of church government focusing on the Annual Meeting led to the appointment of a large (fourteen-member) committee in 1865; its membership included many of the younger and outstanding leaders among the Brethren such as D. P. Sayler, H. D. Davy, and Christian Long. Their recommendations led to a major readjustment in 1866 in church polity. The decisions of the committee have been largely followed to the present.

A major departure was the decision to restrict decision making to ordained elders and elected delegates, rather than to all those present. The greatly increasing number of those attending the Annual Meetings had made the older procedure cumbersome. The plan also codified the practice of District Meetings, often delineated by state, a development which began in 1856. One or two delegates from each organized congregation in the district would gather at these meetings to consider and resolve questions of local interest. Those deemed to be of general interest (or those insoluble at the district level) would be sent on the the Annual Meeting.

Annual Meetings were to begin on the Monday following Pentecost with delegates from congregation and church leaders present. The alternation of locations between East and West was preserved. A Standing Committee composed of elders would be organized at the beginning of the Annual Meeting, with membership proportional to numbers of congregations present in each state. (In 1868 it was agreed that District Meetings would appoint its representatives on the Standing Committee.) The Standing Committee would appoint its officers, including a Moderator, a Reading Clerk, a Recording Clerk, and a Doorkeeper. The Moderator would preside over the meetings of the Standing Committee and the General Council, keeping order and declaring answers to queries passed with general consent. The leading task for the Standing Committee was to prepare the business for the general session beginning on

Tuesday; this took place by organizing the accumulated queries into coherent blocs and preparing suggested answers to the queries.

A significant change was the provision for sending committees from the Annual Meeting to individual congregations to "investigate grievances"; conclusions of the Annual Meeting were to be published and communicated to local congregations. If local elders did not have the decisions "faithfully read and observed in their respective charges," then the Standing Committee could appoint committees to visit these bodies "and see that the Minutes are properly read and observed." They could "set in order things that are lacking." This provision shifted authority and power in the denomination squarely to the centralized body.[25]

Some sense of the rival currents of opinion can be gleaned from the comments of the well-connected editor Henry Kurtz. In 1867 he published a classified selection of the "counsels and conclusions" of the Annual Meetings under the title *The Brethren's Encyclopedia*. In his introduction he described two opposing views on the subject:

> Some perhaps esteem them somewhat too highly, taking them as rules and laws of equal authority as divine writ, and which, like the Persian laws, could not be altered. Others again put perhaps a too low estimate upon them, considering them as a bundle of human traditions, as they are sometimes called as "traditions of elders," which we cannot too soon forget and lay aside, because, they think, they conflict with and are contrary to the word of God, as it is written. They object, when reference is made to these conclusions, and would have rather consigned them to destruction for fear they might obtain an undue influence.

Kurtz laid out the principles (based on research "at once deep and earnest for nearly forty years") upon which he undertook to "put into the hands of my brethren of the present generation those words of peace and union which had been concluded upon by our beloved brethren of past generations under their own trials and difficulties, for our present and future benefit and instruction." These were seven in number:

1. The fundamental principle of the Brethren is "to take the pure word of God, and that alone, as the infallible rule of their faith and practice."
2. "Guided by this principle, they rejected every form of doctrine, every practice, every custom and ordinance contrary to that divine and infallible rule, and united as a church with the sincere object to follow the apostle's converts on Pentecost...."
3. Just as in apostolic times, differences of interpretation arise; Brethren have tried to work for union as the apostles did.
4. If "an express word of God" is found to "cover and decide" a question, this must be followed and is in no way to be considered to be a "human tradition."
5. If there are questions for which the word of God supplies no direct answer, and are not matters of "true faith and morality," then "brotherly love will be liberal and forbearing, without insisting others to be of our opinion." Any expression of opinion on such matters should be withheld if it gives offense to others.
6. On matters of a practical nature, it is necessary to be of one mind "that there be no divisions among you;" in such cases, where the Brethren have unanimously agreed, regardless of whether it was "yesterday or a hundred years ago," by "brethren representing the whole fraternity in Yearly Meeting," then such agreement "is binding on all...."
7. Brethren should "look upon the counsels and conclusions as solemn agreements or covenants" and are to be considered "bonds of love" intended "to bind them together in union of the spirit." Those unwilling to accept these agreements could not be held in fellowship, for they were "disturbers of the peace" and "covenant breakers."

Hence, Kurtz concluded, the minutes of the Annual Meetings should be considered neither laws and rules nor simply human traditions. He emphasized the binding quality of past decisions until altered to suit changed situations. Brethren seeking to preserve unity in love will respect and follow the agreed covenant. Unfortunately for the church, this attempt at moderation and conciliation did not prove successful in rallying the increasingly divergent voices in a united chorus.[26]

ADJOINING ELDERS

The traditional authoritative role of the Annual Meeting makes it clear that the Brethren never had a purely congregational form of polity in which final power rests with the local body. Another aspect of this connectional emphasis lies in the activities of the *adjoining elders*. The meaning of the term is clear, referring as it does to the leading ministers in neighboring congregations.

In practice, Brethren polity insisted on their presence and moderating participation in every critical decision of the local congregation of representatives of the larger body. Thus, whenever leadership was chosen, serious cases of discipline treated, and love feast celebrated, it was imperative to invite elders from area congregations to be present. It was their role to officiate at these meetings, bringing their broader perspective and greater experience to bear on the local issues. It helped to guard against overdominance by leading families or aggressive individuals.

The well-informed Elder Philip Boyle of Maryland explained their duties in a description of the Brethren for a comparative history of American denominations (1836), using the term *bishop* for the wider audience; it was not generally used in Brethren polity: "It is the duty of the bishops to travel from one congregation to another, not only to preach, but to set in order the things that may be wanting; to be present at their love feasts and communions, and, when teachers and deacons are elected or chosen, or when a bishop is to be ordained, or when any member who holds an office in the church is to be excommunicated." Further, "As some of the congregations have no bishops, it is also the duty of the bishop in the adjoining congregation to assist in keeping an oversight of such congregations."[27] Eventually the system of adjoining elders evolved into the formal elders' body, which functioned as a disciplinary and advisory body overseeing ministers and church leaders in each district.

In looking at Brethren polity over the years, it is evident that a considerable amount of pragmatic reorganization and adjustment has taken place. Basic principles of representative leadership and participatory involvement have remained constant beneath transitory arrangements. Without the traditional structures of the presbyterian or episcopal forms of church polity, Brethren have felt free to modify and rearrange as it "seemed good to the believers and the Holy Spirit." While not always neat and tidy, it does reflect a spirit of cooperation and willingness to be flexible that has its own values.

The name of Henry Kurtz was mentioned here, indicative of the rising importance of this figure in the course of Brethren history. The next chapter portrays the innovation he introduced among the Brethren and provides an analysis of some of its impact upon them.

11

Emergence of Publications

As Brethren spread themselves across the continent in the course of the nineteenth century it became more difficult to preserve unity. The changes in church polity by the introduction of District Meetings and delegates to the Yearly Meetings helped to alleviate the problem but did not resolve the problem of ready communication. Some elders sought to fill this gap by extensive travels. John Kline of Broadway, Virginia, is a celebrated example of these leaders. Based on his own records, he covered more than 100,000 miles over the years of his ministry, spending weeks at a time on any one of his trips. It is calculated that he traveled over 30,000 miles alone on his faithful mare, Nell.[1]

It was left to the ingenuity and enterprise of Henry Kurtz to devise another medium of communication for the Brethren. This was to provide a periodical for distribution to the scattered Brethren across the continent. His overriding concern was to preserve unity among the faithful through the medium of the printed page, as signaled by the title he gave to his pioneering effort, *The Gospel Visitor*, first issued in 1851; he articulated the same vision in his greeting to readers in the first number:

> But we are asked: What do you want to print, and what is your object?...We are as a people devoted to the truth, as it is in Christ Jesus. We believe the church as a whole possesses understandingly that truth, and every item of it. But individually we are all learners, and are progressing with more or less speed in the knowledge of the truth. For this purpose we need each other's assistance.

> But we live too far apart. If one in his seeking after a
> more perfect knowledge becomes involved in difficulty,
> which he is unable to overcome, this paper opens unto
> him a channel, of stating his difficulty, and...there will be
> someone, who has past the same difficult place, and can
> give such advice, as will satisfy the other.[2]

KURTZ'S BACKGROUND

Henry Kurtz had an unusual background for a Dunker. Perhaps it
was this different context that provided the ideas and initiative that
brought him, after initial hesitation on the part of the Brethren, to
his innovation, to a position as one of the most influential leaders in
the history of the church. Born in Germany in 1796 of Lutheran
parentage, he enjoyed a solid classical education. At the age of
twenty-one he left home and migrated to the United States, locating
in Northampton County, Pennsylvania, where he won a position as
a schoolteacher. In 1819 he embarked on a career as a Lutheran pastor, soon moving up the ranks to achieve ordination.[3]

He was called in 1823 to the pastorate of a united
Lutheran/Reformed parish in Pittsburgh. After a promising start,
he antagonized lay leaders of the congregation by insisting on rigorous church discipline. This led to bitter factional disputes and his
forced resignation in 1826. During the same period he became interested in communitarianism. After contact with the Scottish reformer
Robert Owen and the German communal leader Georg Rapp of the
Harmony Society, Kurtz attempted to create his own community.
He planned to call it Concordia and to site it in northeastern Ohio.
For two years he edited and published a periodical to spread his
communal ideas and raise funds for the venture, with mixed success. By late 1827 it became clear that he did not have sufficient support, either in recruits or funding to initiate his colony.[4]

Though disappointed in this attempt, he had learned to know
the Brethren in Stark County, Ohio, where he relocated together
with his family. He found in the Brethren a style of genuine
Christianity modeled on the primitive church that his biblical stud-

ies and communitarian dreams had made attractive. In a dramatic gesture, as he was lowered into the water in the three-fold pattern of Dunker baptism, he allowed his Lutheran preaching robe to slip from his shoulders and float downstream, thus symbolizing his rejection of his churchly past. It was not long before the Ohio Brethren recognized Kurtz's ability; they soon called him to the ministry and then assigned him the oversight of the Mill Creek congregation in Mahoning County. This occurred even before he was ordained to the eldership in 1844.

Although he gained his livelihood from farming, Kurtz also was interested in publishing. In 1830 he bought a press and began to issue a modest number of books. The most popular was a small hymnal, *Die Kleine-Lieder Sammlung*, which went through seven editions under his aegis. He used his press to print copies of the minutes of the Yearly Meetings when he became the recording clerk, largely because of his facility with both the German and English languages.

ESTABLISHING A CHURCH PERIODICAL

In addition to the periodical issued during his communitarian phase, Kurtz attempted publication of two journals in Ohio. Two short-lived ventures have been recorded. One was *Das Wochenblatt* (1833-1834), of which no copies are known to exist; the other was the *Zeugnisse der Wahrheit* (1836-1837), a bilingual (German/English) journal, of which volumes one and two are known.

In 1849 Kurtz began to communicate his interest in creating a journal for the Brethren. He contacted a number of congregations and asked for subscriptions. The Yearly Meeting of 1850 tabled a query that sought to ban this activity, clearing Kurtz to print and circulate a trial issue in April 1851. The subsequent meeting decided to permit the continuation of the paper for one year and then decide whether it could be published; the conference of 1852 also took a watch-and-wait-attitude, allowing continued publication: "We cannot forbid its publication at this time, and hope those brethren opposed to it will exercise forbearance, and let it stand or fall on its own merits." Finally, the 1853 Yearly Meeting concluded that it was a personal business and that the meeting, given the divided counsel about it, "should not any further interfere with it." Kurtz's cautious editorial policy, while not without its critics, had succeeded in allaying the most urgent fears.[5]

Those opposed to the project raised these cautions: 1) it was an innovation and therefore suspect; 2) it might lead to division; 3) it could be considered merchandising the Gospel and in that way violate Brethren practice; and 4) it cost too much for subscriptions. Kurtz used the columns of the journal to answer these and similar objections. In answer to the specter of schism, he wrote, "And in order to put at rest every brother, that is afraid of a division, that might be caused by the Visiter, we would humbly yet solemnly assure him, that so far from harboring any thought like that of causing a division in the body of Christ, we would rather pull out our right eye or cut off our right hand, than that through our instrumentality such a calamity should come over our brotherhood."[6]

Distributed with slowly increasing subscription to the brotherhood (along with a German-language version called *Der Evangelische Besuch* continued until 1861), *The Gospel Visitor* soon established itself as a publication issued in the interests of the Brethren but without official sponsorship. Kurtz, with the aid of his family, produced the journal on a monthly basis in attractive form, with modest amounts of advertising on its wrappers; the cost of one year's subscription was one dollar. It was published in a loft of a springhouse on his farm near Poland, Ohio, and carried to the railroad there for further distribution.

He won a valuable ally when in 1856 he recruited as assistant editor James Quinter of Pennsylvania. Quinter had been known as a "boy preacher" and had already garnered a reputation as a moderately progressive and well-informed church leader. In his first editorial, he stated that he regarded "the press as an instrumentality which may advantageously be used by the Church for the accomplishment of those noble ends which her own organization in the world was designed to accomplish...." Quinter went on in later life to become not only a leading editor/publisher but also a highly respected educator and church statesman. He was widely considered to be the most scholarly advocate of the Brethren cause.

Kurtz also employed for a time the ardently reform-minded Henry R. Holsinger, who pressed Kurtz to issue the periodical on a weekly basis. This Kurtz was unwilling to do. For all of his innovative ideas on methods, Kurtz was concerned to preserve the unity of the church and its distinctive beliefs and practices. Holsinger left Kurtz's employ and proceeded in 1864 to create just such a journal, *The Christian Family Companion*. Holsinger went on to become the leader of the "Progressive" faction that eventually became a separate church.[7]

Unlike the daring and aggressive Holsinger, editors Kurtz and Quinter pressed tactfully for reform in the church, attempting to build in a cautious way a coalition that supported changes in the church. Chief among these was the cause of higher education, which will be discussed later. Other issues that caused controversy in the brotherhood were often first raised in the columns of *The Gospel Visitor*. In January 1874, Kurtz died in his chair, one of his well-loved books in his hands, a quiet revolutionary.

OTHER PERIODICALS

Kurtz's pioneering effort found imitators. This was a boom time in the American economy and Brethren were among those who sought to create successful businesses. Publishing was one such possibility, demanding comparatively little investment and start-up capital.

Holsinger's new weekly publication, *The Christian Family Companion* (1864), has already been mentioned. Another sign of his initiative was the publication of the first periodical dedicated to Brethren young people. He called it *The Pious Youth*; it appeared for two years in 1870/71 and then failed because of lack of support. Holsinger in his candid way was forthright about his motivations for publishing the young people's paper, conceding that "business considerations" were among the "foremost" of them. Trusting that this "honest confession" would not be used against him, he continued: "In these days when every public enterprise professes to be conducted for the public good, it might not be amiss to have one based upon a more reliable, and perhaps also a more liberal principle—mutual benefit." He stated his philosophy: "Publishing useful books and papers affords us a living,

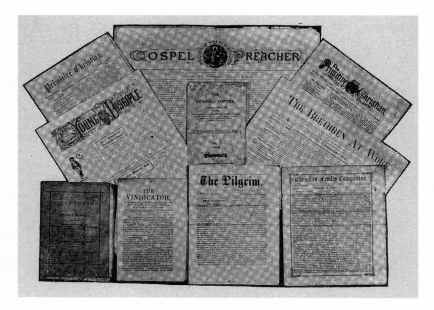

Some of the many Brethren-related periodicals that emerged in the second half of the nineteenth century. *Durnbaugh Collection.*

besides giving us the assurance that we are aiding in the promotion of virtue, happiness, and the dissemination of knowledge."[8]

Although *The Pious Youth* failed, patronage grew for Holsinger's weekly publication, the *Companion*; it began publication with some 380 subscribers and passed the 1,000 mark within the first year, 1,500 the second year, and then increased its circulation by 1,000 in succeeding years until it approached 5,000. His expansive editorial policy created an "open forum" that was both an attraction and a problem. Because contributors (including Holsinger himself) were permitted to express themselves in radical ways, also invoking personalities, the journal became controversial. Holsinger was persuaded to sell his interest in the journal to others; it was merged with *The Gospel Visitor* in 1874 to become *The Christian Family Companion and Gospel Visitor*. Its editors were James Quinter and

Joseph W. Beer. They changed the cumbersome combined name to *The Primitive Christian* in January 1876.[9]

A comparable paper was *The Pilgrim*, first published in 1870 at James Creek, south of Huntingdon, Pennsylvania. Its owners were the brothers Henry B. Brumbaugh and John B. Brumbaugh, members of an influential Brethren family of central Pennsylvania. Because of the similarity of editorial policies, the publishers of *The Pilgrim* and *The Primitive Christian* decided in October 1876 to unite their papers, which was then issued under the combined title. They began a magazine for youth in the same year called *The Young Disciple*.

In 1910, H. B. Brumbaugh reflected on his forty years of writing ministry:

> And if the world is to be saved by being brought into the kingdom, the church must do it by active and aggressive work. So we felt it our duty to place ourselves on the active and aggressive side of the church's work...from the beginning. "Go, work in my vineyard" to us meant "Go to work. Do something!" When we saw something which we thought ought to be done, we did not feel like standing back and watching others do it until it would be safe to fall in with the current and thus float in with the workers to victory, but to take a firm stand on the aggressive side and fight it out to the end, no matter how unpopular it might be....
>
> Since then, editorially and otherwise, we have always placed ourselves on the aggressive side of everything that stood for the advancement, the well-being and the enlargement of our church activities. We have given our sympathy, co-operation and hearty support to our schools and Bible work; our Sunday schools; prayer meetings; our missionary work at home, in our towns and cities and in foreign fields....[10]

In the meantime, other Brethren-related journals had been started. L. A. Plate of Lancaster, Pennsylvania, founded *Der Brüderbote* in 1875. A year later this became *The Brethren's Messenger and*

Brüderbote (1876), a bilingual edition with the English section preceding the German; it was published in Germantown, Pennsylvania. The location soon shifted to Lanark, Illinois, where its name was changed to *Brethren at Work*. The German-language paper continued separate publication for a time, and the editors added a paper for youth called *Children at Work*.

Because *Brethren at Work* was close in editorial policy to the Brumbaugh-Quinter journal, *The Primitive Christian and Pilgrim*, another merger took place in June 1883 to create *The Gospel Messenger*, with James Quinter as the editor-in-chief. This has remained, with a simplifying name change in 1965 to *Messenger*, the official periodical through the years for the mainline Brethren. Ownership passed from a stock company in 1897 to the denomination.

LATER PERIODICALS

With the exception of *The Companion*, all of the periodicals mentioned above took a moderate reform line. As time went on, publications opposed to this approach began appearing, some on the ultra-liberal side and some on the ultra-conservative side. As tensions grew within the church after the close of the Civil War (1865), periodicals emerged which served as the mouthpieces for these developing factions.

The Vindicator of the Ancient Order, and Self-Denying Principles of the Church, As Taught by the Saviour and Held Forth by the Fathers of Our Fraternity became the voice of the very conservative element among the Brethren; its title presents its program. It began in March 1870 as the private enterprise of Samuel Kinsey, a minister in the Lower Stillwater congregation in southern Ohio. Kinsey was the son-in-law of Peter Nead, one of the few Brethren to publish theological treatises and a staunch defender of the older ways of the church. Both Kinsey and Nead felt that the moderate papers edited by Kurtz, Quinter, and the Brumbaughs were not sufficiently supportive of the conservative cause. In 1882 the newly formed Old German Baptist Brethren recognized the work of *The Vindicator* as the official voice of their body and appointed two ministers and a deacon to assist Kinsey in its publication.

H. R. Holsinger had turned over *The Christian Family Companion* to more moderate hands but he could not stay away from the field of periodical publication. He initiated a secular journal, *The Dale City Record*, in 1873, which recalls that his very first printing venture had been with a newspaper, *The Tyrone Herald*, which he published in 1863-64. Holsinger, along with an associate Joseph W. Beer, turned his energies again to religious publishing in 1878 with *The Progressive Christian*. With some interruptions it was merged with *The Gospel Preacher* in 1882, after which it gradually became recognized as the official organ of the Brethren Church, after a name change in 1885, as *The Brethren Evangelist*. Full church ownership came in 1892; it is still published as the denominational organ.[11]

Though Holsinger's publication policies with the *Companion* had proved controversial, he opened the pages of *The Progressive Christian* to a yet more aggressive approach; Holsinger printed (and wrote) scathing criticism of perceived shortcomings in the church, attacks on named leaders, and satires about what the editors considered to be unbiblical and outmoded church practices. Reactions by those offended by this editorial policy were heated, and queries condemning the publication were repeatedly brought to the floor of the Yearly Meetings.

Even more radical was an informal publication issued by Peter H. Beaver, a manufacturer of horse collars in Northumberland County, Pennsylvania. He called his monthly publication *The Deacon*; it appeared between 1877 and 1879. Beaver announced that his periodical would be "an exponent of apostolic church government and for arresting and defeating the gradual and persistent usurpation of power by aspiring elders." Not surprisingly, it was denounced for "slanderous and schismatic" articles at the Yearly Meeting of 1879. Lack of sufficient support brought on its early demise.[12]

Of somewhat different character was the monthly published at Singers Glen, Virginia, by John Flory and Benjamin Funk. This was *The Gospel Trumpet*, issued from 1873 to 1876. It was the organ of a separate group, the Congregational Brethren; core members had been followers of the adventist William C. Thurman. Members of the Congregational Brethren eventually merged with the progressives in the Brethren Church, but the journal itself ceased when Flory returned to the German Baptist Brethren.

Among minor publications emerging in the later decades of the nineteenth century were *The Free Discussion, The Western Star, The Free Gift, The Prophetic Age, The Advocate, The Educator and Companion, Teacher and Student, Golden Dawn,* and several others. In this and some other aspects such as higher education, Brethren were participating in the enterprising and entrepreneurial spirit of the times. This is nowhere more evident than in the several publishing ventures of Peter Fahrney of Chicago, a patent-medicine magnate. His promotional monthly, *The Surprise,* hawked his products, extolled the merits of the Brethren, described his illustrious ancestry, and published scores of testimonials from Dunker elders and sisters.

Perhaps the zenith of varied publications was reached in 1879 when fully ten separate Brethren-oriented periodicals were represented at the Yearly Meeting held in Virginia; these included many of those named above and some minor publications as well. A reporter from *The Baltimore American* commented without fully understanding the informal and private nature of the enterprises (he could also have listed *The Vindicator*):

> The church supports ten papers of its own....They are the Primitive Christian, published at Huntingdon, Pa.; the Brethren at Work, published at Lanark, Ill.; the Progressive Christian at Berlin, Pa.; the Home Mirror at Longmont, Colo., the Free Discussion at Topeka, Kansas; the Deacon at Montandon, Pa.; the Gospel Preacher at Ashland, Ohio; the Brethren's Advocate at Waynesboro, Pa.; and two children's papers, the Young Disciple and Children at Work. The editors of all these are here, and some of them like Henry Holsinger and James Quinter are men of great ability.

One of the progressive-minded leaders of the day reported in more detail about the editors present:

The indefatigable H. R. Holsinger was there; and we are happy to say, he was more calm than usual....Brother J. W. Beer, his associate editor, was there in all his native composure, bordering almost on timidity, the exact counterpart of the impetuous Holsinger. Bashor, the "Gospel Preacher," was there....[J. H.] Moore and [M. M.] Eshelman were both there, doing what they could for the cause in general, and the Brethren at Work in particular, H. B. Brumbaugh was there, attending principally to the obtaining of a full report. Brother Kinsey of the Vindicator was there, and we formed a more intimate and favorable acquaintance with him than formerly. In short, the press was well represented, and all seemed to enjoy the meeting; and we hope they will all (that is, the editors) work in harmony and peace for the upbuilding of Zion. There is ample room for all to work, and there is no call for strife and jealousy, and the less they show of it in the future the better they will be patronized, and the better they will succeed in their calling.[13]

Unfortunately, this pious wish was not to be followed, and the papers and editors named were in the thick of the fray that resulted in a three-way division of the church.

PERIODICALS AND RISING TENSIONS

Although Henry Kurtz had introduced the medium of regularly issued periodicals with the desire to maintain and develop unity, it had become clear that one result of their proliferation was heightening tensions. The columns of the papers gave those discontented with any aspect of the church a vehicle for expressing their grievances and attracting support for their causes. Given the relative lack of overhead machinery for the denomination, editors developed *de facto* power through their access to the membership. Even the most conservative element in the brotherhood, nicknamed the Old Orders, who had opposed the introduction of the press, saw the utility and influence that accrued from it and supported, as we have seen, their own publication, *The Vindicator*.

Stephen H. Bashor who evaluated the 1879 Yearly Meeting and the role of the papers and editors there was known as an outstanding young evangelist, and his gift for telling phrases is evident in the following lengthy excerpt. To dramatize the growing tensions revealed in current articles and expressions of editorial opinion, he used the metaphor of the battlefield (the more striking when applied to a church with nonresistant principles!) in an article entitled "War Is About to Be Declared":

> Last week we stated that everything was quiet, and that general peace prevailed, but from later intelligence we find that our statement was premature. Before and during the harvest the peace principles advocated and instilled by Yearly Meeting seemed to be heeded. But now that harvest is over, the past appears to be forgotten in the exultation over present prosperity, and things are livening up all along the line.
>
> R. H. Miller, in *Brethren at Work*, advocates the new policy of the old brethren withdrawing from actual service, and the young brethren controlling the church. He also annexes a few stray thoughts on the *authority* of the Yearly Meeting and the wisdom of its rulings. Enoch Eby advances to the front in favor of the Standing Committee meeting three days ahead of time and getting a "good ready" for business before Conference sits; and in anticipation impeaches the wisdom of future Standing Committee men, and suggests that they may be allowed to go outside of their own number for a wise moderator. He says the *old brethren* are the ones to do the business.
>
> D. C. Moomaw rushes to the front of the line and scolds Yearly Meeting for slighting the missionary question. Howard Miller flourishes the sword over the dress question and hacks into it upon all sides, and ends the demonstration with a thrust at the gratis ministry of the church, and a broad slash at J. H. Moore, who, in return, explains the construction of his fort of defense, and how he came to fire the first shot. H. B. Brumbaugh loads his

pistol with liberal powder, and sends a buckshot into the camp of rich men, for not giving their wealth to the church and schools when they die. He says he is in dead earnest, and will likely shoot again.

The *Vindicator* is groaning under the wounds received at last Yearly Meeting, and calls for future justice and a fair fight. The *Progressive Christian* empties a full broadside into the secrecy of the Standing Committee and its work, while the *Primitive Christian* smells the battle from afar, and rushes into the *Progressive* with a few musket balls and a full round of ammunition in reserve. The *Progressive* admits that he is wounded, but has loaded and will shoot again this week, not only at the *Primitive* but also at S. Z. Sharp, who has unconsciously stirred up his righteous indignation through the *Gospel Preacher*.

[R. H.] Miller, the moderator, sends a round of grape and canister at the *Progressive* on the dress question, with a small cross-fire at the *Preacher*. The *Progressive*, in return, moves his artillery around and pours shot and shell into Miller's forces, cavalry, infantry, and all. The *Brethren at Work* thinks we ought to make a big paper, and call it the Church organ, hire some smart man to interpret the doctrines of the Church in such a compact legal way that he who disputes it must be court-martialed. Amid all the cross-firing the *Preacher* came very near blazing away at somebody....

Things begin to look stormy, and unless some one is careful, the result will likely be that every editor and special contributor in the church will have about three guardians appointed over him by the next Yearly Meeting to keep him straight.

The people cry for peace and are tired of war, but with all their efforts, protestations, and pitiful pleadings, the war aspect of the head men and leaders grows sterner. What it will amount to none can tell at present....Should the cry for peace not be heeded we fear there is great danger ahead....Feel on these grave matters

> as you please, but stop fighting, and for conscience' sake
> let us have peace.[14]

Tensions continued to heighten, leading to a fateful three-way division in the church in the early 1880s. One of the leading churchmen of the period, Enoch Eby, who had served as moderator eleven times, in looking back some fifteen years after the division, highlighted the role of the periodicals in sharpening tension points:

> What was the cause of this trouble? Let us see. How many papers sprang up in our beloved Brotherhood just prior to these difficulties? We answer, A half dozen at least. These caused trouble by moulding sentiment, which every paper is sure to do. It was generally admitted that our many unauthorized papers were the most prominent, if not the exclusive, factors, in bringing about the unfortunate results.[15]

No doubt the editors and publishers of the papers would have defended themselves by claiming that they were simply articulating and disseminating ideas already present among the church's members, rather than creating them.

BOOK PUBLICATIONS

Although the rise of periodical publications had great impact on the course of Brethren history, the early national period also saw an increase in the release of book-length works. There was understandably some overlap of authors with those active in periodical publication, such as Henry Kurtz and Peter Nead.

Kurtz focused on editing important works calculated to bring increased order and continuity in Brethren church life. Notable here was his edition of the writings of Alexander Mack, Sr. These he published in the original German with side-by-side English translations in 1860. Kurtz explained in an "advertisement of the present edition" that Mack's writings are "of an abiding value," which do not depreciate with age but rather become "more precious" to successive generations for their "efficacy and beneficial tendency." He concluded, "Persuaded that the principles and sentiments, as avowed and explained in the present work, and as adopted and practiced by the Brethren generally, should they become known and prevalent, would make the world much wiser, better, and happier, than what it is, it seems very desirable to give them the utmost publicity."[16]

Mack's writings had been translated into English and published in Philadelphia in 1810, but Kurtz found that a new translation was necessary. He did this himself, translating as literally as possible; this was then revised by his co-editor, James Quinter, to smooth out the English style. Quinter also provided a brief biography (*Memoir*) of Alexander Mack, depending largely on materials secured from Abraham Harley Cassel. He regretted that, despite considerable "trouble and expense," relatively little had been preserved about the first minister of the church.

Kurtz and Quinter supplied these translated titles of Mack's two major treatises: *A Short and Plain View of the Outward, Yet Sacred Rights and Ordinances of the House of God* and *Ground-Searching Questions Answered by the Author Alexander Mack*. Interestingly, in the latter work, the editors dropped the fortieth question and answer, in which Mack expressed warm appreciation for the merits of the Mennonites, although he also considered them to have deteriorated from the courageous stance of their sixteenth-century ancestors. No reason was given for this editorial decision, but it may reflect the denominational troubles then current between the Brethren and Mennonites. That part of the preface or introduction written by Alexander Mack, Jr., for the first American edition which refers to forty questions, however, was reprinted here in unchanged form.[17]

Often bound with the Mack treatises was a collection of minutes from the Annual Meetings of the Brethren, organized by topics and annotated by Henry Kurtz; he called the compilation *The Brethren's Encyclopedia, Containing the United Counsels and Conclusions of the Brethren at their Annual Meetings, Carefully Collected, Translated (from the Original German in Part), and Arranged in Alphabetical and Chronological Order* (1867).[18]

It was the first such venture and was produced without the approval and direction of the Annual Meeting. For this reason and because Kurtz had added what he considered to be "necessary and explanatory notes," the innovative publication was received coolly and never widely used. Ironically, it is exactly the notations by Kurtz that are found most valuable today. Kurtz apologized that illness had prevented a final revision of the book, allowing some materials to slip in that "ought to have been left out."[19]

BRETHREN-MENNONITE DEBATES

The Kurtz press was involved in a long-standing Mennonite-Brethren interchange that stretched over the first half of the nineteenth century. Virginian Peter Bowman had published a German-language treatise on baptism, love feast, and feetwashing in 1817 (*Ein Zeugniß von der Taufe*, reprinted in 1818) upholding these peculiar Brethren practices, in response to a small book published the year previously by a Mennonite named Peter Burkholder. This had evidently been stimulated by the conversion to the Brethren faith of a number of Mennonite families in the Shenandoah Valley. The two denominations had so much in common in belief and practice that it was no large shift to move from one to the other. The Bowman book was translated into English and published in 1831 as *A Testimony on Baptism, as Practiced by the Primitive Christians*.[20]

In 1834 Peter Nead published the first work in what would eventually become the most systematic and broad interpretation of Brethren doctrine of the nineteenth century; this was titled *Primitive Christianity, or A Vindication of the Word of God* (German edition, 1836). Nead described the Brethren views on a range of topics, notably including baptism and feetwashing. It was widely distributed and read among Christians in the area.

Not surprisingly, given the rivalry between Brethren and Mennonites in the Valley, the latter felt it incumbent upon them to publish an answer to Peter Nead's work. This appeared in 1837 and was twice as long as Nead's writings; it was a compilation of works by three authors, including an important Mennonite confession of faith with annotations, material from Peter Burkholder noticed above, and writing by Joseph Funk, who became very active as a publisher.

The running "debate" continued in the 1850s. In 1851 Joseph Funk edited and translated *A Mirror of Baptism*, written by his grandfather Heinrich Funk; it was the first Mennonite book (1744) published in North America. The burden of the text and notes was that baptism by pouring or sprinkling was the preferred, biblical form. Brethren decided that this effort should be answered; they called on a leading figure in Virginia, John Kline, to do so.

His effort, entitled *Defence of Baptism*, was a sixteen-page pamphlet, published on the Kurtz press near Poland, Ohio. It contained a refutation of the arguments included in the 1851 Mennonite publication as well as a brief presentation of Brethren doctrine on baptism, making three main points: 1) the baptism of Christ and his apostles took place in water; 2) biblical baptism is by immersion; and 3) biblical baptism requires three separate actions. His pamphlet had a polemical bite, as revealed by the following quotation:

> What a pity that professed ministers of the gospel of the lowly Jesus, should bring such a stain upon their Master, by representing him as being so careless, as to have given them no landmark how to go, or do, as is indicated in the little work above alluded to. What a pity that professed ministers of the gospel, have to run over all the Old Testament, to seek for terms to contradict, or controvert, the plain order of the baptism of Christ, as given in the New Testament, and to change it into pouring or sprinkling, and that for no other purpose, than that to build up some fancy doctrine of their own.

Kline's effort evidently stung Joseph Funk, because within a year he had written and published a reply over three hundred pages long called *The Reviewer Reviewed* (1857). He found that Kline had not written his review in the "spirit of an humble, self-denying Christian...but to the contrary, in a haughty, arrogant, and assuming spirit...." Funk's own writing, he maintained, was simply to defend the truth, disclaiming any pleasure "in controversy and disputations on the subject of religion and its outward forms." It reiterated and expanded the defense of the pouring or sprinkling forms of baptism on the basis of Old Testament pre-figurations; it went on to rebut the three points that Kline had presented to support the Brethren practice of three-fold forward immersion. Funk also defended the manner of communion favored by Mennonites, which Kline had briefly criticized.

John Kline responded to Funk's book with a seventy-four page booklet entitled *Strictures and Reply to The Reviewer Reviewed, Being a Further Defence of Baptism, And also of Feet-Washing, the Lord's Supper, and Other Ordinances, as Taught in the Gospel and Practiced by the Brethren* (1858). Again, this was published on the Kurtz press in Ohio. Kline considered it to be "a solemn duty both to God and man, enjoined upon him by the most weighty considerations, to publish these strictures and reply" but apologized if his previous pamphlet had offended his "old friend." He contended that the Mennonites had been the aggressors in this published conflict (reviewing the books and pamphlets in question) and regretted the necessity to continue the polemics.[21]

Joseph Funk wrote another extended answer to this second Kline rebuttal but mercifully it never saw publication. In 1862 Kline took the initiative to alleviate the bruised feelings by visiting the aged Funk, recording in his diary that he succeeded in "bringing about a better state of feeling on his part toward me" and effecting a reconciliation. The timing was apt because within two months, the octogenarian Funk died.[22]

About 1840-41 Henry Kurtz published a German translation of a treatise by Menno Simons on baptism—*Menno Symons Erklaerung der christlichen Taufe in dem Wasser aus dem Wort Gottes...*; this may well have been an attempt to undercut the repeated Mennonite efforts to defend their ordinary practice of baptism by pouring or sprinkling. Immersionists such as Brethren and Baptists contended that the important Anabaptist leader urged immersion baptism in this rare work. One of the two known original copies was in the library of Abraham Harley Cassel, who established early contact with Kurtz.[23]

FURTHER PUBLICATIONS

In 1836 Peter Nead had returned to his theological essays with the publication of *An Exposition of Certain Evangelical Truths and a Few Remarks on the Present State of Christendom*...(second edition, 1845), continuing his work on *Primitive Christianity* (1834). About 1845 he presented another installment with *Baptism for the Remission of Sins by the Faith Alone and Prayerless Doctrine Considered*.... He combined these works with additional material in his important book *Theological Writings on Various Subjects; Or a Vindication of Primitive Christianity as Recorded in the Word of God. In Three Parts*...(1850).

The book was often referred to simply as *Nead's Theology*. According to the well-informed editor J. H. Moore, the book was "well-received, widely distributed, and regarded as the best and most satisfactory vindication of Brethren church principles ever published." It was a "standard work," which "did much to stabilize and unify the membership in every part of the Brotherhood." Based on thorough knowledge of the limited previous doctrinal writing of the Brethren, Nead's book drew on a wide range of commentaries, theological works, theological dictionaries, and other sources. He was critical of Brethren openings to higher education, but his own work paradoxically demonstrated to other Brethren the values of broad reading and learning. In the judgment of J. H. Moore, Nead as a "pathfinder" opened "up the way, unintentionally, for every Brethren educational institution west of the Alleghenies."[24]

It was common for the tome to be placed in the hands of inquirers into Brethren faith, although Brethren would first direct those questioning to consult carefully the Brethren "guide of faith and practice," namely the New Testament. Because of the steady demand for Nead's theological study, it was republished in 1866 (and later in 1950 and 1985). In 1866 he produced another volume on important biblical themes: God, creation, redemption, church, and eschatology; it was called *The Wisdom and Power of God, As Displayed in Creation and Redemption*.

Peter Nead and Henry Kurtz were both born in 1796 of staunch Lutheran background, although Nead was born in Hagerstown and Kurtz in Germany. As a young man in Virginia, Nead was a member and then exhorter of the Methodist fellowship but became dissatisfied with its tenets. He embarked on an independent itinerant ministry in 1823; portions of a journal he kept during these travels have been preserved. Nead was also seeking a church based on New Testament principles This he found among the Virginia Brethren and requested baptism in 1824.[25]

By trade a tanner and part-time schoolteacher, Nead was highly disciplined; it was his custom to rise at 3:00 a.m. and to study for three hours. The mastery of the Bible he secured through these efforts served him well when he was called to the ministry in the Lower Linville congregation in 1827. His fluency in the English language, combined with his newly-won dedication to traditional Brethren doctrines and ordinances, brought him great opportunities and influence. In 1848 Nead moved his family to southwestern Ohio, where he served the Lower Stillwater congregation.

An enlightening example of the way in which Nead's books were used is provided by the travel account of a German journalist, first published in Germany in 1854. The author, Moritz Busch, later became famous because of his association with Otto von Bismarck. Busch devoted a lengthy passage in his narrative to a visit to a weekend love feast held at the Lower Stillwater congregation. Although the theologically trained and cosmopolitan writer was condescending in his appraisal of the "rough-hewn" and "rustic" doctrines of the Dunkers, he admitted to being much impressed by "Bishop Nead." He reported that he found in the elder "not only a childlike, loving spirit, but also a man much more informed on theological matters than I had anticipated." On encountering the Brethren and asking them for their religious books, he had simply been referred to the New Testament. Upon further probing, he was provided with a copy of *Nead's Theology*. The visiting reporter esteemed the book as "the most valuable memorabilia of all the souvenirs gathered in beautiful Ohio."[26]

By far the most often printed and most widely distributed books by and for Brethren between 1800 and 1860 were hymnals. These will be discussed elsewhere.

ABRAHAM HARLEY CASSEL

Although he never published a book, the "great antiquarian"
Abraham Harley Cassel must be mentioned in connection with
publications. Born near Harleysville, Pennsylvania, in 1820 of
Mennonite and Brethren parentage, Cassel accumulated through
his passion for books, periodicals, pamphlets, and manuscripts one
of the leading private collections in nineteenth-century America,
totaling over 50,000 volumes. He was an early supporter of Kurtz's
enterprise, sending in articles on Brethren history under the pen
name *Theophilus* for publication in *The Gospel Visitor*. He later had
scores of his articles published, at the urgent request of their editors,
in the various Brethren periodicals and almanacs as well as general
historical journals.[27]

Because his strict Pennsylvania-German parents distrusted education, Cassel had only six weeks of formal schooling; he always felt
insecure about writing in English. Many of his articles were published under the names of educated friends who polished his prose.
As he wrote to the distinguished book collector James Lenox,
explaining his diffidence,

> But hard as my lot was I had such an indomitable desire
> after knowledge that no severity could quench & no obsta-
> cle could check. Although kept from school & tied down
> to work more like a gall[e]y slave than a Pa. German son I
> stole time from the midnight hours to persue my studies.
> In which manner I have accumulated a considerable fund
> of knowledge under almost unsurmountable difficulties
> but while I had no instruction I never learned the gram-
> matical construction of our language and therefore seldom
> appeared in print before the public with any of my articles
> although I have written many 100 pages of interesting
> material...."[28]

Cassel's dedication preserved for Brethren and several other
Pennsylvania-German groups the early records of their history in
America. Bibliographers gave him credit for saving rare and even

unique examples of eighteenth-century German-American imprints. Samuel W. Pennypacker—a collector, historian, and governor of Pennsylvania—wrote of Cassel, "[It] may be said with substantial truth that to the patient research, and unwearied enthusiasm of this unassuming man, we owe the preservation of the history of the Germans of Pennsylvania." He then listed notable scholars of the Pennsylvania-Germans "who have written meritoriously and ably," but concluded that "back at a farm house near Harleysville, in Montgomery Co., is the well from which the waters have been drawn."[29]

Later Brethren authors vied for the privilege of consulting his collection of early Brethren manuscripts and books for contemplated histories of the church. Martin G. Brumbaugh was most successful in this quest because he raised several thousand dollars personally in 1898 to buy a large portion of Cassel's library, which he then donated to Juniata College. The Cassel materials formed the basis for his pioneer *History of the German Baptist Brethren in Europe and America*, published in 1899. The hastily written work concentrated almost exclusively on the eighteenth century.

There had been two earlier purchases. In 1880-81 Cassel sold 27,000 volumes to form the library of the recently founded Mount Morris College in Illinois. When the Brethren school closed its doors in 1932, it transferred the Cassel Collection to Bethany Biblical Seminary in Chicago to be held in trust for the Church of the Brethren. As the seminary moved in 1963 to a new campus in the Chicago suburbs, the collection was transferred as well. In the wake of another relocation of the seminary to Richmond, Indiana, in the autumn of 1994, the nontheological Cassel books from the seminary's holdings were sent to Juniata College, thus rejoining that part of the library placed there by Brumbaugh almost a century earlier.[30]

In March 1900, M. G. Brumbaugh sent out a printed letter appealing to Brethren in the East to report to him any rare books and manuscripts of Brethren provenance they could find. He sought a complete record of Germantown and Ephrata publications and "old church records, letters from or to old brethren, and minutes of meetings (congregational, district, and annual)." He urged his correspondents to help "to secure a complete library," for the "generations to come will bless you for the part you take in this." Evidently there were few responses to his plea. He personally added many rare books to the Cassel Collection at Juniata College, which was substantially augmented in the 1960s by the gift of hundreds of Pennsylvania-German books from the collection of W. Emmert Swigart, a Huntingdon businessman and benefactor of the college.

In 1882 a smaller but select portion of Cassel's library, some 1,200 rare German-American imprints, went by purchase to the Historical Society of Pennsylvania in Philadelphia. Cassel also donated two hundred books to both Ashland College in Ohio and Bridgewater College in Virginia. It had been Cassel's original hope that his impressive library could be preserved for posterity in one location. That was not to be, but by the time of his death in 1908 virtually all of his books were securely held and treasured in several academic and research institutions.[31]

After Kurtz's breakthrough and owing in part to the discussions included in his periodical, the second half of the nineteenth century saw increasing Brethren interest in higher education. In many cases there was a direct connection between publishing and schools, as the same persons involved themselves with both.

12

Rise of Educational Institutions

Hand in hand with the introduction of periodicals came the initiation of academies and schools of higher education. Editors and publishers founded schools, and schools used the print medium to solicit support and students for their institutions. The same voices of caution and disapproval raised against Brethren-related journals were raised against schools, with much the same reasoning. These were novelties copied from the world; they would seduce young people from the strict and narrow path of religious instruction by home and church; they would introduce secular values and ways of thinking that would prove damaging to the Brethren way.

This notwithstanding, the mid-century point brought the first Brethren attempts to introduce higher education. This trickle would become a flood in the second half of the century with a host of new school starts. Fully forty were announced or attempted; although most failed, about one-fourth survived and had a marked effect upon the course of Brethren history.[1]

BRETHREN ATTITUDES TOWARD EDUCATION

It was common in the late nineteenth century and the early part of the twentieth century for educators and historians to make sweeping claims about the advanced educational backgrounds of the early Brethren in the Germanies. They were called "university-trained" and "ripe scholars," who had enjoyed the academic privileges at such universities as Heidelberg and Marburg. It is now known that only a few figures related to earlier Brethren history had university background. These included E. C. Hochmann von Hochenau and Johann Peter Müller; Hochmann never joined the Brethren and Müller was associated with the Ephrata Society.

Little is known specifically of the educational attainments of early Brethren, but it is clear from their writings that they had completed at least elementary schooling and were literate and articulate. Their style was direct and straightforward, lacking the elaborate baroque rhetoric and redundant phrasing of the scholarly manner of the time. It is evident from this that they had never attended institutions of higher learning. The single exception to this generalization appears to be the figure of Johannes Lobach (one of the Solingen Brethren), who conducted a school for small children in Krefeld. But even here a disdain for formal education was revealed in the reflections of his mature years about his time as a student:

> Although one can learn something from Latin, Greek, and Hebrew (which are in themselves very good), the fear of God is little considered in the learning of these languages and it is even forgotten. On the contrary, one learns pride most of all....For my part I admit that when I think of the tricks and sins which I committed at school with my fellow students, I have to marvel at the great patience and forbearance of God that He does not cause the schools to sink into the depths.[2]

Although the first Christoph Sauer never actually joined the Brethren, he attended their meetings from time to time and shared many of their values. He was noted for acerbic reflections on the follies of educated persons, to whom he referred by spelling their title as *Doc-tor* (a play on words in German, using the word *tor* or fool). His comment on higher education was, "Many are offered a whole manure wagon full of arts and sciences, for which many a rich father pays a lot of money, not a small amount of which goes to prevent him [the student] from receiving the proper discipline, to the detriment of his soul;...the true understanding of Christ is eternal life. This knowledge is lacking in the schools and cannot be found there."[3] As we have seen, Sauer played a leading role in blocking the ambitious Charity School scheme in colonial Pennsylvania; he saw it as a device to Anglicize the German-speaking settlers, to make them subservient to the high churches, and to further the aims of a certain political faction. Scholars who have studied their episode conclude that he was accurate in his estimate.

On the other side of the scale could be placed the active participation of his son Christoph Sauer II, an elder among the Brethren, in founding the Germantown Academy. Sauer was one of the school's officers and raised a large sum of money for its operation. The Brethren congregation at Germantown supported a private ("select") school run by Sister Susan Douglas.

There seems to be good evidence for finding that the Brethren in colonial America favored elementary schools that would provide basic skills in reading, writing, and doing sums. Given the Brethren emphasis upon mastery of the Bible, they had a natural tendency to favor that which made for basic literacy. Advanced schooling was considered to be unnecessary and even harmful to the spiritual development of their young people.

This general approach can be clearly documented in the actions of the Annual Meetings of the nineteenth century, and in published articles, when Brethren attendance or sponsorship of high schools and colleges became controversial. In all of the debate this engendered, there is widespread acceptance, almost without questioning, of the value of an elementary level of education. An anonymous writer in 1856, contending against higher education, granted that he would not "attempt to argue against a good, common school education, but believe it to be the duty of parents and others, having children under their care to give them a good common school education, so that they may be able to read, understand, and judge for themselves, between right and wrong."[4]

Henry Kurtz, the Brethren publisher, even called in mid-century the common school a "noble institution" because it provided free education to all (that is, as he noted, "at least of white color"). "Children of the poor as well as of the rich enjoy its privileges without expense to their parents, excepting for books." It is open to all children, he asserted "whether their parents are native citizens, or emigrants from foreign countries, and children, whose native language is English, can obtain there an education sufficient for all the ordinary purposes of life."[5]

The only issues related to attendance of the children of Brethren families, or participation by Brethren teachers, had to do with "worldliness." This was a danger perceived in certain public occasions, when musical instruments were used in concerts and "exhibitions" at the conclusion of school terms. Even participation by pupils in debates in the school setting was deemed acceptable, although parents were advised not to attend such.[6]

There were, however, Dunkers who had no use for schooling at all. A notorious case was the father of the famed antiquarian Abraham Harley Cassel; the parent advocated rearing children in what he called "Pious Ignorance." His position was, "If you give a child learning then you fit, or prepare him for Forging, Counterfeiting, or any other badness that he may choose to do, which an unlearned or ignorant one would not be capable of doing."

The lad was so determined to learn—even to the point of defying his father—and so talented, that sympathetic neighbors interceded with the parent. The father grudgingly gave in, remarking to his son, "I tried to bring you up according to my conscientious convictions, but I see I can't, as you will learn in spite of all my opposition. Therefore learn, and if it leads you to evil, the fault is not mine." This opened the way for the six weeks of formal schooling, which is all that Abraham Harley Cassel ever enjoyed; the rest of his extensive knowledge of languages and scholarly disciplines resulted from his own omnivorous reading in spare hours after his daily work.[7]

THE SABBATH SCHOOL DEBATE

A harbinger of the conflict within the denomination on instituting higher education among the Brethren was the debate on Sunday schools (most often called Sabbath schools in Brethren usage). Early histories of Brethren education pointed to a gathering of young people in Germantown in 1738 as the first Sunday school in North America. These were actually part of a spiritual revival and had much more the nature of prayer meetings or Bible study groups. Under the guidance of Ludwig Höcker, the Ephrata Society developed in 1749 what could fairly be called a Sunday school, but this was a part of that schismatic movement and not within the Brethren mainstream.

An early indication of Brethren concern for the Christian instruction of children and youth was found in the statement of the 1789 Yearly Meeting. They are pictured as falling into a "coarse life," this resulting from a lack of energy by parents and church leaders in providing them with instruction in the faith as directed by Moses (Deuteronomy 6:7) and by Paul (Ephesians 6:4):

> It is (our) opinion (and advice) that there should be used more diligence to instruct our dear youth and children in the word of truth to their salvation, and that it is the special duty of the dear parents, as well as of the pastors and teachers, to be engaged herein,...hence we admonish in heartfelt and humble love all our in God much beloved fellow members...that they would use all possible diligence that our dear youth might be provoked to love God, and to appreciate his word from their childhood. Do not spare any labor and toil to convince them by our teaching and by our life....[8]

Sunday schools as such came to the Brethren as an innovation derived from other Protestant bodies, though much later than their emergence in the early decades of the nineteenth century. It is unclear when the first attempts were made to introduce them in Brethren congregations. A query brought to the Annual Meeting of 1838 asking about the legitimacy of Brethren attendance at a Sabbath school, linked with the advisability of involvement with Methodist class meetings, met with an awkwardly phrased negation: "Considered to be most advisable to take part in no such like things."[9]

The question became more pointed less than two decades later (1857) when a query asked whether Brethren themselves might sponsor Sabbath schools. The answer was cautiously permissive: "Inasmuch as we are commanded to bring up our children in the nurture and admonition of the Lord, we know of no scripture which condemns Sabbath-schools, if conducted in gospel order, and if they are made the means of teaching scholars a knowledge of the scriptures." The phrase "gospel order" had reference to practices in some denominations of linking Sunday schools with picnics, celebrations, and other social gatherings, frowned on by Brethren. Five years later the positive answer was reaffirmed by Annual Meeting.[10]

A Sabbath school organized in 1845 in the area of the White Oak congregation in Lancaster County, Pennsylvania, by Jonas Gibble and his wife is one of the earliest known ventures. Even earlier (1832) the unused Pricetown meetinghouse of the Brethren near Oley, Pennsylvania, was allowed to be used for a community Sunday school. Another step in the process was the decision by Annual Meeting in 1870 that meetinghouses used actively could house Sunday schools if other structures were unavailable. This was to be permitted if good order were maintained and the members all agreed to it.

Despite this growing commitment to education of Brethren children and young people in the Sunday school setting, the innovation remained controversial among much of the membership. It became one of the issues raised during the great division of the early 1880s, an example to conservatively minded Brethren of yet another case where the Progressive element was introducing novelties unknown to the "Old Order" of the Brethren.

EARLY VOICES FOR BRETHREN HIGHER SCHOOLING

It was in the columns of *The Gospel Visitor* and later journals after 1851 that the first advocates of higher education for Brethren were heard. Their most persuasive argument took account of the drive for learning, seen in unusual intensity with Abraham Harley Cassel, shared by many young Dunkers. By mid-century more and more of them were seeking advanced training in academies and normal schools (teacher-training institutions), sponsored by other religious denominations. Kurtz and others argued that Brethren youth were demanding education and would be lost to the church if "safe" schooling were not provided.

This argument has never been put more clearly than in the articles of the association (1870) for the short-lived but ambitious school at Salem College in Indiana. One long sentence revealed that

It has been the intention of the Brethren, organizing and conducting Salem College, to build an institution under the control and patronage of the church that shall be a school where the Brethren can safely place their children with the assurance that they will receive that training and admonition that shall endear the Church of the Brethren to their young hearts and cause their further lives to be spent in the service of the Lord, as believed and practiced by the Brethren in all its purity and simplicity, and as taught by the Scriptures, with nothing of the follies of pride or the frivolities of the world encouraged or tolerated in the school.

Here the argument was presented in clear terms: 1) Brethren young people insisted on advanced learning; 2) if this were done in schools not under Brethren auspices, the youth will be lost to the church; 3) only Brethren-sponsored schools could guarantee education imbued with Brethren values; and 4) this would prepare these young people for lives of service.[11]

The same point of view was expanded upon in an article (May 1870) by elder P. R. Wrightsman; he claimed that "hundreds of our Brethren's children [are now] away from home, receiving their education in the high schools of other denominations, some of the teachers of which are Univeralists, Infidels, Deists, and to say the least, may do their best to explain away the simple commandments of Christ's Church." He asked, "How shall we, who profess to be the true followers of Christ, lie still and suffer these sectarians thus to poison the minds of our dear children? God forbid, Brethren, forbid it." Wrightsman concluded, "The time has come when the young people will have an education." Therefore, "How much better to have such a school among the Brethren and teach them the true Christian doctrine."[12]

Another argument raised on behalf of higher education involved training teachers. A number of Brethren ministers had engaged in public school teaching as a way to support themselves and their families. Several answers to queries raised at the Annual Meetings acknowledged that this was acceptable. The problem came with stiffening standards for teachers in these schools, thus demanding better preparation.

In 1856 Henry Kurtz spoke to this issue in commenting editorially on a communication from his younger colleague (and later collaborator) James Quinter. Kurtz's comment was, "Years ago we had many brethren, who had received only a common-school education, engaged in teaching school, where the Bible and the New Testament was read, and probably both English and German was taught. But now so much is required of school-teachers, that many of those old teachers cannot pass examination any more, and others have taken their places, who need the Bible no longer, and our children are deprived of a vital element of education, namely the moral and religious."[13]

It is striking that a comparatively large number of Brethren leaders from this era had at least for a time been employed as teachers in public schools. These included Kurtz and Quinter, Peter Nead, Isaac Price (a noted preacher from Montgomery County, Pennsylvania), John Wise (for many years reading clerk at the Annual Meetings), Abraham Harley Cassel (the historian and collector), and Enoch Eby (a leading elder in Illinois). Important church leaders from a somewhat later era who taught included J. G. Royer, Henry C. Early, James Sell, Daniel Vaniman, S. Z. Sharp, Robert H. Miller, and Daniel Hays.

Voices Against Brethren Schools

For many years, the face of the church as expressed in the Annual Meetings was set squarely against permitting members to attend higher schools, let alone to permit Brethren to organize them. The first query (1831) bearing on the wisdom of allowing a youth to be educated in college received the answer, "Considered not advisable, inasmuch as experience has taught that such very seldom will come back afterward to the humble ways of the Lord." Similarly a query asking about attendance or teaching at a college was answered, "Considered, that we would deem colleges a very unsafe place for a simple follower of Christ, inasmuch as they are calculated to lead us astray from the faith and obedience to the gospel."[14] One response to the fledgling Huntingdon Normal School in Pennsylvania (later Juniata College) came from a critic in Franklin County. The elder there complained that such exposure to learning would cause students to "come home from college dressed in fine broadcloth, wearing a high bee gum hat, swinging a little cane, and acting like dudes." Brethren were convinced that attendance at high schools and colleges led inexorably to vain conduct and display.[15]

Another standing complaint was that the introduction of higher schools would lead directly to the establishment of Bible departments. This in turn would lead to schools of theology or seminaries and that to the adoption of a salaried or "hireling" ministry: "Some say it is just to make preachers and they will want salary for preaching." Brethren had long memories of the oppression suffered by their ancestors under the clergy of the established churches and wanted no part of it. Brethren practice had long prevailed of choosing ministerial leadership from within their own ranks by a process of discernment. While spontaneous and intermittent material support to these ministers and their families was welcomed (gifts of food, contribution of labor, reimbursement of expense), the prospect of regular monetary support for preachers was anathema. The self-supported or "free" ministry was the only biblical approach.

An editorial in *The Pilgrim* issued by the Brumbaugh brothers in Huntingdon sought to scotch such fears: "There is an idea extant among part of the Brotherhood, at least, that were we to establish schools the design would be to prepare our brethren for the ministry, and that our ministers would finally drift into the same channel with other Churches....We assure you, brethren, that were this so, we would be among the number that would oppose schools." There is no reason to believe that this attitude was anything but sincere, although the actual development was precisely in the direction that conservatives suspected.[16]

This fear explains the otherwise curious feature of the earliest Brethren schools that they by design omitted departments for Bible study. They wished by this omission to reassure the church that religious instruction would remain squarely in the hands of the families and congregations at home. Schools were to be conducted in a religious atmosphere, but formal religious instruction was to be avoided.

The negative posture also explains why formal theological education came late to the Brethren. It was only in 1905 that a training
school for ministers was initiated, known as Bethany Bible School.
Interestingly, some of the strongest opposition to its inception came
from the colleges, which had in the meantime established their own
Bible departments. They saw the new venture as direct competition.

ESTABLISHMENT OF BRETHREN HIGHER SCHOOLS

The first successful Brethren academy was the Kishacoquillas
Seminary in central Pennsylvania; it was operated by Solomon Z.
Sharp, a well-educated man of Amish background who had an
extended career in Brethren higher education. He began his board-
ing school with a staff of five in April 1861, using the facilities of an
earlier Presbyterian school. Despite the problems in provisioning
that the war years brought, the school flourished for five years
under Sharp's direction until the health problems of his wife made
a move necessary. Another Brethren schoolman took over and the
school continued until the Huntingdon Normal College began in
1876, when students from the Kishacoquillas Valley moved the
short distance to the new school. Two of Sharp's students in the
academy went on to become stalwarts at Huntingdon, J. B.
Brumbaugh and W. J. Swigart. Sharp then ran a school in Maryville,
Tennessee, affiliated with the Presbyterian Church, until a later date
when he returned to the field of Brethren schooling, being associated with several new institutions across the country. He also became
the first historian of Brethren higher education, making him the
"grand old man" of this aspect of Brethren life.

The next venture was led by James Quinter, the associate of
Henry Kurtz, in New Vienna, Clinton County, Ohio; it was initiated
in the fall of 1861 with the aid of the local Fall Creek congregation.
It continued for three years "with a reasonable degree of success,"
but was closed in early summer 1864 because of the "disturbed conditions of the country during the Civil War" (Sharp). Despite this
relative failure, Quinter persisted in his editorial championing of
the educational cause in the pages of *The Gospel Visitor*.[17]

Another early effort was the Plum Creek Normal school, established by Lewis Kimmel near Elderton, Pennsylvania, in 1874. A graduate of Allegheny College, Kimmel was one of the first Brethren to complete an academic program. He won as an assistant the young Howard Miller, who was later to play a significant role in the Progressive movement. The efforts of Kimmel and Miller met with success, and the Plum Creek school attracted a number of pupils. When an educational program was introduced at nearby Huntingdon, Pennsylvania, Kimmel's school faded, as a number of students transferred to the better-sited new school.

SALEM COLLEGE

Salem College in Bourbon, Indiana, had the distinction of being the first school established under the auspices of a district. With the financial assistance of business interests of the town, Brethren undertook in May 1870 an ambitious attempt to establish "a first-class institution of learning," professedly along the lines and of the quality of Oberlin College in Ohio. Classes began in December 1870, with eight students, finishing that term with twenty-two. The second term concluded in the spring of 1871 with 87 students and numbers increased in the third term to reach 125.[18]

Conscious of the opposition to the venture among Brethren leaders and laity, the directors of the school sought to reassure skeptics. (An effort early in 1870 to start a school in the Middle District of Indiana had foundered on the stiff opposition it encountered.) The Salem College catalog announced that the school would be "managed entirely by Brethren; having for its object mental and moral excellence instead of external display." Seventeen laws and regulations regulated student contact under a code every pupil had to sign. One rule read,

> Indecent and profane language, rude and boisterous conduct, tippling; frequenting taverns, inns, beer houses, places of mere idle amusements and resorts of bad company, gambling, betting, games of chance, smoking tobacco within the college enclosure, or carrying concealed firearms or deadly weapons, and every other

> species of vulgar and immoral conduct are absolutely
> forbidden, and will subject the offender to punishment.

While undoubtedly meant to convince critical onlookers of the school's dedication to strict behavior, such a listing of possible student conduct may well have alarmed more than it soothed.[19]

The school seemed after its first year to have gotten off to an excellent start, when a difference of opinion between the principal, Oliver W. Miller (formerly of the New Vienna faculty), and the trustees led to Miller's resignation. He immediately opened a rival school nearby. In the meantime the non-Brethren local financiers became increasingly disappointed by the slow progress made toward the promised high standard of education and began demanding repayment of the money they had advanced. There was also a great deal of criticism about the school among Brethren in northern Indiana. Student enrollment fell drastically in the 1872-73 school year. The result of these troubles was the failure of the school in 1873. Individual Brethren who had backed the school found themselves deeply in debt, which took them years to repay. One elder was so embarrassed by the failure that he moved to another location.

Another ambitious effort, this time in Bedford County, Pennsylvania, also failed to produce a school. The chief promoter here was the energetic and creative editor, publisher, and church leader Henry R. Holsinger. Under his leadership a meeting of Brethren interested in education was held in 1872 in Martinsburg, Pennsylvania; those meeting decided to open a school in Berlin, after considering Martinsburg and Huntingdon. Holsinger's plan was to secure a large endowment ($100,000) to ensure the success of the venture before launching out; no funds pledged would actually be due until the entire amount was subscribed. He secured the services of S. Z. Sharp to help raise the awareness of Brethren in the region about the need for the school.

Holsinger and Sharp called on one conservative and well-to-do brother; although Holsinger was aware of the man's opposition to education, he felt that courtesy demanded the visit. To Holsinger's surprise, when the man read the terms of the subscription, he promptly pledged $500. With a mischievous smile, he urged others present to subscribe heartily, saying in German, "Subscribe heartily, brethren; you will never need to pay it." As he foresaw, although substantial amounts were pledged, Holsinger's over-ambitious goal was never reached, and the venture never got off the ground.[20]

HUNTINGDON NORMAL SCHOOL (JUNIATA COLLEGE)

The first truly successful attempt at founding an academy for Brethren began in Huntingdon, Pennsylvania, in 1876. The two Brumbaugh brothers, Henry B. and John B. (both publishers), along with their cousin Dr. Andrew B. Brumbaugh (a physician), were the prime movers. They convinced a brilliant and experienced, though physically frail, young educator, Jacob M. Zuck, to relocate and begin a school. It began quite modestly with three students in a small room on the second floor of the building in which *The Pilgrim* was published.[21]

An early member of the school's faculty, the artist and philanthropist David Emmert, provided a word sketch of the beginnings:

> The little room, 12 by 16 feet [had] two windows to the south....A long pine table in the middle, with three chairs around it...; plain pine shelves, holding the modest but well-selected library of the teacher; at the end of the room, and near by, is his table, with checkered cover and a large inkstand; above these, on the wall, a map of the world; a round backed armchair, with a deerskin thrown over the back and seat, and a long blackboard on stilts leaning against the wall, complete the furnishings and general aspect of the room.

Very soon, the skill and acumen of Zuck became better known, and by the end of the term the class had grown to more than a dozen students. By the start of the fall term, the school moved to occupy a large building nearby, and by the close of this school year, numbered nearly 120 students. They came not only from Pennsylvania but also from Ohio, Missouri, Indiana, Maryland, Virginia, and West Virginia.[22]

Burchinell Hall, a building in Huntingdon, Pennsylvania, used in 1877 by the oldest surviving Brethren-related institution of higher learning, which came to be known as Juniata College. From Juniata College Museum, *BHLA Collection.*

The promising beginning was virtually cut short over the Christmas break of 1877 when a smallpox epidemic broke out in Huntingdon. The wife of one of the students died. Although the attempt was made to begin the new term in January 1878, it was found necessary to send all of the students home. It seemed doubtful to many if the young enterprise could weather this tragedy. Three young male students had come from a distance and decided not to return home. Through school leaders they heard of an abandoned building owned by the Brumbaugh family in the Trough Creek area south of Huntingdon. They decided to camp there and keep up their studies. A young neighbor braved possible contagion to visit them from time to time on horseback to bring them food his mother had prepared; he enjoyed their company and decided to join them at the school when it resumed. The lad was Martin G. Brumbaugh, who became the most famous person ever associated with Juniata College and was twice its president.

Public-spirited citizens of Huntingdon donated land on a hill west of the town to accommodate a new building. This became Founders Hall, finished in April 1879. The staff and students moved in while the plaster was still damp and heating arrangements not yet completed. The frail principal J. M. Zuck became chilled, contracted pneumonia, and soon died, presenting the young institution with another crisis. This was met when Elder James Quinter, an advocate of education and an increasingly respected figure in the church, accepted the newly created position as president of the (recently renamed) Brethren's Normal School. Under Quinter's guidance, the school flourished. Some church leaders complained about the unauthorized use of the denominational name. Finally, in deference to Annual Meeting action recommending place names for colleges, the name Juniata College was officially adopted in 1896.

ASHLAND COLLEGE

In 1877 a committee of Brethren in northern Ohio who favored higher education met to consider establishing a school in their region. The committee recruited S. Z. Sharp from Tennessee to build up support for the idea; after looking at several locations, Sharp and the committee decided to site the proposed school at Ashland. They convinced the citizens of Ashland to raise $10,000 for the cause; Sharp spent a year soliciting contributions from Brethren in Ohio, Indiana, Illinois, and Michigan.[23]

The result of the campaign was a 28-acre campus with a college building which cost $40,000 to erect. Trustees borrowed money to build a three-story dormitory and engaged a well-qualified staff, enabling the school to open in the fall of 1879 with 60 students. At the end of the spring term 102 students were enrolled. This promising beginning was threatened when the college was caught up in the controversy that resulted in a three-way split in the German Baptist Brethren. Ashland College became a center of the Progressive wing, which took the name Brethren Church, and Sharp left.

OTHER COLLEGE CREATIONS

A large number of other schools were created after 1879-80. Most of these failed or were merged with other schools. The beginnings of several of those that maintained longer existence can be sketched.

Mount Morris College in Ogle County, Illinois, took over an older Methodist institution, the Rock River Seminary. A number of Illinois Brethren caught the contagion of higher schooling in 1879; these included M. S. Newcomer, J. H. Moore, M. M. Eshelman, and D. L. Miller. Sixty students were present when class work began in late August 1879. A convert from the Baptists, J. W. Stein, was recruited as president of the new school. He was known as an able and articulate leader who wrote a series of widely circulated tracts explaining the many reasons for his abandoning the Baptists to join the Brethren. By the beginning of the second term, early in 1880, nearly 150 students had signed on. A strong faculty was recruited to staff the school.

Stein was eager to strengthen the library for Mount Morris; to do this he negotiated the purchase of 27,000 books from the expansive collection of Abraham Harley Cassel. Stein had a special catalog published with a checklist of the impressive addition of books and pamphlets. Unfortunately, the coup did not meet with general approval. Many volumes in the collection were rare books in foreign languages, dating from the sixteenth to the nineteenth century. Faculty and students complained that what they needed were the very latest and most scientific books, not old theological treatises.

After two successful years, President Stein announced that he was undertaking a trip around the world. Postcards came back to the campus from several places in Europe and then ceased. The worried college staff alerted the United States diplomatic service but the latter's inquiries proved fruitless. Much later it was learned that Stein had not left the country at all but rather had migrated to the northwestern part of the United States, living there in a common-law marriage with a former ward in his home. He had abandoned family, church, and college. Chicago newspapers learned of the affair and publicized it widely.

The scandal almost ruined the young institution. Those elders who had opposed the venture now demanded its cessation. Only by the exertion of a few men was the school sustained. D. L. Miller threw his considerable influence on the side of continuation, seconded by J. H. Moore. Miller recruited the experienced S. Z. Sharp to join the faculty where he became chairman. At this point, the only member of the Brethren on the faculty, he was given responsibility for the religious instruction of the students. Through his untiring work in leading Sunday school and revival meetings, a large number of young people joined the fellowship. This eased the criticism against the college among some of the constituency.[24]

Bridgewater College began in 1880 as Spring Creek Normal School with D. C. Flory as its founder. In 1881 the location was moved to Bridgewater, but the school was not renamed until 1889. By 1883 sufficient interest had been created among Brethren in various parts of the state to organize a representative board of trustees. A large structure was built in 1883/84 to house the growing institution. Then two catastrophes struck the young institution. First, serious charges of immorality were brought against the principal, A. E. Miller, resulting in factions pro and con, a controversy that reached into congregations across the district. The second blow came on the last day of 1889 when the main building was destroyed by fire. Benefactors, faculty, and students maintained their support, and the college survived the two crises, slowly but steadily growing in numbers and reputation.[25]

McPherson College was created in Kansas in the 1880s. The ubiquitous S. Z. Sharp had moved to Kansas in 1884 and built support for a new school. A committee of interested persons canvassed several possible locations, seeking also support from the local citizens. They found that McPherson offered the greatest inducements and decided on that location. A state charter was secured in August 1887 to establish the McPherson College and Industrial Association. The company determined that the school was to be held in trust for the denomination.

Through the generosity of the citizens of McPherson substantial sums were donated and ten acres of land given to establish the school and requisite buildings. Classes began in the fall of 1888 with S. Z. Sharp as president. An innovation was the introduction of a Department of Agriculture to help train the largely rural Brethren in modern means of farming. Despite a bank failure which cost the young school much of the funds intended for construction, work went forward.[26]

La Verne College (originally Lordsburg College), east of Los Angeles, California, was founded by Brethren residing in the San Gabriel Valley. Several Brethren leaders bought a defunct resort hotel as the first school building in 1889. Classes began in 1891 on a small scale, most of them on a high-school level; only a few students were capable of college-level work. Several faithful supporters covered deficits for several years before the church took over ownership.[27]

What became Manchester College originated in 1889 as a United Brethren school in North Manchester, Indiana, which was ruined financially through fraud. In 1895 Brethren took over the institution under the leadership of E. S. Young, formerly of Mount Morris; he was known for his books and institutes on biblical study. The town offered the campus and its one major building plus $5,000 in cash, matched by Young and his associates who invested another $5,000. School began with a faculty of eight and some 200 students but had to weather financial straits under several short-term presidents. Elder I. D. Parker and some others saved the school by raising enough funds to retire the debt and then turn over the school to the surrounding church districts. The college was deeded to the church in 1902. It finally established itself with real stability under the firm and energetic leadership of Otho Winger, who began his long tenure in 1911 at the age of thirty-three.[28]

Eastern Pennsylvania was slow to catch the fever of higher education. Lancaster County was known as a bastion of conservatism among the Brethren; there was great reluctance to institute a school that might lead members astray from the straight and narrow way of Brethren nonconformity. Thus it was not until 1898-99 that a number of those favoring advanced education coalesced in a cooperative effort.

A catalyst in this action was Jay G. Francis, a talented but erratic figure, who called the first meeting late in 1898. He was suspect to some by his study at Union Theological Seminary in New York under Charles A. Briggs, a champion of higher criticism of the Bible, who had been tried for heresy by the Presbyterian Church. Francis rode a bicycle for miles to develop support for the fledgling institution. As the initiative developed, he lost out in its direction. He later proposed an ambitious rival undertaking for what he called Alexander Mack University, to be sited at Reading. To encourage that ambition he published a short-lived newspaper, *The Flying Eagle*. Several towns competed for the privilege of becoming the home of the new school in eastern Pennsylvania, with Elizabethtown eventually winning preference. I. N. H. Beahm of Lordsburg (La Verne) College in California was called as the first principal (president) but owing to illness was not able to serve for a longer period. Instead George N. Falkenstein, already a member of the faculty, acted as its first head.

Although known through much of his later life as an evangelist, Isaac Newton Harvey Beahm was above all an educator, first at Bridgewater College and often in public schools. He founded Botetourt (Daleville) Normal School (1890), Prince William Normal (1897), and Hebron Seminary (1909), in addition to his short-lived presidencies at Lordsburg and Elizabethtown. A minister said of him, "Brother I. N. H. Beahm did more to make education acceptable to the Church of the Brethren than any [other] single individual." Considered eccentric by some, in part for his habit of speaking of himself in the third person singular as "Brother Beahm," he became a kind of a folk hero among his contemporaries, who enjoyed repeating his witticisms and telling of his exploits. To celebrate fifty years in the ministry, he preached on one day (July 26, 1931) twenty different sermons in a 200-mile dash across the state of Virginia. A decided conservative, he still came down on the side of the unity of the church when schism threatened.[29]

HIGHER SCHOOLS AS A REFLECTION OF THE TIMES

One little explored facet of the wave of Brethren school foundings in the late nineteenth century is the way in which they reflected the times. This was the era of American history marked by boom and bust, a time of great entrepreneurial activity, the era of robber barons and great conglomerates. In a real sense, the wave of school foundings exactly mirrored this development. These Brethren schools were ordinarily organized as private business enterprises and were at first not given church approval as such. They were typically established as joint stock companies, raising money by issuing stocks to shareholders.

Although many of the early Brethren schoolmen sacrificed their personal fortunes in their attempts to start schools, many originally hoped to make money from the enterprise. As had other church leaders, before and since, they meant to do good but also hoped to do well for themselves if possible. The language in which they promoted their initiatives perfectly reflected the aggressive business spirit of the times. It was in part this characteristic which put off conservative opponents of higher education among the Brethren.

Similarly, when the early histories of these schools are studied, it is remarkable how much local boosterism and self-interest was involved among local businessmen. Towns competed as sites for the schools, often donating building lots and large amounts of money for the perceived economic advantages that would accrue to their locality if chosen. School leaders themselves emphasized the economic and cultural advantages that would ensue from their enterprise, with the arrival of hundreds of newcomers, faculty and especially students, who would bring income to the favored town through their purchases.

A history of Mount Morris College in Illinois frankly described these benefits in the language of puffery typical of the time:

> Concerning Mount Morris College, the pride of the town and community, we cannot speak too highly....Here a polished education can be obtained under the most favorable moral and religious influences....A home college is a great thing for the people of the place where the college is located. Viewed from a financial angle, Mount Morris College is very valuable to Mount Morris and vicinity....It saves the expense of sending away to college the young people of the community....All this expense is saved to the people of Mount Morris in the education of their children, and in its stead they receive as an income thousands of dollars brought here by those who come from a distance.[30]

IMPACT OF HIGHER EDUCATION UPON THE BRETHREN

Many studies have been written assessing the impact upon the church resulting from of the introduction of higher education. Critics have emphasized the ways in which this move accelerated the change of the Brethren from a sect to an acculturated, Americanized denomination. They reported the trends of relocation that saw relatively few of the sons and daughters from Brethren farm families and rural congregations returning to their home communities after graduating from college. There was instead a pronounced shift of location from the countryside to towns and cities, with much attendant loss in church membership.

On the other side must be weighed the contribution of the colleges in training the future leadership of the church and perpetuating distinctive Brethren values. College histories abound with the statistics recording the numbers of pastors, professors, missionaries, and church executives produced by their institutions. A comprehensive reflection of this aspect was the *Educational Blue Book and Directory of the Church of the Brethren, 1708-1923* (1923), issued by the General Educational Board of the denomination. The compilers, W.

Arthur Cable and Homer F. Sanger, advised readers that "in the present collaboration may be found the number of graduates and other school people who are ministers; the number who are elders; the number of those who are giving their full time to pastoral or other church work; and the range of occupations represented by our school people and those who have enjoyed the advantages of an education." Over three hundred pages listed graduates with brief biographies, followed by more than one hundred pages of sketches of those "not graduates of college courses, who have been recommended [for inclusion] because of service rendered in educational work."[31]

Although an occasional voice has been raised to contend that the Brethren, on balance, would have done better to have concentrated on elementary and secondary education (parochial schools), rather than higher education, there is no doubt that the present Church of the Brethren is unthinkable without the formative influence of Brethren institutions. Although the Old Order wing of the Brethren adamantly opposed all forms of church-sponsored education (including Sunday schools, academies, and colleges), in very recent years it has accepted parochial schools because of dissatisfaction with the public schools.

Early Brethren attempts at beginning schools of higher education were frustrated by the conditions imposed by the Civil War. This cataclysm in the national history had a tremendous impact on the Brethren as well.

13

The Irrepressible Conflict

Unlike the experience of most American denominations, the fabric of the Brethren church was not torn by the slavery/abolition controversy and the subsequent outbreak of fratricidal violence in the early 1860s. The struggle was so traumatic that it is still called by different names—the Civil War (by Unionists and their descendants) and the War between the States (by Confederates and their descendants).

Members of the Religious Society of Friends (Quakers) are rightly given much credit for taking the lead in the movement to abolish slavery in the United States. The first declaration against the marketing and owning of slaves in the colonies was penned in Germantown in 1683 by several Friends, primarily of Mennonite background. The protest was sent by the Monthly Meeting to the Quarterly Meeting, where it was quietly tabled and forgotten. Despite this, individual Friends such as John Woolman and Anthony Benezet worked in the colonial period to eliminate the practice from Quaker ranks and to increase abolitionist sentiment in the wider society. By the end of the eighteenth century the Quaker discipline forbade members to hold slaves.[1] While this is meritorious, it should not be forgotten that German sectarians such as the Mennonites and Brethren never permitted slavery at all. With but minor exceptions their members never held slaves, and there was thus no struggle within their ranks to ban the practice.

Christoph Sauer, an intimate of the Brethren, as well as his like-named son, a Brethren elder, were vocal opponents of slavery. They aired their critique in editorials published in their Germantown newspapers and almanacs. The second Sauer wrote in dismay in

1761 that some Germans, discarding previous practice, had begun to deal in "black goods":

> It is with the utmost regret that we learn that Germans are to engage in the nefarious slave traffic....This godless traffic could find, up to the present, no safe footing in Pennsylvania, owing to the abhorrence the Germans still have for it....[But] we are assured that three ships have been sent from Philadelphia to the African coast to steal these poor creatures, though this has never happened before. May God be merciful to our country before the measure of iniquity is full and the vials of His wrath are poured out upon it![2]

BRETHREN AND SLAVERY

The first reference to church discipline among Brethren on the subject had to do with a member of the Germantown congregation, Johannes van Laschet. In 1775 he begged forgiveness from his sisters and brothers for "anything where I may have sinned against you or angered you...." He continued, "As far as I know, the greatest complaint was about a Negro woman, that I should let her go." He stated that he had done this for her and her son but that she wished him to retain her other children "until they have earned some money, lest they become wards of the township...."

A statement of the 1782 Yearly Meeting deals with the problem of the "unchristian slave trade," holding unanimously that no member could be permitted to "purchase negroes, or to keep them as slaves." Referring to the ongoing Van Laschet case, the meeting insisted that the woman must be manumitted, and that if she wished to stay with him after being freed, he had to contract for her labor. Because of the presence of her four minor children, however, he should keep them until the age of twenty-one to see to their education and care. When they reached their majority, he had to provide them with new clothes. The Brethren were concerned that their abrupt freeing could result in hardship.[3]

The 1797 Yearly Meeting again addressed slavery, in this case with reference to slave owners who wished to join the church. While restating their policy against slaveholding, the meeting agreed that slaves could be kept until they earned their purchase price (in the judgment of the local congregation). The care of the children of slaves was again a concern. As with the Van Laschet incident, Brethren agreed that such children should be retained as servants for a specified time, in this case until the age of twenty-five. During this time they were to be taught reading and writing, instructed in religion, and when freed, provided with new clothes.[4]

Ironically one of the most prominent of the slaveholders in Virginia in the antebellum period was a descendant of Germantown Brethren. Though William Weaver never became a member of the Dunkers, he was a son of Adam Weaver and Hannah Mack Weaver, and thus a grandson of Sander Mack. He later owned and operated iron forges on his estates of some 20,000 acres in Rockbridge and Botetourt counties. He ran them with a slave force that numbered in 1858 seventy men, women, and children.[5]

The anti-slavery decision was reaffirmed in 1812 and 1813; any member not following the policy was to be disfellowshiped. Brethren ruled in 1845 that members were not permitted to hire slaves owned by outsiders to work on their own property. A common practice in the Shenandoah Valley of Virginia, it was apparently accepted by some Brethren who pointed out that they were not the actual owners and therefore felt that they were not offending against the discipline. The Meeting, however, advised that the practice of hiring slaves was "but little better than purchasing and holding slaves, and that it would be best for a follower of Jesus Christ to have nothing to do with slavery."[6]

When state laws regulating slavery were stiffened in the 1850s as the national controversy grew more heated, it became more difficult for Brethren in the South to adhere to the decisions of Annual Meeting. A committee appointed by the Meeting of 1853 spoke to the issue; the report adopted in 1854 added the new thought that free slaves could "migrate to a land of liberty." This could have simply meant northern states but may also have been a reference to the American Colonization Society (founded in 1817), which favored resolving the slavery problem by settling American blacks in the newly created (1821/22) nation of Liberia in Africa. Many Americans, including Abraham Lincoln, favored this answer to the growing crisis over slavery.[7]

During the war itself, the Annual Meeting repeated its anti-slavery tenet in response to a query concerning a brother who "would preach that slavery was right according to the Scriptures," thus causing discord: "Inasmuch as the Brethren always believed, and believe yet, that slavery is a great evil, and contrary to the Doctrine of Christ, we consider it utterly wrong for a brother to justify slavery, either in public or private, and that he should be admonished, and if obstinate, shall be dealt with according to Matt. 18."[8]

A particularly poignant aspect had to do with the Brethren practice of the holy kiss. As a small number of Negroes sought and won membership among the Brethren, this issue came to the fore. Would church discipline be brought to bear upon white members who hesitated to "salute" their colored Brethren upon meeting or, in particular, when they participated in the love feast in which the kiss played an important role?

Two decisions at the 1835 Annual Meeting revealed somewhat different interpretations. The first, responding to a question on how "to receive colored people into our church," declared flatly, "Considered, to make no difference on account of color." The second answer agreed that "the Gospel is to be preached to all nations and races," hence, repentant sinners and believers of all colors were to be accepted. Yet, in regards to the holy kiss, the answer recognized that "there is a repugnance in some of our white members to salute colored persons in this manner." "Colored members" were asked to "bear with that weakness," and not "offer the kiss to such weak members until they become stronger and make the first offer." The issue was dealt with again in 1845 and 1849, recognizing that the "more perfect way" was to practice "that love, which makes no distinction in the Brotherhood" in the holy kiss, while urging patience with those members "who are weak in the faith and cannot do so." After the end of the Civil War, the counsel of the church remained much the same.[9]

BRETHREN AND THE ABOLITIONIST MOVEMENT

As the sectional dispute about the morality of slave holding grew more intense, even the low-profile Brethren were brought willy-nilly into its sway. Although Brethren were urged to stay far away from political controversy, it became impossible to side-step the issue completely. Unlike the Friends, few Brethren were involved in the Underground Railway, the illicit network of anti-slavery activists who aided escaped slaves from the southern states reach freedom in the northern states or in Canada. A few members in Pennsylvania seem to have assisted, but the illegal procedure was alien to Brethren values and patterns.

Brethren immigrants to the Kansas territory in the 1850s found themselves in the middle of the raging controversy over slavery. The conflict rapidly grew so violent that soon the region was known as "bloody Kansas." Although most of the outrages committed there came from the pro-slavery side, the fanatical abolitionist John Brown sought to redress the balance with his massacre of slavery activists at Pottawatomie in 1856.[10] Brown happened to stay overnight after the raid with a Dunker, Jacob Ulrich. As they discussed slavery at breakfast, Brown said to his host, "Mr. Ulrich, you show me a man that will justify slavery, and I will show you a man that's rotten to the core." During the Civil War, those few Brethren remaining in Kansas suffered severely during the raids of irregular Confederate guerrillas.[11]

Back in the East, one of Brown's closest lieutenants was a young Ohioan with family roots among the Brethren in the Shenandoah Valley. This was John Kagi (Keagy). He taught school among his Dunker kinfolk until he was dismissed by the school board because of his outspoken abolitionist views. When John Brown set about organizing a "provisional government," which he hoped to set up following his raid on the government arsenal at Harpers Ferry, (West) Virginia, Kagi was to become his secretary of war.[12]

To effect the Harpers Ferry raid, John Brown arrived in the vicinity in 1859 using the alias "Isaac Smith"; he rented a house on the Kennedy farm in Maryland within the territory of the Brownsville Brethren congregation. The Kennedy house had been used as a meeting place for Brethren worship from 1848 to 1858, that is, until shortly before Brown's arrival. One of the closest neighbors was a Brethren leader named Jacob Yourtee. It is generally accepted that John Brown preached as "Isaac Smith" at several Brethren meetings in the area; his daughter Annie testified later about these visits. Of course, Brethren knew him only as Smith, a generous and devout neighbor who railed against slavery at every opportunity.[13]

A Brethren preacher from Illinois, Samuel Garber, ran afoul of the controversy about slavery in 1860. On a visit to relatives in Tennessee, he was asked to preach on Isaiah 58:6: "Is not this the fast that I have chosen? To loose the bands of wickedness, to undo the heavy burdens, and to let the oppressed go free, and that ye break every yoke?" Word got about in the community that Garber would preach on that text, with the consequence that at the appointed time the local sheriff and other officials were in the congregation.

As he expounded the text, with evident reference to the slave system, these men "could scarcely keep their seats." Garber was arrested immediately after the conclusion of the service. He was set free awaiting trial on $500 bail. Following the urging of the local Brethren, Garber left for Illinois, and they paid the forfeited bail.[14]

THE SECESSIONIST MOVEMENT

As the threat of war heightened, alert Brethren in the South were aware of the impending dangers. Elder John Kline of Broadway, Virginia, was the leader among them. On the first day of the New Year of 1861, he wrote in his diary:

> The year opens with dark and lowering clouds in our national horizon. I feel a deep interest in the peace and prosperity of our country, but in my view both are sorely threatened now. Secession is the cry further south; and I greatly fear its poisonous breath is being wafted northward towards Virginia on the wings of fanatical discontent. A move is clearly on hand for holding a convention at Richmond, Virginia; and while its advocates publicly deny the charge, I, for one, feel sure that it signals the

separation of our beloved old State from the family in which she has long lived and been happy.

Kline went on to prophesy correctly that secession meant war and that war meant "tears and ashes and blood"; it meant "bonds and imprisonment, and perhaps even death to many in our beloved Brotherhood, who, I have the confidence to believe, will die, rather than disobey God by taking up arms."[15]

Kline had earlier articulated his views on citizenship and patriotism in reflections in his journal on a celebration held at the anniversary in 1849 of the birth of George Washington, a festivity marked by much firing of cannon:

> It is presumable that those who find pleasure in public demonstrations of this sort are moved by what they regard as patriotic feelings and principles....But I have a somewhat higher conception of true patriotism that can be represented by the firing of guns which give forth nothing but meaningless sound....My highest conception of patriotism is found in the man who loves the Lord his God with all his heart and his neighbor as himself. Out of these affections spring the subordinate love for one's country; love truly virtuous for one's companion and children, relatives and friends; and in its most comprehensive sense takes in the whole human family. Were this love universal, the word *patriotism*, in its specific sense, meaning such a love for one's country as makes its possessors ready and willing to take up arms in its defense, might be appropriately expunged from every national vocabulary.[16]

Even earlier his prescience was demonstrated in a journal entry of July 4, 1847. Kline had on his travels heard an eye-witness account of a slave auction held in North Carolina. A family consisting of a mother, daughter, and two sons had been sold separately, thus forced to anticipate that they would never see each other again. The agony of the mother and daughter were "past description."

Kline ruminated, "It is to be hoped that such heart-rending scenes are not often to be witnessed; and I do believe that the time is not far distant when the sun will rise and set upon our land cleansed of this foul stain, though it may be cleansed with blood. I would rejoice to think that my eyes might see that bright morning; but I can have no hope of that."[17]

Not only was Kline well informed, he was also very active in making the views of the Brethren known to leading government officials. He was known and respected by the governor of Virginia, John Letcher (with whom he often corresponded), and by state legislators. Although such highly placed government leaders tended to understand and protect the Brethren, lesser bureaucrats and local figures were often less sympathetic.[18]

It was widely known that Brethren opposed secessionism and slavery; as conscientious objectors to military pursuits, they were unwilling to support the emerging Confederate cause. Another Brethren leader in Virginia, Benjamin F. Moomaw, had been a moving spirit in trying to organize Botetourt County to oppose secession. In the heat of the day, his position lost. Activists used physical violence at the polls to force Brethren to vote for secession. One story records balloting at the Mt. Crawford precinct. The local judge, a Colonel Peter Roller, had confidently predicted a unanimous vote in favor of secession. After a Dunker preacher voted, someone mentioned that he might have cast an opposing vote. They opened the ballot box and found his vote marked "Against secession." Roller mounted his horse, ordered his sons and some others to follow him, pursued the preacher on his way homeward, and overtook him. Drawing their revolvers, the mounted party gave him the option of withdrawing his ballot or dying. He chose to withdraw it, and in this way Mt. Crawford was able to report a solid vote in favor of secession. (Another version has an election judge changing the vote.)[19]

Despite this kind of pressure Kline wrote to Gov. Letcher in January 1861 that the Brethren supported the "General Government of the United States," and "as a church and people, are at heart and soul opposed to any move which looks toward its dismemberment." This stand took courage because emotions ran high in the southern states on the issue.[20]

Understandably, Brethren in the northern states also were opposed to secession, although they usually refrained from making official pronouncements about it. Brethren were advised to avoid political activity, in particular, during troubled times. A query to the Annual Meeting held in Wayne County, Indiana, in 1864 referred to the war currently raging as "the rebellion," obviously taking the northern perspective on it. The answer reasserted the nonresistant position of the Brethren but surprisingly took a decidedly pro-Union view: "And lest the position we have taken upon political matters in general, and war matters in particular, should seem to make us, as a body, appear to be indifferent to our government, or in opposition thereto, in its efforts to suppress the rebellion, we hereby declare that it has our sympathies and our prayers, and that it shall have our aid in any way which does not conflict with the principles of the gospel of Christ."[21]

An outspoken and influential elder from the Pipe Creek congregation in Maryland, D. P. Sayler was even quoted as stating publicly, "I have often prayed God that what he cannot do otherwise, he will do at the mouth of the cannon." It is said that Lincoln once responded to those who criticized him for exempting members of the peace churches from the army in this way: "People who do not believe in war make poor soldiers. Besides the attitude of those people has always been against slavery. If all our people had held the same views about slavery as these people hold, there would be no war." His anecdote is credible because Lincoln knew Brethren while still living in Illinois and had many contacts with Quakers while president.[22]

BRETHREN EXPERIENCES IN THE SOUTH

Although wartime has never been a comfortable period for a peace church, Brethren in the South had more difficulties than their co-religionists in the North. Because of their opposition to secessionism, their discipline, which forbade slave holding, and their nonresistant attitudes, they were bound to face serious problems. Adding to these realities based on their own principles, the situation of the Confederate states brought its own perplexities. The economic and industrial wherewithal in the South was limited; they had a much

Dunkers and Mennonites receiving passes to travel north from General George Crook's headquarters. Drawing by J. E. Taylor, *Western Reserve Historical Society, Cleveland, Ohio.*

smaller pool of manpower; and they had within their borders a large population of the disaffected, namely the slaves. As the fortunes of the war shifted slowly to favor the Union, despite the superior skill of southern military leaders, beleaguered officials of the Confederacy brought more pressure to bear upon dissenters such as the Brethren.

The immediate problem facing the Brethren was the Confederate call for soldiers, issued by the Provisional Congress in March 1861, before the firing on Fort Sumter triggered hostilities; later measures in May and August asked the states to recruit the military. Anticipating these actions, Elder John Kline wrote again in late January 1861 to Governor Letcher appealing for the exemption of church members from military service. The governor's immediate reply was positive, remarking that there were "enough of others who take pleasure in the performance of such duties."[23]

Despite this assurance, there were many instances where Brethren were forced into the military. A letter from Kline directed to a Colonel Lewis, asked him to use his influence on behalf of

Brethren dragooned into duty. After a statement of the Brethren opposition to the "bearing of carnal weapons," Kline wrote that they felt "bound to pay our taxes, [and] fines, and to do whatever is in our power which does not conflict with our obligation to God." Nevertheless, "[w]henever God speaks we think we should obey Him rather than man." Kline protested that nonresistants were being forced into the army. Some Brethren felt compelled to hire substitutes, paying as much as $1,500 apiece.[24]

Brethren and Mennonite leaders in Virginia and North Carolina appealed to state officials, asking for relief. A Virginia law passed in March 1862 granted exemption to members of recognized nonresistant churches, upon payment of a fine of $500 plus two percent of the assessed value of the applicant's taxable property. An earlier law in North Carolina (September 1861) was more generous; those persons "having scruples of conscience against bearing arms" who could prove membership in a nonresistant church would be exempted from mustering or performing military duty "except in cases of insurrection, or invasion, or war," in which case they would be liable for taxation and paying an equivalent in lieu of furnishing a quota of men.[25]

Hardly had these laws come into effect before a Confederate-wide regulation passed in April 1862 superceded the state arrangements. There was no provision for conscientious objectors. A Richmond newspaper commented on the hardship thus entailed:

> Scattered over certain portions of Virginia are a well-known sect called "Dunkards." These Dunkards, in the act of the Legislature calling out militia were exempted....Under the conscript act which is now being put into operation these men will have to enter the army, no provision being made by Congress for their exemption. It seems hard they should be made to pay and fight too, but as the law now stands there is no help to it.[26]

Brethren leaders including elders John Kline and B. F. Moomaw immediately turned their attention to the Confederate Congress, petitioning for relief, aided by a sympathetic legislator. A treatise on biblical nonresistance written by the Baptist William C. Thurman (the later Adventist) proved useful in explaining the peace position to Confederate legislators.

In November 1862, the Confederate Congress passed another law permitting recognized members of the Society of Friends, Dunkers, Nazarenes, and Mennonites to provide substitutes or pay a tax of $500 to secure exemption. Brethren were grateful for this relief and appointed a day of thanksgiving on January 1, 1863, when special services were held across the state. When John Kline preached on that day at Linville Creek, he reminded his hearers that they should not forget the "bare-footed, half-clad and half-fed children in our land," who needed care from the Brethren, in the midst of their rejoicing. Even secular journalists, critical of Brethren and Mennonite pacifism, recognized their willingness to succor the poor. "It has always been a part of their policy to take care of their own poor; but now they go a step beyond this [to help others]...."[27]

Not all went smoothly after passage of the bill. In the first place, raising the money meant great hardship for many Brethren. John Kline led the church in collecting money from those with means to aid those poorer members. In December 1862, for example, he turned over to a Confederate official some $9,000 to pay exemption taxes for young Brethren. Many members had already paid substantial sums to the state government under the Virginia law of March 1862. This was not recognized by some Confederate officials, who tried to collect twice. In some areas, as in Tennessee, the Confederate law was not respected, and Elder P. R. Wrightsman recorded situations where "local authorities arrested many of our Brethren and shut them up in prison and in the stockades in various places, even after they had paid the $500 penalty." Wrightsman was very active in taking up the cause of these Brethren with the authorities, at great risk to himself.[28]

An additional cause of worry was the repeated rumor that the Confederate law would be changed to omit exemptions. At one point Brethren leaders pondered the possibility of petitioning for the right of mass emigration. In late 1863 and especially in 1864 the shortage of available men for the military brought increased pressure on the right of exemption. New converts were specifically excluded from the benefits of the law. Then in March 1865, conscription matters were returned to the states and exemptions were stringently decreased.

BRETHREN RESPONSES TO CONFEDERATE PRESSURE

Just before the passage of Virginia's draft law of March 1862 permitting Brethren to escape the military by paying the fine, nearly one hundred Brethren and Mennonites (in two groups) attempted to flee the Shenandoah Valley to reach the North. They were apprehended and brought back under a minimal guard to prisons in Harrisonburg and Richmond. Officials were impressed by their quiet submission to authority; many could have escaped but voluntarily stayed with the group. A favorable report about them by a representative of the War Department, indicating their willingness to pay the anticipated exemption fee then in legislative process, led to their freeing.

Elder John Kline was himself imprisoned for two weeks in a Harrisonburg guardhouse in April 1862 because of his vigorous efforts on behalf of the prisoners and others faced with the army. His incarceration was memorialized by a hymn written in captivity. Kline's medical skills allowed him to alleviate the sufferings of the young Brethren and Mennonites in the prison. Sickness struck the men early in their stay, while the dampness of the room and the lack of fuel and comfortable bedding added to their distress. Kline himself became ill because of the harsh conditions.[29]

Particularly at risk during the war period were those young men who joined the church after the passage of the exemption laws in the separate states and the Confederacy. They were thought to be opportunists and not given the privilege of paying the fine. Many sought shelter by moving through the lines to safer territory in the northern states, especially in Ohio and Indiana. As the war continued this became more regularized as a kind of Underground Railroad; hiding places referred to as depots were created in the mountains where those escaping could wait until guides, known as pilots, conducted them through the lines. A secret delivery service for correspondence was created, operated by postmasters such as Margaret M. Rhoades; in this way families in Virginia received word about the whereabouts and situation of their sons, brothers, and husbands.

A letter written in Clark County, Ohio, in February 1865 by John W. Eller, one of the refugees from Virginia, to his best friend, another refugee then living in Illinois, witnesses to the heartbreaking trials of this experience:

> Dear Brother in the Lord....the reffugees relations and friends are all well as far as now at present....Brother John i guess you would like to hear Some news from old virginia. i received a letter from some [one] about a month ago and they was all well at that time and they rote that your Father & Mother was well and sent their best respects to you and Brother Benjamin and all enquiring friends and want you to rite to them....my son Joseph died the 23 day of November he died with the croup and my companion [wife] was sick the res[t] was well...i am rite smartly troubled and some times think that i will go rite of[f] home i dont no how much longer i can stand it though if i was their i could do them no good so long as the cruel war is goin on....I am looking for more letters from home every day for i [k]now their is some on the way my wife says in her last letter that [the] common class people will certainly have to sell their land to pay their taxes. The times are hard there....

Three days after the letter was written, Eller's wife Leah died in Virginia.[30]

Others chose not to travel far away but rather hid out near their farm homes, living in the woods and picking up food and clothing from time to time in secret. A communication describing this situation came from Henry Garst, who wrote to his wife Anna in January 1865 from Macoupin County, Illinois, after finally deciding to pass through the lines. Reporting that he was in "reasonable health," he admitted that he missed her and their three sons greatly, deprived of seeing her and "passing off my Loansome hours with my Littley boys":

...I have bin cauled for to go and leave you in fear and distress a many a time not knowing how soon I might be struck the fatal blow for the roar of the musquet and canno[n] was roaring loudley round thoug I have aulways escaped and returned home again affectionate Ann and Little children come meeting me with glad and fondly looks as if they was relased from ther fear and trouble again to see me returning home after a few days of hardship and danger....I no you often feared and treampled when you would her the news that the enemy weas rushing in uppon us but thank god the storm and wars past off with out harm or hurt and by and by I would return home for a while to try and prepare something for my Little family to subsist uppon but alas the time would come that we had to take the parting hand not knowing whether we may ever meet again or not[31]

Yet others were forced into the Confederate army where their treatment varied from extreme harshness to comparative understanding. It was of these Brethren and Mennonites that General Thomas "Stonewall" Jackson wrote, "There lives a people in the Valley of Virginia, that are not hard to bring in the army. While there they are obedient to their officers. Nor is it difficult to have them take aim, but it is impossible to get them to take correct aim. I, therefore, think it better to leave them at their homes that they may produce supplies for the army."[32]

BRETHREN EXPERIENCES IN THE NORTH

Those Brethren living in the North fared better than those in the South. The government was more stable and the demands for manpower less urgent. But there, too, wartime brought stresses and tensions, in particular because of conscription. As in the South, in the early months of the war conscription was the responsibility of the several states. Some, such as Pennsylvania, had precedents for exempting conscientious objectors. Petitions exist from Pennsylvania congregations asking for the retention of the privilege.

A general Federal Militia Act was passed in July and a General Order in August 1862 to regulate military service in the Union Army. The General Order provided that exemption would follow the established state practice, without citing religious scruples as sufficient cause. Indiana and Ohio provided exemption for conscientious objectors by a commutation payment of $200, Pennsylvania by $300. The money was used to hire substitutes and care for the wounded and sick.

Further acts of March and December 1863 had the effect of shifting final responsibility for conscription from the states to the federal government, again with no recognition of religious scruples against service. Friends, Mennonites, and Brethren worked with the federal government to recognize their nonresistant principles. Finally, in February 1864, a new law provided that "members of religious denominations who shall by oath or affirmation declare that they are conscientiously opposed to the bearing of arms" when drafted would be assigned to the care of the wounded or to the Freedmen's Bureaus. Alternatively, they could make a commutation payment of $300 "to be applied to the benefit of the sick and wounded soldiers." This regulation did much to ease the consciences of members of these churches who were unhappy about their money going to pay for substitutes.[33]

Before this took place, individual elders issued statements on behalf of young men of draft age attesting to the Brethren principle of nonresistance and certifying church membership. This resolution to the problem of conscription seemed to have worked rather well in the North, although certain local incidents reveal lack of sympathy for Brethren nonresistance and their reluctance to support the war effort, seen increasingly as a crusade by Unionists.

ACTIONS OF THE ANNUAL MEETING

The actions of the Brethren Annual Meetings in the first half of the nineteenth century were consistently opposed to any participation by members in military activities such as mustering, drilling, and the like. As part of the baptismal service, new members promised to adhere to the longstanding principles of nonresistance. Therefore, the Brethren position was clear and well known at the outbreak of war.

Despite this, the Annual Meetings of 1861 and 1862 were silent on the war issue in the face of the violence sweeping across the nation. In 1863 the first query raised the issue, "How are we to deal with our brethren who have enlisted and gone to the army as soldiers or teamsters, or those who have been drafted, and are gone to the army?" The cautious answer, no doubt reflecting the presence of Brethren on both sides of the battle lines, stated simply, "We think it not expedient to consider (or discuss) these questions at this time. Still it is believed, and was expressed, the gospel gave sufficient instruction." One who was present reported that Kline, as moderator, had requested that he not be asked questions about the South because of the danger involved.

One year later the Meeting warned members and ministers (!) against wearing military clothing; those disobedient to this ruling would face church discipline. The same gathering advised only in extreme circumstances could a soldier still under arms be accepted into the church, and then only when he promised to shed no more blood. Finally in 1865, the last year of the war, the Meeting answered a query whether a brother could be held as a member who will "when put into the army, take up arms and aim to shed the blood of his countrymen?" The succinct answer: "He can not."

The most complete statement came the year before in answer to a query that spoke of the "national troubles" that "tried our nonresistant principles," asking what is to be done about voting, payment of bounty money for substitutes, and the like. The eloquent answer reads,

> We exhort the brethren to steadfastness in the faith, and believe that the times in which our lots are cast strongly demand of us a strict adherence to all our principles, and especially to our non-resistant principle, a principle dear to every subject of the Prince of Peace, and a prominent doctrine of our Fraternity, and to endure whatever sufferings and to make whatever sacrifice the maintaining of the principle may require, and not to encourage in any way the practice of war.
>
> And we think it more in accordance with our principles, that instead of paying bounty-money,...to await

the demands of the government, whether general, state, or local, and pay the fines and taxes required of us, as the Gospel permits, and indeed requires. Matt. 22:21; Rom. 13:7.[34]

UNITY PRESERVED AMONG THE BRETHREN

Although Brethren unity was preserved, there were tension points. Early in 1861, editor Henry Kurtz questioned whether, in the face of impending war, it was wise to continue plans for the Annual Meeting announced for Rockingham County in the Shenandoah Valley of Virginia. He reasoned, "Owing to the present disturbed and excited state of affairs in our country, and especially in the southern states, would it not be well to change the place of holding our next annual meeting?" He mentioned that "fears are entertained from the present indication of things, that should the meeting be held in Virginia, the general brotherhood will be but poorly represented in 1861..., and if so, it would be an occasion of sincere regret."

The leaders of the Brethren in Virginia immediately replied that there were no grounds for fear, no reason to change the location at that late date, and that Northerners had no reason to anticipate danger in traveling to the southern location. When the war did break out in April, Kurtz repeated his warning: "It is presumed under present circumstances, it will be best for all brethren, North and South, to stay at home at this time, and postpone yearly meeting until fall, and some other locality, where they may meet in peace, and without fear of being molested. A great deal may be said, but we forbear."[35] In fact, the Annual Meeting did take place in Rockingham County as planned and enjoyed a large attendance, with over 3,500 participants. Leaders regretted that so few Brethren came from the North; only four congregations were represented from it, and those from the Midwest—Iowa, Indiana, Kansas, and Ohio. The minutes lamented that so few "brethren from distant parts" came "to share in their hospitality."[36]

Elder John Kline and other leading churchmen from Virginia were critical of Henry Kurtz and his associate James Quinter for their counsel against attending, raising the specter of disunity:

And while we believe that such a thing was most foreign
from your intention, yet we cannot be blind to the
deplorable tendency it is likely to have, that of creating a
sectional feeling among the brotherhood, which God in
his mercy forbid should ever be the case with us. For we
say should all other churches divide, should the political
world crumble to atoms, let us by the hope of God, stand
united in the bonds of fraternal love, exercizing charity
and forbearance toward each other until time shall cease,
so that then we may be cemented together in the spirit
world and united to God....

Although somewhat offended by the critique, Quinter wrote on
behalf of both editors that they had received the communication "in
meekness and love, being conscious of our frailty and liability to
err." He assured the Virginia Brethren that their fears about the creation of a "sectional feeling" were "without any foundation."[37]

Annual Meetings were henceforth held each year at Pentecost,
in Montgomery County, Ohio (1862); Blair County, Pennsylvania
(1863); Hagerstown, Indiana (1864); and Lee County, Illinois (1865).
Relatively few Brethren from the Confederate states were able to
attend, although the fact has symbolic importance that Virginian
John Kline served as a moderator through 1864. He was able to
secure passes from both warring sides allowing him to cross the
lines in order to attend the meetings.

Elder Kline expressed his concern for unity in a letter to Kurtz in
June 1864 urging the committee led by James Quinter to work expe-
ditiously to complete the hymnal authorized by the Annual Meeting:
"Tell br[other] James [Quinter] to not delay the hymnbooks any
longer, or we will be almost compelled to make a selection of our
own, which we are opposed to; we want but one Hymnbook, that is
one for all the brotherhood, both North and South." (The letter was
one of the last letters Kline ever wrote; it was dated two days before
his death.) Brethren leaders, therefore, were clearly alert to the dangers of division and eager to preserve church unity.[38]

Brethren Suffering

Clearly, Brethren in the Confederacy suffered more severely than did Brethren in the North, for reasons explained above. Many members were threatened with death for their lack of support for the war. Elder P. R. Wrightsman of Tennessee narrowly missed being killed several times because of his fearless defense of the Brethren position. A book called *The Olive Branch of Peace and Good Will to Men*, compiled by S. F. Sanger and Daniel Hays, is filled with incidents of this sort from the Civil War period.[39]

Some Brethren were able to use the exigencies suffered to witness for their beliefs. One striking incident involves Elder B. F. Moomaw, one of the most active leaders in representing the Brethren peace cause before Virginia and Confederate officials. A southern regiment numbering some eight hundred men had to be billeted in the Roanoke area to undergo training. Local residents, seeking to embarrass Moomaw, suggested to the commanding officer that he choose the Moomaw farm for the purpose.

Moomaw accepted the situation in good grace, setting about to win the friendship of the officers and men. His first step was to invite some twenty officers to his home for a meal. It was at this time that they revealed to him that neighbors had directed them to his farm "with evil intent." The elder was asked to preach for the encampment, which he agreed to do. He described the occasion and his approach to it: "I never felt more solemn, standing alone, and the soldiers seated around me on the ground, and I certainly never preached Christ, a peaceable Savior, a needed Savior, an efficient Savior, the Prince of Peace, with more earnestness than then and there." Shortly thereafter measles swept through the encampment, and the Moomaw family took many soldiers into their home and nursed them to recovery. When the soldiers left after nearly three months, they prepared a strongly worded statement, signed by many, refuting categorically a rumor circulated by "some vile wretch, or wretches" that the Moomaws had charged them for the care received.[40]

Many Brethren settlers in Missouri and Kansas were driven out by pro-slavery zealots. A letter from Jacob Ulrich of Kansas published in *The Gospel Visitor* in late 1861 described their troubles:

Our laboring Brethren [ministers] in Missouri all had to flee; brother William Gish had to come to us, and had lived a while in Kansas but is now moved North. Br. Jacob Kaub with much trouble and distress got his family here, though the best of his team had been taken from him, and his son badly hurt, but has recovered again.

Br. Joseph Kenny and br. John Firestone came to my house on last Saturday, the latter being robbed of his wagon and part of his team, had to leave all his property and some of his family behind; his wife has now gone back, and will try to bring the children, clothing and bedding. Their crop is taken and destroyed....By the last account there were yet 5 families of Brethren in Missouri, who have to make their escape from a merciless rabble.[41]

A deadly raid on Lawrence, Kansas, in August 1863 led by the Confederate guerrilla leader William C. Quantril left behind a town in flames, 150 people dead, and more than one million dollars worth of property damage. The marauders terrorized Brethren settlers on their way back to Missouri. The band burned the house and barn of Jacob Ulrich, causing about six thousand dollars worth of damage. At the nearby farm of the aged Abraham Rothrock more violence took place. When the elder tried to reason with the raiders, one of them threw him down into the cellar and shot him three times, shouting, "That's the way we treat all damned old preachers!" They torched the house as they left.

Neighbors rescued the grievously wounded man, who had sustained injuries to the neck, shoulder, and chin. While he was recuperating a neighboring Baptist minister paid a visit. Anticipating that Rothrock would waver from his peace principles because of his sufferings at the hands of the raiders, he asked, "Mr. Rothrock, what would you do if you had those men in your power now?" The elder quickly responded, "I would convert every one of them." "Well," said the Baptist, "that beats my religion."[42]

Worse was to come in the South. In June 1863, *The Gospel Visitor* reported on two unprovoked murders of Brethren in Barbour County, Virginia. On the pretense of taking Henry Wilson and

Henry Bowman to court as witnesses, a band of men took them from their homes and at short distances from their residences brutally shot them. Wilson was described as "naturally kind and affectionate," with his home "open and his table free for saint and sinner, rich or poor, friend or foe." He was "always ready for every call to visit the sick and the afflicted." In Tennessee, Elder John P. Bowman was murdered by soldiers when he pleaded with them not to requisition a much-needed horse.[43]

The best-known incident involved Elder John Kline of Broadway, Virginia. Kline, the most prominent Brethren figure in the South, had often received death threats because of his well-known anti-slavery and anti-secessionist views. His travels across the battle lines to moderate the Brethren Annual Meetings stimulated dark suspicions of espionage activity.

As Kline left the Meeting held in Hagerstown, Indiana, in May 1864, he expressed a presentiment of his death:

> Possibly you may never see my face or hear my voice again. I am now on my way back to Virginia, not knowing the things that shall befall me there. It may be that bonds and afflictions abide me. But I feel that I have done nothing worthy of bonds or of death; and none of these things move me; neither count I my life dear unto myself, so that I may finish my course with joy, and the ministry which I have received of the Lord Jesus, to testify the Gospel of the grace of God.[44]

On June 15, 1864, while on a visit to a sick neighbor, he was waylaid and killed by two Confederate irregulars, whose names, although well known in the community, were long suppressed. Those who found the body observed a gentle smile on Kline's face. When responding earlier to concerns about his safety, he had commented that enemies might take his life but he did not fear them; they could only kill his body, not harm his soul. Brethren have honored John Kline as a martyr and witness for the faith; the memory of his life and work has inspired many.[45]

Although understood as friendly to the Union cause, Brethren in the valley of Virginia suffered along with their southern neighbors when General Philip H. Sheridan pressed through the area with his commands that his troops should spare nothing. By his own notorious report he "destroyed a thousand barns filled with wheat," drove "in front of the army over 4,000 head of stock," and "killed not less than 3,000 sheep." His summary provided the best-remembered line: "So entire has been the destruction that a crow flying across the Valley must carry its own rations." The devastation was corroborated by a resident who recalled: "The Union army came up the Valley sweeping everything before them like a wild hurricane; there was nothing left for man or beast; neither was there anything needed for beasts, as they left no beast from horse down to chicken; all was taken." Because of these losses and the constant pressure from war-minded neighbors, some Virginia Brethren and Mennonites at this point accepted General Sheridan's offer of transport out of the Valley. The general reported "over four hundred wagonloads of refugees" from the Harrisonburg vicinity. "Most of these people were Dunkers."[46]

Some idea of the extent of Brethren loss can be gleaned from their petitions for reimbursement to the federal government following the war. Joseph Bowman, formerly of Rockingham County, wrote from Ohio about the experiences of the Virginia Brethren: "There were seventy-one or seventy-two members left their homes out of our district, besides friends and children....A great many of the brethren and neighbors had all their buildings burned." Brethren in the North mounted a vigorous campaign to send materials and money to the South to help them recover from the depredations of the war.[47]

Brethren in the Midst of War's Carnage

By the irony of history, two of the most fateful battles of the Civil War raged around Brethren properties—Antietam and Gettysburg. The Mumma meetinghouse of the Manor congregation near Sharpsburg, Maryland—the famous Dunker Church depicted in battle-field photos—was at the epicenter of the bloodiest day of the war, September 17, 1862; over 23,000 on both sides fell as casualties at Antietam.

The Mumma meetinghouse at Antietam (the "old Dunkard meetinghouse"), the epicenter of the bloodiest battle of the Civil War on September 17, 1862, when the Northern and Southern armies suffered nearly 23,000 casualties. Matthew Brady Associates photo by Alexander Garddner, *BHLA Collection.*

A member of General Thomas "Stonewall" Jackson's staff left a record of his experiences in the night after the conflict. He rode through a "dreadful scene" where the "dead and dying lay as thick over it as harvest sheaves." Cries of the wounded for water and aid "were more horrible to listen to than the deadliest sounds of battle." The dead were motionless but "here and there were raised stiffened arms; heads made a last effort to lift themselves from the ground; prayers were mingled with oaths, the oaths of delirium; men were wriggling over the earth; and midnight hid all distinctions between the blue and the grey."[48]

Local Brethren gathered on the next day to aid those still living, using the meetinghouse as a hospital. Although its walls were pockmarked by shells, the building was soon repaired with substantial gifts from northern Brethren, using funds collected by Elder D. P. Sayler of the Pipe Creek congregation in Maryland. He reported in February 1864 that the Manor congregation was again using the meetinghouse for worship and that funds not used for this purpose were distributed among members who had suffered material loss. Many of their household effects had been burned, destroyed, or carried off by soldiers. Some members had not yet recovered from the nervous shock of the battle.[49]

The building stood for many years until it was heavily damaged by a storm in 1921 and torn down. It was rebuilt on the centennial of the battle and stands today on the Antietam National Battlefield, part of the National Park Service. Periodically, Brethren hold religious services there, stressing their peace convictions. The pulpit Bible used in the Mumma meetinghouse was taken as a souvenir by a Union soldier. It was later given to John T. Lewis, a black member of the Meadow Branch, Maryland, congregation, then living in upstate New York. He returned the Bible to Antietam, where it is now displayed in the rebuilt meetinghouse. John T. Lewis was a warm friend of his celebrated neighbor, author Mark Twain, who, it is said, modeled in part his character Jim in *The Adventures of Huckleberry Finn* on Lewis.[50]

Brethren property was also at the heart of the fateful conflict at Gettysburg, Pennsylvania. When Union forces beat back the concerted charges of the Confederate armies in the three-day battle of early July 1863, the turning point in the War between the States was reached. Much of the battle took place on the farm of Jacob Sherfy, a member of the local Marsh Creek congregation of Brethren. Areas now prominent in military history—Little Round Top, Devil's Den, the Wheat Field, Plumb Run, the Peach Orchard—all lay on his land. Members of his son's family (Joseph Sherfy, a minister at Marsh Creek) were driven from their home on that part of the farm that contained the Peach Orchard.

More than a year later a traveling Brethren minister viewed the scene on the Sherfy farm. He described the "sorrowful sight" of the ruins of the burned barn, as well as the "almost numberless marks of shots into and against" the farmhouse. This was caused by the

Union sharpshooters trying to drive out southern defenders inside the house. He saw "where a large shot passed through his house knocking the footboard out of a bed, and the middle drawers out of a bureau in its course."[51]

Marsh Creek records itemize donations of money, bedding, and clothes coming from the Pipe Creek congregation in Maryland and the Codorus congregation in York County. They were distributed to the "sufferers on the Battlefield of Gettysburg" who were "in the estimation of the Marsh Creek church the most needy." Recipients included Brethren, Lutherans, Methodists, German Reformed, and Roman Catholics. Some had lost everything except what they had been wearing.

Though Brethren survived the travail of the war without fracturing the unity of the body, serious strains were yet to come. These were of internal nature, rather than external, and were to prove more difficult to resist than the stress of warfare.

14

Division in the Church

Although Brethren had experienced numerous divisions during the eighteenth and nineteenth centuries—the Ephrata Society and the New Dunkers are cases in point—it was not until the last half of the nineteenth century that schisms completely rent the Brethren fabric. Between 1881 and 1883 tensions that had been heightening since mid-century erupted, creating three major Brethren bodies. A very conservative wing called itself the Old German Baptist Brethren to signal its determination to preserve the traditional church ways; they were nicknamed the Old Orders. The largest and middle body, which retained the legal name German Baptist Brethren (after 1908 known as the Church of the Brethren), attempted to combine both conservative and progressive tendencies; they were called the Conservatives. A forward-looking group wishing to open the denomination to modern methods and programs became the Brethren Church; they were nicknamed the Progressives. Although there were later divisions, nothing approached the trauma of this three-way split of the early 1880s. The divisions were triggered by pressure for change and resistance to that change, pressure that became increasingly insistent after 1850.

Some historians have linked the internal dissension among the Brethren to the effects of industrialization, others to growing acculturation (adapting to the contemporary society), and yet others to the shift from a sectarian to a denominational posture as the Brethren movement matured after 150 years of existence. Another line of interpretation sees the division as derived from the differences between the two movements—Anabaptism and Pietism—that predominantly shaped the formation of the Brethren.[1]

The specific bones of contention that led to the Great Divide of 1881-83 can be readily listed. They included higher education, Sabbath schools, church periodicals, organized missions, fixed compensation for ministers, revival or "protracted" meetings, prescribed dress, the method of feetwashing (single mode or double mode), and the organization and authority of the Annual Meetings. Underlying these specific issues were deeper questions. How were Brethren to relate to the world (nonconformity)? What was the final locus of authority in the church (polity)? How were converts to be won (evangelism)?

Closely linked with these fundamental concerns was the question of control. Would the future of the church be decided by the generally younger Progressives (often termed the "fast element")? by the generally older traditionalists (Old Orders)? by the moderate Conservatives (who were often considered to be carrying water on both shoulders by their opponents on either side)?

Growing Tensions

Once past the agonies of the Civil War, the lurking tensions within the expanding Brethren movement surfaced more openly. During the conflict much attention had been devoted to maintaining church unity despite sectional differences. With the outer struggle over, some leaders decided that it was time to turn their attention inward to perceived problems within the church.

The center of the unrest was in southwestern Ohio, in the Miami Valley. In October 1868, some twenty churchmen, mainly elders, met at the Wolf Creek congregation. The stated aim of the gathered leaders was to consult about the "present digression of the church, in many localities, from the ancient order and practice."[2] Those attending announced a wider consultation to be held at the Stillwater congregation (Peter Nead's church) in November 1868; its purpose was to draft a petition/query to be presented at the Annual Meeting of 1869. The focus of the petition was the current manner of holding the Annual Meeting, which by this time included delegates, a moderator, and an elected Standing Committee with the responsibility of preparing the business for the meeting. The

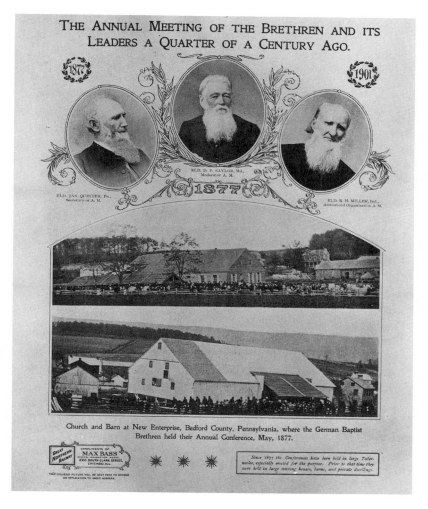

A souvenir keepsake from the Annual Meeting of 1877 held near New Enterprise, Bedford County, Pennsylvania; it was distributed by Max Bass, an agent of the Great Northern Railroad. The three men depicted are (left to right) James Quinter (writing clerk), D. P. Saylor or Sayler (moderator), and R. H. Miller (member of Standing Committee). They were among the most prominent church leaders of the era. *Durnbaugh Collection.*

Brethren of southern Ohio called for a return to the older, informal practice of choosing a group of the most venerable elders to prepare the business and to guide deliberations. They also questioned the current practice of sending Annual Meeting committees to settle differences in local congregations.

This broader consultation was followed by another, held at the Bear Creek church in March 1869, which also produced a petition. The issues here listed became the central controversies of the schisms—protracted meetings, Sabbath schools, prayer meetings, social meetings, Bible classes, and worldly dress. These innovations were held to have come from the "popular religions of the day" and were considered to be inconsistent with the humility and self-denial so cherished by Brethren. The sense of the Bear Creek consultation can be captured in a sentence in their petition, which in the original is strewn with underlining and capitalization to convey emphasis and strong emotion:

> The object of our labors, in short, is by the favor of God, to unite the brotherhood upon the ancient principles of our church, and thus save her from a corrupted Christendom; and in order to awaken us to our duties we would sound the alarm, and that loud and earnestly, and thus cause a reformation or coming back to the original standard of the brotherhood....[3]

Of those attending the March meeting, 126 men signed the petition, which was then extensively circulated and later presented to the 1869 Annual Meeting. Its drafters had suggested that it could also be submitted to District Meetings, but where its reception might be thought unfavorable, then directly to the Annual Meeting. This comment reflected discomfort with the relatively recent church polity which had established the District Meeting as an intermediary between local congregations and the national assembly.

The answer of the 1869 Annual Meeting was a compromise. Although it respectfully received the petition and cautioned all members of the church to avoid the excesses of popular religion, the answer failed to denounce the specific practices to which the petition objected. It called on those responsible to conduct meetings with propriety and with due attention to the virtues of simplicity and humility. Annual Meeting would continue to be organized along the current pattern, with only minor changes. Publishers of church-related periodicals and their writers were cautioned not to dispute church practices.

The controversy about the correct mode of feetwashing emerged in the 1870s as a major irritant. By that time almost all congregations had adopted the so-called double mode. A few congregations near Philadelphia had always followed the single mode, as had Brethren living in the Midwest known as the Far Western Brethren.

Once again, the Miami Valley elders held diversity in this practice to be insupportable and petitioned the Annual Meeting to mandate the universal observance of the double mode, allowing no exceptions. Recent actions of the Meeting had asserted the correctness of the double mode but had failed to prohibit absolutely the single mode. The debate over this issue was carried on with great vehemence and detail in Brethren periodicals. Abraham Harley Cassel of Harleysville, Pennsylvania, the leading Brethren historian of the day (who possessed in his huge personal library all of the early Brethren books and manuscripts still extant), insisted that the single mode had been the original form but failed to persuade the Miami Valley elders. In their view, the double mode was the form they had always followed; they were impatient with arguments from history to the contrary.[4]

In 1879 the Old Order element sent another petition to the Annual Meeting dealing with this and other issues, which, however, was returned by the Standing Committee without conference deliberation. When the elders in the Miami Valley learned this, they perceived the rejection as a kind of a threat. As a historical sketch issued by the Old Order Brethren shortly after the division phrased it, "Now, the treatment that these queries and petitions received impressed the minds of many members with the view that it was useless to expect that the Annual Meeting would adopt any measures by which to rid the church of the things which caused the troubles."

Subsequently, a committee of five elders in southern Ohio began to correspond systematically with leaders in other areas, pressing their grievances and asking for counsel on next steps; this resulted in many communications, queries, and petitions. With this material in hand, the Miami Valley elders convened in late November 1879 to prepare another and more comprehensive petition to the Annual Meeting. This, submitted through the District Meeting, reiterated the concerns of the previous statements and asked that the "fast element" be removed from the church. The five core issues treated were 1) higher education, 2) Sabbath schools, 3) protracted or revival meetings, 4) salaried or supported ministry, and 5) the mode of feetwashing.

The tone of the petition, while sorrowful, was extremely firm. Its signers could "no longer suffer or tolerate those innovations in the church of Christ" and quietly observe the "fast element gaining ground year after year." This course would "lead the church off into pride and the popular customs of the world." Their longsuffering and forbearance had allowed the innovations to creep in amongst them. The only answer to disunity and discord in the church was a firm attachment and adherence to the ancient order of the church, congruent as it was with the principles of the gospel.

The drafters frankly address the issue of power: "Our plain decisions have been disrespected and overruled, and if this state of things shall continue to exist, we will lose all of our power in the controlling of the church." Therefore, the Miami Valley elders concluded, "We...can see no better plan by which to restore brotherly harmony and peace than to direct our efforts at the causes from whence the disunion arises."[5]

When the fateful petition reached the Annual Meeting, without total concurrence from the District Meeting, Standing Committee reworked it and then passed it to the voting assembly. The reworking removed the chief purpose of the query, namely, the condemnation of all of the listed points. Instead, the substitute allowed their continuance while urging moderation and tact in their performance. It urged "liberty of conscience" and asked that agitation cease on these matters. The key paragraph reads,

> Resolved...that while we declare ourselves conservative,
> in maintaining unchanged what may justly be consid-
> ered the principles and peculiarities of our fraternity, we
> also believe in the propriety and necessity of so adapting
> our labor and our principles to the religious world as will
> render our labor and principles most efficient in promot-
> ing the reformation of the world, the edification of the
> world, and the glory of God. *Hence, while we are conserva-*
> *tive, we are also progressive.*[6]

No clearer statement of the contrasting positions can be desired.
The Miami Valley elders called for the extension of the ancient order
as they understood it, with no variance tolerated. Nonconformity to
the world and the popular churches, humility, and faithfulness to
the old ways were central. For those of the Conservative party at the
Annual Meeting who drafted the substitute, central were efficiency,
reformation and edification of the world, and active work for the
glory of God.

THE OLD ORDER BREAK WITH ANNUAL MEETING

Not surprisingly, the elders who sent the petition were frustrated by
the answer. In some ways, the innovations they had attacked so
fiercely were now legitimated by the response, limited only by mild
cautions to conduct schools and meetings in good order. Increasingly
voices were heard in southern Ohio that concluded it was useless to
approach the Annual Meeting for redress of grievances.

The next step for these men was to call another consultation for
November 1880 at the Wolf Creek congregation. Those dissatisfied
with the disposition of the 1879 petition by the Meeting were asked
to foregather "to learn what course would be thought best to be pursued for the good of the church." Those invited were deacons and
ministers known to be in favor of the "ancient and apostolic order
of the church, as set forth in said [1879] petition."

Three days of meetings at Wolf Creek produced yet another
petition; it repeated the conclusions of the 1879 petition and under-
girded them with statements from prior Annual Meetings. In addi-

tion to those points, criticism was included about the recently adopted plan for organizing missions and the ordination of ministers by elders from a distance, without the necessary concurrence of adjoining elders. It was clear to those present at Wolf Creek that the petition represented a final attempt, virtually an ultimatum, to bring the church around to the viewpoint of the Miami Valley.

A fateful decision was taken in regard to procedure. With the advice of several weighty Brethren present, prominent in church affairs, they decided that the 1880 petition should be sent directly to the Annual Meeting, bypassing the District Meeting. When it subsequently came before the 1881 Meeting, Standing Committee rejected it without discussion on procedural grounds. It was held to be out of order, in violation of the standard procedure for receiving queries and petitions. Although one of the leading Brethren explained the reason for bypassing the District Meeting, the petition was disallowed on this point of order and the substitute answer of 1880 reaffirmed. Use of this tactic by those in authority in 1881 made clear that no ground would be conceded to the Old Order element.

THE OLD GERMAN BAPTIST BRETHREN ORGANIZE

The expected then took place. A call went out for a special conference to be held in August 1881 near Arcanum, Ohio. A draft resolution there presented was readily passed. It detailed the course of changes in the church since the inception of *The Gospel Visitor* in 1851, the advent of Sabbath schools in 1857, and permission for revival meetings and academies in 1858. The attempts by traditionalists to secure redress from these innovations from Annual Meeting were rehearsed, followed by a statement of their discouragement and the wounding of their "tender feelings" by reason of their failures. Therefore, they concluded, no one should find fault if this attempt was made to "agree upon some rule or order for the Brethren's Church in the future," that is to say, the creation of a separate branch of the church.

A clear statement lists the innovations that would not be tolerated in their church and positive expectations: "No Sunday-schools, no high schools, no revival meetings, no paid ministry, no missionary plans or mission boards,...no money soliciting or begging to carry out such plans. No single mode of feetwashing, no musical instruments, no pianos, melodeons, and organs, etc. No unlawful interest to oppress the poor." Adherence to "primitive Christianity" necessitated a uniformity of dress for brothers and sisters, which was briefly delineated. Mission work was approved "if carried out in gospel order," and poor ministers could be assisted monetarily in informal ways in carrying out their work.

The resolutions adopted in August 1881 spell out the method by which members and congregations should be asked if they wished to associate themselves with the principles therein stated. After full discussion, those who wished to unite would be welcomed; if they needed more time to consider, that could be granted. Those opposed to the principles, who did not "stand united with us in the apostolic order of our church, would then have to be disfellowshipped from the old brethren's church." In other words, those wishing to stay with the continuing German Baptist Church would be expelled, where a majority of a congregation held to the newly restructured Old Order church.[7]

Full organization took place on November 25, 1881, at the Salem, Ohio, congregation, where they adopted the name Old German Baptist Brethren (the name Old German Baptist Church was also used). There followed a sad and turbulent time. Elders sympathetic to the Old Order movement traveled from congregation to congregation, seeking to rally believers to the cause. Rather quickly the Conservatives (German Baptist Brethren) organized deputations to call special council meetings in these congregations; the meetings proceeded to expel venerable elders and other members who sided with the Old German Baptist Brethren.[8] In a few regrettable cases, the Conservatives took legal action to forbid the Old Orders the use of meetinghouses, even where a majority of the congregation sided with the latter. Sometimes locks were changed on doors to deny Old German Baptist Brethren the use of meetinghouses for their worship gatherings. These unfortunate actions bruised feelings, the hurt of which lived on for decades and is still recalled.

Even before the meeting in August 1881, division had taken place. One year previously some 200 Old Order-minded members withdrew from the Beaver Dam congregation in Frederick County, Maryland. Twenty members from the nearby Pipe Creek congregation joined them. By June 1881 these numbers were enlarged by others coming from the Antietam and Middletown Valley congregations. These Old Order Brethren held a meeting at Beaver Dam on Pentecost (June 1881) to organize themselves.

Minutes of this council meeting covered twenty-two points, both positive and negative, on which they wished to stand. These included affirmations of Brethren ordinances and a list of practices that could not be tolerated. In addition to the points at issue mentioned previously and debated repeatedly at the Annual Meetings, they added required education for ministers, life-insurance policies, secret societies, instrumental music, and political activity. Some 500 of these Brethren from Maryland and Pennsylvania then made common cause with the Miami Valley elders in November 1881.[9]

Historians from the Old German Baptist Brethren have made detailed studies of the process by which individuals and groups "took their stand" with the separating Old Order Brethren. (Of course in their self-understanding, they were not leaving but rather continuing the original Brethren church.) Visits from traditionalist elders helped many of them to form new congregations. Substantial numbers came into the Old Order fold in Ohio, Indiana, Maryland, Pennsylvania, Virginia, and West Virginia. Smaller numbers (at times but two or three) came from North Carolina, Tennessee, Kentucky, Arkansas, Michigan, Wisconsin, Illinois, Iowa, Nebraska, Wyoming, Missouri, Kansas, Texas, Idaho, Oregon, and California. Somewhat later, a few members were to be found in yet other states. In fact, this enumeration demonstrates that the division affected virtually all of those areas where Brethren had members.[10]

Estimates of the number of those who became Old German Baptist Brethren range from 3,000 to 5,000. The Brethren journalist Howard Miller was employed by the United States Census for 1880 to enumerate members of the plain churches. He counted about 3,000 Old Order members in his book *Record of the Faithful* (1882). Historian J. M. Kimmel estimated the early membership to be between 4,000 and 5,000. The first applicable United States Census (1890) counted 4,411 members in 135 congregations.[11]

Another consideration is in play: not all who became Old German Baptist Brethren joined in 1881; there was a continual drift their way from the German Baptist Brethren in the last years of the nineteenth century and the early years of the twentieth. The figure of 4,411 members in 1890 dropped to 3,388 in the 1906 census. The decline was probably due to the deaths of the relatively large proportion of aged persons who had joined the Old German Baptist Brethren at the time of division and to the difficulties of maintaining congregations in districts with very few members.

Personal decisions to go with the Old Orders were often painful, necessitating a break with friends and even family members in many cases. Although leaders on all sides called for kindness and decency, it was difficult to avoid bitterness as the divide took place. James Quinter of the Conservatives urged moderation in the columns of periodical he edited. Prior to the division, Henry R. Holsinger and other Progressives were often accused of using drastic language and sarcasm, but none of the parties seemed to be able to stay free from the temptation.

History has shown that further division was not to be alien to the Old German Baptist Brethren themselves, when newer technological innovations such as the radio and the automobile occasioned different judgments as to their admissibility. Here again the question of the final authority of the Annual Meeting came into play. Smaller schisms took place in 1912 and 1915 (the Old Brethren or Salida and Deer Creek Brethren); in 1921 (the Old Order German Baptists or Petitioners); in 1939 (the Old Brethren German Baptists or Sol Lavy Union); in 1947 (Darstites); in 1967 (Christ's Assembly); and 1971 (Olive Grove). In the 1990s a substantial number of Old German Baptist Brethren in California went over to the Dunkard Brethren.[12]

THE PROGRESSIVE BRANCH

The scene was the Annual Meeting of the German Baptist Brethren held at Pentecost, 1867, in Carroll County, Maryland. The assembled Brethren were discussing a query brought from the Middle Pennsylvania District urging the ordination of deacons. As explained by the district delegate who introduced the business item, it had been initiated by Henry R. Holsinger, then a publisher and minister thirty-four years old.

The moderator of the session, the well-respected Henry D. Davy, asked Holsinger to open the discussion. The young minister did so, asserting that the duties of the deacons in Brethren practice seemed "strikingly similar" to those of deacons described in the sixth chapter of Acts. As the seven there described had been set apart by the laying on of hands, he suggested that it would be good for the Brethren to do so as well.

An aged elder from the Miami Valley of Ohio immediately arose to quash the proposal, relating at length that a now-deceased and much-respected elder had long since treated and rejected the matter. According to Holsinger's recollection of the incident, the elder proceeded in this manner until the "audience was thoroughly aroused." Holsinger quickly rose to his feet and asked why the old brethren did not meet his reasoning with scriptural evidence, or lacking in that, did not present the arguments that the deceased elder had used, instead of "giving shame [to him] for attempting to defend the plain reading of the Word of God?"

At that point, Daniel M. Holsinger, Holsinger's father and an elder in central Pennsylvania, spoke out, cautioning his son to speak carefully lest he "ruin his business." Holsinger, later recalling that the reproof "greatly agitated" him, recounted that he sprang to his feet, threw his hands aloft and cried: "Thank God, I am not bound to truckle to the prejudice of any man or set of men, for the sake of my business, as long as I have the use of these two hands wherewith to labor for the support of myself and family."

This outburst raised excitement to a fever pitch, with many in the audience weeping and some shrieking. Holsinger remembered that he had "never before or since witnessed such intensity of feeling in an assemblage." Officers of the conference appointed a committee to wait upon him and secure his promise of a public apology. After extended discussion, Holsinger consented and made a statement toward the end of the session; his friends later told him that his apology was more offensive than the original incident. He commented on the incident in his periodical, *Christian Family*

Companion: "To our argument no one objected...but we were severely rebuked for daring to differ with the opinions of the old brethren upon this point."[13]

The answer of the Annual Meeting to the query from the Middle District of Pennsylvania stated that the Brethren would continue their previous pattern, making "no change at present in the order of installing speakers and deacons in their offices."[14]

This was the first glimpse that many Brethren had of the fiery young Holsinger, who had become a person of interest through his publishing initiatives. Holsinger himself was clear in his own mind about the cause of church problems. It was aged and incompetent leadership, chosen less for ability than for adherence to the church order (in particular, the dress code). He could be scathing in his public criticism of what he perceived as the inability and weakness of the untrained and unpaid ministers and elders. As an editor and publisher he had extensive contact, through correspondence and in person, with a large representation of the church's ministry. (Typically he remarked that those who did not subscribe to his paper could "be safely set down as prejudiced or uninformed.")

Holsinger was quick to extol the personal qualities of the leaders he attacked; they had sterling characters and enjoyed fine reputations. It they had stayed within the laity, as their modest talents suggested to him, he would have only praise instead of criticism. However, as ministers they lacked proficiency in basic skills and were responsible, he found, for the evident shortcomings in the brotherhood. "The state of affairs described...did not contribute much to the prosperity of the church, either numerically or spiritually." Additions to the church came about primarily from Brethren progeny, with few converts from the outside.

Holsinger concluded that the first corrective task was to remove hindrances to church prosperity by sweeping away the "rubbish of tradition." The problem with the Brethren was that they were held back by the dead hand of the past, seeking to perpetuate the rulings of past leaders set out in minutes of the Annual Meetings and refusing to adopt or adapt new methods to move the church forward. Against the weight of traditional custom and usage, Holsinger and those who rallied to his banner placed the appeal to scripture alone.

He also saw clearly that such initiatives would be resisted. As he wrote, "It is no wonder, therefore, that persons filled with church patriotism were greatly concerned for the welfare of the denomination. Neither is it to be wondered at that those who felt that the salvation of the church depended on the maintenance of the 'order' or peculiar costume and habits of the fathers, should be greatly concerned lest the 'landmarks' might be removed."[15]

REACTIONS TO HOLSINGER'S PROPOSALS FOR CHURCH REFORM

Over time Holsinger developed a clear and specific program for church reform. These measures included 1) training for ministers and other leaders at schools of higher education; 2) regular financial support for ministers; 3) Sunday schools for all age levels; 4) revival or "protracted" meetings; 5) evangelism through organized home missions and foreign missions; 6) reform in the method of holding Annual Meetings, including verbatim reports of its transactions; and 7) relaxation of the strict and uniform dress code (garb), while avoiding extravagant fashions.

By opening his periodicals to free discussion of church problems and by his own vigorous championing of reform, Holsinger hoped to persuade others of the merits of innovation. He did not limit himself, however, to reasoned rhetoric and biblical exposition. He also sought to move the church along by the use of satire and what was taken as personal attack. Not surprisingly, this approach met with opposition. Years later, Holsinger mused,

> The controversies were not confined to the church papers, but they were carried up to the district and national conferences, resulting in bitter personalities, envies, and, it is to be feared, hatred, until, sad to say, Christian affection and brotherly love were strangers in the camp of Israel. While we are not to measure [others] by ourselves, yet I doubt whether any member of the Dunker fraternity deprecates more painfully the unkind expressions and bitter denunciations between brethren than did the writer.[16]

In response to criticism that came both officially and unofficially, in 1873 Holsinger sought out another progressive-minded minister, the scholarly James Quinter, and sold his publishing interests to him. As has been seen, the combined publication eventually became *The Gospel Messenger*, the journal of the Conservatives, later Church of the Brethren.[17]

Holsinger entered the lists again in 1878, after several other business ventures, with his church periodical *The Progressive Christian*. By then there were already six papers in the field, all private efforts and all seeking adequate subscriptions from the Brethren, whose membership at this point may have reached some 60,000 adults. Despite his earlier bruising experience, Holsinger's new paper was more avowedly radical than ever. Three years after it was launched, the editor clarified its purpose: "The reader will notice what we say, The Progressive Christian will advocate an onward movement by the use of all lawful and expedient means. We hold it to be our duty to keep pace with the times. And we mean what we say, an onward movement, not a backward movement." In his view, the Brethren were always several decades "behind the times" in adopting new methods.[18]

In his effort to move the church forward rapidly, he escalated the level of attack in the columns of his journal. One of the most notorious examples was the point-by-point comparison made of the central organ of Brethren polity—the Standing Committee—to secret societies, organizations absolutely forbidden to Brethren. The article making this case, evidently written by Holsinger, appeared in the first volume of his organ *The Progressive Christian*.[19]

In 1879 queries came to the Annual Meeting from five different districts complaining about Holsinger's paper and requesting the meeting to prohibit the publishing of such "slanderous and schismatic articles." The Annual Meeting complied, ruling that the "editors of the Progressive Christian [must] make an humble acknowledgment to the Annual Meeting for publishing erroneous statements in regard to church members; charging a part of the church with idolatry; stigmatizing some of its members with terms of reproach; ridiculing some of the peculiar practices of the church, and admitting into the paper inflammatory and schismatic articles[,] some even from expelled members."[20]

The Annual Meeting broadened its reproach to several other papers, concluding with the admonition "That the editors of all our periodicals be required hereafter not to admit into their papers any articles that will assail the doctrine of the church in regard to non-conformity to the world, the personal character of ministers, or any of its peculiar tenets or practices."

As sternly as this was worded, it was toned down somewhat from the original version suggested by the Standing Committee, which had specifically denounced Henry R. Holsinger by name and called for a committee to enforce the ruling. Holsinger defended himself at the conference by charging that preachers were "continually advocating externals to the neglect of the weightier matters of the laws of God." Because an article in his paper calling the dress order "Idolatrous Clothes Religion" had been found particularly offensive, he spoke to the issue of the garb. Holsinger advocated a "happy medium" on dress, opposing all "sinful extremes" of fashion, as well as a prescribed uniform, but permitting a variety of garments that met the standards of plainness and modesty.[21]

HOLSINGER'S CHARACTER AND PERSONALITY

Henry R. Holsinger was clearly one of the most gifted and energetic figures to emerge among the Brethren in the nineteenth century. He was a good example of the largely self-made and aggressive personalities who marked the expansive period of national history following the Civil War. As a promoter, entrepreneur, and outspoken champion of progress he embodied remarkably well the spirit of the times. Clearly dedicated to the church and its advancement, H. R. Holsinger was impatient with the passive, time-bound patterns of the past and eager to spur the church forward with energy and new ideas.

Most characteristic in Holsinger's attitude was his appeal to intelligence. The word itself appears time and again in his writings. There is evident chagrin at the modest educational attainment that characterized, with few exceptions, Brethren ministers of the time. In describing the program for his periodical, *The Christian Family Companion*, and the necessity of removing the "rubbish of tradition," Holsinger wrote, "It was imperative that this dead weight be removed before the light of intelligence could shine upon the sacred page with such brilliancy as to reflect into the hearts of mankind." Already quoted was his complaint about ministers who could not speak or write intelligently.

In introducing his comprehensive history of the Brethren, he first sketched his life as a son and grandson of Brethren ministers and his attachment to Brethren practice. But, he wrote, "In a few things, however, I did not agree with the average membership of that day. For instance, I never could see that education was a dangerous thing, and had a great thirsting for more of it. I always preferred to hear a man preach who knew more than myself, which did not require anything uncommon."[22]

The latter phrase was an uncommon expression of humility and modesty, which were not Holsinger's major attributes. In relating the circumstances and difficulties encountered in writing his history, characteristically entitled *Holsinger's History of the Tunkers and The Brethren Church*, he commented, "It had been intended to include in this work an autobiography of the author, but when it was observed how frequently my name appeared in every department of my work and how intricately my own history is interwoven with that of my people, all inspiration to write on the subject was lost." In other words, Holsinger expressed surprise at how often his name appeared in *his own text*. After presenting three brief paragraphs on the barebones of his life, he concluded, "The remainder of my history, is it not written in the Chronicles of the Church?"[23]

An historian of The Brethren Church gave three reasons for Holsinger's central role in the Progressive movement of nineteenth century Brethren: first, his "aggressive, outspoken, impatient personality;" second, his papers "published as open forums that discussed both sides of leading questions;" and third, his possession of a "keen prophetic sense." Ten years before his death, Holsinger wrote expressing gratitude for having many good friends. "But," he stated, "it is beginning to be a mystery to me how I came to have them, and to hold them, unamiable, outspoken, sarcastic, and austere, as I feel myself to *have been*."[24]

This may be read both as a belated recognition of the effects of his sometimes abrasive personality on others, or, more charitably, as an expression of humility. By all accounts, Holsinger was a man who did not suffer fools gladly and was not hesitant to let others know that he considered them to be such. He was always candid in his expression.

THE BERLIN "TRIAL" OF HOLSINGER

Because of the tensions that led to the withdrawal of the Old Order movement, coupled with pressure from the Progressive faction, many leaders of the Conservative middle pressed for a stiffening of the authority of the Annual Meeting. The formal action taken in 1882 (Article 5) was to define the decisions of the Meeting as mandatory; discussion likened it to a legislature passing laws.

Correspondingly, whereas earlier committees had been sent from the Annual Meeting when requested by local congregations to settle problems they could not resolve by themselves, increasingly it became common practice for the Annual Meeting to send committees to congregations on its own volition when the congregations were perceived to be out of the order prescribed by the central authority. Thus the Annual Meeting also took on executive power.

In the same year (1882) a firmly stated minute decreed that the order of the church should be upheld by stringent church discipline brought against "any member, whether lay member, elder, teacher, deacon or printer, who shall speak, preach, write, or publish anything disrespectful against the doctrine, order, custom, or usages of the general church." It is striking that the answers to queries were increasingly couched in legal language quite different from the tenor of those issued earlier in the century.[25]

A trial of Holsinger was decided upon at the 1881 Brethren Annual Meeting in response to five queries reminiscent of those that came to the 1879 Meeting. Those of 1881 charged him with agitation, disrespect, untruthfulness, and disorder. A committee organized at the Meeting to deal with the queries found that "Holsinger is publishing a paper in which many articles have appeared criticizing the work of annual meeting, and against the order of our church government, as also against our order of observing the gospel principle of non-conformity to the world in wearing apparel."

According to the committee, he had been "again and again admonished by our annual meeting to be more guarded" in his expressions, had failed to do so, and in fact was "continuing his former course with renewed effort." Consequently, they recommended that a committee be sent to his home congregation in Berlin, Pennsylvania, to "wait on him" and "deal with him according to his transgressions." It seems that in this trial the defendant was already pronounced guilty.[26]

The Annual Meeting concurred and named five church leaders to form the committee, failing to indulge Holsinger's plea that at least one of them should be a regular reader of his pages "through which I might expect an intelligent representation of my cause." Members of the committee arrived in Berlin, Pennsylvania, in August 1881 to carry out this appointed task.[27]

Although the Berlin congregation promptly accepted the committee, its work ran at once into a roadblock. Holsinger had employed a public stenographer to take down a verbatim account of the proceedings. The committee objected to this as not in accord with customary church usage. They also objected to the presence of nonmembers of the congregation, although it had been made clear that the latter were not to participate in discussion or vote.

Holsinger insisted on these two points, stenographic record and presence of nonmembers, speaking in an emphatic and definitive tone. He argued that the discussion and decision of the previous Annual Meeting that condemned him and authorized the committee's visit had been open to the public and had been reported widely. The Berlin congregation unitedly backed its elder. After considerable delay, the visiting committee announced that they could not proceed with the hearing under the given circumstances, concluding,

> In view of the above considerations, especially in view of the fact that brother H. R. Holsinger refused to have his case investigated by the Committee in harmony with the consent of our general brotherhood, and inasmuch as brother H. R. Holsinger and the Berlin church assumed all responsibility in the case, therefore we decided: that brother H. R. Holsinger can not be held in fellowship in

> the brotherhood, and all who depart with him shall be held responsible to the action of the next Annual Meeting.

Only one member of the congregation, an aged elder, accepted the verdict, saying, "*Ich gehe mit den Alten*—I go with the old ones."

The committee left after appealing, unsuccessfully, for contributions from the Berlin congregation to help defray their travel expenses of $126. The Berlin members in an immediately held council reaffirmed their support of their elder, finding him innocent of violating any gospel order of the brotherhood and concluding that he had not received a trial on the charges brought against him at the 1881 Annual Meeting. To the end of his days, Holsinger maintained that he had never received a hearing and therefore considered himself still to be a member of the German Baptist Brethren.

AFTERMATH OF THE BERLIN "TRIAL"

A public worship service held that evening in the Disciples' churchhouse announced that the committee had severed all connections between the Berlin congregation and the German Baptist Church and that their council had reorganized itself as the *Brethren's Church*. A reporter in a local newspaper (possibly a member of the congregation) gave several pages of coverage to the visit of the committee under the title "An Ecclesiastical Court Martial" and likened it to the Inquisition.

He described the service of worship as the "first sermon to an independent Progressive Brethren congregation," predicting that future history will conclude that the Progressive Brethren will have drawn to it everything vital among the Brethren and the Old Order "will crumple to dust." According to the reporter, "five fanatics [the committee members] were the blind instruments in the hands of Almighty God, in organizing a demonstration which will grow in numbers day by day...."[28]

Given the tenseness of the situation and such publicity, it is not surprising that emotions were unleashed by the action of the visiting committee. Editor Holsinger, along with a colleague, published in *The Progressive Christian* an important article titled "Progressive Unity—Our Principles Defined." He also printed biting articles, some circulated as pamphlets, on the case. One called "Where is Holsinger?" was written by S. H. Bashor, a noted evangelist. It reviewed the events of the Berlin "trial" and presented Holsinger's defense.

Another called "The Berlin Situation" was written by Howard Miller. It reviewed all of Holsinger's initiatives so bitterly opposed at first but now accepted by the main body of the church; these included weekly periodicals, full reports of Annual Meeting proceedings, schools of higher education, and a hymnal with melodies. Miller saw Holsinger as a pioneer who metaphorically braved the wilderness, accepted the burdens of innovation, and now saw his work preempted by "camp-followers." He asserted, "Divested of all verbiage, the trouble with Henry is that he is now, and always has been, too far ahead of his day and generation."

Miller continued, claiming that it was really pettiness and pride of place that caused Holsinger grief: "But here comes some poor, miserable specimen of conservative mediocrity with his mouth full of bad grammar and his heart full of suspicion that every line in the paper is specifically designed to pull his little self off the picket fence of local supremacy, and something has to be done—for if he were belittled, it would be just the same as destroying religion in the abstract."

Nevertheless, Miller commented, Holsinger persevered in preaching and publishing his paper. "Contributors without the fear of men before their eyes, characterize the committee as a 'blast of one hundred and twenty-six dollars worth of old-orderism,' and the sun has not failed to rise, the wells have not gone dry, and nobody has been whisked away in a blue blaze by the supreme power of Satan." Curiously, despite Miller's extreme rhetoric, he remained with the main body of Conservatives instead of following Holsinger into the new body.[29]

THE 1882 ANNUAL MEETING

With this kind of language bandied about, it is not surprising that many Brethren looked with apprehension to the forthcoming

Annual Meeting scheduled for the vicinity of Milford, Indiana, in late May 1882. Voices warned that if the committee's decision were upheld and Holsinger expelled, many others would depart. Conversely, others predicted that if the decision were overthrown, then there would be a large defection to the Old Orders.

When the issue was broached at the Annual Meeting, several leading Brethren appealed for leniency and delay in taking action to allow time for reconciliation; Holsinger himself held out the prospect of a categorical apology and even pledged to give up his paper. Both actions, however, were made contingent on the rejection of the committee's report. The mood of the delegates, however, was to back up the committee, thereby sealing Holsinger's expulsion.

D. P. Sayler, a weighty and combative elder from Maryland and a staunch advocate of the authority of the Annual Meeting, argued that the committee must be supported. "Their reputation must be maintained and vindicated. During the entire year the doings of that committee have been slandered and reviled....Tracts have been published and put out to injure the reputation of the committee."[30] He and others suggested that following a vote to uphold the committee, the possibility was then open for Holsinger to apologize and be reinstated as a penitent, expelled sinner. The publisher and his supporters could not accept that, for it would (as Holsinger interpreted it) mean willingness "to truckle to the whims of ignorance and superstition to such an extent as to recognize the righteousness of their cause." Apologize "Yes," but accept the committee report, "No."

By a large majority vote the delegates accepted the committee report, thus definitively disfellowshiping Holsinger. His supporters called for a public meeting in a nearby schoolhouse on the following evening, as the first step toward creating a new church body. Before that, however, an *ad hoc* committee sent a communication to the Standing Committee asking for the decision that expelled Holsinger to be reconsidered in the light of the anticipated division in the church.

Using the precedent of the prior rejection of the Old Order petition at the 1881 meeting for not coming through regular procedure (District Meeting), the Standing Committee refused to accept the present petition. Thereupon, the Progressive gathering called for a convention to be held at Ashland, Ohio, in late June to organize a new church. A set of resolutions adopted at Milford concluded with the motto, "The Bible, the whole Bible, and nothing but the Bible."[31]

ORGANIZATION OF THE BRETHREN CHURCH

A large number of Progressive-minded Brethren gathered at the Ashland convention on June 29, 1882. One of their first actions was to adopt a "Declaration of Principles"; its lengthy sentences, too wordy to quote, consciously paralleled the language of the Declaration of Independence, with the role of tyrant occupied by the Annual Meeting. The declaration's language documented the extent of alignment with modern thought that the Progressives had accepted. An historian of the Brethren Church recently summarized the long declaration in this way:

> 1) The gospel of Christ must be the sole rule of faith and practice for the church. 2) In doctrinal matters there should be universal harmony, but on questions of government and customs the church is to observe congregational polity. 3) The Conservatives had departed from the standard of Scripture "in almost every essential feature of gospel liberty and church rule." 4) The Progressives are the "true conservators and perpetuators of the brotherhood and its original doctrines and principles."[32]

The Ashland meeting also made common cause with smaller Brethren bodies who had earlier separated from the German Baptist Brethren over doctrinal or polity issues, such as the Congregational Brethren and the Leedy Brethren.

After waiting for one year to see if the next Annual Meeting of the Conservatives would offer a palm branch of reconciliation and finding none forthcoming, the Brethren Church proceeded to full organization at its first General Convention, held in June 1883 in Dayton, Ohio. Tellingly, it decided at first to avoid yearly conferences to protect the independence of local congregations. It was not until 1892-93 that annual meetings became the norm.[33]

Henry R. Holsinger was named moderator of the Dayton Convention. In his response to this honor he said that just one year previously he had suffered "the deepest stigma or ignomy that it is in the province of a professed Christian body, in this country of religious liberty, to tender to a fellow man." Now he felt very inadequate to the responsibility placed upon him. Holsinger was also elected moderator of the second conference of the Progressives and later itinerated to raise money for Ashland College. He did not continue in a central role, moving to California in 1887 where he became a pastor.[34]

Henry R. Holsinger died in 1905, not long after writing and publishing his most ambitious work, his Brethren history (1901), despite severe health problems that kept him bedfast and unable to speak. He lost much of his investment in the project, as it did not sell that well among the Brethren Church and hardly at all among the German Baptist Brethren, who refused to advertise it.

The end of the turmoil of the early 1880s saw the creation of three separate denominations—the Old German Baptist Brethren, the German Baptist Brethren (later Church of the Brethren), and the Brethren Church. Most analysts agree that the severity of the tensions after 1850 were such that the Old Order split was inevitable. Because the moderate body, the Conservatives or German Baptist Brethren, in a relatively short time accepted all of the innovations for which the Progressives stood, the second division is seen as avoidable. Less abrasiveness by the Progressive leadership and more patience by the Conservative leadership, it is held, could have spared the Brethren another division. The petition of troubled members to the 1882 Annual Meeting had not prevailed—"by all means to labor in love and Christian forbearance to unite the present conflicting elements in the church at large."

It is also noteworthy that the several decades after the traumatic divisions saw the Conservatives, the moderate German Baptist Brethren, achieve tremendous advances in membership and outreach. Without the enervating and longstanding internal struggle attempting to conciliate the Old Order element on the one side and the Progressives on the other, the majority in the middle could direct its energies toward constructive effort. An historian in

Indiana in 1897 expressed this in a harsh way, when he wrote of the church that "having rid itself of its refuse matter, its progress during the last decade and a half, in the way of building up good schools and establishing missions, both home and foreign, erecting homes for the aged and infirm, and general church extension has been far beyond expectations."[35]

The German Baptist Brethren had still before them many serious debates as they sought to balance progress with tradition, Christian liberty with unity in the ranks. It was a difficult task to work out in detail what the 1880 formula had announced, namely to be concurrently conservative and progressive, in the face of a rapidly changing social context.

15

Industrialism and the Brethren

Although the earliest Brethren in Europe came primarily from the artisan class—millers, weavers, metal workers—after their arrival in North America they devoted themselves primarily to agricultural pursuits. The relatively inexpensive land available in the New World proved to be irresistibly attractive to the immigrants, most of whom would have had little chance in their original homes to possess substantial landholdings. There were always some few exceptions to the generalization that Brethren were farmers—one thinks of the Sauer family of printers in the Philadelphia and Baltimore areas—but the great mass of church members were attached to the soil.

In this they were like other members of the plain people—Mennonites, Amish, River Brethren. All of these German sectarian folk understood almost instinctively that they could more successfully and lastingly pursue their nonconformist ways in the comparative isolation of farm communities, at a distance from the distractions and allures of city life. They could best inculcate their religious and moral values within their children in a setting where all members of the family were rooted in the good earth, earning a livelihood by the sweat of their brow, close to nature.

Moreover, the farm economy was best suited to the style of church leadership, the self-supporting "free ministry." Elders were better able to find time for church duties from that base, as compared, for example, to that of a shopkeeper. This did, indeed, place heavy tasks on the shoulders of their wives, often left at home for days and even weeks at a time; these women had to direct family members in farm operations while their husbands visited other congregations or unchurched areas on preaching missions. Ordinarily, election to church office only came relatively late in life when men had established a solid financial base, allowing them to devote more time to the congregation. Brethren felt, and occasionally said, that success in the economic sphere was a qualification for spiritual office.

Shift Away from the Rural Economy

By 1900 the United States had come to the end of the frontier period. The West Coast had been reached decades earlier, and in the meantime great areas of the trans-Mississippi West had been opened for settlement. This had, all too often, come at the expense of the Native Americans, who had been pushed successively across the continent and confined in inhospitable reservations. As we have seen, Brethren entered energetically into the westward movement, with the first settlers on the Pacific slope by 1850. Those Brethren moving west were largely farmers, seeking inexpensive land when the East and Midwest had run out of that commodity.

The nineteenth century saw increasing urbanization in America. In 1790 only three percent of the nation's population lived in cities of 8,000 or more population; by 1860 nearly seventeen percent were urban dwellers. A century later the proportion was reversed—only one in six lived on farms, the rest in towns and cities. The later nineteenth century saw a rapid rise in industrialization, with the advent of huge factories, the concentration of labor needed to work in them, wide use of steam power, and, especially important, the creation of a mass market through the intercontinental linkage of the nation by railroads.

Brethren began a modest movement toward the city in the post Civil War period. There had been earlier footholds in Philadelphia and Baltimore. These were now expanded in such areas as Washington, D.C.; Hagerstown, Maryland; and Chicago, Illinois. In many cases this resulted from the movement of Brethren from rural areas to seek work. In other cases Brethren were imbued with a missionary spirit.[1]

A scene following worship at the Linville Creek congregation near Broadway, Virginia, at the turn of the century. M. R. Zigler, an outstanding church leader in the twentieth century, stands at the front center of the photograph wearing a white hat. *Durnbaugh Collection.*

RAILROADS AND THE BRETHREN

After 1830 the railroad network expanded so rapidly that within a decade their mileage surpassed that of the canals. By mid-century the nation's 9,000 miles of railroad track had overtaken and nearly supplanted transportation of freight by canal boats and wagon teams. The Atlantic coast was connected with the Great Lakes in 1850, reaching Chicago by 1853. Shortly thereafter the Union Pacific Railroad pushed west from Nebraska and the Central Pacific Railroad pushed east from California, spanning prairies and conquering mountain ranges. When the two tracks met at Promontory Point, Utah, on May 10, 1869, and the final, golden spike was driven, the nation had been successfully connected by rails. Within twenty-five more years four more transcontinental lines had been completed.

Two generous acts of Congress (in 1862 and 1864) that granted vast public lands to railroad companies for the purpose made the link economically possible. Standardization of rail widths and car design in 1887 facilitated the interchange of traffic between railways. The fiscal rapaciousness and political corruption of the big business tycoons of the era were finally checked and regulated by the Interstate Commerce Commission of the same year, enacted by the United States Congress.

Brethren were not slow to use the railroads as a means of travel. Whereas earlier ministers rode horseback or on stagecoaches, it became increasingly popular in the nineteenth century for traveling preachers to take the "cars" to travel long distances. A few Brethren, such as John Kline, were even engaged in companies to establish railroads, although the Annual Meeting advised members in 1849 against investing in railroad stocks because of the possible deception involved, a judgment repeated in 1873.

Beginning in 1853, however, Brethren accepted reduced "clergy fares" (ordinarily half of the regular cost) for travelling ministers. The practice, questioned by some, was encouraged by Henry Kurtz in the columns of *The Gospel Visitor* because of the good accomplished by their journeys. After 1863 successive Annual Meetings appointed rail agents to negotiate with companies for special rates.[2] Because of the large numbers (as many as ten to twelve thousand) of Brethren travelling to Annual Meetings in those years, railroad companies offered special inducements to the church. These included reduced rates, chartered cars, special ticket agents, luggage tags, souvenir literature, and even newly constructed spur lines to the rural sites of the conferences. At least two Annual Meetings, that of Bismarck Grove near Lawrence, Kansas (1883) and Burlington Park near Naperville, Illinois (1889) were held on exhibition grounds owned by railroads. It was customary as late as the early twentieth century for Annual Meeting delegates to pass resolutions of gratitude for favors received from these companies.[3]

BRETHREN COLONIZATION AND THE RAILROADS

Of special interest is the Brethren involvement with the transcontinental railroads in the later nineteenth century. Having once pushed their tracks across the western lands, the rail companies needed to use them. They were not connecting population centers in that part of the nation but rather opening up great tracts of unpopulated territories. They were eager to attract settlers to the areas contiguous to their lines; transporting the settlers to the new locations provided business, as did shipping farm produce created there and bringing in needed supplies. Railroad companies established land departments to solicit business from new immigrants and farmers in the East and Midwest who could be convinced to relocate.

Before long a number of railroad agents discovered the potential of the Brethren as clients. They were attracted to the Brethren because of their reputation as excellent farmers with stable families and also because of what they called Brethren "clanishness." They understood that if they could win a number of Brethren to one of their areas, it was almost certain that relatives and other church members would follow. They began to advertise heavily in Brethren-related periodicals and to direct agents to attend Annual Meetings to spread the word about the possibilities of resettlement along their respective lines.

Some of these agents became well known and trusted among the Brethren. They included George L. McDonaugh, who, working for the Sante Fe and Union Pacific lines, settled Brethren families in Kansas, Texas, California, and North Dakota. Max Bass, representing the Great Northern, succeeded in settling Brethren along that line in North Dakota, Montana, and Washington state. Charles W. Mott, working for the Northern Pacific, urged Brethren to settle in Carrington in North Dakota, the Nez Perce area of Idaho, and the Yakima Valley of Washington. A. M. T. Miller was the immigration agent for the Burlington Route; he successfully encouraged Brethren to relocate in Nebraska. Quite often the agents arranged for free lots to be given to the new Brethren colonies on which to erect meetinghouses, occasionally donating the buildings as well.

A common technique was to persuade Brethren ministers to accept free tickets to the regions in question to look over the new land. If they were sufficiently impressed, they would often attract many other Brethren to settle there with them. In some cases, Brethren ministers were placed on retainers by railroad companies to facilitate the recruitment of Brethren settlers. Among the Brethren ministers active in the resettlement efforts and employed at least for a time by the companies were A. B. Peters (Great Northern), M. M. Eshelman (Sante Fe), Samuel Bock (Oregon Short Line), and R. R. Stoner and David Hollinger (Canadian Pacific).

Typical of the tenor of the times were these excerpts from an elaborate pamphlet published and distributed by the Land Department of the Northern Pacific Railway Company (1896). The occasion was the dedication of the new churchhouse at Carrington, North Dakota, and the love feast that followed:

> The fame of the German Baptists, or, as they are perhaps more often called by outsiders, Dunkards, has gone abroad through the land as standing for industry, honesty, good farming, and all that goes to make up a law-abiding, prosperous, moral community, and recognizing this fact the Land Department of the Northern Pacific was naturally desirous of having some of these excellent settlers located along its road. It knew well that the districts in which the brethren were dwelling in the Eastern and Middle States were becoming badly congested, and that it was practically impossible for the farmers now living there to provide farms for their children anywhere near the old homes.
>
> In view of these conditions Mr. W. H. Phipps, the Land Commissioner of the Northern Pacific, addressed a circular letter to the ministers of the German Baptist Church, calling their attention to the advantages offered by Wells and Foster counties in North Dakota as a place of settlement, and, in order that the brethren might settle together, three townships of railroad land were reserved for them, and the promise was made that when fifty fam-

ilies were located upon this land, the Land Department would donate $500 toward the erection of a church building. This offer was followed up personally by Mr. C. W. Mott, the General Emigrating Agent of the Land Department, who visited Indiana and laid the matter before certain ministers of the German Baptist Church....

The men Mott visited formed a committee to visit North Dakota, which led to the sending of a colony. Its members were housed after arrival in the railroad cars in which they had traveled, until they could make other living arrangements. Within two months after their arrival, the churchhouse was erected.[4]

Carrington had been preceded by two years by Cando (a name chosen to express an optimistic spirit), the mother congregation in North Dakota. It was established along the Great Northern line through the efforts of land agent Max Bass. The settlers there, led by A. B. Peters, were also from Indiana and arrived on a specially chartered train bearing 350 passengers, their equipment, and livestock. Each car was provided with a cookstove on which meals were prepared, using foodstuffs taken along or purchased at the frequent stops along the way.

The train was festooned with banners and routed in such a way that it passed through Indiana, Illinois, and Wisconsin during the day. One of the banners read, "From Indiana, to the Rich Free Government Lands in North Dakota, via the Famous Red River Valley, the Bread Basket of America!" followed by the address of the agent. Two more special trains were sent in 1895 and 1896. Already by 1895 there were 145 Brethren families at Cando who were said to have raised over 400,000 bushels of grain.[5]

Agents of the Great Northern were quite aware of the competing efforts of the Northern Pacific. In internal communications they used this threat to justify their practice of paying influential Brethren leaders retainer fees to promote further migration. As the general traffic manager wrote to the president, James J. Hill,

It has been customary each year since this work began, to employ a number of Elders or Prominent Men to visit their people in Illinois, Indiana, and other States during the Winter months for the purpose of inducing further immigration. For the coming year it will be necessary for us to somewhat enlarge this work, as the competition to control the movement of these people is stronger than ever before; strenuous efforts are being made by the Southern and Western Roads to divert them to other sections; the Northern Pacific has also lately actively entered the field.

The amount of the stipends ranged from $300 for A. B. Peters to $25. President Hill was skeptical of the value of this practice, pointing out that those who did not receive money would tend to be critical and those receiving it would feel underpaid, but he did not stop the program.[6]

A report of Max Bass to Great Northern officials in 1902 referred to the Brethren settlement: "Almost universal success crowned the efforts of these first settlers, and their good reports to Eastern friends coupled with judicious advertising caused our work to grow from spring to spring until now." Beginning with the 350 on the chartered train in 1894, the numbers settled in North Dakota from the eastern and central states increased to over 10,000 in 1900, not all, of course, of Brethren background.

An ad placed by Max Bass in *The Gospel Messenger* (1896) made it clear that almost anyone in the East or Midwest was considered a candidate for resettlement. Running under the title "Who Should Go West?" it described ten categories of potential candidates, ranging from those in poor health to those artisans facing too much competition, from young married people just starting in life to parents who wanted to provide their grown children with farms of their own. Indeed, there were few people who did not fall into one of the categories.[7]

Resettlement efforts were often promoted as church extension. Many new congregations were established in areas where previously Brethren had been unknown. "The railroads, though soulless corporations, are being used wonderfully by the Lord for the spread of the church," stated one supporter in an editorial entitled

"Evangelization by Colonization." In fact, almost all of those Brethren congregations still existing west of the Mississippi stem from this period.[8]

The movement did have its critics. They pointed out that the gain of new congregations in the West had to be balanced by the loss of membership from their former congregations. Many of the colonies failed, either because of the disappointment of those persuaded to move by overly optimistic propaganda or because of crop failures due to drought or recurring insect plagues. Settlers, once having torn up their roots in the East, were much more likely to seek even better land elsewhere, making for instability. Some critics asserted that it was primarily the companies that profited from the colonization. Eventually there were sufficient doubts about the process that an Annual Meeting forbade railroad and colonization ads in Brethren periodicals, solicitation at the conferences, and elders linked with the railroads on Standing Committee.[9]

The sharpest attack came from historian and educator Martin G. Brumbaugh, writing in his history of the Brethren. In his view the "rush to what some well-paid agent represents as more favored territory has greatly complexed the work of the church." He lamented the loss of "home traditions, ancestral graves, good schools" and the abandonment of "convenient churches." Those leaving may find larger acreage but this will not offset the disappointment. Most importantly, the loss to the church is great. "New congregations, small in numbers and financially limited as yet, call for assistance, and the older and more stable congregations are obliged to send more help to those than would have been necessary to aid the same members to comfort and prosperity in the home congregations."[10]

Between 1850 and 1889 sixteen churches were initiated on the Pacific coast. Between 1889 and 1918 there were eighty-five congregations started, of which thirty failed. The scholar who made the most careful assessment of the development, Gladdys E. Muir, concluded, "If the reader adds to the declining churches of California the declining churches of the Northwest, and notes in addition the number of new projects, north and south, which failed to develop into permanent church organizations, he will probably question the effectiveness of the colonizing experiments in bringing about permanent growth."[11]

The Language Shift

A largely overlooked aspect of the Brethren shift toward integration into the broader society was dropping the German tongue and adopting the predominant English language. This transition took many years but was well along by the late nineteenth century. When the official name of the denomination was changed in 1908 from German Baptist Brethren to Church of the Brethren, one persuasive argument was that Brethren in general were no longer fairly described by the adjective German.

On the other hand, one indicator of the extended duration of this language shift was that the Brethren published a German-language hymnal (*Eine Sammlung von Psalmen, Lobgesängen, und Geistlichen Liedern*) as late as 1903. Use of the Pennsylvania Dutch language was still common among many Brethren homes in the East well into the twentieth century. To this day occasional services are held in eastern Pennsylvania that feature hymns and preaching in German.

As might be expected, the first trend toward predominant use of the English language occurred in Brethren congregations in urban settings, that is, in Philadelphia and Baltimore. One notable step was the publication of the first English-language hymnal, *The Christian's Duty, Exhibited in a Series of Hymns*, issued in Germantown in 1791. It was followed in 1810 by the first translation of the writings of Alexander Mack, Sr., also in the Philadelphia area.

The shift from German language to English can be followed in the early nineteenth century in the language used in the Annual Meetings. Minutes of the proceedings were distributed solely in German until this period; for many years thereafter they were published both in English and German. The pioneer publisher for the Brethren, German-born Henry Kurtz, was asked to serve as recording secretary for the Meetings in 1837, largely because of his proficiency in both languages. Beginning in 1837, in order to assure wider circulation, he published the minutes in German and English, usually appearing in the same booklet but also separately. As has been seen, he was already experienced in that kind of publication, through his attempt at a bilingual periodical and his publications in both German and English.

One year after Kurtz began *The Gospel Visitor* in 1851, he began publishing a German version called *Der Evangelische Besuch* to serve those Brethren who were still more fluent in German than in English. He described it in the subtitle as a "companion" and "translator" of the English-language monthly; its contents paralleled but were not completely identical with *The Gospel Visitor*. Because of lack of patronage, however, it was discontinued in 1861.

A rival of Kurtz's periodical, *Der Brüderbote*, was published by the German-born L. A. Plate in Lancaster in 1875; with the fifth issue the place of publication was moved to Germantown, where it became in 1876 *The Brethren's Messenger and Brüderbote*, published in both languages. Later that year it moved to Illinois where it lost its identity through merger with *The Brethren at Work*. Another *Brüderbote* was published in Grundy Center, Iowa, from 1880 to 1892. Even Henry R. Holsinger, the advocate of everything progressive that promised to advance church life, introduced German lessons in his paper for young people, *The Pious Youth* (1871-72).[12]

BILINGUAL WORSHIP AND MUSIC

Another way to track the language shift is to study the language used in worship and hymnals.[13] Through much of the nineteenth century it was common for Brethren hymnals to be issued both in German and English versions, ordinarily bound together. The two most used were *Die Kleine Liedersammlung* (1826ff.) and *The Choice Selection of Hymns* (1830ff.). Small in format, they were convenient to carry; they ran through at least fifteen editions before being stereotyped for extensive republication. Early bound volumes placed the German hymnbook first as that language was still predominant; later on the order was reversed. The last edition of *Die Kleine Liedersammlung* was issued by the Old German Baptist Brethren in 1885.

The first hymnal authorized by the Annual Meeting of the Brethren appeared in 1867—*The Brethren's Hymn Book: A Collection of Psalms, Hymns, and Spiritual Songs; Suited to the Various Kinds of Christian Worship; And especially Designed for, and adapted to, the Fraternity of the Brethren*; its primary compiler was James Quinter.

The only major objection to the hymnal upon publication was that it lacked German hymns. A query brought to the 1868 Annual Meeting reasoned,

> Whereas, there is a difficulty in introducing the new hymn-book among the brethren where the German language is yet used, as there are none that contain both English and German hymns, would it not therefore be advisable to revise the German hymn-book [*Die Kleine Liedersammlung*], and make a small collection of the choicest German hymns, and combine them with the English book [*The Brethren's Hymnbook*], and thus have some books containing both English and German hymns, to meet the wants of our German members and avoid the necessity of having more than one book in the church?[14]

The Meeting agreed and appointed a committee headed by Henry Kurtz to select 200 German hymns. The addition appeared in 1870 as the *Neue Sammlung von Psalmen, Lobgesängen und Geistlichen Liedern*; it actually included 303 hymns. It was thereafter available as a separate volume or bound with the 1867 hymnbook.

The German-speaking Brethren in eastern Pennsylvania were not completely satisfied with the *Neue Sammlung* and issued their own, more comprehensive German hymnals in 1874 and 1879, known as the "Lancaster hymnbooks." In 1891 the Annual Meeting authorized the compilation of yet another German-language hymnal, the committee for which was to include representatives from eastern Pennsylvania. This was *Eine Sammlung von Psalmen, Lobgesängen, und Geistlichen Liedern* and appeared in 1893. It was a revision of this that was published in 1903 as the last German-language Brethren hymnal.

The story of repeated demands for German-language hymnals documents the need for both languages in the worship services of the Brethren throughout much of the nineteenth century. Because Brethren preserved the pattern of multiple ministerial leadership under the free (self-supported) minister system, it was long customary for some ministers to preach in German and some in

English. Some indeed were bilingual but usually favored one language over the other for preaching, but it was not unknown for a sermon in English to be at least summarized in German (or vice versa) by the same speaker.

According to elder Philip Boyle in Maryland, speaking of ministers in 1848, "In travelling and preaching there are in general two together; and very frequently one speaks in German, and the other in the English language, to the same congregation." A query, evidently from German speakers, addressed to the 1841 Annual Meeting, asked whether it was proper for ministers "to speak both German and English in meetings" where the great majority of the church were German. The Solomonic answer was, "Considered, that it is right, and our duty, to preach the gospel to every nation, as far as we are able, yet so that in such a case not too much time ought to be taken up in English." [15]

One of the most vivid and accurate accounts of Brethren worship in mid-century came from the pen of a visiting German journalist, Moritz Busch, mentioned earlier for his respect for Peter Nead. While visiting the Dayton, Ohio, area in 1851 he seized the opportunity to attend a Brethren love feast held at the Lower Stillwater congregation and led by Elder Nead. The vantage point of the reporter was directly across from the trestle table behind which sat some twenty ministers, "mostly elderly men in the sectarian garb and adorned with long Noah-beards."

First came singing in German and English; the singing of English in more parts indicated to the visitor that the language shift was well advanced. Following reading of a scripture in German came the first sermon in English. "He must have spoken about a half-hour in this fashion, when his sermon took a characteristic turn as he suddenly abandoned the lame in the temple at Jerusalem, forgot his English, and in the purest Pennsylvania Dutch complained about the pain in his lungs: 'I could talk much longer on this text, but my lungs won't stand it. Oh, my lungs! (*Mer könnt noch viel schwätze über diesen Text, aber meine Lungs wolln's net stände. Ach, meine Lungs!*) But however...' and then the flow of words poured forth well over another quarter of an hour without period or pause, in its rise and fall similar to that in which we sing the collect [in German churches]."

This was followed by another speaker in German who basically repeated the concepts of his predecessor. Busch continues: "Quite a different impression was made by the following sermon of a preacher who came to the meeting from Southern Ohio. He had a long lean figure with noble, prophet-like features....The apt development of the sermon which he presented in excellent English could have been heard with success by a congregation of intellectuals." After prayer with all kneeling, the service continued:

> Then followed several more preachers who spoke with more or less talent, mostly in English, some in German, almost all disturbed by the screaming of infants and the noise of the fire which cooked their noonday meal and, therefore, seemed to have the right to speak a word along with them. All of them concluded their remarks with the naive sentence that if they had not brought anything to the benefit and edification of the brotherhood, they at least hoped that they had not said anything harmful.

The visiting journalist engaged in a spirited discussion with some of the Dunkers present about distinctive Brethren practices such as feetwashing and the holy kiss. Busch commented, "The ensuing debate, during which my opponents continually had their fingers in their pocket Bibles and were at all times ready to construct a barricade against my objections with an appropriate dictum from the gospels or epistles, was carried out primarily in English, as the majority of the participants understood only *Deutsch*, that is Pennsylvania Dutch, but not German as the Germans speak it." Sometime later, Busch was able to accept an urgent invitation to visit Elder Nead, whom he found to have not only a "childlike, loving spirit" but also "much more information on theological matters" than anticipated.[16]

During the tensions leading to the fateful three-way split in the early 1880s members of the Progressive element were vocally critical of the halting grammar and incorrect speech of many of the free ministers. It is likely that the root of much of the inadequacy in oral and written communication of these men stemmed from the fact that their mother tongue was German; they were never completely at home in the English language.

Abraham Harley Cassel, the premier historian among the Brethren in the late nineteenth century, was always sensitive to the faults in his English prose, and often asked for his writings to be vetted for mistakes before publication. A minority of letters in his extensive preserved correspondence files were written to him in the German language.

The Introduction of Insurance Among the Brethren

Another bellwether in the movement of Brethren into the larger society during the industrial period was the introduction of insurance, first for the protection of property and later for life. For much of Brethren history, it was thought wrong to purchase insurance policies. This was for two reasons: first, it seemed to demonstrate a lack of faith in God's providential care; second, Brethren were expected to care for their own when tragedy struck through the active practice of mutual aid.[17]

Always in the forefront of change, the Philadelphia congregation insured its meetinghouse as early as 1829. A query to the Annual Meeting of 1847 asked whether members could insure their property; the response was equivocal, stating that "we cannot advise Brethren to do so, neither could we forbid its being done, in a mutual way." Similar answers were given to nine other appeals for guidance on fire, livestock, property, and life insurance between the 1847 response and 1875.[18]

A new plateau was reached four years later when the Meeting was asked whether it would be "considered right and according to the Gospel and the old-established order of the Brethren" for members to organize a mutual fire insurance company. The judgment of the conference was that it was permissible so long as members would not be required to "compromise any of our principles."[19]

Since that decision, a number of Brethren have been active in organizing and operating mutual insurance companies, especially in Pennsylvania, Indiana, and Kansas. In 1908 the Brethren Mutual Aid Society of Northeast Kansas became the Mutual Aid

Association of the Church of the Brethren; originally a district endeavor begun in 1885, it has extended its services to all members of the denomination from its base near Abilene, Kansas. Securing permission from the Annual Meeting to buy life insurance policies proved more difficult. Beginning in 1864 numerous queries on the issue were uniformly answered negatively. In fact, decisions of the Meetings of 1873, 1882, and 1886 required new members of the church to terminate life insurance policies. On the other side, the answer to a query asking why insurance on property is permitted but denied on lives frankly states, "Whereas there are different views on the subject of insurance, therefore resolved that we defer this query indefinitely." Attempts to settle the issue in 1896, 1902 and 1903 failed; it was not until 1920 that the Annual Conference permitted the purchase of life insurance policies "where the taking of such policies violates no Gospel principle."[20]

CHURCH ORGANIZATION

One way in which to observe the impact of the broader society is to analyze the forms of organization developed within the church in the late nineteenth century. Many of the initiatives of the period closely reflect the ways in which the secular world went about its business. This, of course, was one of the reasons why these developments were found so objectionable by the traditionalist or Old Order element in the church.

When academies and colleges were instituted on behalf of the Brethren, the usual pattern was to organize them on a joint-stock basis. Solicitors raised money for the ventures by selling shares; holders of the shares were authorized to vote at stated times on personnel and educational policies. The Brethren's Normal School (after 1896 known as Juniata College) was the first educational effort to endure. It was organized in 1876 as a joint-stock company by Henry B. Brumbaugh, his brother John B. Brumbaugh, and his cousin Dr. Andrew B. Brumbaugh. These three men, along with three other trustees, were authorized to solicit funds by selling stocks at $100 per share to "brethren and others friendly to the cause." By March 1878 they had raised $3,000; this enabled them in

1879 to build Founders Hall on a block of donated lots in West Huntingdon. The construction allowed the rapidly growing school to move from temporary accommodations. The College ceased its operations as a joint-stock operation in 1908.[21]

Comparable arrangements were often followed when church-related papers were inaugurated. The rash of mergers among Brethren publication companies in the later nineteenth century was reminiscent of the fervid activities in the larger business world. Publishers sought to enhance their positions by consolidation through buying out competitors, thus securing more subscribers. Although they always spoke of serving the church, self-interest was not absent in these sometimes protracted negotiations.

Following the three-way division of 1881-83 one can observe a flowering of boards and agencies among the German Baptist Brethren (later Church of the Brethren), in part sponsored by specific districts and increasingly by the denomination itself. An almost bewildering number of rapidly changing organizational schemes were created to care for the internal needs of the church and for outreach to those beyond its borders.

The typical pattern that emerged at this time was the creation of a board (often incorporated or chartered), members of which met at regular intervals to set policies; it employed a few partially supported or fully supported staff persons to carry on its work. By the early decades of the twentieth century, the board organization had become common, so much so that it was found necessary to work out some way to coordinate their work. The final step in this process was the creation in 1946 of a centralized and unified board, the General Brotherhood Board of the Church of the Brethren.[22]

The evolution (and subsequent intertwining with other concerns) of an agency sponsoring the printing and dissemination of tracts is a case in point. (The idea of reaching out to a broader public through tracts is in itself a sign of the change in Brethren self-understanding; earlier church leaders would have found this means inappropriate for a nonconformist body.) In 1876 three Brethren active in publishing—J. H. Moore, J. T. Meyers, and M. M. Eshelman—organized the Gospel Tract Association to publish and distribute books, pamphlets, and tracts "ably defending the doctrine and practice of the Brethren." They sought donations to enable distribution of tracts in "the waste places and wherever they will be read by those who are seeking the Truth." This became the Brethren's Book and Tract Work in 1888. In turn this was merged in 1893 with the General Church Erection and Missionary Committee (authorized by Annual Meeting in 1884) to form the General Missionary and Tract Committee. This body took over the Brethren's Publishing Company, a privately owned business that published *The Gospel Messenger* after 1883. The printing establishment became known as the Brethren Publishing House; it issued a wide variety of papers, quarterlies, tracts, and books, and also did general job printing.

The substantial profits realized went into the work of the General Missionary and Tract Committee, renamed the General Mission Board in 1908. It was responsible for both home and foreign missions, the preparation and distribution of all authorized printed materials, and even relief aid to refugees after World War I. The General Mission Board became the most powerful agency within the denomination, developing a small but efficient staff and a large endowment.

THE LIFE AND WORK OF D. L. MILLER

The transfer of the assets of the Brethren's Publishing Company to the church in 1897 was primarily the work of Daniel Long Miller, known universally as D. L. Miller. (Almost all Brethren leaders during this period were known by their initials; this was the custom among businessmen of the day and reflects, in itself, an accommodation to the larger society.) His life and achievements as a self-made man are representative of changes in the church during this era.

Miller was born in 1841 near Hagerstown, Maryland, in the basement of a grist mill owned by his father, a staunch lay member of the Brethren. As Daniel grew up he assisted in the mill and on the family farm; although he received only a few months of winter schooling, he read and studied avidly, seeking to improve himself. Before his twentieth birthday he migrated to Ogle County, Illinois, where he built up a prosperous grocery business in Polo.

Because of his interest in and support of higher education, he became a major investor in the new Mount Morris College, becoming in 1879 a part owner and business manager. Later he served as president and longtime head of the board of trustees. After 1882 he joined in publishing *The Brethren at Work*; Miller was instrumental in merging the journal with eastern papers to form *The Gospel Messenger* in the next year. He served first as managing editor, and after the death of James Quinter, as editor-in-chief of the combined periodicals from 1891 until his death.

During this period D. L. Miller began a series of extensive, world-wide travels, visiting every continent between 1883 and 1906. He combined travel, private study in foreign universities, and groundwork for Brethren foreign missions on these trips, the expenses for which he paid personally. His vivid word-pictures from abroad were eagerly read in *The Gospel Messenger* and were instrumental not only in tripling its circulation but also in broadening the horizons of many Brethren.

The articles, collected in well-illustrated and handsomely bound book form, were distributed widely in many printings. Miller showed lantern slides made from his photographs across the brotherhood to illustrate the necessity for mission programs; his standing as a devoted church leader tended to mute opposition to new media as he itinerated among the Brethren congregations.[23]

BRETHREN ENTREPRENEURS

Some members of the Dunker family during this era were known as inventors and manufacturers. Daniel Houser, originally from Pennsylvania, invented a combined harvester-thresher in 1876 that he produced commercially in California; the huge combine was pulled by as many as thirty-six horses. The teacher-artist-orphanage director David Emmert of Huntingdon, Pennsylvania, offhandedly invented a note tablet upon which a successful business was based. Samuel Fahrney of Maryland perfected an early reaper, some ideas from which aided Cyrus McCormick whose patent brought him immense wealth. Fahrney also invented practical devices such as a garlic press, washing machine, sausage grinder, and molasses faucet.[24]

Peter Fahrney (1767-1837) was known as the "walking doctor" in Washington County, Maryland; a grandson, "Dr." Peter Fahrney (1840-1905), became a millionaire in Chicago with his proprietary (patent) medicines such as Dr. Peter's Blood Cleanser or Panacea. From *The Surprise*, one of Fahrney's many publications. *Durnbaugh Collection.*

Another member of the Fahrney family, Dr. Peter Fahrney, made a fortune in proprietary medicines. A grandson of the famed "walking doctor" Peter Fahrney of Maryland (from whom he inherited his formulas), Fahrney moved from Pennsylvania to Illinois in 1865 and to Chicago in 1869. He developed there a business with an international clientele producing and distributing patent medicines, of which the best known was Dr. Peter's Blood Cleanser or Panacea.

He rebounded from the loss of his laboratory in the great Chicago fire of October 1871, shipping his product again within a few weeks. Fahrney advertised widely in Brethren periodicals, often printing testimonials from Brethren leaders; he also published his own. A typical communication reads, "Having been personally and intimately acquainted with Dr. P. Fahrney for some years, I cheerfully recommend him as a worthy, careful, conscientious and responsible business man. Those who may deal with the Doctor will find him clever and accommodating—a gentleman who will attend to their wishes punctually and on sound business principles....And the Vitalizer advertised is, beyond a doubt, an article of great merit. J. S. Beer."[25]

Peter Fahrney died in 1905 a multi-millionaire, reputedly the wealthiest member of the Brethren. Soon after arriving in Illinois, he had written an article for the *Christian Family Companion* entitled "Dying Rich"; it begins, "Of all the cases of human folly which men are addicted to, few are more common than the desire to hoard up wealth, that they may die rich." It continues, "Think of these selfish, narrow-minded, close-fisted souls at the bar of God, giving an account of their stewardship. They spent their life in hoarding up wealth, and had the honor of dying rich, and now the *Master* [is] auditing their accounts!" And "Better, infinitely better, to lay out their wealth for the glory of God, the advancement of Christ's kingdom, feeding the poor, clothing the naked, and ameliorating the condition of mankind, than hoard it up...."

Perhaps Fahrney recalled these earlier sentiments when, in his last business transaction, he donated his summer home (known as San Mar) in Washington County, Maryland, to the church for use as a home for the aged—now known as the Fahrney-Keedy Memorial Home. Included on the estate was the original office used by his grandfather, which has been preserved. Fahrney's business was inherited by three sons. It continued in Chicago under the name Dr. Peter Fahrney & Sons Co. until 1974 when it was bought by another firm and moved to New York City.[26]

Chicago was also the base of operations for the clothing business of B. A. Hadsell, who specialized in creating and distributing plain dress. Like Fahrney, he advertised widely in Brethren and other periodicals and sold his clothing (in the various styles prescribed by the plain sects) across the nation. Hadsell and Fahrney were instrumental in beginning the first Brethren congregation in Chicago. In the 1880s and 1890s Hadsell was involved in colonization schemes in New Mexico and California.[27] These and others possessed creativity, ingenuity, and business skills. None, however, had such long-lasting success as did the Studebaker brothers of wagon-making and automobile fame and Harry C. Stutz, creator of modern racing and touring automobiles.[28]

STUDEBAKERS AND STUTZ

John Clement Studebaker posted as his motto in his blacksmith shop near Ashland, Ohio, "Owe no man anything but to love one another." He had built a Conestoga-style wagon in Pennsylvania to carry his family to the Ohio farm home in 1835. In 1851 the family migrated farther west to South Bend, Indiana, where his sons Henry and Clement Studebaker began a blacksmith's shop in 1852, with a capital of sixty-eight dollars (forty of which was borrowed from Henry's wife) and two sets of blacksmith's tools. According to family tradition the profits for their first day of work amounted to twenty-five cents. They branched out by constructing wagons, similar to the one their father had built earlier; later on they were joined in this expanding enterprise by their brothers John Mohler, Peter, and Jacob.

John Mohler Studebaker had sought his fortune in the California gold rush, making his way on one of three wagons the brothers made in their first year. He sent back information to his wagon-making brothers on the specifications needed for success on the western trails which they incorporated into their designs. As it turned out, he made his fortune on the West Coast not by panning for gold but rather by using his skills to make desperately needed wheelbarrows for the miners. On his return he had $8,000 to invest in the family business.

In 1868 the Studebaker Brothers Manufacturing Company came into existence with a capital of $75,000. By 1874 annual sales had reached $1,000,000 and by 1878 the Studebaker brothers were considered to be the leading wagon manufacturers in the world. Their wagons were honored at the international exposition in Paris in 1878, attracting the attention of clients such as the Sultan of Zanzibar, who ordered two of their best wagons in 1880. Well known for using high-quality materials and building techniques,

THE STUDEBAKER — Is the Greatest Wagon of the Century.

...CONSTRUCTION...

AXLES, Indiana Black Hickory, straight grained.
SKEINS, Cast or Steel, take in more axle wood than others.
SPOKES, Slope Shouldered, Indiana White Oak.
HUBS, Patent, Oil Mountain Black Birch, are check proof.
TIRES, Patent Round Edge, Welded on.
GEARS, Soaked in Boiling Oil, Moisture Proof.
PAINTING, only Best Oils, handsome finish.

Hitch to a "**Studebaker**" and

SAVE YOUR TEAM, REPAIRS, TIME, MONEY, PATIENCE.

☞Every Wagon guaranteed. Every promise made good. If not on sale in your town, write direct to

Studebaker Bros. Mfg. Co.,
South Bend, Indiana.

Of all Brethen entrepreneurs of the late nineteenth century, the Studebaker brothers were the most successful. They became famous for their line of sturdy wagons and then moved into the production of automobiles and trucks in their factory at South Bend, Indiana. *BHLA Collection.*

the Studebakers prospered by following another of their father's mottoes: "Always give a little bit more than you promise." Giving more than expected pleased customers, but giving too much more harmed profits.

Studebaker wagons became mainstays of the American westward migration. A branch office flourished at St. Joseph, Missouri, the staging ground for the wagon trains heading west, directed by Peter Studebaker. When he entered the company as a salesman, he and his brother Clement drew up a unique agreement. "I, Peter Studebaker, agree to sell all the wagons my brother Clem can make. [Signed] Peter Studebaker." "I agree to make all he can sell." [Signed] Clem Studebaker."

When the United States military bought Studebaker wagons in quantities as part of their war against the Mormons (the Utah War) in 1857-58, Henry Studebaker perceived an ethical conflict. Mormons had bought the same type of wagons for their trek to Utah. He did not want to be in the position of supplying material for a war. As an historian comments, "A good Dunkard could not help to arm one side, much less both." The upshot was that he resigned from the firm, with John Mohler Studebaker taking his place. The father John C. Studebaker refused to let the youngest son,

Jacob, enlist in the Union army during the Civil War, but Studebaker wagons were used in it to transport army goods.

Although not the first to shift from the wagon to the "horseless carriage," when the Studebaker company entered the automobile market with an electrically driven vehicle in 1902 it was a success. This was also the case when they moved two years later into manufacturing gasoline-powered cars and trucks. By the 1920s the Studebaker company had established itself as one of the leaders of the hotly competitive automobile industry. It garnered a reputation for fine workmanship, sturdiness, integrity, and innovative design; a loyal work force, often employed over several generations, and a generally adept management kept the Studebaker brand viable until the car company closed its doors in 1966.[29]

Harry Clayton Stutz grew up in the German Baptist congregation at Donnels Creek, near Dayton, Ohio; he became a member at the age of fifteen. His inventive nature was manifested early on; at the age of ten he attempted to construct a bicycle, and four years later he successfully built a machine to hull beans. While working as a young man in a machine shop, he invented an efficient gasoline engine that enjoyed good sales. It was at this juncture that he became interested in automobiles. He built his first model from old agricultural parts in 1898 and by 1902 had sold several.

His first real success connected with automobiles was his creation of rear-axle-mounted transmissions, which brought him employment in Indianapolis, Indiana, at that time a center of car manufacturing. After working for several different companies for short periods, he won distinction as the designer of an underslung touring car known as the American Car. The real breakthrough, however, came at the first Indianapolis endurance race on Memorial Day, 1911. A car designed by Stutz for the Marmon Company won the race and another, running under his own name, became known as the "car that made good in a day" because of its durability and reliability. It had been constructed in the five weeks prior to the race.

With outside financial backing, Stutz organized several automobile-related companies, finally emerging in 1916 with the Stutz Motor Car Company with himself as president. It was this flourishing enterprise that made the name Stutz synonymous with fine sporting cars. The Stutz Bearcat (first produced in 1912) was called by an authority the "most popular American sports car of that day." Pictures of it are often used to illustrate histories of the period. This success is the more striking when the intense competition of the era is considered. During this period more than 280 different makes of cars and trucks were made in the state of Indiana alone, and more than fifty in Indianapolis.

In 1919 Stutz sold his interest in the car company to the steel magnate Charles M. Schwab. The company continued until 1936 but declined in sales and profits. Stutz created another company, the HCS Motor Car Company, which was active from 1920 to 1926. It specialized in small cars and taxicabs. He then shifted his attention to other matters, including engines for airplanes, but died suddenly in 1930.[30]

The Studebaker brothers and Stutz (and their biographers) credited their success in great part to the sturdy values of hard work, honesty, and integrity implanted by their early home and church training. It must also be reported, on the other hand, that as their ingenuity and hard work brought them high social status and wealth, they tended to transfer their denominational allegiances to more fashionable churches, except for Henry Studebaker who resigned from the family firm. The strict ethic of the conservative Dunkers had instilled useful moral traits, but the church discipline of the time demanded what increasingly seemed to be untenable constraints.

Just as Brethren raised their sights from their plow handles to move into industrial activities, they also started looking farther afield in their religious objectives. Increasingly they reached out to areas in which Brethren had never flourished—the cities—and then to far-flung foreign missions.

16

Home and Foreign Mission

According to historian Kenneth Scott Latourette, the nineteenth century was the "Great Century of Missions." The century, for this purpose, begins in 1792 with the Baptist shoemaker William Carey who caught a fervent vision of taking the gospel to distant places. He had been inspired by the sacrificial work of Moravian Brethren missionaries on several continents and by the overseas exploits of British explorers. Although discouraged by the predestinarian views of his fellow Calvinists (who assured him that God alone would take care of any mission activity needed), he chose as his motto, "Expect great things from God; attempt great things for God."

This Carey effected as he went to India in 1793, where he developed against great adversity a full-orbed mission program of evangelism, education, medicine, and publishing. It was also Carey who called for a world conference on missions, which he thought could best be based on the tip of South Africa and held in 1810. Although this never came to pass, exactly one hundred years later the great Edinburgh missions conference marked the beginning of the modern ecumenical movement.[1]

AMERICAN MISSION SOCIETIES

Many attempts, with varying degrees of success, had been made to bring Christianity to the Native American population in the colonial period. It was, however, in the first decades of the 19th century that American mission societies as such were first organized. The first to be organized was the Connecticut Missionary Society, formed in 1798 as an agency "to christianize the Heathen in North America, and to support and promote Christian knowledge in the new settlements, within the United States." A comparable society was founded in Massachusetts. These efforts culminated in 1826 with the organization of the American Home Missionary Society, whose agents were prominent in the western territories as evangelists and church promoters, and also as educators, civic leaders, and promoters of eastern culture.[2]

The early years of the nineteenth century were also a fertile time for foreign missions in North America. By mid-century a number of mission societies, either interdenominational or denominational, had been created. The movement was sparked by a revival within the student body of Williams College in Massachusetts; while sheltering from a summer rainstorm in 1806 (the "Haystack Prayer Meeting"), Samuel Mills, Jr., and college friends committed themselves to take the Gospels to foreign lands. Mills went with some of his prayer partners to Andover Theological Seminary where their determination deepened.

They inspired the founding in 1810 of the American Board of Commissioners for Foreign Mission, with support derived from Congregationalists, Presbyterians, and Reformed. Within two years the Board sent the first five American missionaries to India and the Far East. Poor health prevented Mills himself from going, so he devoted himself to investigating the needs for missionaries on the western frontier of the United States. His persuasive reports helped to lead to the establishment after his death in 1818 of the American Home Mission Society, mentioned above.

Among the first New Englanders sent to Asia in 1812 by the American Board were Adoniram Judson, Anne Judson (his wife), and Luther Rice. On shipboard as they studied the Bible they became convinced of the necessity of adult baptism. This conviction estranged them from the sending agency but led to the creation in 1814 of a comparable organization, the General Convention of the Baptist Denomination in the United States for Foreign Missions (later known simply as the Baptist Mission Board). The Judsons went to Burma, where they established a mission despite tremendous obstacles. Reports of their struggles did much to popularize the sentiment for foreign missions in the United States. Luther Rice soon returned home from India and through his American travels stirred up further support for the mission enterprise. The American Board was conceived and originated as an interdenominational body, but the mainstream churches soon were convinced that missions belonged squarely within the responsibility of each denomination. By mid-century Baptist, Congregational, Episcopal, Disciples, Lutheran, Methodist, Presbyterian, and Reformed churches all had mission agencies actively at work, sending workers across North America and across the seas.

BRETHREN SENTIMENT FOR AND AGAINST MISSIONS

By the early twentieth century, the General Mission Board of the Church of the Brethren had an endowment of $1,000,000, an efficient staff, and supported Brethren missionaries in India, China, Scandinavia, and France. At the urging of missionary to India Wilbur B. Stover, foreign missions was accepted as the "great first-work of the church." A well-illustrated journal, *The Brethren's Missionary Visitor* (begun in 1894), brought reports from the mission fields and appeals for donations to Brethren homes. Missionary circles in congregations were well attended and active, as were missionary bands on the campuses of colleges related to the Church of the Brethren. There is no question that foreign missions, and to a lesser extent, home missions, had captured the hearts of the Brethren.[3]

In the face of this enthusiasm, it was hard for mission advocates to explain the lack of activity or interest among the Brethren through much of the nineteenth century, to say nothing of the active critique of those few advocates of missions who had come forward. Apologists tended to take one of two lines. One was to state that the Brethren had indeed always been missionary minded, as they pressed for converts in Europe and in colonial America, and then as they spread across the North American continent.

Otho Winger, a college president and mission board chairman, wrote in his survey of Brethren history,

> The history of the Church of the Brethren in Germany
> shows that there was a good missionary spirit existing
> there. Many of the leaders were active in preaching the
> Gospel and endured much persecution in doing so. The colo-
> nial church was also zealous in witnessing to the truth as she
> had received it....[Referring to the 19th century] Was the
> church a missionary church in those days? Most assuredly it
> was. A study of the lives of some of these pioneers like Jacob
> Miller, George Wolfe, John Metzger, James Quinter, Enoch
> Eby and others will show that they possessed the true mission-
> ary spirit. The story of their life and work reads like a romance,
> so full of activity, interest, and wonderful results....It is true that
> they did not organize a foreign missionary society, but their
> hands were full of the work just before them....Had the main
> body of the church manifested the zeal of some of the leaders,
> the church membership today should have been much larger.[4]

Another approach was to portray the nineteenth century as a
"dark ages" when the church backslid from its aggressive and progressive beginnings because of the frontier situation, suspicion of
higher education, and over emphasis upon the traditional order in
dress and church polity. As John S. Flory put it, the church "lost its
breadth of vision," and "lost the cultural atmosphere that formerly
surrounded it." The church had been "plebianized and rusticated
and permeated with the spirit of the frontier and the farm." Starting
with the reform program of Henry Kurtz and James Quinter in *The
Gospel Visitor* in 1851, the inception of colleges and Sunday schools,
the establishment of publishing houses, and better training for ministers, the denomination was seen to be regaining the leading position it had once enjoyed.[5]

The historian of the foreign mission effort, Galen B. Royer,
wrote during the bicentennial year,

> What if the first settlers of the Brethren did not reach out
> in a mission work as does the church today? This is by no
> means an argument that they were anti-missionary in
> heart and life. They were few in number, limited in

means, and confronting a big problem of occupation. Theirs was the formidable task right at their own door, and it is no wonder that there was no special effort in behalf of lands beyond them....

Why the church should degenerate from such high ideals and purposes as clearly seen in educational and religious activities of the first century of great progress into one of greater anti-missionary and anti-educational sentiments, is a problem perhaps no one can solve. Let the mantle of charity and not harsh judgment be spread over this period, for during these decades here and there was a member sensitive to the mute appeal of the unsaved about him, and the obligation of the Commander of the church militant upon him to ring out the clarion note of warning to those who did not go farther than their own doors.[6]

The fact remains that a substantial and, for many years, controlling element within the Brethren during the nineteenth century understood organized mission activity to be false to the gospel. Their objections were both theological and practical. In the first place, they understood that the "Great Commission" of Jesus Christ (Matt. 28:19-20) to go into all the world had been directed at the apostles, who carried it out! That the gospel message was in fact carried everywhere, they contended, was demonstrated by the Pauline words, "But I say, 'Have they not heard? Yes, verily; their sound went into all the earth, and their words unto the ends of the world'" (Rom. 10:18). Inasmuch as the apostles carried out the command of Christ, it was no longer incumbent on later Christians.

The second objection dealt with the implications of an organization carrying out missions; opponents foresaw support for missionaries as an opening wedge for salaries for ministers, collections for missions as a move toward centralization of the church, traveling secretaries as forerunners of a church bureaucracy. If this approach were to be accepted, the Brethren would soon be like the popular churches. With the hindsight of history, it must be admitted that their suspicions were warranted. The developments they feared and opposed all came to pass. The Old Order party, as long as they remained in the brotherhood, were able to block most organized mission activity. After the separation they continued to hold an anti-mission posture in the sense of separate organization.[7]

GROWTH IN MISSION CONCERN

Growth in the concern for mission outreach may be documented in articles in the Brethren-related periodicals but is especially clear in the queries that came before Annual Meeting. One of the first appeared in 1852: "Whether the commission of our Lord and Savior Jesus Christ (Matt. 28:19-20; Mark 16:15) does not require the Church to send brethren to preach the Gospel, where the name of Christ is not known?" The response was affirmative but did not provide any mechanism for carrying it out: "Considered, that the Brethren acknowledge the great commission of Christ to its full extent, and that it is the duty of the church, the ministers, and every private member, to do all that is in their power to fulfill that commission in accordance with apostolic practice." The last phrase was undoubtedly meant to block any attempt to organize a society to perform mission tasks.

In 1856 a letter from Virginia asked for the devising of a plan so that the response of 1852 did not "remain a dead letter," the Annual Meeting answered by commending the subject "to the serious consideration of all the churches." Two years later a specific plan was proposed at the Meeting, which called for the formation of districts in areas where Brethren lived; congregations in each district could contribute to a fund to defray the expenses of two or more ministering brethren in travelling throughout the district. The response was negative, although Brethren were urged to give the subject "serious and prayerful consideration."

The plan was brought up again the next year (1859), leading to the appointment of a committee to propose a plan that the entire church might accept. Its members were leading figures of moderately progressive bent. In 1860 the committee submitted a plan very similar to that proposed in 1858, to be supported by weekly contributions through a district organization. Funds were to be disbursed

A graphic demonstration of the mission outreach of the Brethren in the early twentieth century. *BHLA Collection.*

as districts "judged most conducive to the glory of God and the salvation of souls," with reports at Annual Meeting so that "all such proceedings may be in harmony with the regulations" of the conference. Again, the Annual Meeting postponed decision because of the sparse attendance in troubled Tennessee. The turmoil of the Civil War kept the issue off the Annual Meeting agenda during its duration, although an occasional article in *The Gospel Visitor* tried to keep the subject alive.[8]

Mission proponents reopened the discussion in a query to Annual Meeting in 1867, with evident impatience: "Should not our church adopt some general plan for the spread of the Gospel, as the duty is enjoined upon her by the Savior himself? And does not an efficient plan imply some pecuniary provision?" The answer was, "This Annual Meeting hails the desire to have the Gospel spread and which is growing among the Brethren, as a favorable indication, and it would encourage this and recommend it to the several States to take such measures as a prayerful consideration of the subject would suggest, to engage in this good work." However, its judgment was that no one plan could be agreed upon; hence several different plans should be tried and reported on.

The plan suggested in 1860 was actually adopted in 1868 but evidently little was done because requests came repeatedly—in 1869, 1872, 1873, and 1874—for action. The 1874 query sounds a plaintive note: "Since the Macedonian call is heard from many places over the land, and as the Gospel said, 'go,' and as the Annual Meeting of 1868 has formed a plan, will not this Annual Meeting of 1874 perfect the plan and carry it into effect?" The response was, "We cannot see how we can make a more perfect plan than the one referred to in the query, but we request the churches having such calls to make arrangements to carry out the said plan."[9]

Further appeals came in 1875 and 1879, but it was only in 1880 that an effective arrangement was accepted by the Annual Meeting. Five brethren were made responsible "to superintend the domestic and foreign missionary work of the general brotherhood," to "take over any foreign or domestic work of a general nature," "to make reports," but in no way to interfere "with any present individual church or district missionary efforts among our Brethren."[10]

HOME MISSIONS

From one perspective, as indicated by quotations given above, Brethren had an active record in home missions. Evangelistic zeal has characterized much of Brethren history in North America. Although without central direction or organization, there was a rather remarkable and persistent striving to create new church communities. Many elders understood that it was incumbent upon them to travel extensively to bring the gospel to areas of limited or no Brethren population. Church growth during this period often occurred by the organic process of dividing congregations as they grew larger, usually centering on preaching points and scattered meetinghouses of the mother congregation. Often then these younger congregations themselves spawned a third generation of newer communities. The Conestoga church in Lancaster County is often cited as the model of this development.

As one of the early eighteenth-century congregations, its initial growth was modest; by 1770 there were only 86 members listed. This figure, however, fails to record the more than 400 members who had joined the congregation between its founding and 1770; almost all of them had left its boundaries through outmigration. In contrast, steady growth in the nineteenth century and the process of division and subdivision resulted by 1908 in a total in the original territory of 5,000 adult members in 20 different congregations. Conestoga had "become the mother church of all the congregations in Lancaster, Dauphin, Lebanon, Berks, and Schuylkill counties, and, in fact, of most of the congregations comprising the Eastern District of Pennsylvania."[11]

The other substantial approach was by colonizing, when bodies of Brethren went en masse to another location, ordinarily including a preacher in their midst. This made it possible to organize a new congregation almost overnight. The connection of railroads with this form of church extension has been previously described. Brethren were quick to erect meetinghouses for themselves and were also active in inviting their new neighbors to join with them. Because of the specific requirements of dress and lifestyle for Brethren membership, this was not always easy.

In the later nineteenth century a new form of ministry was developed, which became the usual definition for Home Missions. This ministry entailed planning and an organized effort to focus the resources of a district or the church as a whole on planting new congregations. As has been seen, several specific church-wide programs were discussed by Annual Meetings (1856, 1858, 1860) to effect this, but little actual progress was made with them, in part because of the onset of the Civil War but also because of determined resistance from traditional Brethren.

An early hint at a more structured direction was the recommendation by the 1853 Annual Meeting that members who wished to move westward should locate where they were most needed by the church. This came about because of the repeated pleas from Brethren on the plains and the Pacific Northwest for ministers to move into their areas; these requests were often printed in *The Gospel Visitor* and later in other Brethren periodicals. Seven years later the Meeting named James Quinter and D. P. Sayler as a committee to seek ministers for members residing in the Pacific Northwest. In 1870 two Indiana ministers, Jacob Miller and Daniel Sturgis, were appointed and financed to bring ministerial care to the West, which they did by extended trips but not by relocation.[12]

The Annual Meeting of 1866 approved organization for missions on a district basis; a number of districts then established mission boards to implement the decision. A number of persons became active in mission work, including James R. Gish and Barbara K. Gish, John Metzler, J. M. Neff, John Stump, and George C. Carl. Although the church-wide Brethren's Church Extension Union of 1877 spearheaded by Howard Miller was short-lived, and the Domestic and Foreign Missionary Board of 1880 was abandoned after one year, after 1884 organized mission work through its several permutations did survive and became a powerful force in the church. The board raised and disbursed $900 by 1882 to pay expenses of evangelists. It went on to distribute moneys to help newer congregations erect churchhouses.

Closely connected (both in organization and personnel) with the increasing urgency for mission reach was the parallel concern for the production of tracts and booklets. Brethren began to publish such ephemeral literature in a desire to reach new people in areas where the Brethren were unknown; here, too, they were following in the footsteps of other denominations. A well-organized printing and distributing campaign had been set in motion early in the nineteenth century to cope with the flood of new immigrants and the spread of population westward. Between the years 1829 and 1831 the American Tract Society printed each year an average of five pages for every person living in the nation.

Leading Brethren writers penned these tracts, which varied from a single page to substantial booklets. Topics emphasized distinctive Brethren beliefs and practices—for example, *Plain Dressing, The Christian Salutation, One Baptism, Feet-washing*—but also included more general topics, such as *The Atoning Blood of Christ, Gold and Costly Array, Intemperance.* They were gathered into a substantial volume, *The Brethren's Tracts and Pamphlets, Setting Forth the Claims of Primitive Christianity* (1892, 1900). A very popular tract was *The Brethren's Card,* summarizing in brief compass the Brethren plan of salvation. It begins, *"Be it known to all men,* that there is a people who, as little children (Luke 18: 17), accept the Word of the New Testament as a message from heaven (Heb. 1: 1,2), and teach it in full (2 Tim. 4: 1, 2; Matt. 28: 20)."[13] A particular concern of the advocates of the Brethren's Church Extension Union had been missions to the cities. Several new congregations were begun by local initiative in Philadelphia by 1900, and the work of James Quinlan with orphans in Baltimore was also notable. Nevertheless, an increasing number of voices were heard urging the Brethren to take their message to the rapidly growing urban population. D. C. Moomaw had proposed in 1879 that the church select and support two evangelists to tour all of the major cities to conduct preaching missions. As district mission boards became active, urban ministries came to the top of their agendas.

Two well-known city missions can stand for others. These were the Hastings Street mission on the south side of Chicago and the Brooklyn mission in the New York metropolitan area. They began work by collecting neighborhood children into Sunday schools, hoping that this would also provide an entreé to their families as well. Systematic visitation of the neighborhoods revealed both promise and problems. Linked with the Hastings Street program were students of Bethany Bible School, founded in 1905 across the street from the mission. The school's founders laid great emphasis upon practical work, which the home mission provided, as did ministries in prisons and hospitals. The work in Brooklyn focused on Italian immigrants and led to the formation of a largely Italian congregation under the leadership of the talented immigrant John Caruso, who supported himself as a hod carrier.

Home missions work provided many opportunities for gifted women to take leadership roles. Among those prominent were Alice J. Boone and Bertha Ryan (Shirk) in Chicago and Alice J. Boone, Elizabeth Grater, and Elizabeth Howe (Brubaker) in Brooklyn.

CHRISTIAN HOPE AND THE DANISH MISSION

After nearly three decades of discussion, in 1880 the Annual Meeting did permit a breakthrough for organized missions. What had happened? There are two reasons for the change. In the first place, by 1880 the Old Order faction, which had so strongly opposed missions was for all intents and purposes out of the picture, in the process of withdrawing to set up its own church body. In the second place, Brethren were effectively involved in foreign missions through the initiative of a specific district, that of Northern Illinois. The story is an interesting one.

A Dane (improbably) named Christian Hope, born into the Lutheran state church in 1844, had joined the Baptists in Denmark but found they could not answer his probing questions. He began writing tracts calling for church reform, which soon brought upon him government reprisals. He fled to Norway and then emigrated to the United States, seeking there a church that followed New Testament teachings. He read a description of the Tunkers which interested him but sought them without success in large American cities. Eventually, after becoming the pastor of a Swedish Baptist congregation in Rock Island, Illinois, he learned of their location. He concluded that the Brethren were indeed a New Testament church and sought baptism in 1874 in the Hickory Grove congregation; at this time he supported himself as a harness maker in Lanark. The

Brethren recognized his gifts and called him to the ministry in 1875 in the Cherry Grove church.

Hope was eager to communicate his newly found faith to friends back in Denmark. Together with M. M. Eshelman he began a publication fund to translate Brethren materials into Danish. When these were sent to Denmark, Christian Hansen was convinced of their truth and asked for someone to come to preach and to baptize. The request was taken to a district meeting held at the Cherry Grove congregation in 1875. The decision was to send Christian Hope back to Denmark to prepare for the arrival of two elders and their wives, Enoch and Annie Eby and Daniel and Julia Ann Fry.

Hope and his wife, Mary Katherine Nielsen Hope, went there in 1876, the elders' party in 1877. The procedure followed exactly the traditional Brethren method of sending adjoining elders to organize a new congregation. The only difference here was the greater distance between congregations. It is more properly understood as church extension rather than foreign mission.[14] In 1877 the first congregation was established in Denmark with thirteen members. At great sacrifice, Hope and his family remained in Denmark when the American elders returned home after five months. Some of the American Brethren were disposed to supply him only scantily with money to keep from "spoiling" him. He traveled, gaining adherents in several localities, but not enough anywhere to build a viable congregation. His lower-class status, reputation as a rebel, and lack of education worked against him. Nevertheless, he preached, wrote and distributed tracts, and organized a peace society among young men facing compulsory military duty. Members of the Northern Illinois district tried to support Hope and appealed with little success to the brotherhood for additional financial aid until 1880 when the Domestic and Foreign Mission Board was organized to provide oversight and funding.

At times on his travels Hope had to sleep in open fields at night because of his limited funds, and his family did not always have sufficient food; nonetheless, he persevered until 1886, even extending Brethren work into Sweden. Upon his return to the United States Brethren assisted him in obtaining a farm in Kansas. He traveled extensively to build support for missions, returned to visit Brethren congregations in Denmark and Sweden three times, and worked with Scandinavian settlers in Kansas before he died in 1899 while on a mission tour in Texas.[15]

The mission program in Scandinavia (Denmark and Sweden) persisted despite difficulties through the first half of the twentieth century. The focus of work shifted from Denmark to southern Sweden after Christian Hope began a mission in Malmo in 1885. At its height, there were five congregations in Sweden with 171 members, and only 91 in two congregations in Denmark. The most success in Denmark came through the work of Niels Esbensen, a native-born minister who had been educated at Bethany Seminary in Chicago.

Although the investment of missionary personnel in Scandinavia was always modest (six in Denmark between 1913 and 1924; nine in Sweden between 1901 and 1947), interest continued until the program was officially closed in 1947. Jacob F. Graybill was the senior in authority and length of service. Many of the staunchest members found it necessary to migrate, in particular because of government pressure on young men who refused military service. There were also internal squabbles, inadequate funds, and lack of training for national ministers. Two of the American missionaries in Denmark were accused of immorality. Finally, the disruption of World War II made it virtually impossible to continue.

There had been one informal case of Brethren mission activity in Europe prior to the work of Christian Hope. Henry Kurtz had returned to his German home in late 1838. He wanted to visit his aged parents, to acquaint himself with some of the newer religious movements there, and to "preach the word wherever there was an open door." He found the latter in Switzerland among the followers of Samuel Froelich. They rejected the established Reformed Church, military service, infant baptism, and other accepted church rites, and for this suffered severe repression.

Kurtz visited these *Neutäufer*, preached to them, and convinced nine of the group of the validity of immersion baptism. Although their leader Samuel Froelich won back some of the nine, others held firm to their new belief, emigrated to the United States, and united with the Brethren. Kurtz was also later in close correspondence with a dissenting group in Germany that he hoped would accept conversion to the Brethren, but this initiative finally failed to be consummated.[16]

MISSION BOARDS AND THE INDIAN MISSION

In response to the Annual Meeting action of 1880 the Domestic and Foreign Mission Board was created, with Enoch Eby (president), S. T. Bosserman, James Quinter, J. Leedy, and D. E. Brubaker as its five members. Response to the board's request for funds was limited. The board was reorganized in 1884 as the General Church Erection and Missionary Committee with only $8.69 in its treasury. After going through several more changes it became known in 1908 as the General Mission Board. Five years later it had over $1,000,000 in funds and endowments. The major figure in its phenomenal growth was D. L. Miller, the businessman, educator, editor and publisher, philanthropist, world traveler, and author described earlier.

After the first overseas response by Brethren to the "Macedonian Call" of Christian Hope and Christian Hansen in Denmark, the growing Brethren interest in missions awaited new directions. This came through the agency of a thrusting newcomer to the church, Wilbur Brenner Stover, a native of Franklin County, Pennsylvania, whose family moved to DuPage county west of Chicago.[17] D. L. Miller recruited Stover as a student of Mount Morris Academy and College, where he worked his way through several years of study. While a student he was caught up in what became the Student Volunteer Movement (SVM), led by the layman John R. Mott, later to become the foremost American ambassador of missions and ecumenism. The famous slogan of the SVM was "the evangelization of the world in this generation." Under its stimulus, thousands of college students pledged either to become foreign missionaries or to support sacrificially those who did.

Stover caught fire with missions fervor, preaching it in and out of season. After leaving college (he wrote in 1894), he had preached within forty months nearly 600 times, speaking "every night and twice on Sundays, with but four or five exceptions." He had a pleasant manner and met people readily. Stover won his way, although not completely kosher according to the Brethren order: he wore a mustache as well as beard and a tie under his plain-cut coat. In 1892 he went to Philadelphia to study at Temple College, and then became a pastor at the mother Germantown Church, evidently sup-

A gathering in 1912 of Brethren missionaries in India. The tireless promoter of missions, Wilbur B. Stover, sits on the right in the second row. *BHLA Collection.*

ported by Mary Geiger, a generous widow and member of the Philadelphia congregation.

Using Germantown as his home base, he stumped the brotherhood promoting the missions cause; one technique was to organize Missionary Reading Circles. He preached missions so much at Germantown that members asked if he expected them to go. He replied, "Someone has to go." Many years later he wrote of this period that he was tempted to leave the Brethren because of their slowness to adopt the missions cause: "When I was talking missions at first, and no one gave a very sympathetic ear, when I was counted by a good many as rather an unsafe venturer and theorist on this subject, and even a crank about missions, then it came hard to stand with the Church...."[18]

In 1893 he married Mary Emmert, who shared his missionary passion; her uncle, George Zollers, was a friend of missions and had baptized Christian Hope. A year earlier Stover had offered himself to the General Church Erection and Missionary Committee as a missionary to India. When the Meyersdale, Pennsylvania, congregation offered to underwrite the Stovers' expenses, the church board gave its approval at the 1894 Annual Conference. Stover at age 28, his wife at 22, and Bertha Ryan at 23, sailed for India in October 1894. "Three lone young people, a man and two women, to be set adrift, as it were in a non-Christian world numbering hundreds of millions; it was a gigantic proposition and it is not remarkable that in the face of it stout hearts quailed." The Stovers stayed in India for three terms (26 years), returning twice on home leaves, which they spent interpreting their work and promoting the mission cause.

The three volunteers went first to Bombay; in that teeming city they took counsel with veteran missionaries, who advised them to concentrate on the Bulsar area under the comity principle. Under this plan Christian missions from several denominations apportioned areas of work so as to avoid direct competition. Stover travelled to Bulsar and asked if there was anything of interest for a visitor. A local resident thereupon took him to view the cemetery established for foreigners.

The new missionaries spent several years learning the Gujarati language, although Stover began evangelistic work already in 1895. After two years they counted only sixteen converts. Their courageous response to a famine and plague of 1897 created the breakthrough. They undertook the tasks of housing, feeding, and clothing scores of orphans. The orphans they raised became the nucleus of the Brethren congregations in India.

By the time the Stover family returned permanently to the United States in 1920 because of Mary Stover's illness, the membership in the Indian church had risen to nearly 1,500, by 1930 totaling 4,000. The Stovers itinerated for several years after their return, working hard to maintain and increase the interest in missions as the "great first work of the church." This was the title of one of Stover's influential books, some five in all, predominantly focused on missions. He wrote unceasingly in the church periodicals, using a clear and attractive style with many photographic illustrations.

In his last years, Stover served as a pastor, first in Cleveland, and then in Seattle and Olympia, Washington. Ever energetic, Stover also preached regularly on the radio and published a magazine *The Little Brother*. Because of his expansive and friendly personality, he developed a wide acquaintance. At his funeral, Stover was given credit by Charles D. Bonsack, secretary of the General Mission Board, along with D. L. Miller and Galen B. Royer, as the three who "sold missions to the heart of the Church of the Brethren."[19] As the church sent many missionaries to India in the twentieth century, more mission stations were established in the Gujarati-speaking areas and after 1902 in the Marathi language areas as well. By 1945 there were 22 congregations and more than 8,000 members. This number had doubled by 1970, when the Brethren in India united with Christians from five other denominations to form the Church of North India. (A minority of Indian Brethren refused to join the united church.)

Brethren missionary work in India was characterized by the creation of strong educational and medical institutions. The achievements of the Vocational Training School and Rural Service Center at Anklesvar were particularly noted; carpentry, agriculture, public health, literacy, teacher training—these practical forms of Christian service were taught there. The indigenous leadership, in particular Govindji K. Satvedi, Premchand G. Bhagat, Naranji Solanki, and Jivanji K. Satsangi, and their families, demonstrated faithfulness, ability, and wisdom and won the respect of other denominations.[20]

FAILED MISSIONS

Relatively unsung in Brethren literature were the missionary efforts at the turn of the century that failed, despite considerable investments of personnel and funds. G. J. Fercken was sent to Smyrna in Turkey in 1895 to open an orphanage on Christian principles. Fercken was one of the most unusual personalities ever connected with the Brethren, in a sense a reverse version of the Christian Hope story.[21]

A Dutch national, Fercken was born in 1855 in Aleppo, Syria; his father was a Dutch nobleman and his mother a Frenchwoman.

He was educated in Lebanon, Turkey, and Connecticut. With this background, it is no great surprise to learn that he became fluent in seven languages. He had served for ten years as an Episcopalian clergymen in Washington state when he received correspondence from David M. Brower, a pioneer Brethren minister in Oregon. Becoming convinced of the validity of Brethren tenets, in 1894 Fercken traveled to Mount Morris, Illinois, where he was baptized. Brethren mission leaders were impressed by his qualifications and in the following year sent him to initiate the mission in Turkey. Funds for the project were collected through the sale of D. L. Miller's book, *Seven Churches of Asia*, which described Asia Minor in detail. Brethren understood this mission venture as "simply reestablishing primitive Christianity among the seven churches spoken of in Revelation."[22]

Fercken's early efforts were promising. After not quite three years, he had established two congregations (Izmir and Aydin), one out-station, with a total membership of 39 and five church leaders, all of Armenian and Greek ethnic background; he also began an orphanage. When several of the orphans were baptized in 1898, suspicious Moslem authorities closed the orphanage because of complaints of proselytizing. Fercken was forced to leave the country. The indigenous leadership continued church activities until 1909.

After leaving Asia Minor, Fercken was asked by the mission board to investigate work in Switzerland. In 1899 he moved to a location in France just outside of Geneva and by the end of the year had organized a small congregation there and another in Geneva. American funds enabled him to erect a churchhouse in the French village in 1900, but it was so poorly sited that it was later sold. Mission work was then concentrated in Geneva itself, with both French and Swiss members. When the mission board in America learned in 1906 (through several of his book-length publications) that Fercken had converted to the Swedenborgian faith, financial support was terminated. An associate, Adrian Pellet, who came to the Brethren from the Salvation Army, continued the mission; an American missionary couple sent to further the project in 1911 found that Pellet had "proved unworthy" and the mission was in such disrepute that the work was closed in 1912.

Fercken was for six years a minister of the General Convention of New Jerusalem on the island of Mauritius, before soliciting membership in the Swedenborgian New Church (General Church of the New Jerusalem), a process that took two years. He left Mauritius in 1914, thereafter serving as a Swedenborgian minister in Lausanne, Switzerland. Because of dissatisfaction with the support he received from church headquarters, he resigned his membership in 1919.

The *New York Times* announced his death in 1930 as a "noted American theologian," listing his place of residence as Yverdon, near Lausanne. A Swedenborgian publication observed his death, likening him to the category of comets, "men who enter swiftly into the ministry at one point, stay a while, and pass out again...." the author concluded that Fercken "came into the church; impulsively sought some field in which to work; could not see his way clear to accept certain propositions covering English and French methods; and presently stepped aside." Brethren records list him as restored to membership in 1917 (?) but not to the ministry.[23]

THE CHINA MISSION

Fourteen years after opening the mission in India, Brethren began work in China. Here the pioneer figures were Frank Crumpacker and Anna Newland Crumpacker, George Hilton and Blanche Cover Hilton, and Emma Horning, all of whom arrived in Shanghai in September 1908. They established work in the Shansi province of North China, extending over nine districts. Before the work was terminated by internal unrest in 1948, more than one hundred missionaries had served as evangelists, educators, and medical specialists. Of particular interest was a program of rural service, created in the 1920s and 1930s, that dealt with agricultural extension, mass education, and industrial cooperatives.[24]

A smaller but intensive field was opened in Kwangtung province in South China by Martha Shick in 1916. To this area also came a Chinese minister, Moy Gwong Han, who had joined the Brethren in the United States. Although born in China, he emigrated to Chicago as a young man and there was educated in a Sunday school for Chinese initiated by Brethren. After study at Manchester

College and Bethany Bible School, he returned to China in 1920 and served faithfully there until his death in 1950. Two other able Chinese converts of the Sunday school in Chicago were Moy Way and Moy Wing Lum. Both were licensed to the Brethren ministry; the former led Sunday schools and churches for Chinese in Detroit and Chicago, the latter in Riverside, California.

As in India, Brethren workers were active in China in alleviating suffering from plagues (1918), famines (1920-22), and war (1937ff.) Three missionaries—Alva C. Harsh, Mary Hykes Harsh, and Minneva J. Neher—disappeared during the time of the Sino-Japanese war after they answered an appeal for help late one night; they were never heard from again. The Japanese invasion of China eventually forced the evacuation of all Brethren workers from the Shansi province in 1940. Several survived internment in Japanese prison camps during the war.

Brethren personnel were actively involved in internationally sponsored reconstruction efforts after 1945. Missionaries were able to return to the Shansi province in 1946, only to be forced out again by the success of the Communist revolution of 1948. Some were able to work for a time in other parts of China, but by 1951 all had to leave. A number moved to other Brethren mission fields; for example, George Mason and Rae Hungerford Mason went to India. Daryl Parker and Martha Neiderhiser Parker, who had served during the World War II years with the Masons in Puerto Rico, were later medical missionaries in Nigeria.

Chinese Brethren persisted in their faith in house churches, despite massive Communist pressure, until a shift in government policy in 1979 permitted more public activity. Some of their ministers played leading roles after this time in the national leadership of the united Christian church. The pastor of the Beijing (Peking) Protestant church in the 1980s, Yin Ji Tzeng, was the son of the first Chinese elder of the Church of the Brethren in China.[25]

THE NIGERIAN MISSION

Fourteen years after the China mission was inaugurated, the General Mission Board opened a mission field in Nigeria. There had been earlier exploratory visits. D. L. Miller and Wilbur B. Stover had investigated South Africa in 1905. On a world-wide trip in 1921 mission executive J. H. B. Williams was on his way to study the possibilities of an African mission when he fell seriously ill of typhus fever on shipboard between India and Africa. Williams died soon after reaching port and was buried in Mombasa, East Africa (now Kenya).[26]

The pioneers in Nigeria in late 1922 were H. Stover Kulp and Albert D. Helser; leaving their wives temporarily in England, they pressed ahead to Garkida in the Bornu province of northeastern Nigeria, suggested by other missionaries. They had to overcome considerable obstruction from the British imperial officials, who preferred to leave the indigenous Bura people with their animistic religious beliefs. Ruth Royer Kulp and Lola Bechtel Helser rejoined their husbands in 1923; tragically the former died of dysentery along with her infant son in the spring of 1924.[27]

Following the pattern earlier used by missionaries in India and China, as the Brethren organized mission stations in Nigeria they created school systems and medical institutions. Especially famed was a leprosarium (1929ff.) that achieved an international reputation. Brethren expatriate missionaries took the lead in reducing the Bura language to writing, enabling biblical translations and primers. Work was expanded to the Margi-speaking people in 1927, and later among those speaking other tribal languages.

Numerical growth was modest until after World War II when numbers exploded. By 1981 the membership reached 40,000, with double the number attending worship services; by 1995 it had tripled to 120,000 and promised to exceed the membership of Brethren in the United States by the year 2000. The expansion of the church in Nigeria has been used as an example of mass conversion by experts in the church growth movement. The *Ekklesiyar 'Yan'uwa a Nigeria* (*EYN*, or Church of the Brethren in Nigeria) became autonomous in 1972.

As numbers increased, the educational system expanded as well. First came a training school for primary teachers at Garkida (1932); then a school for the children of expatriates called Hillcrest (1942); then the Waka Teacher Training Schools (1952, 1960); then the innovative Kulp Bible School (1960), where adult students received vocational training (in agriculture and domestic science) to support themselves during the time they studied religious subjects and to ensure a livelihood afterwards; and finally, with the cooperating of other mission bodies, the Theological School of Northern Nigeria (1969). A people-based and decentralized program of preventive health was awarded international attention; it was called *Lafiya* from a West African greeting wishing health and well being. It featured village-based education, para-professional health workers, and a drilling program to provide clean drinking water. Its successful approach has been followed by agencies in other nations in Africa.

LATER MISSIONS

A mission program in Ecuador evolved from social service work by conscientious objectors during World War II. The first assigned missionaries were J. Benton Rhoades and Ruby Frantz Rhoades, who began work with a rural Indian population in 1946. It centered on the Calderón Valley for many years, with evangelistic outposts in other parts of the country. By 1964 six congregations formed the *Iglesia Evangélica de los Hermanos* (Evangelical Church of the Brethren). In the ensuing year it combined with other congregations to form the *Iglesia Evangélica Unida del Ecuador* (United Evangelical Church of Ecuador). The rural and medical work was turned over to the Brethren and United Foundations.[28]

A shift in mission philosophy after 1955 toward indigenization changed the denominational approach to missions. Those younger churches created by Brethren missionaries were encouraged to become independent. Instead of sending missionaries to other countries, the policy led to the seconding of personnel to indigenous churches, such as to Indonesia.

Since then, sending expatriate personnel has drastically declined. By 1985 there were no American Brethren serving in India, none in Ecuador, none in China, and only sixteen in Nigeria in fraternal and advisory positions. It was illustrated by the attempt after 1975, called *Misión Mutua en las Américas*, to practice "mutual mission" with Latin American Protestants; Brethren worked with a

Pentecostal church in Cuba, trying to develop joint work in Nicaragua.

A comparable approach had more impact in the Sudan mission in Africa. In 1980 Carolyn and Roger Schrock went there as a support ministry for the Sudan Council of Churches. Their immediate project was to develop in the Upper Nile region a broad-scale, village-based health care system based on the successful Lafiya model that Roger Schrock had coordinated in Nigeria. The Schrocks were in the United States from 1985 to 1991 but returned again to the Sudan with Schrock as acting executive secretary for the New Sudan Council of Churches until 1995. The assignment was supported by the Presbyterian Church (USA) and the Reformed Church as well as by Brethren.

Work was located in the southern section of the nation within the area controlled by the armies opposed to the central government, all part of the drawn-out civil war that brought untold agonies to the civilian population. Jan and Roma Jo Thompson also served in the Sudan during this period, replaced later by Phil and Louise Reiman. Lester and Esther Boleyn worked on a project with the Presbyterian Church, coordinating a team of Sudanese translating the Old Testament into the Nuer language; the Boleyns were based in Nairobi, Kenya, where other Brethren workers had to relocate when it became too dangerous to stay permanently in Sudan. One of their efforts has been to provide information about the great need in southern Sudan, largely ignored by the western media.[29]

The policy of indigenization was hotly debated in the church over several years, and in the 1990s the church began efforts to develop Brethren congregations in South Korea, Brazil, and the Dominican Republic, in the first two cases by linking with indigenous independent churches.

As Brethren recognized a broader horizon for missions in the United States and abroad, they also realized that there were social issues that they could no longer ignore. Attention to them did much to change the character of this once withdrawn body.

17

Expanding Concern for Social Problems

As Brethren answered the call of domestic and foreign missions, they were brought face to face with a host of social issues. Their workers in the slums of Chicago and Brooklyn quickly found that evangelism was impossible if attention was not paid to the results of alcoholism and poverty. Brethren missionaries in India, China, and the Near East faced catastrophes of famines and plagues; the loss of adult life there led to the creation of hordes of orphans. Their creative responses to these horrendous challenges laid the groundwork in large part for the Indian and Chinese congregations.

The withdrawn and nonconformist character of the Brethren through the nineteenth century made it difficult for Brethren to respond forthrightly to social problems in the surrounding society. Given their self-understanding as a "peculiar people," having as little to do as possible with the world, Brethren were reluctant to engage themselves in broader societal issues. They saw themselves as a "colony of heaven," primarily responsible for keeping themselves uncontaminated by the world and its quandaries.

The response of the Annual Meeting in 1875 to a request for cooperation with a peace association testifies to this stance. They rejected the bid, reasoning, "Our church itself being a peace association, we need not, as a body, cooperate with others." Instead, the Meeting asked members as individuals to use their influence for peace.[1]

THE TEMPERANCE CAUSE

Interestingly, it was the issue of temperance that broke through this separatist position. By the second decade of the twentieth century, the Church of the Brethren was urging the government to legislate a ban on the production and sale of liquor. Shortly thereafter the Annual Conference hailed the passage of the Eighteenth Amendment that established prohibition (ratified 1919). This stance reversed the long-standing Brethren position that held to a strict barrier between the church and the state.

Early agitation of the temperance issue among Brethren focused naturally on the involvement with alcohol by church members. As early as 1783 the Yearly Meeting acted to restrict distilling by members; repeated reference to the issue indicates that not all members accepted the discipline. Because the cost of transporting grain was excessive, farmers found its distillation into the more compact whiskey or other liquor economically advantageous. Brethren store-keepers were not to retail spirits. Tavern keeping, because of its involvement with excessive drinking, was soon pronounced "entirely unbecoming" for members (1835).[2]

Early liquor-related issues involved social customs that Brethren were asked to avoid—the widespread expectation that employers would provide farm workers with strong drink or the celebration with whiskey of the raising of the rafters of a building. In 1822 the Annual Meeting forbade Brethren to provide liquor at public auctions. Minutes from the Meetings of 1841, 1857, and 1867 urge Brethren to avoid "intoxicating drinks as a beverage"; brewing beer was not absolutely forbidden, though discouraged. There is good reason to believe that Brethren, like other German sectarians, continued to drink beer and wine in moderation. These were ordinarily prepared at home for family consumption.[3]

Quite a different issue was the use of fermented wine at love feasts. The Bible-loving Brethren held strongly to the use of home-brewed wine for these liturgical occasions; the Annual Meeting of 1858 insisted on the use of "the purest article." When Brethren influenced by the burgeoning American temperance movement questioned this use, their efforts were for many years resoundingly rejected. When the 1875 Meeting permitted the use of unfermented grape juice as an option, the following meeting was faced with holding off a concerted move by the traditionalist faction to declare the use of wine mandatory. *The Vindicator*, as an organ of the Old Order movement, argued passionately that the use of fermented wine was alone biblical, and after the Old German Baptist Brethren organized as a separate body, it ruled in 1883 that wine must be used at love feasts "as the fathers understood it."[4]

The formation of the Prohibition Party in 1869, the Women's Christian Temperance Union (WCTU) in 1874, and the activist Anti-Saloon League of 1893 created more pressure for change, adding to organized efforts in the country that began in the first half of the nineteenth century. Although temperance efforts originally tried to moderate but not eliminate drinking, a shift to total abstinence soon took place, along with the politicization of the movement. Instead of urging voluntary commitment, the temperance movement pushed strongly for government intervention, winning an early victory in Maine where statewide prohibition was enacted in 1851.

In 1842 the Annual Meeting ruled that Brethren were not to sign the pledge of total abstinence because this would "meddle with the proceeding and excitement of the world on this subject"; they were also to avoid delivering public lectures specifically on the topic. Brethren members were not to join temperance associations; instead they were urged to use their personal influence to restrict the abuse of intoxicating beverages. The answer of the Annual Meeting of 1867 to a request permitting members to join a temperance society was forthright:

> As our brotherhood has, again and again, taken decided ground against intoxicating drinks as a beverage, and recommended to the brethren to abstain from their use as such, we see no necessity of joining ourselves to any other organization; and, therefore, we cannot allow brethren the privilege of doing so, but renew our solemn protestation against the use of intoxicating drinks as a beverage, and consider it the duty of every member of the church to use his influence against them.[5]

The last two decades of the nineteenth century saw repeated unsuccessful queries to the Annual Meeting urging the Brethren to go on record on behalf of the temperance movement. The First District of Virginia in 1881 and the Southern Indiana District in 1884 called on the Annual Meeting to petition the US Congress for prohibition laws. Although both initiatives were rejected, the dissatisfaction with the 1884 decision was such that the Meeting of 1885 returned to the issue.

It declared that the action of the previous year had been "misconstrued to the detriment of the Church, and her position on the temperance question misunderstood and misrepresented." It reaffirmed the long-standing Brethren position against the manufacture and sale of intoxicating beverages and vowed that the church should "use all lawful Gospel means to suppress and eradicate this great evil from our land." Four years later the Annual Meeting returned to the issue, restating its anti-intoxicant stance and pledging the church "to the extent of [its] influence" to share in the effort "to secure practical prohibition." It still advised against its members participating in the "public agitation."[6]

The sea change in attitude toward the problem began in 1900 when conference delegates were urged to help "mould temperance sentiment," without which "no law can become operative." It was furthered in 1908 when the Annual Conference established a permanent (General) Temperance Committee charged with developing literature for members to educate them about the evils of strong drink. That Brethren attitude was changing was seen in that part of the committee's mandate "to assist State Districts and local congregations to organize and maintain aggressive movements toward counteracting and stamping out the evil of intemperance." The 1907 query that led to the committee's formation spoke of the "duty of Christians to endeavor to suppress all forms of evil that imperil the morality of the people...." By 1916 the committee had distributed one million pages of literature. District-wide and state-wide committees became active in the effort.[7]

Though the Brethren were still reluctant to cooperate closely with temperance agencies (cautioning against this in 1912 and 1913), this soon changed. An important step was the election in 1914 of

Brethren educator and minister, Martin G. Brumbaugh, an outspoken prohibitionist, to the post of governor of the Commonwealth of Pennsylvania. The Annual Conference commended Brumbaugh for the "high ground" he had taken "upon all moral issues," with special attention to his efforts to "secure local option in Pennsylvania as a stepping stone to speedy elimination of the legalized traffic in intoxicating liquors from our nation." The sweeping quality of the rhetoric indicates the extent to which Brethren now understood it appropriate to link church and state issues. When Prohibition itself was enacted with the ratification of the Eighteenth Amendment in 1919, it met with official approval by the Annual Conference.[8]

Brethren continued after 1920 to press the cause of temperance. It became common for its leaders to call the church a temperance church since its organization. A church board in 1933 urged members to "support and cooperate fully" with temperance movements. The church as a body should "pray dry, preach dry, and vote dry"; they could also "buy dry" by patronizing only those stores which "sell dry." Some of its members became officers in the WCTU. Virgil Finnell of the Midwest became active in the anti-tobacco and anti-alcohol cause in Indiana and chaired the national Prohibition Party in the late 1940s.[9]

PEACE CONCERNS

Following the crucible of the Civil War, little attention was given by Brethren to peace issues. New members were still asked if they accepted nonresistance at the time of baptism, but little effort was made to explain why that was important. The Annual Meeting records some attention to issues related to veterans' organizations and pensions.

Only a few scattered pieces of literature were produced to strengthen the Brethren position of nonresistance. Shortly after the end of the war the Virginian Benjamin F. Moomaw published a brief "Dialogue on the Doctrine of Non-Resistance" (1867); it was appended to a published debate he had with a Dr. J. J. Jackson, which as the subtitle indicated, resulted "in the conviction of the latter and change of his religious association." The articulate convert from the Baptists, J. W. Stein, included nonresistance in a series of booklets he published, as one of "twenty reasons for a change" in his "church relations." The well-reasoned effort was entitled *Christianity Utterly Incompatible with War and Retaliation*...(1876).[10]

The local historian James Y. Heckler of Montgomery County, Pennsylvania, included nonresistance in a curious and extensive rhymed exposition, *Ecclesianthem, or A Song of the Brethren, Embracing Their History and Doctrine* (1883), of quite different nature and intent than Walt Whitman's *Song of Myself*, first issued in 1855. Under the "peculiarities of the Brethren," Heckler describes their pacific qualities:

> They are a non-litigant people you see;
> They go not to war nor engage in its service;
> They claim a non-combatant people to be.
> They fight but the battles of life in the Spirit;
> Their weapons are not of the carnal, whate'er,
> But mighty through God to discomfit the devil
> When he and his imps or his angels appear.

The northerner Heckler used the recent "Rebellion" as a case in point. Whereas most American churches fought on both sides ("members were murdered by those of their kind"), Brethren were "united in spirit and purpose":

> And on this great question were all of one mind,
> They took not the sword but they paid for exemption,
> The church was in peace and it was not disjoined.

When Brethren became active in publishing tracts later in the century, several mentioned the peace position. The succinct treatise by Daniel Hays called *The Path of Life, or Gospel Facts for the People* (1884) included four pages on nonresistance. Daniel Vaniman wrote a one-page tract *Christ and War* (n.d.) contrasting the two: "Christ says, 'Do them good. War says, 'Do them harm.' Christ says, 'Pray for them.' War says, 'Slay them.'"[11]

Because the Spanish-American War (1898) was concluded so quickly, there was no conscription, and therefore the church did not have to take a stand on military service. Some young Brethren were caught up in the excitement that the military victories caused in the country. Peace activist M. R. Zigler recalled as a boy posting portraits of the military heroes on his bedroom wall—Admirals Dewey, Schley, and Sampson. An older brother reduced their mother to tears by expressing his wish to join the United States Navy.

After the turn of the century, the Annual Meeting became more active in peace-related affairs. In 1902 it agreed to petition the king of Denmark on behalf of those young Danish men who had been converted by Brethren missionaries; their conscientious objection resulted in stern punishment. Seven years later the Meeting acted to petition the United States Congress, protesting increased military expenditures. This type of activity would have earlier been unheard of, given Brethren views of noninvolvement with the state.

How much the Church of the Brethren had changed was sharply revealed in 1911 when the Annual Conference, as it was now called, appointed a Peace Committee. It was charged with caring for conscientious objectors and distributing peace literature. It was asked to keep the brotherhood apprised of the work of organized peace movements and further given the astounding mandate "to use every lawful gospel means in bringing about peaceful settlement of difficulties when such may arise *between governments or societies.*" The fact that the Conference did not see fit to provide a budget for the committee ensured that little could be accomplished. Nevertheless, the change in the interpretation of appropriate church activity, as revealed in these directions, is significant.[12]

The shift in attitude continued in resolutions and actions of Annual Conferences through the 1910s. In 1915 an expression of appreciation for his peaceful foreign policies was directed to President Woodrow Wilson, describing the Brethren as a church which was "a peace-promoting and peace-observing body from its founding...." After restating Brethren allegiance to peace and the brotherhood of man, the resolution encouraged the United States government to enlarge opportunities for judicial arbitration of international disputes. The Church of the Brethren pledged to exert greater zeal to spread the peace gospel of Jesus Christ "to the end that it may be an increasingly effective power in the hands of the

Master for the maintenance of peace and goodwill among men and among the nations of the world." Again the change in language from the aloof posture of a withdrawn fellowship to that of an involved and liberal Protestant church is startling.

Some Brethren had welcomed Wilson's presidency for its peaceful potential. Shortly before he was inaugurated, a young instructor at Manchester College wrote to a friend at Juniata College, "Hurrah for Wilson! Don't you admire the way he takes his time to everything, uses his head instead of a 'big stick' and doesn't allow personal obligations to restrict him in his performance of public duties? I surely wish for a prosperous four years from him." The obvious comparison is with the blustering Teddy Roosevelt; the writer expected more from the reformer and one-time president of Princeton University.

In 1916 the National Peace Committee warned against the spread of militarism, which it blamed upon commercial interests. It urged the United States government to send monetary aid to war sufferers:

> Since God has so richly blessed this land with great abundance, we believe that our Government should take this Christlike act as an initiative [sic] step toward the ending of all war, and the bringing in of the Reign of Peace, and Good Will Towards All Men. May "Righteousness exalt our nation" (Prov. 14: 34).

As the United States moved rapidly toward its own involvement in the Great War in Europe, which it entered in the spring of 1917, the Church of the Brethren had moved to a position that identified the United States government as an agent of God.[13]

HOMES FOR THE AGED AND ORPHANAGES

The late nineteenth century saw a flowering of Brethren interest in two segments of the population with special needs—the aged poor and children without parents. This renewed a concern demonstrated in Germantown as early as the late colonial period. The Yearly

Meeting of 1793 cautioned against those going from church to church collecting alms, as they may be frauds; each congregation should care for the needs of its own members, seeking support from neighboring congregations if necessary. This was affirmed in 1812 in response to a query about the care of widows and orphans and later throughout the century. [14]

Primarily on a district level, Brethren began to create institutions to care for both older men and women and orphans who needed homes; at times the same buildings were used to care for both age groupings. Between 1883 and 1910 the German Baptist Brethren erected fourteen homes for both categories. One of the first, started in the mid-1880s, was the Honey Creek Orphans' and Old Folks' Home located near Sulphur Springs in the Southern Indiana District.[15] A typical development took place in 1889 in Mexico, located in central Indiana, when Levi Miller donated land and a building for a home. When confronted with Miller's generous action, the district agreed to assume responsibility and seventeen residents were admitted in the first year. Brethren in the area soon voiced concern for orphans and Miller again responded, constructing an orphanage building at his own expense in 1892. (In 1873 the Middle District of Indiana had earlier queried the Annual Meeting about establishing a home for orphans; although the Meeting did "not see the propriety of adopting such measures," it did not block the district from proceeding on its own.) A visitor in 1890, writing in *The Gospel Messenger*, describes the work of the home in glowing phrases and recommends that each district provide a similar facility.[16]

In the bicentennial volume of 1908, the director of the Mexico home, Frank Fisher, put forth the claim that child rescue work was not only mandated by Christian charity but could also be justified as a form of mission work. By 1917 more than 1,500 children had been admitted in the Indiana home. Because of changes in philosophy and governmental regulations, the orphanage was phased out in 1943. The combined facility was known after 1936 as the Mexico Welfare Home. Following a national trend, the home for the aged was closed in 1968, making way for a modern retirement home in another location. Comparable changes took place with most of the other facilities for the aged operated by Brethren.[17]

A venture that attracted attention was the orphanage created by David Emmert at Huntingdon, Pennsylvania, in 1881. An artist and educator, Emmert had a passion for aiding indigent children. While teaching at the Brethren's Normal School (later Juniata College), he provided a benevolent atmosphere for needy children nearby, with the aid of a number of students. In 1882 he was able to construct a house for use as an orphanage, located across from the campus. Emmert published a magazine, *Helping Hands*, to solicit support for the project; it is remarkable for the many original illustrations he created to add interest. In 1907 he initiated another orphanage in Hagerstown, Maryland. Emmert placed strong emphasis upon moving his orphans to settled situations with families as soon as possible.[18]

An alternative strategy to the creation of orphanages was to place needy children directly in Brethren homes. This emphasis was pioneered by the District of Oklahoma and Indian Territory in the early 1900s. The Annual Conference of 1908 urged other districts to create comparable programs and appointed a committee consisting of Frank Fisher, David Emmert, and George C. Carl to provide direction. They reported two years later, urging each district to create an orphan's agency; they recommended the name be The Children's Aid Society of the Church of the Brethren. Although they discouraged the construction of homes, the influenza pandemic which followed some years thereafter produced more orphans than could be housed with available families, so more orphanages were instituted as emergency shelters, again often in conjunction with homes for the elderly. By 1923 seventeen states had work with homeless children.

There is evidence that some Brethren participated in the program of the late nineteenth century known as "Orphan Trains." In an effort to care for abandoned children in Eastern cities, trainloads of orphans were sent to the Midwest and Plains states, stopping along the way to permit interested families, mostly of rural background, to select children. With somewhat similar motivation as the care for orphans and the aged was the creation of a denominationally-supported hospital on the west side of Chicago. It was a spin-off and neighbor of Bethany Bible School. In 1921 a charter was secured for the Bethany Sanatorium and Hospital, which quickly won church support. Funds thus realized enabled the construction in 1930 of a new building housing fifty beds. It developed a fine reputation for community health service. To avoid confusion with other hospitals it was renamed Bethany Brethren Hospital in 1962. Six years later it was merged with a nearby hospital as Bethany Brethren-Garfield Park Hospital. It then became part of the larger Evangelical Hospital Association, and under these auspices constructed in the 1980s a new building (with 212 beds) on the former site of Bethany Biblical Seminary.[19]

ROLE OF WOMEN

As Brethren sought to answer human needs in the communities about them, a rising tide of concern developed about the position and potential of half of the Brethren membership—its women. Following the patriarchal nature of German society and the Pauline admonitions about the place of women, Brethren, like most other denominations of the time (except for Quakers), accepted a generally subordinate role for women in church affairs for much of the first two centuries of Brethren existence. This was the case, despite the fact that three of the first eight members in 1708 were women.

This is not to say that women had no significant roles to play. Women, along with men, had a voice and vote in congregational meetings for business; their counsel was sought in the process of choosing ministers. During the solemn service of ordination, they stood with their husbands and were installed with them. They had the primary role in arranging for and preparing the love feasts, so crucial in Brethren church life. Women served actively as deaconesses. Though too often taken for granted, the contribution of women made possible the extensive service of men under the self-supported pattern of ministry; it was the womenfolk who held things together in their absence, which often involved lengthy journeys.[20]

There were exceptions to the generalization of female subordination. One is mentioned in the diary of a traveling evangelist, Christian Newcomer, one of the early leaders of the revivalist movement among the German-speaking population in the late eighteenth

A portrait of Sarah Righter Major, the first woman to gain partial recognition as a Brethren minister. *BHLA Collection.*

century that eventually took form as the *United Brethren in Christ*. (Recorded in the diary are several instances of overnight hospitality given to him by Brethren). On October 8, 1798, he reported a meeting near Middletown, Pennsylvania, where, before the close of the meeting, an unnamed "Dunker sister gave an exhortation with astonishing power."[21]

The chief exception was the life and ministry of Sarah Righter (Richter) Major. Born near Philadelphia in 1808 as the daughter of a devoted Brethren family, she was converted under the eloquent preaching of the eccentric itinerant Harriet Livermore, the self-styled "Pilgrim Stranger," who, though not a member of the church, was admitted to the pulpit in Germantown and other Philadelphia-area Brethren congregations. She had preached in the halls of Congress to great acclaim and traveled to Jerusalem for a time to await the millennium. As a young woman, Sarah Righter also felt a strong call to preach and was given encouragement in this by several area ministers, despite its unusual character.[22]

When the Annual Meeting heard of the innovation, they ruled negatively in 1834 on the propriety of a woman preacher, judging "such sister being in danger, not only [of] exposing her own state of grace to temptation, but also causing temptations, discord, and disputes among other members." In an essay she sent to a brother who questioned her right to preach, citing the Pauline injunction against women speaking publicly, she writes: "I conceive it would be very inconsistent in an apostle who laid his hands on men and women, and pray'd over them, that they might receive the Holy Ghost, to quench the Spirit of God, because it was given to a woman." In 1859 the Annual Meeting drew a distinction between teaching and preaching, forbidden to women, and prophesying and testifying, permitted to them.[23] In 1842 she married Thomas Major, a minister, and shortly thereafter the couple moved to southern Ohio. The Majors often held preaching missions in Ohio and Indiana; Thomas would ordinarily open the meeting and then invite Sarah to speak. In those congregations that were not open to her preaching ministry, she would often lead in eloquent prayer.

A description of her appearance, manner, and preaching was recalled in 1901; it deals with an earlier visit by the Majors to northern Indiana. She was pictured as "in dress...neat and plain" with a "very plain bonnet, which she soon laid aside, and a little shawl around her neck and over her shoulders....Her face showed marks of age and care and labor. She was the picture of meekness and humility, completely subject to the will of her husband." When invited by Thomas Major to preach, she arose and "slowly announced her text...an old, plain, simple one." The observer continues,

> I was disappointed in the text, but was interested in the preacher, and I gave attention. It did not take long to discover that out of the common came forth the sublime. I could see a wonderful unfolding of the text. I think I am safe in saying that I never heard a text so expounded, illustrated and so transformed into newness of life as was done in that discourse.

He was convinced by the sermon that Sarah Major had been "specially and divinely set apart for the Lord's work."[24]

A committee was sent from the Annual Meeting to silence Sarah Major but returned without fulfilling its duty. One committee member explained, "I could not give my vote to silence someone who could outpreach me." She was even permitted to speak at the Annual Meeting of 1878. Besides her preaching, she was also known for her devotion to the cause of temperance work, ministry to minorities, and home visitation. She died in 1884.

A few women were involved in preaching and evangelism in the late nineteenth and early twentieth centuries; included among them are Mattie A. Lear, Catherine Beery Van Dyke, and Bertha Miller Neher. Mattie Lear taught for many years, including a position on the faculty of Mount Morris College, and wrote articles for Brethren publications. She was noted as a Bible student and a skilled speaker. Her home congregation, at Hudson, Illinois, licensed her to the ministry in 1897.

Catherine (Cassie) Van Dyke also taught at Mount Morris College, and after she married and moved to Chicago, taught at Bethany Bible School. She was a licensed minister and directed the Mothers' and Daughters' Association of the Church of the Brethren for twenty years. Bertha Neher was licensed to preach by the Milford, Indiana, congregation in 1908, and served as a pastor and evangelist. Also a writer, she was known for her Sunday school materials and for a children's book, *Among the Giants* (1895), that was often reprinted.[25]

Despite these exceptions, there were still definite limits to the ways in which women could provide leadership in the church. One avenue was by writing for Brethren publications or editing them. One of the earliest was Wealthy Agnes Clark Burkholder, who assisted the publishing business of the Brumbaugh brothers in Huntingdon, Pennsylvania. She edited their publication for youth, *The Young Disciple*, and was active in literary affairs at the forerunner of Juniata College; she even served on its board of trustees. Later she worked in the publication office of *The Brethren at Work* in Illinois before returning to Pennsylvania and marrying. She wrote an autobiographical account, *Some Things I Remember* (1929). A comparable career was achieved by Adaline Hohf Beery, who edited the Huntingdon literary magazine issued for a Brethren readership called *The Golden Dawn* and wrote memorable texts for hymns. Others who wrote prolifically were Julia Wood (*Close Communion, My Northern Travels*), Maud Newcomer, and Anneta C. Mow.[26]

During this era sisters could develop and deploy their talents most readily in the missions outreach of the church. Their involvement began with assistance in an unofficial home mission board, the Brethren's Church Extension Union (1877-78). Beginning in 1885 Sisters' Aid Societies sprang up across the country, which raised funds for the mission program. The initiative was frowned on and scotched in 1886 by the church's male leadership but was revived ten years later and flourished thereafter.

From the beginnings of both home and foreign missions, women were fully engaged. In the case of the domestic missions, usually located in cities, women had access to private homes that men could rarely match. They proved expert in leading Sunday schools and family counseling. Among the leading home mission workers were Elizabeth Howe (Brubaker) and Alice J. Boone.

In overseas settings, women likewise had possibilities of ministries barred to men by cultural taboos. Because, for example, modesty forbade the examination of female nationals by male missionary doctors, Brethren women desiring to serve in the medical missions were motivated to secure training as physicians and nurses. There were many outstanding examples of such service, such as Laura Murphy Cottrell who served in India from 1913 to 1949, Clara Harper who served in Nigeria from 1926 to 1960, and Bessie Crim, who served in China from 1940 to 1950.[27]

Women missionaries played active roles in other aspects of the mission program. They were usually freed from much domestic responsibility by the presence of servants in the home. Among the earliest examples were Bertha Ryan Shirk and Mary Quinter of India. They taught, directed the training of girls and women, and were active in writing, both for use in the field and in the necessary reports back to the sponsoring congregations. Returning female missionaries could serve as talented, energetic, and even daring role models for girls and women among the American membership.[28]

Another women's issue surfaced in the mid-nineteenth century; this involved the role of women in the love feast. By tradition, women were not allowed to break bread for or pass wine to each other as the eucharist was taken, as was long customary for the men. Rather, the presiding elder broke bread for each communing sister and handed each the cup of wine. In 1849 a query asked whether "it would not be more consistent with the Word if, at the communion, the administrator [elder] would give the bread and cup to the sisters, and they divide it, like the brethren, among themselves...?" The response was to preserve the status quo. The Far Western Brethren had allowed sisters to participate fully, but this was one of their innovations that the larger church frowned on.

The issue was raised again bluntly by a query in 1857: "Why do not the sisters break the bread and pass the cup to each other in the same manner as the brethren do at the communion?" The answer was really based on tradition, rather than on scripture, unlike usual Brethren practice: "Man being the head of woman and it having been the practice of the church, from time immemorial, for the officiating brethren to break the bread to the sisters, we know of no scriptural reason for making the change in our practice."[29]

The issue continued to be raised throughout the remaining decades of the nineteenth century, in the columns of church papers and in discussions at Annual Meetings. After 1894 the leading advocate for women's equality at love feast was Julia A. Gilbert, originally of the Wolf Creek congregation in Ohio, who had been crippled by childhood diseases. In 1883 she responded to an article in *The Gospel Messenger* by I. J. Rosenberger who contended for the traditional practice; in her published letter she asked why sisters could wash each other's feet and offer the holy kiss but not pass the bread and cup. Her efforts to change the pattern by sending queries through the Wolf Creek congregation and the district were rejected.

In 1897, following the death of her parents, she moved to Grundy County, Iowa, where she lived with a brother. She continued to press the cause of equality. In 1899 the Iowa district passed her query on to the Annual Meeting, which appointed a study committee. The issue was debated vigorously in 1900 and succeeding Annual Meetings. Finally, a committee in 1910 sought to finesse the question by recommending that the presiding elder administer the bread and cup to *both* brothers and sisters. Julia Gilbert then made an eloquent statement, recalling that when she was baptized, a strong current flowed in the river. The elder who baptized her said, "Don't be afraid, Jesus went before." She then and there committed herself "to live faithful to Christ Jesus until death." But, she continued, "When we come down to the breaking of bread and the passing of the cup, however, then man steps in between us and our Savior. Though man never suffered for us, or shed a drop of blood for us, he takes his hand to break the bread as if God hadn't given us any hands." The conference passed a substitute motion giving sisters the same privilege of passing the bread and cup enjoyed by the brethren.[30]

Whether women members of the Brethren could participate actively in the Annual Meetings was debated throughout the nineteenth century. In 1881 their right to vote was denied, but the decision was overturned the following year. By 1889 women were pressing for the right to be named as delegates to the Meetings; although at first disapproved, within ten years the names of women were appearing on the lists of delegates.[31]

The character of the Church of the Brethren was changing. Social needs pressing in from the outside, as well as desire for changes in long-accepted practices, forced the church to react. These shifts usually took long years to accomplish, but they were effected in time. More change was on hand in the first decades of the twentieth century.

18

Change in the
Early Twentieth Century

The last chapter portrays the shift away from the long-standing Brethren posture of aloofness to one of increasing engagement. Whereas previously Brethren were content to be known as a "peculiar people," a plain group shielded by a codex of rules and regulations from untoward contact with the "world," by the second decade of the twentieth century Brethren were aligning themselves with reform movements for temperance and peace. They began to urge the United States government to take vigorous action on moral issues.

The change in the legal name of the Brethren symbolizes this alteration. It was as late as 1836 that the Annual Meeting recommended an official name for legal documents—Fraternity of German Baptists; the brethren were so determinedly informal that they were even reluctant to accept a specific designation. In 1871 the name was changed by conference action to German Baptist Brethren. After lengthy discussion over several years, during the bicentennial year 1908 delegates at the Annual Conference adopted the name Church of the Brethren. Whereas earlier the use of the word church had been conscientiously avoided—as smacking of the establishment the first Brethren had rejected—by the early twentieth century Brethren wished to be identified as a respected Protestant body.

Home missions advocates argued that the tag German was misleading and hampered outreach; others wished to distance themselves from the Baptist label to avoid confusion with that aggressive denomination. Two queries reached the Annual Meeting of 1902 asking that the "derisive" names of Dunker or Dunkard or the "national" appellation of German Baptist be dropped because they were "detrimental to the work of the Brethren church." A committee of three assigned to study the issue reported that, in their judgment, such a change would be advisable and pose no legal problems, but they asked for another year to be absolutely safe about the latter. In 1904 the committee reported that legal counsel assured them that there were no obstacles to a change. They recommended the name be changed to the New Testament Church.

Discussion on the matter continued for four more years. A vote in 1906 found a majority favoring Dunker Brethren but it failed to achieve the required two-thirds. Another committee appointed in 1906 submitted three recommended names in 1908 for the delegates to choose from; they were The Brethren, The Dunker Brethren, and The Christian Brethren. After a long debate the Annual Meeting chose none of the suggested names but rather Church of the Brethren. Some of the discussants were influenced by the use of the last name by M. G. Brumbaugh in his bicentennial address earlier in the day.

Some still staunchly championed the alternative Dunker Brethren in 1908, such as the outspoken and colorful evangelist I. N. H. Beahm, but most felt the nickname Dunker (or worse Dunkard) had derogatory and infelicitous connotations. Hence the choice of Church of the Brethren, popularized in the mid-nineteenth century by Progressive leader Henry R. Holsinger and also used by other publishers.[1]

CULTURAL EVOLUTION OF THE BRETHREN

As the Brethren reshaped themselves in the course of the first half of the twentieth century, they struggled to remain faithful to their historic principles but found it imperative to recast these time-honored values in more acceptable forms to contemporary life. In a well-documented and convincingly argued book, sociologist Carl F. Bowman has demonstrated how venerable Brethren wine skins were filled with the new wine of twentieth-century affirmations. Thus the long-standing emphasis on nonconformity was transformed into the doctrine of the simple (or spiritual) life; then nonresistance was translated into the peace position; Brethren insistence on doctrinal uniformity was changed to emphasize the freedom of the individual conscience; the free ministry was transformed into the professional pastorate; and unity gave way to tolerance.[2]

As Brethren entered the twentieth century they were torn between loyalty to traditional Brethren beliefs and the appeal of contemporary Protestantism. The pressure of change had brought them by 1920 to adopt much of what Henry R. Holsinger and his colleagues had championed (with the notable exception of the congregationalist polity of the Progressives), but in their self-understanding they had held true to the ancient principles of the Brethren. "At stake were conflicting commitments to self-denial versus personal growth, preservation versus progress, primitivism versus practicality, submission versus liberty, church authority versus democracy, uniformity versus diversity, and separation versus inclusion." The Brethren response was often to keep the wording of traditional phrases but invest them with new content.[3]

NONCONFORMITY

The twelfth chapter of Romans with its appeal for nonconformity to the ways of the world had long been a favorite of the Brethren and the focus of many sermons. While nonconformity implies a wide range of behaviors and attitudes, in the debates of the late nineteenth century it had largely become equated with the order of plain dress. Advocates of a regulated style of dress for all members argued that this formed the clearest boundary between the church and the world. Members could instantly recognize each other by their style of dress and be recognized by others. It provided a clear witness to their faith commitment. Some also reasoned that wearing plain dress protected the individual, who would not wish to be seen in questionable places such as taverns wearing this costume, as it would bring dishonor to the church.

The defection of the Old German Baptist Brethren tempered but did not eliminate lengthy discussions at the Annual Meetings on the garb issue. Most of the moderate German Baptist Brethren party

(Conservatives) wished to adopt cautiously progressive methods in church life, but they also wished to maintain the distinctive Brethren practices. This notwithstanding, calls began to come for relaxation of the prescribed costume, many proceeding from dismay on the loss of valued members who no longer saw a biblical rationale for the dress code. The Standing Committee of 1898 drew up a comprehensive statement intended to provide direction on the controverted issue but found inconsistency in Annual Meeting rulings. "Upon examination seventy-four decisions regarding the various phases of non-conformity to the world in dress and in adorning the body are found on our Minutes....[More] decisions will not remove the inconsistency...but a more intelligent understanding of the important gospel principles of non-conformity to the world, plain dressing and plain living is what is needed."[4]

Continued confusion climaxed in a call in 1909 for a "clear and concise restatement of our position on this vexed question, so that all may understand alike and be unified and dwell together...in love and peace and harmony." A committee balanced between conservative and liberal church leaders brought back a well-reasoned and articulate report, basically restating past conference decisions in clear language.

Despite its merits the Annual Conference of 1910 was not satisfied with it. They appointed another committee, composed largely of liberal thinkers (although the answer suggested by the Standing Committee and accepted by the delegates specified "five faithful, intelligent, *conservative* brethren," who brought back an altered statement to the conference held at St. Joseph, Missouri, in 1911. While restating eloquently the biblical and practical rationale for plain dress, it for the first time failed to insist absolutely on adherence to plain dress as a test of membership.

Crucial language stated that "those who do not fully conform to the methods herein set forth, but who manifest no inclination to follow the unbecoming fashions, and whose life and conduct is becoming a follower of Christ, be dealt with in love and forbearance; and that every effort be made to save all to the church until they see the beauty of making a larger sacrifice for Christ and the church." The minute did call for church discipline for those who "in an arbitrary spirit" followed the "foolish fashions" of the world; in practice, however, many leaders chose to ignore that part of the statement.[5] The result was that, after 1911, congregation after congregation abandoned the requirement of plain dress until by 1940 only a minority of Brethren clung to it, largely in eastern and southern Pennsylvania and Maryland, with pockets elsewhere. A minority of Brethren led by Elder B. E. Kesler of Missouri were so aggrieved by the change that they left the Church of the Brethren to form the Dunkard Brethren (1926).

Not wishing to depart completely from the teaching of biblical nonconformity, church leaders began to speak of the simple life. Members could emphasize the virtues of plainness, economy, and modesty of dress by avoiding conspicuous and flashy costumes; Brethren would refrain from standing out in society either by their studied adoption of a regulated nonconformist style or by extravagances of fashion. An outline of doctrine published in 1912 for new converts by Philadelphia pastor and Yale graduate D. W. Kurtz dealt with fashions in dress in a section on worldliness. Kurtz explained that "no modest Christian women can for a moment think of following" the latest modes of fashion because most of them "are invented by lewd women of Paris, whose business it is thus to advertise their profession." Instead, "the whole life and teachings of Jesus show that the Christian life is the SIMPLE LIFE." This, however, does not mean a prescribed garb: "There is not a word in the Scriptures that demands absolute likeness or uniformity in dress, as to cut or form, for the Gospel is intended for all races and climates, and it is not a matter of form but of spirit." Good stewardship of financial resources would also militate against spending lavishly for clothing.[6]

FREEDOM OF CONSCIENCE

In comparable manner, the earlier Brethren insistence on doctrinal uniformity was now changed to enfold the right of individual conscience. Whereas a plethora of decisions of the nineteenth century Annual Meetings were devoted to creating and maintaining unity of doctrine (as on such issues as universal restoration, for example),

Martin G. Brumbaugh, governor of Pennsylvania, at the executive mansion. J. W. Replogle photo, *BHLA Collection.*

by the mid-twentieth century the church was reluctant to speak authoritatively on doctrinal issues. The unity of doctrinal expression expected by earlier Brethren gave way to individualized interpretation.

Two mottoes were repeatedly invoked to justify the change. One was *no force in religion*, the other *no creed but the New Testament*. The former was popularized by Martin G. Brumbaugh in his lengthy history of the Brethren movement. Brumbaugh had abandoned in his own personal lifestyle many Brethren restrictions and attitudes; he was, for example, an inveterate cigar smoker, a member of sophisticated social clubs, and, at least for a time, a member of a "secret society" (the Masons), all forbidden by Brethren codes. He interpreted *no force in religion* to mean that exercise of church discipline was a departure from traditional Brethren practice. It was wrong from the heritage, according to Brumbaugh's interpretation, to force "anyone to join *or to leave* the church of Christ."[7]

Although the motto itself is not found in early Brethren sources, it is an accurate projection of Brethren conviction, stemming from both Anabaptist and Pietist teaching, that coercion dare never be used by the state in matters of faith. It is decidedly wrong to reason, as did Brumbaugh, that the early Brethren did not practice strict church discipline. It loomed large not only in their practice but also in their few extant writings. For one example, we have seen that the open letter to the Palatine Pietists which served as an announcement and invitation to their first baptisms clearly declared that church discipline was foundational.

It was at this time that the phrase *no creed but the New Testament* became popular and often quoted. It was used to justify individual interpretations of doctrine jarring with traditional Brethren readings. Brethren had always resisted the elaboration of creedal statements and therefore could be accurately called noncreedal. They understood this as a protection against scholastic dogma and sterile formulations that became hidebound.

Another quotation often quoted at this time (using its supposed author as a spokesman for the Brethren) came from the early Ephrata figure Michael Wohlfahrt (Welfare) of colonial Pennsylvania, as reported by Benjamin Franklin. The free-thinking Franklin was said to have asked Wohlfahrt why the Ephrata Society did not publish their "articles of belief and rules of practice" to put a stop to the outrageous rumors about them that often circulated. His answer, which pleased the deist Franklin greatly, runs,

> When we were first drawn together as a society, it had pleased God to enlighten our minds so far as to see that some doctrines which we once esteemed truths were errors, and that others which we had esteemed errors were real truths. From time to time he has been pleased to afford us further light, and our principles have been improving and our errors diminishing. Now we're not sure that we are arrived at the end of this progression, and at the perfection of spiritual or theological knowl-

> edge; and we fear that if we should once print our confession of faith, we should feel ourselves as if bound and confined by it, and perhaps be unwilling to receive further improvements, and our successors still more so, as conceiving what their elders and founders had done to be something sacred, never to be departed from.

Franklin called this "modesty in a sect" perhaps "a singular instance in the history of mankind." Given Franklin's well-known penchant for literary invention, the anecdote may be fictional, recorded as congenial to the printer's distrust of religious orthodoxy. The veracity of the story is immaterial in this context; what is important is that it was used by Brethren seeking greater doctrinal freedom.[8]

A more accurate way to speak of Brethren noncreedalism is to put the phrase in this more complete way: We have no creed, but the New Testament is our rule of faith and practice. The late eighteenth-century description by Robert Proud is indicative; in describing the Brethren, he writes: "They have a great esteem for the New Testament, valuing it higher than the other books; and when they are asked about the articles of their faith, they say they know of no others but what are contained in this book; and therefore can give none."[9]

As D. L. Miller explains the Brethren position on this point, "They mutually agreed to lay aside all existing creeds, confessions of faith and catechisms, and search for the truth of God's Book, and having found it, to follow it wherever it might lead them. They were led to adopt the New Testament as their creed and to declare in favor of a literal observance of all the commandments of the Son of God....The Brethren hold the Bible to be the inspired and infallible Word of God, and accept the New Testament as their rule of faith and practice." Understood this way, Brethren were actually hyper-creedal in attempting to follow exactly all of the directions of the entire New Testament, as explicated by the decisions of the Annual Meetings.[10]

MINISTRY

During this same period, Brethren experienced a major change in ministerial leadership. Since 1708 Brethren had called out leaders from within its ranks by a process of discernment of gifts of biblical knowledge and character. Those chosen by election to the various ranks of ministry understood this as a life-time commitment without stated remuneration. Often congregations gave love gifts to their leaders or assisted with unusual financial needs. It was common for members, for example, to assist in harvesting crops for their farmer-preachers, and it was not unknown for ministers to receive farms as gifts, enabling them to settle as preachers in a new community. The scholarly James Quinter, for example, was asked to become a minister at the George's Creek congregation, in Fayette County, Pennsylvania. Members gave him a small farm from which he was to earn his living. A later publishing associate of his, J. H. Moore, related that he had only seen his dignified friend laugh once. That was when Quinter recalled the "good brethren...who undertook, by locating him on a farm none too desirable, to make a creditable farmer of him." They found out, said Quinter, that he was not cut out to be a farmer. More usually, men were not called to the ministry who had not first achieved at least a modest, or more often, a substantial fiscal competency.[11]

As the membership came to include a larger number of college-educated persons, pressure grew for an educated and well-prepared ministry. An unusually high percentage of Brethren became teachers in the public schools. As these and other professional lay members began to become impatient with the efforts of relatively uneducated and self-trained ministers, more voices were heard advocating advanced training for church leaders.

Earlier Brethren had been very suspicious of the motives of what they called the "hireling"—that is, salaried—ministry. The nineteenth century attitude toward the ministry was well expressed by Henry Kurtz, himself once a Lutheran pastor with a fixed income. In a sermon at the 1845 Annual Meeting recorded by John Kline, Kurtz emphasizes,

> There is one feature particularly in the order of our ministry that I have always advocated...and that is an *unsalaried* ministry. The world will say to me right here: "You are working against your own interest...." In answer

to this I have to say that God never meant for the Gospel to be used as a means of getting water to the preacher's mill, or grain into his garner. When the Gospel is converted into merchandise, the preacher becomes a merchant, and like all other merchants it becomes his interest to handle his goods in a way that will please his customers, and put them in such shape and procure for them such kinds, whether good, bad, or indifferent, as will suit their fancies and please their tastes. "The love of money is a root of all evil," no less in the ministry than anywhere else.[12]

The first regular financial support for a Brethren minister emerged in the Philadelphia congregation, always a fount of innovations. It seems to have been initiated in the 1860s. In 1861 and again in 1866 Annual Meetings spoke against any "treasury for the exclusive benefit of the ministry" and any "stated salary," while encouraging the membership to support their ministers "in all cases of necessity." These pronouncements may well have been directed at Philadelphia. For years there were rumors that the pastor at Philadelphia received $1,000 per year.[13]

The first known full-time salaried pastors were Tobias T. Myers at Philadelphia (1891) and J. W. Cline at the Geiger Memorial church, also in Philadelphia (1896); Myers' yearly income (counting the rental value of a free parsonage) approximated $1,000, Cline's, $600. The name Geiger in the latter congregational title refers to the generous Mary Schwenk Geiger, widow of the physician Henry Geiger, who paid the salary of Cline from her own substantial means and provided much of the budget for the Philadelphia congregation as well. Pastors in Sterling, Cerro Gordo, and Chicago (all in Illinois) also were salaried in the 1890s. One of them, John W. Lear, who later was a faculty member at the Bethany Bible School, did much to promote the cause of the professional, salaried ministry.[14]

In the bicentennial year a report came to the 1908 Annual Conference from a committee charged with considering the matter of financial support of ministers and evangelists. It basically viewed with concern "unequaled distribution of our ministry" and "financial hindrances." It urged the church toward greater generosity in supporting its ministers. Primarily, however, it registered the changes from the former free ministry system to that of a salaried ministry and urged patience "while this conscious change is taking place," leading to an "entire transformation coming over us...."[15]

A substantial change began with a committee report (culminating discussion since 1911) that recommended to the 1915 Annual Conference that young men be allowed to volunteer for the ministry. Previously, this was considered to be prideful and self-promoting; the best way to ensure that one would not be called to the ministry would be to let it become known that one had ambitions in that direction. The same 1915 action urged the establishment of educational standards for ministers. Ministers were to be encouraged to provide their services free of charge, but congregations were to be given permission to employ pastors. The committee report was tabled and again recommitted during the following year, but in 1917 it was adopted by Conference, save for naming specific educational standards. Throughout the 1920s virtually every Annual Conference tinkered with the ministerial system.[16]

BETHANY BIBLE SCHOOL / BETHANY BIBLICAL SEMINARY

Linked with this development was the creation of a seminary for the denomination. This had been vehemently denounced well into the later nineteenth century, never more clearly than in the Annual Meeting of 1882; its legal-sounding statement reads:

> We also declare distinctly that our loyal and faithful Brotherhood should neither fellowship, countenance nor tolerate those who would undertake to establish, under any pretence or color whatever, theological schools, or theological departments of schools or colleges, having in contemplation or purpose the training or graduation of any youth specially for the ministry of the Brotherhood or elsewhere, but we should faithfully adhere to our long-established practice of calling brethren to the ministry.[17]

P R E P A R E

Grounds and Buildings Bethany Bible School

The harvest indeed is plenteous but the laborers are few.
(Matt. 9:37)

"Whom shall I send, and who will go for us?
Here am I send me." (Isa. 68)

"Study to show thyself approved unto God,
a workman that needeth not to be ashamed,
handling aright the word of truth."
(2 Tim. 2:15)

Bethany Bible School

is the specialized institution in which the Church of the
Brethren provides opportunity for

Bible Study	Sacred Music Training
Pastoral Preparation	Missionary Preparation
Religious Education	Training in Actual Religious Work

Courses to meet the needs of all grades of students

For particulars, address

BETHANY BIBLE SCHOOL
3435 VAN BUREN STREET   **CHICAGO, ILLINOIS**

S E R V E

Student Ministers' Association Spring of 1925

Advertisement for Bethany Bible School at Chicago in the mid-1920s; only later did
the school take the name Bethany Biblical Seminary, eventually changing it to
Bethany Theological Seminary. *Durnbaugh Collection.*

Despite this firm disavowal, in the 1890s colleges did begin Bible courses and institutes and later there came Bible schools, such as those of E. S. Young. The real breakthrough, however, came in 1905 when two Brethren, Emanuel B. Hoff and Albert Cassel Wieand, began Bethany Bible School on the south side of Chicago. They had agreed on the venture in 1891 as they sat on the hillside overlooking the Palestinian Bethany.[18]

The immediate motivation for founding the small enterprise was their realization that more than a few young Brethren men and women were enrolling in Moody Bible Institute in Chicago. Following the lead of Dr. W. W. White's Bible Training Institute in New York (where Wieand had taught), they proposed to center the school on the Bible rather than on theology, using the inductive method. They also intended to stress practical work, using the teeming city as a laboratory.

With some of the means brought to Hoff by his wife, in 1905 the two began their school on Hastings Street in a house located across the street from a home missions outpost of the Brethren, where E. B. Hoff was pastor. Starting with twelve students in these improvised quarters, within three years the enrollment swelled to more than 150. A city block on the west side of Chicago was purchased (after complex negotiations) and the first of a number of buildings was erected in 1908. By the 1919-20 school year the student body notched 376 in number, most of these studying in the training school with only a few in the seminary.

Although the denomination recognized the school in 1909 and took complete ownership and governance in 1925, Bethany did have its detractors. These came from two sources; the first was made up of the Brethren colleges, whose leaders correctly saw Bethany as a rival, recruiting as it did high-school graduates for its training school. Several offered Wieand teaching positions, hoping to stop the school that way; others hoped to transform their Bible departments into full-fledged seminaries. The second source was the camp of conservatives in the church, who continued the long-standing criticism of theological schools per se. Interestingly, however, some conservatives believed that Bethany might perpetuate, as a Bible school, traditional Brethren belief more faithfully than the modernistic colleges.[19]

Gradually, the graduates of the school took their places as pastors of Brethren congregations, until the norm for pastoral leadership became a Bethany-trained minister. The stated goal for the denomination, as articulated by A. C. Wieand, consisted of two trained and supported workers in each congregation, a pastor and a Christian education director. At this point it was understood that the first would be a man and the second a woman.[20]

CHANGE IN CONGREGATIONAL CLAIMS

A significant change in the concept of membership took effect between 1926 and 1931. The traditional practice had been for geographical boundaries demarcating the limits of a congregation. All Brethren residing within those lines belonged to the congregation and were under its discipline. If they happened to move to a residence within the boundaries of another congregation, the procedure was to bring with them a "church letter" that certified that they had been in "good standing" and therefore could be readily accepted. The effect of this procedure was to make impossible a shift in residence from a more strictly disciplined fellowship to one more liberal. By rulings of Annual Meeting as late as 1907, letters were to be withheld from those considered to be unfaithful to church regulations, and members without them were not to be accepted in a new congregation.

In the early decades of the twentieth century, the question of transfer of membership became one of the most troublesome in the church. Some church leaders issued letters of transfer for members whom they thought questionable, but indicated on the backs of the letters problems of disciplinary nature they considered serious; this proved to be an unsatisfactory solution. In 1926 a new ruling decided that "membership in a local congregation is to have membership in the general body"; consequently, requirements for transfer of membership must not be greater than those for general membership. Because conservative church leaders understood that the logic of the ruling led to force each congregation to be as liberal as the most liberal, they pushed for a change. It came in 1930-31 with the proviso that each congregation should have the right to judge whether a letter of transfer should be granted and also whether letters would be received. The effect was to undercut the long-standing Brethren drive toward complete unity within the total church by facing the reality of different congregational identities, some more conservative, others more liberal. In essence, congregationalism triumphed over connectionalism.[21]

THEOLOGICAL STRUGGLES

Although most observers have explained the transformation of the Brethren during this period in sociological or socio-economic categories, it is important to recognize that theological issues were also at the forefront. At least three distinct strands can be identified in the Brethren fabric of the late nineteenth and early twentieth centuries: primitivism, liberalism, and fundamentalism.

PRIMITIVISM

This is the doctrine that church belief and practice is best based on the life and thought of the early Christian church. To the extent possible, true Christianity is to be expressed by following the pattern of the first Christians. Seen by some as the key concept for understanding the sixteenth-century Anabaptists during the Radical Reformation, primitivism has appeared and re-appeared as a perennially popular engine of radical reform.[22]

Those adopting this principle can "sit loose" with church tradition, appealing as they do to Christian origins. The first followers of Jesus Christ are understood to be the best reflection of his intent, unencumbered by the overlay and admixture of the centuries since then. In contrast to the concept of Roman Catholic apostolic succession—church authority based on the presumption of an unbroken chain through the descendants of Peter in the bishop's office—primitivism seeks to ground itself directly on the experience of "the first and best Christians," as it was expressed by Sander Mack.[23]

In the controversies of the later nineteenth century, Brethren polemicists consistently argued that not only had they taken their faith and ordinances from the early church, they actually were the direct continuation of the one true church (in essence, a different kind of apostolic succession). A classic example of this attitude was found in a German-language concordance of the New Testament published in 1878 at Ephrata, Pennsylvania, by a Brethren printer named John Eby Pfautz. In a series of thumbnail sketches of all American denominations, Pfautz describes the German Baptist Brethren:

> The denomination arose as follows: John, the forerunner of Jesus, was the first Baptist, then Jesus Christ and his apostles; in this way the Church of Christ on earth was founded and organized in Palestine, then planted elsewhere under heavy persecution and martyrdom. [At this point Pfautz presents a long line of martyrs through sixteen centuries.] In the 17th century, the persecuted Christians [i.e., the Waldensians] found a refuge in the valley of the Alps in the western part of the Piedmont, where they lived unharmed for a short time. However, they were soon again atrociously persecuted.
>
> Then in the 18th century, in the year 1708, a place of freedom was found near Schwarzenau, where some of the apostolic Christians assembled and again organized a church; but soon afterwards they were again persecuted and dispersed, a part to Holland and Crefeld, the rest to Friesland. Then in the year 1719 they came from Friesland to America and landed at Philadelphia. Then in the year 1729 their brethren from Holland and Crefeld followed. In this way the Church of Jesus Christ arose and came to America which at this time has been extended over almost all of the United States.[24]

The same self-understanding was shared by the well-educated Henry Kurtz, who began a long series of articles in his periodical on the history of the Brethren. Although never actually coming to the eighteenth-century beginnings, Kurtz gave extensive coverage to the persecuted sectarians such as the Waldensians, considered to be the direct forerunners of the Brethren. He gave his series this title: "The

Church in the Wilderness: Testimonies of the existence of the apostolical church from the beginning of the Gospel up to our time."[25]

When the German journalist Moritz Busch visited Peter Nead's congregation in the Miami Valley of Ohio and asked about Dunker origins, he was given to understand by a venerable elder with impressive beard that the "rise and progress of the church began with the apostles and was the history of the invisible church of God."[26] Not all of the critics of the Brethren accepted this primitivist self-portrayal. A Baptist elder named M. Ellison challenged the Brethren claim in an extensive work called *Dunkerism Examined* (1869), maintaining that it was the Baptists who were the current perpetuation of the early church. Having learned of their founding in 1708, he maintained that the Brethren "were about 1675 years too late to be the church founded upon a rock, against which the gates of hell never were to prevail." Brethren journalists noticed the rebuttal and attempted to refute the "impudent elder." John S. Flory explained the 1708 date for the Brethren as a "re-organization" rather than as a founding.[27]

An exemplar of the primitivist approach was John Henry (J. H.) Moore, whose long life from 1846 to 1935 was devoted to the Brethren cause. In early life a poor lad in the recently settled Illinois territory, he had little formal education but a tremendous desire for self-improvement. He earned his living as a house painter and carpenter but studied and read voraciously. Moore was keenly desirous of becoming a leader in the church despite deafness and a speech defect caused by medical malpractice; he resolved to make his mark as a writer and editor.[28]

He first won a reputation among the Brethren with a defense of their form of baptism, *Trine Immersion Traced to the Apostles*; published in 1,000 copies in 1872, it attracted large sales and necessary republication because it supplied the Brethren with voluminous citation of sources demonstrating the validity of three-fold forward immersion. A later booklet, *One Baptism* (1876) was written as a dialogue between a Dunker and six other denominational representatives; in the words of the subtitle, it showed that "trine immersion is the only ground of union that can be conscientiously occupied by the leading religious denominations of Christendom." It is said to have enjoyed the largest sale of any book or booklet released by the Brethren in the nineteenth century.

In 1876 J. H. Moore associated himself with M. M. Eshelman in issuing the periodical *The Brethren at Work*; when this was amalgamated with the eastern Brethren papers in 1883 to become *The Gospel Messenger*, Moore became the office editor. Although he moved to Florida for a time, where he busied himself in creating new Brethren congregations, most of his life was devoted to editing and writing.

Moore had a keen historical interest. Besides his urgent desire to prove that the Brethren were the representatives in modern times of the early church, he was dedicated to discovering everything he could about Brethren history in the USA. In his book *Some Brethren Pathfinders* (1929), he gathered information about the pioneers in the Midwest. Through his collection of material, requests for biographical data, and his own articles and books, he laid the foundation for the current Brethren Historical Library and Archives in Elgin, Illinois.

During this swing period, before Brethren had developed a central administrative office and staff, editors such as Moore played strong roles in directing the course of the church. They were trusted gatekeepers for soliciting, receiving, and passing on information; moreover, by their control of the columns of the Brethren periodicals, they steered the course of doctrinal thinking. Often penning polemics, Moore and other editors were ardent defenders of Brethren ways. H. C. Early wrote of Moore, "He knew the genius of the Brethren faith as few men knew it. He knew the people he served. He could sense trends and anticipate situations with remarkable correctness. He knew the kind of paper the church wanted and did his best to provide it without sacrificing his independence as editor and leader."[29]

J. H. Moore's most popular later work, *The New Testament Doctrines* (1914), is an anthology of his topical articles. Its orientation is revealed by Moore's observation about the Brethren beginnings in Schwarzenau: "After studying the Word for months, it became evident that there was no body of people in all Europe...who, in their faith and practice lined up with the form of doctrine enjoined upon the followers of Christ." After brief chapters on God, the Bible, Jesus, atonement, repentance, conversion, and other basic topics, Moore devoted most attention to chapters on the Brethren ordinances of trine immersion baptism, the Lord's Supper, and feetwashing. This simple, sensible, and straightforward exposition of Christian doctrine reflected mainstream Brethren belief during this period.[30]

LIBERALISM

As Brethren opened themselves to the winds of doctrinal change during this era, many of the younger leaders were caught up in the dominant Protestant liberalism. Among its core understandings were the goodness of God, the presence of the Holy Spirit in human activities, the basic goodness of humankind, and an active optimism about the resolution of all societal problems. A later and unkind caricature said liberalism taught that a "God without wrath brought men without sin into a kingdom without judgment through the ministration of a Christ without a cross." Liberals favored a "spirit of open-mindedness, of tolerance and humility, of devotion to truth wherever it might be found." They understood that the pursuit of truth could only be of assistance to the Christian faith, which itself consisted of the truth.

Among the more specific themes of liberalism were 1) respect for science and the scientific method; 2) acknowledgment that the possibility of acquiring knowledge of the ultimate reality is only tentative; 3) emphasis upon the principle of continuity, the close connection of the divine and the natural; 4) the essential similarity of all world religions; and 5) confidence in the future of humankind. Liberals stressed the humanity, not the divinity of Jesus Christ; the immanence of God's action in the world; the dignity and potential of every human being; and the importance of human experience. It was linked with, but not the same as, the Social Gospel movement, the attempt to relate Christianity to actual human needs in an increasingly industrialized society.[31]

As younger Brethren leaders went on to graduate schools to secure advanced training, they gravitated to the centers of liberal

Protestant thought—the University of Chicago, Yale University, Vanderbilt University, and Boston University, including their respective divinity schools. None went to Princeton Theological Seminary, a bastion of orthodox Calvinist theology. It was only later that some young Brethren found their way there, such as Calvert N. Ellis, later the longtime president of Juniata College, who wrote the first American thesis on the neo-Reformation theologian Karl Barth.

A Brethren exemplar of the liberal mindset was Daniel Webster Kurtz, usually known as D. W. Kurtz. He was a pastor, educator, college and seminary president, and perhaps the pre-eminent orator of his time among the Brethren (rivaled only by M. G. Brumbaugh, who died in 1930). Born of solid northeastern Ohio stock in 1879, he was among the first Brethren to pursue graduate training in the Ivy League, taking BA and BD degrees from Yale University. Kurtz pastored a small Congregationalist parish to support his education. He won a traveling fellowship from the university which allowed him to study in Germany at Marburg, Leipzig, and Berlin, where he heard the great liberal theologian Adolf Harnack.[32]

Back in the United States, he took up pastoral work in Philadelphia in 1910, studying also at the University of Pennsylvania. While in Philadelphia he intervened actively in the dress question then under review by Annual Conference, arguing that for Brethren to have success in ministering to urban areas, it was imperative to drop unnecessary rules. He also pressed for the creation of the new Southeastern Pennsylvania district, the boundaries of which were drawn so as to include the more progressive congregations around Philadelphia; this was to free them from the control of the conservative congregations in Lancaster County.[33]

In 1924 Kurtz was called to the presidency of McPherson College, where he labored for three years to achieve academic credibility for the small school. Speaking widely on a variety of topics, he addressed hundreds of high-school commencements and service clubs, making McPherson College known across the region. He was reputed to have more than 100 eloquent lectures he could deliver on a moment's notice. His repeated claim on hearing of a topic was "I've read a hundred books on the subject." It is known that it was his custom to speed-read a book every morning before breakfast.

Kurtz helped to launch a trend in the church (initiated in 1923 by Otho Winger) to call educators to the honored position of moderator of the Brethren. He himself was elected to serve in this capacity four times between 1926 and 1939. Until 1960 college and seminary presidents and deans virtually dominated the position. He served as pastor of the Long Beach, California, congregation from 1927 to 1932, when he was called to take up the presidency of Bethany Biblical Seminary. In the heart of the depression years, Kurtz labored valiantly to keep the school afloat, ruining his health in the process. Faculty were often paid in part during this period in foodstuffs, donated by supportive Brethren farmers. Forced to resign in 1937 by ill health, he returned to California where he was pastor of the La Verne congregation until shortly before his death.

As an educator, he chaired the General Education Board of the Brethren from 1915 to 1928 and took leading positions in international Sunday school associations. He attended their world conferences in Zürich (1913), Tokyo (1920), Glasgow (1924), and Los Angeles (1928), speaking at the last three. As a noted orator, he lectured widely at Chautauquas and lyceums; he was one of the speakers in the Federal Council of Churches Preaching Mission of 1936-37.

Although he called himself an evangelical, Kurtz was frankly liberal in his theological positions. He wrote the pamphlet *Ideals of the Church of the Brethren* in the 1930s, which is still kept in circulation. It portrays the Christian life not in terms of doctrine but rather in terms of ethical principles Brethren cherish: peace, temperance, the spiritual (or simple) life, brotherhood, and "a religion of the good life, fellowship, and harmony with Christ, as against mere creeds and cultus of the churches from which [the Brethren] came." More importantly, he authored the doctrinal section of the influential book sponsored by the Church of the Brethren *Studies in Doctrine and Devotion* (1919), which is characterized by liberal definitions of God, Jesus Christ, the church, revelation, and other doctrinal themes.

For example, God is defined as "the personal Spirit, perfectly Good, who in holy love, creates, sustains, and orders all." Also "God is the perfect Person, the spiritual Person who is over all things." Further, "God has revealed himself through nature,...through the great prophets..., through Jesus" and through the Bible. The scriptures are understood as the "Record of how God has gradually revealed himself to the world through the Hebrew race."

On human nature: "God made man in his own image, hence man is like God in personality. God is the Personal Spirit, who made all things, and man, the image of God, is likewise personal spirit." Man is a growing personality, going through stages of growth. Sin is defined in several different ways, but is principally understood as "missing the mark, or aim," falling short of God's purpose in human life. "The will of God is this perfect standard of life, which sin misses, and thus brings discord into the world."

Jesus Christ aimed to bring in the kingdom of God, open to all. The law of life is love and love is the supreme ethic. "Christ is our Authority, because he is the Eternal Truth and Goodness. We should therefore acknowledge him as our Teacher, our Guide, our Lord and Savior." Christ's role in salvation is through revelation. He revealed the gospel through his teachings, through his deeds, through his own life, and through his death. "The Holy Jesus died the most shameful death to show how much love will do to save a lost world." Atonement is understood as reconciliation, as "at-one-ment." Conversion is the whole process of the soul, intellect, feeling, and will—"a will that turns away from sin unto righteousness."[34]

Kurtz had earlier written an even more liberal work, which he daringly called *An Outline of the Fundamental Doctrines of Faith* (1912), as a brief introduction to doctrine for new converts in his Philadelphia congregation. A Brethren fundamentalist named Paul Mohler attacked it as dangerous, claiming that Kurtz's God was near-Unitarian, that he accepted evolution, and that he denied the existence of Satan and eternal punishment. According to Mohler, Kurtz avoided such terms as propitiation, redemption, salvation, justification, and sanctification. In the denominational book, Kurtz did use these words but with liberal connotation and definition. After a long and influential career, he died in California in 1949.[35]

FUNDAMENTALISM

Although not often understood in this way, fundamentalism among the Brethren represented quite as much acculturation to the world as had liberalism; in this case it marked an importation of conservative theology. Though the Church of the Brethren was not buffeted as severely by the fundamentalist/modernist conflict as most other Protestant denominations in the first half of the twentieth century, it did encounter shock waves.

This battle is clearer within the broader Brethren movement in the struggles of the Brethren Church, where intramural debates on these issues resulted in a raging controversy. The upshot was that half of the membership left in 1939 to form the Grace Brethren (National Fellowship of Brethren Churches). The greater involvement of the Brethren Church in the struggle may be explained by recalling that the Brethren Church, as the inheritor of the Progressive movement of the 1880s, was more open to the winds of doctrine, of outside pressure, than was the Church of the Brethren.[36]

Fundamentalism turned its face against everything that liberal Protestantism favored; it bitterly opposed any accommodation of the faith to scientific innovations, being most sharply opposed to the Darwinian theory of the evolution of the species and Freudian concepts of psychology. It rejected the application of scientific methods to biblical study, the so-called "higher criticism." Any attempt to use a comparative method of studying Christianity along with other world religions was decried as syncretism. It understood itself as fighting for the preservation of orthodox doctrine at a time when those tenets were fast crumbling.

There are various ways of listing the "fundamentals," some containing no fewer than fourteen points. By one popular reckoning they include 1) the inspiration and verbal inerrancy of scripture; 2) the virgin birth and deity of Jesus Christ; 3) the substitutionary theory of atonement; 4) belief in the bodily resurrection and imminent return of Jesus Christ; and 5) Christ's performance of miracles during his earthly ministry. The tag "fundamentals" was derived from a series of publications under that name (1910-15) given wide distribution by two California businessmen, concerned by what they saw as religious decline in the nation.

Vital to the fundamentalist position was insistence on the authority and verbal inspiration of the Bible. Although minor errors could be conceded in the process of copying scriptural manuscripts, the "original autographs" (unfortunately no longer preserved) were inspired by God in such a manner as to preclude any distortion or error. Therefore, the scriptures must be understood as the absolutely reliable and authoritative source of detailed knowledge about God and God's activity in the world.

The methods of biblical study accepted by liberal scholars, which tended to treat the scriptures on the same level as other ancient documents, undermined its trustworthiness.

> As soon as we have questioned the authenticity of any of the recorded sayings of Jesus or the validity of Paul's theology; as soon as we have said that the Bible is in part a result of the natural working of the human mind, without the full inspiration of the Holy Spirit; then, we have left the solid rock of truth and embarked upon a hopeless sea of uncertainty. Either the words of the Bible are infallibly the words of God or we have no basis for faith. It is all or none.[37]

Given this mindset, fundamentalists could grant no concession on even minor points of doctrine, for that would imply that human judgment is involved. Fundamentalism could be likened to a fortress, the defenders of which fought fiercely from its ramparts to prevent the displacement of a single stone, for fear that the entire structure would fall. In essence fundamentalism was a hardening of Reformed scholasticism of the seventeenth and eighteenth centuries; it wished to pin down every facet of orthodox Christian belief to provide security for believers in an increasingly chaotic world.

Fundamentalists were a tiny but aggressive minority within the Church of the Brethren. The most vocal did not appear until the 1940s; this was Harold Snider, born in 1900 in Waynesboro, Pennsylvania. Following a pastorate in Martinsburg, West Virginia, he was called to the pulpit of the Church of the Brethren in Lewistown, Pennsylvania. This was in 1941, shortly before the United States entered World War II. He attacked Brethren pacifism as unbiblical and unpatriotic in his book *Does the Bible Sanction War?* (1942) and reproved the church for its cooperation and then affiliation with the Federal Council of Churches—*Modernism, the Federal Council, and the Church of the Brethren* (1944).

An ardent follower of the arch-fundamentalist Carl McIntire, he imitated that activist's militant style and tone in a monthly periodical called *The Brethren Fundamentalist* (originally called *The Gospel Trumpet*), which Snider published after 1945. He contended that he could not get his articles published in the denominational paper, *The Gospel Messenger*, then edited by the strongly peace-minded Desmond Bittinger. Snider opened his columns to Carl McIntire and to dissident Brethren, attempting to create support for his position across the church. Snider ridiculed the social action programs of the Brethren in jarring and sarcastic ways, claiming, for example, that support of the Heifer Project proved that the Brethren worshiped sacred cows. On his letterhead as pastor of the Lewistown congregation, he identified it as "The Church of the Brethren—Dispensational, Premillennial, Fundamental."

Having won most of the members to his independent point of view, Snider attempted to take the congregation out of the Church of the Brethren. The Middle District of Pennsylvania responded with litigation in a dispute that was spread across local newspapers. The district won the case and kept the church property for the minority of members who wished to remain loyal Brethren; Snider and his followers proceeded to erect a new building, calling their congregation the Calvary Independent Church of the Brethren. In 1959 Snider left the congregation and was employed as a chaplain by an oil company in Venezuela. He died in 1993.[38]

Juniata College and Conservative Theology

Much more influential for the conservative theological cause in the Church of the Brethren than the flamboyant Snider was another resident of middle Pennsylvania. This was Charles Calvert Ellis, who lived from 1874 to 1950, the long-time president of Juniata College.[39]

He was won as a lad to the Brethren cause in a Baltimore Sunday school taught by James Quinlan. His studies at Juniata College were funded by an active layperson of Waynesboro, Pennsylvania, J. F. Oller. After further graduate study, Ellis was associated for a time (as the director of the educational system) with the "prophet" John Alexander Dowie in his abortive theocracy at Zion, Illinois. This linkage later embarrassed Ellis.

After completing a second doctorate at the University of Pennsylvania in 1907, C. C. Ellis was called back to Juniata College, where his talent as an educator won advancement to the vice presidency in 1917 and the presidency in 1930 upon the death of M. G. Brumbaugh. He was known as a brilliant orator, lecturing in the summers at teachers' institutes and Chautauquas in several states. The church called him to be moderator three times (1935, 1944, and 1950), and he was also named as chairman of the General Education Board.

Ellis made no secret of his conservative theological views. He was a strong premillennialist and was openly critical of articles in *The Gospel Messenger* that spoke of bringing in the kingdom through social action. He strongly criticized a publication of the General Education Board called *The Social Message of Christianity* (1922), which set forth a program of action akin to the Social Gospel. For many years he wrote articles every week for *The Sunday School Times*, a conservative paper, which also published an influential book by Ellis on religious psychology. In 1922 he became a contributing editor of *The Bible Companion*, the organ of the fundamentalistic Bible League of North America. He taught in the summer school of the Moody Bible Institute in Chicago, which sought to place him on their permanent faculty.

Ellis issued a creedal statement for Christian colleges, largely following the fundamentalist line. The tenor of the document may be sensed from the first affirmation: "The unique and infallible inspiration of the Bible (by this is meant inspiration different in kind as well as in degree from that of every other book in the world); and every part of the entire Bible equally inspired and infallibly accurate, both in matters of fact as well as of doctrine, in the original manuscripts."[40]

J. Oliver Buswell, president of Wheaton College in Illinois, wrote to Ellis in 1933, asking if he wished to be identified with the World's Christian Fundamental Association and be present at its convention slated for Chicago. Ellis responded to Buswell's associate, assuring him of his desire to cooperate with the association, though not considering it essential to join officially or to be represented. "As an institution we are essentially at one with the positions of the Association and personally I believe increasingly that the only salvation for our education is to maintain it on the basis of the Christian fundamentals."

Although C. C. Ellis shared doctrinal views with fundamentalists, he did not appreciate its characteristic militancy. This Ellis clearly articulates in a letter he wrote to a conservative Brethren figure who wished to recruit him to join an effort to oppose Brethren affiliation with the Federal Council of Churches. Writes Ellis, "I must confess that though my doctrinal attitudes are far more in line with the attitudes of the fundamentalists, so-called, than perhaps with any other group, I have been frequently disturbed in spirit at the intolerant attitude which certain ones of them seem to manifest; and I have taken occasion sometimes to suggest that important as it is to accept the doctrine of Christ, it is quite as important to manifest the spirit of Christ, for if one [does] not have this spirit, he is none of His." For this reason Ellis preferred to be known as an evangelical Christian.[41]

The theological position of this academic leader became more important with the creation at Juniata of the School of Theology in 1918, shortly after Ellis became vice president. It emerged because of dissatisfaction with the liberal theological slant of the faculty of Bethany Biblical Seminary. When the Church of the Brethren took ownership of the seminary in 1925, Juniata's theological school was terminated "in deference to the request of the church that the denomination have but one seminary."[42] For the first time in 1927 the Bethany catalog listed a nine-point doctrinal statement, introduced by the phrase "The Board of Directors have determined the following as doctrinal tenets of the school." It seems to have been the case that this was instituted to ease the concerns of conservative church leaders; it is possible that Juniata agreed to drop its school if Bethany introduced a doctrinal statement.

While containing many traditional doctrinal points, the spirit of the Bethany statement was different than classic fundamentalist creeds. The first item of tenets to be believed reads, "The Personality and Eternal Sovereignty of God, the Creator and Upholder of all things"; the second, "The Deity as well as the humanity of Jesus

Christ our Lord." At any rate, the demise of the conservative Juniata school removed a center which could have proved divisive for the denomination. Given a different temperament on the part of C. C. Ellis, the fundamentalist story for these decades could have been quite different.

During this period conservatives from Middle Pennsylvania tried to make the so-called *Brethren's Card* mandatory for church workers such as missionaries. First published in the late 1880s by the Brethren's Book and Tract Work, it was widely circulated as a succinct statement of Brethren belief. In 1923 the Annual Conference, persuaded by liberal church members, refused to endorse a revised version of the Brethren's Card as an official summary of Brethren doctrine, so as to avoid creedalism, but recommended it for widespread distribution by the Tract Committee.[43]

Brethren were engaged in serious internal struggles in the first decades of the twentieth century. As it happened, an equally serious threat was to come from the outside, the onslaught of American participation in World War I.

19

World War I and Its Aftermath

Most Brethren at the beginning of the twentieth century had become complacent about peace issues. Memories of the agonies of the Civil War had faded. As has been seen, the Spanish-American War of 1898 had been quickly won by professional military men and had not raised the conscription issue. If anything, Brethren, along with other Americans, basked in the success of the war, which was pictured by a crusading press as a righteous conflict between the declining yet cruel power of autocratic colonial Spain and the reforming zeal of a democratic United States. That the United States emerged from the brief fray with its own colonial empire was rationalized as a necessary tutorial step on the path of emancipation. Most Americans joined John Hay in thinking it "a splendid little war."

One member of the Church of the Brethren who was definitely not complacent was the now-forgotten George Fulk. Born in 1878 in the Shenandoah Valley, he moved as a lad with his family to Cerro Gordo, Illinois. After graduation from De Pauw College (where he organized a peace movement among students) and a brief stint teaching the classics in Kentucky, he moved to Chicago where he put himself through law school, specializing in international law.

In 1907 Fulk was appointed to represent American colleges and universities at the Second International Peace Conference held at The Hague; he also attended the 16th Universal Peace Conference in Munich. He stayed in Europe through 1907 and 1908 to study and teach at the University of Geneva. During this period he was commissioned to negotiate a merger between European and American student federations. He was elected National Secretary of the

Intercollegiate Peace Association of America.

In 1908 he continued to visit European universities to press for the merger of student federations. While in London to attend the 17th International Peace Congress, he was recognized by the British king and the House of Commons for his educational work for world peace among students. In 1909 he chaired the American delegation attending the International Student Congress at The Hague. For his services he was elected a "Life Member of Honor" of the International Federation of Students.

After returning to the United States he spent four years working with students in colleges and universities (sponsored in part by the Brethren), seeking to train leaders active in arbitration and judicial work as a means of solving international conflicts without resort to war. During this period he participated for three years in the historic Lake Mohonk [New York] Conferences on International Arbitration.

Although he was offered several prestigious positions in law firms and universities, as well as a post as a private secretary directing Andrew Carnegie's peace work, Fulk's health failed. He returned to the family farm in Cerro Gordo, Illinois, where he became, in his words, a "dirt farmer" active in farmers' cooperatives. He provided the full financial support for the congregation's first full-time salaried pastor and was active in district work.

Still passionately interested in international affairs, he served on the executive committee of the celebration in 1915 of "One Hundred Years of Peace between the United States and Canada," was a journalist at the Washington Conference on the Limitations of Armaments in 1921-22, and was appointed by President Warren G. Harding to participate in the National Agricultural Conference of 1922. He twice ran unsuccessfully for the United States Congress in the 1920s, defeated largely through the influence of the Ku Klux Klan, which he had vigorously opposed because of his peace convictions.

After 1945 Fulk resettled many refugees in his area and as late as 1951 was chairman of the Macon County Crusade for Freedom. A neighboring farmer commented dourly, "He could have had three times as much land if he had stayed home and tended to business." He died in 1964.[1]

THE ONSET OF THE WAR

Fulk's striking peace activism was an anomaly in the first decade of the new century among the Brethren, who took little interest in world affairs. This changed abruptly in April 1917, when the United States Congress, at the behest of President Woodrow Wilson, declared war against Germany and its allies. The declaration of war caught the Brethren unprepared. With Annual Conference resolutions on peace to back them up, Brethren supported the attempts made by Wilson to keep the nation out of the war, as well as his attempts to act as an "honest broker" to negotiate an end to the horrendous Great War.[2]

In the wartime crisis the president reluctantly bowed to the weight of financial, diplomatic, and propagandistic pressure of the Allies (United Kingdom, France, and Russia), compounded by the fateful decision of the German high command to resume unrestricted submarine warfare on the high seas. Wilson sought, nevertheless, to justify United States involvement in the war as required "to make the world safe for democracy." He proclaimed that this would be a "war to end all wars," one that promised "peace without victory." It was his declared intention to use the power and influence of the United States to end the fighting and then to bring about a confederation of nations that would be willing and able to contain and arbitrate future international conflicts.

In the short run, however, he and his associates found it expedient to whip the nation into a bellicose spirit. Committees of communication specialists (led by George Creel) organized widespread campaigns to shape public opinion. Clergymen were recruited to lend their moral influence to the cause and university officials added their weighty authority. At the same time, rigorous laws with sweeping provisions were passed to control any potential subversion and opposition.

The war became a crusade, a holy war against the enemy, dehumanized as the spike-helmeted and jack-booted Hun. Reports of war events, already controlled by the British through their command of overseas cables, throbbed with reports of actual and manufactured German atrocities, ignoring the starvation of German civilians by the British naval blockade. Zealous mobs of patriots mounted a reign of terror against any American suspected of pro-German sentiments or of simply being unenthusiastic about the war ("slackers"), while government officials winked at such activities. Accounts of this period often speak of war hysteria, an accurate characterization.

Peace groups such as the Mennonites and Brethren were suspect on two counts—they were of German origin, and as nonresistant pacifists they were unwilling, with some exceptions, to join the war effort. Many Brethren and Mennonite families still spoke the German language in their homes. National leaders, especially Theodore Roosevelt, had long fulminated against "hyphenated Americans"—those who retained a specific ethnic identity such as German-Americans. President Wilson now climbed on this bandwagon.

Mennonites suffered more than did Brethren, especially in Kansas, where mobs of patriots raided homes to force those suspected of resistance to the war to kiss the flag and subscribe large amounts to war bond and Red Cross drives. Some Mennonites were tarred and feathered and otherwise abused and several lynchings were narrowly averted by moderates. One Mennonite minister in Whitewater, Kansas, turned the tables on the tormentors who invaded his home by suggesting that they sing together the anthem "America." He led the singing of the first verse in a vigorous manner and proceeded to sing the following three. Members of the mob joined in the first verse, but were visibly embarrassed when it became evident that they did not know the words of the remaining stanzas. They departed in discomfited fashion, forgetting their violent intent.[3]

CONSCRIPTION

Congress passed the Selective Service Act on May 18, 1917. It provided that members of a "well-recognized" and already-existing "sect or organization" having principles against participation in war were exempt from fighting cadres, but in no case would they be relieved of service in a military unit designated as noncombatant by presidential order. Unfortunately for conscientious objectors (COs), President Wilson delayed issuing this definition for almost one year. This was not solely because of other pressing wartime duties. It became evident that government policy was calculated to reduce the number of COs by pressures brought upon them in the camps.[4]

By order of the government in August, 1917, all drafted men, including potential COs, were to be forwarded to mobilization camps. Treatment meted out to those who declared themselves COs upon arrival in the camps and refused to don the uniform varied widely in this extended interim before the president defined non-combatancy.

Some camp commanders ordered the COs to be set apart and treated with fairness. In other cases, treatment was brutal. Many commissioned and especially noncommissioned officers were frustrated and increasingly furious at those who, from their point of view, stubbornly and willfully rejected normal military discipline. Their efforts to resolve this problem ranged from tossing the COs with blankets, to standing them at attention for hours in the hot sun, to lengthy showers under cold water with the victims scrubbed raw with brooms, to prodding with bayonets on forced runs, to "baptisms" in the fecal filth of latrines, to beatings, to mock executions.

In October 1917, camp commanders were ordered to isolate the COs in their camps and to treat them humanely, in the hope that greater numbers of them would voluntarily agree to accept full or noncombatant military service. Officers encouraged COs to "police"—that is clean up—the barrack areas or to assist in the dining halls. Having once agreed to accept such orders, it was difficult for them to draw the line in resisting further orders. A considerable number of men, including many Brethren, were won over by this policy, if by nothing else from unhappiness at enforced idleness and also from the lingering sense that they owed something, after all, to their country when so many of their mates were willing to die for it. One acute observer noted that students from small church colleges were particularly open to this rationale.

News of the violent treatment to which COs were subject leaked to the press, who reported on the excesses. The newly formed forerunner of the American Civil Liberties Union took up the cause.

Bowing to this adverse publicity, the War Department appointed a special three-man panel to interview COs in the camps and recommend disposition of their cases. It was composed of a major, a judge, and the dean of a law school. Their usually hasty procedure to identify sincere COs mitigated some flagrant cases of injustice.

Generally, however, the panel found most religious objectors to be of a low class of mentality and morality. The chairman of the panel, Walter G. Kellogg, called COs "dull and almost bovine." In the words of Frederick P. Keppel, the official in the War Department charged with handling these cases, "the great majority of the objectors were men from about the most isolated social groups in the United States, and consisted of men of the most limited social outlook."

He reflected the attitude of his superior, Secretary of War Newton D. Baker, who as a Progressive, had embraced the Wilsonian philosophy of the "New Freedom," which saw in the war the possibility of worldwide extension of enlightened democratic principles. For Baker, the "war was the purest mission that a nation ever espoused." Those who failed to share this altruistic vision, thought Secretary Baker, must be be mentally lacking, socially isolated, or determinedly corrupt.[5]

When the classification of noncombatancy finally emerged in March 1918, COs were bitterly disappointed by its restrictiveness. Noncombatant options were defined solely as service in the medical, quartermaster, and engineering corps, all of which had close connection to combat. The several hundred COs who still remained firm at this point were given direct orders to elicit their disobedience and then were court-martialed for it. Their convictions were automatic (there was one acquittal). According to War Department records, of the 504 court-martials of conscientious objectors, the sentences meted out included 17 death sentences and 142 sentences of life imprisonment; the average sentence at hard labor given to 345 cases was 16½ years. Most of these draconian punishments were sharply reduced at war's end.

BRETHREN AND WORLD WAR I

Every student of the period has concluded that the Church of the Brethren was not prepared in 1917 to face this crisis. Although new members were still asked whether they shared the peace witness as they accepted baptism, the doctrine was not strongly taught or preached.

More importantly, the change in the Brethren relation to the broader society (detailed in an earlier chapter) had moved the Brethren from the status of a withdrawn plain people to that of an involved Protestant body. Beginning with the temperance issue, Brethren began to believe that they should work with others to reform society, and, increasingly, that the government should dictate moral behavior.

Brethren were now voting and a few even holding office. Given this shift in posture, how could they now simply stand aside in the face of the nation's crisis? Influential Brethren leaders such as D. L. Miller, H. C. Early, and Otho Winger advised young men seeking their counsel to enter the military in a noncombatant capacity. More traditional leaders, however, advised that members should stay aloof from all participation in the military. Statistics are lacking for this period, but the best estimate is that most young Brethren who were drafted accepted noncombatant service, a small number performed regular military duties, and several hundred refused all military participation.

Although atypical, the success in politics of a Brethren minister just at this time is symbolic of the change of the Brethren attitude toward the state. Martin G. Brumbaugh, a graduate and president of Juniata College, was elected governor of the Commonwealth of Pennsylvania in the autumn of 1914. He had made his mark in public affairs as a reforming superintendent of schools in Philadelphia, serving also as the first commissioner of education in Puerto Rico after the United States seized the commonwealth in the course of the Spanish-American War. While some Brethren thought it inappropriate for a member to hold an office that involved coercion, others felt honored that one of their own had won such acclaim. H. C. Early, the highly respected church leader (who had been elected moderator seven times) wrote to a friend in 1916: "The feeling of the general brotherhood as to Brother Brumbaugh serving his state as governor is much divided. There is dissatisfaction and there is pleasure among the members with his position...."[6]

At a dedication in May 1916, of a new building for the Walnut Grove Church of the Brethren in Johnstown attended by thousands of Brethren, Governor Brumbaugh devoted a large section of his sermon to the church and peace. First asserting that the church provides inner peace for individuals, he went on to portray the church as "the militant organized body praying for peace at all times" in the world. Moreover, the church is the "beacon...for arbitration that will bring about a reign of reason, of love, of fair play for all of humanity...." In this great work, the Church of the Brethren, which "from its inception stood for peace," has a role: "The church from the beginning has pleaded and prayed and worked for peace giving due respect to every man and his property." Further, "The church not only promotes peace, but I pray God I may hope to live to see the day come when the church will be strong enough and willing to offer its services in the arbitration of industrial difficulties and help settle strikes that so disorder the peace of the common people."[7]

Brumbaugh took office as governor in January 1915—affirming, not swearing, to uphold his duties—to begin his four year term. He was thus in the executive chair when war was declared and, as governor, became commander of the state militia, which he called out. Photographs exist of Brumbaugh astride a horse reviewing his troops. One of his first public actions was attending the launching in Newport News, Virginia, of the battleship Pennsylvania in March 1915. Some Brethren leaders were put off by Brumbaugh's willingness to serve in such roles, instead of resigning on a point of conscience. He was never ordained an elder and never called to the office of moderator. Young Brethren draftees from Pennsylvania, who sought to remain faithful to the nonresistant principle of the church, found his willingness to hold this office detrimental to their attempts to follow a consistent anti-war position.[8]

Brumbaugh took the position that as a patriotic and loyal citizen it was his duty to persist as governor, even in wartime. He had once given a lecture at the University of Pennsylvania with the title

"The Patriotism of Jesus Christ." According to Brumbaugh, "that man is the noblest American who believes in universal education, Christian religion, and the sovereignty of the individual, and who puts the whole force and pressure of his life to working out these institutions."[9]

BRETHREN IN THE MILITARY CAMPS

In the meantime, young Brethren men were marched off to the camps where they faced varying degrees of pressure from the military machine. Brethren were sent to camps such as Meade in Maryland, Lee and Belvoir in Virginia, Sherman in Ohio, Funston and Riley in Kansas, Greenleaf in Georgia, Jackson in South Carolina, Taylor in Kentucky, Shelby in Mississippi, and Dodge in Iowa.

The church tried to provide camp visitors, ordinarily local pastors. They varied widely in their usefulness and acceptability to the men; ordinarily camp visitors confined themselves to conducting religious services in the camps but on occasion they were able to secure better conditions for the men or to resolve problems. Brethren tended to fare better in camps where there were relatively large numbers of COs. They were usually assigned to separate barracks and often largely left to their own devices, either cooking for themselves or drawing bulk rations from the mess hall for preparation and distribution in the barracks.

An unknown number of Brethren died in the camps, either through illnesses that swept the camps or because of ill treatment. Charles W. Bolly, a "Dunkard" from Mungo, Indiana, died at Fort Leavenworth. Old Order member Maurice Hess wrote of five members of his church in the "damp, dark guard house at Ft. Riley at one time." Of them, "two were seriously sick in the hospital and one died as a result of the unhealthful conditions."

Hess was able to preserve a piece of tissue paper on which he wrote a draft of the statement he made at his court martial. It has often been reprinted because of its eloquence. After recounting the details of his case, in which he was promised a farm furlough, he stated,

I do not believe that I am seeking martyrdom. As a young man, life and its hopes and freedom and opportunities for service are sweet to me. I want to go out into the world and do my work and make use of what little talent I may have acquired by long and laborious study.

But I know that I dare not purchase these things at the price of eternal condemnation. I know the teaching of Christ, my Savior. He taught us to resist not evil, to love our enemies, to bless them that curse us, and do good to them that hate us. Not only did He teach this, but He practiced it at Gethsemane, before Pilate, and on Calvary. We would, indeed, be hypocrates [*sic*] and base traitors to our profession if we should be unwilling to bear the taunts and jeers of a sinful world, and imprisonment, and torture, and death, rather than to participate in war and military service. We know that obedience to Christ will gain for us the glorious prize of eternal life. We cannot yield, we cannot compromise, we must suffer.

Two centuries ago our people were driven out of Germany by religious persecution, and they accepted the invitation of William Penn to come to his colony where they might enjoy the blessing of religious liberty which he promised them. This religious liberty was later confirmed by the Constitution of Pennsylvania and by the Constitution of the United States.

If those in authority now see fit to change those fundamental documents, and to take away our privileges of living in accordance with the teaching of the Scriptures of God, then we have no course but to endure persecution as true soldiers of Christ. If I have committed anything worthy of bonds of death, I do not refuse to suffer or die. I pray to God for the strength to remain faithful.[10]

He was sentenced to imprisonment for life. Along with 40 other COs, Hess was sent to the disciplinary barracks at Fort Leavenworth, Kansas, to begin his sentence. Because he could not accept commands given there to work—seeing no difference between accepting orders on a military base or in a military prison—he was thrust into solitary confinement. Some prisoners were shackled by their wrists to the bars of their cells in such a way that they could not support their weight by standing; Hess was chained with his hands just below the level of his shoulders. This lasted nine hours a day (for as long as other prisoners were working) and continued for 23 days until Secretary of War Baker outlawed the practice. His action came after news of the practice reached the outside press. Hess wrote his father shortly thereafter, saying, "There is much less probability of a physical breakdown now that they [the shackles] are no longer used."

Prisoners slept at first on the concrete floor, later on blankets on planks; Hess said, "I never did mind a hard bed." He received a diet of bread and water, saying, "We prefer crusts when we can get them"; this was alternated every 14 days with the regular fare. He later summarized his experience in Fort Leavenworth: "I was chained up 23 days, in solitary 38 days, lived on concrete floors 109 days, was in confinement 121 days, was away from home fifteen months."[11]

His sentence had been reduced on review to 25 years but Hess was actually released in January 1919, along with others. After release, Hess taught for many years at McPherson College, recounting when asked his wartime experiences. Among his prison friends was one of the four Hutterites whose brutal treatment elicited some of the harshest criticism of the government's policies. Because they refused to put on military clothing in prison, they were treated so abominably that two of them died in captivity. As a final indignity their corpses were clothed in uniforms and sent to their families.

A document drawn up by a Mennonite minister listing "Religious C.O.'s Imprisoned at the U. S. Disciplinary Barracks, Ft. Leavenworth, Kansas" in March 1919 included 24 men from the Church of the Brethren, Old German Baptist Brethren, and Brethren Church. The sentences listed ranged from ten to 25 years. Two Brethren COs served time in Alcatraz, including Jesse C. Beery, later a long-time educator at La Verne College.[12]

A few Brethren were able to win assignment to constructive projects; some were allocated to the Farm Furlough project, initiated in the spring of 1918, in which they helped farmers caught short-handed for labor. Those assigned to these jobs returned their wages to the army or to the Red Cross. Eventually, some 1,200 COs were released to the farms. This was generally satisfactory, although in some localities, super-patriots made life hellish for COs.

Many other COs had asked for overseas assignments, in particular with the Friends Ambulance Unit in France, but few were permitted to join it. Among those joining the AFSC in France were four Brethren, of whom John C. Baker became the most prominent in later life. Of nearly 4,000 recognized COs during World War I, only 99 were assigned to Friends' reconstruction work.[13]

THE GOSHEN CONFERENCE

Because of the varying positions adopted by church leaders and increasing calls for guidance from conscripted men, Brethren thought it wise to take the unusual step of calling a specially delegated conference to seek and find a consensus on response to the military draft. Some 400 people attended the conference held on January 9, 1918, in Goshen, Indiana. Of these, about 100 were voting delegates, consisting of members of the Standing Committee, camp visitors and members of the Peace Committee, and congregational representatives. An advance party had drafted a comprehensive statement in three sections, which was adopted by the conference.[14]

The first section consisted of a resolution setting forth the church's position, designed for presentation to government leaders; President Wilson sent a gracious response, as did Secretary of War Baker. The second section contained a concise biblical and theological rationale for the Brethren peace position; the third, an outline for an organizational procedure for the church to follow during the crisis.

The stance worked out at Goshen is suggested by this passage: "We believe that war or any participation in war is wrong and entirely incompatible with the spirit, example, and teachings of Jesus Christ; [we] cannot conscientiously engage in any activity or perform any function contributing to the destruction of human life." The statement specifically recommended that Brethren, when drafted, should "refrain from wearing the uniform" and should avoid military drilling.

Church members were urged to give freely to relieve war-sufferers through several named agencies in gratitude for their protection from war's devastation. Two new committees were formed: a Special War Relief and Reconstruction Work Committee and a Central Service Committee to handle liaison with the state; the latter replaced the Peace Committee.[15]

The second and third sections of the Goshen statement were soon published in pamphlet form and distributed through the congregations to young men facing the draft. Several pamphlets submitted by young Brethren to local boards and to the military when entering camps were forwarded through channels until they reached the War Department, which secured advice from its Advocate General. Third Assistant Secretary of War F. P. Keppel called W. J. Swigart and J. M. Henry, both members of the newly appointed General Service Committee, to his office on July 8, 1918. They were told that the officers of the Goshen conference were guilty of treasonable obstruction of the Selective Service Act. The government was ready to prosecute them. The penalty was imprisonment up to 20 years and/or a fine of $10,000. Keppel was willing to give them a short period of time in which to think over their response.

They summoned other Brethren to join them; I. W. Taylor, along with H. R. Gibble, came hurriedly from Pennsylvania to the nation's capital to help draft a reply. When the men took this to Keppel, he had an Assistant Judge Advocate meet with them to go over their statement, point by point. After rehearsing the background of the Goshen conference and its resolutions, they assured the official that the Brethren were loyal citizens and that the statement had never been circulated clandestinely; they pledged their influence to have it withdrawn by the denomination. Finally, they "humbly prayed" that the threatened prosecution be dropped.[16]

The strategy worked. Urgent statements printed in *The Gospel Messenger* directed pastors and drafted Brethren to refrain from using the Goshen statement. Committee members were relieved that they had been able to protect church leaders from sanctions. Later commentators have provided more critical comment, concluding that the historic peace position of the church had been seriously weakened by the abrupt withdrawal of the Goshen statement.[17]

A resolution passed at the Annual Conference in June 1918, inoffensively thanked the government for its generosity in making noncombatant service available to those "called to the colors," and prayed for divine guidance for the "President and his advisors." It renewed a "pledge of loyalty" and urged Brethren to support liberally "those organizations that are engaged in furthering the moral and religious welfare of the men in camps in service," that is, such groups as the YMCA and the Red Cross. It also encouraged Brethren to support "the alleviation of suffering and the reconstruction of devastated lands."[18]

There has been speculation that the charge of prosecution was actually a bluff to secure Brethren cooperation. That the threat was real is evidenced by similar prosecutions actually pressed at the time by the government. Officers of the Jehovah's Witnesses (then disparagingly called Russellites) were imprisoned, as were other peace-minded men such as labor leader Eugene V. Debs. During this period more than 50 clergymen were arrested on comparable charges.[19]

Just before moderator H. C. Early rose to address the Annual Conference in June 1918, he was informed that members of the Secret Service were seated in the large auditorium at Hershey, Pennsylvania, to monitor his words. Had he spoken anything that could have been interpreted as critical of the government he would have been held for questioning.

The true attitude of Assistant Secretary Keppel is revealed in an internal document directed to a colleague in which he flippantly spoke of putting "the fear of the Lord" into a Mennonite peace advocate. He continued, "As you doubtless know, the Dunkards were similarly warned of the error of their ways, by Colonel Call [Goff?] of the Judge Advocate General's office and myself last month."[20]

Brethren leaders were unaware of his real feelings. They praised the courtesy, patience, and understanding of Assistant Secretary Keppel in their report to the 1919 Annual Conference, evidently still grateful that the threatened prosecution had not taken place. In fact, W. J. Swigart sought Keppel's advice at that time about the advisability of the Church of the Brethren associating itself with a petition under circulation that urged the state to free the relatively large number of COs still incarcerated at Fort Leavenworth. Keppel reacted negatively and the potential Brethren support of the petition was dropped.[21]

The activities of Swigart were even less appreciated by the military itself. A report from the military intelligence officer of Camp Sherman, Ohio, was highly critical of COs who justly deserved their harsh sentences, in his judgment. Yet, he asserted, Swigart and others like him among Mennonite and Quaker leaders were more dangerous: "It has been impossible to nail the chief troublemakers because they have been without [i.e., outside] the military jurisdiction. Such people as Swigart, of Huntingdon, Pa...deserve punishment far more severe than any given conscientious objectors." His reasoning was that the propaganda of these leaders misled many drafted men who would not otherwise have taken the CO position. They influenced parents and relatives, who in turn guided their young men to become COs, "inspired either by fear for the draftee's safety or pro-Germanism."[22]

HARASSMENT OF THE BRETHREN

It was not only men in the army who faced pressures. Because of the wartime hysteria many congregations experienced harassment. This happened ordinarily for two reasons: first, if resistance to conscription were noticed, and, second, if members seemed less than enthusiastic about buying bonds to subsidize the war, the so called Liberty Bonds, then sold in highly public and pressured ways.

J. A. Robinson, pastor of the Des Moines, Iowa, congregation, was indicted under the espionage law, but his case was eventually dropped. Dr. J. S. Geiser of Froid, Montana, and a local minister in Kansas were both charged with treasonable attempts to obstruct conscription. David Gerdes of Illinois was indicted and sentenced to ten years in prison for obstructing the draft but was released after serving ten months in Leavenworth prison. Some Brethren were beaten, others threatened with lynching, and many had their homes and church buildings splashed with yellow paint, to publicize their supposed cowardice.

Judge Kenesaw Mountain Landis sentenced a Church of the Brethren pastor to ten years at Leavenworth "for advising people not to buy Liberty bonds and [for] attacking the activities of the Red Cross." Under severe pressure most Brethren bought war bonds or deposited money in local banks that was then used for the same purpose.

A well respected and able Latin professor, a 20-year veteran of teaching at Indiana Normal College, Terre Haute, Indiana, lost his position in January 1919, in part because his wife was a member of the Church of the Brethren; he had earlier taught Latin at Mount Morris College for two years. Trouble started for John J. Schlicher in the late spring of 1918 when he delivered a chapel talk, characterized by a colleague as a "mild and thoughtful warning" motivated by concern "lest super-heated American citizens...use undemocratic methods at home" to pursue war objectives. He urged his audience to permit a variety of viewpoints as one of America's ideals. A drumbeat of criticism from patriotic clubs, the press, and critical colleagues, sealed his fate despite his long and meritorious service.[23]

Several cases have been documented where agents of military intelligence monitored Brethren worship services, alert to possible anti-war comments; letters of Brethren ministers and laity were intercepted in the mails and checked for "treason." A teacher in Mayfield, California, the fiancee of a Brethren CO, often wrote to him and to other pacifists; she became the subject of a massive military investigation.

She once wrote to a young Brethren man who was working as a noncombatant in a military hospital in the state of Washington. In her letter she expressed a simple wish that he would not be sent overseas; she also complained that as a teacher she was expected to volunteer to teach at night as well as during the day. In a report summarizing the gravity of her misconduct, an officer in the Military Intelligence Branch (which had intercepted the letter) wrote, "I would recommend that the facts in this case be laid before the proper school authorities at Mayfield. You will note the young woman finds sufficient time to write frequent letters to a rabid conscientious objector given to aiding alien enemies and slackers, yet she is averse to doing more toward helping along educational lines."[24]

The Impact of the War

A number of young Brethren who experienced these struggles and the equivocations of the church's top leaders decided to dedicate their lives to strengthening the peace testimony of the Brethren. They were disappointed by the divided counsel they received from the church and determined to prepare themselves and the church better for the next test. Especially prominent among these men were M. R. Zigler, Dan West, and Rufus D. Bowman. All took prominent roles in the inter-war period, in educational or staff positions. Zigler went to Elgin in 1919 as home missions secretary and became one of the leading churchmen of the interwar period; West was a teacher and church staff worker, known for his prophetic vision and ability to challenge and motivate young persons; Bowman was a successful pastor, then president of the seminary at Chicago, long active in peace circles.

Brethren Relief Efforts

Another result of the war was the renewed dedication of the Brethren to relieve suffering caused by war. This was in part motivated by a desire to show others that their reluctance to support the war effort was not derived from unwillingness to give. By contributing generously to relief drives they demonstrated their positive spirit for constructive, rather than destructive actions.[25]

The Goshen statement of January 1918 encouraged Brethren to acknowledge their blessings by sacrificial sharing of their means with those suffering from the horrors of war. Beyond that it urged members of the church to "practice the greatest economies in clothing, food, and all supplies which may, mechanically or otherwise, aid in the production and transportation of food, clothing and fuel, so that a suffering and hungering world may be clothed, warmed and fed." Contributions could be channeled to the Red Cross, YMCA, Friends Relief Work, or "through our own Service Committee."[26]

The last organization named marked something new for the Brethren. Mutual aid had been a mainstay for Brethren since the inception of the movement; generous aid to neighbors in need had been almost taken for granted; and mission fields in Asia had been noted for their charitable efforts; but to have an organized relief committee was an innovation.

In 1917 Brethren heard of the plight of those Armenians in Asia Minor who had survived genocidal attacks in Turkey. The Annual Conference of that year authorized congregations to collect moneys "for the relief of these unfortunate sufferers." This work was taken over by the Special War Relief and Reconstruction Work committee appointed by the Goshen Conference.

Some of the church's leaders had hoped that the committee might be able to develop a framework that could employ some COs in a kind of alternative service. In fact, the new committee never was able to develop a substantial program. This changed in 1919, when the committee was reorganized and two able church leaders were added; they were Edward Frantz, editor of the church paper, and J. H. B. Williams, the energetic executive of the foreign mission program. J. E. Miller chaired the committee. In 1920 M. R. Zigler, newly appointed to the staff at Elgin, was added.

The expanded committee decided on a complete canvas of the church membership to raise money for the needy Armenians, with the goal of raising $250,000; in fact they more than met the goal within three years. For that time, this was an amazing feat. In March 1919, Miller was invited by the American Committee for Relief in the Near East (ACRNE) to go on a fact finding mission to Palestine, Syria, and Turkey; he did so, taking with him A. J. Culler, the pastor of a large Kansan congregation. Culler was assigned by the ACRNE to administer relief in the Marash region of Syria, with particular attention to orphanages.

The church was gratified by the success in raising this substantial sum for the Armenians but felt that a continuing organization was not needed. In 1921 the Relief and Reconstruction Committee was dissolved, with relief needs placed under the jurisdiction of the General Mission Board. The board asked M. R. Zigler, H. Spenser Minnich, and J. E. Miller to study the problem and suggest what could be done. The recommendation was to continue raising funds for Armenian relief and to add support for Russians suffering famine during their civil war. This aid was sent through the AFSC.

In 1923 some $6,000 was raised to send relief to suffering Germans in the Erzgebirge region; it was administered by German Mennonites. Certificates could be redeemed at relief centers for food; the certificates bore the legend *Hilfswerk der Gemeinde der Brüder in Amerika.* At his own expense, Minnich visited the area to observe the work.[27]

It was possibly in connection with this program that Maynard L. Cassaday, who was in graduate study at the University of Heidelberg, undertook to administer some relief work for the Brethren. A note in a Juniata College publication (May 1924) refers to Cassaday's plans for study, then states, "His work as relief administrator for the Church of the Brethren in Germany will be continued during the summer." In correspondence from Heidelberg, Cassaday reported on the great need for food and fuel among the citizens and students.[28]

INCREASED ECUMENICAL ACTIVITY

The tensions of the war years brought together in tentative ways officials of those denominations with heritages of peacemaking. They realized that they shared common problems; it made sense to take counsel as to effective ways to approach government.

In May 1917, an unofficial meeting of representatives of the Friends, Brethren, and Mennonites met in Washington, DC. Those who met called for the three groups to appoint delegates to a central committee to work together with various government offices on war and peace issues. Little of consequence, however, occurred because of the meeting,

Despite this, younger leaders of these peace churches moved after war's end to make common cause. At the initiative of Elmer E. S. Johnson of the Schwenkfelders and Wilbur K. Thomas of the recently organized AFSC, a series of conferences were called beginning in 1922. Preparatory material for the first conference explained the motivation behind it:

> A number of these groups have been sadly misunderstood during the past six years. Because of their isolation

> they have frequently had no knowledge of what other like-minded groups were doing. Not infrequently one or the other of these groups or individual members of them have suffered more or less persecution....The thought of their inability to prevent war or even utter an effective protest against it, was so overwhelming that they either compromised or suffered in isolated silence. Under these conditions these groups have not been able to effectively demonstrate that love, as it was revealed in Christ Jesus, is capable of meeting such situations as arose in 1914 and 1917.

With this background, a conference was called with the following objectives: first, "To bring together for a season of Conference and Prayer representatives of all who profess discipleship of Jesus Christ and who hold that war has no place among Christians"; second, "To discuss ways and means of furthering this Christian principle outside the respective denominations participating in the Conference."[29]

Although a wider span of churches was invited to the first conference, held at Bluffton College in Ohio (General Conference Mennonite) in early August 1922, those actually attending were from the Church of the Brethren, Religious Society of Friends, Mennonite Church, and the Schwenkfelder Church. Clerical work in preparing for the conference was in the hands of the AFSC. The name of the conference was National Conference of Religious Bodies Who Hold that Peace between Nations Can Be Maintained by Following the Teachings of Jesus. Brethren addressing the meeting were J. M. Henry and W. J. Swigart, both veterans of the Central Service Committee; the former spoke on "Christianity and Patriotism," the latter on "Methods of Developing Peace Sentiment through Schools and Colleges."

Response was favorable enough (although conservative Mennonites were reluctant to cooperate) to schedule another conference, this one held at Juniata College during late December 1923. (Quaker sponsorship is indicated by the program's announcement giving the dates as Twelfth Month 28th-30th.) Participants were welcomed to Juniata College by President I. Harvey Brumbaugh; on the first evening J. M. Henry, at that time president of Blue Ridge College in New Windsor, Maryland, spoke on the question "Is War Justifiable According to Christian Principles? A Review and a Forecast." His approach was that of a liberal Protestant pacifist: "The Church may have failed. Christian principles have not failed. The war has only emphasized the world's need of them." President Brumbaugh was mortified that the Brethren presence was woefully lacking, except for those on the program and a few local Huntingdon people.

A Continuation Committee, which included I. Harvey Brumbaugh, was named to plan future meetings; it used the title Conference of Pacifist Churches. These took place in Lancaster, Pennsylvania (1924), and in Wichita, Kansas (November 1925). The committee then urged the calling of two retreats of church leaders to gather to become better acquainted with each other. Ten Friends from different bodies were to be invited, ten Brethren from different branches, as well as ten Mennonites, representing the Mennonite Church and the General Conference Mennonites. There is no record that these ever took place.

The fifth major meeting was held at a General Conference Mennonite congregation in Carlock, Illinois, from August 30 to September 1, 1926. The statement of findings for the conference was prepared by a committee co-chaired by Wilbur B. Stover and Merlin G. Miller, Brethren from Mount Morris, Illinois; it gave a long list of practical measures for peace and emphasized Christian education. "We believe our churches, collectively and individually, are under obligation to continue faithfully their witness against participation in war and preparation for war, and to continue their works of good will, such as have been carried out by their service and relief committees." J. M. Henry and Wilbur B. Stover were named to the Continuation Committee.[30]

The sixth conference was held at Elizabethtown College in late December 1926. This was followed by a seventh at Manchester College, Indiana, in November 1927, which drew the largest attendance since the first conference at Bluffton. It was addressed by the well known peace leaders Frederick J. Libby of the National Council for the Prevention of War and Dorothy Detzer of the Women's International League for Peace and Freedom. Dan West for the

Brethren led a discussion of the peace plans of the denominations represented.

The next in the series was a small meeting (under thirty persons) of Brethren, Mennonites, and Friends peace workers to discuss problems and methods; it was held at Bethany Biblical Seminary in Chicago during March 1928. This was followed by the ninth conference, held among the Quakers in Wilmington, Ohio, in March 1929. It featured a report by H. P. Krehbiel (of the General Conference Mennonites) on his personal survey of European peace work in 1927.

Following Wilmington came a major conference at Mount Morris, Illinois; its date was late March 1931. Much of the planning was done by the relevant Brethren staff in Elgin; at this point it consisted of Rufus D. Bowman and Dan West. The title of the sponsoring group was changed slightly to the Conference of Pacific Churches. The theme of the conference was "The Meaning of Pacifism"; it attracted 47 people, with attendance limited by a severe winter storm. Rufus D. Bowman was named to the Continuation Committee.

The Pacific coast was the site of a significant meeting; it is not clear whether it was considered to be part of the foregoing series. Friends, Mennonites, and Brethren came to a well attended three-day peace conference, held at La Verne, California, in early March 1932. Then the impact of the Depression seems to have thwarted the sponsorship of continuing meetings for several years.

THE NEWTON CONFERENCE OF 1935

This hiatus was broken by the most important of all of these meetings in the interwar period. It was the Conference of Historic Peace Churches held at North Newton, Kansas, from October 31 to November 2, 1935. It was called by H. P. Krehbiel, then 78 years old, who had been active in the previous series of peace conferences, as a representative of the General Conference Mennonites. He had a vision for grand cooperation of peace churches world-wide and issued in 1929 an "Overture to the Historic Peace Groups of the World." The 1935 conference owed its existence partly to the

CHRISTIAN PATRIOTISM

Statement of Position.

We, Friends, Brethren and Mennonites, assembled in the Conference of the Historic Peace Churches at Newton, Kansas, October 31 to November 2, 1935, remembering in gratitude to God the historic war testimony of our churches desire, in absolute renunciation of war for the wholehearted practice of peace and love, to state the basis of our common position.

1. Our peace principles are rooted in Christ and his Word.

2. Through Jesus Christ, who lived among men as the incarnation of the God of love, we become partakers of the spirit and character of our Lord, and thereby are constrained to love all men, even our enemies.

3. Christ has led us to see the value of human life and personalities, and the possibilities in all men, who by spiritual rebirth from above may become sons of God.

4. The spirit of sacrificial service, love, and goodwill promotes the highest well-being and development of men and society, whereas the spirit of hatred, ill will, and fear destroys, as has been demonstrated repeatedly in human experience.

5. Since good alone can overcome evil, the use of violence must be abandoned.

6. War is sin. It is the complete denial of the Christian spirit of love and all that Christ stands for. It is wrong in spirit and method, and destructive in results. Therefore, we cannot support or engage in any war or conflict between nations, classes, or groups.

7. Our supreme allegiance is to God. We cannot violate it by a lesser loyalty, but we are determined to follow Christ in all things. In this determination we believe we are serving the interests of our country, and are truly loyal to our nation.

8. Under God we commit ourselves to set forth in the true way of life this statement of position and assume the obligations and sacrifices attending its practice.

Our Concept of Patriotism.

As members of the historic peace churches we love our country and sincerely work for its highest welfare. True love for our country does not mean a hatred of others. It is our conviction that only the application of the principles of peace, love, justice, liberty, and international goodwill will make for the highest welfare of our country; and the highest welfare of our country must harmonize with the highest welfare of humanity everywhere. Our faith is in security through love, protection through goodwill; and for such we are willing to make the necessary sacrifice. We are opposed to war as a method of settling disputes because it is unchristian, destructive of our highest values and sows the seeds of future wars. We feel that we are true patriots because we build upon the eternal principles of right which are the only foundation of stable government in our world community.

A tract issued by the Brethren following the landmark conference of the three Historic Peace Churches at Newton, Kansas, in 1935. *Durnbaugh Collection.*

Brethren Dan West and C. Ray Keim, who repeatedly urged Krehbiel to convene it.[31]

The term Historic Peace Churches here introduced was chosen by Krehbiel in a (successful) effort to attract members of the (Old) Mennonite Church. They were currently caught up in fundamentalist controversy; important figures led by the historian John Horsch and Daniel Kauffman attacked the modernism of general Protestantism. The terms "pacifism" and "pacifist" for these Mennonite conservatives were linked with modernistic liberalism, while the word peace was redolent of Anabaptist nonresistance.

(Actually Krehbiel preferred the term "amity" for the theme.) Since 1935 the term Historic Peace Churches has had wide currency.

The purpose of the conference was to consider "ways and means to strengthen and co-ordinate the peace position and testimony of the three groups in the face of the approaching World War II" (Bender). The North Newton meeting attracted nearly eighty persons, including virtually all of the important peace leaders of the Brethren, Friends, and Mennonites. There were few formal addresses; extensive discussion time made it possible for these men (there were few women in attendance) to deepen their friendships. They debated the wording of an extensive conference statement, which was then adopted unanimously.

More importantly, they agreed to form an active Continuation Committee, with two representatives from each of the three groups mandated to go beyond sponsoring conferences to cooperative efforts on a wide range of peace education and action. They also agreed to make common cause in contacts with the US government; conference-goers were alert to the dangers of the international situation, then marked by a series of threats to the security mechanism of the League of Nations established after World War I.[32]

The Church of the Brethren created and circulated the pamphlet *Christian Patriotism*, quoting part of the conference findings. Those Brethren most active in the continued cooperative work after the Newton meeting were Rufus D. Bowman, Dan West, C. Ray Keim, L. W. Shultz, and M. R. Zigler. The leading figures in the Brethren peace movement of the time, they were committed to cooperative effort with Friends and Mennonites.

The close relationships developed at the Newton conference presaged and made possible intense unified work during and after World War II. But first the Church of the Brethren had to cope with the impact of the depression years.

20

The Depression Years

The intrusion of fresh American military might into the bloody attrition of World War I trench warfare brought the war to a victorious conclusion and occasioned national euphoria. This was matched by the fervor with which President Woodrow Wilson was greeted by war-weary Europeans. They looked to him as a savior, able to bring to reality a new world order based on his famous Fourteen Points, which included open diplomacy, freedom of the seas, ethnic self-determination, democracy, and international security.

The American president was sobered as he and soon the rest of the world learned of the secret promises of territorial gains promised by his French and British allies during the war to lure other nations to their side, which directly contradicted his announced principles. His idealism was further undermined by the cynicism and *Realpolitik* of his European allies revealed in the packet of peace treaties ending the war. He took heart, nevertheless, by the expectation that the new League of Nations (which he predominantly crafted) could over time redeem many of the compromises made in the peace process.

When Wilson was unable to persuade the United States Senate to ratify the treaties and enter the League of Nations, the war-inspired balloon of American enthusiasm was pricked. National disillusionment deepened when postwar journalists exposed the hypocrisy of Allied diplomacy, the trafficking of avaricious munitions-makers with both sides of the conflict, and the manufacturing of atrocity stories by English and American propaganda mills. Even voluntary agencies such as the Red Cross were accused of profiting from wartime contributions, when it was reported that they charged soldiers in France for coffee and doughnuts.

The election in 1920 of the genial but ineffectual Warren G. Harding as president symbolized a "return to normalcy" and the end of Wilsonian Progressivism. It was not actually a return, because it was marked by widespread cynicism, relaxed morals, and disenchantment on a scale unknown heretofore in American history. The endemic corruption introduced by Harding's cronies was symbolic of national decay. Skeptics such as the journalist H. L. Mencken scoffed at religious leaders (numbering them among the *booboisie*) and mocked their opposition to the teaching of evolution in public schools. Widespread evasion of Prohibition laws and the attendant surge of mobster violence soured many on government-led attempts to regulate moral issues.

The 1920s saw an upsurge of easy economic prosperity, aided by the status of the United States as the only world power not impoverished by the costly war. It had become the world's banker and manufacturer. The racy lines of the Stutz Bearcat sports-car, crafted by the Brethren-born designer, symbolized for many the age of the "roaring twenties."

This boom time came to an end with the collapse first of the stock market and then of the entire overheated economy in 1929. The Wall Street plunge soon extended itself to the world economy; the ensuing depression of the 1930s effectively ruined the remaining hopes of the postwar European democracies. This crisis led directly to the rise of Fascist and Nazi totalitarianism. The throes of the depression brought down everything which the Wilsonian era had stood for.

This was a tough period for American churches. Widespread retrenchment in the 1930s became the order of the day, even harder psychologically because of the expansive era just preceding it which had seen the building of new church edifices and educational plants. Newly popular radios had brought the sermons of leading churchmen into millions of American homes and made preachers Harry Emerson Fosdick and S. Parkes Cadman household names.

Now hundreds of missionaries serving overseas had to be brought home. This reduction was also caused in part by the influential *Re-Thinking Missions: A Laymen's Inquiry After One Hundred Years* (1932), which questioned the basic rationale for evangelism abroad, while still encouraging educational and medical programs. Attendance at church services and Sunday schools fell, ministers had lower prestige, and revivalists won fewer converts.[1]

SHIFTS IN BRETHREN CHURCH ORGANIZATION

With thousands of church members struggling to survive financially after 1930, the expansive programs that the Church of the Brethren had initiated in the first two decades of the century had to slow down. The denomination had launched a Five Year Forward Movement in January 1919, endorsed five months later by the Annual Conference; it was directed by C. D. Bonsack and J. W. Lear. The ambitious numerical goals of the program sought annually to add 15,000 new members and 300 "aggressive" and "spiritual" young men to the ministry. Some 100 new Sunday schools would serve 15,000 new pupils. Brethren colleges would enroll 3,500 students, with half of the graduates committing themselves to ministry or missions. The General Mission Board would receive $250,000, helping to sponsor 15 additional missionaries, while district mission programs would receive $200,000. Although these goals were never actually reached, the decade of the 1920s was a time of dramatic growth for the Church of the Brethren.[2]

Brethren had known energetic evangelists before, such as S. H. Bashor who won many converts as the "boy preacher," but these efforts had been largely individual initiatives. The church moved now toward a more structured program of evangelism under the Forward Movement. A Committee on Evangelism, composed of John H. Cassady, J. W. Lear, and M. R. Zigler, prepared a concise *Manual for Special Evangelistic Meetings* (ca. 1920) for preparing, capitalizing on, visiting homes, and following up evangelistic campaigns. Written materials, including suggested sermon outlines, were prepared and distributed from Elgin. Cassady wrote booklets of *Evangelistic Sermons* in a series issued by the New Ideas Publishing Company for distribution to possible converts.

In 1921 the church added another agency, the General

Members of the General Mission Board in the first half of the twentieth century; they are (first row, left to right) Charles D. Bonsack, Otho Winger, Henry C. Early, Joseph J. Yoder; (second row) Clyde M. Kulp, Harry H. Nye, H. Spenser Minnich, Jesse B. Emmert, M. Robert Zigler, Albert P. Blough. *BHLA Collection.*

Ministerial Board, to guide and promote the growing trend for each congregation to have its own professionally trained and salaried pastor. This tended to replace the older pattern of guidance by the district-based elders' body. The executive of the board had considerable responsibility in locating (or transplanting) pastors for congregations, providing for ongoing training, and streamlining the procedures involving ministerial leadership. For the first time, congregational leadership was expected to provide regular and comprehensive statistical information to church headquarters. The Board for Religious (later Christian) Education, through its small employed staff, was responsible for providing curricular materials for Brethren Sunday schools; it was also charged with providing peace education. The board had the additional task of liaison with the colleges related to the Brethren.[3]

The same board also gave leadership to the rapidly expanding program of summer camps for children and young people. Initiated as an organized movement in the period 1916-1920, among the earliest and most active were Camp Beatrice in Nebraska (1917), Camp Harmony in western Pennsylvania (1923), and Camp Alexander Mack in northern Indiana (1925). Brethren districts began to purchase camp sites in scenic areas.

Adults volunteered their time to teach, chaperone, and care for hundreds of Brethren children and youth in summer camps of one to two weeks length. Many campers received lasting spiritual formation and stimulation in these natural settings, away from the distractions of normal life. The national church provided top leadership to these camps, often on an itinerate basis. Four talented younger educators with an impressive range of leadership skills began in 1929 to barnstorm all summer long from camp to camp, with significant impact. The "four horsemen" were Dan West, Alvin Brightbill, Chauncey Shamberger, and Perry Rohrer.[4]

Camping fell under the youth department of the Board of Christian Education, organized separately in 1928. At that time Chauncey H. Shamberger, its executive, was also given responsibility for youth ministry. Dan West became the first full-time youth director two years later; at the same time a panel of young people was organized as an advisory commission for the staff. This assignment helped to identify emerging leadership in the denomination.

Already in 1927 the pages of *Our Young People*, the church's publication for youth, used the name Brethren Young People's Department (BYPD); the name was used to identify denominational programs directed at young people until 1948, when the term Youth Fellowship was adopted. The BYPD was guided by the National Youth Cabinet. Following the end of World War II, the major task of the cabinet was to plan the National Youth Conference (NYC), which was held on a four-year schedule, allowing every Brethren young person of high school age the possibility of experiencing it. The conferences came to bear much of the same

emotional and conversionist weight for young Brethren that summer camps held in the 1920s and 1930s. NYC was held in 1954,
1958, and 1962. Controversy surrounding the liberal agenda and
lax discipline of the 1966 conference almost killed the program,
but it was reinstated in 1971 and after 1974 went back to a four-
year cycle.

FURTHER SHIFTS

During the depression, congregations did well to provide adequate
sustenance for their pastors, most often by gifts in kind of food, fuel,
and clothing. Communications from the Elgin staff reminded them
that pastors and their families needed some cash income as well,
even as they tried to make do with little.

As funds dried up in the 1930s, church programs were pared;
the number of Brethren on foreign mission fields declined and new
missionary candidates deferred. The Elgin staff itself was cut back.
By 1934 one staff person, M. R. Zigler, had been asked to direct the
boards for Home Missions, Ministries, and Christian Education.
While a compliment to his executive abilities, it also testified to
stringent budget restrictions as well. A brochure announcing the
change described this "United Program of the Church of the
Brethren in Ministry and Education, including Home Missions."
Zigler was awarded the new title of executive secretary, a term likely borrowed from other denominations. Zigler also acted as the
chairman of the staff under the (Joint) Council of Boards, the function of which was to coordinate the work of the several independent
church boards and the seminary.[5]

Zigler took the opportunity of guiding the work of the Board of
Christian Education to establish close ties to the six Brethren colleges
and the seminary. He saw them as potential research centers for the
denomination, each with a pool of trained analysts. In his vision, the
church could tap their combined expertise to provide guidance on
current issues. Somewhat arbitrarily, he assigned research areas to
the schools: family life to Juniata; economics to McPherson; peace to
Manchester; rural life to Elizabethtown; temperance to Bridgewater;
the problems of individuals to La Verne; and the message of the

church to Bethany. The schools took up the assigned tasks with varying degrees of energy, as might be expected.

Several significant publications emerged from the research. Most successful was the book *Home Builders of Tomorrow* (1938) by Warren D. Bowman of Juniata; it was widely distributed and often reprinted, and brought Bowman a reputation as an expert on family life. He carried this interest with him as he went on to become pastor of the Church of the Brethren in Washington, DC, and then president of Bridgewater College.

The research project was even more impressively fulfilled at Manchester College with its focus on peace. Through the leadership of C. Ray Keim and L. W. Shultz, Manchester developed a program of peace education and action that influenced the entire denomination and beyond. An early project was an anthology of Annual Conference pronouncements on peace issues, compiled by L. W. Shultz. Both Shultz and Keim worked closely with other peace churches to sponsor oratorical competitions on peace, conferences on international relations, widely-performed peace plays, and other innovative projects.[6]

Manchester College was the launching pad for the brilliant career in international relations of historian Andrew W. Cordier, who lectured widely on foreign affairs, chaired the early Brethren Service Committee, and later became one of the prominent architects and chief administrators of the United Nations (UN). He was executive assistant to the first two secretary generals of the United Nations and was the administrator of the General Assembly. He acted as well for the UN in trouble spots such as Israel, the Suez Canal, and the Congo. In 1962 he became dean of the Graduate School of International Affairs at Columbia University, and then took over as president from 1968 to 1970 to calm the university after tumultuous student unrest.[7]

It could thus be said that the 1930s, though placing the Brethren in real straits for resources, was a formative and creative period in the life of the denomination. The church was blessed with talented and innovative leaders, who had a vision for what their religious body could achieve. Most lay members were willing to accept the guidance of their chosen leaders, who generally took care not to lose touch with this supportive constituency by moving ahead too rapidly.

DUNKARD BRETHREN SCHISM

There were of course strains. One was the schism of 1926, which saw several hundred members leave the Church of the Brethren to follow Elder B. E. Kesler of Missouri into what the dissidents called the Dunkard Brethren. He had rallied supporters for some years with his periodical *The Bible Monitor* (1923ff.).

Tensions heightened when the credentials committee at the 1923 Annual Conference refused to seat Elder Kesler, sent as a delegate from his home congregation. Unhappy with slackening discipline on the dress code, impatient with the increasing emphasis upon higher education, critical of the growing acceptance of divorce, and restive with the liberal theological bent of most church leaders, conservatives within the church voted with their feet.

At a meeting in Plevna, Indiana, in late June 1926, the decision was made to leave. They declared "as part of the loyal and faithful of the present Church of the Brethren, [we] see no other remedy for relief than to obey the gospel, and to declare ourselves independent, and to reorganize, and to reestablish the true faith of the gospel among us." In their self-understanding they were the true continuation of the Brethren, who had sadly drifted from their nonconformist moorings.[8]

The division can be understood as a kind of "delayed" Old Order split. Many of the same dynamics that tore the garment of the church in the 1880s were present in 1926. The Dunkard Brethren were among that wing of the mainstream German Baptist Brethren who expected the church to retain much of its conservative character. They were dismayed that the denomination moved rapidly to accept everything for which the "fast element" had contended; in fact, in one of the ironies that church history often offers, the Church of the Brethren leadership by the late 1920s was more liberal theologically than the Progressives, that is those who formed the Brethren Church in 1883. Because the leaders of the Brethren Church had been earlier more open to contemporary doctrinal currents, they had been more influenced by the rising tide of conservative thought.

If the Dunkard Brethren represented a kind of Old Order split, why, the question is raised, did they not simply unite with the Old German Baptist Brethren? The Old Orders had retained the plain dress, self-supported and untrained ministers, and nonconformity to the world which the Dunkard Brethren demanded.

The explanation is that in over four decades between the Old Order departure and that of the Dunkard Brethren, certain changes had occurred that the latter favored. These included, for example, Sunday schools and missions (home and foreign), both of which innovations the Old German Baptist Brethren still adamantly rejected. There was some conversation between Dunkard Brethren and Old Order leaders. When the latter made it clear that Dunkard Brethren would need to repent and enter their church by rebaptism, the Dunkard Brethren lost interest in that option.

There was real danger that the plainly dressed elders of eastern and southern Pennsylvania might take their congregations into the Dunkard Brethren movement. They shared many of the same concerns about the direction in which the church was headed, and both districts brought queries asking the 1926 Annual Conference to take a conservative stand. If these were flatly rejected by the delegates, as was recommended by the Standing Committee, the Pennsylvania elders would be offended. Otho Winger—president of Manchester College, chairman of the General Mission Board, and several-times moderator of the church—spent most of one night at the conference crafting language for a substitute answer that satisfied the Pennsylvania elders.

Although deeply troubled by some of the current church practices and programs, these conservative leaders were not ready to break with their church family. Three of the most influential elders of the Eastern District of Pennsylvania—I. W. Taylor, J. H. Longenecker, and Samuel H. Hertzler—sent a mimeographed letter to all of the district leaders; they warned against division because that would "bring back again as from the grave all the dark record, the painful experiences, and horrors of things that happened some forty years ago." Experience had taught that "division was no cure then" and "we have no reason to believe it will mean a cure now." Encouraged as they were with the attitude of church leaders at the recent conference, they concluded that "it would be very unfortunate to agitate or disturb the church with a spirit of division at a time when there is hope of a check to the worldly trend in the main body of the church."[9]

A delegation of Dunkard Brethren visited the area but met with little positive response. By the end of 1927 there was one meeting with about twenty members in a new church house at Sinking Springs near Reading. I. W. Taylor wrote J. H. Moore at Elgin that "matters are rather quiet," although Dunkard Brethren were attempting to "find openings for services with the view of proseliting." In his informed judgment the "present indications are that their prospects are not favorable" for gaining members in eastern Pennsylvania. The Lower Cumberland congregation of the Southern Pennsylvania District lost members, including those in leadership positions, to the Dunkard Brethren.[10]

A similar crisis was averted in the same districts in the late 1930s after a loose coalition of conservative-minded lay and ministerial leaders began meeting privately to confer about leaving the Church of the Brethren. They agreed with the ideas expressed in a booklet entitled *The Gist of the Church of the Brethren* (1936), drafted by Grant Mahan, who had been associated in the 1920s with B. E. Kesler as an associate editor of *The Bible Monitor*. At a large meeting this group called in 1939 or 1940, I. N. H. Beahm spoke strongly against schism.

Beahm, an outspoken and idiosyncratic personality, contended on the floor of Annual Conference and elsewhere for traditional Brethren values and practices. A near-fundamentalist in theological position, he lent comfort to many in the denomination who were at odds with its progressive-minded leadership. He repeatedly intervened, for example, without being asked, in the legal disputes in the Middle Pennsylvania District involving the Lewistown and Altoona congregations, taking the side of the fundamentalist dissidents. He was, nevertheless, reluctant to break the bonds of fellowship with the church.

This rebuff and some behind-the-scenes effort by district and denominational leaders dissipated the momentum of the dissident parties, who abruptly ceased their meetings.[11]

ECUMENICAL INVOLVEMENTS

Part of the shift from sectarian withdrawal to churchly involvement that has been repeatedly noticed was the markedly different attitude that Brethren now adopted toward other Christian bodies. Long suspicious of the worldly and fashionable churches, Brethren were also stand-offish with groups similar to them, such as the Mennonites. By the end of World War I, Brethren were prepared to grant that heaven would not be inhabited solely by Dunker saints.

Contributing to this was the experience of Brethren on the mission fields. As they began work as newcomers in India and China they were glad to accept the guidance of missionaries from other denominations long present in these areas. In a phenomenon often noted in the history of ecumenical relationships, doctrinal divergences that loomed large in the homeland waned to insignificance as Christians contemplated the awe-inspiring task of converting millions of indigenous people who were completely ignorant of the Christian faith. Brethren had also cautiously cooperated in the United States since the late nineteenth century with the commissions providing common Sunday school curricula and had thus been exposed to Christians of other backgrounds.

Unfortunately, as they waded from their beach of isolation to try the waters of the larger Protestant world, Brethren were bowled over by an unexpected wave. In 1919 the joint Brethren boards voted to join the Interchurch World Movement. Spurred by the cooperation of mainstream churches in ministering to servicemen during World War I and also reflecting the Wilsonian philosophy of the bright new opportunities for world betterment, Protestant leaders plotted a new strategy for church advance. By pooling resources and talents, they anticipated that the immediate post-war era could be a great epoch for churches, both in their American context and in foreign outreach.

The plan of the Interchurch World Movement was to harness business methods of promotion and efficiency with the research of skilled social scientists to launch a tremendous leap forward in evangelization and service. They anticipated that hordes of sympathetic business people as well as the broader public would gladly contribute millions to an ecumenical plan for world mission. They confidently expected such fund raising to reach the goal of $336 million. The huge staff of 2,000-plus workers headquartered in New York would be initially supported by borrowing against denominational pledges. The IWM movement encouraged these bodies to pledge five percent of their asking budgets, which were to be greatly expanded in anticipation of the much-increased income.

Brethren leaders were persuaded to link their Forward Movement (which had some of the same go-getter spirit as the IWM) with the ecumenical plan. Unfortunately, the Annual Conference of 1920 censured the staff and boards for committing the denomination to the scheme and mandated withdrawal from the IWM after paying its obligation. To their surprise and dismay, Brethren were held to a percentage of their inflated askings rather than to their actual receipts; this amounted to $135,000.

The Interchurch World Movement itself soon collapsed. It had been tremendously over-staffed and expensive. It lost the support of business by taking positions seen as partisanly pro-labor. The ambitious funding projections were never realized. Brethren were sadly burned by this first venture into large scale interdenominational cooperation. It would take several decades before the church would be willing to try again.[12]

M. R. Zigler, as has been seen, had emerged by the mid-1930s as the single most powerful church executive. From the beginning he had been open to ecumenical work, dating from his days in World War I as the head of a YMCA program for Marines on Parris Island, South Carolina. Soon after reaching Elgin, he began meeting informally with the Home Missions Council of America. As his responsibilities grew, he began also to attend as an observer meetings of the Federal Council of Churches (FCC), the overall ecumenical body. This was made more palatable to some Brethren because of the strong pacifist position that the FCC took during the inter-war years. J. H. B. Williams of the General Mission Board had inquired of the FCC back in 1916 what the procedures were for gaining membership but of course the Interchurch World Movement debacle closed that door.

In 1938 the Council of Boards authorized church agencies to cooperate with the Federal Council of Churches, especially in the areas of peace, temperance, relief, missions, and evangelism; they also approved a small block grant to the council to support these areas of work. M. R. Zigler was then named as the Brethren fraternal delegate to FCC biennial meetings.

With this background, Zigler was eager for the Church of the Brethren to secure full membership in the FCC. He took counsel on strategy with a Brethren minister, J. Quinter Miller, who had become an associate secretary of the Council. They agreed that they would initiate a move toward membership at the 1941 Annual Conference, which met at La Verne, California. A resolution proposing that the Brethren apply for Federal Council of Churches membership was sent by the Joint Council of Boards at Elgin to the Standing Committee. As the body that prepared business for conference action, it was empowered in Brethren polity to receive such proposals, although the normal procedure for any question of magnitude was for it to come as a query through a local congregation and the related district meeting.

At Zigler's prodding, wording in the proposal also provided that the action, if approved, would authorize the Brethren to secure charter membership in the World Council of Churches (WCC), then in the process of formation. Zigler had represented the Brethren at both world conferences in 1937—the Oxford Conference on Life and Work and the Edinburgh Conference on Faith and Order—from which emerged the plans for the creation of the WCC. He had subsequently been authorized by the church to monitor its progress.

Standing Committee voted after lengthy debate to send the recommendation for FCC and WCC affiliation to the floor of the Annual Conference for action. The resolution emphasized the peace orientation of the FCC, and pointed out that because of its federative polity its actions could not bind the Brethren to any unwanted decision; the church would retain its complete freedom and would "in no way compromise its doctrinal position by this action."

Despite the heated objections of a fundamentalist minority present at La Verne—who anathematized the FCC as a communist front—and the hesitations of traditionalist-minded Brethren, delegates approved the initiative by a substantial majority. Five leading churchmen were appointed as the Brethren representatives to the FCC when its application had been processed and accepted. The Asheville, North Carolina, Annual Conference of 1942 officially joined the Council.[13]

Opponents complained that the motion had been sprung upon them without due notice, and, moreover, that the West Coast location had been selected for this motion because there were usually fewer delegates attending than in locations in the East or Midwest and also because the West Coast tended to be more liberal theologically.

Because of the enabling action of 1941, when the World Council of Churches was inaugurated at Amsterdam in 1948, a full contingent of Brethren was there to participate in its solemnities with hundreds of other Protestant and Orthodox dignitaries. Since that time, Brethren have been fully represented at each of the world assemblies of the WCC, ordinarily held at an interval of six or seven years. The Church of the Brethren was honored in 1954 when M. R. Zigler was elected to the Central Committee, the executive body that meets annually between world assemblies to direct the affairs of the ecumenical body. (Subsequent to this appointment, general secretaries of the church—Norman J. Baugher, Robert W. Neff, and Donald E. Miller—received similar appointments.)

REACTION TO THE FCC/WCC AFFILIATION

Following 1941, the conservative critics of the action kept up a drumfire of polemics against what they considered to be an unnatural linkage of the Brethren with modernists and subversives. Pastors Harold Snider (Lewistown, Pennsylvania) and Fred A. Flora (Los Angeles, California) led the fundamentalist charge. Although not as extreme in language, veteran churchmen I. N. H. Beahm (Nokesville, Virginia) and Grant Mahan (Rehoboth, Maryland) wrote and circulated tracts against the conciliar movements, accusing them of harboring heretical and anti-Brethren positions. Fundamentalists and traditionalists alike sought but failed to enlist C. C. Ellis of Juniata College into their anti-ecumenical camp.

Successive Annual Conferences saw agitation of the issue. In 1943 Paul Haynes Bowman, moderator of the Church of the Brethren, published a firm and pointed "Statement for the Benefit of the Ministry of the Church of the Brethren," replying to the charges of the fundamentalist critics of conciliarism. He found the source of most accusations against the FCC as communist and modernist in Carl McIntire's periodical. Bowman wrote, "Such wholesale condemnation of Christian leaders whom the world accepts as loyal and faithful and on such flimsy evidence as is submitted shakes one's confidence in the criticism and judgments against the Federal Council and places a serious question mark on the motives and purposes of those who make such rash judgments." Again, "It is my opinion that these publications against the Federal Council which have come to my attention are born of prejudice and bitterness. They are unreliable and it seems to me are the products of unhealthy minds and of spirits which are not in harmony with Brethren tradition." Further, Bowman found,

> Most of them, if not all, belong to a school of militant theologians who love controversy more than they love the truth. They represent the type of mind which wrote the creeds and dogmas of the Middle Ages and then in their intolerance and bitterness burned at the stake those who claimed the right to disagree with them. Our Brethren forefathers suffered too much at the hands of demigogs in other ages to fail to recognize their spirit in 1943.

It was clear that Bowman, known for his courtly ways as a southern gentleman, was repelled by the manner and tone of fundamentalist debate. Harold Snider published the statement in *The Christian Beacon*, followed by his own long rebuttal, with a brief answer from Bowman; some 2,800 copies of this issue were mailed by Snider to every Brethren minister and elder.[14]

In the spring of 1944, the combative Snider circulated to the church's ministry a booklet called *Modernism, the Federal Council, and the Church of the Brethren.* It repeated the attacks on the FCC as communist and blasphemous because of its willingness to address social problems and the liberal theological position of some church leaders associated with it. The booklet concluded with a checklist of 27 questions about the FCC and the Elgin staff that amounted to a battery of indictments against both bodies. His last question summarizes Snider's attack:

> After bringing evidence to prove that the Federal Council is not helping the cause of Christianity but rather is aiding mightily in destroying the Bible, which is the cornerstone of the TRUE church, and helping with its ungodly literature to destroy even the morals of our youth, we ask this: HOW LONG ARE TRUE BRETHREN GOING TO STAY IN THE FEDERAL COUNCIL?

The Lewistown pastor was given a hearing by the Standing Committee of the 1944 Annual Conference at Huntingdon, Pennsylvania, moderated by C. C. Ellis. Influenced by Snider's complaints, members introduced a query that begins, "[It] appears that the church became affiliated with the Federal Council of Churches of Christ in America without adequate study by the church in general...." Because of its concern that "the church...move forward with as complete unity as possible," they recommended, and the conference concurred, that a study committee be appointed to bring a report to the 1945 Annual Conference. It did so, agreeing that the decision to join had been made without sufficient study. Most of the report was a description of the actual makeup and intent of the FCC. It admitted that some individuals connected with the FCC were not completely orthodox in doctrine but concluded that the Brethren experience with the council was "too brief to warrant a change" in relationship to it.[15]

The 1945 conference tried to defuse the ongoing issue by appointing a committee of three to work for increased understanding and in three years to bring back recommendations "as may seem wise for the peace and unity of the church." Its equivocal report to the Standing Committee submitted in June 1948 concluded that members of the Church of the Brethren are evangelical Christians, who take the New Testament as their only creed. On those matters not clearly delineated in scripture, as for example, eschatology, the church allows freedom. "Our fraternity should be willing to cooperate with other Evangelical denominations to increase understanding and goodwill, to promote the evangelization of the lost, and to disseminate Christian ethics. In doing so, we will come into contact with men and organizations whose ideas and doctrines we cannot accept. This should not disturb our church as long as we maintain our Brethren principles and heritage."

Then to the critical point, "If or when our relationship with such organizations as the Federal Council leads us to compromise these principles and this heritage, or promotes major division in the church, the church should then consider withdrawal therefrom." FCC affiliation should continue, but Brethren representatives to it should be alert to possible problems. "In the meantime let us practice Christian tolerance and strive to create a fellowship of love and goodwill." The report did not appear in the minutes of the 1948 conference.

The Standing Committee of 1949 appointed a Committee on Understanding and Reconciliation, chaired by pro-FCC church leader Paul Haynes Bowman. The hope was that it could visit congregations where controversy was rife and seek alleviation of conflict. The committee reported back to the Standing Committee of 1950, citing minimal progress: "The experience of the committee suggests that the churches which seek help really do not need it and those which need it do not seek it."

The report refers to the litigation of the Middle District of Pennsylvania against Harold Snider's independent congregation in Lewistown, as well as a second case in the same district, that of the Twenty-Eighth Street Church of the Brethren at Altoona, taken independent by its pastor Henry R. Kulp. The district lost this suit because of errors it made in following due process. Kulp took eighty percent of the congregation with him to form the fundamentalist Altoona Bible Church in 1949.[16]

LATER DEVELOPMENTS

The ecumenical affiliation has continued to be a lightning rod of controversy for Brethren, attracting criticism over the years. A few congregations left the denominational fold, particularly in the South, over this and related issues (for example, the Bible Brethren of York County, Pennsylvania, and the Fundamental Brethren Church, drawn from four congregations in North Carolina in 1962). A sizable number of members individually or in groups left their congregations and joined independent Bible churches or Grace Brethren congregations for the same reasons; this was especially true in Eastern Pennsylvania but occurred elsewhere as well, as in Florida. Despite this, Brethren delegates have consistently voted by large majorities to retain conciliar memberships when the issue has been raised at Annual Conference.

Many Brethren have been active in the ecumenical movements on several levels, from local to international. Among them, to name only some of the more prominent, have been Zigler, J. Quinter Miller, Minor C. Miller, Jesse D. Reber, Kurtis Friend Naylor, John D. Metzler, Sr., Andrew W. Cordier, Edward K. Ziegler, Ira W. Moomaw, J. Benton Rhoades, Melanie A. May, Warren F. Groff, Lauree Hersch Meyer, and H. Lamar Gibble, as well as the general secretaries mentioned before. It has even been argued that, proportionate to its membership, Brethren have had more individuals in local and state conciliar staff positions than any other denomination, but that would be difficult to prove. Nevertheless, the quantity is what one author called a "startling number."[17]

One of the later fundamentalist controversies centered on the ministry after 1955 of William H. Freed, Jr., at the Broadfording congregation near Hagerstown, Maryland. His work was frankly patterned upon that of Jerry Falwell of Lynchburg, Virginia. Through busing, gimmicks to increase attendance, radio and television broadcasts, and other devices, Freed was able to greatly increase the membership at Broadfording until it became the largest congregation in the denomination, nearing 1,800 members by 1978.

The energetic pastor greatly enlarged the church plant in 1971, adding facilities to house a parochial school, Broadfording Christian

Academy. He added the Broadfording Christian College (1976), and the Broadfording Bible Seminary (1979), purchasing for the purpose an unused public school building in Hagerstown. In 1978 Broadfording dropped its Brethren affiliation. The precipitating issue in 1976 was the action of the congregation to license a number of its own ministers without the consent of the district, a violation of basic Brethren polity. Rather than contest the issue, the district did not pursue litigation but instead supported the minority of the congregation wishing to remain with the denomination.

The separating majority took the name Broadfording Bible Brethren Church. In 1982 there was a major dispute among the Broadfording leadership group over Freed's management style, leading to the defection of almost all of the ministers and deacons. The ambitious educational program had to be sharply downsized and the public school building sold; there was considerable loss of membership.[18]

FRATERNAL RELATIONS

Also ecumenical in nature were the series of conversations and cooperative activities with other Brethren bodies. In 1934 a permanent Fraternal Relations Committee was established under the Annual Conference, supplanting previous short-term arrangements. It sent fraternal delegates to give greetings or simply be present at the annual conferences of the other Brethren bodies stemming from Schwarzenau, returning the gesture by inviting their representatives to bring greetings at the Church of the Brethren Annual Conferences.

The most sustained and serious exchanges took place with the Brethren Church, headquartered at Ashland, Ohio. As previously stated, the Church of the Brethren had accepted most of the innovations for which the Progressives had contended in the 1880s. Ecumenically-minded leaders on both sides saw, therefore, no insuperable obstacles to a reunion of the two; they worked through their respective Fraternal Relations committees to effect that goal.

As early as 1904 a representative of the Brethren Church appeared before Standing Committee; H. C. Early reported in 1916 that "fraternal relations have been alive in some form from that day to this." Two years before Early's report, Standing Committee had appointed a three-member committee to receive communications from the Fraternal Relations Committee of the Progressive [Brethren] Church. In the years since 1916 several queries urged further movement toward conversations looking toward unity but little concrete action followed.

The response of the 1925 Annual Conference to a query asking for work looking to unity with the Brethren Church was cool: "Since the most precious and practically vital part of Christian unity is that within the denomination itself, we believe that present conditions in the brotherhood call for the use of this method of promoting Christian unity rather than for the appointment of a church unity commission." In the wording of the minutes, "all sincerely seeking fellowship with the Church of the Brethren [may] be welcomed and received in the regular way."[19]

C. H. Ashman, a minister from the Brethren Church, was invited to speak on denominational church life at the 1933 Annual Conference held in Hershey, Pennsylvania. Following him on the program was M. R. Zigler, whose topic was "Wholesome Denominational Cooperation." After citing the prayer of Jesus Christ for unity (John 17) he asserted that peace churches should especially emphasize those things they hold in common rather than those about which they differ. He pointed out that there were at least 72 communities that had both Church of the Brethren and Brethren Church congregations, hence inevitable competition and unnecessary cost.[20]

Zigler arranged for Brethren leader Otho Winger to speak at the August 1933, conference of the Ashland Brethren, an address that was very well received. Shortly thereafter, members of the Fraternal Relations committees of both groups met, during which warm appreciation was expressed for Winger's message. Neither side was yet ready to talk about merger, but there was strong interest in cooperation. Some of the areas identified were 1) local communities where congregations of both were weak and cooperation would benefit both; 2) urban sites such as Columbus and Cleveland, Ohio, where both had a few members but not enough to form viable congregations, suggesting a joint congregation; and 3) the possibility of joint publications. In 1936 the suggestion was made of holding their annual conferences simultaneously.

Zigler pursued these openings vigorously in the following years. His opposite number was Charles A. Bame, who pressed for cooperation from the Ashland side. He often visited Elgin, Illinois, staying in Zigler's home. Bame published and circulated a tract titled *A Working Agreement with the Church of the Brethren* urging practical cooperation. In 1938 the fourth annual union services were held in northeastern Ohio among members of both bodies, with 22 congregations represented and some 900 persons attending. Zigler was invited to speak and assigned the title "Our Merging Highways."[21]

Unfortunately, the increasing traffic on the churchly highway met a roadblock. Tensions had been growing during these years in the Brethren Church between those favoring traditional Brethren doctrines and a younger group of outspoken fundamentalists led by California pastor Louis S. Bauman, well known for his premillennial dispensational views. Among his converts was the theologian Alva J. McClain, who precipitated the 1939 division in his role as dean of Ashland seminary. The fundamentalist faction held as one of their major grievances the openness of some of the Ashland leadership to relationships with members of the Church of the Brethren, seen as liberal apostates. The friction led to a full-scale and bitter division and the creation of the Grace Brethren Church (National Fellowship of Brethren Churches) with perhaps half of the membership of the Brethren Church.[22]

When the acrimony died down, it was just possible for relationships between the Ashland Brethren remnant and the Church of the Brethren to be reinstated. This took place in 1943 through a joint meeting of the two Fraternal Relations committees; a list of cooperative possibilities was created, many of which were effected. They included cooperation on the mission fields (which took place in Nigeria), exchanges of speakers, sharing of articles in church publications, and consolidation of small congregations. Not foreseen in this meeting, but carried out in several places, was the development of joint affiliation; several congregations adopted dual Church of the Brethren/Brethren Church alignment. Comparable efforts continued in the post-war years.

The depression years were thus a time of troubles, in which the church struggled to find its direction. Denominational leaders guided the church into broader ecumenical vistas but were beleaguered by a small but vociferous cadre of fundamentalists and traditionalists who fought a rear-guard action. This confused many of the rank-and-file members, eager to follow trusted leaders but also wary of entanglements that would divert the Brethren from traditional paths.

21

World War II and the Brethren

Those attending the Historic Peace Churches Conference at North Newton, Kansas, in the autumn of 1935 saw clearly the war clouds on the horizon. Adolf Hitler, who had come into power legally in Germany in January 1933, had recently renounced the Treaty of Versailles and, in defiance of its provisions, was preparing to militarize the border Saar area, which had just come to Germany by plebiscite. Italy, under the dictator Benito Mussolini, had just invaded Ethiopa despite the protests of the League of Nations. The Fascist leader Francisco Franco was developing a power base from which he would attack the Spanish Republic in late 1936, thus precipitating the Spanish Civil War.

Peace Programs

A series of fifteen short articles by Kermit Eby on "What Causes War?" was published in *The Gospel Messenger* in 1934-35, alerting its readership to growing international tensions: "War is coming closer not because of deliberate acts, but because of ignorant drift. It is not yet too late to turn toward peace." Church leaders were determined not to repeat the mistakes of 1917-18 when Brethren were unprepared for the crisis that wartime and conscription brought to them.[1]

Youth director Dan West also carried staff responsibilities for peace education and action. Reviving the nickname Dunkers, frowned on by older churchmen as undignified, he began in January 1932 to recruit young adults for a project called One

Hundred Dunkers for Peace; recruits were to commit themselves to sacrifice as much for peace as soldiers did for war.

The initiative grew out of an article he published in *The Gospel Messenger* in 1931 challenging the church to provide positive outlets for youthful energy instead of trying simply to squelch it; he anticipated that their efforts could also change society. He wrote, "Find me one hundred Dunkers between the ages of twenty-one and thirty who will give as much for peace as a soldier gives for war and we will change the thinking of Congress in three years' time."[2]

By 1934 West knew of at least twenty-five youth who were "hunting for the moral equivalent of war" and expected the number eventually to reach the projected one hundred. The publication *Brethren Action*, published irregularly after 1937 to keep the fellowship in touch with each other, often carried articles critical of American political and economic systems. Some pastors and laity expressed alarm at the sweeping nature of West's prophetic vision.

A frequent contributor to *Brethren Action* was Kermit Eby (1903-1962), a native of northern Indiana and then a schoolteacher in Ann Arbor, Michigan. While there he engaged in the struggles of the labor movement as a friend of the Ruether brothers. Eby was executive secretary of the Chicago Teachers' Union from 1937 to 1942, after which he joined the national staff of the Congress of Industrial Organizations (CIO) as assistant director and then director of its educational department. In 1948 he became a professor of social sciences at the University of Chicago. Eby wrote four books and more than one hundred articles for scholarly and popular journals, often bringing to bear upon national issues the values of integrity and honesty derived from his childhood training in the Baugo congregation. At the same time, he was a vocal critic of Brethren institutions, which he challenged to remain loyal to their Dunker heritage.[3]

An early evidence of the sacrificial spirit of the young Brethren led by West was their success in raising sufficient funds during the depths of the depression to send Kermit Eby to Japan on a goodwill mission (1935) and J. Harman Bjorklund to England for study (1935-36). In 1929 West had made it possible for Ben Stoner to study international relations in Geneva for one year and also observe Hitler's youth movement. Already in 1925 West had singled out Japan as critical; he encouraged Brethren students to make friends with Japanese and "discuss freely with them the relations between the two nations."

A corollary to these projects was the drive in the 1930s to enroll a larger body of Brethren in the peace cause known as "Twenty Thousand Dunkers for Peace." The idea emerged from a caucus of young people at the 1932 Annual Conference. Robert J. Noffsinger became the leader of the project, which sought to secure the signatures of thousands of Brethren to a pledge that they would not participate in any form of militarism. In 1935 the goal was changed in an attempt to reach "Two Hundred Thousand Dunkers for Peace."[4]

The plan seems similar to, but is evidently independent of, the Oxford Pledge issuing from that university's debate on the resolution that "this House will not fight for King and country in any war." The vote of the Oxford Union was 275 to 153 in favor. Though much criticized, the Peace Pledge cause circulated widely among student and socialist groups in the United Kingdom and the United States. In 1935 these groups, augmented by the Methodist Youth League and the Inter-Seminary Movement, recruited 175,000 American students to abandon classes for a one day anti-war strike, during which many signed the Oxford Pledge.[5]

The 1935 Annual Conference passed a sweeping resolution declaring that "all war is sin"; from that premise it reasoned that it was "wrong for Christians to support or to engage in it." The resolution committed the church to prepare a program of general peace education, to support mechanisms to settle international conflicts, and to engage in the resolution of class tensions. Brethren declared themselves opposed to military appropriations and supportive of "every effort by our own nation to promote peace in the world...." At the same time, the statement recognized that not all members agreed with the conscientious objector stand and urged Brethren to display compassion and forgiveness toward each other, "enabling all to live in harmony."[6]

The 1935 conference created an advisory Committee on Legal Counsel for Conscientious Objectors to lay plans for anticipated future conscription. The committee reported back in 1938, advocating that in time of war conscientious objectors should perform alternative service of a constructive nature under civilian direction. It listed types of wartime activities "not consistent with the historic position of the church"; these included combatant service and work as military chaplains, medical attendants under military direction, YMCA staff, and Red Cross posts under military supervision. The committee further called on members to avoid the purchase of war bonds, renounce wartime profits, and refuse to pay direct war taxes. The chairman of the committee, Rufus D. Bowman, admitted that these recommendations ran well ahead of the attitude of many church members.[7]

COOPERATION WITH THE AFSC

Brethren cooperated closely with the American Friends Service Committee (AFSC) during these years. The church sent young people to participate in work camps—pioneered in the United States by the AFSC on the model of those developed after World War I in France by the Swiss pacifist Pierre Ceresole. The American work-camps brought students and other young adults to inner-city ghettos and Appalachian villages to help poor families repair homes and church buildings. West saw this experience as training for missions of wartime relief.

In 1936 Dan West was released from his work with young Brethren under the Board of Christian Education to assist, at their specific request, the AFSC in the Emergency Peace Campaign designed to bring the crisis home to the American populace. His primary task was to visit colleges and universities to recruit, train, and organize youth caravans to travel in twenty states in the interest of peace. More than 500 able young people from many denominations volunteered (including fifteen Brethren), so many that only half could be used.[8]

West's experience led to more cooperation with the Friends in extending relief to both sides of the Spanish Civil War (1936-1939). The able Florence Fogelsanger Murphy in Philadelphia was asked to become the Brethren liaison with the AFSC, a task she performed with distinction. The Board of Christian Education mounted an educational program to alert the church membership to the possibility of relief work in Spain. The response was positive.

Again Dan West was requested by the AFSC staff to join their relief effort in Spain for four months in late 1937, working on the side controlled by Franco (it was a condition of AFSC assistance that they brought aid to those suffering on both sides of the conflict). He was followed by three able young people—David E. Blickenstaff, Paul Hoover Bowman, and Martha Rupel, all of whom subsequently gave distinguished service in several areas of overseas relief during and after World War II. Blickenstaff later became a career officer for the United Nations.

During the same period that Brethren were engaged in relief work in Spain, they also sought to bring relief to the other side of the world. The Sino-Japanese War, which began in 1937, brought with it great need. Brethren appeals went out in 1938 for "Neutral Relief Work for China and Spain." Twenty-one-year-old Howard E. Sollenberger was sent to China to carry on relief work alongside the Brethren missionaries stationed there, using funds raised by Brethren; the church sought to raise $3,000 per month for the purpose.

Seeing already by the late 1930s the broader implications of relief work, Dan West urged the Brethren to create what he termed a "relief machine" under civilian control. This could provide the much sought after "moral equivalent to war." He maintained that if the church were to "get busy on jobs such as these," it could "earn the right to ask for exemption from military duty....Our record...will be a better argument than our intentions, however sincere, without that record." Although not fully implemented before World War II, West's concepts were remarkably prescient for the later development of alternative service for Brethren conscientious objectors.[9]

HEIFER PROJECT

Dan West communicated vividly through articles in the *Messenger* miseries suffered by the civilian population in Spain, especially by hungering children. It was while he was in Spain that West developed the concept, later actualized as the Heifer Project, of contributing livestock to those suffering from war and natural disasters.[10]

Forced by the limited food supplies at his disposal (principally dried milk) to make agonizing decisions about which children should receive aid and which not—actually deciding over life and death—he saw the potential of ongoing sources of nourishment through the donation of milkcows. If recipients of animals were themselves to donate offspring to others in need, a geometric progression of food supply would ensue.

He discussed his idea with neighbors in northern Indiana in 1939, who formed a "Heifers for Relief" committee. In 1941 West won the support of the Northern District of Indiana for the project and in 1942 that of the Brethren Service Committee. In 1943 young Claire Stine began caring for the first heifer, named Faith, donated by Virgil Mock; within one year 1,000 heifers had been given but could not yet be sent abroad because of the war. The first shipment of animals, therefore, went to Puerto Rico and others to sharecroppers in the southern United States. *Time* magazine took notice of the plan as early as July 1944, and praised it as "A Down to Earth Project." After war's end the program expanded greatly. The first major overseas shipment went to France in 1945, consisting of 160 Holstein and Guernsey heifers, distributed there to children's homes.[11]

Heifer Project staff worked out an arrangement with the United Nations Relief and Rehabilitation Administration (UNRRA) that proved useful to both sides. The former supplied attendants (dubbed "sea-going cowboys") for UNRRA shipments of cattle and horses; in return UNRRA supplied overseas transportation for Heifer Project animals. Eventually more than 7,000 students, teachers, preachers, and others, a mix leavened by some experienced farmers, volunteered for the task. In the beginning, sea travel was still risky because of the hazard of maverick floating mines; a few ships in fact experienced collisions or explosions at sea but without major casualty. After they returned to their homes, these volunteers did much through their enthusiastic reports to popularize the program. The Heifer Project-UNRRA coalition worked well until January 1, 1947, when the United Nations agency abruptly ceased operations.[12]

Ben Bushong (called by *Time* the Brethren's "chief red-tape cutter") and Thurl Metzger took leading roles in developing the Heifer Project. Under their shrewd administration, cattle and bulls were sent to many areas, including Ethiopa and Eastern Europe. (A shipment even went to the Soviet Union in 1956.) One animal was presented to the Vatican, prompting the pope to quip that this represented a unique kind of "papal bull." M. R. Zigler's saying was that "you can go anywhere on the back of a heifer."[13]

Although initially sponsored, directed, and supported largely by Brethren, Heifer Project soon became an ecumenical project; it was incorporated in 1953 as a nonprofit agency and was henceforth known as HPI (Heifer Project Incorporated, later renamed Heifer Project International). Members of other denominations were attracted by the earthy practicality of sending animals, some offspring of which would be passed on, thus creating what was once called a "chain reaction of love." Personal connections established between donors and recipients also enhanced support. Already by 1951 more than 11,000 heifers, bulls, goats, and horses had been sent to 20 foreign countries.

By 1994 more than 1,000,000 families in 110 nations and 35 states in the United States had been helped by HPI projects. As they "passed on the gift" to others in need, this aid was extended. In 1994 supporters and staff of the project celebrated the 50th anniversary of the first shipment of heifers from the United States to Puerto Rico. In the late 1990s HPI, with headquarters since 1979 on a ranch near Little Rock, Arkansas, was a highly respected, well-organized voluntary agency, with trained staff members working on agricultural and community development in many nations. It distributed internationally an "ark" of more than twenty different kinds of animals, ranging from bees to camels. In an unusual award, HPI was given an honorary degree by Manchester College in May 1995.[14]

THE LEGISLATIVE EFFORT OF THE HISTORIC PEACE CHURCHES

The sense of impending war and the necessity of timely preparation for it marked the cooperative agenda of the Continuation Committee of the Historic Peace Churches, established in 1935 at the Newton conference. This attitude was exemplified by the representatives of the Historic Peace Churches who twice went as unified delegations to call on the highest levels of national government, including President Franklin D. Roosevelt. This access was largely made possible by good Quaker connections.

The first interview with the president took place in February 1937. Members of the delegation wanted to place on record their history of peace witness, current peacemaking activities, and their understanding of Christian citizenship. They concluded their presentation by stating, "We earnestly solicit your co-operation, Mr. President, now, and if, or when a war comes in discussing and dealing with the types of service in which those of us with deep religious convictions on peace may serve in the spirit of Christ with constructive benefit to humanity and without compromise of conscience."

As the international situation worsened in late 1939, with the outbreak of World War II following Hitler's invasion of Poland, the Historic Peace Churches sought a second interview. This took place in January 1940. Members of the Continuation Committee worked out a common statement that included provision for alternative service under civilian direction if conscription occurred. The statement pointed to their extensive record of peacetime reconstruction and relief, as evidence of the sincerity of the peace churches.

Shortly before the interview was to take place, AFSC staff members raised serious objections, demanding that the delegation include in its statement support for absolutist objectors who would refuse to register if conscription were imposed. Both Mennonites and Brethren balked at this; from their point of view, the government had the right to expect registration of conscientious objectors.

The impasse was resolved shortly before the meeting by an agreement that two statements would be presented. The first highlighted the historic peace witness of the churches and the difficulties experienced in World War I. A second, confidential statement detailed procedures the government should use in dealing with COs, including one paragraph on the absolutist position and another on COs who were not members of the peace churches.

The interview seemingly went well; the president put the delegation at ease with his affable manner. Although of symbolic value, the interview had no lasting importance for peace concerns because the president did not engage himself in these issues until late in the process, and then in a negative way. Subsequent interviews by members of the delegation with other high ranking officials failed to achieve lasting gains. Some scholars believe that the peace church representatives were purposely misled. Paul Haynes Bowman and Rufus D. Bowman were the Brethren representatives on these two delegations.[15]

As the Nazi juggernaut continued to roll over European nations in the late spring of 1940, representatives of the Historic Peace Churches met often with government officials, seeking to prepare the way for the anticipated conscription, despite the assurances of administrative officials that this was not foreseen. In fact, the Burke-Wadsworth Selective Service bill to enact the first peacetime conscription in American history was introduced in late June of 1940.

The bill had to overcome strong isolationist sentiment in the country and even resistance from top figures in the military establishment who feared that its unpopularity would harm their ability to secure more support for their budgets. The determination of President Roosevelt to swing the nation to the support of England and Free France (following the defeat of French forces in late spring 1940), aided by the skillful efforts of the Anglophile eastern elite to influence public opinion through the press, proved to be successful. The conscription bill became law on September 13, 1940.

Sensing that this would happen, leaders of the Historic Peace Churches worked feverishly through the summer of 1940 to influence the legislative process; within a few weeks they had talked to 75 senators and some 250 representatives, military men, and members of congressional committees. Their concern was to introduce language into the bill to guarantee that COs would find equitable and enlightened treatment once conscription took effect. They had only partial success; in the law finally passed, alternative service was established, but there was no provision made for absolutists. The agents of the Historic Peace Churches also failed to have the procedure placed totally under civilian control, as was the case in the United Kingdom.

The final language of the law provided that drafted men who by "religious training and belief" were opposed to military service, if found sincere by local draft boards, were to be assigned to "work of national importance under civilian direction." What was eventually achieved was a new departure—the creation of alternative service for COs in camps with work projects provided by the government. This began the novel and controversial experiment in church/state relations called Civilian Public Service (CPS).[16]

THE EVOLUTION OF CIVILIAN PUBLIC SERVICE

Although the American Friends Service Committee was prepared and also desired to take the lead in setting up the new work program, a meeting of the Historic Peace Churches held in Chicago in October 1940 decided to organize a cooperative agency to perform this task. It was called (after an early name change) the National Service Board for Religious Objectors (NSBRO), still in operation in the 1990s as the National Interreligious Service Board for Conscientious Objectors (NISBCO). M. R. Zigler was named chairman of the board of NSBRO, which found an able director in the Quaker journalist Paul Comly French.[17]

Prior to the Chicago meeting, the Church of the Brethren staff called together representatives from the other four Brethren bodies to assess their attitudes toward the crisis, with the hope of a coordinated effort. The chairman asked someone from each body to express his opinions. When Elder J. W. Skiles of the Old German Baptist Brethren was called on, he demurred, explaining that the Old Orders were from the country and had no suggestions. When the chairman replied that Skiles should go ahead anyway, for, after all, quite a few sitting around the table were from the country, Skiles responded, "But we came from the country this morning!"

In fact, the conscription crisis brought the divided Brethren together in significant ways for the first time since the divisions of the 1880s. Good will built up through mutual assistance at this time built bridges of understanding that persisted long after the end of the war and made possible certain cooperative projects, if carried out informally.

Following the creation of the NSBRO, its executive and peace church leaders negotiated with government officials to flesh out how this work "of national importance" by COs under "civilian direction" was to be effected. The work camps of the 1930s were suggested as models. Brethren proposed to Gen. Lewis B. Hershey (who emerged at this time as the key administrator of the Selective

Leaders of the peace churches who directed the National Service Board of Religious Objectors, Washington, D.C. They include Paul Comly French (kneeling on left), W. Harold Row (kneeling in the middle), M. R. Zigler (standing at left), and Orie O. Miller (standing second from left). *BHLA Collection.*

Service agency) that three kinds of camps be established: 1) those run solely by the government, with maintenance and wages paid by it; 2) those run cooperatively by a peace church and the government, with the church administering the camp and the government responsible for the work project and maintenance; and 3) those run solely by the church for COs who preferred this option, with costs borne by the church itself.

A plan incorporating something very close to these three options was agreed upon by the NSBRO and Selective Service; the proposal was taken to President Roosevelt in late November for his approval. Unfortunately, the president took violent exception to the plan, which had to be scrapped. The administrator of Selective

Service then asked the peace churches if they would be willing to administer *all* of the camps for COs, bearing all of the costs except for the transport of drafted men to and from them and the direction of the actual work projects. The only other alternative, he said, was to seek congressional appropriations for the camps, in which case they would then be run solely by the government.

Faced with this dilemma, the peace churches agreed to try to administer and finance the camps for a six-month trial period, to the extent of their financial capabilities. President Roosevelt approved this plan; thus memoranda of agreement were signed between the NSBRO and the Selective Service Administration in late 1940 to establish the Civilian Public Service program.

This was the genesis of what proved to be a troubled arrangement. The churches thought that they were engaged in a sacrificial enterprise of cooperation between church and state with shared authority; the government understood that the churches had become its agents, with authority remaining solely in government hands. This led over time to sharp differences, precipitated by absolutist COs who were convinced that the peace churches had sold out to the state to save the skins of their own young men. These absolutists either refused to register or walked out of the CPS camps to protest their "incarceration"; this ensured federal prosecution and lengthy prison sentences, for the most part.

In the course of these high level church/state transactions, M. R. Zigler had to secure the approval of the Church of the Brethren for the enormous financial obligation of the projected camps. A special meeting of the Standing Committee was held in Chicago on December 18-19, 1940, to respond to the proposed agreement with Selective Service. After being apprised of the situation, delegates accepted the proposal:

> Voted to assume financial responsiblity for training our young men, with or without government aid (it not yet being clear what position the government will take as to financial aid), in projects of national importance under civilian control which are in harmony with our convictions regarding military training and service.

The committee prophetically noted about the financial obligation, "This may run into large amounts." By the belated end of the CPS program in March 1947, it had cost Brethren over $1,300,000 to care for some 3,000 men, not counting great quantities of donated food and clothing. As it transpired, Brethren supported far more than their own young men, because COs of every description were sent to the CPS camps. Some of them were able to support themselves, and some denominations sent payments to support their own COs, but a great burden still fell on the peace churches administering and supporting the camps.[18]

BASE CAMPS AND DETACHED CAMPS

Early camps were established in former barracks of the Civilian Conservation Corps, a New Deal program to provide work and training for unemployed young men. Many of these CPS projects were located in state and national parks, devoted to construction or maintenance; others worked at soil conservation. The Forestry Service directed many. From the point of view of Selective Service, these base camps were well sited, for they were in isolated locations, and, thus, far from public scrutiny and possible objection.

Some of these projects were devoted to firefighting in the West; the exploits of these "smoke-jumping" COs and the attendant danger received positive public attention. In the course of the CPS program, Brethren administered fourteen such base camps, sited in Virginia, Pennsylvania, Indiana, Arkansas, Michigan, California, and Oregon.

To ease the feeling of many CPS men that they were being stockpiled and were simply wasting time, Brethren administrators developed special schools in the base camps, with classes organized after work and on weekends. They included the "School of Cooperative Living" at Walhalla and Wellston, Michigan; a "School of Pacifist Living" at Cascade Locks, Oregon; a "School of Race Relations" at Kane, Pennsylvania; and a "School of Foods Management" at Lyndhurst, Virginia.

The most unusual was a "School of Fine Arts," at Waldport, Oregon. Authors and artists stationed there issued books of poety and short stories printed on their own hand press; their imprint was the Untied Press. Historians give the school credit as the early foundation of the Beat poetry movement in San Francisco. William Everson, who later was a Dominican lay brother with the name Brother Antonius, was the best known of these Waldport poets.

Another CPS man, William Stafford (of Brethren background), was even more famous in later years as the award-winning poet laureate of Oregon and poetry consultant to the Library of Congress. His memoir of the CPS experience, *Down in My Heart* (1947), described life in Camp Magnolia, Arkansas, and the anger directed at COs by local residents.[19]

Through the urging of CPS men, NSBRO developed in the later years of the program "detached units," special projects that involved more direct human assistance. Among the most significant were assignments of groups of CPS men to mental hospitals, caught badly short-handed by wartime labor shortages. Brethren administered thirteen of these projects. Conscientious objectors in these units found many examples of negligent, even brutal treatment, and provided documentation for a series of exposés by the media. Although resulting in short-term reprisals by staff and administrators revealed as incompetent or worse, the long-term contribution thus made was great. Experts give credit, in fact, to CPS participation in mental hospital work during World War II as the basis for whole-scale national reform of mental health. A substantial number of CPS men devoted their subsequent professional careers to this field.[20]

Other special assigments also involved medical programs. Some CPS men worked on public health projects; others volunteered as "human guinea pigs" for medical experiments. The best known of the latter was a unit that imposed near starvation on subjects to examine the physical and psychological ills caused by insufficient diet. The experiment, conducted by scientists at the University of Minnesota, proved to be of great assistance in planning the rehabilitation of war-sufferers after the end of World War II. It received much favorable public attention because of the sacrifice involved, but was achieved at the cost of some long-term damage to the health of the participants. Other CPS men, including 400

Brethren, were assigned to agricultural projects such as dairy testing or farm work under the Emergency Farm Labor program.

Assignments as mental hospital attendants, medical experimentation subjects, and agriculture workers were accompanied by the payment of wages. CPS men agreed that they would receive nothing beyond maintenance. Excess payments went to a special fund in the United States Treasury, amounting by 1947 to nearly $1,400,000. The clear arrangement with Selective Service was that the fund would be transferred after war's end for the use of service agencies in relief and reconstruction. The NSBRO also attempted to secure a portion of the funds to relieve the emergency needs of dependents of CPS men. Because of technical regulations (and ill will) neither of these legitimate uses was permitted.

Treasury officials insisted that an act of Congress was needed to release the funds, despite the original agreements with Selective Service. Repeated attempts made until 1958 through Congress to free this "frozen fund" for appropriate uses were blocked by a minority of unsympathetic legislators, despite considerable support elicited from fair-minded congressional members. It finally proved impossible to recover this money, which disappeared into the maws of the federal government.[21]

Another disappointment in the course of CPS was the inability to place men in overseas projects. Intensive training programs preparing them to administer relief and rehabilitation work in war areas were conducted on college campuses related to the Historic Peace Churches. With Selective Service approval, the first contingent of men headed by ship to China in 1943. While they were still in transit, however, a right wing columnist named Westbrook Pegler learned of the project. He stirred up such a ruckus that the United States Congress attached a rider to an appropriations bill for the War Department that forbade any CPS men to serve outside the country. The shipload of workers bound for China had to turn back in mid-course at the Cape of Good Hope.

As second best, the peace churches established CPS projects in Puerto Rico; as a United States commonwealth, it could not be excluded by the above cited legislation. After careful investigation, Brethren initiated the Martin G. Brumbaugh CPS Unit in the isolated mountain setting of Castañer in 1942 (thus honoring the early contribution of Brumbaugh as the first United States commissioner of education on the island). It brought badly needed medical and social services to a deprived area.

Following the end of CPS in 1947 the project at Castañer was continued under the auspices of the Brethren Service Commission; later a Brethren congregation was established. The hospital was turned over to the community in 1967. Its contribution to the general welfare of an entire region was honored by the Puerto Rican government.[22]

BRETHREN AND THE WAR

Although the CPS experiment had serious defects, as even its strongest champions would grant, it did provide a more positive answer to the question of conscience than had World War I. Of the 12,000 men enrolled in the program between 1941 and 1947, about half were Mennonites; Brethren came next with nearly 1,400, followed by the Friends with nearly 1,000.

The figure of some 1,400 Brethren in CPS camps, of course, indicates that most of drafted Brethren went into the military. One of the CPS men wrote in January 1944, "When we went to CPS camp we were prepared to face an unfriendly community, but we were unprepared for the number of people in our own church who would no longer support our position." Figures are not precise, but it is reliably estimated that ninety percent of Brethren men of military age accepted the uniform; of this number about 1,400 chose noncombatant service. This reveals that fewer than twenty percent of those members drafted followed the church's peace position.[23]

Recognizing this fact, the Church of the Brethren assigned a staff person the task of communicating with Brethren men (and a few women) during their time in the military; a regular printed bulletin was sent to all those for whom addresses were available, at its peak some 12,000. Personal correspondence followed for those desiring it, some 1,000 in all. In addition church representatives, about 80 in number, paid visits to members in the camps where possible.[24]

According to a survey of these representatives conducted by Rufus D. Bowman, the following reasons were most often given for the large percentage of young Brethren who entered the military: 1) the war was to preserve freedom; 2) lack of peace education in the home and local church; 3) the social pressure of the community, family, and friends; and 4) the compensation offered by the military services. These reasons were corroborated by replies from local churches, recording statements from the young men themselves. According to Bowman's summary of these findings "duty to country, social pressure, the economic problem, inadequate peace teaching, the feeling that the war was forced upon them, indifference to the church, and lack of sympathy to the CO position were the primary reasons why Brethren boys went into the army."

The Church of the Brethren developed a system of Brethren Service certificates that were designed to give an alternative to members to purchase of war bonds and stamps. In some cases the Brethren Service Commission certificates were readily accepted by employers in lieu of the latter. It seems, however, that a majority of members went along with the drives to fund the war effort.

Bowman's conclusion was that, although the Church of the Brethren remained officially pacifist, "in reality during World War II [it] moved some distance from its historical peace convictions."[25]

Brethren had been alert to the prospect of war in the 1930s and worked, in cooperation with other peace churches, to negotiate a better solution to the problems of the conscientious objector than had been the case in World War I. Their efforts led to the creation of the Civilian Public Service experiment in church/state relations. While roundly criticized by some, it did provide a positive alternative for some 1,400 Brethren men. Many of them sought to demonstrate their willingness to serve in humanitarian projects overseas. This possibility came with the expanded program of the Brethren Service Commission after 1945.

22

The Brethren Service Explosion

The ambitious Civilian Public Service program was operated from the Brethren side by the Brethren Service Committee (later known as the Brethren Service Commission—in both cases referred to as BSC). During these war years and those immediately following, it grew from a modest enterprise into the dominant activity of the Church of the Brethren. It commanded major funding, thus rivaling and even surpassing the support that Brethren had given to missions earlier in the half-century.

The origins of the BSC program lie in the Special Neutral Relief Board of 1938-39 that sought to deal with several crises—aid to those suffering from the Spanish Civil War, those suffering in the wake of the Sino-Japanese War, and refugees fleeing Nazi Germany. Brethren were able to place some Jewish refugees in positions and assist some while they stayed in Cuba, waiting to emigrate to the United States.

Soon, burgeoning relief needs impelled the creation of a new committee to integrate Brethren efforts. Members of the General Mission Board and Board of Christian Education came together in 1939 to form the Peace and Relief Commission of the Church of the Brethren, the executive committee of which was to be called the Brethren Service Committee.

M. R. Zigler was the key staff figure in these efforts, with Andrew W. Cordier and L. W. Shultz from Manchester College playing leading roles in the policy-making committee. In 1940 Brethren established an Advisory Committee for Conscientious Objectors to represent Brethren peace interests in the nation's capital. M. R. Zigler, Paul Haynes Bowman, and Ross D. Murphy were named as committee members. The committee took over the concerns previously addressed by the Committee on Legal Counsel for Conscientious Objectors appointed in 1935.[1]

BSC WARTIME EFFORTS

During the war years, the primary, almost sole duty of the Brethren Service Committee was to administer the expanding Civilian Public Service Program. Zigler recruited a hard-working staff to assist in this huge undertaking, securing as his chief aide W. Harold Row, an able young pastor from West Virginia. Some CPS men were also assigned to the BSC office.

The special meeting of the Standing Committee that approved the CPS program also called for a study of the status of the Brethren Service Committee (BSC). Although some voices recommended that the committee secure independent standing, committee members recommended, and the 1941 Annual Conference voted for, establishing the Brethren Service Committee as one of the permanent and major boards of the church. Its sweeping charter was given the biblical basis (Matthew 25) of serving the hungry, thirsty, sick, and naked "least of these."

The primary function of the BSC was foreseen as "personal rehabilitation and social reconstruction" in four fields of service. The sweeping nature of the objectives are noteworthy. They included 1) "To arrest and eliminate, insofar as possible, those forces in human society which contribute to the disintegration of personality and character, and to social instability"; 2) "To relieve human distress and suffering around the world without regard to barriers of race, creed or nationality"; 3) "To represent the church in the area of creative citizenship and Christian testimony on issues of national and international significance" with specific reference to CPS and peace issues; and 4) "To develop, organize and apply the spiritual and financial resources of the church to the above areas of service...." In 1946-47 the entire framework of the church was reorganized, at which time Brethren Service became one of five commissions set up to carry out the denominational program. The five commissions made up one overarching unit called the General Brotherhood Board.[2]

Although almost all BSC attention went to the CPS program during the war years, some modest overseas programs were carried out. David E. Blickenstaff worked with refugees from Spain in Vichy-controlled Southern France. John W. Barwick was seconded to work with the World's YMCA in England, arriving in the middle of the blitz of German air raids; he became the director of the entire YMCA program for German prisoners of war (POWs) held in English camps.

His extensive program included recreation, education, and spiritual care. An unusual development was the creation of three institutions in the camps to prepare the prisoners for work in postwar Germany: a teacher's training institute, a youth training center, and a seminary to train both Protestant and Catholic clergy. He was later assisted by Luther H. Harshbarger and Dwight B. Horner.

Kurtis Friend Naylor and Paul Hoover Bowman were sent to Quito, Ecuador, in 1942; they established a boys club that served 2,000 underprivileged boys until 1947 when city officials took responsibility for the program. A small project in a mountain village near Mexico did community outreach and first aid work. Short-term work camps pursued projects in other parts of Mexico.[3]

On the home front, there were two significant developments. The first was the development of relief centers; they served as collecting and processing points for material aid such as food, medicine, soap, and clothing. The principal centers were located at New Windsor, Maryland; Nappanee, Indiana; and Modesto, California; others were at Houston, Texas; Denver, Colorado; Seattle, Washington; and St. Louis, Missouri.

New Windsor was the largest and most important. It was sited on the former campus of Blue Ridge College, for many years one of the Brethren schools. After passing through a number of owners, it came on the market in 1944. M. R. Zigler saw its possibilities as a base for Brethren Service work and raised the money for its purchase. At war's end, he offered its facilities to the ecumenical Church Committee on Overseas Relief and Reconstruction (later restructured as Church World Service).

Within a year's time, nearly 2,500,000 pounds of clothing had been received for processing and shipment. A fleet of semi-trucks with trailers collected donated materials throughout the region. Since 1945 the New Windsor center has been an important site for both for Brethren and ecumenical social action of the most varied nature, including refugee resettlement, material aid, medical supplies, student exchange, conference center, and other programs.[4]

The other notable effort was the Japanese Relocation Project. In what has been generally recognized as one of the most shameful actions of the United States government during World War II, 120,000 Japanese-Americans, both citizens and residents, were abruptly rounded up early in 1942 and shipped to internment centers in isolated (often desert) areas of the West. These camps were fenced in by barbed wire and guarded by armed military, leading some critics to call them "concentration camps, American style." This arbitrary measure was justified by a supposed threat to internal security. The injustice of the action and injury to civil rights was finally recognized in 1988 when an act of the United States Congress provided for limited reparation.

Brethren on the West Coast, especially Ralph E. Smeltzer and Mary Blocher Smeltzer, became active on behalf of these Japanese-Americans. By mid-war, government regulations permitted the internees to leave the camps if housing and jobs could be found for them in the Midwest and East. Under the direction of the Smeltzers, Brethren set up hostels in Chicago and Brooklyn, New York, for the temporary housing, primarily of young people, until permanent locations could be found for them. Several thousand people were aided in this way; a number of them became members of the Church of the Brethren through gratitude for this assistance and respect for Brethren values. A Japanese woman who had been assisted in resettlement said of the project, "I felt as if I had found a beacon in a dark night."[5]

POSTWAR PROJECTS

The long pent-up desire of Brethren to demonstrate their willingness to work for the benefit of others in times of crisis was given free

One of the most ambitious of the Brethren Service projects in post-World War II Europe was the reconstruction of the noted Karls School (*Karlsschule*) in the central city of Vienna, Austria, repairing severe war damage. Young Brethren and Mennonite conscientious objectors performing alternative service worked here from 1954 to 1961, with funds for building materials donated by the Protestant church. Placards explaining the pacifist motivations of the workers attracted many viewers. *BHLA Collection.*

rein at war's end. A remarkable outpouring of energy, funds, and personal commitment took place, now largely forgotten. Ecumenical records document that the Brethren led American denominations in relief giving not only proportionately to their numbers but also quantitatively; they gave more than the large Methodist Church and more than twice as much as the Presbyterians.[6]

One statistic will illustrate the volume of the response. The fiscal year concluded in February 1947 recorded the total value of materials received and distributed through Brethren as nearing $7,200,000, though not all of this had been given directly by Brethren; the administrative cost had been kept under two percent through the work of many volunteers. The work done at this time earned for Brethren a reputation for concern and effectiveness.

With the close of fighting in Europe (May 8, 1945) it became possible for Brethren to extend work from England to the Low Countries. Attention was first directed to Belgium and the Netherlands and staff moved to these countries. In the immediate postwar months, the central office for BSC in Europe was located in Brussels, directed by Dr. Eldon R. Burke. Brethren sent relief goods to Belgium, where they were distributed through local agencies. Work in the Netherlands began with assistance to war orphans. Later a four-person unit went to the island of Walchern, which had been devastated. BSC staff distributed goods there and began to develop a nursing service. Work in Belgium and the Netherlands was phased out in 1947 because of the rapid recovery of these two nations.

Brethren began work in France soon after the end of the war. There again, assistance consisted principally of shipping relief goods to meet immediate needs and livestock to replenish the diminished herds. Charles and Ruth Webb went to Dunkerque to do community work, with special attention to children. Aid to France was terminated in 1948.

Work in Italy for Brethren Service started in 1946, at first in cooperation with the UNRAA and the AFSC. Material aid distribution was first featured, and then the Heifer Project directed by John H. Eberly was introduced with great success. A team of five workers created an effective children's club in Carrara called *Il Circolo OK*. Through its activities, underprivileged children learned about personal hygiene and group living. Later activities of the Italian unit included health education, supplemental feeding, and a summer camping program. This work was closed in 1949.

An extensive relief operation was opened in Poland in December 1946. The country had suffered severely during the German invasion and occupation and the Russian advance. Again, immediate distribution of food, clothing, and medicine had first priority, with a Brethren team led by Bruce and Clara Wood operating from the town of Ostroda. Beyond that BSC workers sought to develop projects to rehabilitate Polish agriculture. A program to send Polish graduate students to the United States to learn new agricultural methods was initiated in 1947 by Thurl Metzger. Although interrupted for a time for political reasons in 1949 when Brethren workers were forced out of the country, the program was reinstated in 1957 as an exchange program and still continues with great success. A 1987 celebration in Poland to mark the program's 30th anniversary reported that more than 1,000 Polish individuals had studied in the United States; they now occupied high places in government and technical schools; more than 200 Americans had served in Poland, primarily teaching English in Polish agricultural institutes.[7]

GERMANY AND AUSTRIA

The longest lasting programs developed in Germany and Austria. Though Allied occupational policies delayed early relief efforts in Germany, by late 1946 Brethren were able to send the first material aid supplies there for distribution through German church agencies. Dr. Eldon R. Burke was appointed to direct the operation of the Council of Relief Agencies Licensed to Operate in Germany, best known by the acronym CRALOG. With headquarters in Bremen, Burke and his staff oversaw the reception and distribution of tons of relief goods for the entire western part of the country but could not operate in Russian-controlled Eastern Germany. Material aid was distributed by five German agencies and also directly by Quakers, Mennonites, and Brethren. Burke later received an award from the German Federal Republic for his services.[8]

Burke also saved a former German military installation (*Friedehorst*) in the Bremen area from destruction by the occupation forces, securing it for use by the German church as a social institution. He developed there the Christopher Sauer Workshop to provide vocational training for crippled veterans. His wife Cecile Burke, after working for a year in Holland, rejoined him and organized the distribution of material aid in the Bremen area.

Members of the early Brethren Service Committee at New Windsor, Maryland. They are (left to right) W. Newton Long, Paul W. Kinsel, Lawrence W. Shultz, Florence Fogelsanger Murphy, Andrew W. Cordier, Paul Haynes Bowman, George L. Detweiler. *Durnbaugh Collection.*

As earlier in England, a wide-scale program of work with POWs was carried on together with the World's YMCA, directed by Luther Harshbarger. Under the guidance of Ruth and Byron Royer, a youth village (*Jugenddorf*) for homeless boys, operated on a democratic basis, was developed in 1948 at Kaltenstein Castle near Vaihingen in Württemberg. This work was also later honored by the German government.[9]

After 1948 Brethren work in Germany was centered in the Hessian city of Kassel, one of the most badly destroyed of Germany's urban areas. In time a large staff was housed there in a multi-storied building known as the Kassel House, constructed in 1952-53 by volunteer labor. In the fall of 1949 the first contingent of volunteers under the newly organized Brethren Volunteer Service program had arrived in Germany; they came from the third training unit of the program for young adults adopted at the 1948 Annual Conference.

One of the significant German BSC programs involved student exchange; it began in 1948. At first limited to mature students who were enrolled in Brethren-related colleges, after 1949 it was extended to high-school-age youth. The Food and Agricultural Agency (FAO) of the United Nations was involved in the early planning stages, alerted by M. R. Zigler, who had told them of the Polish agricultural exchange. Byron P. Royer developed the first contacts with the American High Commissioner for the Occupation of Germany (HICOG) to begin the program, but it was John H. Eberly who became the major figure in the high school exchange program. Some 300 young Germans, many from refugee families in rural areas, were recruited in 1949, transported on United States Army ships and planes, and placed in Brethren homes in the United States during the first two years. So positive was the reaction to the project that it was continued under ecumenical auspices after 1957-58 as the International Christian Youth Exchange (ICYE). As early as 1952 six other agencies, including the American Field Service and American service clubs, took up the idea and extended it to other countries.[10]

Many other programs centered at Kassel—the Heifer Project, international workcamps and institutes, peace education—continued for many years, long after the worst immediate postwar needs were met. Brethren saw Germany as a key place to demonstrate their long-range commitment to peace and reconciliation. BSC staff there worked closely with European pacifist organizations such as the International Fellowship of Reconciliation (IFOR).

No Brethren Service country program in Europe had greater proportional impact than that developed in Austria after late 1946. By 1947 four BSC workers, led by Ralph E. Smeltzer, were located in Vienna, where they worked closely with the *Evangelisches Hilfswerk*, the social action arm of the minority Protestant church. Early efforts involved the distribution of material aid but soon it was possible to branch out into agricultural programs, especially importing breeding stock to improve the depleted state of cattle, sheep, and poultry.[11]

By 1950 the center of the work had shifted to Linz in Upper Austria in the American zone of occupation. The reason for this was that the bulk of refugees had fled ahead of the advancing Russian army, not stopping until they had passed the Enns River, the demarcation line between the American and Russian zones.

As in Germany, BSC developed a rich gamut of relief programs, focusing primarily on refugees of German ethnic origin, the so-called *Volksdeutsche*. Through 1953 material aid shipments, totaling nearly 1,500,000 pounds and valued at $750,000, had been received and distributed. Among the most effective of the programs was that directed at health; tuberculosis was rampant among the refugee population in Upper Austria because of their miserable living conditions. To counteract this, BSC workers set up the Thalham Tubercular Sanitorium in a former barracks camp in the Salzkammergut, securing supplies and furniture for it from the US military and staffing it with refugee physicians.

Especially effective here was the legendary Helena Braun Kruger (1902-1978), herself a German ethnic refugee from an aristocratic family who left Russia after the Revolution. She and Peter Kruger, her Mennonite husband (by arranged marriage) were helped in 1924 by the Mennonite Central Committee to resettle near Hershey, Pennsylvania. Later on they were invited to join the Spring Creek Church of the Brethren and did so.

Toward the close of World War II, M. R. Zigler spoke in their congregation about plans to open relief work in Europe; they needed workers with language skills. A member suggested that the Krugers should go. She was sure that was impossible because of their dairy herd. The next morning her husband told her, "You should go." They sold their cows and bought steers (which entailed less work), and then she applied to Elgin and was accepted. In 1945, leaving her husband at home, she went to Brussels where she did relief work for six months, before transferring to Austria for two years.

Helena Kruger was a whirlwind of enterprise there in 1946 and 1947. Always impatient with regulations, be they from the military government or church administrators, she largely went her own way throughout the Allied and Russian zones of occupation, helping any one in need. An American general once stated ruefully, in recalling how Helena Kruger "requisitioned" army material for the TB sanitorium, "I could have been court-martialed for giving her those supplies, but how can you say 'No' to Mrs. Kruger?"

After being away from home for more than two years, she returned home determined to stay put. Her husband informed her that the Geneva office had contacted him, asking if Helena could return for another assignment. He told her that he had already agreed. So, after four months home leave, Helena Kruger went back to Brethren Service work in Europe. Later on, Peter and Helena Kruger worked together for Brethren Service, at the last in Greece. They returned home in 1956 only to discover that Peter was not well; he died in 1957. Though grief stricken, Helen soon moved to the Brethren Service Center in New Windsor, Maryland, where she worked as a translator for the large numbers of refugees then passing through the center in the process of resettlement.[12]

In 1950 the Austrian BSC team erected a modest barracks in the harbor area of Linz to house its personnel. Workers at this Brethren Haus administered material aid, health clinics, vocational training, refugee resettlement, student exchange, Heifer Project, international workcamps, and other projects. One of the most substantial was the total renovation of the famed Karlsschule in the center of Vienna; teams of Brethren and Mennonite alternative service workers from 1954 to 1961 provided volunteer labor using materials and funds raised by the small Protestant Church. In 1956, when the Hungarian Revolution broke out, BSC workers in Austria mounted an emergency campaign to meet the needs of thousands of refugees who made their way across the border after Russian tanks put down the uprising.

ADMINISTRATION OF THE PROGRAM IN EUROPE

Directors of the first years in Europe were Dr. Eldon R. Burke and then John E. Bowman. In 1948 M. R. Zigler was assigned to Europe to direct the program and also represent the Church of the Brethren with the newly established World Council of Churches (WCC). For this reason, Zigler chose Geneva as the center of Brethren Service work. He secured two rooms in a barracks office building on the grounds of the ecumenical movement's headquarters. This location allowed him ready contact both with the executives of the WCC and also with the executives of other church agencies whose head offices were located there as well.

Besides maintaining the effectiveness of the ongoing relief and rehabilitation programs in several countries (at times requiring debate with US administrators), Zigler had two major concerns. The first was to promote the peace cause in Europe in cooperative fashion, then using this to influence the ecumenical movement. The second was to extend work into the Orthodox world, especially into Greece. He succeeded in both efforts.

Soon after M. R. Zigler arrived in Europe he sought to create a Continuation Committee of the peace churches, comparable to that developed in the United States after 1935. He did this by bringing together American Mennonites working in European countries with Mennonite Central Committee (or former aid workers then studying in European universities such as John Howard Yoder and Paul Peachey), English Quakers, Brethren Service workers, visiting Brethren academics, and European pacifist members of the IFOR. Although not a theologian himself, he was able to cajole them into drafting peace statements for presentation to the World Council of Churches. At first these were produced separately, but then, at the urging of W. A. Visser 't Hooft, WCC general secretary, Zigler brought about an important combined statement called *Peace Is the Will of God* (1953).

In a further step, the peace churches and IFOR began in 1955 a significant series of high-level consultations on issues of war and peace involving scholars from their own ranks and leading European theologians. The series was referred to as the Puidoux Conferences, a name taken from the Swiss retreat that hosted the first meeting. In time the meetings were merged into the ongoing study consultations on peace of the German church, directed by its research institute (FEST) located at the University of Heidelberg. Selected papers given at these conferences were published in the book *On Earth Peace* (1978). These conferences have been credited with positively influencing the legislation of European governments, specifically in Germany, to permit alternative service for young European conscientious objectors.[13]

Zigler was also able to win an invitation from Spyridon, the Archbishop of Athens and All Greece, to begin relief and rehabilitation work in the isolated villages of the Ioannina district of northern

Greece near the Albanian border. He first sent two Brethren service workers, Edson Sower and Dean Neher. Soon other team members from several nations and churches arrived to form an innovative ecumenical team, taking the name Interchurch Service to Greek Villages. (Zigler always treasured a note he received from the austere Lutheran leader, Franklin Clark Fry: "The Lutheran World Federation at its meeting today approved $5,000 and the appointment of a man for the Greek team, without a murmur. Yours for peace, Franklin Fry.")

Team members fanned out to the mountain villages during the week to teach better farming methods and ways to preserve food. The team introduced the raising of poultry to the area, which by the 1990s was supplying most of Greece with this meat and in the process had revolutionized the area's economy.[14]

OTHER BRETHREN SERVICE WORK

Although most attention went to Western Europe, Brethren Service work was extended to other continents as well. Much of the relief work in China was organized under the General Mission Board using experienced missionary personnel. An interesting project began in 1946 when BSC recruited fifty young men to supervise an UNRAA project to introduce mechanized equipment into Chinese agriculture. This Tractor Unit, directed by veteran relief worker Howard E. Sollenberger, worked in several provinces (as far north as Manchuria) to train indigenous personnel how to use the equipment. Personnel attempted under difficult circumstances to work both in Communist and Nationalist occupied territory. Despite frustrating bureaucratic, political, and technical problems, the unit managed to reclaim more than 50,000 acres and to train 660 tractor operators. The project attracted considerable media attention.[15]

Material aid to other Asian countries, such as India and Japan, was sent through ecumenical intermediaries. During the Korean War, BSC sent supplies for distribution and encouraged a Brethren physician, Franklin Cassel, to join the staff of the World Health Organization for public health work among war victims. A successful agricultural exchange program was initiated in China under

Brethren auspices in 1982, based on the long-standing Polish exchange initiated in 1947. By 1995 some 40 Chinese scientists had been placed in US academic institutions to learn advanced methods; during each year of the exchange two American language teachers have gone to China.

Attention shifted to the home scene from Europe and Asia as immediate postwar needs were met. A lengthy list of North American projects was developed and carried out, many of a short term nature. One of the most significant was the Christian Rural Overseas Program (CROP); this involved the mass collection and shipment of foodstuffs from American farmers to the world's hungry. The material aid director for the Brethren, John D. Metzler, Sr., was the first executive of CROP. It began in 1947 through the cooperation of Brethren, Mennonites, and members of the Evangelical and Reformed Church; some fifty train-car loads of flour were collected for sending to the Netherlands. Soon the Lutheran World Relief and Catholic Relief Service agencies joined the project, and then many other denominations.

With the aid of national publicity from the columnist Drew Pearson, Friendship Trains were organized; they crossed the North American continent, adding train cars filled with grain as they traveled. At each stop ceremonies and worship services took place, even in the early morning hours. Shipments of food on the West Coast went mostly to Japan; those from the East Coast, Great Lakes, and the Gulf area went to Europe. Not only wheat, but also corn, rice, cotton, peanuts, and dried fruits were collected by the ton under the program.

Because of its inclusive-religious base, many firms were glad to cooperate. The value of materials given has mounted into the millions of dollars. It is impossible to calculate the exact amount of the contributions because so much of the handling, transportation costs, pier charges, tariffs, and other ordinary expenses were donated or waived.

In 1952 CROP was placed administratively under Church World Service, the social action arm of the National Council of Churches (the successor to the Federal Council of Churches). It has continued since then to be a major resource for ecumenical relief. It is most often known locally through Walks for Hunger, in which donors pledge so much per mile for those participating in the fundraising effort.[16]

One of the largest programs to emerge from Brethren Service activity was the Sales Exchange for Refugee Rehabilitation Vocations, understandably usually referred to by the acronym SERRV. It began in 1949-50 when returning service commission workers brought home some handcrafts to sell in the United States to assist refugee friends; they placed some items for sale at the New Windsor Service Center. W. Ray Kyle, director of the material aid project there, saw the possibility of expanding the concept to aid craftworkers in developing countries. He arranged through Church World Service for the plan to be publicized in other denominations.

By 1981 the nonprofit program had mushroomed to employ 30 full-time workers and sales of more than $2,500,000, with gift shops sited across the nation; sales doubled by 1995 through over 3,500 cooperating churches. Many patrons were attracted by the self-help philosophy underlying SERVV Handcrafts. In 1995 it changed its name to SERRV International and announced a new partnership with Catholic Relief Services.

VOLUNTEER PROGRAMS

The most creative venture aligned with Brethren service activity came in 1948, at the behest of impatient young people. They pressed the Church of the Brethren to develop a positive social program for them, so that they could balance a "Yes" of sacrificial service with their "No" to military obligations. It emerged from three channels: a summer (1947) work camp/peace institute at Salinas, Kansas; a peace caravan sparked at Salinas that toured congregations during the next year; and a meeting of Brethren students at Bethany Seminary in April 1948.[17]

The Annual Conference of 1948 held in Colorado Springs, Colorado, provided the setting for their initiative. Many of the young people gathered early each morning to pray for guidance; they decided to ask the church to institute a voluntary service program. Dan West helped them to write the proposal. There was in fact a forgotten precedent: in 1942 the Annual Conference had asked

BSC to prepare a plan for voluntary service without remuneration "in normal times as well as [in] crisis times." Some initial work was done but the demands of the CPS program made it impossible to pursue.

The young adults at Colorado appealed directly to the delegates, using as their spokesman Ted Chambers, who was so short that he stood on a box to reach the microphone. This appeal bypassed the normal lengthy procedure that entailed first passing a query in a local congregation, then securing the blessing of a district for its submission to Standing Committee, which could then send it on to the conference itself. Calvert N. Ellis, moderator in 1948, decided that the urgency of the request justified the irregularity in church order. He permitted a vote about introducing the request on the agenda; it passed, and after discussion the delegates approved the proposal by a large majority. In this way the innovative Brethren Volunteer Service (BVS) program was born.

Since its inception in 1948 to the present over 6,000 young Brethren (and those from other church affiliations and none) have enrolled in BVS; this begins with three-week-long training sessions (originally two months), first held at the relief center at New Windsor, Maryland, later in the Chicago area. Volunteers are then sent out to projects across the country (or to foreign lands in some cases) for one to two years of volunteer labor.

Later, older adults were also admitted to the program, typically those taking early retirement and wishing to give volunteer service; the first orientation session organized for older volunteers occurred in 1973. In 1976 the conservative Brethren Revival Fellowship began cooperating with BVS to administer its own orientation sessions and group projects. Many observers have commented that BVS is at least as important as an educational experience for volunteers as it is as a service to others.[18]

With the outbreak of the Korean war (1950-53), the United States government again initiated conscription. It was, however, possible this time for the church to develop a more satisfactory form of alternative service than had been the case in World War II. Those young men considered sincere by local draft boards in their conscientious objection were declared "1-W"; they were then free to apply directly to recognized service agencies for assignment to a wide variety of placements. The agencies only reported to the government the initiation and termination of service; thus under civilian direction, the system avoided most of the problems that had plagued the CPS program. This influx in personnel demanded substantial increase in the BVS program, particularly in the United States but also in overseas assignments.

Based on BVS and comparable concepts, the peace churches worked together to create the International Voluntary Service (IVS) agency, largely at the initiative of W. Harold Row, who succeeded M. R. Zigler as executive secretary of Brethren Service in 1948 when Zigler went to Geneva. International Voluntary Service was incorporated and Brethren educator John S. Noffsinger was called to be its first executive in 1953; the agency received its first government contract later that year. Early IVS projects were in Egypt and Iraq; later work was extended into Indochina. Most of the projects involved agricultural reform. By 1979 some 57 IVS staff personnel were working in seven nations. A Brethren volunteer, Chandler Edwards, was killed by insurgents in 1969 while working in Laos; another young Brethren man, Ted Studebaker, was killed two years later in Vietnam while working with Vietnam Christian Service. It is widely recognized that IVS provided the direct model for the United States Peace Corps initiated in 1961. Noffsinger became one of its senior staff members.[19]

A comparable program was *Eirene* (the Greek word for peace), founded in 1957 in Europe by the Historic Peace Churches and the IFOR. It was created to provide a channel through which European conscientious objectors could volunteer their time in the cause of peace and reconciliation. As European governments increasingly recognized the validity of conscientious objection, there was need for alternative service possibilities. Early project sites were in North Africa, especially in Morocco. An expanded program continues in the late 1990s under ecumenical sponsorship, with headquarters in Neuwied, Germany.[20]

OTHER ASPECTS OF BRETHREN SERVICE

While the direct response after 1945 to the staggering needs of war-sufferers worldwide demanded most attention and resources, the

Brethren Service Committee did not forget that its original charter also directed the office to give attention to broad issues of societal problems. These included racial injustice, economic inequity, militarism, political corruption, social instability, and especially the need for peace education. As the CPS program wound down, increasing staff time of Ora Huston, Ralph E. Smeltzer and others was directed at programs to address these issues.[21]

Brethren Service Committee staff workers developed a series of peace institutes and workshops, often sited on college campuses across the country. This was particularly active between 1947 and 1950. Emerging from one of these institutes in 1947 was the idea of Peace Caravans. They involved car loads of young people who traveled from congregation to congregation to present programs on peace. BSC staff members wrote or commissioned peace literature of several kinds, distributing these pieces primarily through the congregations. Articles appeared regularly in *The Gospel Messenger* and the monthly *Brethren Service News*.

Special institutes on race relations were also developed during this era; particularly significant were interracial camps held in the South in Brethren campgrounds. BVS workers were assigned to projects serving minorities in the South and Southwest. One long-standing BSC project was in Falfurrias, Texas, where a ranch provided a base for work with Hispanics. Other personnel worked with Native Americans at Lybrook, New Mexico, and taught in reservation schools.

One of the most successful projects was the organization since 1949 of seminars on Christian citizenship. This meant bringing groups of church members, with particular attention to youth, to visit the federal government in Washington, DC, and the United Nations in New York City. Speakers from government and private agencies oriented the seminar participants to current issues facing the nation and world. A Washington office to represent the Brethren to government agencies and to inform Brethren of legislative initiatives was first established in 1946-47 under Paul Haynes Bowman, then reestablished permanently in 1962 with Ruth Early and John H. Eberly as the first representatives.[22]

Throughout this period, BSC staff members were instrumental

in drafting early versions or providing materials undergirding a series of Annual Conference pronouncements on social issues. They then took responsibility in communicating these resolutions to legislators and other appropriate offices, at the same time working to acquaint the broader membership with the official position of the church. It must be admitted that in some cases the statements of Annual Conference were in advance of the feelings of the membership, limiting the effectiveness of the resolutions.

BRETHREN-ORTHODOX EXCHANGE

Among the most intriguing of Brethren Service initiatives during the Cold War era was the series of exchanges between the Russian Orthodox Church and the Church of the Brethren. Begun when relationships between Soviet and American citizens were still very restricted and strained, it marked a successful effort to establish bridges across ideological and ecclesiological boundaries. The chief architect of the exchanges was W. Harold Row, executive secretary of the Brethren Service Commission. The unlikely meeting of two such dissimilar churches was made possible by the peace witness of the Brethren and its record of relief aid that included Eastern Europe.

Developed only after protracted negotiations and the surmounting of extensive bureaucratic red tape on both sides, the exchange featured delegations of Russian church leaders visiting American churches and institutions and reciprocal delegations of Brethren church leaders visiting Russian churches and institutions. These exchanges of delegations took place in 1963 and 1967. Right-wing demagogues picketed events attended by the visiting Russian delegations, led by Metropolitan Nikodim; the visitors were called communist agents. The US-USSR exchanges were followed by two joint peace seminars, one held in Geneva in 1969 and another in Kiev in 1971.[23]

The explosion of Brethren Service activity after 1945 represents one of the great achievements of members of the Church of the Brethren. It put them on the map in national and international church circles with a prominence never seen before. In fact the out-

The Church of the Brethren/Russian Orthodox Church exchange was led by W. Harold Row (executive of the Brethren Service Commission) and Metropolitan Nikodim, head of foreign affairs for the Russian Church. They are shown conferring here, along with translator/consultant Paul B. Anderson (at left). *BHLA Collection.*

side perception of Brethren character is still largely shaped by that remarkable burst of energy and commitment. Yet, in the minds of some in the denomination, this was something of an aberration, which should rightfully give way to a more sober and steady attention to ongoing realities of church life.

23

Changes in Church Structure

Partly in direct reaction to the overwhelming response of the church to the Brethren Service program during and after World War II, the early postwar years (1946-47) brought great changes in the polity of the denomination. Thoughtful church leaders expressed concern that less popular yet necessary causes and institutions within the Church of the Brethren were being short-changed in emotional and financial support. They envisioned a rationalized structure that would grant deserving but less dramatic programs appropriate slices of the financial pie.

They also had serious reservations about the spontaneous and freewheeling administrative style of BSC leaders M. R. Zigler, Dan West, and Ben Bushong; these men tended to see urgent needs, then immediately set out to meet them in energetic and direct manner with less-than-perfect regard for authorization and careful communication with all related offices.

Changes in the postwar period also represented the culmination of many decades of appeals for the unification of overhead structures of the church. As we have seen, the church had responded to felt needs in the late nineteenth and early twentieth century by organizing a multiplicity of boards. Predominant among these was the General Mission Board, which throughout this period—at least until the heyday of Brethren Service—had the most emotional support in the pew, largest endowment, best publicity, and most efficient staff. In 1935 the church's budget approved by Annual Conference was $275,000, of which the General Mission Board received $215,000. With the exception of the General Educational Board, all of the other boards and committees until "well into the the twentieth century were directly or indirectly controlled by the General Mission Board."[1]

As the boards proliferated, both the constituency and the staffs of these boards articulated the need for coordination and cooperation. During the introduction of the Forward Movement of 1919, delegates at the Annual Conference directed the three current boards—General Mission Board, General Educational Board, and the General Sunday School Board—to present a plan that would "fully correlate the goals of the three boards, emphasizing the budget."[2]

The Council of Promotion created in 1923 was charged with designing coordination of the boards in their interpretive materials and funding requests. Five years later the boards created the (Joint) Council of Boards intended to facilitate the development of a collective budget, the elimination of duplicate efforts, and a consistent policy for all boards. Staff members met monthly to pursue these goals.

In 1930 J. W. Lear, the secretary of the joint council, pressed for more complete integration: "...until such time as Conference shall see fit to authorize one board of administration...the Council of Boards may well undertake some of the functions of the one board." In his view the church would do well to elect one board for the church; this board could then organize to care for the "departmental functions." The only response to Lear's plea was the selection a committee to study the issue, in an attempt to determine what the church objectives should be and what organization could best achieve those objectives; this did not lead to any real change.[3]

In the same year the Women's Work organization suggested that the work of the boards could be better integrated, commenting that "there should be one General Board to supervise all the activities of the church." By 1942 and 1943 queries brought to Annual Conference indicated restiveness among the church membership along the same lines. The 1943 query asked for the appointment of a committee of five people to study the function of the moderator and "the over-all organization of our church with a view to simplification and integration."[4]

This led in 1945 to the decision of Annual Conference to appoint a blue-ribbon Committee of Fifteen. It was charged with a total review of church polity, looking at "her present organizational needs...." They were asked to formulate a "constitution and a church discipline which will provide a minimum amount of organizational machinery and a maximum efficiency in performing the task set before the church." The committee, consisting of seasoned church leaders, took up its work.[5]

THE GENERAL BROTHERHOOD BOARD

The committee submitted the first part of its report to Standing Committee in 1946, basically calling for the principle of one board at each level of the church—congregation, district, region, and denomination—with a unitary structure throughout and clear linkage between all of the parts; they expected to complete the report during the following year. To their apparent surprise, the Standing Committee recommended that this part of the report be presented to the conference for its review; again surprisingly, the delegates adopted this part of the report, authorizing an immediate reorganization of the board structure at Elgin.

For the sake of "unity, efficiency, and economy," it created a new central structure called the General Brotherhood Board (GBB) to coordinate the work of the denomination; it consisted of 25 members, with a chairman, vice chairman, and executive committee. The former galaxy of independent boards were now realigned as "commissions" under the board; each of the board members also served on a commission. Each commission had a chairman, who sat on the executive committee. The five commissions were the Foreign Missions Commission, Ministry and Home Missions Commission, Christian Education Commission, Christian Service Commission (later renamed Brethren Service Commission), and Finance Commission. (The original names actually read Commission on Foreign Missions, etc., but were changed in common usage without formal action.)

A general secretary served as the executive for the General Brotherhood Board, aided by an executive secretary for each commission, treasurer, manager of the Brethren Publishing House, and other needed staff workers. The Board would have the authority and responsibility to "consider the entire brotherhood program, evaluate all phases of the program, and determine the general policies and budget needs in each area of its work." Further, it would "correlate and unify the work of all commissions."

The Annual Conference retained its final authority to initiate, constitute, and revise policy and polity, but the GBB was given the authority within Annual Conference guidelines to develop program and administrative policies. It employed staff and, by virtue of controlling the budget, set priorities.[6]

It was clear that this centralization would have the effect of clipping the wings of the former executives of the separate boards, who, though under the direction of policy-making boards, in reality had considerable freedom. Personnel decisions made at the time underscored the intent of the power shift. M. R. Zigler was the senior administrator, had served for most of the previous years as the coordinator of the joint boards, and was thus logically in line for the new position of general secretary. Nevertheless, he was passed over in favor of a younger man he had himself recruited, Raymond R. Peters, secretary of Christian Education. The attempt to scuttle the name of Brethren Service, though not successful, also illustrates the strains experienced during this period.[7]

In November 1947, Zigler was "bumped upstairs" as director of Brethren Service work in Europe and Brethren representative to the World Council of Churches in Geneva. This opened the way for W. Harold Row, his former lieutenant in the Brethren Service office, to become secretary of the Brethren Service Commission, and, in that capacity, Zigler's boss. Both Peters and Row represented a more highly organized, less charismatic style of administration than that of Zigler. In 1952 Peters resigned and was replaced by Norman J. Baugher, a pastor from California, who was in his mid-forties and wielded strong administrative skills.[8]

It is of some interest to note that 16 of the 25 members (all men) of the newly elected General Brotherhood Board were professors at or presidents of institutions of higher education. The new chairman of the board was Rufus D. Bowman, president of the seminary; Calvert N. Ellis, president of Juniata College, was the vice chairman and then long-time chairman after the early death of Bowman in 1952. Both Bowman and Ellis had been members of the Committee of Fifteen. This choice reflected a period when leading positions in the church, including the moderatorship, were often given to educators. This would soon give way to the domination of the office of moderator by pastors after 1960.

Under the new board alignment, many of the current personnel at Elgin were retained, but there was turnover there as well. The overall effect of the structural shift was to move toward greater rationalization of procedures and goals with less dependence upon personal connections. The church no longer saw itself as a family but was to be operated more like a bureaucratized business enterprise. It was an example of what the sociologist of religion Max Weber defined as the "routinization of charisma."

As observers noted at the time, the quite intentional effect of the reorganization was to refocus the energies of the denomination on the local work of parish and institutions and away from the mission fields and service projects, although never stated so bluntly. In its own way, it was an appeal for a "return to normalcy," much like that which took place after World War I. It reflected in this way the pent up demand of American society to return to the home and hearth, the concerns of the family and community.

Denominational Polity

The realignment at Elgin was but the capstone of the new polity. In 1947 Annual Conference adopted the second part of the recommendation of the Committee of Fifteen. It contained a comprehensive organizational plan for all other levels of the church besides the central offices—congregations, districts, and regions—and revised procedures for Annual Conference; the latter involved the roles of Standing Committee, delegate body, conference officers, and locations committee. Again the unitary board plan was strongly encouraged but not absolutely demanded on the congregational and district levels.

Finally, this part of the report dealt with institutions related to the church—Bethany Biblical Seminary, the colleges, Bethany Hospital, and the Pension Board.

This plan was also adopted as recommended by the 1947 conference. Many congregations and districts, but not all, quickly revised their charters to follow the plan of having one board with several commissions.[9]

In the 1946-47 plan, the role of the regions was regularized and standardized. They had first emerged informally from among the constituencies served by each of the Brethren-related colleges, with the first employed person in the Southeastern Region in 1941. In time, a sense of identity came to be felt in five regions: Eastern, Southeastern, Central, Western, and Pacific Coast. Because of the concentration of Brethren congregations in the East and their relative scarcity west of the Mississippi River, the difference in the sizes of the regions was great.

According to the new plan, each region would consist of a number of districts. A unitary regional board constituted by district representation was to employ professional staff, located on or near the respective college campus. The role of the regional personnel was to provide liaison between the districts and the denomination on all aspects of the church program, with particular attention to pastoral placement, home missions, Christian education, work with youth, men's and women's work, peace education, and denominational fund raising.

In time districts developed their own full-time staffs, with correspondingly less need for the regional offices. The 1958 Annual Conference appointed a study committee, which recommended two years later, with conference approval, that the regions be gradually eliminated. The last regional staff person, working in the Central Region, closed out work in 1966. In the 25-year period of regional level workers, 24 men and one woman held appointments as regional administrators or associates.[10]

The former regions still function informally in regard to the geographical areas for election of members of the denominational and seminary boards, the rotation of locations for Annual Conference, and in at least two cases (Southeastern, Central), in continuing youth meetings.

A Second Reorganization

It took just 20 years for another sweeping reorganization of the denominational machinery. It is more difficult to assess the dynamics behind this change than was the case in 1945. Restlessness on the part of some influential leadership, especially on the West Coast, seems to have played a major role. The philosophical basis behind the change emphasized the individual, with expressed distrust of "canned" programs created at the top level and "sold" to the congregations.[11]

Instead, staff members were now expected to develop a leadership style as facilitators and consultants, assisting congregations and their members to carry out initiatives developed at the "grass roots." During this same period Christian educators downplayed specific curricular materials and worked hard at developing resources from which congregations could pick and choose.

This was the era of "sensitivity groups," "encounter groups," and "group dynamics," in which participants were encouraged to let their emotions of frustration and anger as well as joy and elation "all hang out." Church leaders on all levels were subjected to training exercises, which their organizers promised would result in greater creativity and deeper inter-relationships.

This individualizing mood was reflected in the Church of the Brethren by the Mission Twelve program developed by the Christian Education Commission in 1962. Defined as "basically a vital depth experience in Christian community," it was directed at "congregations and individuals who willingly commit themselves to explore the deeper meanings of faith, personhood, human relationships, and the nature and mission of the church...." By 1971 nearly 6,000 Brethren had participated in these group dynamics retreats. Underlying the effort "to equip persons to function with flexibility, creativity, and freedom," was the conviction that everyone needs "periodic experiences in the renewal of self, as well as opportunities for updating skills."[12]

The Mission Twelve program was reminiscent in some ways of the earlier Brethren program of Hilltop Retreats, also encouraged by religious educators. The retreats were largely based on Dan West's camping and discussion models of the 1930s; they sought to elicit trusted interactions in small groups and focused on personal growth through hearing the "truth spoken in love." Retreats reflected as well the popularity among more than a few Brethren of the contemporary Ashram movement spearheaded by E. Stanley Jones and the Camps Farthest Out of Glen Clark.[13]

That the highly individualistic philosophy of the later 1960s was not completely shared by all constituents is evident from the expressions of distrust in the central leadership at "Elgin" during this period, by no means restricted to those aligned with the Brethren Revival Fellowship. Symbolic of this mistrust was the sustained protest raised across the denomination after the 1966 National Youth Conference held at Cornell University. The diversity of program presentations shocked many adult youth advisors present. More disturbing yet was the laissez faire attitude of the conference planners to discipline issues. The result was turmoil, excess, and evident capitulation by conference managers. The reaction to Cornell was such that responsible staff workers lost their positions and youth conferences were dropped for a time.

Further evidence of the uncertain nature of the philosophy was presented by the continual tinkering with the denominational structure following its implementation in 1967-68. Unlike the blueprint adopted in 1946-47, the one introduced two decades later needed continual updates.

An eight-point statement of purpose and function was drafted for the reconstituted General Board (the word brotherhood was dropped as sexist). Under the guidance of the Annual Conference, the board was mandated to seek to

> 1) Assist the Church of the Brethren to be oriented around manifestations of Christian mission so that all persons, their relationships, their social structures, and the world may be reconciled to God;
>
> 2) Assist the congregations and the church at large in self-examination of their life, their world, and their witness in accord with their understanding of the intention of God and the Lordship and mission of Jesus Christ;
>
> 3) Encourage manifestations of the oneness of the whole

church of Jesus Christ in the world by cooperative ministry and united witness...;

4) Encourage study and research of biblical and other
sources in the continuing quest for truth;

5) Encourage personal commitment and the nurture of
the Christian life;

6) Extend ministries of Christian love, service, and justice
to persons in need...;

7) Study, speak, and act on conditions and issues in the
nation and the world which involve moral, ethical, and
spiritual principles inherent in the Christian gospel;

8) Help interpret and appreciate the current relevance of
the identity, heritage, and unity of the Church of the
Brethren.

The non-directive and open-ended spirit underlying the shift is
evident in this language, seen also in its sweeping character—all
persons, manifestations, their social structures, the world, the whole
church, and the like. The basic liberalism of the philosophy is
betrayed by the fourth point, which looks to unnamed "other
sources" in addition to the Bible in the "continuing quest for
truth."[14]

In the name of greater integration the five GBB commissions
were here compacted into three: 1) the World Ministries
Commission; 2) the Parish Ministries Commission; and 3) the
General Services Commission. Basically, World Ministries was to
administer all of the outreach ministries of the church; Parish
Ministries was to deal with domestic ministerial, congregational,
and educational ministries; and General Services was to provide the
financial, publishing, and logistical needs for the denomination and
the other two commissions. In practice it was impossible to draw
lines neatly between the commissions, for example between World
Ministries and Parish Ministries on missions, or between Parish
Ministries and General Services on publications. Quite foreseeable
tensions were the result.

Although never emphasized in the discussion that introduced
this change in polity, paring five commissions into three, with the

new World Ministries Commission now bearing responsibility for outreach, effectively wiped the name Brethren Service from church structures. It marked a belated success of those church leaders who had been unhappy about the dominance of Brethren Service in the immediate post-World War II years; they had attempted to drop the name in the 1946-47 change, but it had not worked. The lasting power of the older label was seen in its retention in the continuing European office (down-sized) in Geneva and the decision in recent years to return the designation of the New Windsor Service Center to its older name of Brethren Service Center.

The General Board retained 25 members, distributed over the three commissions. Their terms were shortened to three years, intended, it was said, to broaden representation on the board of the membership. The possibly unintended effect, however, was to strengthen the role of the staff executives and to weaken the board. Although board members could be reelected once, they often were just finding their feet in the complicated arena of board participation by the time their terms were over.

S. Loren Bowman, heretofore secretary of the Christian Education Commission, was named as general secretary upon the death of Norman J. Baugher in 1968. Executives of the three commissions were named associate general secretaries, to highlight the sense of unified work. Together with the treasurer and later the director of human resources (personnel), they formed an administrative council—a staff executive committee.

An innovation was the creation of a Review and Evaluation Committee elected by Annual Conference. It was asked to assess the work of the board every three years and to share its findings with the conference and the board. A powerful body was created in the Goals and Budget Committee; this consisted of the executive committee of the board and the administrative council of the staff (members of which had voting rights—unique in Brethren polity). Its assigned tasks included "unifying and coordinating the related functions of goal setting, program evaluating, and budget building as specifically defined from time to time by the Board." In other words, its responsibilities duplicated almost exactly those of the board; if the key staff members and best-informed board members agreed, the approval of the entire board was virtually assured.[15]

Although not part of the central restructuring, another major change in polity of this era must be mentioned. This was the elimination of the office of elder in 1967. It reflected the increasing centrality of authority of the full-time professional pastor and the expanded role of the denominational and district ministerial boards. In an earlier era, the ruling elder (sometimes called the householder or housekeeper) really ran the congregation, presiding at congregational business meetings, directing the deacons and other ministers. He was a beloved and respected figure, noted for long and sacrificial service. The district gathering of elders, commonly called the Elders' Body, had the power to discipline ministers held to be delinquent in doctrine and/or behavior, and did so in energetic style. Only elders could serve on Standing Committee, the central body preparing business for the Annual Conference, and assume the duties of moderator or clerk.

By the late 1960s almost all of these prerogatives had been lost. Elders' bodies had become ministerial committees with lay membership. Lay members were increasingly used as moderators of local congregations. In 1966 the first layman, Dan West, served in the position of moderator. Ministerial regulations defined ordination in functional terms; those no longer active in ministerial capacities were expected to resign their ordained status. In the light of these changes, many in the Church of the Brethren thought that the position of elder was an anachronism. For that reason, the Annual Conference of 1967 dropped the office but permitted those men ordained as elders for life, who so wished, to retain the title. There were to be henceforth only two levels of ministry—the licensed (for those testing the call to ministry or moving toward ordination) and the ordained. Some observers have questioned this decision, feeling that something valuable was lost in the process. Although sometimes abused in the past, the experience and wisdom of the elders collectively had much to commend it.[16]

EFFECT OF THE UNIFIED BOARD STRUCTURE

One way to determine the impact the changes in board structure had on the life of the denomination after 1946-47 is to look at the issues raised at Annual Conference. Earlier, it was understood that business at Annual Meetings would come primarily from queries raised in congregations and directed to national attention, if thought worthy, by district meetings or, on special occasions, by Standing Committee. After 1947 it became increasingly common for conferences to be presented with issues or resolutions brought directly by the General Brotherhood Board or General Board, for the most part, initially generated by Elgin staff members. The range of issues thus presented is striking.

The most direct analysis of this change is found in S. Loren Bowman's study of Brethren polity (1987), based on personal involvement as board member and staff executive for over a quarter of a century. He summarizes, "The records reveal that the boards have been comfortable in calling the church to a prophetic role in the life of the church and in society." Granting that the boards occasionally overstepped their prerogative by usurping the authority vested by Brethren polity in the Annual Conference, on balance Bowman believes that the board has played an appropriate role: "A board that refuses to take initiative in program formulation and implementation actually denies the reason for its existence. *Boldness, not timidity, is the mark of a useful board.*"[17]

Among the "bold thrusts" he identifies as board initiatives are the Polish Agricultural Exchange, the Cooperative Foundations in Ecuador to assist poor farmers, the innovative Lafiya public health program in Nigeria; the New Call to Peacemaking, and the SERVV marketing program to assist cottage industries among refugees and the Third World. In fact these initiatives arose from dispersed projects under Brethren Service or Brethren mission personnel, or in the case of the New Call to Peacemaking, from another denomination. The Elgin-based board can rightly claim credit for providing additional denominational funding or guidance that allowed these programs to expand. They were not originated by the board.

Where the General Board, prodded by the staff, has taken most initiative is in the area of resolutions and pronouncements on theological, social, and political issues. They include, to name representative examples, statements on criminal justice, urban ministries, evangelism, economics, tobacco, war, the church and state, government (including nonviolence and justice), world hunger, labor unions, nuclear arms race, human sexuality, victims of crime, housing, sanctuary of refugees, aging, and noncooperation with conscription.

In some of these cases, although majority Annual Conference approval was secured, it is evident that the statements were overly "distant from the views of the general membership" (S. Loren Bowman). This was clearly the case with the statement on human sexuality (including the sections on abortion and homosexuality), on noncooperation with the government, and on war taxes, for they were brought back into discussion several times.

In the judgment of some veteran church leaders, the activism of the board departed from its appropriate role as implementer of church policy and polity determined by Annual Conference. The correct balance between these organs of the church is, of course, not always easy to determine. This apparently was one of the motivations behind a third proposal for restructuring of church polity developed by an Annual Conference committee beginning in 1987; four different queries ranging from specific consideration of district boundaries to a sweeping review of polity inter-relationships were assigned to a committee of five people. Members of the committee understood their task to be not only a review but rather a thoroughgoing revamping of total church governance (an assumption that was sharply challenged when their report was debated).

An analysis of the complicated proposal the committee presented to the Orlando, Florida, Annual Conference in 1989 makes clear that they held strong reservations about the current operation of the General Board. They recommended that the role of Annual Conference be strengthened by extending the moderator's term to three years and giving it executive functions.

They found certain aspects of the current functioning of the board to be "dysfunctional"; it was generally understood that this referred especially to a sharp division of opinion between staff members of the Parish Ministries Commission and the World Ministries Commission about the validity of new Brethren missions abroad—PMC strongly favoring, WMC strongly opposed. They also saw a problem in the proliferation of agencies and organizations outside the purview of the General Board, which they wished to coordinate.

It is unnecessary to sketch in detail the restructuring proposal the committee advanced, because it was solidly rejected in 1989 and the committee dismissed. The original concerns were reassigned to a newly constituted committee; its report, when adopted, made only minor changes in church structure. The committee report of 1989 did clearly surface disenchantment with the current board structure.[18]

Having looked at the organizational changes in the polity of the denominational church, it is time to see what was happening during this same era on the level of the local congregations.

24

Changes in Church Life

The sweeping victory of the Allied forces in the European and Asian theaters of World War II was followed in the United States by a booming era of prosperity, positive thinking, and population growth. A built-up demand for consumer goods fueled an economic upswing that saw new houses, new cars, and new appliances reaching new markets. A rapid demobilization of soldiers, sailors, and airmen swelled the pool of workers, in many cases replacing the women and black Americans who during the war had been given access to well-paying jobs for the first time. The G. I. Bill enabled college degrees to be earned by thousands of veterans from socio-economic backgrounds that had never before anticipated such advances.

Church membership increased dramatically across the nation, from an estimated fifty percent in 1940 to seventy percent in 1960. The Roman Catholic Church alone baptized some million infants per year, and the Southern Baptists annually increased their adult members between 1945 and 1949 by 300,000. During the war the National Association of Evangelicals had been formed, distancing itself from strident fundamentalism on the one side and the liberal Protestant establishment on the other. In 1950 the National Council of Churches of Christ was formed, incorporating the Federal Council and other interdenominational organizations. Parachurch bodies, such as Campus Crusade and Youth for Christ flourished; from the latter emerged Billy Graham's Hour of Decision radio programs and his national and then international evangelistic crusades.

The Church of the Brethren was also affected by this expansive trend. Radical changes in church polity in the post-World War II era paralleled comparable shifts in the life of local congregations. As has been seen, one of the driving forces behind the original creation of the General Brotherhood Board in 1946-47 was to rein in the dominance of outreach ministries. Increasingly, personnel in the top leadership of the church changed from educators to pastors of larger congregations. The parish rather than the project became the focus of Brethren attention.

CONGREGATIONAL DEVELOPMENTS

One evidence of the higher priority given to congregational concerns in the 1950s and 60s is the surge of construction that took place during those decades. This was a time when many congregations undertook substantial renovations of their church plant, or more commonly, erected entirely new and expensive facilities. During these years the staff at Elgin included an architect whose assignment was to assist churches in building or renovating.[1]

The architectural trend for the design of the central meeting room for worship, often curiously (from the perspective of Brethren heritage) referred to as the sanctuary, was to move away from the pattern of a raised pulpit centered in the chancel area; this itself had supplanted the former style that featured a long preacher's table at floor level, oriented to the long axis of the unadorned meeting-house. In the postwar era, most Brethren church buildings dropped the centered pulpit and adopted the classical Protestant order of "divided chancel," with a lectern on one side, a pulpit on the other, and a communion table (often confusedly referred to as an altar) in the middle between the two in the raised chancel area.

A committee reporting to the 1952 Annual Conference on "symbolism in worship," after stating general principles of worship, gave equal lists for the virtues of the central pulpit and the divided chancel. It recommended that the conference not "attempt to set rules governing the exact arrangement and design of chancels," evidently assuming there should always be chancels. The report was adopted.[2]

The move to a divided chancel occasioned hearty disagreement in many congregations, more, it must be admitted, from unthinking

Dedicated in September 1966, the First Church of the Brethren of York, Pennsylvania, features the traditional church architecture favored by Brethren building or rebuilding campaigns following World War II. *BHLA Collection.*

nostalgia for the past than from thoughtful theological considerations. Provision for one central Brethren ordinance—baptism—was not forgotten; a baptistry was invariably included in the chancel area, usually so designed that it was covered until needed several times a year for immersion baptisms when pastor and baptismal candidate entered its well-tempered water.

Congregations or the architects they hired gave little attention to the central liturgical act for Brethren—the love feast. This was often relegated to the basement or all-purpose fellowship hall. Some congregations used removable shelves across the back of benches in the main worship room, permitting what one wag called "back of the neck" love feasts. Earlier meetinghouses of the nineteenth century had designed ingenious benches with pivoted backs that could be converted into tables for the love feast ordinance.

Expansive educational wings provided comfortable quarters for Sunday school classes, although some critics complained that it was poor stewardship to build such expensive edifices to be used for one hour per week. Modern Brethren were unhappy with the crowded settings of older meetinghouses, adapted for church school by holding classes in different parts of the main room with attendant noise pollution. Gleaming stainless-steel kitchens provided facilities for meals at social occasions that Brethren congregations enjoyed attending. Some congregations justified this extensive building of educational facilities by permitting classrooms to be used by neighborhood nursery schools and halls to be used by community groups such as the Boy and Girl Scouts or Alcoholics Anonymous.

The overall building style tended in this period toward colonial Georgian, with white interiors, brick walls, and massive steeples ("to look like a real church"). Some introduced stained glass, at times with distinctive Brethren symbols. There was little evidence of real engagement either with Brethren heritage or Brethren doctrines in the planning of these church houses, except for extraneous decor. The distinct impression, rather, was that congregations wished to have a facility that would look much like the substantial buildings of mainstream Protestant churches around them.[3]

Although the introduction of pianos in churches had occasioned sharp struggles in earlier years, these newer buildings often featured expensive pipe organs. There are cases of congregations in eastern Pennsylvania that went directly from a ban on all instruments to the installation of pipe organs in their newly erected church buildings. Congregations of lesser means contented themselves with electric organs. It became common for public address systems to be installed. No longer were ministers required to develop booming public voices so that they could be heard in larger structures, which by the way had been one argument against permitting women to be ministers.

A comparable trend was to enlarge the staffs of these expanded facilities. Larger congregations, no longer using a plural, free ministry plan, began employing associate and/or assistant pastors along with the "senior" pastor. Most pastors had at least part-time secretarial support who helped prepare the worship bulletin, at times an extensive affair. Lengthy published liturgies and responsive readings became common. Emphasis was placed on dignified and well-orchestrated services, timed to the minute. Increasingly, Brethren pastors in the larger congregations wore clerical preaching robes, although only the more high-church oriented introduced stoles over the robes to mark the church year.

Of course many congregations, particularly smaller ones in rural areas, remained with the older patterns of leadership and worship. Many of them in this period struggled with the issue of retaining ministers. Out of these concerns, the denomination developed strategies to assist the smaller congregations. One was called Education for a Shared Ministry (EFSM), initiated in 1977 by the General Board and Bethany Seminary; it was designed to help congregations with membership of fewer than one hundred develop part-time leadership from within its own ranks by a variety of training experiences and consultation. This proved to be effective and in some cases sparked renewal in the congregations.

Another had the acronym TRIM, standing for TRaining in Ministry. It was developed to guide those men and women not able to follow the recommended process of four years of college education and three years of theological study to prepare for ministry. Through college classes, short-term continuing education, and mentoring, the TRIM program readied candidates for ordination.

Larger congregations moved away from the older informality of Brethren worship, when Deacon Bowman or even Sister Huffman would not be surprised to be called on spontaneously by the minister to lead in prayer, with all worshipers kneeling facing the benches; increasingly congregations no longer considered such informality to be appropriate. The somewhat uneven skills of those providing "special music" gave way to trained musicians leading well-rehearsed and handsomely-robed choirs. By the end of the period it was not unknown to see liturgical dance in some urban and urbane Brethren congregations, although most Brethren were still uncomfortable with that. Experiments along this line at some Annual Conferences were not well received.

The last vestige of Brethren nonconformity in dress, the prayer covering for women, might still be made available for sisters at love feasts but were hardly ever seen on Sunday mornings. This generalization did not hold true for areas of the Atlantic Northeast District and especially not in the Southern District of Pennsylvania, where a substantial number of congregations held the line on plain dress as a requirement for all members, men and women.

CENTRAL INSTITUTIONS

Not to be outdone by the trend toward new church buildings, the General Brotherhood Board itself decided on a new headquarters building. For many years it had occupied cramped and inefficient quarters in the upper stories of the Brethren Publishing House at 22 South State Street in Elgin, by the Fox River and the railroad. In the late 1950s, under the careful guidance of general secretary Norman J. Baugher, a handsome and roomy new headquarters building was constructed on the outskirts of Elgin near an expressway.

By shrewd negotiation the planning committee was able to secure the land without cost by selling off unneeded acreage to the expressway. The printing and publishing activities were carried on in a spacious area behind the offices. The facility was basically on one floor, except for storage space (and the historical library and archives) in a basement. It featured an austere chapel of stone, as well as extensive parking space.

After formal dedication in 1959, the careful scheme of interior decoration prescribed for each office was rigidly controlled for an extended period, but eventually the individual tastes of office occupants began to assert themselves. As well expressed by S. Loren Bowman, "The building symbolized the coming of age of the Board—and perhaps the denomination—as it gave support to a modified version of a bureaucratic structure. While the building exhibited elements of creativity, simplicity, and flexibility congenial to the one board concept, organizationally it suggested a carefully planned departmental structure." It marked a triumph of bureaucracy. The new building symbolized a shift in the pattern of denominational guidance to a more thoroughly rationalized and systematized approach patterned quite directly upon that used by the mainline Protestant bodies with which Brethren were now more closely interacting.[4]

Shortly thereafter, Bethany Biblical Seminary moved from its increasingly crowded and unsafe location on Chicago's racially-changed west side to a spacious suburban site in Oak Brook, 18 miles west of the city's loop. Some critics charged that the move was tantamount to abandoning the inner city, but supporters, led by seminary president Paul Minnich Robinson, explained that the city's demand for off-street parking, combined with the need to repair or replace aging buildings at the 3435 West Van Buren site, made it almost impossible to remain. Moreover, the school was losing students who hesitated to bring their families into a crime-ridden area.

The seminary moved in 1963 to its new 60-acre campus, with 11 substantial buildings including a stone chapel. The entire campus—buildings, furnishings, and landscaping—were completed by astute contracting for the surprisingly low figure of $3,000,000. The Lutheran architect Charles E. Stade studied the Brethren for several years before completing his plans. He tried to represent Brethren values by using simple but elegant materials—stone, brick, wood—to create a prize-winning design.[5]

Its new campus served the school very well, until financial problems forced the seminary in the fall of 1994 to move from Oak Brook to Richmond, Indiana, where it formed a partnership with Earlham School of Religion, a theological school of the Religious Society of Friends. The relocation went hand in hand with a shift in curricular emphasis toward a more congregationally-based and decentralized operation. Increasingly seminary classes were based in Brethren communities and near a satellite in Pennsylvania.

During the period of physical transition from Chicago to Oak Brook in the early 1960s, there had been also transition in the faculty. Because of retirements, most faculty members had to be replaced. Whereas many of the earlier professors had been educated at the liberal University of Chicago, most of the new teachers had taken their graduate degrees at Ivy League schools—Princeton, Yale, Harvard, University of Pennsylvania. They combined a moderate theological liberalism with great respect for the authority of the scriptures and intense loyalty to the church's heritage.

During their tenure, the roots of the Brethren faith in Anabaptism and Pietism, with the radical implications of that perspective, came to the fore. The curriculum was changed to reflect a communal style of education. This core of faculty members stayed at the seminary for most or all of their teaching careers, providing a unity and stability of orientation that was influential in shaping the theological direction of the church.[6]

Shortly after the move to Oak Brook, the seminary changed its name from Bethany Biblical Seminary to Bethany Theological Seminary, which was about the same time the General Brotherhood Board became the General Board. Concurrently, the church's periodical changed its name from *Gospel Messenger* simply to *Messenger*. These changes prompted one critic to complain that the Church of the Brethren had lost the Bible, brotherhood, and gospel in one fell swoop! While the comment is overdrawn, the name changes do tell us something about the shifts in self-understanding the denomination was undergoing.

Evangelism and Church Growth

During the post World War II years, the church gave much attention to expanding its rolls. Staff positions were created at Elgin to give this attention. They directed the Brethren to the growth possibilities in expanding metropolitan areas; by cooperating with local church councils and developers under the comity system, Brethren were assigned areas for new congregations. During this period, church leaders were eager to attract new members by downplaying some of the traditional expectations for membership. A significant departure in this regard was a paper on church extension, adopted in 1958, that permitted congregations to accept new members by transfer of letter from other denominations without requiring baptism (or rebaptism) in traditional Brethren manner. The change was made more palatable by the condition that the decision was not made binding on all congregations.[7]

Partly in response to this attention to church growth, membership of the Church of the Brethren in the United States reached an all time high of some 200,000 at this time. Between 1948 and 1960, when Charles E. Zunkel was responsible for home missions, there were 72 new congregations initiated in 25 states. Six of them, primarily those located in suburbs, failed.

Analysts concluded that the lack of Brethren name-recognition, in addition to its challenging positions on contemporary issues, made it difficult for Brethren to attract new membership from the general population. Some newcomers, on the other hand, were attracted precisely by the Brethren convictions on peace and justice issues. Since that peak, the trend has been downward in membership, causing concern among the leadership, repeated queries to Annual Conference, and renewed concern for evangelism.

ORDINANCES AND WORSHIP

The church extension paper of 1958 also authorized Brethren congregations to institute "bread-and-cup" communions during Sunday morning worship services, comparable to the practice of mainstream Protestants, in addition to the traditional love feasts. "This procedure serves not only as a bridge to unite those who come from other traditions and makes more inclusive the ministry of the church, but also provides more frequent remembrance of the death of our Lord and enriches the love feast and communion observance for all." Although resisted in more conservative congregations, in many Brethren churches it became customary to have two of these abbreviated communions each year as well as love feasts in the fall and spring.[8]

One argument for the change was the need to increase participation in the ordinance. Instead of attracting at love feasts the largest number of congregational members for the entire year, as had previously been the case, in many churches attendance dwindled to a fraction of the membership. Some pastors attempted to renew the traditional love feasts by changing the way in which it was carried out—by seating families together, by substituting handwashing for feetwashing, by introducing meals reminiscent of those that Palestinians might have eaten—with mixed success.

During this period a new manual of polity and worship for pastors was released (1964, revised 1978), marked by greater attention to the church year and to formal liturgical services. It became common for some pastors to follow an ecumenical lectionary in their preaching. They contended that this innovation actually kept the sermons more biblical, as it tended to decrease the possibility of pastors riding "hobby-horses" in their choice of sermon topics.[9]

Greater attention given to preaching during this period was signaled by the release of sermon collections and the submission of sermons by Brethren pastors for publication in general homiletical periodicals. The generalization could be made that whereas earlier Brethren preaching had been characterized by emphasis upon practical application of scripture to daily living, in this period more emphasis was placed on literary and rhetorical excellence.

A new *Brethren Hymnal* of 1951 (the "red book") revealed the same trend toward greater formality and congruence with standard Protestant worship patterns. It replaced *Hymnal, Church of the Brethren* of 1925 (the "blue book"), which for the first time had introduced liturgical materials and choir responses. That in turn had supplanted *The Brethren Hymnal* of 1901 (the "black book"), characterized by shape notes and gospel songs, many composed by Brethren such as George B. Holsinger, J. Henry Showalter, and William Beery, who had compiled the book. Its popularity had kept it in print until 1947.

The 1951 hymnal had been compiled by committees that worked intensively for six years on doctrine, music, literary quality, and worship values. Nevin W. Fisher was the music editor and editor in chief. Paul Minnich Robinson directed the worship subcommittee. It included what became the most popular Brethren hymn of the era, "Move in our Midst," with text by Kenneth I. Morse and melody by Perry Huffaker. Morse was a veteran editor of Brethren publications and Huffaker a pastor, both active in the camping movement from which the hymn sprang.

The hymnal committee made a conscious effort to include more hymns by a range of Brethren writers and composers than had been the case in earlier hymnals, including a number by eighteenth century Brethren (both Alexander Macks, Johann Naas) long forgotten in Brethren hymnody. Ora W. Garber translated some of these into English, retaining a metrical form.

Sensitive to the affection that many Brethren had for gospel songs but critical of what they considered their inferior musical and textual quality ("They distract from genuine worship and are psychologically disintegrating in their effects upon groups and individuals"), editors included a section of 57 of these "Songs of Salvation," but dropped most of their choruses. Because of this change, a minority of congregations clung to the 1901 or 1925 editions or introduced hymnals from independent publishers. Some congregations resolved the issue of differing tastes in hymnals among their members by using the older editions for Sunday school exercises and the 1951 hymnal for church services.[10]

A member of the hymnal committee, Alvin F. Brightbill, faculty member at Bethany from 1927 to 1968, toured the denomination to conduct hymn festivals and workshops to introduce the new hymnal. He was well known to, even beloved by, many Brethren because of his stirring leadership of singing at Annual Conferences.[11]

He often teamed with the venerable William Beery, who died at the age of 103. As a young student at Huntingdon, Pennsylvania, Beery was one of three young men who went to the Forge to continue their studies, thus helping to ensure that the school that became Juniata College would continue. After re-enrolling he was asked to teach music, which he continued to do until 1885 while studying for an advanced degree that he completed in 1882; in 1888 he returned again and taught there until 1908.

Beery sang on the WLS radio station in Chicago to celebrate his last fifteen birthday anniversaries. His best known hymn tunes were "Lo, a Gleam from Yonder Heaven" (for which his wife Adaline Hohf Beery wrote the text) and "Take My Hand and Lead Me, Father." His last melody, composed for the poem "I Shall Not Be Afraid," was written at the age of ninety-eight; some musicians consider it to be his strongest. Nelson T. Huffman of Virginia was another much-respected musician of the period, known for conducting large male choruses.[12]

LITERARY ACTIVITY

A Brethren writer, whose poem received wide attention although often without attribution, was Myra Brooks Welch of La Verne,

California. First published in *The Gospel Messenger* in February 1921, her poem told the story of a battered violin that was about to bring only a pittance at an auction, when a skilled musician coaxed beautiful music from it. It then sold for a thousand times the original bid—the difference was "The Touch of a Master's Hand." Her moral was that often a person's wasted life was often considered worthless until "the Master comes, and the foolish crowd / Never can quite understand / The worth of a soul and the change that's wrought / By the touch of the Master's hand."

By the 1930s the poem was widely reprinted, often with the tag "author unknown." In 1941 the Brethren Publishing House published a collection of Welch's poems advisedly entitled *The Touch of the Master's Hand*; this publication stemmed, but did not completely stop, further unattributed publication. The poem has often been set to music and still appears in books and periodicals; among the more recent reprintings was one by Norman Vincent Peale in 1980 and another in *Ideals* magazine. It is the single most famous literary composition by any Brethren author.[13]

Another popular author whose fame reached past Brethren boundaries was Anna Beahm Mow, one of the first women to be fully ordained (1960) within the church. A daughter of the colorful evangelist I. N. H. Beahm, she was a missionary for 17 years in India with her husband, the brilliant but retiring Baxter Mow. While there they became lifelong friends of Madame Pandit of the prominent Nehru family, later India's ambassador to the United States.

Upon their return home in 1940, Anna Mow became a professor at Bethany Biblical Seminary, much beloved for the personal interest she took in her students and for her spiritual depth. In some ways it was after retirement in 1958 that "Sister Anna" made her greatest impact on a wide number of people, not only through her preaching missions but also especially by means of her publications.

The range and intent of her work can be seen in the titles of some of her many books, a majority of which were published by the conservative Zondervan Press: *Say "Yes" to Life* (1961); *Your Child from Birth to Rebirth* (1963); *Going Steady with God* (1965); *So Who's Afraid of Birthdays?* (1969); *The Secret of Married Love* (1970); *Your Experience and the Bible* (1973); *Find Your Own Faith* (1977); *Springs of*

Love (1979). They found a devoted readership because of their marks of deep spirituality, common sense, rich experience, and sense of humor.[14]

Surpassing even Anna Mow in the number of published books and articles was Vernard Eller, professor of religion and English at La Verne College (later University of La Verne), California. After early work as an editor of Brethren youth publications at the church offices in Elgin, Illinois, in 1958 he entered his life career as an educator.

Eller's doctoral thesis, published as *Kierkegaard and Radical Discipleship: A New Perspective* (1968), drew parallels between the Danish philosopher-theologian and the Brethren. His later books followed year after year, finding acceptance from major publishers. They dealt with ethics, sacraments, the simple life, pacifism, and ecclesiology from the perspective of radical Christianity. Biblical studies on Revelation and the Gospel of John also came from his facile pen. He wrote major interpretations of church/state relations and pacifism.

Eller's racy style was marked by word games and humor in an attempt to communicate his serious concerns to a wide audience. This was especially evident in his popular books, *The Mad Morality* (1970), which used excerpts from *Mad Magazine* to illustrate the Ten Commandments, and *The Sex Manual for Puritans* (1971).

Brethren Press issued his *Cleaning Up the Christian Vocabulary* (1976) and *Towering Babel: God's People Without God's Word* (1983). They demonstrated his increasing disenchantment with the policies of the Church of the Brethren, which, he contended, was losing its biblical base and drifting into shallow humanitarianism. He criticized the feminist movement in *The Language of Canaan and the Grammar of Feminism* (1982). Accompanying these books were numerous articles by Eller in a wide variety of popular and scholarly journals.

Many other members of the Church of the Brethren published books during this era. Faculty members of Bethany Theological Seminary were productive, especially Donald E. Miller, Warren F. Groff, Graydon F. Snyder, Dale W. Brown, and D. F. Durnbaugh. The independent quarterly journal *Brethren Life and Thought*, edited for 25 years by pastor, author, and former missionary Edward K.

Ziegler, published a host of articles of "opinion, scholarship and interpretation."[15]

250TH ANNIVERSARY

A highlight of this period was the observance in 1958 of the 250th anniversary of the birth of the Brethren movement. Under the guidance of general secretary Norman J. Baugher and church statesman Paul Haynes Bowman, a multi-faceted celebration was carefully planned and executed. It began with an inaugural service and love feast at the Germantown congregation on January 1, 1958, focused on the theme "The Mind of Christ." It continued with a specially expanded anniversary quarterly for use in Brethren Sunday schools, interrupting the usual focus on the International Sunday School Lessons. An "Anniversary Call" sought to deepen the spiritual base of the church and to increase denominational giving.[16]

The Annual Conference held at Des Moines, Iowa, in late June featured a series of 250th anniversary addresses by church leaders. They were published in a book edited by Bowman, *The Adventurous Future*. The address with the longest lasting impact was delivered by the moderator, Desmond W. Bittinger, entitled "How Shall the Brethren Be Recognized?" Drawing on Brethren history and his experience as a missionary in Nigeria, his answer was threefold: 1) by the praying, searching, open mind; 2) by the loving heart; and 3) by serving hands. In sum, Brethren will be recognized, said Bittinger, "by the manner of their living." It was later published as a pamphlet.[17]

Released at the same conference was a book of translated source documents on Brethren beginnings, edited by D. F. Durnbaugh with the aid of Hedda Durnbaugh; entitled *European Origins of the Brethren*, it was the fruit of research in one hundred European archives and libraries in 1955-56. Much of the material had been previously unknown to the Brethren.

M. R. Zigler and other BSC staff organized a large-scale celebration of the 250th anniversary in Germany; its site in early August was the Brethren center at Kassel. A highlight was the outdoor service on August 6 at the village of Schwarzenau where the Brethren movement originated. Delegations from the United States, Ecuador, India, Nigeria, Denmark, along with Brethren Service workers and many German visitors, gathered along the Eder Brook to hear addresses by German dignitaries, American church leaders, and W. A. Visser 't Hooft, WCC general secretary. Over 150 people took part at Kassel in the love feast that concluded the anniversary observance. Arranging this event was the last major task of M. R. Zigler in Europe, who was completing ten years of service and looking forward to retirement in the United States at the end of the summer.[18]

Unfortunately two tragedies marred the European celebration. Shortly after it ended, while on the way to a meeting of the WCC Central Committee, Zigler and his wife, Amy, were involved in a two-car crash in Sweden; the accident took the lives of two people in the other car and of Amy Zigler. He was himself severely injured in the crash, which he had accidentally caused. Scores of Brethren rallied to his bedside and hundreds of communications expressing sympathy arrived from ecumenical and stateside friends. The WCC meeting, which received a special anniversary message from the Brethren delegation, announced a $10,000 gift from Church World Service toward the construction of a new WCC center, given in Zigler's name. He fought back from his injuries and returned home. He was determined to find a new cause to champion, but he never drove a car again.[19]

The second tragedy involved members of a tour group who had visited Europe and the Schwarzenau celebration. Twenty people (of whom thirteen were Brethren) were among 99 passengers and crew members who died in the early hours of August 14, shortly after leaving Ireland, in an unexplained plunge into the Atlantic Ocean of KLM flight 607E from Amsterdam to New York. Among those who died was Max Snyder, a former Brethren Service worker and one of the tour organizers. The airline arranged for a solemn memorial service at Galway after which unidentified bodies were interred. Most bodies were never recovered.[20]

Despite these tragedies, the anniversary year focused the attention of the church on its rich past, which affected the Brethren attitude toward developing issues.

CONSULTATION ON CHURCH UNION

One of the sharpest of these issues was whether the Church of the Brethren should join the ongoing Consultation on Church Union (COCU) as a full member, upgrading its previous role as observer-consultant. This ecumenical venture was initiated in 1961 by an appeal from the stated clerk of the Presbyterian Church, Eugene Carson Blake, for the union of Protestant churches in the United States. He painted the vision of a united church that would be "truly evangelical, truly reformed, and truly catholic" (that is, universal). Six major Protestant communions joined in a process designed to lead to this united church. In 1963 the Church of the Brethren began involvement by sending two representatives to observe and advise.[21]

In 1965 an invitation came to the Standing Committee to upgrade the Brethren role to full participation. Its response was basically positive; however, because there was not enough time to consider the matter thoroughly or for the "church to be fully informed," the committee said that it would respond officially at the next Annual Conference. Standing Committee members may have recalled the troubles following the precipitate move to join the Federal Council in 1941.

Responsibility for replying to the COCU invitation was assigned to the Fraternal Relations Committee, which had been reconstituted in 1960 as a permanent Annual Conference committee. Since then it had carried on a series of bilateral conversations with the American Baptist Church, Brethren Church, Church of God (Anderson), Churches of God in North America (Winebrennarian), Moravian Church, and United Presbyterian Church (USA).

The committee entered into a heavy schedule of meetings, interviews with church leaders, and exchange of correspondence. This was the background for its recommendation, submitted to the 1966 Annual Conference held at Louisville, Kentucky, that the Church of the Brethren *not* enter into full participation in COCU but rather continue in its observer-consultant status. Some members of the committee personally favored joining the consultation but sensed that, as the church was not ready for it, a positive decision would bring too much disunity.[22]

It also recommended more intentional conversations with denominations understood to be closer in doctrine and heritage to the Brethren. The article reporting its findings in the *Messenger* (June 23, 1966) was titled "Report Urges Ecumenicity—But Outside Consultation," a good brief characterization.

Sentiments expressed prior to the Kentucky meeting, during the conference, and following it, were among the most heated and sustained in recent memory. Among the fervent advocates of joining the COCU process were educators, influential pastors, and church administrators. They argued that Brethren had consistently moved toward greater ecumenical involvement and had worked closely with the churches already involved in COCU; the potential of a united church promised enrichment for Brethren. To reject the invitation to full participation would be a step backwards toward sectarianism. DeWitt L. Miller and Jesse H. Ziegler were among the most articulate proponents.

Those ardently opposing, or at least questioning, the change were a disparate grouping of academics (who were sometimes called "Neo-Anabaptists"), conservatives, and members who could not bear to entertain the thought of the demise of their beloved church as they knew it. These opponents worried that the Brethren peace position and practice of believers baptism might be lost, and also raised concerns about episcopal church polity. Dale W. Brown, Vernard Eller, and C. Wayne Zunkel were among the most active critics of COCU. Both proponents and opponents of the decision sensed that the outcome would be pivotal for the future direction of the church.

The recommendation of the Fraternal Relations Committee was accepted by delegates at the Annual Conference after spirited debate; those calling for full COCU involvement lost. In the aftermath some previously influential pastors resigned their parishes in disappointment; a few left the church. Inez Long, a free-lance writer and the wife of a pastor of a large Pennsylvania congregation, filed a scathing report on the conference and its outcome with *The Christian Century* entitled "Brethren Take to Hills and the Alleys." She reported that COCU critics, characterized as "parochial planners and scriptural literalists," had left Louisville "convinced that they are capable of designing a new road" of denominational direction.

Long asserted that the "main risk involved in the decision against COCU lies with those urban parishes which have built steepled churches since World War II and have had growing memberships since 1958 when the denomination first accepted non-Brethren without rebaptism." She warned that if "these parishes see their denomination continue to deny participation in mainstream Protestantism as it moves toward a unified and uniting church, they could well lose all sense of belonging—certainly to a denomination that takes to the hills in extremism and returns to the alleys with parochialism."[23]

A letter of response by a journal editor to a Brethren critic of the article revealed that it had been "checked by a number of Brethren officials prior to publication" and that some "strong 'pro-Long' communications" had been received after it appeared from "Elgin headquarters and elsewhere." Because of the widespread interest nationally in COCU the Brethren decision was discussed in several churchly journals.[24]

COCU proponents raised the issue of full involvement at the next two Annual Conferences (1967-68) but failed to overturn the 1966 decision. The continuing division impelled M. Guy West, in his 1968 moderator's address to exhort his listeners to move "from Diatribe to Dialogue." He identified one "strong minority" as sensing that the church is "too sectarian and provincial, too pietistic and moralistic, too rigid and unrealistic in its ethical standards, too exclusive, too self-righteous, too hesitant to trust involvement with others, too small to be effective, too naive and impotent to be realistic." Those holding this view tended to despair about the future of the church after the COCU defeat.

At the other pole, he found, was another minority who believed that the church in the past two decades had "gone too far and too fast." They were concerned about the conciliar connections and "unhappy about our 1958 open membership decision." They disapproved of any Brethren involvement with COCU and "any talk of merger was abhorrent to them." They saw most of the church's institutions—Elgin staff, colleges, seminary—and most of the church's program as "distressingly liberal." The moderator granted that a majority in the denomination would be found in the middle between these extremes, basically satisfied with the direction and character of the church. He encouraged honest and caring dialogue as the answer to the problem.[25]

The intense discussions about COCU presaged an era of greater tension and division in the Church of the Brethren, marked by the emergence of organized and vocal minority groupings.

.

25

Rise of Denominational Minorities

With the last third of the twentieth century came a trend that, while not unknown to Brethren previously, took on greater importance. This was the rise of minorities in the church. It can be understood in two ways: first, in the emergence of movements that in some sense stood apart from the mainline denomination; second, in the emergence of ethnic minorities in more than minimal numbers, accompanied by a correspondingly greater focus by the church on their specific concerns.

As has been seen, from early on Brethren have experienced the rise of movements that in some significant ways did not follow majority expectations. In most cases, these groups were either expelled or left on their own accord, thus forming schisms. An early example was the Ephrata Society; later came the Far Western Brethren and the New Dunkers. As it happened, the Far Western Brethren were reconciled with their Eastern brothers and sisters, whereas the New Dunkers were not. Tensions in the latter half of the nineteenth century led to the painful trifurcation, from which sprang the Old German Baptist Brethren, Brethren Church, and Church of the Brethren. The roll call of separating movements can be extended into the later twentieth century.

Following 1960 a new reality within the church came about through the formation of fellowships that chose not to depart as separate entities though differing from the mainstream. Instead, they remained within the church as loyal oppositions, seeking to become the majority. They consistently opposed certain aspects of the program and direction of the denomination. At times they selectively denied financial support, also often generously underwriting those budget lines they thought worthy.

They tended to create their own distinctive structures, complete with annual meetings, publications, schools, and even salaried staff. Individuals speaking for their point of view were noticeable in discussions of controverted points on the floor of Annual Conference. Attention to the most active of these groups will thus also highlight leading controversies of the period.

Of those fellowships dissenting in some important way or ways from the agreed denominational line, the most important are, or have recently been, the Brethren Revival Fellowship, the Brethren Peace Fellowship/Brethren Action Movement, the Neo-Pentecostal or Charismatic Movement, the Womaen's Caucus, and the Brethren/Mennonite Council for Lesbian and Gay Concerns.[1]

BRETHREN REVIVAL FELLOWSHIP

The Brethren Revival Fellowship (BRF) was founded at the Ocean Grove Annual Conference in 1959, when some 50 men and women came together to share in prayerful fashion their concerns about the church's direction. Actions of the 1958 conference had alienated many of them. Although 250th anniversary events had focused on Brethren heritage, there was as well strong support for ecumenism, seen as providing "new frontiers." This conference passed pivotal measures in a paper dealing with new churches; also, the conference agreed to permit membership by transfer of letter rather than by baptism or re-baptism, and approved Sunday morning bread-and-cup communions in addition to the traditional love feasts. Though women had been admitted to ordination in 1952, it was not until 1958 that "full rights" to every form of ministry were in fact authorized.

Those gathering in 1959 chose a committee of five people (later enlarged to nine) to carry forward the causes articulated; they also scheduled a mass meeting to be held later that summer in southern Pennsylvania.[2] The movement soon took the name Brethren Revival

Brethren

Revival

Fellowship

Witness

The BRF Witness is prepared and distributed by the Brethren Revival Fellowship of the Church of the Brethren, in the interest of proclaiming and preserving Biblical values for living today. We believe the Bible is the infallible Word of God, the final authority for belief and practice, and that to personally accept Jesus Christ as Lord and Saviour, is the only means of salvation.

BRF WITNESS   Vol. 1, No. 1   1966

The first issue of the Brethren Revival Fellowship periodical. *Durnbaugh Collection.*

Fellowship to signal the conviction of those associated with it that the church needed renewal. Specific concerns were raised about the church's curricular material, the theological positions of seminary and college faculty, Brethren affiliation with ecumenical (NCC/WCC) conciliarism (it favored the National Association of Evangelicals or NAE), and the perceived liberal orientation of the church's leadership. An early statement of goals announced a determination to "help stem the tide of unbelief and compromise in the Church of the Brethren, and to encourage the return to a sound biblical position."

In recent years, the acceptance within the Church of the Brethren of women's rights and a moderate position on homosexuality has been adamantly contested by BRF members. In addition, the BRF has consistently questioned those Annual Conference and General Board resolutions that have criticized or sought to influence governmental policies. For this reason, some critics have found the BRF to be unduly and perhaps unwittingly influenced by American right-wing politics. They saw this bias reflected, for example, in a summary statement of its concerns in a 1984 BRF periodical:

> [Our] General Board and its staff are largely committed to liberation theology, mutuality in mission, uncertainty about man's need, the push for women's rights, reluctance to criticize massive violations of human rights in communist countries, and support for non-Christian ideologies implying that God is at work among all people and in all religions to bring about his reign of justice.[3]

A more positive self-description of the BRF was given by Harold S. Martin in 1983: "The Brethren Revival Fellowship is a concern movement *within* the Church of the Brethren seeking to call the Church to a firm stand for the authority of the Scriptures and to an emphasis upon the teachings of the New Testament as historically understood by the Brethren."[4]

A BRF publication—*A Handbook of Basic Beliefs within the Church of the Brethren*—lists in brief compass with relevant scriptural basis the beliefs held essential by members of the BRF, while clearly stating that it is not to be considered a creed. It contains all of the points considered essential by fundamentalists but also adds traditional Brethren principles such as nonresistance, plain dress, and trine immersion baptism. BRF tracts and pamphlets speak of the Anabaptist foundation of the Brethren. One BRF leader described the BRF as trying to be "fundamental without being fundamentalistic" (W. Hartman Rice).[5]

The BRF articulates its position through *The BRF Witness*, published at regular intervals since 1966 (now bimonthly). Each issue focuses on a different theme or question, and also includes news, announcements, and regular columns by BRF writers. The fellowship conducts summer and winter Bible institutes (often on the campus of Elizabethtown College) for high school graduates and schedules inspirational and business meetings of supporters each September; it has also recruited, trained, and placed BVS units since 1976. The BRF took major initiative in establishing two new congregations in Maine.

There is no official membership, but by 1980 it counted about 5,000 active supporters, largely but by no means exclusively, resident in the East. Contact people in local congregations distribute BRF literature and serve as liaison; by 1972 fully a quarter of Brethren congregations had liaisons in place. In 1988 more than 10,000 copies of the newsletter were distributed to congregations in all 24 districts. In 1988 the BRF budget was about $80,000.

Harold S. Martin, a former mathematics teacher in the public schools, has contributed much of the published material for BRF— books such as *Sermons on Eternal Themes*, articles, and tracts; he conducts many preaching missions and since 1977 has been employed as a staff person. James F. Myer has also been employed part-time since 1986 and travels widely to provide evangelistic services. BRF staff members have attended the meetings of comparable renewal-minded conservatives in other Protestant denominations. There is some evidence that BRF leaders have played informal but effective roles in pastoral placement, bypassing the usual denominational procedures.

Although early statements by the BRF implied the potential for schism, that possibility has been disavowed by the Fellowship's leadership. One of their stated goals is "to offer hope to our people and to discourage individual scattering into other churches"; one of their concerns is "saving the Church of the Brethren and not fragmenting it by splintering and dividing into many small independent groups." The divisive potential was also lessened by the studied inclusion of BRF supporters in the nomination process for denominational positions—Annual Conference study committees, General Board members, and the like. This was highlighted by the nomination and election of James F. Myer as moderator of the 1985 Annual Conference of the Church of the Brethren.[6]

Robert B. Blair, a sociologist who studied the BRF movement, concluded that it has appealed largely to Brethren coming from rural areas, most of whom have not pursued formal higher education. Its leaders at the time of organization lacked access to "significant decision making bodies in the church," and their attempts to gain a hearing to express their concerns had generally been ignored. This has changed dramatically.[7]

Brethren Peace Fellowship/Brethren Action Movement

The Brethren Peace Fellowship (BPF) and the Brethren Action Movement (BAM) with associated groups, can be considered together. Although of different origin, they shared many common values, organizational styles, and, in some cases, personnel.

The Brethren Peace Fellowship had its first meeting in Elizabethtown, Pennsylvania, in April 1967; those attending were 125 "Brethren Service veterans." This fact best describes the orientation of the group. The fellowship grew from among those who had been powerfully shaped in their beliefs and attitudes by their BSC or BVS experience and those who were dissatisfied with the direction of the church.

They had observed with distrust the strong movement within the church structure toward a bureaucratic and highly rationalized organization. They correctly understood the creation of a unified board in 1946-47 as designed to limit and channel the Brethren Service agenda. Earlier they had responded with enthusiasm to the charismatic visions of M. R. Zigler and Dan West. They now saw these leaders and others like them moved from the center of church influence to the margins.

In the opinion of Robert B. Blair, the author of a sociological study of Brethren subgroups, the "BPF represents an opposition group protesting the way goals of elites have deviated away from traditional service ministries stressing 'fellowship,' spontaneous youth-centered programs (Brethren Volunteer Service), and toward objectives centering around 'establishment' ecumenical relationships and 'mainline' Protestant values."[8]

Donna Forbes Steiner was BPF's first president; she worked with a coordinating committee of six members. In this grouping James C. Gibbel, J. Kenneth Kreider, and Walton Z. Moyer have been mainstays over the years. BPF's major responsibility has been to publish and distribute the *Brethren Peace Fellowship Newsletter*, which began monthly publication in May 1968. C. Wayne Zunkel, an area pastor, became and has remained, despite pastoral relocation to California after 1976, the editor of the plainly formatted four-page periodical. The circulation peaked at some 1,000, with readers in every district of the church.

Under Zunkel's editorship, the newsletter has carried as its motto since 1979 some variation of "Dedicated to realizing SchwarzeNOW—letting the ideals of the earliest Brethren find expression today." Consistent with that agenda, it has ranged far beyond peace and justice concerns to discuss issues such as church merger, church growth, foreign missions, tax refusal, Annual Conference controversies, and national/international events.

The editor has pushed issues that he felt were not being adequately covered in the denominational journal *Messenger*, becoming at times an irritant to members of the General Board staff. A particularly volatile issue was the newsletter's partly successful campaign to change the policy of Brethren-related colleges that permitted military recruiters on their campuses.

Comparable peace fellowships emerged in other areas, including Southern Pennsylvania and the Mid-Atlantic District. The latter has persisted over the years, with major leadership from peace activist and author Dale H. Aukerman. It has published a newsletter since 1974, with a consistent focus on peace issues.

Beyond the newsletters, the peace fellowships seek to promote peace awareness and action through workshops and conferences, peace evangelists, publication and distribution of *Shalom Tracts*, demonstrations, and personal witness. For many years the original BPF has annually chosen a member of the Church of the Brethren as the "Peacemaker of the Year."

The Brethren Action Movement originated in 1967 from the desire of several people largely centered at first at Manchester College, Indiana, to react to the Vietnam War with a revitalized peace witness. The movement took on momentum through correspondence between Kenneth L. Brown of Manchester and Dale W. Brown and Arthur G. Gish of Bethany Seminary that sought "a way to transform a historic peace witness into life."[9]

A tract describing the movement states, "The Brethren Action Movement is not a membership organization and has no official status within the Church of the Brethren. It is made up of members and friends of the Church, working together to carry out the concerns that grow from the teachings of the Church and our fellowship within it....The love of Christ constrains us to positive rather than passive witness. One who stands against the vast impinging chaos calls us to stand with Him. Let us act together!"[10]

Though a mailing list was maintained at Manchester College, where a group of faculty and students served as a clearinghouse, very quickly ad hoc groups developed outside Indiana in the Shenandoah Valley of Virginia, Ohio, Illinois, Iowa, Kansas, and Washington state, almost all naming themselves by attaching a geographical prefix to BAM. Participants raised $14,000 from 1968 through 1971 for the personnel expenses and publications and for gifts toward medical aid for the Vietnamese people.

Although never highly organized—in fact, they maintained an absolutist anti-institutional posture—the various groups developed a wide variety of initiatives; these included hospitality lists, yearly conferences, deputation teams, peace counselors at summer camps, workshops on nonviolence, vigils, draft and tax resistance, witness at Annual Conferences, and participation in large-scale anti-war demonstrations. Members published a newsletter from 1968 to 1974. More than 25 original tracts and booklets were written, published, and distributed, several by the two Browns and Gish. When the Vietnam war finally came to an end in 1973, the BAM movement disbanded. BAM activists linked New Left concerns with the radical Anabaptist heritage of the Brethren. This was worked out in great detail in Arthur G. Gish's book, *The New Left and Christian Radicalism* (1970), which began as an independent study at Bethany Theological Seminary. It won wide attention in evangelical, Brethren, and Mennonite circles and was even translated into Japanese. A comparable effort was Dale W. Brown's *The Christian Revolutionary* (1971).

Most BAM participants were young men and women, largely students, who were consciously rejecting the liberal, middle class values of their parents by the lifestyles and ideas they adopted. They were attracted to the sectarian origins of the Brethren and disliked the move toward Protestant respectability then regnant, as they saw it, in the church. Whereas the BPF sought to bring pressure on the Elgin staff to be more pro-active on peace, the BAM groups took direct action themselves. They were deeply impatient with the peace programs of designated Elgin staff. As an informed observer phrased it, those who began the movement "rationalized their emergence as requisite to keeping alive an active peace witness of the Brethren peace heritage which otherwise might 'get lost on the desks of the staff at Elgin.'"[11]

Although the BAM movement was in many ways on the opposite end of the theological spectrum from the BRF, both groups found some similarities in their shared criticism of the mainline church body and appreciation of Anabaptist roots. In 1969 representatives from BRF and BAM met at Milford, Indiana, to discuss their commonalities and differences. An observer commented: "The responses made clear that one decisive dream the two bodies share in common is to take the main body of the Church of the Brethren and reorient, reform, and reshape it into a more vital, disciplined being."[12]

The name of the BAM movement inadvertently repeated, it seems, the comparable effort by young Brethren of the interwar generation under the banner of One Hundred Dunkers for Peace, who published from 1937 to 1945 the *Brethren Action* newsletter.

THE NEO-PENTECOSTAL OR CHARISMATIC MOVEMENT

Ever since the early Brethren were challenged by the charismatic leaders of the Inspired, they have tended to find this spirit uncongenial. Little could they have imagined that in the mid-twentieth century a powerful charismatic movement would sweep through the Church of the Brethren, creating both renewal and congregational struggles. This was part of a larger phenomenon in American Christianity, which impacted both Protestants and Catholics, low church Baptists as well as high church Episcopalians.

Pentecostalism has been defined as a "post-conversion experience of Spirit baptism evidenced by speaking in tongues." It emerged from the Wesleyan Holiness movement in the United States in the early twentieth century—Topeka, Kansas (1901, Charles F. Parham and his Bible school), and Los Angeles, California (1906, William J. Seymour and Azuza Street). The movement gradually moved through camp meetings and ministerial linkages into separate institutionalized form as the Assemblies of God, International Church of the Foursquare Gospel, Church of God (Cleveland, Tennessee), and other bodies.[13]

The late twentieth century neo-Pentecostal or charismatic movement was different. This developed within denominations and, while often divisive within local congregations, did not (with some exceptions) result in the wholesale creation of new denominations, though it did create parachurch structures. The Pentecostal spirit was communicated to Protestant churches after 1953 through the Full Gospel Business Men's Fellowship, initiated by Californian Demos Shakarian and encouraged by Pentecostal evangelist Oral Roberts.

Generally conceded as the beginning of the modern charismatic movement was the announcement in 1959 by the pastor of an Episcopalian parish in Van Nuys, California, that he had received the Holy Spirit baptism of speaking in tongues. By the mid-1960s charismatics had become active within the Roman Catholic Church, in particular around university campuses in Ann Arbor, Michigan; Notre Dame, Indiana; and Pittsburgh, Pennsylvania. Many Lutherans joined the movement, although the Missouri and Wisconsin Synods stolidly opposed it. Charismatic fellowships developed among

One of the extended households of the early Reba Place Fellowship in Evanston, Illinois. *Durnbaugh Collection.*

members of the Baptist, Methodist, United Church of Christ, Mennonite, Presbyterian, and other denominations.

The charismatic movement among Brethren has had several quite different foci; they include the ministries of R. Russell Bixler based in the Pittsburgh, Pennsylvania, area; the Communion Fellowship in Goshen, Indiana, led by Douglas Fike; in a moderate form, the Reba Place Fellowship of Evanston, Illinois; the work among ethnic Filipinos in the Chicago area by Roger El Cruz; the Christ's Assembly movement largely active among the Old German Baptist Brethren in the Dayton, Ohio, area; and the Faith Assembly of Northern Indiana.[14]

The charismatic movement took on reality as a Brethren sub-grouping through the organization of the Holy Spirit Renewal Group in 1974, which has held since that year well-attended national and then regional Conferences on the Holy Spirit for members of the Church of the Brethren and others. R. Eugene Miller, a pastor in central Pennsylvania, was the convenor of the planning committee in the early years. Invited speakers came both from the ranks of Brethren and non-Brethren. Among them was the television personality Graham Kerr (the "Galloping Gourmet"); influenced by the Pentecostal conversion of his wife Treena and by personal crises, Kerr sought baptism in the Church of the Brethren at Easton, Maryland. Former Bethany Seminary faculty member and Nigeria missionary Chalmer E. Faw emerged as a leader in the charismatic movement, often working to reconcile congregations troubled by the charismatic influx.[15]

The Holy Spirit Renewal Committee changed its name to Brethren Renewal Services and in 1987-88 joined forces with the charismatic Mennonite Renewal Services (organized in 1977), to create Empowered Ministries, "linking Brethren, Mennonites, and other Anabaptists in a vital network of renewal"; Douglas Fike became its executive director. Although both bodies kept their separate identities, they wished to cooperate closely because of their common background in the Believers Church tradition. This became evident as members of both groups met at huge charismatic conferences, such as those organized in New Orleans in 1986 and 1987. Increasingly resource people at the Holy Spirit conferences had come from Mennonite ranks, leading to this cooperation.

By the testimonies of R. Russell "Russ" Bixler and other pastors in the Church of the Brethren, their breakthrough charismatic experiences followed a profound sense of failure in ministry and inadequacy in personal spiritual growth. After they were baptized by the Holy Spirit and introduced to glossolalia, evident power infused their ministries.[16]

In 1972 Bixler moved from the full-time pastorate of the Pittsburgh Church of the Brethren, where perhaps a fourth of the membership followed his new charismatic stance, to a non-salaried position as associate pastor. This allowed him to devote his time to a ministry of speaking and writing; he developed contacts in at least eighty Brethren congregations across the nation. Bixler introduced a "Prayer and Praise" service on Sunday evenings in the Brethren church house that consistently attracted over four hundred people. The three-hour-long service included folk gospel songs, testimonies, speaking in tongues with interpretation, and healings. He organized the Greater Pittsburgh Charismatic Conference, which annually brought together 10,000 participants.

Beginning in 1976 Russ Bixler and his wife, Norma Bowman Bixler, developed the Western Pennsylvania Christian Broadcasting Company, which constructed and operated a Christian-oriented television station. Bixler told his story in the autobiographical book *It Can Happen to Anybody!* (1970), which had gone through five printings by 1973. It is filled with anecdotes of miraculous healings, unusual resolutions of plumbing problems through prophecy, and portrayals of the gift of tongues.

Also active in the series of Holy Spirit conferences were Donald L. and Shirley Fike, formerly pastors at Castañer, Puerto Rico. Together with their son Douglas Fike, they developed the Communion Fellowship in Goshen, Indiana, with the son assuming major direction. A core leadership group of a dozen people coordinated the work of the community that resisted being called a church. It began as a Bible study group for students; in 1982-83 it became more permanent as college graduates settled in the Goshen area to preserve their ties with the community. The fellowship is jointly affiliated with the Church of the Brethren and the Mennonite Church.[17]

Another combined Mennonite and Brethren community is Reba Place Fellowship, located in urban Evanston, Illinois, adjacent to Chicago. It began in the 1950s among Mennonite students and faculty members at Goshen College, who were caught up in the "recovery of the Anabaptist vision" and wished to realize it anew. Though frowned on by college officials, the group persisted and in 1957 began communal life in Evanston, at first as a project of Mennonite Voluntary Service.[18]

Several individuals with backgrounds in the Church of the Brethren joined them, including Julius and Peggy Belser and

Conrad Wetzel. In 1975 the fellowship officially began a relationship with both the Mennonite Church and the Church of the Brethren as a recognized congregation. Though for many years all members were completely committed to the communitarian principle of full economic sharing, after 1980 the fellowship restructured itself to permit over half of its membership to become congregational members; they live as families controlling their own finances. Virgil Vogt has functioned as a leading elder.

Reba Place Fellowship experienced charismatic renewal in 1972 through the influence of Graham Pulkingham, the rector of an Episcopalian charismatic parish in Houston, Texas. This change brought revival and increased communal membership. Since then Reba Place has continued with a moderately charismatic orientation, most notably in a free flowing yet structured style of gathering that includes singing, instrumental music, testimonies, biblical dramas, dance, and teaching, characterized by an elder as "gentle charismatic worship."[19]

A charismatic movement related to the Church of the Brethren, largely among immigrants from the Philippines, was developed by Roger El Cruz. He graduated with a masters degree in theology from Bethany Seminary and was ordained by the Illinois/Wisconsin district in 1985. He had already developed an expansive ministry after 1976 in inner city Chicago (later receiving aid from the Illinois/Wisconsin District) under the names of Charismatic Prayer Tower Ministries, Inc. and the Charismatic Christian Center International, based at the Charismatic Cathedral (Filipino Fellowship).

A fiery preacher, Cruz found a devoted following among ethnic minorities (many of them Filipinos connected to medical institutions in the urban area) through his parish work, his newspaper and tapes, and his radio and television ministries. Tensions resulting from internal differences and district polity expectations led to a rupture of the relationship in 1992 between Cruz and the Church of the Brethren.[20]

Christ's Assembly was organized near Eaton, Ohio, in August 1967, when Johannes Thalitzer (formerly Thalbitzer) of Denmark celebrated a love feast with nine young Brethren, several from the Old German Baptist Brethren. He was the elder of an assembly in

Copenhagen that saw itself in direct line of continuation with the Schwarzenau Brethren; members had contact with remnants of the Danish Brethren mission that existed from 1876 to 1948. In the 1950s and 1960s Thalitzer contacted each of the five largest Brethren bodies in North America by correspondence or personal visits but found something lacking in each one sufficient to block full affiliation. For a time in 1966 the Dunkard Brethren had two missionary couples in Denmark seeking union.

Within five years of the first love feast, Christ's Assembly grew to number some 70 adult members, attracting Brethren and Mennonite converts as well as other Protestants. Members built an attractive meetinghouse near Eaton, Ohio, with another group assembled near Berne, Indiana. As described by observers, "Christ's Assembly is Brethren in ordinances, eschatological in outlook, Inspirationist...in theology and polity, and Pentecostal in spirit." In the 1980s the movement was disrupted because of accusations of mismanagement and financial abuse by American leaders.[21]

Some Brethren living in northern Indiana, including two former pastors (one of whom became the associate pastor of the new movement) became members of the Faith Assembly led by Hobart Freeman. For a time a professor of Old Testament at the Grace Theological Seminary at Winona Lake, Indiana, Freeman developed first a house church and then a relationship with the charismatic Glory Barn near North Webster, often visited by students from Manchester College.

In 1978 Freeman established the Faith Assembly north of Warsaw, Indiana. The movement grew rapidly under his eloquent preaching and confident pronouncements. Followers were kept under strict discipline, forbidden contact with any form of mass media, and permitted no contact with outsiders, including their own families and relatives. The Assembly erected a large window-less, warehouse-like meeting place seating 2,200 near Wilmot, Indiana, to accommodate its members.

Freeman rejected all traditional health care, linking it historically with witchcraft. He insisted that if members had positive faith, their prayers and those of fellow members would suffice to cure disease. In his view, illness and death were signs of the lack of faith.

Critics charged that as many as 90 people—largely infants, children, and mothers in childbirth—died as the result of the rejection of outside health care by Faith Assembly members. This precipitated, beginning in 1982, prosecution by local authorities, which led to the conviction for "reckless homicide" of several members who had allowed their children to die without medical attention.

In October 1984, Freeman was personally indicted on similar felony charges. He died two months later at the age of 64 of broncho-pneumonia, gangrene, and heart failure, free (as he had taught) from medical attention. Some members confidently expected his resurrection.[22]

Womaen's Caucus

The Womaen's Caucus is the organized form within the Church of the Brethren of the feminist movement. At the 1970 Annual Conference Carole Ziegler and Nancy Peters presented a resolution to Standing Committee asking that the Annual Conference direct the General Board to appoint a committee to study the role of women in the church; the resolution was passed by delegates at the conference. In the following year a newsletter called *Femailings* was started and a caucus of women began to sponsor events at Annual Conference to promote women's concerns.

In 1972 the requested paper entitled "Equality for Women" was adopted by the Annual Conference. In that year two coordinators, Mary Cline Detrick and Mary Blocher Smeltzer, were named to form a new group by and for women, Womaen's Caucus; the name *Womaen* was coined to signify interest in each woman as well in as all women. In 1973 the caucus was formally established at the Fresno Annual Conference and a steering committee appointed. Since that time through formal and informal discussions the caucus has energetically pressed women's concerns to members of the General Board and its staff and has been especially active at Annual Conferences to influence appointments and nominations for elective positions. The board adopted an affirmative action program in 1975 to increase women's participation in staff and board positions. The trend was enhanced by a paper adopted by the 1977 conference updating the 1972 resolution on equality.[23]

The Womaen's Caucus was instrumental in the creation in 1976 of a half-time staff position on "person awareness" at the Elgin offices; the goal was to work for equality among women and men in the church. Beth Glick-Reiman filled this position until the end of 1978; Mary Cline Detrick and Ralph Detrick were then jointly appointed to the office. An early effort was the organization of a Conference on the Role and Status of Church of the Brethren Women, held at Elizabethtown, Pennsylvania, in May 1977. Some 250 women from 21 districts attended the meeting, which focused on "Women as Persons," "Women in the Church," and "Church Women in the World."

This conference was followed by a somewhat larger one, the Women's Gathering, held at Manchester College, in July 1978, designed to celebrate the diversity of women. A highlight was the address by Ruthann Knechel Johansen, which she called "Giving Birth to a New World." In it she challenged women in the Historic Peace Churches to adopt a self-imposed tax on "every non-essential purchase" for distribution in needy areas of the world. "What sense of solidarity might arise if a transnational group of women distributed our self-collected taxes directly, none siphoned off for bureaucratic expenses, to women, men, and children somewhere in that bottom twenty percent of the world's economy?" Such a discipline could also raise awareness of over consumption, encourage a simpler lifestyle, and heighten consciousness of justice issues around the world.[24]

The challenge was met with enthusiasm by conference-goers, and from it emerged the Global Women's Project, approved in October 1978 by the General Board. A volunteer steering committee chose projects for the funds, which were administered through the Persons Awareness staff.

Another highpoint of the women's movement was the conference Empowered by Our Birthright. Billed as the "first Church of the Brethren international women's conference," it was held at Bridgewater College in August 1985 to celebrate the 100th anniversary of the first organized women's group among the Brethren. Women at the 1885 Annual Meeting brought their gifts totaling

nearly $300 for the new foreign missions program, then began orga-
nizing local missionary bands.

Fourteen participants from other countries were enabled to
attend the 1985 meeting through a fund collected in memory of
Ruby Frantz Rhoades, executive of the World Ministries
Commission, who died at the beginning of the year.[25] A pointed
attempt was made at this conference of 900 women (and a few men)
to include the entire spectrum of women across the denomination,
including those sisters uncomfortable with the strong feminist orientation of earlier gatherings planned by the Womaen's Caucus.
The conference was directed by Melanie A. May, who was appointed in January 1985 to the denominational staff to represent women's
concerns.

In a sense, she followed the earlier position of the director of the
Women's Fellowship, held for many years by Anna Warstler. The
organization was disbanded in 1964, along with the parallel Men's
Work association, under the theory that men and women should be
encouraged to work together, not separately. The National Women's
Work movement itself had been organized in 1929 by the
redoubtable Florence Fogelsanger Murphy to combine the
Missionary Society, the Mothers and Daughters Association, and
the Sister's Aid Societies. The program raised substantial sums of
money for mission projects. All of these groups were celebrated at
the 1985 conference.[26]

One of the long-time goals of the women's movement was realized with the election of Elaine Sollenberger as the first woman
moderator of the Church of the Brethren. She presided efficiently
over the 1989 Annual Conference held at Orlando, Florida, which
rejected the controversial restructuring paper.[27]

BRETHREN/MENNONITE COUNCIL FOR LESBIAN AND GAY CONCERNS

A lightning rod for several of the above subgroupings was the
Brethren/Mennonite Council for Gay Concerns (BMC), after
October 1986 renamed the Brethren/Mennonite Council for Lesbian
and Gay Concerns. It was founded in October 1976 by Martin Rock,
a member of the Church of the Brethren in Washington, DC; he had

worked for the Mennonite Central Committee for eleven years in Akron, Pennsylvania, and in Vietnam, but was dismissed when his homosexual orientation became known. He served as the first BMC coordinator until June 1984. In 1990 the council hired its first part-time staff member.

The council began to distribute an attractively produced newsletter in May 1978, published variously two, three, or four times per year; from the second issue of 1978 on it was called *Dialogue*. (There was a gap of publication between December 1987 and May 1989.) Since the second issue it has carried this self-description:

> The Brethren/Mennonite Council for Gay Concerns (BMC) was founded in October, 1986, to provide support for Brethren and Mennonite gay people, and their parents, spouses, relatives, and friends; to foster dialogue between gay and nongay people in the churches; and to provide accurate information about homosexuality from the social sciences, biblical studies, and theology.[28]

In the first year Rock traveled widely (largely spending personal funds) to visit denominational leaders, informing them of the council and its aims. The council paid special attention to the national assemblies of the Church of the Brethren and Mennonite Church, seeking to inform delegates and others attending of their concerns. Its leaders repeatedly sought representation in the exhibit booths of Brethren conferences; though this was consistently denied, their literature was displayed for several years by the Womaen's Caucus.

In 1986 for the first time the council was assigned by conference officers a separate room adjacent to the exhibit area where BMC members could be present to engage conference-goers in dialogue and display literature; this was in response to the Human Sexuality paper adopted by the 1983 conference that encouraged the discussion of controversial issues, including homosexuality. The arrangement has continued since then, with a few exceptions. BMC views have also been given exposure at conferences in the late evening

Insight Sessions. Liaison with the General Board was established through the Parish Ministries Commission.

BMC leaders took the initiative in organizing regional and national meetings, largely attended by homosexuals but also by family members and others who supported their aims. In October 1986 BMC sponsored a conference in Chicago, attended by more than 100 people from the United States and Canada. This was followed by other large conferences on a two-year cycle: Toronto in 1988; Philadelphia in 1990; Denver in 1992; and Indianapolis in 1994.

Homosexuality became a controversial topic in the Church of the Brethren after 1977, reflecting in part the increasingly bitter debate within American society. The report adopted on marriage and divorce in that year by Annual Conference recommended that the General Board appoint a committee "to address itself in a comprehensive way to the basic issues of human sexuality from a Christian perspective." It did so. A five-person committee began work and conducted a hearing at the 1978 conference but requested more time to complete its study. An article published in *Messenger* (June 1978) by Graydon F. Snyder, a member of the committee, reported in an interim way upon the committee's findings.

Continual attention to the subject was given through letters to the editor published in *Messenger*. They tended to be either harsh condemnation of homosexuality as a sin clearly defined by scripture or appeals for tolerance and love. A number of communications came from men and women identifying themselves both as homosexuals and as Brethren in leadership roles; to protect these authors because of the intense feelings aroused by the issue, the letters were published anonymously.

In 1979 the committee presented its report ("Human Sexuality from a Christian Perspective") to the General Board; after extended discussion the board dismissed the committee and appointed a new committee from its own ranks, chaired by Guy E. Wampler, Jr., charged to prepare a new paper. In 1981 this version was accepted, upon recommendation of Standing Committee, as a study document to be circulated within the church for two years (a study guide was prepared to facilitate the process). The committee was asked to gather reactions and submit the paper, revised in light of them, to the 1983 conference.

At that conference held in Baltimore, there was extensive and heated discussion of the paper, centering almost entirely on that section dealing with homosexuality. Three lifestyle options were outlined in the paper for Christians with homosexual orientation: celibacy, conversion to heterosexuality, and a covenant (life-long) relationship. The committee suggested that the church was not of one mind about accepting the last option. By a narrow margin, the third option was rejected through amendment as unacceptable to the delegate body.

A special issue (Winter 1991) of *Brethren Life and Thought* was devoted to the subject of human sexuality. It published presentations made at an insight session sponsored by the Parish Ministries Commission at the 1986 Annual Conference, as well as six additional statements from a variety of perspectives. Several contributions in the issue came from Brethren men and women who were avowedly homosexual. One from a former executive of the Parish Ministries Commission acknowledged his bisexuality. Another from a young minister in Michigan and later campus pastor affirmed "same-sex covenants" and alluded to a covenant service for two women she had conducted.

In February 1993 a *Messenger* article profiling Charles L. Boyer, that year's moderator, quoted him as saying: "I have written very straightforwardly to individuals and said that I personally am ready to accept gay, lesbian, and bisexual people into positions of leadership in the church."[29] About the same time, the campus pastor mentioned above was announced as one of the speakers at a youth rally for young people scheduled to be held at Bridgewater College. Also announced were two actions of the General Board protesting limitations upon homosexual rights in Colorado and in the Boy Scouts.

These three developments provoked a fire storm of protest, especially in but not limited to the Southeast; this culminated in a mass meeting held in April 1993 at the Greenmount Church of the Brethren in Virginia. This meeting was attended by the moderator and the general secretary of the General Board, both of whom clarified the intent of their statements and board actions.

The Greenmount meeting led to further responses coordinated by a group reflecting (in their own words) "Concerns of the Grass Roots." Some congregations threatened to leave the Church of the Brethren; some members demanded that the moderator resign. Upon the recommendation of the Standing Committee's "Words of Guidance," the Indianapolis Annual Conference of 1993 began with a special service of reconciliation and unity. As part of Charles Boyer's "state of the denomination" address as moderator, he led in a service of anointing for forgiveness of sins and for restoration of unity.

A panel at an insight session (which included BMC representatives in its planning) was crowded by some 500 people. Later, during the business session, an open forum on the issues surrounding human sexuality heard more than 30 speakers express a range of views from those condemning homosexuals to those calling for greater openness to them. A report in *Messenger* concluded, "All these opportunities to present hurts, to confess sins, to seek healing and forgiveness found eager participants. Brethren reached out to one another. It was a Conference like none other of recent memory."[30]

The 1994 Annual Conference at Wichita also heard heated debate on the issue, often expressed in harsh terms. The Standing Committee recommended to the delegates that the Church of the Brethren "refrain from requesting additional policy statements on the homosexual issue for the next five years." It proposed naming a committee to create and implement a plan for dialogue on the issue "at every level of the denomination," using those skilled in conflict resolution in its design. This recommendation and proposal were accepted. Several sessions at the conference were designed to work toward reconciliation; members of the newly formed Ministry of Reconciliation moved among those participating in the debate, seeking to restore relationships.

Added to this mix and, at places, intertwined with it was the new reality of diversity in Brethren ethnic background. This increasingly demanded the attention of the members and leaders of the denomination in the latter half of the twentieth century.

26

Ethnic Minorities Among the Brethren

During the same time frame that saw the development of dissenting fellowships within the denomination, Brethren saw the emergence of Black, Hispanic, Korean, Haitian, and, to a slight extent, Filipino and Native American congregations.

There had been African-American congregations of Brethren already in the second half of the nineteenth century. Work with other ethnic minorities came in the first half of the twentieth century. Among the most successful early ministries were those among Asians. Brethren began mission work with Chinese in several urban settings, typically by organizing Sunday schools. The longest lasting of the Brethren Sunday schools for Chinese began in Chicago in 1908. Elgin S. Moyer was a devoted leader of the school, and the congregation that grew from it in Oak Park, for over fifty years. Three able Chinese leaders—Moy Wing, Moy Way, and Moy Gwong—were educated there; the first two served as ministers and teachers in the United States and the last named as a missionary in his native China.[1]

By 1915 Brethren were directing Sunday schools for Chinese not only in Chicago, but also in Los Angeles and Riverside, California; Detroit, Michigan; Washington, DC; South Bend and Elkhart, Indiana; Bluefield, West Virginia; and (aptly) in Canton, Ohio. Four of these were still functioning in 1940.

Brethren also initiated Sunday schools for Japanese laborers in Rocky Ford, Colorado, and La Verne, California, but these were of short duration. A small but noticeable influx of Japanese-Americans found membership among the Brethren in the wake of the Japanese Resettlement Program during World War II, producing at least one member of both the Standing Committee and the General Brotherhood Board, Sim Togasaki, called by a biographer a "most unlikely Dunker." Following the end of World War II there were plans to open Brethren service work in Japan but they did not materialize. Brethren have been active in the World Friendship Center at Hiroshima since its establishment in 1964 and in the International Christian University.[2]

Likewise, Brethren had prized contact with leaders of Brethren mission congregations in India, China, Nigeria, and Ecuador who often sojourned among Brethren in the United States on deputation visits.

The difference in the modern period is that Brethren self-understanding has changed dramatically through encounters with a new reality. In metaphoric terms, the historic Dunker tree with deep roots in the German ethos was now experiencing new growth through multiethnic grafts on its branches. The solidly familial character of Brethren, based not entirely but substantially on intermarriage of Germanic clans over generations, was in a process of change. The family reunion character—so noticeable at Brethren Annual Conferences—was being politely challenged by newcomers who wished to break into the circle.

Increasingly new members questioned the "Brethren game"— that is, the long-accustomed manner of a member, upon meeting someone new, proceeding to engage in a series of questions to establish common relatives or, at least, connection through shared experiences in institutions—colleges, BVS or BSC, and the like. The shift can be illustrated by the anecdote in which a new convert encountered a friendly soul at Annual Conference; the latter, noticing the name tag, commented, "Why, Garcia is not a Brethren name." The reply promptly came, "Well, it is now!"

BLACK BRETHREN

The first black members of the church seem to have been slaves of Elijah Padgett who was baptized by Daniel Martin in 1770 southwest

Members of the Second Church of the Brethren, Colored, at Denver, Colorado, in 1910; the short-lived congregation grew out of a Brethren-sponsored orphanage. *BHLA Collection.*

of Charleston, South Carolina. Padgett is thought to have organized the first integrated congregation, which consisted of his family and his slaves. African Americans began voluntarily to seek membership with the Brethren in the southern states in the early nineteenth century. Though little is known about their numbers, their presence is documented by the discussion about the holy kiss at Annual Meeting, as mentioned in describing the onset of the Civil War.

Writers in Brethren periodicals agitated in 1857, 1878, and 1880 for evangelization among African Americans. They were answered by Landon West—who had a longstanding "burden" for people of color. He related the story of Samuel Weir in periodicals and in a much-reprinted pamphlet. Born a slave in Botetourt County, Virginia, Weir was freed in 1843 by his master when the latter joined the Brethren. With the aid of other Brethren, Weir made his way across the Mason-Dixon line to Ohio where he became a member of the Painter Creek Brethren congregation.

Ralph E. Smeltzer, director of Peace and Social Education for the Brethren Service Commission, played an active role in mediating the civil rights struggle in Selma, Alabama, from 1963 to 1965. He is pictured here with his friend Andrew Young, a close associate of Martin Luther King, Jr. *BHLA Collection.*

Ohio Brethren helped Weir to learn to read and write. In 1849 he was licensed to preach among resident blacks, advanced in the ministry in 1872, and ordained an elder in 1882. His first convert, Harvey Carter, was also later licensed to preach. The congregation organized by Weir was known under the name of the Frankfort Colored Church; though never large, it created a daughter congregation at Circleville, Ohio.[3]

Carter and another black minister, James May, continued Weir's work when the latter died in 1884, but both congregations eventually ceased their work. Another black minister, Wiley Dolby, pastored a black Brethren congregation in Jeffersonville, Ohio.

Southern Ohio has continued over the years to have black members, some of whom became ministers.

Brethren pastors in Maryland and Philadelphia attempted ministries among African Americans in the late nineteenth century with mixed success. After 1900 interest grew among the Brethren to develop further ministries. In 1903, with support given through the mission board by her father, Mattie Cunningham (Dolby) from Indiana began a black mission in Palestine, Arkansas. The local white congregation was willing to support the project. Mattie Cunningham had been converted in Flora, Indiana, by Elder A. G. Crosswhite and baptized there by a local minister. Soon thereafter, Elder Crosswhite admonished her in a kindly manner to be "a good soldier for Jesus, because after you get a little older the church will need you. It won't be long till the church will want to do something for your people and will want to use you." So impressed was she by this that two years later she volunteered her services to the mission board. She completed high school and studied at the Bible school at Manchester for three years; her tuition was paid by her father and by interested Brethren.[4]

James May, a black minister from southern Ohio, went to the Arkansas mission on several preaching tours, and was then asked to relocate there by the mission board. This move was protested in 1903 by Landon West, a long-time supporter of the Frankfort church of black Brethren in Ohio, because to "starve out the weak points here, to help start up new points in other states is not Mission Work and cannot be a success." He complained that the Ohio ministers were neglecting the congregation. The team in Palestine had a good initial response, and a local convert, D. C. Clark, was called to the ministry. A meetinghouse was built with contributed funds. May, however, did not stay long. Clark died, and in 1906 malaria forced Mattie Cunningham to return to her home; the mission was closed in 1908.[5]

Mattie Cunningham went to southern Ohio, where in 1907 she met and married Newton Dolby, the son of Wiley Dolby; she and her husband were installed in the same year as deacons of the Frankfort congregation. She was called to the ministry in 1911, becoming the first woman to appear on the Brethren ministerial list.[6]

When she and her husband moved to Urbana, Ohio, they joined the nearest Brethren congregation, although it was some distance from their residence. After several years, when a different minister was put in charge, they were encouraged to find a church closer to their home, effectively expelling them. They then joined the Methodist Church, where she was able to serve as a minister, later also ministering in the Church of God.

H. C. Early urged in many articles the creation of an industrial institute along the lines of the Tuskegee Industrial Institute led by Booker T. Washington, which he inspected. Although some funds were received, the response was insufficient to begin it. A combined orphanage and home for the aged, serving African Americans, was developed in the early twentieth century in Denver, Colorado, by William Rhodes; it attracted substantial support from congregations in Kansas and Colorado. One of the charter members of Bethany's first class in 1905, a black student named Nellie Morgan (Rainey), went to Denver to work in the institution. Springing from this home was Denver's Second Church of the Brethren, Colored, organized in 1910 and disbanded by 1920. Early in 1918 Nellie Morgan offered to open a mission for blacks in the South but the General Mission Board declined the offer.[7]

At mid-century, Brethren in the South made some moves toward better race relations. Although an attempt failed in the 1940s to hold an integrated camp at Camp Bethel, Virginia, Brethren in West Virginia sponsored one at Harpers Ferry in 1945 and another near Terra Alta in 1946. Bridgewater College was one of the first predominantly white private schools in Virginia to admit black students, beginning in 1953. In May 1954, the faculty voted overwhelmingly to ask the trustees of the college to approve admission of black students on the same basis as whites. Trustees subsequently directed the admissions office to admit any student, including those of color, who met published admission requirements. Incoming black students were accorded a friendly reception from other students.

A number of Brethren congregations in the Dayton, Ohio, area developed significant black membership in the twentieth century. To them could be added the First Church of the Brethren in Chicago.

For many years the home church of Bethany Seminary faculty and students, First Church increasingly reflected the ethnicity of the surrounding neighborhood, becoming substantially black in its membership and leadership following the relocation of the seminary to the western suburbs, although always remaining an integrated congregation. One of its black ministers, Thomas Wilson, accepted a staff position in Elgin, serving from 1967 to 1982. Additional congregations with black membership were found in Illinois, Pennsylvania, Florida, and California.

Seminary students were active in the ministry of the West Side Christian Parish, devoted to pastoral care of the black population of inner-city Chicago. Other students became active in the civil rights movement. Paul Laprad, while a student at Fisk University of Nashville, was beaten when he participated in one of the very first nonviolent sit-ins when young blacks sought to be served at a restaurant. As a white man, Laprad was singled out for especially rough treatment by the mob that disrupted the demonstration.

Other Brethren were arrested and jailed in 1965 in Mississippi for demonstrating against police brutality. Juniata College students and faculty were in the Montgomery, Alabama, demonstration of 1965 that was forcibly broken up; two faculty members were injured. Ralph E. Smeltzer of the Brethren Service staff played a key role in the drive for voter registration at Selma, Alabama, by acting as a liaison between the government and civil rights activists. Many Brethren were active participants in the great civil rights marches, such as the March on Washington for Jobs and Freedom in August 1963.

Over the years Brethren Service organized or supported a large number of projects serving black communities. One of the most successful was the Pilot House project initiated in the 1940s that assisted black families in Baltimore, Maryland, to renovate and upgrade their housing; a series of BVS workers came to Baltimore to further the project. In later years Brethren supported financially and with BVS personnel the work of the Voice of Calvary mission in Mississippi, organized in 1964 by John M. Perkins.

The Church of the Brethren initiated a program in 1969 called the Fund for the Americas in the United States (FAUS) in response to the Black Power movement. It sought to encourage self-help projects among African Americans and other minorities by financial and educational support. Later renamed SHARE, by 1981 it had disbursed over $1,000,000 to aid 55 projects.

In 1987 A. William Hayes, pastor of the First Church of the Brethren in Baltimore made history when he was installed as the first black moderator of the Church of the Brethren, going on to guide the deliberations at the 1988 conference. Although he came to the Brethren in mid-career after ministry in the United Church of Christ, he was soon elected to the General Board of the denomination and then to its highest elective office. Hayes was critical of the slow pace of the integration of minorities as full participants in the life of the church but was noted for his adept ministry to both black and white members of the Baltimore congregation and his irenic spirit.[8]

HISPANIC BRETHREN

The story of Brethren relationships with Spanish-speaking peoples goes back to the first decade of the twentieth century. Following the Spanish-American War the United States took over Cuba as a protectorate; the island nation was established as an independent republic in 1902, but the United States, under the Platt Amendment, reserved the right to intervene in Cuban affairs. The appeal was made to United States citizens to migrate there to aid in stabilizing the country.

Some Brethren followed the appeal, and in 1906 three families established a small colony at Omaja in the Oriente Province. Others joined them and in 1907 they organized a congregation; its highest number of members was about 30. An economic downturn motivated the Brethren to begin returning to the mainland in 1910. The colony persisted with a few members, however, until 1937. The leading figure in Cuba was Grant Mahan, formerly an editor of the Brethren publication *The Inglenook*, a literary magazine.[9]

The La Verne congregation in California supported mission work among Spanish-speaking people from 1918 to 1928, as did the Garden City congregation in Kansas at much the same time, 1918-1925. Brethren operated a Brethren Industrial School for Mexicans in Falfurias, Texas, from 1921 to 1927. A congregation was organized in 1928 that integrated white and Mexican families under C. D. Fager as pastor. When he moved away, a Mennonite minister continued the work for twelve years.

Work at Falfurias was revitalized after 1948 as a project of the newly organized BVS, with major investments of funds and personnel going there for several decades to pursue work with Hispanic residents in the areas of agricultural development, youth work, and education. When the BVS/BSC project was virtually terminated in 1964, membership dwindled again, but a charter member became the lay pastor, serving from 1965 to 1975. In 1980 some 30 members were counted in the bilingual congregation.

The First Church of the Brethren in Chicago developed an Hispanic congregation under the leadership of Fabricio Guzman that transferred in 1965 to the Douglas Park Church of the Brethren, also in Chicago. Two services were held there for many years for the convenience of both English-speaking and Spanish-speaking congregations.

Mention has previously been made of the extensive community program that was developed by the CPS project in Castañer, Puerto Rico. Services there for CPS workers and interested Puerto Ricans led to the development of a congregation; this was initiated in 1948 with 12 charter members. It was recognized as a congregation by the District of Georgia and Florida in 1954 and received its first Hispanic pastor in 1956. By 1982 three more congregations had been organized in Puerto Rico.

A General Board report to Annual Conference in 1993 noted that of the 30 new congregations established in the last decade, one-third had been Hispanic. There were five in 1988, twenty by 1992. Over this period an Hispanic Steering Committee has functioned to represent the needs and concerns of Spanish-speaking congregations to the broader denomination. Tensions arising out of Brethren openness to feminist concerns and its struggles with the homosexuality issue have caused some of the newer Spanish-speaking congregations to move away from Brethren connections.

Through the efforts of Jorge Toledo of the Puerto Rican church, congregations were developed in the Dominican Republic. The first congregation was established in the late 1980s at Los Toros, with

Santos Mota as pastor. Toledo explained his motivation: "Every time I went there I saw the people hungry for the gospel, hungry for interrelationships, and I started to dream. I wanted to start churches in small villages where there are no churches."[10] By April 1991, five congregations and five mission points had been started. In 1994 the third annual assembly of the Brethren was held in that poor nation. At that point there were ten congregations. Hispanic speakers from the United States, including Gilbert Romero, pastor of the Bella Vista congregation in California and George Rivera from Puerto Rico, spoke. Guillermo Encarnación, pastor of the Alfa y Omega congregation in Lancaster, Pennsylvania, served as moderator. He has played a major role in the church as a representative of Hispanic concerns.

HAITIAN BRETHREN

Brethren have been concerned about meeting needs in Haiti for many years. Particular support from 1965 to 1991 flowed to a program called *Aide-aux-Enfants* in the nation's capital, Port-au-Prince, established and directed by Pastor Luc Nérée. The original contact had been made by John W. Barwick, the veteran Brethren relief worker in England, Europe, and later in the Near East, at that point directing the Church World Service work there. A government official, describing the work of the charismatic pastor, reported that Protestant churches were held in low esteem in that poverty-stricken Roman Catholic country. The one exception he made was that of the Church of the Brethren: "The Brethren live what they believe rather than just talking about it."[11]

The pastor's program was dedicated to feed malnourished children. Later he added an out-patient clinic and a school. For many years, Brethren volunteer Mona Lou Teeter worked on the pastor's staff as the English language secretary. Other volunteers came on shorter-term stints. In 1980 Pastor Nérée asked for his church, Eglise Baptiste des Cités, to be affiliated with the Church of the Brethren; it responded with a covenant of understanding. The pastor died in 1992 after failing health and political turmoil caused the termination of the Aide-aux-Enfants program.

The *Eglise des Frères Haitiens,* a Haitian Church of the Brethren, was created in Miami, Florida, to serve Haitian refugees who have flocked to the United States in a number of desperate ways to escape the grinding poverty and political unrest in their homeland. Their pastor, Ludovic St. Fleur, was one of the "boat people" himself, surviving a risky 20-day voyage on a crowded sailboat in 1979. The multi-ethnic First Church of the Brethren in Miami chose him as a person to train as a pastor to reach out to other Haitians. For his part he appreciated the concern for the poor demonstrated by the Brethren. St. Fleur completed the training for ministers through the denominational EFSM program.[12] By 1983 the young church movement was recognized by the district as a fellowship and ten years later as a congregation of one hundred members. There is in addition a new Haitian fellowship in Brooklyn, organized in the early 1990s.

Brazilian Brethren

The connection of Brethren with Brazil came through the pilgrimage of a young Brazilian named Onaldo Pereira of Rio Verde. As a teenager he discovered the Bible and dedicated his life to Jesus. He began to gather young people like himself into a community, working together on a farm, and developing an independent church. Through his reading of the New Testament he became a convinced pacifist and refused to serve in the military when he was called. The government told him that if he could find a church that supported his position, he would receive an exemption.

He discovered the Brethren through reading church history and sought contact with several groups; the Church of the Brethren responded and sent a representative to visit him. He was baptized by a member of the Old Brethren, one of the divisions within the Old German Baptist Brethren with members in Brazil. Pereira came to the United States in 1984-1985 to study at Bethany Theological Seminary, with the aid of the Old Brethren, and while there received Brethren ordination in the Virlina district.

Back in Brazil he gathered another group about him; they called themselves first the *Igreja dos Irmaos* (Church of the Brethren in

Portuguese), later the *Comunidade Pacifista Christa* (Pacifist Christian Community), and sought affiliation with the Church of the Brethren. The General Board passed a resolution in 1988 affirming the relationship with the Brazilian community. This had the advantage for them of securing exemptions from military service. The Annual Conference of 1992 recognized and accepted the Brazilian church. Contact with the very poor group was strengthened by the visits of Brethren from North America. In 1995 there was turmoil in the Brazilian community, and Onaldo Pereira was removed as the minister.[13]

KOREAN BRETHREN

Although Brethren knew of Korea primarily through the work of Brethren Service and the Heifer Project during and after the Korean War (1950-53), their interest took a new turn in the 1980s. An independent Korean Christian church in the Los Angeles area was provided space for services in the Pomona Church of the Brethren. Through conversations of the two pastors, C. Wayne Zunkel and Dan Kim, interest grew on the part of the Korean congregation to seek closer contact with the Brethren.

This contact led to the affiliation of several Korean congregations with the Church of the Brethren. By 1992 one-third of new congregations within the denomination were of Korean ethnic origin. By their testimony, the quality of the Brethren that attracted them was the combination of inward evangelical commitment to Christ matched with intense social concern, which they had not seen elsewhere among American Protestants.

A new stage began with the growing interest of these Korean Brethren, supported by others in the Pacific Southwest Region, to develop mission work in the South Korean homeland. The General Board sent a delegation to the Republic of Korea in 1988 to study this possibility. They returned with a strong recommendation from the Korean Christian leaders with whom they spoke that there was no need for yet another denomination in the nation; they already suffered from a proliferation of small, splinter churches. While these leaders spoke of their appreciation for the contribution that

Brethren could make in the area of peace, service, and justice issues, they urged that this be done within an ecumenical context. On this basis the staff of the World Ministries Commission recommended and the General Board decided against beginning a mission there. This paralleled an earlier decision in 1984. The matter, however, did not rest.

This specific discussion about beginning a mission in Korea was entangled in a broader denominational debate about mission philosophy referred to earlier. In 1955 the church recognized a changing world by adopting a policy which stressed indigenization—"helping nationals establish indigenous churches," those that are "self-propagating, self-governing, self-supporting," and identify with the local culture. The churches were encouraged to join with other Christians in their respective lands as soon as possible. This took place in India, China (of necessity), Nigeria (in part), and Ecuador.[14] When these recommendations were implemented, it had the effect of reducing the presence of expatriates in former mission fields, that is missionaries from abroad; those who were sent to the mission areas were to be there only at the request of the indigenous churches and under their direction. In an ecumenical age, it was thought to be no longer necessary for Brethren personnel to be present in other lands. As a mission executive from this era exhorted, "Is the task to build the church? Yes, Christ's church....But the day is coming when Brethren will need to decide if they will support the continued growth of Christ's church through the support of a Mexican Methodist teacher in Ecuador, an Indonesian youth worker in India, an Egyptian Coptic medical doctor in Nigeria."[15]

The executive of the World Ministries Commission from 1969 to 1977, Joel K. Thompson, vigorously promoted this new policy of ecumenical cooperation and decrease of Brethren personnel in the field. He and his wife Phyllis Yount Thompson had lived it as educational missionaries in Indonesia (1960-1963). When he left General Board employment in 1980 he told an interviewer, "They'll remember me for indigenization. Ecuador, India, Nigeria...indigenization took up a lot of my time as WMC exec[utive]."[16]

The year 1981 saw the adoption of a comprehensive policy statement on world mission theology, in which mission was defined globally as "all God-motivated efforts to make Christ known, loved, and obeyed...to redeem, heal and lift *all* of life." A distinction was drawn between *missions*, considered inappropriate in some settings, and *mission*, always appropriate. The Great Commission is intended for the next door neighbor as well as the distant national. Correctly understood, world mission is a two-way street. The statement specifically reiterated that "indigenization and mutuality should guide" Brethren efforts.[17]

A growing undertone of dissent surfaced at several Annual Conferences as members noted that the numbers of foreign missionaries were rapidly shrinking by attrition and by policy. As one example, Laura Sewell, who for some time had been the last Brethren missionary to work in India, returned in 1985 after 36 years of service. An additional complication was the agitation of some Brethren in the United States who were sympathetic to the petitions of a dissenting group of "separated Brethren" (who opposed the 1970 merger of the Church of the Brethren in India with other bodies to form the United Church of North India). The separated Brethren asked for the American church to reestablish direct relations with them.

These issues led to the appointment of a study committee, which brought their policy proposal to the 1988 Annual Conference. A key recommendation contained therein states, "It does not appear to be the best expression of mission at this time...to seek or encourage a structured connection between (new churches in other countries) and the Church of the Brethren in the U.S.A." Although for procedural reasons, much of the paper was never discussed, dissatisfaction with it was sufficiently great that the paper was rejected, the committee dismissed, and a new committee selected to redraft a mission philosophy.

It was clear from the discussion that a significant number of delegates and others wanted to see at least partial return to something that could clearly be identified as Church of the Brethren missions, as opposed to ecumenical cooperation, seconding personnel, a mission of presence, and the like. A new statement, suggesting a more "pro-active stance" to missions overseas by Brethren was presented and accepted at the 1989 conference; it was described as a revision of the 1981 statement that was to remain authoritative.

At the 1990 Annual Conference, delegates endorsed two some-what conflicting actions: first, planting new Brethren congregations in Korea, and second, pursuing a partnership with the Korean Evangelical Church (KEC), a small indigenous Korean church with strong peace concerns. Pastors of Korean Brethren congregations in the United States differed among themselves as to which was the better approach. In late spring 1991, a "discernment team" of Brethren, including three Korean pastors, was sent to Korea to investigate the potential for Brethren mission work there.[18]

In October 1991, the General Board approved a five-point strategy developed by the discernment team; it included the appointment of a Korean field director to initiate contacts with Korean churches and to act as liaison with the denomination. This was effected in September 1992, when the appointed field director, Dan Kim, arrived in South Korea. Existing Korean congregations wishing to affiliate with the Brethren were to be assisted through a process of orientation and information. A goal was suggested of planting seven new churches by 1995.

Two of the three districts of the Korean Reformation Presbyterian Church, representing about thirty congregations, voted in October 1994 to join the Church of the Brethren. Measures were beginning in 1995 to organize training and orientation of the pastors under the guidance of Dan Kim and with the assistance of visiting Brethren leaders from the United States. A delegation of Koreans from this church body visited the Elgin offices in March and the Annual Conference in June 1995.

Brethren briefly had a Filipino congregation within its ranks in the 1980s; this was discussed under the rubric of the charismatic movement in the preceding chapter.

NATIVE AMERICAN BRETHREN

Early Brethren encounters with indigenous peoples seem to have been friendly, except when raiding Indians from other areas made no distinctions between nonresistant settlers and others in their massacres. Christopher Sauer II, following the lead of his father, spoke out in his Germantown newspaper against mistreatment of Native Americans. Although individual encounters on the nineteenth century frontier seemed to have been peaceable, there seems to have been very little concern expressed by Brethren in the nineteenth century about the injustice suffered by the American Indians in the course of the sweep of American migration across the West. They took advantage of the presence of new land to colonize and purchase inexpensive land.[19]

An enigmatic figure affiliated with the Brethren in some way named Adam Paine (Payne) traveled among Indians in the Illinois Territory in the first decades of the nineteenth century. Although trusted by many, he became embroiled in the war mounted by the Chief Black Hawk, who reacted to the Indian Removal Act of 1830. Paine was killed in 1832.

In the late nineteenth century there were passing references to the "Indian Problem" and some reprints of descriptive articles from other sources in Brethren periodicals, but nothing of sustained interest. The same can be said of the mission agencies of the church, which several times (1882, 1896, 1908, 1916, 1917) discussed the possibility of opening missions to the Native Americans without any result.

Otho Winger, the energetic president who put Manchester College on its feet after his election in 1911, took a special interest in the local Miami tribe. He wrote several books covering its history; the most popular was the true tale of Frances Slocum, the "lost sister among the Miamis," a white child captive from a Quaker family who, when grown, married a chief and spent all of her days with the Indians. She was rediscovered by her family as an old woman.

According to a brief reference in a Brethren publication, there existed in 1880 a "Dunkard Church of Indians" in California. The evangelist S. H. Bashor reported that one of their number had been baptized by Brethren, had taken the Brethren message to his tribe in the mountains, and had succeeded in baptizing a number of his fellows. There is otherwise no knowledge about the existence of this grouping.[20]

The first calls for Brethren missions to the Native American population came in 1882, but there was little official response. In 1924 the denominational paper ran an obituary titled "Our Only

American Indian Member Gone to Rest"; this was Betty Rathbun, who had joined the Los Angeles congregation in 1910. After the BVS program was introduced in 1948, a number of volunteer workers were assigned to projects serving American Indians, primarily of an educational nature, in South Dakota, Utah, and Arizona.

The major project over the years has been the Lybrook Navajo Mission near Cuba, New Mexico, begun in 1953. Several individuals suggested the mission, which attempted holistic attention to the needs of the community, stressing evangelism, education, health care, in addition to Sunday school and worship services. Ernest and Olivia Eikenberry, longtime China hands, were the first directors. Later more emphasis was placed on community service, especially the rehabilitation of alcoholics. Turnover of personnel hampered the progress of the project, but it has continued through the local congregation, which chose the name Tok'ahookaadi when it reorganized in 1984.

Native American members of the Church of the Brethren came into more prominence in the early 1990s with the discussion at Annual Conference of the study paper "Community: A Tribe of Many Feathers." It was adopted as a study document in 1993 and accepted with slight revision in 1994. Some critics objected that the paper did not clearly spell out the uniqueness of Jesus Christ and his role in salvation.

Although fraught with possibilities for misunderstandings and even tension, after the changes brought to the denomination by the diversity of new ethnic congregations, the character of the denomination had been changed permanently.

27

Brethren Approaching Their Tricentennial

In the summer of 1979, Jimmy Carter called together his staff at the presidential retreat at Camp David, near Thurmont, Maryland. Following their ten-day deliberations, he broadcast to the country a speech widely remembered as the "malaise" speech, although that word was never used. He graphically portrayed the problems facing the nation, naming it a "crisis of confidence." He called for renewal, for a "rebirth of the American spirit," much like a revival preacher out of his Southern Baptist past. He appealed for disparate and warring groups to come together, to share in a reawakening sufficient to meet the challenges of the day.

Unfortunately for the president, a cynical press (who mocked this "born-again" southerner) and a jaded political opposition twisted his intentions by complaining that he was badmouthing the great American populace. Some political commentators register that speech and the disappointing reaction to it as the true beginning of the precipitous decline in fortunes of the Georgia-born politician. Americans, they pontificated, do not cotton to gloom and doom. They want their leaders to smile and to be upbeat. Carter lost his bid for reelection to a former governor from California who followed that recipe.

In some ways the Church of the Brethren at the end of the twentieth century stands in a place like that of President Carter at Camp David. There have been many oracles of malaise and gloom, not without foundation. This has occasioned appeals for renewal and revival but not all have met with sympathetic reception. In 1995 it is not yet clear what the outcome of the perceived crisis will be.

BRETHREN IN THE LATE TWENTIETH CENTURY

The careful statistics of sociologist Carl F. Bowman published in 1986 make discouraging reading. He found that four out of five Brethren live in 12 districts that extend over only ten states, all east of Mississippi River—Pennsylvania, Maryland, Delaware, New Jersey, Virginia, West Virginia, North Carolina, Ohio, Indiana, and Kentucky. Of this four-fifths, six states in themselves comprise eighty percent of that number. "The Brethren are largely a mid-Atlantic phenomenon, with extensions into the Midwest," Bowman concluded.[1]

The problem with these statistics is not just the waning of the once vigorous Brethren membership in the trans-Mississippi West. It is also that these eastern states are in the "rust belt" where the industrial-economic base is evaporating, negatively affecting population growth, as opposed to the "sun belt" where the industrial-economic base is thriving, positively affecting population growth. Moreover, Brethren live predominantly in the rural areas of the states rather than in urban areas where the population is growing. Bowman concluded that "many younger Brethren don't have the opportunity to remain in the church, because their careers take them to the job centers of the city, and away from the rural Brethren centers."[2]

In addition, the membership of the Brethren is marked by age. The median age of Brethren interviewed by Bowman was 53, with 30 per cent of his scientific sample aged 65 or older. In 1983 the corresponding ratio of all United States residents in that age range was sixteen percent. Although the average age of the entire population of the country is rising rapidly, to an anticipated twenty-one percent over 65 by the early part of the next century, the aging of the Brethren is both striking and troubling.

This reality is illustrated in a backhanded way by a recent program in the church that has won great popularity. The reference is to the two national conferences held thus far for older Brethren. The Association of Brethren Caregivers (ABC), recognizing the realities just cited, sponsored together with the General Board the first National Older Adult Conference (NOAC) at Lake Junaluska, North Carolina, in October 1992. Taking as its theme "Say Yes to Years," conference attenders with an average age of 70 enjoyed a full schedule of addresses, interest groups, workshops, recreation, and worship services. More than 600 people made their way to what was called a "mini Annual Conference."

So positive was the response that it was repeated as NOAC II in September 1994 with an even greater attendance, some 900 in all; it was limited to those over the age of fifty. Its theme was "Yes to Years: The Best Is Yet To Be." Vigorous speakers affirmed the faith, life, heritage, the church, and the future and received hearty response. The spirit was overwhelmingly positive. The point is that the denomination finds it necessary to create special programs for the aging, recognizing at the same time that these are the most supportive of the denomination both in attendance and giving. A reporter noted, "Clearly, too, the NOACers make up a core group of staunch supporters of Annual Conference and of denominational programs."[3]

Brethren membership has been declining since 1960, dropping from a high of over 200,000 to about 165,000 by 1983. Since then it has dropped further to about 150,000. In fact, in 1989 an Annual Conference Committee on restructuring calculated in its paper that the active Brethren membership, as opposed to the numbers on the rolls, was really only 70,000. They used this number to argue that the current organization and staff levels were excessive for the size of the denomination.

Bowman pointed out that in the same period (1960-1983) when the Brethren were rapidly declining in numbers, the United States population was increasing by thirty percent. It was of little comfort for Brethren that most mainstream Protestant churches had similar problems. The United Methodist Church lost 2,000,000 members since 1965 and the Christian Church over thirty percent of its membership.

In October 1991, a team of faculty members at Bridgewater College called together a conference of scholars and church leaders to consider the "20th-century directions and dilemmas" of "Brethren in transition." They pointed to individualism, membership loss, theological failure and drift, pluralism, ethical relativism, and other factors making for change. "The forces at work pull us in different directions, and we wonder if we are losing our identify and our morale as a denomination." They understood the conference as way of taking stock of the situation, though "no easy solutions" were anticipated by the planners.[4]

The sense of crisis considered by the Bridgewater College consultation had been underscored a year earlier when the General Board interrupted its usual business at its autumn 1990 meeting to issue a church wide "Call to Spiritual Renewal." Impelled by many of the concerns listed above, it was sparked by an "almost despairing" statement by board member Wayne Fralin; this had been prompted by a report from a committee studying strained relationships in the church. He cited the committee's report that Brethren "are in too many places experiencing a lack of trust, both in the institution and the people who they feel are running it." Fralin lamented that the report only hinted at the underlying ailments such as aging and declining membership: "We are presiding over a dying organization." Thus challenged, the general secretary Donald E. Miller, moderator Phillip C. Stone, and four other leaders called the membership to a time of sustained prayer and spiritual revival. The 1991 Annual Conference at Portland, Oregon, began its sessions with six church leaders on their knees.[5]

A comparable flurry erupted in the spring of 1995 when the board released word of several downsizing options precipitated by the prospect of a serious shortfall in revenues. Included was a suggestion to close the general offices at Elgin, Illinois, and relocate to the Brethren Service Center in New Windsor, Maryland. Instead of choosing any one of the proposed options, the board decided that any restructuring should flow from rethinking the basic vision of what the church should be in the future. Therefore, they elected an "Envisioning" committee to produce such a document, focusing on the work of the General Board.

The committee's product was accepted in amended form at the June 1995 meeting of the General Board. It reads, in part,

We envision a General Board that:
— equips congregations to make faithful disciples to carry on the ministry of Jesus Christ, locally and around the world;
— works in partnership with Church of the Brethren pastors, congregations, districts, and agencies, as well as other denominations and organizations;
— participates in the Annual Conference discernment process and then faithfully implements the will of the delegate body;
— facilitates denominational ministries through a unified structure and vision of shared ministry;
— acts as compassionate employer, calling together gifted staff in a nurturing environment and encouraging excellence among its employees;
— constantly pursues simplicity, clarity, focus, and good stewardship in its structure and functions;
— anticipates and prepares for the future mission of the church and is informed by the strengths of our Brethren heritage.

The process of implementing these objectives was assigned to a "Redesign Committee," with change in programming, decision on location of the headquarters, and redesign to be completed by January 1998.[6]

THE EVANGELICALISM/EVANGELISM THRUST

In part motivated by the issues above, the 1990s have been marked by a growing movement among Brethren that labels itself evangelical. It emerged in most visible form at a hastily called and well attended breakfast meeting at the 1990 Annual Conference, billed as an "exploratory meeting to examine 'network/support' needs among Church of the Brethren evangelicals" by its initiator Terry Hatfield. The early morning meeting intended to "pray for trends in our denomination toward Christ-centered, biblically-based, evangelistic mission in the Anabaptist/Pietist tradition," looking toward the twenty-first century.

A "Statement of Concern" formulated earlier in 1990 by an ad hoc group was distributed to those attending. Also represented were some of those pressing for a new school of evangelical bent, who had publicly deplored the "lack of evangelical training in Bible, leadership, and missions" in the Church of the Brethren.[7] Expressing a clear wish not to create another pressure group in the church, those attending called for means to maintain fellowship for Brethren with evangelical concerns on district and denominational levels. As one means of fulfilling this desire, Hatfield began in the fall of 1990 a publication called *Evangel 21*. An advisory committee to provide counsel to the undertaking was announced in the second issue (Winter 1991); it was later expanded. Names included pastors, district executives, teachers, representatives of ethnic minorities, and one Brethren Church leader. What had begun as a modest newsletter blossomed by the second volume into a slick-paper magazine of more than 36 pages with ambitious subscription goals, which, however, ceased publication after several issues.

Agreeing with the view most sharply articulated in a host of books and articles by Vernard Eller of the University of La Verne, the Brethren evangelicals were convinced that the denomination went off the rails following World War II. In its drive to meet the needs of the world through social action programs, it forgot the foundations of its faith, becoming broadly humanistic and relativistic in its beliefs. The answer to the bewildering diversity of subgroupings and the decline in membership, they said, lies solely in recovery of the church's basis, which is evangelical faith in Jesus Christ as Lord and Savior. A query brought to the 1991 Annual Conference from this direction asked the Church of the Brethren to define the essential nature of the church; it was returned for fear that this could establish a creed, but a statement was accepted that affirmed that "Jesus Christ is the Son of God, the Savior of the world, and the Head of the Church, according to the Scriptures."[8]

The increasingly vocal and at points disruptive tactics of some in the evangelical camp, in particular on the floor of several recent Annual Conferences, have created unease in the minds and hearts of those Brethren advocating tolerance. They charge some evangelicals with personal attacks, threats of separation, and an intolerant spirit foreign to the Brethren character.

In the late 1980s the denomination sought guidance from local congregations on its direction. The result was the "Goals for the 90s." One of the clear goals emerging from this process was more attention to evangelism. It emphasized a recurrent Brethren concern, most recently seen in the 1960s. Driven in part by the eroding numbers on membership rolls, it also reflected a growing concern, felt most keenly by the evangelicals, that long attention to the pressing needs of peoples in this country and abroad had eroded basic attention to the care for the local congregation.

A new church publication, begun in 1983, highlighted the renewed denominational efforts at evangelism. Called *New Beginnings*, it both charted and provided resources for new congregations and revival of established congregations. In 1992 the Annual Conference accepted a "Call to Evangelistic Outreach" with measurable goals. Between 1993 and 1995 congregations were challenged to increase attendance at worship services and Christian education groupings by ten percent each year, adding new members equal to ten percent of average church attendance. This was symbolized by a "Tree of Life" erected at each Annual Conference since 1993; it grew in size as names of new members were placed on leaves attached to it.[9]

To aid in these evangelistic efforts, the Church of the Brethren created a center to provide resources for evangelism and congregational growth. It was launched in 1993 as the Andrew Center and opened its doors on March 1, 1994. It was organized to assist congregations (on a contracted basis) in four areas: resourcing, training, consulting, and networking. It was directed by Paul E. R. Mundey and staffed by full- and part-time consultants. Although initiated by Brethren, its resources were declared open to members of any denomination.[10]

The Andrew Center took over administration of a popular program called the Evangelism Leaders Academy, developed to promote evangelistic efforts. This was a series of well planned regional workshops designed to inspire and train congregational leaders in effective conversion. It began in 1985 with 35 participants. Within six years it had grown to encompass more than 1,200 attenders from American Baptist, (Ashland) Brethren, United Methodist, Presbyterian, United Church of Christ, and Mennonite churches, as well as the Church of the Brethren. Many of the leaders came from other denominations.

The Andrew Center continued an emphasis promoted by a longstanding denominational program, Passing on the Promise. It was developed in the evangelism office of the General Board staff. First tested in the Southern Ohio District in 1986, it was extended to other districts with considerable success. It was designed to integrate the resources of local, district, and national leadership, providing an overall framework but avoiding cut and dried structures. The Brethren Church of Ashland, Ohio, cooperated in some phases of the program.

A study of the program noted that although its focus was evangelism, in many congregations the evangelistic process provided the impetus for new social ministries. The effectiveness of the unique manner in which Brethren at their best have blended social outreach and personal faith was again documented.[11]

Most Brethren engaged actively in evangelistic efforts have distanced themselves from the "church growth" orientation associated with Fuller Theological Seminary. One exception is Brethren pastor C. Wayne Zunkel, who has written prolifically from this perspective. They have characterized Brethren evangelism as "holistic," involving engagement with the world as well as personal conversion and enrichment.[12] At the same time that the evangelical movement and concern for evangelism were exercising the Brethren, this period was notable for a rise in working alliances with longtime confederates, the other Historic Peace Churches.

ALLIANCES: FRIENDS AND MENNONITES

After the controversy over the Consultation on Church Union (COCU) of the later 1960s, the work of the Fraternal Relations Committee, created by and answerable to Annual Conference, was transferred to General Board direction as the Committee on Interchurch Relations (CIR); this move was seen by some as reaction to the decision of the former committee to recommend that the church abstain from full membership in the COCU scheme. A change, however, had been asked for by the Fraternal Relations Committee itself to deal with the "growing concerns in such areas as church unity, faith and order, ecumenical involvements, ecumenical education, and fraternal conversations," specifically in discussions of church merger. Since that time the CIR committee has been active on a variety of fronts.[13]

Most sustained attention was initially given to a deeper relationship with the American Baptist Churches. Intensive Baptist/Brethren conversations after 1960 directed at possible church union issued in 1968 in a document *Principles for a Plan of Union*; when it became clear that neither denomination was ready for actual merger, a less demanding "associated relationship" was agreed upon in 1973. Practical outcomes of this understanding included cooperative relations in theological education (between Bethany Theological Seminary and Northern Baptist Theological Seminary in Oak Brook, Illinois), shared staff in some yoked parishes and districts, and exchange of representatives on national program boards. In 1993 a meeting was made to attempt to further these relationships.

The 1991 Annual Conference, as part of its effort to further the cause of people of color, mandated the CIR to seek a relationship with a black denomination. Conversations were held with the Progressive National Baptist Convention, without any actual covenant being established. The CIR continued the program of sending and receiving representatives to other religious communions. It instituted an annual award for the individual who or congregation that had distinguished itself in ecumenical affairs. M. R. Zigler won the first award.

In a recent development, because of financial pressures, Bethany Theological Seminary was forced to leave its spacious Oak Brook, Illinois, campus and seek partnership with another graduate school of theology. After talking to several seminaries, the board of directors decided to relocate on the campus of Earlham School of Religion (ESR) in Richmond, Indiana, serving the Religious Society of Friends.

The transfer took place in the fall of 1994, with Bethany occupying a newly constructed building next to that of ESR. This had the effect of bringing together two institutions of the Historic Peace Churches. In the course of the realignment, both sides expressed appreciation for new possibilities. Bethany and Earlham, along with Associated Mennonite Biblical Seminaries in Elkhart, Indiana, had already cooperated on peace studies programs over the years. A popular example was a combined peace seminar that involved a field trip to Washington, DC.[14]

A lengthy series of theological conferences arose in part from a significant meeting of members of the three faculties held in 1964 in Richmond, Indiana. These have used the title *Conferences on the Concept of the Believers Church* or, more simply, *Believers Church Conferences*. Faculty members at the Southern Baptist Seminary in Louisville, Kentucky, brought together the Richmond initiative with one developed by Mennonites and Baptists in the Netherlands by calling an elaborate conference at Louisville in June 1967 on the "Concept of the Believers Church." Several hundred professors and church leaders of many denominations, as well as ecumenical observers, heard addresses and discussed all aspects of the issues.

Members of a findings committee prepared a resolution of "Consensus and Commitment," which reads in part, "...as heirs of various Free Church traditions, we profess to have discovered in history and in our present fellowship a common scripturally based heritage, which is relevant to contemporary life and which is developing in churches of other traditions."

Conference-goers had agreed that those in the Believers Churches come together around specific concerns and issues and were thus opposed to bureaucratic arrangements, such as an office, newsletter, or coordinator. The sole concession made to pursue the call to seek to "multiply contacts with one another" was the informal agreement of several attending to serve as a Continuation Committee. If a call were to come for another such conference, this group agreed to give guidance as desired.[15]

To the surprise of many, such calls have continued to come every two or three years until the present. They have often had some connection with the Historic Peace Churches (whose members have made up the largest single grouping of those attending) but have also come from other church bodies as well. Individuals or groups—most often related to academic institutions—have organized self-funding conferences since 1967, asking for and receiving guidance from the informal Continuation Committee, largely given by correspondence. The twelfth conference in the series is scheduled for McMaster Divinity College in October 1996. Following the intent of the original meeting, the themes chosen and discussions at the meetings have sought to engage the broader ecumenical movement. Through the conferences, publications derived from them, and discussion about them, the term *Believers Church* has come into general parlance.[16]

All three of the Historic Peace Churches were involved in a North American-based effort to revitalize their peace testimonies. This came through the New Call to Peacemaking, a cooperative venture since 1976. It was inspired by the renewal-minded Faith and Life Movement within the Friends (1970-74). A series of New Call regional meetings culminated in an important national gathering in Green Lake, Wisconsin, in October 1978. Follow-up national conferences continued for several years, resulting also in several significant publications. New Call cosponsored a major conference on "Church and Peacemaking in the Nuclear Age" at Pasadena, California, with a largely evangelical audience. The peace effort has persisted on a more modest scale under the part-time leadership of John Stoner, formerly of the Mennonite Central Committee.

Brethren worked with other peace churches to draft a statement titled "In God's People the World's Renewal Has Begun," as part of the process leading up to the large WCC-sponsored gathering in Korea, March 1990, focused on "Justice, Peace, and the Integrity of Creation." Mennonites, Brethren, and Friends worked together on a related effort. The result was the publication of *A Declaration of Peace* (1991) written by Douglas Gwyn (Friends), George Hunsinger (Fellowship of Reconciliation), Eugene F. Roop (Brethren), and John Howard Yoder (Mennonite). It grew from a series of theological consultations sponsored by the several denominational agencies charged with peace education and action.

All of these pale, however, in numbers and depth in comparison to the working relationships formed in recent years by the Church of the Brethren with various agencies and constituencies of the Mennonite churches, that is the Mennonite Church and the General Conference Mennonite Church (in the 1990s moving toward some form of union). This ranges from the cooperation of charismatic bodies to financial entities.

The most striking evidence lies in the publication of a shared hymnal, called simply *Hymnal: A Worship Book*. It was released in 1992 by Brethren Press, Faith and Life Press, and the Mennonite Publishing House after a long (and sometimes painful) gestation since 1983, as a cooperative effort of the Church of the Brethren, the Mennonite Church, and the General Conference Mennonite Church.

Nancy Rosenberger Faus chaired the hymnal committee, with original editorial work by Mary Oyer; Rebecca Slough was the managing editor. Slough writes in an introduction, "Our singing reveals much about who we have been and who we are as Anabaptists and Pietists. *Hymnal: A Worship Book* was prepared with the goal of continuing and expanding our singing tradition."

The new hymnal was well received by congregations and critics, selling far more prepublication copies (140,000) than had been expected by its publishers. Related publications are *Hymnal Companion*, written and compiled by Joan Fyock, and *Hymnal Accompaniment Handbook*, edited by Kenneth Nafziger, the hymnal's music editor.

A number of other church programs have seen growing Brethren/Mennonite cooperation. In curricular design, there have been the successful *Foundation Series*, *Jubilee: God's Good News*, and the recently announced *Generation Why*, a curriculum for youth. Churches of the Anabaptist tradition joined in developing a manual (and video) for deacons in their congregations. In physical and mental health care, it is now customary for the relevant groups to meet together, at times under the sponsorship of the Association of Brethren Caregivers (a merger of the Brethren Health Foundation and the Brethren Health and Welfare Association), which maintains an associated relationship with Mennonite Mental Health Services. Brethren and Mennonite retirement homes formed a common association in 1989.

In March 1995, the Brethren Church, the General Conference Mennonite Church, and the Mennonite Church agreed to enter into partnership with the Church of the Brethren's Andrew Center for evangelistic outreach, jointly publishing the journal *Together*. When the denomination decided to establish a foundation as a core for fund raising activities, it chose to work with an already established Mennonite body; a member of the Brethren sits on the board of a Mennonite mutual aid fund. Leaders of the denomination meet regularly with the Council of Moderators and Secretaries of Anabaptist Groups. In 1991 Brethren agreed with other churches "in the Anabaptist tradition" to form a new Anabaptist Deaf Ministries Board. The rapidly growing area of conflict resolution has seen much cooperation between Brethren and Mennonites, with the latter taking the lead in both theory and practice. In Pennsylvania the two churches cooperated for many years in the Keystone Bible Series, providing training for congregational members and ministers.

An expanding line of well-received biblical commentaries, known as the Believers Church Commentary Series, is planned by a joint editorial committee, with representatives from the Brethren Church, Brethren in Christ, Church of the Brethren, General Conference Mennonite Church, Mennonite Brethren, and Mennonite Church; this committee oversees the work of the individual authors. Those published before 1994 by Church of the Brethren authors were *Genesis* by Eugene F. Roop, *Matthew* by Richard B. Gardner, and *Acts* by Chalmer E. Faw.

In the arena of academic research, the most vigorous current enterprise is the Young Center for the Study of Anabaptist and Pietist Groups, an agency of Elizabethtown College; it is directed by Donald B. Kraybill of Mennonite background, now a member of the Church of the Brethren. Since the Center was established in 1989, it has sponsored a series of summer conferences on Anabaptist/Pietist themes; one of the largest and most significant was that in June 1993, which looked at the future of Harold S. Bender's life work, tagged the "Recovery of the Anabaptist Vision." Many of the visiting fellows of the Center have been leading Mennonite and Brethren academics and writers. The numerous publications of the Center staff have often compared Brethren and Mennonite developments, as have lecture series sponsored by the Center.[17]

Although without a center, Bridgewater College's Forum for Religious Studies has planned a number of conferences centered on Anabaptist/Pietist themes. The first, on "Brethren in Transition" in 1992, was cited previously. Another, held in the fall of 1993, dealt with "Anabaptism: A Heritage and its 21st Century Prospects," and was equally attended by Mennonites and Brethren. The latest, on "The Holy Spirit and the Gathered Community," focused on the role of Pietism in the lives of Mennonites and Brethren; it took place at Harrisonburg and Bridgewater, Virginia, in late September 1995. Publications derived from the conferences spread their messages to a wider audience.[18]

Brethren have joined with Mennonites (and the related Brethren in Christ) in peace action. At the 1984 Mennonite World Assembly convened at Amsterdam, a speaker was Ronald J. Sider, a leader in the New Call to Peacemaking movement, founder of Evangelicals for Social Action, and best known for his book *Rich Christians in an Age of Hunger* (1977), which calls Christians to a simple life of sharing. In the Netherlands, Sider challenged his hearers to create teams of peacemakers ready to intrude themselves in areas of conflict to seek reconciliation. Pacifists should risk as much as the military often do, he asserted.

In May 1989, Brethren and Mennonites taken by this concept met in Chicago for a Christian Peacemaker Teams Training/Action Conference. Church of the Brethren peace consultants were involved in early planning but greater engagement has come from individual Brethren, of whom Cliff Kindy of Indiana, Janice Kulp Long of Virginia, and Dale Aukerman of Maryland have been most active. A publication, *Signs of the Times*, informs supporters of its work.

Christian Peacemaker Teams (CPT) composed of Brethren and Mennonites have gone to tension spots in Israeli-occupied Palestine, in Haiti (before and after the engagement that replaced President Aristide in power), and in ghetto areas of Washington, DC, in short-term or longer engagements. In May 1995, CPT along with New Call to Peacemaking called together in Chicago members of Mennonite, Brethren, and Brethren in Christ churches to a Peacemaker Congress.[19]

ALLIANCES: OTHER BRETHREN BODIES

Inspired most directly by M. R. Zigler, the ecumenical orientation of the Brethren has also been focused in recent years on other Brethren bodies. The concerted attempts of the 1930s and 1940s failed, as has been seen, to reunite the Brethren Church (Ashland, Ohio) and the Church of the Brethren, but they elicited some areas of cooperation, as on the mission field in Nigeria. Shared work during wartime in meeting the challenge of the Civilian Public Service program engendered warm friendships, especially between the leading Brethren personage during this period, M. R. Zigler, and his counterparts in other Brethren bodies.

The remembrance of this fellowship stimulated Zigler in the 1960s to seek renewed contact. His aim was not to promote organizational unity but rather to have the Brethren come together simply "to shake hands." He often expressed his view that the restorative practices outlined in Matthew 18 had never been fully employed during the times of strain that produced division. With a small grant from Brethren lay leader W. Newton Long of Baltimore, Zigler began traveling to visit the leadership of the five largest continuing Brethren churches—the Brethren Church, the Church of the Brethren, the Dunkard Brethren, the Grace Brethren, and the Old German Baptist Brethren.

He invited these people to a meeting held at the former home of Peter Nead in Broadway, Virginia, which was also his boyhood home. This building, called the Tunker House, had been restored by Samuel and Pauline Lindsay and served not only as their residence but also as a historical museum. Zigler secured enough commitments to schedule the meeting in June 1973 with speakers from all five church bodies. During some mealtimes, seating was by vocation; at one of these, a gathering of historians and writers, the suggestion arose that it would be good to have another such meeting.

Joseph R. Shultz, president of Ashland Theological Seminary, invited those present to convene at Ashland, Ohio, the following year. This meeting took place and began a series of smaller meetings to investigate shared historical developments. At the third, held at Bethany Theological Seminary in May 1976, Zigler broached the idea of a huge collection of primary sources, to tell the story of all of the churches. That idea met with resistance, but out of the suggestion came the proposal to create and publish *The Brethren Encyclopedia* (1983/84).[20]

The board to accomplish this ambitious project, which was incorporated and won nontaxable status, was composed of members of the five Brethren bodies, serving not as their church's official representatives but in their own names. This informal arrangement was made necessary by the polity of the more conservative groups, who do not organize formally. In addition to publishing the three-volume reference work, they undertook other publications, in particular a monograph series to enable publication of important manuscripts, especially dissertations too technical for mass sale.[21]

By default—for there is no other body containing representatives from the five Brethren bodies—planning for a suggested Brethren World Assembly fell to the encyclopedia board. It cosponsored, along with the Young Center at Elizabethtown College, this unusual event in the summer of 1992. (The date was chosen because it was 250 years after the first known Brethren Yearly Meeting that met not far away.) The assembly brought to the college campus several hundred sisters and brothers, again from all five major Brethren groups, meeting first in smaller academic-type sessions where papers were read (later published), and then in a larger gathering to hear Brethren preaching. Evenings were devoted to talks by representatives of Brethren congregations in Latin America and Africa.[22]

On Earth Peace Assembly

Also inspired by M. R. Zigler was a movement he called On Earth Peace, which held its first assembly in December 1974. He gave credit to W. Newton Long for pressing him to see how the New Windsor center could be used in the cause of peace. As Zigler described it, "One morning at 4 o'clock I recalled Newton Long's concern. Suddenly, the message that came at the birth of Christ, 'On earth peace and goodwill among men,' alerted me. I thought, let the Church of the Brethren implement this message, and search for peace through conferences at New Windsor, Maryland, as a natural thing to do."[23]

In fact, back in 1944 when he had managed to buy the unused campus for the church, he was not thinking solely of its usefulness for the relief effort. Even then he saw its potential as a place of education and renewal along the lines of the Quaker-sponsored Pendle Hill retreat center outside of Philadelphia. The pressure of Brethren Service work and his years in Europe had prevented that concept from taking material form.

Given this vision and who he was, it was but a short time until he was on the road buttonholing old friends and supporters to raise funds for the new project. Within several weeks he had in hand $30,000 worth of pledges. As he thought of those who should come to the conferences, he first reached out to former co-workers in Brethren Service and even earlier to the days of CPS.

In the series of conferences he held at New Windsor, he used some ideas that had been developed in Germany by the lay academies of the German church. These brought together individuals by vocational categories to discuss the implication of the Christian ethic for their workplaces. Zigler brought together farmers, physicians, pastors, veterans, and others to discuss how they could work for peace. His most creative move was to focus on the youth of the church in intensive weekends. This continued as the On Earth Peace Assembly (OEPA).

Although some of his closest advisors urged him to keep OEPA independent, Zigler was eager to maintain a relationship with the Church of the Brethren, which he sought through the General Board in March 1975. This affiliation led to endless complications and even conflict, distressing to those who were working to bring about a more peaceful world. What M. R. Zigler most wanted was the blessing of the church and the assurance that On Earth Peace was considered part of the denominational program. For the Elgin staff, however, this meant that both Zigler and the program would fall under the same management constraints as all other offices and agencies. It took many troubled years until the On Earth Peace program came in 1983 to rest more or less congenially within the framework of the denominational structure. In the fall of 1994 OEPA celebrated 20 years of existence at its New Windsor offices.

A useful program developed jointly by the General Board and OEPA in 1992 was the Ministry of Reconciliation. It was designed to teach members of the Church of the Brethren conflict resolution skills needed in personal, family, church, and societal situations. Beyond that it provided practitioners who are used to help solve conflicts within congregations and in the course of debates at Annual Conferences. It published *Crossroads* three times a year and issued a *Discipleship and Reconciliation Committee Handbook* in 1995 for use by district committees.

One of the initiatives of On Earth Peace was the creation late in 1980 of a peace bookstore at New Windsor. This gradually developed until it evolved into the Peace Place, a bookstore with teaching resources for children, adults, families, and churches in the area of peace education and conflict resolution. It mailed its first catalog in the late spring of 1995.

Members of the Brethren Church participated actively in On Earth Peace activities, some serving on its board. During this same period the Brethren Church also cooperated with the Church of the Brethren in the Passing on the Promise program, as well as with projects such as Disaster Aid. The latter provided volunteers to give immediate as well as long-term aid to residents living in sites struck by natural catastrophes—floods, fires, earthquakes, hurricanes, and tornados. Besides cleanup and reconstruction, Brethren concentrated particularly on distraught and worried children.

OTHER PEACE INITIATIVES

The underlying, and often forthrightly, stated rationale of such movements as On Earth Peace, Brethren Peace Fellowship, and the rest was that the denomination was not doing enough in the area of peace. For part of the post-World War II era, the Church of the Brethren thought it could dispense with direct staff support of the peace cause. For much of the time, however, there were those—such as Wilbur Mullen, Charles Boyer, David Radcliff, and H. Lamar Gibble—assigned to strengthen the Brethren peace witness. They carried on regular peace-related activities, such as draft counseling, peace education, organizing seminars, and the like, in the United States and to some extent abroad.[24]

Other church-related institutions were working on peace as well. It has become well known that Manchester College developed the first undergraduate major in peace studies in 1948; since then two hundred such programs have been launched in American higher education. The concept was first suggested as early as 1927 by the prophetic Dan West when he wrote to Otho Winger urging the Manchester College president to establish a chair in peace studies. Winger was not impressed; in a crusty reply he stated, "My own opinion is that what the Church of the Brethren needs more than convention speeches and professionalized instructions is some practical capable men to present this business where it will count for results. We have talked much. We have done little. We should do more." As recent history has shown, both West's vision and Winger's desire for practical results came to pass.[25]

West himself instituted a course in 1947 called "Bases for Enduring Peace," but the real peace studies emphasis came to Manchester one year later when Gladdys E. Muir joined the faculty. While in residence in 1947 at Pendle Hill on a study leave, Muir sent Manchester's president, Vernon F. Schwalm (Otho Winger's successor), an essay dealing with "The Place of the Brethren Colleges in Preparing Men and Women for Peace Leadership." While clearly pointing out the pressures against the teaching of moral values in colleges, she called for Brethren schools to dare to teach their deepest convictions.

She challenged the myth of objectivity and the related fear of "indoctrination," correctly noting that some form of indoctrination always takes place in education. Pointing out that only a minority of Brethren students enrolled in Brethren schools had taken the conscientious objector position during the war, she remarked dryly, "The record would seem to indicate that the colleges could hardly be charged with indoctrination." She concluded her searching essay with these words:

> Probably if Brethren educators would feel less hesitancy about departing from conventional patterns, often set up by the larger schools, and were willing to experiment along lines which they feel would best meet the needs of

> our generation, they would find that they could trust
> their own religious intuitions and judgment more, and in
> the end the results achieved would merit approval and
> not criticism.

Schwalm liked the proposal so much that he asked Gladdys Muir to join the Manchester faculty and put her plan into action. She did so, although this meant leaving La Verne College where she had taught for 32 years.[26]

Gladdys Muir was born (in 1895), raised, and educated in McPherson, Kansas, where her father taught music at McPherson College. He was also a gifted artist and when he left McPherson in 1915 he took his family to California where he painted landscapes. His daughter was employed at La Verne College to teach Spanish and history, soon concentrating on the latter. She was challenged by the effects of World War I to concentrate on international affairs and studied in Geneva and Edinburgh after completing graduate study at the University of California at Berkeley.

During the 1930s Gladdys Muir was influenced by institutes on international relations sponsored by the Society of Friends. She looked increasingly for renewal to the great saints and seers, especially the mystics of East and West. Among contemporary authors, the Quaker Douglas Steere (a personal friend), the mystic Gerald Heard, and the sociologist Pitirim Sorokin were influential.

At Manchester in her own quiet and personalized way, she influenced hundreds of students both during and after her stimulating and demanding classes. For years she circularized former students with newsletters, complete with reading lists, always including long, personal, handwritten notes. Many of them had entered careers of teaching or social service with a peace orientation. She returned to La Verne College in 1959, where she died in 1967.[27]

If Gladdys Muir and the Peace Institute at Manchester College demonstrated the academic side of West's vision, the practical side came with the striking involvement of Manchester graduates in the Brethren Service empire. This sprang up, as has been shown, from the struggles of the CPS days and the challenges of the immediate postwar era. Though the administrators, M. R. Zigler and W. Harold

Row, were graduates of Bridgewater College, most of the leading BSC figures were associated with Manchester College. M. R. Zigler gave the credit for this outpouring to the assignment he gave to Manchester College in the 1930s to concentrate on peace. This resulted, as already mentioned, in the early peace activities of C. Ray Keim, L. W. Shultz, and especially of Andrew W. Cordier at the United Nations, and the readiness of Manchester graduates to volunteer for BSC assignments.

In later years, other Brethren-related colleges (Bridgewater, Elizabethtown) also developed peace emphases in their curricula, with Juniata College's Peace and Conflict Studies taking a prominent place. Under the guidance of director M. Andrew Murray it has moved to a leading role in the subject area among American higher education. Murray was one of the founders of the Peace Studies Association, has served on its executive committee since 1988, and is co-chair of its Emerging Programs Committee.

The Juniata program was strengthened by the creation of the Baker Institute for Peace and Conflict Studies, funded by Elizabeth Evans Baker and John C. Baker, a distinguished educator and long-time chairman of the Juniata board of trustees. After World War I he worked with the AFSC in France. Another Baker-funded project, the open-air Peace Chapel was dedicated in 1989 and won national attention. It was designed by Maya Lin, the architect for the Vietnam Memorial in Washington, DC, and honors Elizabeth Evans Baker who died in 1990.

The Juniata program took an additional step forward, beginning in 1993, with a series of annual International Seminars on Arms Control and Disarmament, jointly sponsored by the International Association of University Presidents, the Baker Institute, and the United Nations Centre for Disarmament Affairs. This marked the first time that this United Nations agency contracted with an American school.[28]

BRETHREN IDENTITY

In the face of declining membership and rising factionalism, matched with increasing concern for evangelism, it was probably inevitable that many in the Church of the Brethren struggled in the 1980s and 1990s with the issue of identity. Brethren sociologist Carl F. Bowman struck a nerve in a series of articles sketching a profile of the Brethren in 1986. The award-winning series ended with a section titled "Church of the What?"

The identity issue was illustrated by the revived debate about the name of the denomination. Critics of the current name, the Church of the Brethren, come from different corners. Some concerned about growth in membership contended that the "sectarian" name was a handicap to their efforts. Church of the Brethren, they claim, signifies to the public an unknown quantity, perhaps a cult, and certainly one in which women are not valued.

Members of the women's movement had for many years expressed frustration about the name. They called their periodical of worship resources *The Cistern* (1980ff.), referring to the need for a source of fresh and non-sexist material; they added wryly, "If readers also see 'cistern' as a pun on the absence of Sisters in the name of the church,...so be it."[29]

In 1975 a task-force appointed by the Parish Ministries Commission concluded, as part of its larger study on language in the church, that to suggest a new name considered to be more inclusive would not be advisable. They recommended that individuals and groups work to develop congregational awareness that might result later in a changed name.

Standing Committee, replying to numerous requests, appointed a committee in 1992 to study a name change. This action stimulated an outpouring of letters to the *Messenger* magazine, rather evenly balanced between those who found the name Brethren biblical and inclusive in meaning and those who found it limiting; most correspondents expressed strong feelings on the issue. The study committee reported to the Standing Committee of 1993, suggesting no action at that time but rather a process and timetable for addressing the matter of a name change leading up to 2008, the 300th anniversary of the founding of the movement and the 100th anniversary of the acceptance of the present name.

An unofficial group of members of the Church of the Brethren (20 women and one man) announced at the controversial feminist-oriented RE-imagining Conference held in Minneapolis in late 1993 that they were rejecting the old, sexist name and claiming a new one—The Church of Reconciliation. It is likely that the issue will remain before the denomination at least until 2008.[30]

In recent years the General Board and its staff have followed management concepts common to American businesses; it was, therefore, not surprising that its response to the question of Brethren identity was to seek the aid of an outside consulting firm from Georgia. After conducting a number of interviews, arranging "focus groups," and visiting an Annual Conference, the firm's representatives presented a report called the *Review and Reflection Paper* to the October 1994 meeting of the General Board, receiving a generally favorable reaction.

The paper recommended the following phrases to the Brethren for identification: "Another way of living" (to be followed either by the denominational logo or selected scriptures); then "Continuing the work of Jesus. Peacefully. Simply. Together." By late summer 1995 the Media Outreach Committee of the Elgin staff had developed packets of materials based on this "identity line" for use in local congregations. General secretary Donald E. Miller explained their rationale saying, "These media outreach resources present no contrived or imported messages, but a message drawn from within, based on what Brethren profess and instinctively pursue. The resources encourage self-disclosure, not self-promotion."[31]

The Schwarzenau eight in the first decade of the eighteenth century sought their identity through studying the Bible and church history. Leaders of the Church of the Brethren in the last decade of the twentieth century sought to sharpen their sense of identity by hiring outside consultants who listened to focus groups and then fed back in a simple formula what they had heard. For better and worse this can stand as a parable of the Brethren at the end of a century.

EPILOGUE

Given the tenacity of all religious organizations, there is little reason to fear, as some seem to, the immiment demise of the Church of the Brethren. For the reasons detailed above, there is indeed basis for concern about the decline in numbers and the general aging of the membership. Renewal is called for.

Reflection on the course of Brethren history of the last decades suggests that the way forward will follow these directions: 1) continued efforts to balance evangelism and social outreach in a way that will retain present members and attract new ones; 2) intensified cooperation with sister churches of Anabaptist/Pietist orientation; 3) deepened fellowship with other Brethren bodies; and 4) strengthened peace witness and action to serve a world freed from many of the dangers of the Cold War but bedeviled by murderous ethnic hatreds and increasing levels of familial and societal violence.

Creative ventures in peacemaking—understood both in the sense of broader social issues as well as the resolution of personal and family conflicts—provides an arena for activity and service that Brethren seem destined by heritage and aptitude to play. Although surveys indicate that not all members adhere strongly to the official Brethren pronouncements against war (one-third would accept full military service if conscripted), it is significant that two-thirds of the membership support some form of pacifism—from noncompliance with registration or conscription, to alternative service, to noncombatant military service. About two-thirds of Brethren polled said that too much money in the United States national budget is devoted to military purposes.[1]

The challenge is clear. It remains to be seen how Brethren will respond in the rapidly approaching twenty-first century. We recall the haunting wish of the prominent physician Benjamin Rush of Philadelphia, a reformer and signer of the Declaration of Independence, who proposed in 1790 that what the new nation urgently needed was a department of peace, not the customary department of war. The year previously he urged the Pennsylvania legislature to "cherish" the peace churches with "peculiar tenderness" and relieve them from the "absurd and unnecessary militia laws." They should be respected as "repositories of a truth of the gospel, which must spread hereafter over every part of the world."[2]

In the same year, after describing the Brethren, Mennonites, Moravians, and others, he penned a similar appeal:

> Perhaps those German sects of Christians who refuse to bear arms for the shedding of human blood may be preserved by Divine Providence as the center of a circle which shall gradually embrace all nations of the earth in a perpetual treaty of friendship and peace.[3]

Enlarging the circle of peace—here is a vision reclaimed from the past that is worthy for Brethren to pursue in the twenty-first century, recognizing at the same time that the future is not held in human hands but rather in the hands of God.

REFERENCE ABBREVIATIONS

To save space in the endnotes, those references often cited will be given in abbreviated form. Their more complete bibliographical forms are listed here. Those materials published at Elgin, Illinois, had as publisher the Brethren Publishing House (for earlier imprints) and the Brethren Press (for later imprints). Other references are given complete citation upon their first use in a chapter, then cited by short title later.

BB (1964) = Donald F. Durnbaugh and Lawrence W. Shultz, comps., "A Brethren Bibliography," *Brethren Life and Thought* 9 (Winter/Spring, 1964): 3-177.

BE (1983-84) = *The Brethren Encyclopedia*, ed. Donald F. Durnbaugh (Philadelphia/Oak Brook, Ill.: 1983/84), three volumes.

C. F. Bowman, *Brethren Society* (1995) = Carl F. Bowman, *Brethren Society: The Cultural Transformation of a "Peculiar People"* (Baltimore: 1995).

R. D. Bowman, *Brethren and War* (1944) = Rufus D. Bowman, *The Church of the Brethren and War* (Elgin, Ill.: 1944).

S. L. Bowman, *Power and Polity* (1987) = S. Loren Bowman, *Power and Polity Among the Brethren* (Elgin, Ill.: 1987).

BLT = *Brethren Life and Thought* (1955ff.).

Brubaker, *Women's Participation* = Pamela Brubaker, *She Hath Done What She Could: A History of Women's Participation in the Church of the Brethren* (Elgin, Ill.: 1985).

Brumbaugh, *History GBB* = Martin G. Brumbaugh, *A History of the German Baptist Brethren in Europe and America* (Elgin, Ill.:1899).

Chronicon Ephratense (1889) = Lamech and Agrippa [pseud.], *Chronicon Ephratense; A History of the Community of Seventh Day Baptists of Ephrata, Lancaster County, Penn'a.*, trans. J. Max Hark (Lancaster, Pa.: 1889).

Colonial America = Donald F. Durnbaugh, ed., *The Brethren in Colonial America: A Source Book on the Transplantation and Development of the Church of the Brethren in the Eighteenth Century* (Elgin, Ill.: 1967).

Durnbaugh, *Brethren Beginnings* = Donald F. Durnbaugh, *Brethren Beginnings: The Origin of the Church of the Brethren in Early Eighteenth-Century Europe* (Philadelphia: 1992).

Durnbaugh, *Pragmatic Prophet* = Donald F. Durnbaugh, *Pragmatic Prophet: The Life of Michael Robert Zigler* (Elgin, Ill.: 1989).

Eberly, *Complete Writings* (1991) = William R. Eberly, ed., *The Complete Writings of Alexander Mack* (Winona Lake, Ind.: 1991).

European Origins (1958) = Donald F. Durnbaugh, ed., *European Origins of the Brethren: A Source Book on the Beginnings of the Church of the Brethren in the Early Eighteenth Century* (Elgin, Ill.: 1958).

Fitzkee, *Mainstream* (1995) = Donald R. Fitzkee, *Moving Toward the Mainstream: 20th Century Change Among the Brethren of Eastern Pennsylvania* (Intercourse, Pa.: 1995).

Flory, *Flashlights* (1932) = John S. Flory, *Flashlights from History: A Brief Study in Social Development* (Elgin, Ill.: 1932).

GM = *Gospel Messenger* (1883-1965); the name was then changed to *Messenger*.

GV = *The Monthly Gospel-Visitor* (1851-73). Until December 1856 the name was *The Monthly Gospel-Visiter*.

Holsinger, *Tunkers* (1901) = Henry R. Holsinger, *Holsinger's History of the Tunkers and the Brethren Church* (Lathrop, Calif.: 1901).

Industrial America (1985) = Roger E. Sappington, ed., *The Brethren in Industrial America: A Source Book on the Development of the Church of the Brethren, 1865-1915* (Elgin, Ill.: 1985).

Kaylor, *Brumbaugh* (1995) = Earl C. Kaylor, Jr., *Martin Grove Brumbaugh: A Pennsylvanian's Odyssey from Sainted Schoolman to Bedeviled World War I Governor, 1862-1930* (Cranbury, N.J.: 1995 [listed as 1996]).

Kimmel, *Chronicles* (1951) = John M. Kimmel, *Chronicles of the Brethren, Comprising a Concise History of the Brethren or Dunker Church...and the...History of the Old German Baptist Church* (Covington, Ohio: 1951).

Mallott, *Studies* (1954) = Floyd E. Mallott, *Studies in Brethren History* (Elgin, Ill.: 1954).

MQR = *Mennonite Quarterly Review* (1927ff.)

Minutes (1909) = General Mission Board, *Minutes of the Annual Meetings of the Church of the Brethren* (Elgin, Ill.: 1909).

Minutes (OGBB) (1956) = Willis A. Hess and others, eds., *Minutes of the Annual Meetings of the Old German Baptist Brethren from 1778 to 1955 and Appendix...*(Covington, Ohio: 1956).

Minutes (1910-22) = *Minutes of the Annual Meeting of the Church of the Brethren...*(Elgin, Ill.: 1910-22), published annually.

Minutes (1923) = Otho Winger and others, eds., *Revised Minutes of the Annual Meetings of the Church of the Brethren from 1778 to 1922* (Elgin, Ill.: 1923).

Minutes (1946) = H. L. Hartsough and others, eds., *Minutes of the Annual Conferences of the Church of the Brethren, 1923-1944* (Elgin, Ill.: 1946).

Minutes (1956) = Ora W. Garber, ed., *Minutes of the Annual Conferences of the Church of the Brethren, 1945-1954* (Elgin, Ill.: 1956).

Minutes (1965) = Ora W. Garber, ed., *Minutes of the Annual Conferences of the Church of the Brethren, 1955-1964* (Elgin, Ill.: 1965).

Minutes (1970) = William R. Eberly, ed., *Minutes of the Annual Conferences of the Church of the Brethren, 1965-1969* (Elgin, Ill.: 1970).

Minutes (1975) = William R. Eberly, ed., *Minutes of the Annual Conferences of the Church of the Brethren, 1970-1974* (Elgin, Ill.: 1975).

Minutes (1980) = Phyllis Kingery Ruff, ed., *Minutes of the Annual Conferences of the Church of the Brethren, 1975-1979* (Elgin, Ill.: 1980).

Moore, *Pathfinders* (1929) = J[ohn] H. Moore, *Some Brethren Pathfinders* (Elgin, Ill.: 1929).

Moyer, *Missions* (1931) = Elgin S. Moyer, *Missions in the Church of the Brethren: Their Development and Effect Upon the Denomination* (Elgin, Ill.: 1931).

New Nation (1976) = Roger E. Sappington, ed., *The Brethren in the New Nation: A Source Book on the Development of the Church of the Brethren, 1785-1865* (Elgin, Ill.: 1976).

Past and Present (1971) = Donald F. Durnbaugh, ed., *The Church of the Brethren: Past and Present* (Elgin, Ill.: 1971).

Peters, *Foothills* (1990) = Raymond R. Peters, *Foothills to Mountaintops: My Pilgrimage to Wholeness* (Elgin, Ill.: 1990).

Reichmann and Doll, *Contemporaries* = Felix Reichmann and Eugene E. Doll, eds., *Ephrata As Seen by Contemporaries* (Allentown, Pa.: 1953).

Royer, *Thirty-three Years* (1913) = Galen B. Royer, *Thirty-three Years of Missions in the Church of the Brethren* (Elgin, Ill.: 1913).

Sappington, *Social Policy* (1961) = Roger E. Sappington, *Brethren Social Policy, 1908-1958* (Elgin, Ill.: 1961).

Stoffer, *Brethren Doctrines* (1989) = Dale R. Stoffer, *Background and Development of Brethren Doctrines, 1650-1987* (Philadelphia: 1989).

Two Centuries (1908) = D[aniel] L. Miller, ed., *Two Centuries of the Church of the Brethren, Or the Beginnings of the Brotherhood* (Elgin, Ill.: 1908).

Willoughby, *Counting the Cost* (1979) = William G. Willoughby, *Counting the Cost: The Life of Alexander Mack, 1679-1735* (Elgin, Ill.: 1979).

Yesterday and Today (1986) = Donald F. Durnbaugh, ed., *Church of the Brethren: Yesterday and Today* (Elgin, Ill.: 1986).

ENDNOTES

Endnotes used in this book will provide brief orientation, sources of quotations, and recent literature not included in previous works.

Endnotes for the Preface and Acknowledgments: Pages vii-xi
1. Preface or Introduction to *A Short and Plain View of the...Rights and Ordinances of the House of God...Also Ground Searching Questions...* (Columbiana, Ohio: 1860), 23.
2. For information on these and later books see Donald F. Durnbaugh, "Historical Writing," *BE* (1983/84), 610-13. Interestingly, the best study of Brethren historiography was written by a German Mennonite seminarian, Rainer Burkart, "Die Kirche der Brüder (Church of the Brethren, Schwarzenauer Täufer, Neutäufer, Dompelaars, German Baptist Brethren, Dunkers, etc.): Geschichte ihrer Erforschung vom 18. Jahrhundert bis zur Gegenwart," (MATh thesis, Friedrich-Alexander-Universität Erlangen-Nürnberg, 1986).

    The Brethren Encyclopedia contains articles on all phases of Brethren history, life, practices, and thought; great care was taken in its preparation to provide each article with extensive bibliographies. Those wishing to delve further may consult the relevant encyclopedia articles and the extensive bibliography in its third volume.

Endnotes for the Prologue: Page xiii
1. *European Origins* (1958), 120-24. See also the article "Baptism, First," in *BE* (1983/84), 82.
2. Numbers are taken from David B. Barrett, ed., *World Christian Encyclopedia* (Nairobi: 1982), esp. 825. The total number of Brethren and those affiliated with them in 1980 was calculated at 619,068, projected to increase to 675,958 by 1985.

Endnotes for Chapter 1: Pages 1-22
1. The first two chapters are drawn in large part from three previous publications of the author: *Brethren Beginnings* (1992); *European Origins* (1958); and "250 Years—Church of the Brethren (1708-1958)" in *Brethren Adult Quarterly*, ed. A. Stauffer Curry (Elgin, Ill.: 1958), 15ff.
2. The classic description is Kurt von Raumer, *Die Zerstörung der Pfalz von 1689*, 2nd ed. (Bad Neustadt a. d. Saale: 1982).
3. See the discussion in Willoughby, *Counting the Cost* (1979), 14-18.
4. There is a voluminous literature on Anabaptism. Three useful intro-

ductory interpretations are: C. J. Dyck, *An Introduction to Mennonite History*, 3rd ed. (Scottdale, Pa.: 1993); William R. Estep, *The Anabaptist Story*, rev. ed. (Grand Rapids, Mich.: 1975); and J. Denny Weaver, *Becoming Anabaptist* (Scottdale, Pa.: 1987). The most comprehensive scholarly overview is George H. Williams, *The Radical Reformation*, 3rd rev. ed. (Kirksville, Mo.: 1992). For a discussion placing Anabaptism within a larger framework of radical Christianity, see D. F. Durnbaugh, *The Believers' Church: The History and Character of Radical Protestantism*, (Scottdale, Pa.: 1985), originally published (New York/London: 1968).

5. See *European Origins* (1958), 30-31.

6. An accessible introduction to Pietism is Dale W. Brown, *Understanding Pietism* (Grand Rapids, Mich.: 1978). More detail is found in two volumes by F. Ernest Stoeffler, *The Rise of Evangelical Pietism* (Leiden: 1965) and *German Pietism During the Eighteenth Century* (Leiden: 1973). Concise descriptions of the various forms of Pietism are provided in Stoffer, *Brethren Doctrines* (1989), 5-43. An anthology of Pietist literature is given in Peter C. Erb, ed., *Pietists: Selected Writings* (New York: 1983).

A definitive four-volume history of Pietism has begun publication in Germany, edited by Martin Brecht; the first volume is *Geschichte des Pietismus: Der Pietimus vom siebzehnten bis zum frühen achtzehnten Jahrhundert* (Göttingen: 1993); the second is *Geschichte des Pietismus: Der Pietismus des 18. Jahrhunderts* (Göttingen: 1995).

Pietism is placed within a broader context by two recent works: W. R. Ward, *The Protestant Evangelical Awakening* (Cambridge, UK: 1992) and Ted A. Campbell, *The Religion of the Heart* (Columbia, S.C.: 1991).

7. The standard work is Johannes Wallmann, *Philipp Jakob Spener und die Anfänge des Pietismus*, 2nd ed. (Tübingen: 1986); a biography in English is K. James Stein, *Philipp Jakob Spener: Pietist Patriarch* (Chicago: 1986). A recent English translation of Spener's programmatic treatise is *Pia Desideria* (Philadelphia: 1964).

8. Erich Beyreuther has written two helpful biographical works: *August Hermann Francke: Zeuge des Lebendigen Gottes* (Marburg/Lahn: 1956) and *August Hermann Francke und die Anfänge der ökumenischen Bewegung* (Hamburg/Bergstedt: 1957). See also Gary R. Sattler, *God's Glory, Neighbor's Good: A Brief Introduction to the Life and Writings of August Hermann Francke* (Chicago: 1982).

9. On Radical Pietism, see the expert articles by Hans Schneider, "Der radikale Pietismus in der neueren Forschung," *Pietismus und Neuzeit* 8 (1982): 15-42 and 9 (1983): 117-51; "Der radikale Pietismus im 17. Jahrhundert," in Brecht, *Pietismus* (1993), 391-437; and "Der radikale

Pietismus im 18. Jahrhundert," in Brecht, *Pietismus* (1995), 94-179. A comprehensive study of Radical Pietist literature is Hans-Jürgen Schrader, *Literaturproduktion und Büchermarkt des radikalen Pietismus* (Göttingen: 1989). The most complete study in English is C. David Ensign, "Radical German Pietism, c. 1675-c.1760," (PhD diss., Boston University, 1955).

10. The best recent study is Andrew Weeks, *Boehme: An Intellectual Biography of the Seventeenth- Century Philosopher and Mystic* (Albany, N.Y.: 1991).

11. See Peter C. Erb, *Pietists, Protestants, and Mysticism: The Use of Late Medieval Spiritual Texts in the Work of Gottfried Arnold* (Metuchen, N.J./London: 1989) and Jacob Boehme, *The Way to Christ*, ed. Peter C. Erb (New York: 1978).

12. The definitive biography is Heinz Renkewitz, *Hochmann von Hochenau* (1670-1721), rev. ed. (Witten: 1969); this has been translated and published (without footnotes) by William G. Willoughby (Philadelphia: 1993).

13. These activities are described in Durnbaugh, *Brethren Beginnings* (1992), ix, 7-18; translated source documents for the same events are given in *European Origins* (1958), 36-105.

14. Durnbaugh, *Brethren Beginnings* (1992), 7.

15. Information on these Lambsheim residents is found in Heinrich Rembe, *Lambsheim, Die Familien von 1547 bis 1800...: Beiträge zur Bevolkerungsgeschichte der Pfalz, Band 1* (Kaiserslautern: 1971), 63ff.; see in connection with this, Don Yoder, "Emigration Materials from Lambsheim in the Palatinate," *Pennsylvania Folklife* 23 (1973-74): 40-48.

16. See on these developments, Willoughby, *Counting the Cost* (1979), 33-42. A recent book published in Germany describes Mack's involvement but must be used with caution: Gernot G. Lorsong, *Taufe Uns, Alexander: Kurpfälzer Geschichte der Dunker (German Baptist Brethren)* (Karlsruhe: 1990). A basic source for the Mack family of millers has been reissued in an enlarged edition: Hermann Brunn, *Schriesheimer Mühlen* (Schriesheim: [1989]); see also his *Ueberblick über die Entwicklung der Schriesheimer Bevölkerung* (Schriesheim: [n.d.]), printed from a manuscript of 1951.

17. *European Origins* (1958), 72-73.

Endnotes for Chapter 2: Pages 23-50

1. *Studien zur Wirtschafts- und Sozialgeschichte der Grafschaft Sayn-Wittgenstein-Hohenstein* (Marburg/Lahn, 1935).

2. Cited in Geoffrey Rowell, "The Marquis de Marsay: A Quietist in 'Philadelphia,'" *Church History* 41 (1972): 61-77 (65).
3. *European Origins* (1958), 121.
4. *European Origins* (1958), 121.
5. *European Origins* (1958), 111-15.
6. *European Origins* (1958), 115-20 (119). It is republished as "The First Brethren Tract" in Eberly, *Complete Writings* (1991), 9-14, on the assumption that the unknown author was actually Mack.
7. Durnbaugh, *Brethren Beginnings* (1992), 23.
8. *European Origins* (1958), 124-28 (126), 206-10 (209).
9. On Gruber, see D. F. Durnbaugh, "Eberhard Ludwig Gruber and Johann Adam Gruber: A Father and Son as Early Inspirationist Leaders," *Communal Societies* 4 (1984): 150-60. Other Inspirationists also criticized the Brethren, asserting that they over-emphasized outward behavior and neglected the leadings of the spirit: see, for example [Johann Samuel Carl], *Historische Umstände zur Prüfung des Geistes der so genannten Inspirirten und Inspiration* ([n.p.]: 1715).
10. The most recent publication is Eberly, *Complete Writings* (1991), 21-42, taken from *European Origins* (1958), 325-44.
11. Eberly, *Complete Writings* (1991), 43-105, taken from *European Origins* (1958), 344-405.
12. *Chronicon Ephratense* (1889), 2; it was reprinted (New York: 1972).
13. *European Origins* (1958), 151-57 (152); see Matthias Benad, "Toleranz und Oekonomie: Das Patent des Grafen Ernst Casimir von 1712 und die Gründung der Büdinger Vorstadt," *Büdinger Geschichtsblätter* 11 (1983): 11-272, published also in his *Toleranz als Gebot christlicher Obrigkeit: Das Büdinger Patent von 1712* (Hildesheim: 1983).
14. *European Origins* (1958), 160-61.
15. The latest publication of the letter is Eberly, *Complete Writings* (1991), 15-20, taken from *European Origins* (1958), 161, 163-67.
16. See D. F. Durnbaugh, "Peter Becker (1687-1758)," in *Chronik Düdelsheim, 792-1992*, ed. Willi Luh (Düdelsheim: 1991), 116-27.
17. *European Origins* (1958), 180-81 (180).
18. A brief overview of the Inspired, with extensive bibliography, is Hans Schneider, "Inspirationsgemeinden," in *Theologische Realenzyklopädie* 16: 203-06; the most recent monograph is Ulf-Michael Schneider, *Propheten der Goethezeit: Sprache, Literatur und Wirkung der Inspirierten* (Göttingen: 1995). The earlier histories of the Inspired by Gottlieb Scheuner have been published in English translation: *Inspirations-Historie, 1714-1728 and Inspirations-Historie, 1728-1817*, trans. Janet W. Zuber (Amana, Iowa: 1977-78).

See also W. R. Ward, *The Protestant Evangelical Awakening* (Cambridge, U.K.: 1992), 160-73, 183-84, 191-92, and Hillel Schwartz, *The French Prophets* (Berkeley, Calif.: 1980).

19. *European Origins* (1958), 187-88 (188).

20. *European Origins* (1958), 215-16.

21. For detailed information on the Brethren in Krefeld, see the articles by Charlotte Boecken: "Early Brethren in Krefeld, Lists and Documents: Some Supplements to Previous Research," *BLT* 35 (1990): 122-39 and 36 (1991): 102-14; "Die ehemaligen Jülicher Festungshaftlinge Grahe und Henckels als Krefelder Einwohner," *Zeitschrift des Bergischen Geschichtsvereins* 95 (1993): 21-40; and "1716—Zwei Krefelder Namensregister," *Die Heimat* 60 (1989): 187-90. See also Dieter Hangebruch, ed., *Hausshaltsvorstände und Hausbesitzer in Krefeld im 18. Jahrhunderts* (Krefeld: 1993), and Pieter Kriedte, "Äußerer Erfolg und Beginnende Identitätskrise: Die Krefelder Mennoniten im 18. Jahrhundert (1702-1794)," in *Sie kamen als Fremde: Die Mennoniten in Krefeld von den Anfängen bis zur Gegenwart*, ed. Wolfgang Froese (Krefeld: 1995), 61-104, esp. 84-88.

22. Thomas Story, *A Journal of the Life of Thomas Story* (Newcastle/Tyne: 1747); see Durnbaugh, *Brethren Beginnings* (1992), ix-x.

23. [Alexander Mack, Jr.], *Apologie; Oder schriftmässige Verantwortung etlicher Wahrheiten* (Ephrata, Pa.: 1788), 80-81; see also Samuel Smith, *History of the Province of Pennsylvania*, ed. William M. Mervine (Philadelphia: 1913), 182-83 and Durnbaugh, *Brethren Beginnings* (1992), 33.

24. [Alexander Mack, Jr.], *Anhang zum Widerlegten Wiedertäuffer* (Ephrata, Pa.: 1788), 7-12; see also Durnbaugh, *Brethren Beginnings* (1992), 33-34.

25. Ingun Montgomery, "Der Pietismus in Norwegen im 18. Jahrhundert," in *Der Pietismus im achtzehnten Jahrhundert*, eds. Martin Brecht and Klaus Deppermann (Göttingen: 1995), 486-87; Fridtjof Valton, *De Norske Vekkelsers Historie* (Oslo: 1942).

26. *European Origins* (1958), 313-14 (314).

27. "Brethren in Switzerland," *Brethren at Work* (October 28, 1876): [2].

28. Recent portrayals of early Brethren doctrinal convictions are found in Vernard Eller, "Beliefs," in *Past and Present* (1971), 39-51; Dale R. Stoffer, "Beliefs," in *Yesterday and Today* (1986), 43-60; Stoffer, *Brethren Doctrines* (1989), 74-85; C. F. Bowman, *Brethren Society* (1995), 23-50 (26).

29. *European Origins* (1958), 335, 355.

30. *European Origins* (1958), 117, 120.

31. Franklin H. Littell, *The Anabaptist View of the Church: A Study in the Origins of Sectarian Protestantism*, 2nd rev. ed. (Boston: 1958), esp. 79-108

(79); republished as *The Sectarian Origins of Sectarian Protestantism: A Study of the Anabaptist View of the Church* (New York/London: 1964).

32. *European Origins* (1958), 120, 121; emphasis added.
33. *European Origins* (1958), 215-16.
34. *European Origins* (1958), 341.
35. *European Origins* (1958), 118.
36. See the discussion in Peter Brock, *Freedom from Violence: Sectarian Nonresistance from the Middle Ages to the Great War* (Toronto: 1991), 192-93.
37. These are discussed in C. F Bowman, *Brethren Society* (1995), esp. 27-35.

Endnotes for Chapter 3: Pages 51-70

1. *European Origins* (1958), 217.
2. Quoted from an account by Abraham Harley Cassel in R. D. Bowman, *Brethren and War* (1944), 45- 46 (45).
3. Samuel Smith, *History of the Province of Pennsylvania*, ed. William M. Mervine (Philadelphia: 1913), 188-89.
4. The Liebe story is narrated in Durnbaugh, *Brethren Beginnings* (1992), 44-46, based on documents, many of which are given in translated form in *European Origins* (1958), 217-40.
5. Pierre Barthel, "Die 'Lettre Missive' (1717) des Nicolas S. de Treytorrens," *Pietismus und Neuzeit* 11 (1959): 1-39; the author was not aware of the nobleman's connections with the Brethren.
6. *European Origins* (1958), 234-35.
7. Durnbaugh, *Brethren Beginnings* (1992), 46-50; *European Origins* (1958), 240-80. See also Kenneth I. Morse, "In Heart and Conscience Free," *Messenger* (May 1979): 20-21.
8. *European Origins* (1958), 252.
9. *European Origins* (1958), 263, 274. Although not specified, the "mal-treatment" mentioned may be a reference to sexual abuse.
10. *European Origins* (1958), 268.
11. The tricentennial of the arrival of the *Concord* stimulated the publication of new research; among the newer studies are Helmut E. Huelsbergen, "The First Thirteen Families: Another Look at the Religious and Ethnic Background of the Emigrants from Crefeld," *Yearbook of German-American Studies* 18 (1983): 29-40; John Ruth, "A Christian Settlement 'In Antiguam Silvam': The Emigration from Krefeld to Pennsylvania in 1683 and the Mennonite Community of Germantown," *MQR* 47 (1983): 307-31; Guido Rotthoff, "Die Auswanderer von Krefeld nach Pennsylvanien im Jahre 1683," *Die Heimat* (1983): 2-11.
12. Abraham H. Cassel, "Anecdotes of the Brethren," *Brethren's Almanac for*

1871 (Tyrone, Pa.: 1870), 23.

13. *European Origins* (1958), 283.

14. Charlotte Boecken, "The Krefeld Congregation of the Brethren: Some New Archival Finds," *BLT* 37 (1992): 231-36.

15. Durnbaugh, *Brethren Beginnings* (1992), 54.

16. *Chronicon Ephratense* (1889), 1-2; *Geistliche Fama* 1/10 (1733): 86-87.

17. Durnbaugh, *Brethren Beginnings* (1992), 55; the latest study of the Collegiants has no reference to the Brethren: Andrew C. Fix, *Prophecy and Reason: The Dutch Collegiants in the Early Enlightenment* (Princeton, NJ: 1991). The Dutch Collegiants were also involved in the early history of the English Baptists.

18. *European Origins* (1958), 291.

19. *European Origins* (1958), 55.

20. *Colonial America* (167), 605.

21. Smith, *History* (1913), 189-90.

22. Durnbaugh, *Brethren Beginnings* (1992), 59-60.

23. *Colonial America* (1967), 174. There may have been more relationship of the Brethren with the Socinians than thus far discovered. Their main group, the Polish Brethren, were an Anabaptist movement that baptized by immersion. It is known that they had contacts with the Collegiants in the Netherlands. There is, however, no evidence that Brethren accepted an Unitarian view of the Trinity, one of the leading tenets in Polish Brethren belief.

24. Published in English translation in *European Origins* (1958), 310-12 (306-07, 308).

Endnotes for Chapter 4: Pages 71-86

1. A useful resource for this topic is Jean R. Soderlund, ed., *William Penn and the Founding of Pennsylvania, 1680-1684: A Documentary History* (Philadephia: 1983).

2. Recent treatments on Pastorius are John David Weaver, "Francis Daniel Pastorius (1651-c.1720): Early Life in Germany with Glimpses of his Removal to Pennsylvania," (PhD diss., University of California, Davis, 1985); Rüdiger Mack, "Franz Daniel Pastorius—sein Einsatz für die Quaker," *Pietismus und Neuzeit* 15 (1989): 132-71; Marianne S. Wokeck, "Francis Daniel Pastorius," in *Lawmaking and Legislators in Pennsylvania: A Biographical Dictionary. Volume One, 1682-1709* (Philadelphia: 1991), 586-89.

3. The complicated story of German involvement in Pennsylvania politics can be traced in many books; see especially, Dietmar Rothermund, *The*

Layman's Progress: Religious and Political Experience in Colonial Pennsylvania, 1740-1770 (Philadelphia: 1961) and A. G. Roeber, *Palatines, Liberty, and Property: German Lutherans in Colonial British America* (Baltimore: 1993).

4. Frank R. Diffenderfer, *The German Immigration into Pennsylvania Through the Port of Philadelphia from 1700 to 1773. Part II: The Redemptioners* (Lancaster, Pa.: 1900), 33.

5. *Colonial America* (1967), 24-32; *European Origins* (1958), 301-12.

6. *Chronicon Ephratense* (1889), 15.

7. Durnbaugh, *Brethren Beginnings* (1992), 52.

8. *Chronicon Ephratense* (1889), 21-23.

9. *Colonial America* (1967), 62-63.

10. [Anonymous], "Gestalt des Reiches Gottes unter den Deutschen in Amerika," *Evangelisches Magazin* 2 (1813): 22-24 and 3 (1814), 65-69, 129-38 (130-32); see also Martin E. Lodge, "The Crisis of the Churches in the Middle Colonies, 1720-1750," *Pennsylvania Magazine of History and Biography* 94 (1971): 195-220; John B. Frantz, "The Awakening of Religion among the German Settlers in the Middle Colonies," *William and Mary Quarterly*, 3rd series, 33 (1976): 266-68 (274); Sally Schwartz, *"A Mixed Multitude": The Struggle for Toleration in Colonial Pennsylvania* (New York: 1987).

11. *Chronicon Ephratense* (1889), 24-25; *Colonial America* (1967), 66-67.

12. Walter C. Klein, *Johann Conrad Beissel: Mystic and Martinet* (Philadelphia: 1942), 57; Peter C. Erb, ed., *Johann Conrad Beissel and the Ephrata Community: Mystical and Historical Texts* (Lewistown/Queenstown: 1985), 12-13; E. G. Alderfer, *The Ephrata Commune: An Early American Counterculture* (Pittsburgh: 1985), 40. All of these books use the name "Johann," but the birth records list the first name as "Georg."

13. *Chronicon Ephratense* (1889), 26; *Colonial America* (1967), 67-68.

14. Brumbaugh, *History GBB* (1899), 298-317; S. R. Zug et al., *History of the Church of the Brethren in the Eastern District of Pennsylvania* (Lancaster, Pa.: 1915), 325-68.

15. *European Origins* (1958), 296-99; Durnbaugh, *Brethren Beginnings* (1992), 58; R. B. Strassburger and W. J. Hinke, eds., *Pennsylvania German Pioneers* (Norristown, Pa.: 1934), I: 27-30.

16. Willoughby, *Counting the Cost* (1979), 123-43.

17. Robert Ulle, "Materials on Mennonites in Colonial Germantown," *MQR* 57 (1983): 354-87 (381), based on Henry S. Dotterer, "The Church at Market Square," *Perkiomen Region* 2 (June 1899): 39-46.

18. Information on the colonial congregations is found in a number of

places; see, for example: *Colonial America* (1967), 171-231; Mallott, *Studies* (1954), 59-98; and district histories. On the Stony Creek (Glades, Brothersvalley) area, see *The Berlin Area...*, 4th ed. (Berlin, Pa.: 1977); Lois Ann Mast, *The Peter Leibundgutt Journal* (Elverson, Pa.: 1991); and H. Austin Cooper, *Two Centuries of Brothersvalley Church of the Brethren, 1762-1962* (Westminster, Md.: 1962).
19. Morgan Edwards: *Materials Towards a History of the Baptists in Pennsylvania both British and German* (Philadelphia: 1770); *Materials Towards a History of the Baptists in [New] Jersey* (Philadelphia: 1792).
20. Roger E. Sappington, *The Brethren in Virginia* (Harrisonburg, Va.: 1973).
21. Roger E. Sappington, *The Brethren in the Carolinas* ([Kingsport, Tenn.]: [1971]).

Endnotes for Chapter 5: Pages 87-102
1. *Chronicon Ephratense* (1889), 50.
2. *Chronicon Ephratense* (1889), 31.
3. *Chronicon Ephratense* (1889), 36.
4. *Chronicon Ephratense* (1889), 35.
5. *Colonial America* (1967), 74-85.
6. *Colonial America* (1967), 86-89 (88); *Chronicon Ephratense* (1889), 29.
7. *Colonial America* (1967), 90-99.
8. This development is treated fully in Julius F. Sachse, *The German Sectarians of Pennsylvania [1708- 1742; 1742-1800]: A Critical and Legendary History of the Ephrata Cloister and the Dunkers,* 2 vols. (Philadelphia: 1899-1900. Unfortunately it is not dependable in every detail. The work in progress by Jeffrey A. Bach, [working title] "The Voice of the Solitary Turtledove: The Mystical Language of Ephrata," (PhD diss., Duke University), should bring clarification to these problems.
9. Reichmann and Doll, *Contemporaries* (1953), 198.
10. See the discussion in Ernst Benz, "Die protestantische Thebais: Zur Nachwirkung Makarios des Ägypters in Protestantismus des 17. un 18. Jahrhunderts in Europa und Amerika," in *Abhandlung der Geistes- und Sozialwissenschaften Klasse, Jahrgang 1963, Nr. 1* (Wiesbaden: 1983), 101-17. On the attractiveness of the cloister for women, see Patricia U. Bonomi, *Under the Cope of Heaven: Religion, Society, and Politics in Colonial America* (New York: 1986), 109-11.
11. Reichmann and Doll, *Contemporaries* (1953), 190.
12. Reichmann and Doll, *Contemporaries* (1953), 191.
13. Reichmann and Doll, *Contemporaries* (1953), 84.
14. On the life of Müller, see several articles by Leo Schelbert, especially

"From Reformed Preacher in the Palatinate to Pietist Monk in Pennsylvania: The Spiritual Path of Johann Peter Müller (1709-1796)," in *Germany and America: Essays on Problems of International Relations and Immigration*, ed. Hans L. Trefousse (New York: 1980), 139-50.

15. On the Eckerlins, see Klaus Wust, *The Saint-Adventurers of the Virginia Frontier: Southern Outposts of Ephrata* (Edinburg, Va.: 1977).

16. For the struggle between Israel Eckerlin and Conrad Beissel for dominance in the Society, see James E. Ernst, *Ephrata: A History*, ed. John Joseph Stoudt (Allentown, Pa.: 1963), 211-34, 265-82.

17. The most recent study of the martyrology is John S. Oyer and Robert S. Kreider, *Mirror of the Martyrs* (Intercourse, Pa.: 1990). On the labor involved in its production over three years, see *Chronicon Ephratense* (1889), 209-10, 213-14.

    For a listing of the Ephrata imprints, consult Eugene E. Doll and Anneliese M. Funke, eds., *The Ephrata Cloisters: An Annotated Bibliography* (Philadelphia: 1944), 83-126. This can be augmented by K. J. R. Arndt and Reimer C. Eck, eds., *The First Century of German Language Printing in the United States of America*, 2 vols. (Göttingen: 1989).

18. *Chronicon Ephratense* (1889), 173; Alderfer, *Ephrata Commune* (1985), 92.

19. Wust, *Saint-Adventurers* (1977), 15ff.; *Colonial America* (1967), 149-69.

20. *Chronicon Ephratense* (1889), 218ff.; Alderfer, *Ephrata Commune* (1985), 124-25.

21. John Joseph Stoudt, *Pennsylvania German Poetry, 1685-1830* (Allentown, Pa.: 1956), xxii-xxiii, xxx.

22. Guy Hollyday and Christoph Schweitzer, "The Present State of Conrad Beissel/Ephrata Research." *Monatshefte* 68 (1976): 171-78.

23. Donald A. Shelley, *The Fraktur-Writings or Illuminated Manuscripts of the Pennsylvania Germans* (Allentown, Pa.: 1961), 101.

24. Reichmann and Doll, *Contemporaries* (1953), 94; *Colonial America* (1967), 113.

25. Reichmann and Doll, *Contemporaries* (1953), 101-02.

26. *Colonial America* (1967), 121.

27. *Chronicon Ephratense* (1889), 280; Ernst, *History* (1963), 332, 336-38.

28. Reichmann and Doll, *Contemporaries* 1953), 115.

29. *Chronicon Ephratense* (1889), 242ff. See also Charles M. Treher, *Snow Hill Cloister* (Allentown, Pa.: 1968); Freeman Ankrum, *Sidelights of Brethren History* (Elgin, Ill.: 1962), 35-50.

Endnotes for Chapter 6: Pages 103-126

1. *Colonial America* (1967), 122-25 (123-24). J. B. S. had arrived in

Pennsylvania about 1750 as the leader of a dissenting group. Though aided by generous residents, their colony in Lancaster County soon failed. Some of the number returned to Germany. A manuscript written by J. B. S. was published posthumously in Altona, Germany, as *Der durch Europa und Amerika aufmerksame Residende* (1777); it was issued in English translation at Ephrata under the title *Anonimus' Travels through Europe and America* (1793).

2. Noted in the account of the Solingen Brethren, in *European Origins* (1958), 268.

3. *Colonial America* (1967), 124; Richard K. MacMaster, *Land, Piety, Peoplehood: The Establishment of Mennonite Communities in America, 1683-1790* (Scottdale, Pa.: 1985), 147. A study of the impact of Pietism upon German sectarian groups is found in Stephen L. Longenecker, *Piety and Tolerance: Pennsylvania German Religion, 1700-1850* (Metuchen, N.J./London: 1994).

4. *Colonial America* (1967), 186; *Minutes* (1909), 150.

5. The story of the houses used for worship can be followed in George N. Falkenstein, *The German Baptist Brethren or Dunkers* (Lancaster, Pa.: 1900); see also *Colonial America* (1967), 192-231. Of the many articles on Germantown, see especially "A Generous Gift: New Church Edifice for the Brethren in Germantown," *The [Philadelphia] Public Ledger* (Feb. 27, 1896); Martin G. Brumbaugh, "Has an Interesting History: The Oldest German Baptist Brethren (Dunker) Meeting House in America," *The Philadelphian* (June 4, 1898).

6. The publications of Martin G. Brumbaugh helped to make Germantown a place of pilgrimage for Brethren and popularized the use of the phrase "mother congregation." See especially his pioneer *History GBB* (1899), 155-90; *Dedication of Plaque and Monument...* ([n.p.]: 1955).

7. An extensive article on the history of the Pricetown meetinghouse is reprinted in the district history: S. R. Zug and others, *History of the Church of the Brethren in the Eastern District of Pennsylvania* (Lancaster, Pa.: 1915), 476-80. See also Nancy Kettering Frye, "The Meetinghouse Connection: Plain Living in the Gilded Age," *Pennsylvania Folklife* 41 (Winter 1991/92): 50-82 (56-59).

8. Frye, "Meetinghouse," (1991/92), 64-65; "Meetinghouse Revisited," *Messenger* (Nov. 19, 1970): 13- 15; Isaac Clarence Kulp, Jr., "Meetinghouses of Montgomery County," *Bulletin of Historical Society of Montgomery County* 21 (1977): 73-86 (84).

9. Kulp, "Meetinghouses," (1977), 77.

10. R. H. Miller, *The Doctrine of the Brethren Defended, or the Faith and Practice of the Brethren* (Indianapolis, Ind.: 1876), 332-33; the book was republished in a condensed version in 1899 and 1907.

11. *European Origins* (1958), 76.

12. There is an excellent description of Brethren worship services of the nineteenth century in Holsinger, *Tunkers* (1901), 244-48.

13. *Colonial America* (1967), 175.

14. *Colonial America* (1967), 175.

15. *Colonial America* (1967), 127.

16. Two standard biographies are A. J. Lewis, *Zinzendorf, the Ecumenical Pioneer* (Philadelphia: 1962) and John R. Weinlick, *Count Zinzendorf* (New York/Nashville: 1956).

17. *Chronicon Ephratense* (1889), 245. See also the documents in *Colonial America* (1967), 267-320.

18. *Colonial America* (1967), 286.

19. *Colonial America* (1967), 312-15.

20. *Colonial America* (1967), 259-66 (266); S. R. Zug, *Eastern District* (1915), 370-73.

21. *Colonial America* (1967), 463-69 (468); emphasis was added.

22. *European Origins* (1958), 118.

23. *Colonial America* (1967), 238-39, 275.

24. For a general discussion, see Dale W. Brown, "Worship," in *Yesterday and Today* (1986), 61-78; see also Kenneth I. Morse, *Move in Our Midst* (Elgin, Ill.: 1977).

25. For a description of the nineteenth century practice, see Holsinger, *Tunkers* (1901), 249-55. There are many journalistic accounts of love feasts by interested observers.

26. *Colonial America* (1967), 174. Yearly meeting rulings in 1812, 1844, 1850, 1852, and 1860 regulated the Brethren practice of anointing—*Minutes* (1909), 30ff.

27. A thorough study of early hymnody is Hedwig T. Durnbaugh, *The German Hymnody of the Brethren, 1720-1903* (Philadelphia: 1986); a useful bibliographical listing is Donald R. Hinks, *Brethren Hymn Books and Hymnals, 1720-1884* (Gettysburg, Pa.: 1986). These supplant, in part, Nevin W. Fisher, *The History of Brethren Hymnbooks* (Bridgewater, Va.: 1950).

28. *Minutes* (1909), 27. The most complete study is Esther Fern Rupel, *Brethren Dress: A Testimony to Faith* (Philadelphia: 1994). See also Mallott, *Studies* (1954), 245-65.

29. Rupel, *Dress* (1994), 29.

30. Roland L. Howe, *The History of a Church (Dunker), with Comments Featuring the First Church of the Brethren of Philadelphia, Pa., 1813-1943* (Philadelphia: 1943), frontispiece. For material on Keyser, see pages 18-22.

31. *Colonial America* (1967), [opposite page 304].

32. Frances Lichten, "John Landis: 'Author and Artist and Oriental Tourist,'" *Pennsylvania Folklife* 9 (Summer, 1958): 8-17.

33. *Colonial Brethren* (1967), 174, 336. In several studies Don Yoder has emphasized the influence of the Quaker dress on the German sectarians: see, for example, "The Costumes of the Plain People," in *Pennsylvania Dutchman* 4/13 (1953): 6-7; "Men's Costumes Among the Plain People," *Pennsylvania Dutchman* 4/15 (1953): 6-7, 9; "Sectarian Costume Research in the United States," in *Forms Upon the Frontier: Folklike and Folk Arts in the United States*, eds. Austin Fife and others (Logan, Utah: 1969), 41-75. See also Brumbaugh, *History* (1899), 546-48.

Endnotes for Chapter 7: Pages 127-142

1. There is a tremendous literature about the Sauers; a compilation in the late 1980s listed more than 500 books and articles with significant reference to them. A recent survey article is D. F. Durnbaugh, "The Sauer Family: An American Printing Dynasty," *Yearbook of German-American Studies* 23 (1988): 31-40; the most recent book is Stephen L. Longenecker, *The Christopher Sauers: Courageous Printers Who Defended Religious Freedom in Early America* (Elgin, Ill.: 1981).

2. Although often claimed as a Brethren member, the evidence is overwhelming that he never belonged, although very close to them in other ways; see D. F. Durnbaugh, "Was Christopher Sauer a Dunker?" *Pennsylvania Magazine of History and Biography* 93 (1969): 393-91.

3. D. F. Durnbaugh, "Christopher Sauer, Pennsylvania Printer: His Youth in Germany and Later Relationships with Europe," *Pennsylvania Magazine of History and Biography* 82 (1958): 316-40.

4. The latest comment on the origin of Sauer's press is found in Hans-Jürgen Schrader, *Literaturproduktion und Büchermarkt des radikalen Pietismus* (Göttingen: 1989), 223-27. He accepts the older account that the press was sent from Berleburg; see Brumbaugh, *History GBB* (1899), 354, 357.

5. Durnbaugh, "Christopher Sauer," (1958), 329.

6. Edward W. Hocker, "The Founding of the Sower Press," *Germantown History* 2/6 (1938): 137-55 (143-44).

7. The best discussion is William R. Steckel, "Pietist in Colonial Pennsylvania: Christopher Sauer, Printer, 1738-1758," (PhD diss., Stanford University, 1949).

8. Theodore G. Tappert and John W. Doberstein, eds., *The Notebook of a Colonial Clergyman* (Philadelphia: 1959), 30.
9. Tappert and Doberstein, *Notebook* (1959), 114-15.
10. Dietmar Rothermund, *The Layman's Progress: Religious and Political Experience in Colonial Pennsylvania, 1740-1770* (Philadelphia: 1961), 171.
11. Edward W. Hocker, *The Sower Printing House of Colonial Times* (Norristown, Pa.: 1948), 37-38.
12. Durnbaugh, "Christopher Sauer," (1958), 335.
13. *Colonial America* (1967), 380.
14. Hocker, *Printing House* (1948), 66-75.
15. *Colonial America* (1967), 202-06.
16. *BB* (1964), 3-177.
17. Published in English translation in *Colonial America* (1967), 428-47.
18. His poetry is studied in Samuel B. Heckman, *The Religious Poetry of Alexander Mack, Jr.* (Elgin, Ill.: 1912); see also *Colonial America* (1967), 459-63.
19. Published in English translation in *Colonial America* (1967), 469-524.
20. Many of them are published in English translation in *Colonial America* (1967), 224-66; see also Brumbaugh, *History GBB* (1899), 219-26, 228-43, 245-51.
21. Some are published in facsimile and translation in Brumbaugh, *History GBB* (1899), 257-62, 271, 273.
22. See *Colonial America* (1967), 447-59 (453); see also Brumbaugh, *History GBB* (1967), 300-03. Vernard Eller used Frantz's writings extensively in portraying Brethren beliefs in *Kierkegaard and Radical Discipleship: A New Perspective* (Princeton, N.J.: 1968), 80ff.
23. Alexander Mack, *Kurtze und enfältige Vorstellung der äussern, aber doch heiligen Rechten und Ordungen....Zweyte Auflage* (Germantown: 1774); *Eberhard Ludwig Grubers Grund-forschende Fragen....Zweyte Auflage* (Germantown: 1774).
24. On this representative of the third generation of printers, see D. F. Durnbaugh, "Samuel Saur (1767- 1820): German-American Printer and Typefounder," *The Report: A Journal of German-American History* 42 (1993): 65-80 (with a checklist of imprints).
25. See on Frey and his publications, *Colonial America* (1967), 291-302; the recent history citing Frey is Ronald A. Knox, *Enthusiasm: A Chapter in the History of Religion* (Oxford, U.K.: 1950), 408-16.
26. An early biography of Dock was Martin G. Brumbaugh, *The Life and Work of Christopher Dock: America's Pioneer Writer on Education* (Philadelphia: 1908); see also Gerald Studer, *Christopher Dock: The Biography and Writings of Christopher Dock* (Scottdale, Pa.: 1967).

27. John Joseph Stoudt, *Pennsylvania German Poetry, 1685-1830* (Allentown, Pa.: 1956); see also *New Nation* (1976), 444-53.
28. John S. Flory, *Literary Activity of the German Baptist Brethren in the Eighteenth Century* (Elgin, Ill.: 1908), 161.

Endnotes for Chapter 8: Pages 143-164

1. A survey of the early Anabaptist view of coercion is James M. Stayer, *The Anabaptists and the Sword*, rev. ed. (Lawrence, Kans.: 1975). For another analysis, which also traces the development of the position, see Peter Brock, *Freedom from Violence: Sectarian Nonresistance from the Middle Ages to the Great War* (Toronto: 1991). The quotation is from Richard K. MacMaster and others, eds., *Conscience in Crisis: Mennonite and Other Peace Groups in America, 1739-1789: Interpretation and Documents* (Scottdale, Pa.: 1979), 29.
2. *European Origins* (1958), 343.
3. Brock, *Freedom from Violence* (1991), 192-93; Heinz Renkewitz, *Hochmann von Hochenau (1670- 1721)*, 2nd ed. (Witten: 1969), 331; *European Origins* (1958), 76.
4. Jean R. Soderlund, ed., *William Penn and the Founding of Pennsylvania, 1680-1684: A Documentary History* (Philadelphia: 1983), 99; Samuel Smith, *History of the Province of Pennsylvania*, ed. William M. Mervine (Philadelphia: 1913), 180; *Colonial America* (1967), 174.
5. On these developments see MacMaster, *Conscience in Crisis* (1979), 61-83.
6. Klaus Wust, *The Saint-Adventurers of the Virginia Frontier: Southern Outposts of Ephrata* (Edinburg, Va.: 1977).
7. Wust, *Saint-Adventurers* (1977), 37.
8. Wust, *Saint-Adventurers* (1977), 37.
9. See D. F. Durnbaugh, "The Brethren in the Revolution: Neutrals or Tories?" *BLT* 22 (1977): 13-23.
10. *Minutes* (1909), 5-6.
11. Theodore G. Tappert and John W. Doberstein, eds., *The Notebook of a Colonial Clergyman* (Philadelphia: 1959), 198.
12. *Colonial America* (Elgin, Ill.: 1967), 349-51.
13. See the discussion in MacMaster, *Conscience in Crisis* (1979), 213-25; the quotation is from Document 117 (236).
14. Durnbaugh, "Brethren in the Revolution," (1977), 15-16.
15. Durnbaugh, "Brethren in the Revolution," 1977), 16.
16. *Colonial America* (1967), 361-62.
17. *Colonial America* (1967), 389.
18. *Minutes* (1909), 7; *Colonial America* (1967), 365-76.

19. Henry J. Young, "The Treatment of the Loyalists in Pennsylvania," (PhD thesis, Johns Hopkins University, 1955); *Minutes* (1909), 5-6.
20. Documents on the Revolutionary War experiences of Sauer II and III are found in *Colonial America* (1967), 377-423; MacMaster, *Conscience in Crisis* (1979), 204ff..
21. Information on Sauer III is found in James O. Knauss, *Christopher Saur the Third* (Worcester, Mass.: 1931); J. Russell Harper, "Christopher Sower, King's Printer and Loyalist," *New Brunswick Historical Society Collections* 14 (1955): 67-109; *Colonial America* (1967), 386-423.
22. Carl Van Doren, *Secret History of the American Revolution* (New York: 1941), 129-31, 220-23, 430; the quotation is from Knauss, *Saur* (1931), 12.
23. *Colonial America* (1967), 405.
24. *Colonial America* (1967, 408-19 (411).
25. *Colonial America* (1967), 411.
26. *Colonial America* (1967), 413.
27. J. M. Henry, *History of the Church of the Brethren in Maryland* (Elgin, Ill.: 1936), 80-81.
28. On this see: D. F. Durnbaugh, "Religion and Revolution: Options in 1776," *Pennsylvania Mennonite Heritage* 1 (July 1978): 2-9; Van Doren, *Secret History* (1941), 130ff..
29. Published in *Colonial America* (1967), 407-08.
30. MacMaster, *Conscience in Crisis* (1979), 492-99; Dorothy Mackay Quynn, "The Loyalist Plot in Frederick," *Maryland Historical Magazine* 40 (1945): 201-10; Peter G. Yackel, "Criminal Justice and Loyalists in Maryland: *Maryland v. Caspar Frietschie*, 1781," *Maryland Historical Magazine* 73 (1978): 46-63. Persistent oral traditions among Brethren of the area tell of the original sentence being carried out, with mutilated parts of bodies posted at different locations; these stories are accepted by Emmert F. Bittinger, *Allegheny Passage: Churches and Families, West Marva District Church of the Brethren, 1752-1990* (Camden, Maine.: 1990), 220-26, and H. Austin Cooper, *The Church of the Singing Hills* (Hagerstown, Md.: 1988 [1989]), 327-67. Peter Suemans had been a local constable which casts doubt on his Brethren affiliation.
31. *Colonial America* (1967), 401.
32. Sauer's own account of his suffering and questions about it are given in *Colonial America* (1967), 400-405.
33. S. F. Hotchkiss, "Ancient Germantown," *Germantown Telegraph* [n.d.], a clipping in the Historical Society of Pennsylvania.
34. MacMaster, *Conscience in Crisis* (1979), 513-15 (513).
35. An early version of this widely-circulated story was printed by "A

Visiter," in *Pencillings of Ephrata* (Philadelphia: 1856), 18-24 under the heading "The Nobility of Christianity;" on his appeal on behalf of Mennonites, see MacMaster, *Conscience in Crisis* (1979), 508-09.

36. The statement has been published many times; for recent instances, see MacMaster, *Conscience in Crisis* (1979), 266-67; *Colonial America* (1967), 363-65 [illustration across from page 326].

37. On this connection, see D. F. Durnbaugh, "Nineteenth-Century Dunker Views of the River Brethren," *MQR* 67 (1993): 133-51; documents are found in *New Nation* (1976), 112-14.

38. William Duke, *Observations on the Present State of Religion in Maryland* (Baltimore: 1795), 33-34.

Endnotes for Chapter 9: Pages 165-190

1. "Quite a few Mennonites in the 1720s and 1730s were won over by the Dunkers' more aggressively experiential and Pietistic form of Christianity" — Richard K. MacMaster, *Land, Piety, Peoplehood: The Establishment of Mennonite Communities in America, 1683-1790* (Scottdale, Pa.: 1985), 147. On these connections, see D. F. Durnbaugh, "Relationships of the Brethren with the Mennonites and Quakers, 1708-1865," *Church History* 35 (1966): 35-59.

2. *Geistliche Fama* 1/10 (1733): 86-89 (88).

3. *Colonial America* (1967), 286; Johann David Schoepf, *Travels in the Confederation, 1783-1784*, trans. Alfred J. Morrison (Phladelphia: 1911), 1: 122. See on Schoepf, Roger E. Sappington, "Eighteenth-Century Non-Brethren Sources of Brethren History III, *BLT* 2 (Summer 1957): 75-80 (77-79).

4. *Colonial America* (1967), 529.

5. Durnbaugh, "Relationships," (1966), 52; the interchange is briefly discussed in *New Nation* (1976), 131, as preface to the later debate in Virginia.

6. See Don Yoder, "Plain Dutch and Gay Dutch," *Pennsylvania Dutchman* 8/1 (1956): 34-55: "Certain outward influences from the Quaker world penetrated into the German dialect-speaking plain world. The Quaker Meeting house with its two doors, the axis through the short side of the house, its shutters and general resemblance to a Georgian house rather than a church, was copied by Mennonites and Brethren and spread west, south, and north with the Dutch [German] Diaspora" (43).

7. E[manuel] Howitt, *Selections from Letters Written During a Tour Through the United States in the Summer and Autumn of 1819* (Nottingham, U.K.: [1820]), 197-98. This and other contacts are discussed in D. F.

Durnbaugh, "Brethren and Friends in a New Land: A Shared History," *BLT* 39 (1994), 227-40.

8. Robert Sutcliff, *Travels in Some Parts of North America, in the Years 1804, 1805, & 1806* (Philadelphia: 1812); on Sutcliff see Sappington, "Non-Brethren Sources III," *BLT* 2 (Summer 1957): 79- 80.

9. *Memoirs of Samuel M. Janney, Late of Lincoln, Loudon County, Va.: A Minister in the Religious Society of Friends,* 4th ed. (Philadelphia: 1880), 46-47.

10. For documents on the Brethren/Universalist links, see *Colonial America* (1967), 321-39, and *New Nation* (1976), 103-12. The history of Universalism by Russell E. Miller, *The Larger Hope: The First Century of the Universalist Church in America, 1770-1870* (Boston: 1979) has superseded the older work, Richard Eddy, *History of Universalism* (New York: 1894).

11. *European Origins* (1958), 399-400 (399).

12. *Colonial America* (1967), 127, 174.

13. The latest biographical sketch of DeBenneville is in Philip E. Pendleton, *Oley Valley Heritage: The Colonial Years, 1700-1775* (Birdsboro, Pa./Oley, Pa.: 1994), 21, 48, 118; this supplements Albert D. Bell, *The Life and Times of Dr. George de Benneville* (Boston: 1953).

14. *Colonial America* (1967), 325-26.

15. *Colonial America* (1967), 139-40 (140).

16. See *New Nation* (1976), 104-07; *Colonial America* (1967), 327.

17. *Minutes* (1909), 16-18, 20-21, 22-23.

18. See two articles by David B. Eller: "John H. and the Spread of Universalism West," *BLT* 28 (1983): 209-28; "The Pietist Origins of Sectarian Universalism," *The Old Northwest* 2 (1986): 41-64; *Minutes* (1909), 358; J[ames] Q[uinter], "Who Are the Dunkards?: Corrections," *GV* 8 (1858): 240-43 (241).

19. G. Wayman McCarty, "A History of the Universalist Church in the Mid-South," (MA thesis, Mississippi State University, 1964).

20. See on Restorationism, Alfred T. DeGroot, *The Restoration Principle* (St. Louis: 1960); Monroe Hawley, *The Focus of Our Faith: A New Look at the Restoration Principle* (Nashville, Tenn.: 1985); and C. Leonard Allen and Richard T. Hughes, *Discovering Our Roots: The Ancestry of the Churches of Christ* (Abilene, Tex.: 1988).

21. *Minutes* (1909), 45.

22. J[oseph] H[ostetler], "A Restoration to the Ancient Order of Things. No. XI," *The Christian Baptist* 3 (March 1826): 163-67. See also Madison Evans, *Biographical Sketches of the Pioneer Preachers of Indiana* (Philadelphia: 1862),

56-74; C. W. Cauble, *Disciples of Christ in Indiana* (Indianapolis: 1930), 30ff.; Henry K. Shaw, *Hoosier Disciples* (St. Louis: 1966), 21ff.; and, especially, David B. Eller, "Hoosier Brethren and the Origins of the Restoration Movement," *Indiana Magazine of History* 76 (1980): 1-20. Some of these sources are reprinted in *New Nation* (1976), esp. 33-35, 44-46, 114-22.

23. Moses Ryan, "News from the Churches," *The Millennial Harbinger* (December 1842): 560.

24. Eddy, *History* (1894), 39-40.

25. D. R. Lucas, "Sketches of Indiana Pioneers," *The Christian-Evangelist* (March 19, 1903): 229-30; Mary Margaret Kern Garrard, *The Kern Family of Rowan County, North Carolina; Nicholas County, Kentucky; Boone, Clinton, Lawrence, Monroe Counties, Indiana; Hancock County, Illinois, Lee County, Iowa* (Noblesville, Ind.: 1968).

26. C. L. Loos, "News from the Churches," *The Millennial Harbinger* (February 1851): 114-15 (114).

27. *Waynesboro* (Waynesboro: 1900), 209-33; David B. Eller, "Church of Jesus Christ of Latter-Day Saints," *BE* (1983/84), 298; Glenn Willett Clark, "The Woman in the Wilderness: Reflections on a Mormon Family's Dunkard Roots," (McLean, Va.: 1986), on Margaret Harley Randall (1823-1919).

28. Joshua Henry Clark, Diary, copy deposited at the Brethren Historical Library and Archives (BHLA), Elgin, Illinois.

29. Special Collections, MS 19, Juniata College Library, Huntingdon, Pa.

30. *New Nation* (1976), 64.

31. Flory, *Flashlights* (1932), 61.

32. M. M. Eshelman, "Two Sticks. Papers One—Fourteen," *GM* (Feb. 1, 1887—May 10, 1887): 69ff.; *Two Sticks: or, The Lost Tribes of Israel Discovered, The Jew and the Israelite Not the Same* (Mount Morris, Ill.: 1887), 13. On the plan to publish the book, see *GM* (April 5, 1887): 219.

33. Flory, *Flashlights* (1932), 59-62; Stoffer, *Brethren Doctrines* (1989), 160-61. See also: Peter Brock, *Pacifism in the United States* (Princeton, N.J.: 1968), 814-815; Clarence E. May, *Life under Four Flags* (Verona, Va.: 1976), 474-76.

34. Henry Kurtz, "Br. Thurman's Work on the Prophecies," *GV* 13 (1863): 289-90 (290); R. H. Miller, "Inquiry Answered," *Christian Family Companion* 1 (1865): 139ff.

35. William C. Thurman, *The Sealed Book of Daniel Opened: A Book of Reference for Those Who Wish to Examine the "Sure Word of Prophecy"* (Philadelphia: 1864). It was published by John Goodyear, a member of the Philadelphia congregation. Kurtz's apology was published in *GV* 14 (1864): 331.

36. Letters about Thurman are contained in the Special Collections, MS 109, Juniata College Library, Huntingdon, Pennsylvania.

37. Roger E. Sappington, *The Brethren in Virginia* (Harrisonburg: 1973), 190-91; Nancy B. Hess, ed., *The Heartland "Rockingham County"* (Rockingham: [n.d.]), 55-56.

38. Daniel Hays to J. H. Moore, n.d., n.p., J. H. Moore Papers, Brethren Historical Library and Archives, Elgin, Illinois; J. Harman Stover, *GM* (Dec. 25, 1909): 820-21.

39. There are two articles by J[ames] L. Switzer, "Elder Daniel P. Sayler," *GM* (Sept. 25, 1909): 610-11; "More About Elder D. P. Sayler," *GM* (Oct. 9, 1909): 643.

40. *Minutes* (1909): 130.

41. Holsinger, *Tunkers* (1901), 383-85.

42. Mary N. Quinter, *Life and Sermons of Elder James Quinter* (Mount Morris, Ill.: 1891), 44-46; Dennis D. Martin, "Debates," *BE* (1983/84), 370-71.

43. *New Nation* (1976), 165-67; Roger E. Sappington, "Brethren Preaching During the Years Before the Civil War," *BLT* 22 (1977): 89.

44. *Minutes* (1909), 203, 267, 327, 350, 357.

45. Frances Trollope, *The Domestic Manners of the Americans*, 2 vols. (New York: 1901), 1: 149-55; quoted in Milton B. Powell, ed., *The Voluntary Church* (New York: 1967), 69-70.

Endnotes for Chapter 10: Pages 191-218

1. The early discussion of this movement was by J. H. Moore in his book, *Pathfinders* (1929); he also collected manuscripts and memoirs of early settlers. The foundational recent research work in untangling the complicated strands of this story has been reported by David B. Eller in his study "The Brethren in the Western Ohio Valley, 1790-1850: German Baptist Settlement and Frontier Accomodation," (PhD thesis, Miami University, 1976), and in several articles, including; "Hoosier Brethren and the Origins of the Restoration Movement," *Indiana Magazine of History* 86 (1980): 1-20; (with John Scott Davenport), "John H. and the Spread of Universalism West," *BLT* 28 (1983): 209-28; "George Wolfe: Giant In Illinois," *Messenger* (May 1984): 25-27; "The Pietist Origins of Sectarian Universalism," *The Old Northwest* 12 (1986): 41-64; "George Wolfe and the 'Far Western Brethren,'" *Illinois Historical Journal* 60 (1987): 85-100. See also the documents in *New Nation* (1976), 15-102.

2. Roger E. Sappington, *The Brethren in Virginia* (Harrisonburg, Va.: 1973).

3. Roger E. Sappington, *The Brethren in Tennessee and Alabama* ([n.p.]: [1989]).

4. Jesse O. Garst and others, eds., *History of the Church of the Brethren of the*

Southern District of Ohio, 2nd ed., (Dayton, Ohio: 1921); a new history is in preparation.

5. Isaac Leedy, *Leedy Chronicles* ([n.p.]: 1906), 3-4.
6. John S. Eilar, *A Genealogical History of the Eiler, Eilar, Eyler, Iler, Oyler and Associated Families* (Albuquerque, N.M.: 1973), 38-48. Information on American nonresistant immigrants to Ontario is found in Frank H. Epp, *Mennonites in Canada, 1786-1920: The History of a Separate People* (Toronto: 1974), 47-65.
7. David Benedict, *A General History of the Baptist Denomination in America and Other Parts of the World* (Boston: 1833), cited in Roger E. Sappington, "Nineteenth-Century Non-Brethren Sources of Brethren History, I," *BLT* 3 (Winter 1958): 71-74 (73).
8. Mallott, *Studies* (1954), 127; see also John Heckman and J. E. Miller, *Brethren in Northern Illinois and Wisconsin* (Elgin, Ill.: 1941), 129-30.
9. Moore, *Pathfinders* (1929), 15-122; Eller, "Ohio Valley," (1976), 106ff.; Eller, "Wolfe," (1987).
10. Moore, *Pathfinders* (1929), 52.
11. Moore, *Pathfinders* (1929), 119.
12. Elder D. B. Gibson in Moore, *Pathfinders* (1929), 121.
13. The story of the pioneers in Oregon and other West Coast territories is recounted in Gladdys E. Muir, *Settlement of the Brethren on the Pacific Slope* (Elgin, Ill.: 1939).
14. *Pictorial and Biographical Memoirs of Elkhart and St. Joseph Counties...* (Chicago: 1893), 440-42.
15. K. J. R. Arndt, ed, *A Documentary History of the Indiana Decade of the Harmony Society, 1814-1824* (Indianapolis: 1975), 1: 77; W. W. Sweet, ed., *Religion on the American Frontier, The Baptists, 1783- 1820* (New York: 1931), 185-200, reprinted in *New Nation* (1976), 35-42; Edwin S. Gaustad, ed., *A Documentary History of Religion in America to the Civil War* (Grand Rapids, Mich.: 1982), 386-87.
16. *Autobiography of Peter Cartwright*, ed. Charles L. Wallis (New York/Nashville: 1956), 179-80; see also *New Nation* (1976), 59-60.
17. Shirley S. McCord, ed., *Travel Accounts of Indiana, 1679-1961* (Indianapolis: 1970), 161-63.
18. *Minutes* (1909), 45, 51, 55.
19. The latest discussion is in Steve Bowers, *Planting the Faith in a New Land* (Nappanee, Ind.: 1992), 267-68. See also: Flory, *Flashlights* (1932), 37-42; *Minutes* (1909), 103-04, 107, 113.
20. A good general discussion of the Old Order mentality in several Anabaptist groups, including the Brethren, is Beulah Stauffer Hostetler,

"The Formation of the Old Orders," *MQR* 66 (1992): 5-25. On dress specifically, see the thorough exposition in Esther Fern Rupel, *Brethren Dress: A Testimony to Faith* (Philadelphia: 1994), esp. 139-55.
21. *Minutes* (1909), 27.
22. *Minutes* (1909), 40.
23. *Minutes* (1909), 63.
24. *Minutes* (1909), 95.
25. *Minutes* (1909), 245-49; see also Mallott, *Studies* (1954), 173-75.
26. Henry Kurtz, *The Brethren's Encyclopedia, Containing the United Counsels and Conclusions of the Brethren, at Their Annual Meetings* ... (Columbiana, Ohio: 1867), iii-viii.
27. Philip Boyle, "History of the German Baptists, or Brethren," in *History of All the Religious Denominations at Present Existing in the United States*, ed. John Winebrenner (Harrisburg: 1836), 91-94 (93); republished (1848, 1861).

Endnotes for Chapter 11: Pages 219-242
1. The diary of Kline has been preserved, albeit in greatly altered form, in Benjamin Funk, ed., *The Life and Labors of Elder John Kline, the Martyr Missionary* (Elgin, Ill.: 1900); see also the biography, Roger E. Sappington, *Courageous Prophet: Chapters from the Life of John Kline* (Elgin, Ill.: 1964).
2. [Henry Kurtz], "Address to the Reader," *GV* 1 (April 1851): 2.
3. Biographical information is found in D. F. Durnbaugh, "Henry Kurtz: Man of the Book," *Ohio History* 76 (Summer 1967 [1968]): 114-31, 173-76; reprinted, *BLT* 16 (1971): 103-21.
4. W. H. Oda, "Reverend Henry Kurtz and His Communal Plans," *Pennsylvania Dutchman* 3 (April 1, 1952): 1, 5-6; Robert H. Billigmeier and Fred A. Picard, eds., *The Old Land and the New: The Journals of Two Swiss Families in America in the 1820s* (Minneapolis: 1965), 268-69.
5. *Minutes* (1909), 129, 134. See also Mallott, *Studies* (1954), 186-97; William R. Eberly, "The Printing and Publishing Activities of Henry Kurtz, *BLT* 8 (Winter 1963): 19-34. Documents are given in *New Nation* (1976), 419-39.
6. [Henry Kurtz], "Correspondence," *GV* 1 (May supplement 1852): 252.
7. Mary N. Quinter, *Life and Sermons of Elder James Quinter* (Mount Morris, Ill.: 1891), 31-34 (33); see also Moore, *Pathfinders* (1929), 217-34. Holsinger, *Tunkers* (1901), 352-54.
8. Henry R. Holsinger, "Introduction," *The Pious Youth* 1 (1870): 8; see also *New Nation* (1976), 439-44.
9. A useful overview of these changes is provided by one of the partici-

pants: H[enry] B. Brumbaugh, "The Publications of the Church: History of Growth and Development," in *Two Centuries* (1909), 343-60. See also, Glen McFadden, "Dunkers as Publishers," *Schwarzenau* 3 (1941): 5-22; special issue, *GM* (April 5, 1941); special issue, *GM* (June 10, 1951), 2-23; Earl C. Kaylor, Jr., *"The Gospel Messenger*: Literary Legacy of a 19th Century Awakening," *Messenger* (July 1983): 17-19, 24, with added material.

10. Henry B. Brumbaugh, "Forty Years in the Chair," *GM* (June 16, 1951): 10-12, reprinted from Feb. 5, 1910.

11. Special issue, *The Brethren Evangelist* (August 1978), 4-33.

12. *Minutes* (1909), 368.

13. M. R. Zigler, "The Press Was There in 1879," *GM* (June 27, 1964): 18-21.

14. [S. H. Bashor], "Gospel Preacher's Sermon, Headed: War About To Be Declared," *The Progressive Christian* 1 (August 1, 1879); quoted in Zigler, "Press," (1964): 18-21.

15. Auburn A. Boyers, "The Brethren, Annual Conference, and Education: Denominational Publications," *BLT* 16 (1971): 75-87 (78).

16. *A Short and Plain View of the Outward, Yet Sacred Rights and Ordinances of the House of God...Also Ground Searching Questions Answered by the Author Alexander Mack* (Columbiana, Ohio: 1860), [5].

17. James Quinter, "Memoir," in *Short and Plain View* (1860), 7-14 (9), 27.

18. (Columbiana, Ohio: 1867).

19. Kurtz, *Encyclopedia* (1867), iii.

20. Discussed in Roger E. Sappington, *The Brethren in Virginia* (Harrisonburg, Va.: 1973), 54-55, 177- 86, and *New Nation* (1976), 131-64.
    Bibliographical data on the Brethren books may be found *BB*, 3-177; the Mennonite books are listed in Harold S. Bender, *Two Centuries of American Mennonite Literature* (Goshen, Ind.: 1929).

21. Quoted in Sappington, *Virginia* (1976), 179-86.

22. Funk, ed., *Kline* (1900), 457.

23. *BB* (1964), 33.

24. Moore, "Our First Book," *Pathfinders* (1929), 181-89 (85-87). There is a thorough analysis of the content of Nead's doctrinal writings in Stoffer, *Brethren Doctrines* (1989), 114-31.

25. D. F. Durnbaugh, "Vindicator of Primitive Christianity: The Life and Diary of Peter Nead," *BLT* 14 (1969): 196-223; Fred W. Benedict, "The Life and Work of Elder Peter Nead," *BLT* 19 (1974): 63-79.

26. D. F. Durnbaugh, "The German Journalist and the Dunker Love Feast," *Pennsylvania Folklife* 18 (Winter 1968/69): 40-48, reprinted in *New Nation* (1976), 186-92; separately translated in Moritz Busch, *Travels Between the*

Hudson and the Mississippi, 1851-1852, ed. Norman H. Binger (Lexington, Ky.: 1971), 77-87.

27. See Marlin L. Heckman, "Abraham Harley Cassel, Nineteenth-Century Pennsylvania German Book Collector," in *Publications of the Pennsylvania German Society, Volume VII* (Breinigsville, Pa.: 1973), 105-224, and D. F. Durnbaugh, "Abraham Harley Cassel and His Collection," *Pennsylvania History* 26 (1959): 332-47.

28. Marlin L. Heckman, "James Lenox and Abraham Harley Cassel: A Nineteenth-Century Vignette," *American Book Collector* 19 (November/December 1982): 14-22.

29. Samuel W. Pennypacker, ""Abraham H. Cassel," in *Lives of the Eminent Dead and Biographical Sketches of Prominent Living Citizens of the Montgomery County, Pa.,* ed. Moses Auge (Norristown, Pa.: 1879), 324-28 (327-28).

30. Kaylor, *Brumbaugh* (1995), 116-19.

31. Kermon Thomasson, "Abraham Harley Cassel Cut a Wide Swath," *Messenger* (October 1978): 17-21.

Endnotes for Chapter 12: Pages 243-264

1. One of the prime movers in Brethren higher education, S. Z. Sharp, wrote its first full history: *The Educational History of the Church of the Brethren* (Elgin, Ill.: 1923); a recent biographical sketch is John E. Sharp, "Solomon Zook Sharp: Educator and Optimist," *Pennsylvania Mennonite Heritage* 2 (January 1979): 8-11. See also: James H. Lehman, *Beyond Anything Foreseen: A Study of the History of Higher Education in the Church of the Brethren* (Elgin, Ill.: 1976); Robert V. Hanle, "A History of Higher Education among the German Baptist Brethren, 1708-1908," (PhD diss., University of Pennsylvania, 1974); Allen C. Deeter, "Education," in *Yesterday and Today* (1986), 97-117.

   A series of articles by Auburn A. Boyers was based largely on his doctoral study in education, "Changing Conceptions of Education in the Church of the Brethren," (DEd diss., University of Pittsburgh, 1969); they are listed in his later article, "The Brethren's Educational Stance: The Early Roots," *BLT* 35 (1990): 140-47.

2. *European Origins* (Ill.: 1958), 191-93 (191).

3. Lehman, *Beyond Anything Foreseen* (1976), 4.

4. Rufus [pseud.], "On Education," *GV* 5 (1855): 9-12 (10-11).

5. H[enry] K[urtz], "German English School on Gospel Principles," *GV* 6 (1856): 159-60 (159).

6. Auburn A. Boyers, "The Brethren, Annual Conference, and Education," *BLT* 16 (1971): 35-47.

7. D. F. Durnbaugh, "Abraham Harley Cassel and His Collection," *Pennsylvania History* 26 (1959): 332- 47 (334-35).

8. *Minutes* (1909), 12-13.

9. *Minutes* (1909), 67.

10. *Minutes* (1909), 163.

11. Sharp, *Educational History* (1923), 64.

12. Sharp, *Educational History* (1923), 65.

13. [Henry Kurtz], appended to a communication from James Quinter, *GV* 6 (1956): 76.

14. *Minutes* (1909), 54, 138-39.

15. Earl C. Kaylor, Jr., *Truth Sets Free: A Centennial History of Juniata College, 1876-1976* (South Brunswick, N.J.:1976), 30.

16. *The Pilgrim* (April 1, 1873): 103.

17. Sharp, *Educational History* (1923), (Kishacoquillas) 47-52, (New Vienna) 52-56.

18. Sharp, *Educational History* (1923), (Plum Creek) 70-71, (Salem) 59-68; Steve Bowers, *Planting the Faith in a New Land: The History of the Church of the Brethren in Indiana* (Nappanee, Ind.: 1992), 132- 35.

19. Bowers, *Planting the Faith* (1992), 133-34.

20. Sharp, *Educational History* (1923), 67-70; Holsinger, *Tunkers* (1901), 270-71.

21. See Kaylor, *Truth Sets Free* (1976) for the history of Juniata College; Kaylor, *Brumbaugh* (1995), 38- 43.

22. Sharp, *Educational History* (1923), 75-77.

23. Sharp, *Educational History* (1923), 96-103.

24. Sharp, *Educational History,* (1923), 103-21; Moore, *Pathfinders* (1929), 262-70; H. J. Kable and H. G. Kable, *Mount Morris: Past and Present* (Mt. Morris, Ill.: 1900), 95-117.

25. Sharp, *Educational History* (1923), 121-43; Francis F. Wayland, *Bridgewater College: The First Hundred Years, 1880-1980* (Bridgewater, Va.: 1993).

26. Sharp, *Educational History* (1923), 146-68.

27. Sharp, *Educational History* (1923), 183-92; Herbert W. Hogan and Gladdys E. Muir, *The University of La Verne: A Centennial History, 1891-1991* (La Verne, Calif.: 1990).

28. Sharp, *Educational History* (1923), 192-205; Bowers, *Planting the Faith* (1992), 135-42; Tim Jones, *Manchester College: A Century of Progress* (North Manchester, Ind.: 1989). See also Tim Jones, "Otho Winger: He Lived 'With the Throttle Wide Open,'" *Messenger* (October 1989): 24-27.

29. Sharp, *Educational History* (1923), 251-68; Ralph W. Schlosser, *History of Elizabethtown College, 1899-1970* (Elizabethtown, Pa.: 1971). On Beahm, see

Baxter M. Mow, "Elder I. N. H. Beahm," *GM* (Jan. 13, 1951): 11-13, substantially reprinted in *Brethren Builders in Our Century* (Elgin, Ill.: 1952), 11- 16.

30. Kable and Kable, *Mount Morris* (1900), 234, 237.

31. W. Arthur Cable and Homer F. Sanger, eds., *Educational Blue Book and Directory of the Church of the Brethren, 1708-1923* (Elgin, Ill.: [1923]), 12, 449; included in the directory is a useful overview of Brethren education: John S. Flory. "A History of Education in the Church of the Brethren," 21-112.

Endnotes for Chapter 13: Pages 265-290

1. A concise overview is given in Margaret Hope Bacon, *The Quiet Rebels: The Story of the Quakers in America* (Philadelphia: 1985), 94-121.

2. *Colonial America* (1967), 207-08; see also Stephen L. Longenecker, *The Christopher Sauers* (Elgin, Ill.: 1981), 113-18.

3. *Colonial America* (1967), 208-09; *Minutes* (1909), 7-8.

4. *Minutes* (1909), 18-19.

5. Charles B. Dew, *Bond of Iron: Master and Slave at Buffalo Forge* (New York/London: 1994), 15-18,

6. *Minutes* (1909), 30, 31-32, 85.

7. *Minutes* (1909), 142-43.

8. *Minutes* (1909), 219.

9. *Minutes* (1909), 58, 60, 85, 110-11.

10. Stephen B. Oates, *To Purge This Land with Blood: A Biography of John Brown*, 2nd ed. (Amherst, Mass.: 1984), 112-77.

11. Elmer L. Craik, *A History of the Church of the Brethren in Kansas* (McPherson, Kans.: 1922), 22-23; Myrtle Crist Porter, "Brethren Heritage in Kansas," *GM* (Oct. 7, 1961): 6-8, 21.

12. John W. Wayland, *John Kagi and John Brown* (Strasburg, Va.: 1961); Franklin Keagy, *A History of the Kagy Relationship* (Harrisburg, Pa.: 1899), 248-52.

13. Oates, *John Brown* (1984), 274-89; National Park Service, *John Brown's Raid* (1973); Kermon Thomasson, "John Brown's Coming to Conference," *Messenger* (June 1986): 14-18; *New Nation* (1976), 333-34 (Sappington doubts the story of Brown preaching in Dunker churches).

14. Roger E. Sappington, "Brethren Preaching During the Years Before the Civil War, *BLT* 22 (1977): 89-97 (90); the account, taken from an unpublished manuscript, lists the event as taking place in 1858. The date of 1860 is supplied by J[ames] Q[uinter], "Remarks," *GV* (July 1861): 213; the preaching took place prior to the Yearly Meeting held there.

15. Benjamin Funk, ed., *Life and Labors of Elder John Kline, Martyr Missionary* (Elgin, Ill.: 1900), 438; Sappington, *New Nation* (1976), 334.

16. Funk, *John Kline* (1900), 246.
17. Funk, *John Kline* (1900), 213.
18. On this, see two books by Roger E. Sappington: *Courageous Prophet: Chapters from the Life of John Kline* (Elgin, Ill.: 1964), 75-112 and *The Brethren in Viriginia* (Harrisonburg, Va.: 1973), 60-86. See also Klaus Wust, "Elder John Kline," *Virginia Cavalcade* 14 (Autumn 1965): 25-32.
19. C[larence] E. May, *Life Under Four Flags In North River Basin of Virginia* (Verona, Va.: 1976), 383- 84.
20. *New Nation* (1976), 339-40; Sappington, *Virginia* (1973), 68.
21. *Minutes* (1909), 231-32.
22. R. D. Bowman, *Brethren and War* (1944), 121; Peter Brock, *Pacifism in the United States: From the Colonial Era to the First World War* (Princeton, N.J.: 1968), 713-821.
23. *New Nation* (1976), 340; Sappington, *Virginia* (1973), 70.
24. *New Nation* (1976), 345-46; R. D. Bowman, *Brethren and War* (1944), 132-34.
25. R. D. Bowman, *Brethren and War* (1944), 135.
26. *New Nation* (1976), 349; Sappington, *Virginia* (1973), 72-73.
27. *New Nation* (1976), 349-52, 390-91; Sappington, *Virginia* (1973), 76. *New Nation* (1976), 352-61, includes a lengthy excerpt from Thurman's treatise.
28. S. F. Sanger and Daniel Hays, *The Olive Branch of Peace and Good Will to Men* (Elgin, Ill.: 1907), 86-93; reprinted in *New Nation* (1976), 367-68; R. D. Bowman, *Brethren and War* (1944), 144.
29. *New Nation* (1976), 377-86; Funk, *John Kline* (1900), 452-53.
30. Lowell Beachler, "Eller and Beckner," *Fellowship of Brethren Genealogists Newsletter* 22 (Spring 1990): 11-12.
31. Geraldine Plunkett Collection.
32. D. H. Zigler, *History of the Brethren in Virginia* (Elgin, Ill.: 1914), 98; a parallel (original?) version is found in *New Nation* (1976), 348-49. It was not unknown for Brethren drafted into the Confederate army to desert to the Northern side; see the account by Amos B. Peters in Edward L. Peters, *Some Descendants of Michael Peters* (Manson, Wash.: 1993), 29-30.
33. *New Nation* (1976), 370-74; R. D. Bowman, *Brethren and War* (1944), 126.
34. *Minutes* (1909), 218, 227, 231-32, 237; *New Nation* (1976), 397-98.
35. [Henry Kurtz], "The Annual Meeting of 1861—A Suggestion," *GV* 11 (February 1861): 62; "Correspondence," (April 1861): 126; Senior Editor [Henry Kurtz], "Our Next Yearly Meeting," (May 1861): 157. See also *New Nation* (1976), 335-37.
36. *Minutes* (1909), 200; *New Nation* (1976), 337-39.
37. John Kline and six others, "The Editors' Offence," *GV* 11 (July 1861): 212; J[ames] Q[uinter], "Remarks," (July 1861); 212-14.

38. John Kline, "Latest Letter from Brother John Kline," *GV* 14 (August 1864): 238.

39. Sanger and Hays, *Olive Branch* (1907); see also *New Nation* (1976), 388-89.

40. Sanger and Hays, *Olive Branch* (1907), 58-59; J. E. Miller, "Winning the Enemy," *Stories from Brethren Life* (Elgin, Ill.: 1942), 146-48.

41. Jacob Ulrich, "News from Kansas," *GV* 12 (March 1862): 91-92; Craik, *Kansas* (1922), 23-24.

42. Craik, *Kansas* (1922), 24-25; Miller, *Stories* (1942), 140-41.

43. "Communicated," *GV* 13 (June 1863): 191; Sanger and Hays, *Olive Branch* (1907), 96-97; *New Nation* (1976), 387-88. Bowman had led a group (the "Bowman Brethren") that was expelled from the church for a time; it was later reconciled—Flory, *Flashlights* (1932), 49-52.

44. Funk, *John Kline* (1900), 477.

45. Besides the references cited, see also Ray A. Neff, *Valley of the Shadow* (Terre Haute, Ind.: 1987), 150-75, which lists many details about the slaying of Kline, said to be derived from manuscript collections of local families. See also *New Nation* (1976), 393-95.

46. Samuel Horst, *Mennonites in the Confederacy: A Study in Civil War Pacifism* (Scottdale, Pa.: 1967), 106; *New Nation* (1976), 391-93.

47. [Letter], *Christian Family Companion* 1 (1865): 118; see also *New Nation* (1976), 392-93, 400-04.

48. Henry Kyd Douglas, *I Rode with Stonewall* (St. Simons Island, Ga.: 1983), originally published (Chapel Hill, N.C.: 1940), 172-73. Stephen W. Sears, *Landscape Turned Red: The Battle of Antietam* (Boston: 1983).

49. D. P. S[ayler], "Correspondence," *GV* 14 (March 1864): 93-94.

50. Freeman Ankrum, *Sidelights on Brethren History* (Elgin, Ill.: 1962), 117-22; Kermon Thomasson, "Mark Twain and His Dunker Friend," *Messenger* (October 1985): 16-21; "Marking the Spot," *Messenger* (June 1992): 4; Shelley Fisher Fishkin, *Was Huck Black? Mark Twain and African-American Voices* (New York: 1993), 87ff.; Herbert A. Wisbey, Jr., "John T. Lewis, Mark Twain's Friend in Elmira," *Mark Twain Society Bulletin* 7/1 (1984): 1-5.

51. John Hunsaker, "A Brief Synopsis of Br. Hunsaker's Journal," *GV* 14 (May 1864): 156-58; Norman Utz, *History of Piney Creek Church of the Brethren* (Hanover, Pa.: 1080), 27-28.

Endnotes for Chapter 14: Pages 291-316

1. Some of these interpretations are found in John L. Gillin, *The Dunkers: A Sociological Explanation* (New York: 1906), 161-99; Mallott, *Studies* (1954), 149-63; Kerby Lauderdale, "Division among the German Baptist

Brethren," (independent study, Bethany Theological Seminary, 1968); Albert T. Ronk, *History of the Brethren Church: Its Life, Thought, Mission* (Ashland, Ohio: 1968), 125-68; Stoffer, *Brethren Doctrines* (1989), 133-56; C. F. Bowman, *Brethren Society* (1995), 95-131. Documents are provided in *Industrial America* (Elgin, Ill.: 1985), 357-477.

2. The series of meetings and petitions are reviewed in the Old Order publication *The Brethren's Reasons for Producing and Adopting the Resolutions of August 24th [1881]* (1883), reprinted in *Minutes OGBB* (1956), "Appendix"—11-58, and *Industrial America* (1985), 357-403. See also John M. Kimmel, *Chronicles of the Brethren: A Concise History of the Brethren or Dunker Church* (Covington, Ohio: 1951), 168ff.; Holsinger, *Tunkers* (1901), 415-59.

3. *Brethren's Reasons* (1883), 16-19 (19).

4. *Brethren's Reasons* (1883), 24.

5. *Brethren's Reasons* (1883), 24-28; *Minutes* (1909), 378-81.

6. *Minutes* (1909), 381-83; emphasis added.

7. *Brethren's Reasons* (1883), 38-40; Kimmel, *Chronicles* (1951), 240-43.

8. *Brethren's Reasons* (1883), 41-58; Kimmel, *Chronicles* (1951), 244-51, 266-69, 270-74, 281-87.

9. *Minutes: A Consulting Council Held at Pentecost, 1881, in the Meeting-house of the Old Brethren of the Beaver Dam Congregation...June 4 to 6, '81* ([n.p.]: 1881).

10. Lowell H. Beachler, "The First Years—A Beginning," *Old Order Notes* 1 (Summer 1978): 29-38, 2 (Fall 1979): 17-29.

11. Howard Miller, *Record of the Faithful; For the Use of the Brethren: Being a Statistical Record and a Complete Directory of the Brethren Church, for the Years 1881-1882* (Lewisburgh, Pa.: 1882); Fred W. Benedict, "An Overview of the Brethren in 1850; A Difficult Time, 1850-1883," in *Brethren History Lectures* (Ripon, Calif.: 1993), 1-23; Kimmel, *Chronicles* (1951), 270; Mallott, *Studies* (1954), [360].

12. Fred W. Benedict, "The Old Orders and Schisms," *BLT* 19 (1973): 25-32.

13. Holsinger, *Tunkers* (1901), 476-78; *Christian Family Companion* (June 26, 1867): 210. There is no full biography of Holsinger but he is discussed in every history of the modern Brethren movement; for recent assessments, see Robert G. Clouse, "Henry R. Holsinger," *BLT* 24 (1979): 134-41; D. F. Durnbaugh, "Henry R. Holsinger: A Church of the Brethren Perspective," *BLT* 24 (1979): 142-46; Stoffer, *Brethren Doctrines* (1989), 148-56.

14. *Minutes* (1909), 262.

15. Holsinger, *Tunkers* (1901), 473-76.

16. Holsinger, *Tunkers* (1901), 476.

17. Holsinger, *Tunkers* (1901), 478-79.

18. Ronk, *History* (1968), 90-91.

19. Reprinted in Holsinger, *Tunkers* (1901), 489-90.

20. *Minutes* (1909), 368.

21. Holsinger, *Tunkers* (1901), 485-86.

22. Holsinger, *Tunkers* (1901), 3, 473.

23. Holsinger, *Tunkers* (1901), 7-8.

24. Ronk, *History* (1968), 132-33; *The Brethren Evangelist* (May 8, 1895).

25. *Minutes* (1909), 405-06. This trend was noted by Peter G. Mode, *The Frontier Spirit in American Christianity* (New York: 1921), 143-45, who concluded, "Through the same process of centralization the Standing Committee which, at first, was a means whereby trivial and local questions were kept out of the deliberations of the Annual Meeting, became, in the course of a few years an instrument by which discussion was stifled and the will of a small minority imposed upon local churches...."

    C. F. Bowman, *Brethren Society* (1995), 120-26, explains the shift as an attempt to maintain unity by formal means whereas earlier unity had been secured by informal measures. Rather than being a move toward greater rigidity and legalism, it was a way of sustaining significant practices in a changed milieu. "Ironically, rather that denoting withdrawal, this so-called legalism was the cautious Brethren way of moving into the world."

26. *Minutes* (1909), 391-94. The meeting also dealt with Samuel Kinsey, the publisher of the *Vindicator*, but the committee assigned to treat with him was directed to "deal with him as the case demands," not according to his "transgressions." Holsinger was quick to note the discrepancy, writing, "There is a discrimination here that looks to me not exactly fair. You see Brother Kinsey confesses he is trying to maintain the old order and gets into trouble, and I am trying to maintain the gospel order, and get into trouble." —Holsinger, *Tunkers* (1901), 299-300.

27. These events are given in great detail in Holsinger's *Tunkers* (1901), 495-514. See also: *Stenographic Report of the Proceedings of the Committee for the Trial of Eld. H. R. Holsinger, for Insubordination to the Traditions of the Elders* ([Berlin, Pa.]: [1881]).

28. G., "An Ecclesiastical Court Martial," *The Somerset Democrat* (August 24, 1881).

29. Holsinger, *Tunkers* (1901), 508-14; Ronk, *History* (1968), 145-48. The text of "Progressive Unity—Our Principles Defined" was reprinted as a tract; see also Ronk, *History* (1968), 135-41. Bashor's tract, "Where Is Holsinger?" was republished in *Industrial America* (1985), 436-44. A

rebuttal followed, written by S. S. Mohler, *Partial Review of "Where Is Holsinger?"* [1882], also republished in *Industrial America* (1985), 446-50.

30. Holsinger, *Tunkers* (1901), 514-25 (519).

31. Holsinger, *Tunkers* (1901), 527-29; Moore, *Pathfinders* (1929), 325-41; the original report was in *Brethren at Work* (June 6, 1882): 5.

    Members of the Church of the Brethren and the Brethren Church met at the Arnold Grove site in May 1991, to engage in a service of reconciliation: Monty Keeling, "Arnold's Grove Revisited: Healing for the Past, Medicine for the Future," *Evangel* 21 1 (Fall 1991): 8-11.

32. Dale R. Stoffer, "Keeping Pace with the Times," *Messenger* (July 1882): 27-29; the text is given in *Industrial America* (1985), 461-66.

33. Material on the Congregational Brethren and the Leedy Brethren is found in *Industrial America* (1985), 467-76.

34. Special issue of *The Brethren Evangelist* (August 1983): 4-20 (6).

35. Owen Opperman, *A Brief Sketch of the Brethren Generally Known as "Dunkards" of Northern Indiana* (Goshen, Ind.: 1897), 40.

Endnotes for Chapter 15: Pages 317-342

1. Documented in *Industrial America* (1985), 22-41.

2. *GV* 3 (Jan., 1854): 192; (March 1854): 240; (April 1854): 264.

3. *Industrial America* (1985), 198-210; see also Gladdys E. Muir, *Settlement of the Brethren on the Pacific Slope* (Elgin, Ill.: 1939), 108-16, 153-56, 175-218.

4. *Northern Pacific Railway Company. Land Department* (St. Paul, Minn.: 1896).

5. Roy Thompson, "The First Dunker Colony in North Dakota," *Collections of the State Historical Society of North Dakota* 4 (1913): 81-100; reprinted in *Industrial America* (1985), 10-19. See also Herbert Strietzel, *My Father and the First Dunker Colony in North Dakota* (La Verne, Calif.: 1979); Edward L. Peters, *Some Descendants of Michael Peters* (Manson, Wash.: 1993). In the 1970s an effort was being made to preserve the graveyards of the Cando settlement: "Cando: An Ongoing Effort to See that 'The Graves Not Be Forgotten,'" *Messenger* (June 1970): 44-45.

6. H. L. Shute to J. J. Hill, Jan. 6, 1896 and Nov. 28, 1896, St. Paul, Minn.; J. J. Hill to W. J. Newman, Dec. 16, 1896, [n.p.]—Great Northern Railway Papers, File 2950, Minnesota Historical Society.

7. *GM* (September 1896): 624; in *Industrial America* (1985), 199-200; Muir, *Settlement* (1939), 163.

8. Muir, *Settlement* (1949), 164-65.

9. Muir, *Settlement* (1939), 165-66.

10. Brumbaugh, *History GBB* (1899), 532-33.

11. Muir, *Settlement* (1939), 325.

12. *BB* (1964): 169-71.

13. *New Nation* (1976), 406-19; *Industrial America* (1985), 270-83. Nevin W. Fisher, *The History of Brethren Hymnbooks* (Bridgewater, Va.: 1950); Donald R. Hinks, *Brethren Hymn Books and Hymnals, 1720-1884* (Gettysburg, Pa.: 1986); Hedwig T. Durnbaugh, *The German Hymnody of the Brethren, 1720- 1903* (Philadelphia: 1986).

14. *Minutes* (1909), 272.

15. Philip Boyle, "History of the German Baptists, or Brethren," *History of All the Religious Denominations in the United States*, ed. John Winebrenner (Harrisburg, Pa.: 1836), 91-94 (93), republished (1848, 1861); *Minutes* (1909), 72.

16. D. F. Durnbaugh, "The German Journalist and the Dunker Love Feast," *Pennsylvania Folklife* 18 (Winter 1968-69): 40-48; reprinted in *New Nation* (1976), 186-92. Another translation is found in Moritz Busch, *Travels Between the Hudsom and the Mississippi, 1851-1852*, ed. Norman H. Binger (Lexington, Ky.: 1971), 77-87. See also Roger E. Sappington, "Brethren Preaching During the Years Before the Civil War," *BLT* 22 (1977): 89-97.

17. *Industrial America* (1985), 195-97.

18. *Minutes* (1909), 95ff.

19. *Minutes* (1909), 368.

20. *Revised Minutes* (1922), 192-93.

21. Earl C. Kaylor, Jr., *Truth Sets Free: A Centennial History of Juniata College, 1876-1976* (South Brunswick, N.J.: 1976), 36.

22. S. L. Bowman, *Power and Polity* (1987), 55-80; *Industrial America* (1985), 236-45; Mallott, *Studies* (1954), 178-82.

23. Bess Royer Bates, *Life of D. L. Miller* (Elgin, Ill.: 1921).

24. Jesse Helene Winder, "Genius in Everyday Life," (MRE thesis, Bethany Biblical Seminary, 1931); J. M. Henry, *History of the Church of the Brethren in Maryland* (Elgin, Ill.: 1936), 228-29.

25. *Fahrney's Pamphlet for Eighteen Hundred and Eighty (1880)* (Chicago: [1879]).

26. Peter Fahrney, "Dying Rich," *Christian Family Companion* 2 (1866): 261; Jesse P. Weybright, ed., *History of Fahrney Memorial Home for the Aged of Washington County, Maryland* (Hagerstown, Md.: 1946), 10-12; Walter Fahrney and Omer Long, *The Descendants of Dr. Peter Fahrney (1767-1837)* (Frederick, Md.: [1994]).

27. D. F. Durnbaugh, "Hadsell, B. A," *BE* (1983/84), 577.

28. D. F. Durnbaugh, "Studebaker and Stutz: The Evolution of Dunker Entrepreneurs," *Pennsylvania Folklife* 41 (1992): 118-26.

29. *Industrial America* (1985), 185-91; Marvin F. Studebaker, "The

Studebakers of South Bend," *The Studebaker Family in America, 1736-1976* (Tipp City, Ohio: 1976), 74-100.
30. Dave Emmanuel, "Harry Clayton Stutz, 1876-1930," *Automobile Quarterly* 20 (1982): 235-55.

Endnotes for Chapter 16: Pages 343-366
1. D. W. Bebbington, "William Carey," *Eerdmans Handbook to the History of Christianity* (Grand Rapids, Mich.: 1977), 548.
2. Sydney E. Ahlstrom, *A Religious History of the American People* (New Haven: 1972), 423.
3. Standard histories are Royer, *Thirty-three Years* (1913) and Moyer, *Missions* (1931). A recent overview is given in B. Merle Crouse and Karen Spohn Carter, "Mission," in *Yesterday and Today* (1986), 135-59. Documents are presented in *Industrial America* (1985), 115-49. The most recent discussion is in C. F. Bowman, *Brethren Society* (1995), 132-40.
4. Otho Winger, *History and Doctrines of the Church of the Brethren* (Elgin, Ill.: 1919), 117-18.
5. Flory, *Flashlights* (1932), 141-42.
6. Galen B. Royer, "The Development of Missions in the Church," in *Two Centuries* (1909), 273-90 (273).
7. "If we believe that the Scriptures are divinely inspired, we will have no difficulty in accepting the fact that all nations received the gospel....Though the great barriers of time, space, and the then existing means of transportation seem to present insurmountable barriers to the mind of men, let us remember that with God nothing is impossible. Neither is it impossible for mankind to perform that which God commands them to do." —*Doctrinal Treatise: Old German Baptist Brethren*, 3rd ed. (Covington, Ohio: 1970), 57-60 (58-59).
8. *Minutes* (1909), 129, 158-59, 179-80, 187-88, 192-94.
9. *Minutes* (1909), 265-66, 319.
10. *Minutes* (1909), 372-74.
11. J. G. Royer, "The Growth to the Mississippi," *Two Centuries* (1908), 78; B. Merle Crouse, "Mission," in *Yesterday and Today* (1986), 135-42; Moyer, *Missions* (1931), 73-105.
12. Crouse, "Mission," *Yesterday and Today* (1986), 141-42.
13. *The Brethren's Tracts and Pamphlets, Setting forth the Claims of Primitive Christianity. Vol. I* (Dayton, Ohio: 1892); republished (Elgin, Ill.: 1900).
14. Glen E. Norris, "The First Brethren Overseas Mission: Scandinavia," *Messenger* (February 1976): 12- 13.
15. Royer, *Thirty-three Years* (1913), 47-62; *Industrial America* (1985), 116-27;

John Heckman and J. E. Miller, *Brethren in Northern Illinois and Wisconsin* (Elgin, Ill.: 1941), 126-29; Terrie Miller, "The First Brethren Overseas Missionary, Christian Hope," *Messenger* (February 1976): 14-15; Niels Esbensen, "My Life and Work," ([La Verne, Calif.]: [1969]), mimeographed.

16. D. F. Durnbaugh, "Henry Kurtz: Man of the Book," *Ohio History* 76 (1967 [1968]): 114-31, 173-76; Perry A. Klopfenstein, *Marching to Zion: A History of the Apostolic Christian Church of America, 1847- 1982* (Fort Scott, Kans.: 1984), 39-62.

17. J. E. Miller, *Wilbur Stover: Pioneer Missionary* (Elgin, Ill.: 1931); Galen Stover Beery, "Wilbur B. Stover: India Pioneer," *Messenger* (October 1994): 10-14.

18. Wilbur B. Stover to John W. Wayland, Sept. 8, 1911, Ankleshwer, India—John W. Wayland Papers, Swem Library, College of William and Mary, Williamsburg, Virginia.

19. Charles D. Bonsack, "Let Us Follow On," *The Little Brother* (December 1930): [8-9], part of a special memorial issue.

20. Anet D. Satvedi, "History of the Church of the Brethren in India, 1894- 1993," (DMin thesis, Bethany Theological Seminary, 1993).

21. Royer, *Thirty-three Years* (1913), 193ff.; Moyer, *Missions* (1931), 160-68.

22. *GM* (July 24, 1895): 464; Crouse, "Mission," *Yesterday and Today* (1971), 145.

23. *New Church Messenger* (May 21, 1930).

24. Royer, *Thirty-three Years* (1913), 253-60; Moyer, *Missions* (1931), 179-90.

25. Karen S. Carter, "Coming Full Circle," *Messenger* (January 1989): 11-13; Dorotha Winger Fry, "The Saga of China's Pastor Yin," *Messenger* (January 1989): 14, 16; Cheryl Cayford, "Pilgrim on a Perilous Road," *Messenger* (April 1991): 10-11.

26. Moyer, *Missions* (1931), 190-95; Chalmer E. Faw, ed., *Lardin Gabas: A Land, a People, a Church* (Elgin, Ill.: 1973); Nvwa Dzarma Balami, "Fifty Years of the Brethren Mission in Nigeria (1923-1973): A Nigerian Perspective," *BLT* 29 (1984): 102-08, derived from his study (MATh thesis, Bethany Theological Seminary, 1983); special issue, *Messenger* (February 1973).

27. Mary Ann Moyer Kulp, *No Longer Strangers: A Biography of H. Stover Kulp* (Elgin, Ill.: 1968).

28. Crouse, "Mission," *Yesterday and Today* (1986), 131-52; Ralph Detrick, "Ecuador: A Transformed Relationship," *Messenger* (January 1980): 21-23.

29. Paula Wilding, "Making a Difference in a War-Torn Land," *Messenger* (February 1995): 16-17.

Endnotes for Chapter 17: Pages 367-384

1. *Minutes* (1909), 325.
2. *Minutes* (1909), 8, 59. See on this Richard V. Pierard, "The Church of the Brethren and the Temperance Movement," *BLT* 26 (1981): 36-44. Some documents are included in *Industrial America* (1985), 80-87.
3. *Minutes* (1909), 48, 74, 162, 262.
4. *Minutes* (1909), 175, 323, 337; *Minutes OGBB* (1956), 516.
5. *Minutes* (1909), 75, 262.
6. *Minutes* (1909), 431, 436, 497. See the discussion in C. F. Bowman, *Brethren Society* (1995), 176-81, 219-21
7. *Minutes* (1909), 719, 857, 871-72.
8. *Minutes* (1915), 30; see also Sappington, *Social Policy* (1961), 35-37; Pierard, "Temperance," (1981), 41-42.
9. Pierard, "Temperance," (1981), 42-43.
10. Peter Brock, *Pacifism in the United States From the Colonial Era to the First World War* (Princeton, N.J.: 1968), 907-11; *Industrial America* (1985), 51-66, including a large excerpt from Stein's booklet (54- 66).
11. James Y. Heckler, *Ecclesianthem, or A Song of the Brethren, Embracing Their History and Doctrine* (Lansdale, Pa.: 1883), 46-47; Brock, *Pacifism* (1968), 909-10; R. D. Bowman, *Brethren and War* (1944), 159-60.
12. *Minutes* (1909), 67-68, 898; *Minutes* (1911), 7; emphasis added.
13. *Minutes* (1915), 29-30; *Minutes* (1916), 31-32. Eldon E. Barnhart to Holmes S. Falkenstine, Dec. 27, 1912, North Manchester, Ind., Juniata College Archives, RG 3, JC Early Records, Box 3.
14. *Minutes* (1909), 30, 69.
15. This development is surveyed in Mary Sue H. Rosenberger, *Caring: A History of Brethren Homes, 1889-1989* (Elgin, Ill.: 1989).
16. Rosenberger, *Caring* (1989), 19-21.
17. Frank Fisher, "The Philanthropies of the Church: The Church's Care for the Aged and Orphans," in *Two Centuries* (1909), 363-69.
18. Earl C. Kaylor, Jr., *Truth Sets Free: A Centennial History of Juniata College, 1876-1976* (South Brunswick, N.J.: 1977).
19. See Mary Sue Rosenberger, *The Gift of Life: The Brethren and Bethany Hospital* (Elgin, Ill.: 1995); for a broader perspective, see Graydon F. Snyder, *Health and Medicine in the Anabaptist Tradition* (Valley Forge, Pa.: 1995).
20. The most complete study of women in the denomination is Brubaker, *Women's Participation* (1985).
21. Samuel W. Hough, ed., *Christian Newcomer: His Life, Journal and Achievements* (Dayton, Ohio: [n.d].), 31.

22. *New Nation* (1976), 228-39; Brubaker, *Women's Participation* (1985), 137-38, 140-41, 175-78; D. F. Durnbaugh, "She Kept On Preaching," *Messenger* (April 1975): 18-21; "Sarah Major," *Brethren Family Almanac* (Elgin, Ill.: 1909): 13, 15.

23. *Minutes* (1909), 58, 183; Brubaker, *Women's Participation* (1985), 175-78 (177).

24. J. H. Warstler, "Sister Sarah Major," *Brethren's Family Almanac* (Elgin, Ill.: 1901): 5.

25. Brubaker, *Women's Participation* (1985), 72ff.

26. Brubaker, *Women's Participation* (1985), 63ff.

27. Mary Sue H. Rosenberger, "Indigenization of Missions: Closing a Door on the Sisters," *BLT* 37 (1992): 179-93.

28. Brubaker, *Women's Participation* (1985), 95-114.

29. *Minutes* (1909), 111, 163.

30. Marlene Moats Neher, "The Woman Who Wanted to Break Bread," *Messenger* (June 1976): 20-24; Brubaker, *Women's Participation* (1985), 45-60.

31. *Minutes* (1909), 497.

Endnotes for Chapter 18: Pages 385-412

1. *Minutes* (1909), 766, 777-78, 792, 830, 872-73; *Full Report of the Proceedings of the Annual Meeting of the Church of the Brethren Held at Des Moines, Iowa, June 9-11, 1908* (Elgin, Ill.: 1908), 75-96; M. G. Brumbaugh, "The Church in the Fatherland: The Conditions in Germany About 1708," in *Two Centuries* (1908), 17-26 (17). See the discussion in C. F. Bowman, *Brethren Society* (1995), 225-32.

2. C. F. Bowman, *Brethren Society* (1995), esp. 340-81.

3. C. F. Bowman, *Brethren Society* (1995), 342.

4. *Minutes* (1909), 669-70. Discussions of this issue are found in Mallott, *Studies* (1954), 245-65; Esther Fern Rupel, *Brethren Dress: A Testimony to Faith* (Philadelphia: 1994), 139-55; C. F. Bowman, *Brethren Society* (1995), 73ff., 198-210, 238-44; special issue, *BLT* 31 (1986): 132-91.

5. *Minutes* (1909), 895-96; *Minutes* (1911), 4-5; emphasis added. The documents presented in *Industrial America* (1985), 94-113, include some frank personal correspondence regarding the members of the two committees involved in deciding the question.

6. D. W. Kurtz, *An Outline of the Fundamental Doctrines of Faith* (Elgin, Ill.: 1912), 48.

7. Brumbaugh, *History GBB* (1899), 356, emphasis added; for its inception, see Kaylor, *Brumbaugh* (1995), 115-18. On the Masonic issue, see Kaylor,

Brumbaugh (1995), 131-32; Fitzkee, *Mainstream* (1995), 187-88; Jay G. Francis, "Martin Grove Brumbaugh: Part of a Review Before the Lebanon Ministerial Association," *Bible Monitor* (May 5, 1930): 15-19. Francis quoted Brethren leaders D. L. Miller and Christian Bucher as accusing Brumbaugh of perjuring himself on his Masonic membership.

8. From Franklin's *Autobiography*, reprinted in Reichmann and Doll, *Contemporaries* (1953), 138-40.

9. Robert Proud, *The History of Pennsylvania...*(Philadelphia: 1798), 2: 345-48; see Roger E. Sappington, "Eighteenth-Century Non-Brethren Sources of Brethren History, IV," *BLT* 2 (Autumn, 1957): 65-75.

10. D. L. Miller, "The Brethren, or Dunkers," in *The Brethren's Tracts and Pamphlets* (Elgin, Ill.: 1900), 2, 3.

11. Moore, *Pathfinders* (1929), 231; Mary N. Quinter, *Life and Sermons of Elder James Quinter* (Mount Morris, Ill.: 1891), 30.

12. Benjamin Funk, ed., *The Life and Labors of Elder John Kline, The Martyr Missionary* (Elgin, Ill.: 1900), 185-86; see Mallott, *Studies* (1954), 275-76.

13. *Minutes* (1909), 203, 257; Mallott, *Studies* (1954), 275-95.

14. Roland L. Howe, *The History of a Church (Dunker), with Comments Featuring the First Church of the Brethren of Philadelphia, Pa., 1813-1943* (Philadelphia: 1943), 62-68; Mallott, *Studies* (1954), 278- 79.

15. *Minutes* (1909), 870-71.

16. *Minutes* (1915), 1-4; *Minutes* (1917), 1-6. See also C. F. Bowman, *Brethren Society* (1995), 232-38.

17. *Minutes* (1909), 407.

18. For one example of the much-told story, see V[ernon] F. Schwalm, *Albert Cassel Wieand* (Elgin, Ill.: 1960), 37-39.

19. Schwalm, *Wieand* (1960), 49-51.

20. Further information on early years and development is provided in *Golden Jubilee: Bethany Biblical Seminary, 1905-1955* (Chicago: 1955); special issue, *Bethany Biblical Seminary Bulletin* 34 (July/September 1946): 1-22.

21, *Minutes* (1909), 841; *Minutes* (1946), 74-81. Consult the enlightening discussion in C. F. Bowman, *Brethren Society* (1995), 195-98, 263-73.

22. See the discussion in Franklin H. Littell, *The Anabaptist View of the Church: A Study in the Origins of Sectarian Protestantism*, 2nd rev. ed. (Boston: 1958), 46-108.

23. *European Origins* (1958), 121-22.

24. J. E. Pfautz, *Eine Deutsche Concordance über das Neue Testament...Auch eine kurze Anmerkung von allen Religions-Verfassungen in den Vereinigten Staaten von Nord-Amerika* (Ephrata, Pa.: 1878), 199- 201, as translated in

D. F. Durnbagh, "The Descent of Dissent," *BLT* 19 (1974): 125-33 (127); see also John Eby Pfautz, "The Pennsylvania Churches and Sects (1878)," [ed. Don Yoder], *Pennsylvania Folklife* 17/2 (1967/68): 44-46. Pfautz was confused in his chronology on the 1719 and 1729 migrations.

25. Henry Kurtz, "The Church in the Wilderness," *GV* 1 (May 1851): 17-20 through 3 (June 1853), 21- 24; see Durnbaugh, "Descent," (1974): 125-26.

26. D. F. Durnbaugh, "The German Journalist and the Dunker Love Feast," *Pennsylvania Folklife* 18 (Winter 1968/69): 40-48.

27. Elder M. Ellison, *Dunkerism Examined* (Parkersburg, W.V.: 1869), 8-14; rebuttals came from John S. Flory in the *Christian Family Companion* 6 (1870): 456ff., and from Henry R. Holsinger, "An Impudent Elder," *Christian Family Companion* 5 (1870): 586.

28. J[ohn] H. Moore, *The Boy and the Man* (Elgin, Ill.: 1923).

29. H[enry] C. Early, "Elder J. H. Moore," *GM* (Jan. 18, 1936): 12-13; J[ohn] E. Miller, "Elder J. H. Moore as I Knew Him," *GM* (Jan. 11, 1946): 1, 3-5.

30. J. H. Moore, *The New Testament Doctrines* (Elgin, Ill.: 1914), 5.

31. John Dillenberger and Claude Welch, *Protestant Christianity, Interpreted Through Its Development*, 2nd ed. (New York: 1988), 188-200; William R. Hutchison, *The Modernist Impulse in American Protestanism* (Cambridge, Mass.: 1976).

32. Floyd E. Mallott, "Daniel Webster Kurtz," in *Brethren Builders in Our Century* (Elgin, Ill.: 1952), 113-18.

33. Fitzkee, *Mainstream* (1995), 23-29.

34. D. W. Kurtz: *Ideals of the Church of the Brethren* (Elgin, Ill.: [c. 1932]); "Studies in Doctrine," in *Studies in Doctrine and Devotion* (Elgin, Ill.: [1919]), 9-55.

35. Herbert Hogan, "Fundamentalism in the Church of the Brethren, 1900-1931," *BLT* 5 (Winter 1960): 25-36, drawn from his study "The Intellectual Impact of the Twentieth Century on the Church of the Brethren," (PhD diss., Claremont College Graduate School, 1958).

36. This bitter controversy is well delineated in Stoffer, *Brethren Doctrines* (1989), 215-31; an overview by one of the protagonists is Albert T. Ronk, *History of the Brethren Church* (Ashland, Ohio: 1968), 395- 447. A professor at the Grace Brethren seminary at Winona Lake, Indiana, John C. Whitcomb, Jr., became a key figure in the "Creation Science" controversy. See Ronald L. Numbers, *The Creationists* (New York: 1992), 184-212; Christopher P. Toumey, *God's Own Scientists: Creationists in a Secular World* (New Brunswick, N.J.: 1994), 31ff.; and George E. Webb, *The Evolution Controversy in America* (Lexington, Ky.: 1994), 159-60. A member of the Church of the Brethren, William J. Tinkle, was also prominent

in the creationist controversy.

37. Dillenberger and Welch, *Protestant Christianity* (1988), 203-08 (205); George M. Marsden, *Fundamentalism and American Culture: The Shaping of American Evangelicalism, 1870-1925* (New York: 1980).

38. Earl C. Kaylor, Jr., *Out of the Wilderness, 1780-1980* (New York: 1981), 266-76. Snider was offended by Kaylor's assessment and wrote a long rebuttal of more than 100 pages, which he placed in the denominational archives in Elgin, Illinois.

39. Tobias F. Henry, "Charles Calvert Ellis, 1874-1950," *Builders* (1952), 65-70.

40. Kaylor, *Wilderness* (1981), 256-65 (262).

41. C. C. Ellis to Rev. Clarence H. Benson, June 17, 1933, Huntingdon, Pa.; C. C. Ellis to Grant Mahan, Feb. 4, 1943, Huntingdon, Pa.—Juniata College Archives, RG 4, President's Papers, Boxes 14, 16.

42. Charles C. Ellis, *Juniata College: The History of Seventy Years, 1876-1946* (Elgin, Ill.: 1947), 68-69.

43. *Full Report of the Proceedings of the Annual Conference of the Church of the Brethren Held at Calgary, Alberta, Canada, June 14 to 20, 1923* (Elgin, Ill.: 1923), 28-31; D. F. Durnbaugh, "Brethren and the Authority of Scripture," *BLT* 13 (1968): 170-83; C. F. Bowman, *Brethren Society* (1995), 186-87. The revision of the card was more conservatively worded than the original text, and could be read in a fundamentalistic way.

Endnotes for Chapter 19: Pages 413-436

1. Minnie S. Buckingham, ed., *Church of the Brethren in Southern Illinois* (Elgin, Ill.: 1950), 213-14, 326-27; Mallott, *Studies* (1954), 279; J. M. Henry, "Diary—Peace Work," *GM* (Nov. 21, 1925); Bob Wilson, "Editorial: God's Innocent," *Prairie Publications* (May 7, 1964); [campaign pamphlet], *The Man We Need in Congress* (Bethany, Ill.: 1924).

2. *Minutes* (1915), 29-30; *Minutes* (1916), 31-32.

3. James C. Juhnke, *Vision, Doctrine, War: Mennonite Identity and Organization in America, 1890-1930* (Scottdale, Pa.: 1989), 208-29; on the anthem incident, see his article, "Mob Violence and Kansas Mennonites in 1918," *Kansas Historical Quarterly* 43 (1977): 334-50, esp. 341, 343.

4. A basic study is R. D. Bowman, *Brethren and War* (1944), 169-233. See also Sappington, *Social Policy* (1961), 39-46; Albert N. Keim and Grant M. Stoltzfus, *The Politics of Conscience: The Historic Peace Churches and America at War, 1917-1955* (Scottdale, Pa.: 1988), 32-55.

5. Charles Chatfield, *For Peace and Justice: Pacifism in America, 1914-1941* (Knoxville, Tenn.: 1971), 72-73, 82; Juhnke, *Vision, Doctrine, War* (1989),

230, 232; Paul Comly French, *We Won't Murder* (New York: 1940), 62-64. The Keppel comment is taken from his communication to the Secretary of War, June 13, 1919, in [Col. J. S. Easby-Smith], *Statement Concerning the Treatment of Conscientious Objectors in the Army* (Washington, D.C.: 1919), 9.

6. Kaylor, *Brumbaugh* (1995), 325.

7. "Thousands at Walnut Grove Church Event," *[Johnstown] Daily Tribune* (May 1, 1916): 8.

8. Kaylor, *Brumbaugh* (1995), 288ff.; C. C. Ellis, "Contribution of Dr. M. G. Brumbaugh to the Church of the Brethren," *GM* (July 12, 1930): 434-35; C. F. Bowman, *Brethren Society* (1995), 245-51; Fitzkee, *Mainstream* (1995), 184-89.

9. Kaylor, *Brumbaugh* (1995), 322-23.

10. Stephen M. Kohn, *American Political Prisoners: Prosecution under the Espionage and Sedition Acts* (Westport, Conn.: 1994), 183. Much of the correspondence of Maurice Hess has been published as "The Hess Letters," [ed. Fred W. Benedict], *Old Order Notes* 6 (Autumn 1982): 7-32, extending to 12 (Summer 1993): 7-43, with brief description of letters not printed in full. His statement at the court martial is found in 11 (Spring 1990): 51-53. See also Norman Thomas, *Is Conscience a Crime?* (New York: 1927), 25-26, originally published as *Conscientious Objection in America* (New York: 1923); R. D. Bowman, *Brethren and War* (1944), 227-28; *BE* (1983-84), 1371.

11. [Fred W. Benedict, ed.], "The Hess Letters," *Old Order Notes* 12 (Summer 1993): 7-43 (13-14, 28).

12. J. D. Mininger, *Religious C.O.'s Imprisoned at the U. S. Disciplinary Barracks, Ft. Leavenworth, Kansas* (Kansas City, Kans.: 1919); Nicholas C. Polos, "A Historian's Vignette of Jesse Christian Brandt: A Christian Gentleman of La Verne," *BLT* 32 (1987): 93-103 (96-97).

13. On the AFSC program, see Hugh Barbour and J. William Frost, *The Quakers* (New York: 1988), 250- 53; J. William Frost, "'Our Deeds Carry Our Message': The Early History of the American Friends Service Committee," *Quaker History* 81 (1992): 19-29.

14. Much has been written about the conference; see especially, R. D. Bowman, *Brethren and War* (1944), 180-89; Sappington, *Social Policy* (1961), 41-48; Robert G. Clouse, "The Church of the Brethren and World War I: The Goshen Statement," *Mennonite Life* 45 (December 1990): 29-34.

15. *Minutes of the Special General Conference of the Church of the Brethren, Held at Goshen, Indiana, January 9, 1918* (Elgin, Ill.: 1918), 15.

16. J. M. Henry, *History of the Church of the Brethren in Maryland* (Elgin, Ill.: 1936), 525-532, subtitled as the "Tragic Experience of the Church in the World War."

17. W. J. Swigart, "The Central Service Committee," *GM* (July 27, 1918): 468-69. See Sappington, *Social Policy* (1961), 44-45; Dale W. Brown, *Biblical Pacifism: A Peace Church Perspective* (Elgin, Ill.: 1986), 30-31.

18. *Minutes* (1918): 10.

19. Ray W. Abrams, *Preachers Present Arms*, 2nd ed. (Scottdale, Pa.: 1969), 211-29. The Acting Judge Advocate General to the Adjutant General of the War Department held the appended Goshen Statement to be "covertly seditious" and "subversive of military discipline and efficiency." He urged the War Department to instruct the Department of Justice to initiate prosecution, holding it "absurd to suggest that religious freedom permits the violation of the law of the land in such a bold and flagrant manner." —James J. Mayes to the Adjutant General, July 1, 1918, Washington, DC, Military Intelligence Division, War Department, RG 165, National Archives.

20. Allan Teichroew, "Military Surveillance of Mennonites in World War I, *MQR* 53 (1979): 95-127 (116).

21. *Minutes* (1919), 33-35.

22. Gordon K. MacEdward to Director of Military Intelligence, Feb. 4, 1919, Camp Sherman, Ohio, Military Intelligence Division, War Department, RG 165, National Archives.

23. Abrams, *Preachers Present Arms* (1969), 213; Timothy R. Crumrin, "Holding a Course: Professor John J. Schlicher's Dismissal from Indiana State Normal," *Indiana Magazine of History and Biography* 88 (1992): 26-48.

24. Polos, "Jesse C. Beery," *BLT* (1987), 96-97.

25. Sappington, *Social Policy* (1961), 48-52.

26. *Minutes* (1918), 5.

27. Durnbaugh, *Pragmatic Prophet* (1989), 112-13.

28. D. F. Durnbaugh, "Ernst Correll and Juniata College," *MQR* 67 (1993): 481-88 (483-84).

29. Keim and Stoltzfus, *Politics of Conscience* (1988), 63-64. The qotation is from Wilbur K. Thomas to I. H. Brumbaugh, April 3, 1922, Philadelphia, Juniata College Archives, RG 4 President's Papers, Box 9.

30. "Carlock Conference on Pacific Action," *Mennonite Weekly Review* (Sept. 13, 1926): 5.

31. A good overview of the conference is Robert Kreider, "The Historic Peace Churches Meeting in 1935," *Mennonite Life* 31 (June 1976): 21-24.

See also Keim and Stoltzfus, *Politics of Conscience* (1988), 64-65; Juhnke, *Vision, Doctrine, War* (1989). 298-99; Paul Toews, "The Long Weekend or the Short Week: Mennonite Peace Theology, 1925-1944," *MQR* 60 (1986): 38-57.

32. Harold S. Bender, "Continuation Committee of the Historic Peace Churches," *The Mennonite Encyclopedia* (1955/59), 1: 703-04.

Endnotes for Chapter 20: Pages 437-458

1. For an overview of the period, see Edward Robb Ellis, *A Nation in Torment: The Great American Depression, 1929-1939* (New York: 1970), republished (New York: 1995); on the churches, see Robert T. Handy, *A History of the Churches in the United States and Canada* (New York: 1976), 376-92.

2. *Minutes* (1919), 15.

3. S. L. Bowman, *Power and Polity* (1987), 69-80.

4. Raymond R. Peters, *Let's Go Camping* (Elgin, Ill.: 1945); see also his autobiography, *Foothills to Mountaintops: My Pilgrimage to Wholeness* (Elgin, Ill.: 1990), 108-12; Glee Yoder, *Passing On the Gift: The Story of Dan West* (Elgin, Ill.: 1978), 33-46; special issue, *BLT* 24 (1979), 7-59; Jacob F. Replogle, "'Look to the Hills': Beginnings of Brethren Camping in Maryland and Delaware," *BLT* 28 (1983): 229- 34.

5. Durnbaugh, *Pragmatic Prophet* (1989), 74-85. An eloquent account of Brethren life during the depression years is provided in the autobiographical book by Inez Long, *Lord's Day Morning* (Lititz, Pa.: 1989;

6. L. W. Shultz, comp., *Minutes of the Annual Conferences of the Church of the Brethren on War and Peace* (Elgin, Ill.: 1936), supplemented by a comparable collection for 1936/40 (1940).

7. Obituary, *New York Times* (July 13, 1975); Kermon Thomasson, "Andrew Cordier: Hope and Reality, Hand-in-Hand," *Messenger* (September 1995): 14-15.

8. Alyson Lee Greiner, "Geography, Humanism, and 'Plain People' in Missouri: The Case of the Dunkard Brethren," (MA thesis, University of Missouri-Columbia, 1991); Roger E. Sappington, "Otho Winger and the Dunkard Brethren Movement," unpubl. paper (ca. 1980); Sappington, *Social Policy* (1961), 55-57.

9. V[ernon] F. Schwalm, *Otho Winger, 1877-1946* (Elgin, Ill.: 1952), 128-37; Fitzkee, *Mainstream* (1995), 125-28.

10. I. W. Taylor to J. H. Moore, Nov. 12, 1927, Ephrata, Pa., J. H. Moore Collection, Brethren Historical Library and Archives, Elgin, Ill.

11. C. F. Bowman, *Brethren Society* (1995), 406-07. The Brethren Revival Fellowship would later speak favorably of the *Gist* booklet.

12. See the long discussion in *Full Report of the Proceedings of the Annual Conference of the Church of the Brethren Held at Sedalia, Missouri, June 14 to 17, 1920* (Elgin, Ill.: 1920), 131-61; Durnbaugh, *Pragmatic Prophet* (1989), 86-88. The Forward Movement may have been inspired by an earlier, conservatively-based interdenominational movement known as the *Men and Religion Forward Movement* of 1911/12.

13. Durnbaugh, *Pragmatic Prophet* (1989), 90-94; Sappington, *Social Policy* (1961), 117-19; *Minutes* (1946), 162, 174. See the explanatory article by Paul Haynes Bowman, "The Church of the Brethren and the Federal Council," *GM* (Nov. 15, 1941): 5-6, and the response by Fred A. Flora, "The Word of God and the Federal Council, *GM* (Feb. 7, 1942): 9-10.

14. Paul H. Bowman, Sr., "A Statement for the Benefit of the Ministry of the Church of the Brethren," *Christian Beacon* 8 (Dec. 30, 1943).

15. *Minutes* (1956), 14-19. The report moved I. N. H. Beahm to print a stinging reply, called "A Second Edition."

16. Charles D. Bonsack, James M. Moore, and J. W. Lear, "Report of 'Committee on Understanding' to Standing Committee, June 1948"; J. W. Lear, Rufus P. Bucher, and Moyne Landis, "Committee on Understanding to Standing Committee, Ocean Grove, New Jersey, 1949;" Paul H. Bowman, J. W. Lear, W. H. Yoder, and Burton Metzler, "The Church of the Brethren: Report of the Committee on Understanding and Reconciliation." See also Earl C. Kaylor, Jr., *Out of the Wilderness, 1780-1980: The Brethren and Two Centuries of Life in Central Pennsylvania* (New York: 1981), 277-95.

17. Edward K. Ziegler, "Ecumenical Relations," in *Past and Present* (1971), 129-41 (134).

18. Bill Freed, "Broadfording: Busing Them In," *Messenger* (September 1973): 24-25.

19. *Minutes* (1925), 11-13.

20. "Echoes from the Hershey Conference," *GM* (June 17, 1933): 4; Durnbaugh, *Zigler* (1989), 107-43.

21. Otho Winger, "Fraternal Relations," *GM* (Sept. 16, 1933): 5-7; Charles A. Bame, *A Working Agreement with the Church of the Brethren* (Milledgeville, Ill.: [ca. 1935]).

22. The story is told from the Grace side in Homer A. Kent, Sr., *Conquering Frontiers: A History of the Brethren Church,* rev. ed. (Winona Lake, Ind.: 1972), 129-70; from the Ashland side in Albert T. Ronk, *History of the Brethren Church: Its Life, Thought, Mission* (Ashland, Ohio: 1968), 395-437.

Endnotes for Chapter 21: Pages 459-476

1. Kermit Eby, "What Causes War?—No. 1," *GM* (Dec. 29, 1934): 6, extending to (April 13, 1935): 7 (which contains the quotation). The articles have an anti-capitalist slant.

2. Glee Yoder, *Passing on the Gift: The Story of Dan West* (Elgin, Ill.: 1978), 47-52 (48).

3. Kenneth I. Morse, "Kermit Eby: The Man and His Ideas," *BLT* 8 (Spring 1963): 40-48. Many of his books and articles had an autobiographical character, especially *Protests of an Ex-Organization Man* (Boston: 1961).

4. Roger E. Sappington, "Some Reflections on the Activities of Dan West in the 1920s and 1930," unpublished paper; Sappington, *Social Policy* (1961), 62-64; *Brethren and War* (1944), 256.

5. Charles Chatfield, *For Peace and Justice: Pacifism in America, 1914-1943* (Knoxville, Tenn.: 1971), 260-61.

6. *Minutes* (1946), 110-12. See the discussion in C. F. Bowman, *Brethren Society* (1995), 350-61.

7. R. D. Bowman, *Brethren and War* (1944), 258-61.

8. Chatfield, *Peace and Justice* (1971), 107ff., esp.267-69; Sappington, *Social Policy* (1961), 74-75.

9. Sappington, *Social Policy* (1961), 75-80; Yoder, *Dan West* (1978), 89-99; Dan West, "Cooperation with the AFSC in Spain," in *To Serve the Present Age: The Brethren Service Story*, ed. D. F. Durnbaugh (Elgin, Ill.: 1975), 107-10.

10. Yoder, *Dan West* (1978), 100-14; Sappington, *Social Policy* (1961), 111ff.; Kermit Eby, *The God in You* (Chicago: 1954), 43-54; Thurl Metzger, "The Heifer Project," in *Present Age* (1975), 144-47.

    It is not generally known that there had been an earlier project after World War I very similar to that initiated by West (but no doubt unknown to him). German-American farmers from the Plains states donated cows to Germany—in all four shiploads totalling well over 2,000 animals from 1920 to 1922— despite harassment from super patriots inflamed by the American Legion. See on this program two articles by La Vern J. Rippley: "Gift Cows for Germany," *North Dakota History* 40 (Summer 1973): 4- 15, 39; "American Milk Cows for Germany: A Sequel," *North Dakota History* 44 (Summer 1977): 15-23.

11. "Down to Earth Project," *Time* (July 24, 1944).

12. Bill Beck and Mel West, eds., *Cowboy Memories...1944-1994* (Little Rock, Ark.: 1994).

13. Rebecca Bushong, "Ben Bushong—Apostle of Mercy," *BLT* 24 (1979): 71-88.

14. Clio Research Associates, *From Relief to Development: The Evolving Mission of Heifer Project International, Inc.* ([n.p.]: 1993); Manchester College, *Manchester College Celebrates Heifer Project International, May 20, 1995* (North Manchester, Ind.: 1995).

15. A succinct account of these events is found in Albert N. Keim and Grant M. Stoltzfus, *The Politics of Conscience: The Historic Peace Churches and America at War, 1917-1955* (Scottdale, Pa.: 1988), 66-83; see also R. D. Bowman, *Brethren and War* (1944), 271-82.

16. Keim and Stoltzfus, *Politics of Conscience* (1988), 84-102; Durnbaugh, *Pragmatic Prophet* (1989), 125-27; John W. Chambers II, *Draftees or Volunteers: A Documentary History of the Debate Over Military Conscription in the United States, 1787-1973* (New York/London: 1975), 301-41.

17. The CPS program is heavily documented. For the Brethren part of it, see especially: Leslie Eisan, *Pathways of Peace: A History of the Civilian Public Service Program Administered by the Brethren Service Commission* (Elgin, Ill.: 1948); Lorell Weiss, *Ten Years of Brethren Service, 1941-1951* (Elgin, Ill.: [1952]), 13-29; Sappington, *Social Policy* (1961), 85-99; R. D. Bowman, *Brethren and War* (1944), 293-318; Durnbaugh, *Pragmatic Prophet* (1989), 129-37; Albert N. Keim, *The CPS Story: An Illustrated History of Civilian Public Service* (Intercourse, Pa.: 1990). See also Richard A. Anderson, *Peace Was In Their Hearts* (Watsonville, Calif.: 1994) and Cynthia Eller, *Conscientious Objectors and the Second World War: Moral and Religious Arguments in the Support of Pacifism* (New York: 1991).

18. "Minutes of Business Transacted by Standing Committee in Special Session Dec. 18, 19, 1940, First Church of the Brethren, Chicago, Ill.," *Minutes of the 155th Recorded Annual Conference of the Church of the Brethren, Held at La Verne, California, June 18-24, 1941* (Elgin, Ill.: 1941), 53-54.

19. Craig Enberg, "Everson at Waldport," *BLT* 19 (1974): 135-39; Glenn Wallach, "The C. O. Link: Conscientious Objection to World War II and the San Francisco Renaissance," *BLT* 27 (1982): 15-34; William E. Stafford, *Down in My Heart* (Elgin, Ill.: 1947) reprinted 1971; "A Poet for Brethren," *Messenger* (September 1981): 10-11; Stafford obituary, *New York Times* (Aug. 31, 1993): A18.

20. Alex Sareyan, *The Turning Point: How Men of Conscience Brought About Major Change in the Care of America's Mentally Ill* (Washington, D.C./London: 1994).

21. Steve Nolt, "The CPS Frozen Fund: The Beginning of Peace-Time Interaction Between Historic Peace Churches and the United States Government," *MQR* 67 (1993): 201-24.

22. Mary Sue H. Rosenberger, *Light of the Spirit: The Brethren in Puerto Rico,*

1942 to 1992 (Elgin, Ill.: [1992]); Rae Hungerford Mason, *The Inimitable George Mason* (Centralia, Wash.: 1991), 1-53.

23. Rufus D. Bowman, *Seventy Times Seven* (Elgin, Ill.: 1945), 38.
24. Weiss, *Brethren Service* (1952), 28-29.
25. Bowman, *Seventy Times Seven* (1945), 42ff.

Endnotes for Chapter 22: Pages 477-496

1. Sappington, *Social Policy* (1961), 72-84; R. D. Bowman, *Brethren and War* (1944), 257-67; Durnbaugh, *Pragmatic Prophet* (1989), 112-22; David B. Eller, "Social Outreach," in *Yesterday and Today* (1986), 119-34; L. W. Shultz, "The Formation of the Brethren Service Committee," in *To Serve the Present Age: The Brethren Service Story*, ed. D. F. Durnbaugh (Elgin, Ill.: 1975), 111-15.
2. *Minutes* (1941), 52-53.
3. Harshbarger, "Work with Prisoners of War," in *Present Age* (1975), 131-43.
4. Kenneth I. Morse, *New Windsor Center* (New Windsor, Md.: 1979); Harold E. Fey, *Cooperation in Compassion: The Story of Church World Service* (New York: 1966), 76ff..
5. Ralph E. Smeltzer, "Report on the Japanese-American Relocation from Lindsay, California, 1942," ed. Craig Enberg, *BLT* 21 (1970): 71-77; Mary Blocher Smeltzer, "Japanese-American Resettlement Work," in *Present Age* (1975), 123-30; Florence Date Smith, "Days of Infamy," *Messenger* (December 1988): 9- 12.
6. M. R. Zigler, "Part One: The Brethren Service Story," in *Present Age* (1975), 15-100; Fey, *Cooperation in Compassion* (1966), 36; Sappington, *Social Policy* (1961), 101-78; Durnbaugh, *Pragmatic Prophet* (1989), 154-79; Eldon R. Burke, "The Development of BSC in Europe," in *Present Age* (1975), 164-71. There was extensive regular reporting on Brethren Service projects in the *Gospel Messenger*; this was supplemented by the monthly publication *Brethren Service News*, issued between 1946 and 1966. The impressions of a visitor are given in Peters, *Foothills* (1990), 150-63.
7. Opal Stech, "Brethren Service in Poland," in *Present Age* (1975), 181-84; Kermon Thomasson, "A Pebble in a Pond," *Messenger* (December 1987): 10-11, 13-15.
8. Eileen Egan and Elizabeth Clark Reiss, *The CRALOG Experience* (Philadelphia: 1964); Paula Sokody, "An Eye on History," *Messenger* (November 1993): 2; "Professor Burke Dies," *Manchester College Bulletin* (March 1994): 2.
9. Byron P. Royer, "The Kaltenstein Project," in *Present Age* (1975), 185-87; Horst Mönich, *Jugenddorf: Reise in eine neue Welt* (Munich: 1984), 171-81.

10. John H. Eberly, "The High School Exchange Project," in *Present Age* (1975), 200-07; Cheryl Cayford, "ICYE: Fostering Service 40 Years," *Messenger* (October 1989), 9.

11. Ralph E. Smeltzer, "Brethren Service in Austria," in *Present Age* (1975), 172-80; Ralph E. Smeltzer, "The History of Brethren Service in Austria, From Its Beginning (November 1946) to July 1949," (research paper, Bethany Biblical Seminary, 1949); Merlin G. Shull, "History of the Brethren Service Commission in Austria...," (research paper, Bethany Biblical Seminary, 1953).

12. *Messenger* (April 15, 1971): 12-15; Kenneth I. Morse, "'To Help Others as We Were Helped,'" *BE* (1983/84), 708.

13. D. F. Durnbaugh, ed., *On Earth Peace: Discussions on War/Peace Issues Between Friends, Mennonites, Brethren and European Churches, 1935-75* (Elgin, Ill.: 1978); John Howard Yoder, "40 Years of Ecumenical Theological Dialogue Efforts on Justice and Peace Issues by the Fellowship of Reconciliation and the 'Historic Peace Churches,'" in *A Declaration on Peace,* Douglas Gwyn and others (Scottdale, Pa.: 1991), 93-108; Durnbaugh, *Pragmatic Prophet* (1989), 204-06.

14. M. R. Zigler, "Interchurch Service to Greek Villages," in *Present Age* (1975), 188-95; Durnbaugh, *Pragmatic Prophet* (1989), 201-02.

15. Howard E. Sollenberger, "The UNRRA Brethren Service Unit," in *Present Age* (1975), 155-63; Sappington, *Social Policy* (1961), 133-36.

16. John D. Metzler, Sr., "The CROP Idea," in *Present Age* (1975), 148-54.

17. Much has been written about BVS: Sappington, *Social Policy* (1961), 168ff.; special issues of *BLT* after ten (1958), twenty (1968), and twenty-five years (1973); see especially, Janice M. Martin, "25th-Year Statistics—Brethren Volunteer Service," *BLT* 18 (1973): 229-32.

18. On BVS as educator, see Don Fitzkee, "Brethren Volunteer Service: Launchpad for Leadership," *Messenger* (December 1988): 20-24.

19. "Ten Years Service As Agents of Change," *GM* (July 18, 1964): 23.

20. Durnbaugh, *Pragmatic Prophet* (1989), 202-04,

21. Weiss, *Ten Years* (1952), 49-80.

22. Special issue, *BLT* 32 (1987): 198-255.

23. Galen A. Heckman, "Russian Orthodox Church," in *BE* (1983/84), 1132, with citations to reports on the exchange in *Messenger*.

Endnotes for Chapter 23: Pages 497-510

1. The most recent comprehensive study of church government is S. L. Bowman, *Power and Polity* (1987); the quotation is from page 72. See also the extended analysis in C. F. Bowman, *Brethren Society* (1995), 290-314.

2. S. L. Bowman, *Power and Polity* (1987), 81.

3. S. L. Bowman, *Power and Polity* (1987), 82-83.

4. *Minutes* (1943), 5.

5. *Minutes* (1945), 7-9.

6. *Minutes* (1946), 5-9; see S. L. Bowman, *Power and Polity* (1987), 84-85, 105-10; Sappington, *Social Policy* (1961), 144-51.

7. Durnbaugh, *Pragmatic Prophet* (1989), 180-83.

8. Peters, *Foothills* (1990), 141-85.

9. *Minutes* (1947), 4-23.

10. Harold Z. Bomberger, "The Regional Program in the Church of the Brethren," *BLT* 27 (1982): 157- 64.

11. See the extensive discussion in S. L. Bowman, *Power and Polity* (1987), 88ff.

12. *Mission Twelve Handbook* (Elgin, Ill.: 1965), 2; Ronald D. Petry, "Mission Twelve and Beyond," *Monthly Report from the Office of Stewardship Enlistment* (March 12, 1971).

13. Glee Yoder, *Passing on the Gift: The Story of Dan West* (Elgin, Ill.: 1978), 51-52.

14. S. L. Bowman, *Power and Polity* (1987), 85-86.

15. S. L. Bowman, *Power and Polity* (1987), 90.

16. Allen C. Deeter, "Recent Developments Within the Church of the Brethren: Their Influence on the Future," in *Brethren in Transition: 20th Century Directions & Dilemmas*, ed. Emmert F. Bittinger (Camden, Maine: 1992): 59-71.

17. S. L. Bowman, *Power and Polity* (1987), 91-98 (93); emphasis added.

18. Wendy Chamberlain McFadden, "Restructure: An Idea Whose Time Had Not Come," *Messenger* (September 1989): 16-17.

Endnotes for Chapter 24: Pages 511-530

1. See, for example, the heavily illustrated article by Leland Wilson and Howard E. Royer, "Churches for New Times," *GM* (Dec. 16, 1961): 9-22; Arthur L. Dean, "Form, the Outgrowth of Function," *The Brethren Leader* (February 1960); Arthur L. Dean, "New Trends in Church Architecture," *GM* (July 9, 1960): 6-9; "New Structures Dedicated to the Glory of God and Neighbor [!]," *Messenger* (16-19); *Building the Temple of God* (Elgin, Ill.: [1946]). On Dean, see Donald J. Shank, "Arthur Dean: Architect for the Lord," *Messenger* (July 1980): 3.

One report saw some value in the older meetinghouse style: "Special Report: Will Mission Reshape Church Design," *Messenger* (June 24, 1965): 17. It suggested that "the early Brethren meetinghouses, designwise, better served corporate participation" than did the long, narrow church structure. The Harrisonburg, Virginia, building, built in 1978, was designed so that seating can be arranged in a semi-circle around a raised front platform, which also has movable furniture. C. F. Bowman, *Brethren Society* (1995), 163-67, describes the shift in building style from meeting house to church house of the late nineteenth century/early twentieth century.

2. *Minutes* (1956), 182-85.
3. Linda L. Fry, "A Study of Architecture and Worship in the Church of the Brethren," (MATh thesis, Bethany Theological Seminary, 1986), with extensive bibliography, including many articles on the dedication of new church houses. The process of new church building is well caught in the memoir by Inez Long, *Lord's Day Morning* (Lititz, Pa.: 1989), 172-82.
4. S. L. Bowman, *Power and Polity* (1987), 111.
5. John Eichelberger, Gerald Harley, and E. Floyd McDowell, "Bethany: The Buildings at Oak Brook and Richmond," *BLT* 39 (1994): 16-19.
6. See the special issue of *BLT* 39 (1994): 2-72.
7. *Minutes* (1965), 106-13 (111).
8. *Minutes* (1965), 111. For a discussion of the changes in holding the love feast, see C. F. Bowman, *Brethren Society* (1995), 368-74.
9. Earle W. Fike, Jr., et al, *Book of Worship: Church of the Brethren* (Elgin, Ill.: 1964).
10. Nevin W. Fisher, *The History of Brethren Hymnbooks* (Bridgewater, Va.: 1950), 90-100.
11. Kenneth I. Morse, ""Still Pointing the Way," *Messenger* (March 1974): 14-16; Guy E. Wampler, Jr., "Grace Actualized," *Messenger* (March 1976): 26-27
12. Nevin W. Fisher, "William Beery," in *Brethren Builders in Our Century* (Elgin, Ill.: 1952), 17-22; "William Beery, 103, Elgin's Oldest Citizen Is Dead," *Elgin Daily Courier* (Jan. 30, 1956).
13. Kermon Thomasson, "A Poem for Lives Out of Tune," *Messenger* (February 1981): 26.
14. Dorothy Garst Murray, *Sister Anna: God's Captive to Set Others Free* (Elgin, Ill.: 1983).
15. On the journal see two of Edward K. Ziegler's writings: "Twenty-Five Years of the Brethren Journal Association," *BLT* 24 (1979): 243-46; *A Tapestry of Grace* (Elgin, Ill.: 1980), 144-46, an autobiography.
16. "The Anniversary Is Launched at Germantown," *GM* (Feb. 8, 1858): 10-11; A. Stauffer Curry, ed., *250 Years, 1708-1958, Church of the Brethren: Brethren Adult Quarterly* (Elgin, Ill.: 1957—writers: D. F. Durnbaugh, Floyd E. Mallott, Lorell Weiss, Ira Frantz, William G. Willoughy.
17. Paul H. Bowman, ed., *The Adventurous Future* (Elgin, Ill.: 1959).
18. *250th Anniversary of the Church of the Brethren/Die 250-Jahrfeier der*

Brüderkirche, 1708-1958 ([Kassel]: 1958); special issue, *Gospel Messenger* (Sept. 20, 1958): 8-19.

19. Durnbaugh, *Pragmatic Prophet* (1989), 233-43.

20. *In Memory of All Those Who Lost Their Lives in the "Hugo de Groot" on August 14th, 1958* (Galway, Ireland: 1959), memorial booklet; "Brethren Lost in Accidents," *GM* (Aug. 30, 1958): 17.

21. James E. Weaver, "Brethren Response to the Consultation on Church Union," *BLT* 14 (1969): 227-47; Fitzkee, "The Divisiveness of Unity," *Mainstream* (1995), 223-53; Edward K. Ziegler, "Ecumenical Relations," in *Yesterday and Today* (1986), 195-96; C. F. Bowman, *Brethren Society* (1995), 364-68. Background is provided by Nevin H. Zuck, "Cornerstone, Cooperation, Conversation, Consultation, Communion: A Historical Survey of Church of the Brethren Involvement in the Ecumenical Movement," *BLT* 11 (1966): 24-36.

22. *Minutes* (1970), 147-53; Peters, *Foothills* (1990), 250-51; Ziegler, *Tapestry of Grace* (1980), 126.

23. Inez Long, "Brethren Take to the Hills and Alleys," *Christian Century* (July 20, 1966): 916-17; see also her *Lord's Day Morning* (1989), 183-84.

24. Dean Pearman to Vernard Eller, July 29, 1966, Chicago, Ill.; C. Wayne Zunkel, "Reply from the "Hills,'" *Christian Century* (Aug. 17, 1966): 1010-11; H[oward] E. R[oyer], "Profiles Drawn of Brethren," *Messenger* (Dec. 22, 1966).

25. M. Guy West, "From Diatribe to Dialogue," *Messenger* (July 18, 1968): 10-12; the characterizations were drawn from a report drafted by Harold Z. Bomberger for the General Brotherhood Board on the mood of the denomination.

Endnotes for Chapter 25: Pages 531-552

1. The most comprehensive study of these movements is Robert B. Blair, "Modernization and Subgroup Formation in a Religious Organization: A Case Study of the Church of the Brethren," (PhD diss., Northwestern University, 1974). Much of the dissertation was published under the same title (with J. Henry Long as co-author) in *BLT* 21 (1976): 5-36, 69-103, 215-32.

2. Elmer Q. Gleim, *Change and Challenge: A History of the Church of the Brethren Southern District of Pennsylvania, 1940-1972* (Harrisburg: 1973), 152-53; Harold S. Martin, *What Happened to the Church of the Brethren?* (Hanover, Pa.: [1963]), 2nd ed. (1965); Linford Rotenberger, "Issues and Concerns in the Church of the Brethren, for Presentation at the Staff Meeting," (March 1-2, 1966), mimeographed document.

3. Dale Aukerman, "A Subtle Version of Conformity," *Messenger*

(February 1988): 25-26; Dale W. Brown, "The BRF Has Pros and Cons," *Messenger* (August/September 1988): 43-45; Harold S. Martin, "Questions and Answers Related to the Council of Churches (WCC and NCC)," *BRF Witness* 19/4 (1984): 3-14 (9-10).

4. Harold S. Martin, "Questions Often Asked About the Brethren Revival Fellowship," *BRF Witness* 18/4 (1983): 2.

5. [Harold S. Martin?], *A Handbook of Basic Beliefs within the Church of the Brethren* ([n.p.]: [1971]); Gleim, *Change and Challenge* (1973), 153.

6. Martin, "Questions," (1983), 3. See also Don Fitzkee, "Who's Afraid of the BRF?" *Messenger* (July 1988): 9-11, (August/September 1988): 14-16.

7. Blair, "Modernization," (1974), 81-86 (86).

8. Blair, "Modernization," (1974), 86-91 (90).

9. Blair, "Modernization," (1974), 91-95.

10. *Brethren Action Movement* (North Manchester, Ind.: [ca. 1970]).

11. Blair, "Modernization," (1974), 95.

12. H[oward] E. R[oyer], "The Actionists and the Revivalists," *Messenger* (Nov. 20, 1969).

13. R. G. Robins, "Pentecostal Movement," in *Dictionary of Christianity in America*, ed. Daniel G. Reid (Downers Grove, Ill.: 1990), 885-91 (885); Donald W. Dayton, *Theological Roots of Pentecostalism* (Grand Rapids, Mich.: 1987).

14. Blair, "Modernization," (1974), 95-100. Some reactions from Brethren writers were Leland B. Emrick, "The Gifts of the Holy Spirit," *Messenger* (April 1973): 14-15; David B. Lehigh, "What About Speaking in Tongues?" *BRF Witness* 8/1 (1973): 3-8; Robert Kintner, "The Brethren Heritage and the Radical and Charismatic Movements," *BLT* 18 (1973): 159-64;

15. Some articles on the conferences were: Edward G. Lyons, "The Holy Spirit at Vaparaiso," *Messenger* (October 1976): 36-38; Bill Faw, "The Spirit Moves Us...," *Messenger* (November 1977): 10-11, 25; Mary and Chalmer Faw, "Holy Spirit Conferences: Continuing Renewal," *Messenger* (November 1978): 10-11; Rowan K. Daggett, "Church United by Love Is Holy Spirit Theme," *Messenger* (October 1979): 5.

16. Russell Bixler, *It Can Happen to Anybody!* (Pittsburgh: 1970); Fred W. Swartz, "The New Russell Bixler Comes Forward," *Messenger* (July 1973): 14-17.

17. Timothy K. Jones, "A Church with No Back Pews," *Messenger* (October 1986): 11-14.

18. Dave and Neta Jackson, *Glimpses of Glory: Thirty Years of Community. The Story of Reba Place Fellowship* (Elgin, Ill.: 1987), 161-71.

19. Julius H. Belser, "Reba Place Fellowship," *BE* (1983/84), 1084-85.

20. See the church's quarterly paper, *The Charismatic Messenger*, initiated in 1987.

21. Fred W. Benedict and William F. Rushby, "Christ's Assembly," *BLT* 18 (1973): 33-42.

22. D. F. Durnbaugh, "Freeman, Hobart," in *Dictionary of Christianity in America* (Downers Grove, Ill.: 1990), 453.

23. Brubaker, *Women's Participation* (1985), 154-67. See also Pamela Brubaker, "Women," in *Yesterday and Today* (1986), 161-80.

24. Ruthann Knechel Johansen, "Giving Birth to a New World," duplicated typescript (July 29, 1978).

25. Howard E. Royer, "A World Ministry for the 80s: Ruby Rhoades shares the vision of the early church — simply sharing the good news it has," *Messenger* (January 1980): 10-13, 33; Robert W. Neff, "Ruby Rhoades: Fighter in a Peace Church," *Messenger* (February 1985): 9.

26. Inez Long, "Florence Murphy," in her *Faces Among the Faithful* (Elgin, Ill.: 1962), 122-27; Fran Clemens Nyce, "Brethren Women: A Century of Work," *Messenger* (November 1984): 8-9; Brubaker, *Women's Participation* (1985), 77-79.

27. Guy E. Wampler, Jr., "Elaine Sollenberger: Quiet Revolutionary," *Messenger* (May/June 1989): 12- 15.

28. Brethren/Mennonite Council for Gay Concerns, *Dialogue* (December 1979): 8. See Martin Rock, "As God's Children, Not Stepchildren," *Messenger* (September 1978): 28-29.

29. George Keeler, "Moderator Chuck Boyer: What You See Is What You Get," *Messenger* (February 1993): 14-18 (15); Messenger staff, "Indianapolis, '93," *Messenger* (August/September 1993): 11-14.

30. Messenger staff, "Living Waters at Wichita, '94," *Messenger* (August 1994): 11-16 (17).

Endnotes for Chapter 26: Pages 553-570

1. *50th Anniversary Brethren Chinese Church and Sunday School* (Chicago: 1958).

2. Vernard Eller, "Sim Togasaki: Most Unlikely Dunker," *GM* (Dec. 30, 1961): 4-7, 14.

3. The pamphlet is reprinted in *New Nation* (1976), 265-72; on Weir and Carter, see Kermon Thomasson, "Black Brother," *Messenger* (June 1977): 32.

4. Mildred Hess Grimley, "No Sound of Trumpet," *Messenger* (January 1976): 16-20; J. Gilbert Ware, "The Afterglow of Mattie Dolby," *Messenger* (April 1976); "Mattie Makes the Comics," *Messenger* (February 1993): 4.

5. Royer, *Thirty-three Years* (1913), 203-04.

6. Brubaker, *Women's Participation* (1985), 140-41.

7. Kermon Thomasson, "Being Black and Brethren," *Messenger* (June 1988): 1, 17-20.

8. On Smeltzer, see Stephen L. Longenecker, *Selma's Peacemaker: Ralph Smeltzer and Civil Rights Mediation* (Phladelphia: 1987); Charles E. Fager, *Selma 1965* (New York: 1974), an excerpt was printed as "A Peacemaker's Role at Selma," *Messenger* (September 1974): 24-27. On Hayes, see Don Fitzkee, "The Two Worlds of Bill Hayes," *Messenger* (June 1988): 10-13.

9. Rolland F. Flory, "The Cuba Colony," *Lest We Forget and Tales of Yester-Year* (Orlando, Fla.: 1976), 89-95; Crouse, "Mission," *Yesterday and Today* (1986), 147-48.

10. Kermon Thomasson, "A People Hungry for the Gospel," *Messenger* (April 1991): 14-17 (14).

11. James H. Lehman, "Haiti's Theological Warrior and the Brethren," *Messenger* (September 1982): 34- 37 (36).

12. Karen S. Carter, "Eglise des Freres Haitiens: The Church of Contagious Joy," *Messenger* (July 1994): 22-26.

13. Karen S. Carter, "Onaldo Pereira: He Came to His Own," *Messenger* (June 1986): 26-29; Karen S. Carter, "As Sheep Among Wolves," *Messenger* (July 1987): 23-26; Cheryl Cayford, "Brethren in Brazil: Fragile as a Petal, Determined as a Thorn," *Messenger* (April 1993): 17-21.

14. Special issue on missions, *BLT* 29 (1984): 67-127.

15. Joel K. Thompson, "Is the Task to Build a Church?" (June 25, 1970), presentation at Annual Conference.

16. [Kermon Thomasson], "Page One," *Messenger* (December 1980): 1. Thompson died in a tragic airplane crash on Sept. 8, 1994, while on church business—*Messenger* (October 1994): 8.

17. *World Mission Philosophy and Program* (Elgin, Ill.: 1981).

18. "Delegates Endorse Overseas Church-Planting," *Messenger* (August/September 1990): 15; Cheryl Cayford, "Discernment Team Returns from 'Positive' Korea Trip," *Messenger* (August/September 1991): 6.

19. On the California tribe of "Dunkard Indians," see *Brethren at Work* (Aug. 2, 1881): 457. An historical overview of this topic is given by John W. Lowe, Jr., "Brethren and Native Americans: An Unfulfilled History," 38 *BLT* (1993): 137-50. See also: Benjamin E. Simmons, "The Beginning of Church of the Brethren Work Among Indian Americans," *BLT* 14 (1969): 183-86; George Keeler, "Lybrook and Its Changing Roles," *Messenger* (May/June 1994): 20-25.

20. *GM* (March 1924): 171.

Endnotes for Chapter 27: Pages 571-594

1. Carl F. Bowman, *A Profile of the Church of the Brethren* (Elgin, Ill.: 1986, derived mainly from a series of articles in the *Messenger* (1986). See also his essay, "Brethren Today," in *Yesterday and Today* (1986), 201-24.

2. C. F. Bowman, *Profile* (1986), 4.

3. Eric Bishop, "Springtime in the Heart: National Older Adult Conference," *Messenger* (January 1991): 18-20; Kermon Thomasson, "NOAC II: Choosing Between Lake and Hills," *Messenger* (December 1994): 16-21 (21); *Transcripts of Sermons and General Sessions: Church of the Brethren National Older Adults Conference (NOAC II)* (Elgin, Ill.: [1995]).

4. Emmert F. Bittinger, ed., *Brethren in Transition: 20th Century Directions & Dilemmas* (Camden, Maine: 1992), 4.

5. Cheryl Cayford, "General Board Receives Call to Spiritual Renewal," *Messenger* (December 1990): 6, 10; Messenger staff, "Portland," *Messenger* (August/September 1991): 16.

6. "Redesigning General Board Ministries," *Messenger* (August 1995): 16-18.

7. Concerned Brethren, "Our Salt Has Lost So Much Savor." *Messenger* (August/ September 1990): 35- 37; Don Fitzkee, "Evangelical Brethren Talk About Starting New School," *Messenger* (July 1991).

8. "Portland," *Messenger* (August/September 1991), 18.

9. Don Fitzkee, "Setting Evangelism Goals," *Messenger* (Aug./Sept, 1992): 20; Don Fitzkee, "Evangelism Events," *Messenger* (August/September 1993): 20.

10. *The Andrew Center* (Elgin, Ill.: 1994); Andrew Center Staff, *Evangelism: Good News or Bad News* (Elgin, Ill.: 1995).

11. Steve Clapp, *Promising Results: Passing on the Promise and Pilgrimage Toward Growth* (Elgin, Ill.: 1993), based on a study by George Mendenhall, *Passing on the Promise: Evaluation Guide* (Elgin, Ill,: 1993).

12. Two expressions of this orientation are Paul E. R. Mundey, "A Prophetic—Yet Inviting—People," *Messenger* (November 1983): 12; Richard B. Gardner, "Brethren and Evangelical: Is the Fit a Good One?" *Messenger* (February 1992): 18-20.

13. "Report of the Fraternal Relations Committee," *Minutes* (1970), 147-53 (152).

14. Paula S. Wilding, "Bethany Welcomes New Beginnings in Richmond," *Messenger* (November 1994): 6-7.

15. James Leo Garrett, Jr., *The Concept of the Believers' Church: Addresses from the 1967 Louisville Conference* (Scottdale, Pa.: 1969), 314-24 (324)

16. John Howard Yoder and D. F. Durnbaugh have served as co-convenors

of the Continuation Committee; both have written brief surveys of the series of conferences: Yoder, "Introduction," in *Baptism & Church: A Believers' Church Vision,* ed. Merle D. Strege (Grand Rapids, Mich: 1986), 3-7; Durnbaugh, "Origin and Development of the Believers' Church Conferences," in *Servants of the Word: Ministry in the Believers' Church.* ed. David B. Eller (Elgin, Ill.: 1990), xvii-xxx (printed in incomplete fashion).

17. Don Fitzkee, "[Rufus P.] Bucher Center Teaches Brethren Who They Are," *Messenger* (August/September 1987): 10-11, and Fitzkee, *Mainstream* (1995), 252-53.

18. Presentations at the 1993 conference were published in Carl F. Bowman and Stephen L. Longenecker, eds., *Anabaptist Currents: History in Conversation with the Present* (Camden, Maine, 1995).

19. Cheryl Cayford, "Christian Peacemaker Teams: What are they and what do they do?" *Messenger* (August 1989): 9.

20. Durnbaugh, *Pragmatic Prophet* (1989), 291-92.

21. See the special issue, *BLT* 30 (Autumn 1985): 132-84; Edward K. Ziegler, "Ecumenical Relations," in *Yesterday and Today* (1986), 191.

22. D. F. Durnbaugh, ed., *Report of the Proceedings of the Brethren World Assembly, Elizabethtown College, Elizabethtown, Pennsylvania, July 15-July 18, 1992* (Elizabethtown, Pa.: 1994). The preparatory steps for both the Encyclopedia project and the World Assembly are traced in the first essay, D. F. Durnbaugh, "The Brethren World Assembly: Background and Basis," (1-18).

23. Inez Long, *One Man's Peace: A Story of M. R. Zigler* (New Windsor, Md.: 1983), 120-33; Durnbaugh, *Pragmatic Prophet* (1989), 274-88.

24. H. Lamar Gibble, "European Origins and Relevant Contemporary Connections," *Messenger* (October 1993): 11-13.

25. Roger E. Sappington, "Some Reflections on the Activities of Dan West in the 1920s and 1930s," unpublished paper.

26. Gladdys E. Muir, "The Place of the Brethren Colleges in Preparing Men and Women for Peace Leadership," *Manchester College Bulletin of the Peace Studies Institute* 19/1-2 (1989): 9-19 (14, 18).

27. Herbert Hogan, "Gladdys Esther Muir: Teacher, Mystic, Peacemaker," *MC Bulletin* (1989): 5-8; Harry A. Brandt, "Meet Gladdys E. Muir: Portrait of a Beloved Teacher," *Messenger* (March 3, 1966): 9-11; Gladdys E. Muir, *La Verne College: Seventy-five Years of Service* (La Verne, Calif.: 1967); Karla Boyers, "Gladdys Muir: Peace Pioneer," *Messenger* (July 1991): 20.

28. Karla Boyers, "Peace That Poses Understanding," *Messenger* (July

1991): 17-19, plus 22-23; special issue "Waging Peace at Juniata College," *Juniata College Bulletin* (Spring 1989): 2-9.

29. *The Cistern* 1 (Spring 1980): 1.

30. "Group Expresses Frustration with Denominational Name," *Messenger* (January 1994): 9. See on the issue of name-change the perceptive comments of C. F. Bowman, *Brethren Society* (1995), 396-99.

31. Paula S. Wilding, "General Board Focuses on Brethren 'Identity Lines,'" *Messenger* (December 1994): 6-7; Donald E. Miller, "Another Way of Living," *Messenger* (January 1995): 22.

Endnotes for the Epilogue: Pages 595-596

1. Carl F. Bowman, "Brethren Today," in *Yesterday and Today* (1986), 201-25 (213).

2. Devere Allen, *The Fight for Peace*, ed. Charles Chatfield (New York: 1971), 1: 245-46, originally published (New York: 1930); Peter Brock, *Freedom from Violence: Sectarian Nonresistance from the Middle Ages to the Great War* (Toronto: 1991), 212-13.

3. Benjamin Rush, "An Account of the Manners of the German Inhabitants of Pennsylvania," *The Columbia Magazine, or Monthly Repository* 3 (January 1789): 22-30, reprinted in his *Essays, Literary, Moral and Philosophical*, 2nd ed. (Philadelphia: 1806), originally published (Philadelphia: 1798).

INDEX